Elihu Samuel Riley

The Ancient City

History of Annapolis, in Maryland.

Elihu Samuel Riley

The Ancient City
History of Annapolis, in Maryland.

ISBN/EAN: 9783337289010

Printed in Europe, USA, Canada, Australia, Japan

Cover: Foto ©ninafisch / pixelio.de

More available books at **www.hansebooks.com**

"THE ANCIENT CITY."

— ▲ —

HISTORY

— OF —

ANNAPOLIS, in Maryland.

1649—1887.

BY ELIHU S. RILEY.

ANNAPOLIS.
RECORD PRINTING OFFICE.
1887.

In pursuance of the Act of 1886, Chapter 150, entitled "an Act to provide for a State subscription to Riley's History of Annapolis," the undersigned, designated by said Act, to examine said History, hereby certify that we have examined said History, as prepared by said Riley, and find that it contains much valuable and interesting matter, a considerable portion of which has not hitherto appeared in any published history ; and believing, as we do, that the book will be of interest to the people of the State, we, therefore approve the same.

Henry Lloyd,
R. H. Alvey,
E. P. Duvall.

PREFACE.

——:o:——

This History of Annapolis has been written in hours taken from the days of a very busy life. They have been hours of labor, but hours lightened by the pleasures of the task.

The annals of the brave, intelligent, chivalrous people who made the City of Annapolis celebrated, are part of the history of the nation.

In the early days of the capital, the sturdy Puritans represented the austere and religious in its annals : the political and aggressive period followed the removal of the capital from St. Mary's to Annapolis ; the third stage was the golden age of Annapolitan history. Its people, polished in literature, skilled in politics, energetic in business, experienced the benefits of literary culture, maintained their rights against encroaching proprietaries, pushed their commerce into many seas, and enjoyed the opulence that active trade returns to intelligent enterprise. Then came the Revolutionary epoch. In it, no city in the colonies was more prompt and decisive in resisting the aggressions of the crown, and in supplying troops and sinews of war for carrying on active operations in the field against the British forces. After the Revolution, Annapolis declined in importance, but the location of the Naval Academy here in 1845 restored its national character. The connection by Short-Line railroad with Baltimore renews its ancient hopes of commercial importance. To gather the rays of light from their varied sources and to form them into one prism of information has made it necessary to search many volumes of history, trench on the memory and patience of numerous citizens, and to record, out of our own limited store-house of recollection, things new and old.

In this task we have had the aid of the following public documents, journals, and histories :

Maryland *Gazette*, William Parks, Publisher, Annapolis, 1727, 1728, 1729.

Maryland *Gazette*, Jonas Green and descendants, publishers, 1745 to 1839.

Ridgely's Annals of Annapolis, 1841.

Historical View of the Government of Maryland, John V. L. McMahon, 1831.

History of Maryland, John Leeds ~~~~~ 2 vols., 1837.

Scharf's History of Maryland, 3 vols., 1879.

Archives of Maryland, 3 vols., 1883.

Appleton's Encyclopedia.

Laws of Maryland, 1637 to 1763.

Allen's History of St. Anne's Parish. 1857.
Eddis' Letters from Annapolis, 1769 to 1776.
Lord Baltimore's Rent Roll for Anne Arundel.
MSS. in the Land Office.
Surveys in Annapolis, MSS. in the Land Office.
Journals of Proceedings of the House. MSS., in the Land Office,
Annapolis and
Maryland Historical Society, Baltimore.
Proceedings of the Provincial Court, MSS. in the Land Office.
Proceedings of the Governor's council, MSS. Land Office.
Marshall's Life of Washington.
Terra Mariæ.
Force's Tracts.
Register of St. John's College.
Report of the Legislature on St. John's College.
A Puritan Colony in Maryland, Dan'l. R. Randall.
A French Officer's Letters from America.
Soley's History of the Naval Academy.
House and Senate Documents, 1861.
Proceedings of the Corporation.
Docket of the Mayor's Court of Annapolis.
The Annapolis *Gazette.*
The Maryland *Gazette.* (New Issue.)
The *Record,* Annapolis.
The Revised Code of Annapolis.
Laws of Maryland of 1884.

I am indebted greatly to Senator Nicholas Brewer, of this county, for the loan of a valuable volume—Eddis' Letters from Annapolis; also, a French Officer's Letters from America. The former has been invaluable and without it the History of Annapolis would have been wanting in much important information.

To Mr. Geo. H. Shafer, Deputy in the Land Office, Dr. E. P. Duvall, State Librarian, and Mr. S. M. Gatchell, Librarian of the Maryland Historical Society, I am indebted for their many courtesies in granting me full access to the numerous sources of history in their respective offices.

To my venerable and esteemed relative, Mrs. Eliza Bonsall, now in the 84th year of her age, of sound mind, keen memory, and well-ordered intellect, I hereby gratefully acknowledge my great indebtedness for much valuable information, especially in the location of former landmarks and the identification of ancient houses in our city.

To Dr. George Wells, whose unremitting and unsolicited efforts were largely instrumental in securing the option of a State's subscription to this History, I here record my high appreciation of his friendly and invaluable services, that were rendered in that lofty spirit which, when conferring a favor, seems to be receiving one.

I am indebted to the members of the Legislature who voted to sustain the work. Had it not been for them this volume had possibly not been written.

My thanks are particularly due to the unwearied assistance the Anne Arundel delegation gave in securing State aid to this work.

To the many friends whose interest has encouraged and whose helpful efforts have aided in the preparation of this work. I am gratefully indebted. and none the less to those, in many quarters, who were instant in season and out of season in bringing to the attention of Legistors, the merits of the proposed work, and in urging upon them the propriety of encouraging the publication by a State subscription!.

The author has endeavored to make the work essentially one of fact. and to present those facts in the language of those who lived this history, or who first chronicled the events to which they were cotemporary. He conceives that the plan will convey to the reader a better picture of the people and the times of which he wrote than any style he might adopt.

If the halo of a State's glory is brightened by this work : if any service has been rendered the commonwealth: if something valuable has been preserved from partial or total destruction by the History of Annapolis. the members of the Legislature who voted for chapter 150, Acts of 1886, are entitled to a large share of the credit to be accorded this volume. These members are :

IN THE SENATE.

President Edwin Warfield, Senator from Howard.

Nicholas Brewer,	"	"	Anne Arundel.
William D. Burchinal.	"	"	Kent.
Charles T. Claggett.	"	"	Prince George.
R. Johnson Colton,	"	"	St. Mary's.
Griffin W. Goldsborough,	"	"	Caroline.
Thomas G. Hayes,	"	"	Baltimore City.
Clinton McCullough.	"	"	Cecil.
A. Beall McKaig.	"	"	Allegany.
George Peter,	"	"	Montgomery.
Isidor Rayner.	"	"	Baltimore City.
Harry W. Rusk.	"	"	"
C. Bohn Slingluff,	"	"	Baltimore county.
Theophilus Tunis,	"	"	Talbot.

IN THE HOUSE OF DELEGATES.

Speaker Joseph B. Seth,	of	Talbot county.
Francis V. King,	"	St. Mary's county.
Charles F. Norris,	"	"
Lewis C. Justice, Jr..	"	Kent.
John Ireland,	"	Anne Arundel.
E. E. Gott, Jr..	"	"
M. Tilghman Howard,	"	"
Geo. N. Potee,	"	"
Francis Gantt,	"	Calvert.

John Hubner,	"	Baltimore county.
William Pole, Sr.,	"	"
Joseph S. Baldwin,	"	"
Michael O'Hara,	"	"
James J. Lindsay,	"	"
F. A. Benson,	"	Talbot county.
Paul Winchester,	"	"
DeWilton Snowden,	"	Prince George's county.
Fillmore Beall,	"	"
William W. Busteed,	"	Queen Anne's county.
Edward C. Legg,	"	"
William Dudley,	"	"
R. Harris Archer,	"	Harford county.
Charles W. Wright,	"	Caroline county.
John Y. Graham,	"	"
James R. Willing,	"	Baltimore City.
Edward D. Fitzgerald,	"	"
John Rooney,	"	"
Peter J. Campbell,	"	"
Richard J. Penn,	"	"
Charles H. Evans,	"	"
C. Dodd McFarland,	"	"
Patrick Reilly,	"	"
L. W. Gunther,	"	"
Timothy Hayes,	"	"
Charles A. Hoffman,	"	"
Lewis Reitz,	"	"
Harry A. Schultz,	"	"
John E. Durding,	"	"
Henry C. Seebo,	"	"
Lewis C. McCusker,	"	"
Geo. M. Stonebraker,	"	Washington county.
E. C. Gaskill,	"	Allegany "
Albert Holle,	"	" "
Samuel H. Hoffacker,	"	Carroll "
Michael Buckman,	"	" "
Elias B. Arnold,	"	" "

Annapolis, June 8, 1887.   ELIHU S. RILEY

CONTENTS.

————(:o:)————

CHAPTER.		PAGE.
I.	Settlement of Annapolis	17
II.	Formation of Anne Arundel County	20
III.	The Puritans Refuse to Send Delegates to the Legislature of 1651	23
IV.	The Animosities of the Old World Transplanted in the New	24
V.	Providence Sends a Petition to the Commissioners of the Commonwealth	26
VI.	Gov. Stone Proclaims the Puritans to be Rebels	27
VII.	An Indian Treaty Made on the Severn	28
VIII.	Preparations for War	31
IX.	The Battle of the Severn	33
X.	Quakers and Indians Disturb the Colony	37
XI.	Colonial Life	40
XII.	An Indiscreet Representative from Anne Arundel	48
XIII.	The Courageous Spirit of the Maryland Settlers	50
XIV.	Providence Changed to "The Town at Proctors"	52
XV.	The Impeachment of Major Thomas Truman	54
XVI.	Removal of the State Capital from St. Mary's to Annapolis	55
XVII.	Chronicles of Annapolis from 1694 to 1700	62
XVIII.	First State House in Annapolis	66
XIX.	St. Anne's Parish	68
XX.	King William's School	77
XXI.	The Second State House in Annapolis	80
XXII.	The Attempt of Richard Clarke, in 1707, to Burn Annapolis	81
XXIII.	Annapolis is Made a City	85
XXIV.	The Annapolis Delegates Denied Admittance to the House	92
XXV.	The First Newspaper in Maryland	94
XXVI.	Chronicles of Annapolis from 1707 to 1740	96
XXVII.	The Second Newspaper Printed in Maryland	96
XXVIII.	Annapolis in 1745	102
XXIX.	Annapolis a Century Old	108
XXX.	Chronicles of Annapolis from 1746 to 1773	109
XXXI.	Customs and Characters of the Capital	122
XXXII.	The First American Theatre Erected in Annapolis	146

10   *CONTENTS.*

XXXIII.	THE STAMP ACT IN ANNAPOLIS	149
XXXIV.	GOV. EDEN, OF MARYLAND, THE LAST ENGLISH GOVERNOR TO LEAVE THE REVOLTED COLONIES	152
XXXV.	SHIPYARDS, RACE COURSES, AND INDIANS	157
XXXVI.	THE THIRD STATE HOUSE IN ANNAPOLIS	161
XXXVII.	ANNAPOLIS IN THE DECLARATION OF INDEPENDENCE	164
XXXVIII.	ANNAPOLIS DURING THE REVOLUTIONARY WAR	165
XXXIX.	A POLITICAL PRISONER IN ANNAPOLIS DURING THE REVOLUTION	189
XL.	ANNAPOLIS AFTER THE REVOLUTION	192
XLI.	ANNAPOLIS WANTS TO BE THE CAPITAL OF THE UNITED STATES	198
XLII.	GENERAL WASHINGTON RESIGNS HIS MILITARY COMMISSION AT ANNAPOLIS	200
XLIII.	ST. JOHN'S COLLEGE	208
XLIV.	PRESIDENT WASHINGTON'S VISIT TO ANNAPOLIS	218
XLV.	CHRONICLES OF ANNAPOLIS FROM 1777 TO 1810	220
XLVI.	THE ANCIENT REGIME DISAPPEARS	228
XLVII.	WILLIAM PINKNEY BANQUETTED IN ANNAPOLIS	230
XLVIII.	ANNAPOLIS DURING THE WAR OF 1812	233
XLIX.	LAFAYETTE'S VISIT TO ANNAPOLIS	239
L.	"THE GLORIOUS NINETEEN"	244
LI.	"JOE MORGUE"	250
LII.	CHRONICLES OF ANNAPOLIS FROM 1810 TO 1839	253
LIII.	LOCATION OF THE UNITED STATES NAVAL ACADEMY AT ANNAPOLIS	264
LIV.	A RIOT IN ANNAPOLIS	268
LV.	CHRONICLES OF ANNAPOLIS FROM 1845 TO 1847	272
LVI.	A RETROSPECT OF TWO CENTURIES	274
LVII.	A GALAXY OF ILLUSTRIOUS ANNAPOLITANS	275
LVIII.	CHRONICLES OF ANNAPOLIS FROM 1860 TO 1861	280
LIX.	OPENING OF THE CIVIL WAR—ANNAPOLIS SEIZED BY THE FEDERAL GOVERNMENT	281
LX.	PUBLIC BUILDINGS, CHURCHES, AND ANCIENT LANDMARKS	302
LXI.	ELECTIONS IN ANNAPOLIS DURING THE CIVIL WAR	310
LXII.	CHRONICLES OF ANNAPOLIS FROM 1863 TO 1887	311
LXIII.	A DISASTROUS ACCIDENT	321
LXIV.	ANNAPOLIS OF THE PRESENT	323

GOVERNORS

—: o :—

Of the Province and State of Maryland from the First Settlement in 1633 to 1887.

——: o :——

UNDER THE PROPRIETARY GOVERNMENT.

Leonard Calvert	1633.	John Hart	1715.
Thomas Greene	1647.	Charles Calvert	1720.
William Stone	1649.	Benedict L. Calvert	1727.
Commissioners under Parliament	1654.	Samuel Ogle	1732.
		Charles Lord Baltimore	1733.
Josiah Fendall	1658.	Samuel Ogle	1735.
Philip Calvert	1661.	Thomas Bladen	1742.
Charles Calvert	1662.	Samuel Ogle	1747.
Charles Lord Baltimore	1676.	Horatio Sharpe	1753.
Thomas Notley	1678.	Robert Eden	1769.
Charles Lord Baltimore	1681.		

UNDER THE ROYAL GOVERNMENT.

Government seized by the crown of England	1689.	Nathaniel Blackiston	1699.
		John Seymour	1704.
Lyonel Copley	1692.	John Hart	1714.
Francis Nicholson	1694.		

PRESIDENT'S OF THE PROVINCE.

Thomas Tench	1703.	Benjamin Tasker	1752.
Edward Lloyd	1709.		

UNDER STATE GOVERNMENT.

Provisional Government	1776.	Elected under Constitution of 1851, for four years.	
Thomas Johnson	1777.		
Thomas Sim Lee	1779.	Thomas Watkins Ligon.	1853.
William Paca	1782.	Thos. Holliday Hicks	1857.
William Smallwood	1785.	Augustus W. Bradford.	1861.
John Eager Howard	1788.	Elected under Constitution of 1866, for four years.	
George Plater	1791.		
Thomas Sim Lee	1792.		
John H. Stone	1794.	Thos. Swann, of Balto. City	1865.
John Henry	1797.		
Benjamin Ogle	1798.	Elected under Constitution of 1867, for four years.	
John Frances Mercer	1801.		
Robert Bowie	1803.		
Robert Wright	1806.	Oden Bowie	1869.

Edward Lloyd........1809.
Robert Bowie.........1811.
Levin Winder ....1812.
Charles Ridgely, of
  Hampton...........1815.
Charles Goldsborough.1818.
Samuel Sprigg........1819.
Samuel Stevens, Jr....1822.
Joseph Kent..........1825.
Daniel Martin........1828.
Thomas King Carroll..1829.
Daniel Martin........1830.
George Howard.......1831.
James Thomas........1832.
Thomas W. Veazey...1835.
William Grason.......1838.
Elected under the
  amended Constitution
  of 1838, for three years
William Grason.......1838.
Francis Thomas......1841.
Thomas G. Pratt......1844.
Philip F. Thomas.... 1847.
Enoch Louis Lowe....1850.

Wm. Pinkney White..1872.
Resigned March 4, 1874,
  to take seat as U. S.
  Senator.
James Black Groome..1874.
Gov. Groome, elected
  by the Legislature.
John Lee Carroll......1875.
Wm. T. Hamilton.....1879.
Robert M. McLane....1883.
Resigned March 27,
  1885, to take the
  position of U. S.
  Minister to France.
Henry Lloyd........1885-7.
On resignation of Gov.
  McLane, Hy. Lloyd,
  of Maryland, (by vir-
  tue of being President
  of the Senate, became
  Governor,) and was
  re-elected by the
  Legislature, Jan. 20,
  1886.

MAYORS

Amos Garrett	1708.	Burton Whetcroft	1807.
Thomas Larkin	1720.	John Kelly	1808.
Benjamin Tasker	1721.	Burton Whetcroft	1809.
Vachel Denton	1722.	John Johnson	1810.
Benjamin Tasker	1726.	Nicholas Brewer	1811.
Vachel Denton	1727.	Gideon White	1812.
William Rodgers	1745.	John Randall	1813.
John Ross	1749.	Nicholas Brewer	1814.
Benjamin Tasker	1750.	John Randall	1815.
Michael Macnamara	1753.	Nicholas Brewer	1816.
Benjamin Tasker	1754.	John Randall	1817.
John Brice	1755.	Nicholas Brewer	1818.
Benjamin Tasker	1756.	Lewis Duvall	1819-1822.
John Bullen	1757.	James Boyle	1823-4.
John Ross	1758.	Richard Harwood, of	
George Stewart	1759.	Thos.	1825-7.
Michael Macnamara	1760.	Dennis Claude	1828-1836.
Stephen Bordley	1761.	John Miller	1837-9.
John Brice	1762.	Alex. C. Magruder	1840-2.
George Stewart	1763.	Richard Swann	1843-4.
Daniel Dulany	1764.	William Bryan	1845.
John Ross	1765.	Richard Swann	1846-7.
Walter Dulany	1766.	Richard R. Goodwin	1848.
Upton Scott	1767.	Abram Claude	1847-50.
Allen Quynn	1778-9.	B. T. B. Worthington	1851.
John Brice	1780.	Richard R. Goodwin	1852.
John Bullen	1781.	Dennis Claude	1853.
James Brice	1782.	Abram Claude	1854.
Jeremiah T. Chase	1783.	N. Brewer, of Nich.	1855.
Nicholas Carroll	1784.	Richard Swann	1854-7.
Robert Couden	1785.	Joshua Brown	1858.
Allen Quynn	1786-7.	William Harwood	1859.
James Brice	1788.	John R. Magruder	1860-1.
John Bullen	1789.	J. Wesley White	1862.
Nicholas Carroll	1790.	John R. Magruder	1863.
Robert Couden	1791.	Solomon Phillips	1864.
Allen Quynn	1792.	Richard R. Goodwin	1865.
John Bullen	1793.	Richard Swann	1866.
James Williams	1794.	Abram Claude	1867-8.

William Pinkney......1795.
John Davidson........1800.
James Williams.......1801.
Allen Quynn.....   ..1802.
Samuel Ridout........1803.
John Johnson..... ...1804.
James Williams.......1805.
Samuel Ridout........1806.

Augustus Gassaway...1869.
John T. E. Hyde......1870.
James Munroe.......1871-4.
Arthur W. Wells....1875-6.
James II. Brown....1877-8.
Thomas E. Martin..1879-82.
Abram Claude... ...1883-7.

ANNAPOLIS CITY GOVERNMENT.

——: o :——

1 8 8 7 .

Mayor,
DR. ABRAM CLAUDE.
Counsellor,
JAMES REVELL.
Alderman,

1st Ward,	JOHN H. THOMAS,	DAVID O. PARLETT.
2nd "	JOHN B. FLOOD.	WM. E. BROOKS.
3rd "	JULIAN BREWER.	GRAFTON MUNROE.

Clerk,
ELIHU S. RILEY.
Treasurer,
LOUIS H. REHN.
City Commissioner.
EDGAR HUTTON.
Market Master,
MARTIN F. REVELL.
City Police,
ARTHUR MARTIN, Chief.
EZEKIEL A. MITCHELL, JAMES WATKINS,
C. N. STINCHCOMB, JOHN R. TYDINGS.

——: o :——

ANNAPOLIS VOLUNTEER FIRE DEPARTMENT.

Chief Marshal—WASHINGTON D. BASIL.
Engineer—ROBERT BELLIS.
Fireman—JAMES D. JOHNSON.

——:o:——

RESCUE HOSE COMPANY.

Assistant Marshal—FRANK MYERS.
Foreman—JOHN H. RAWLINGS.
1st Assistant Formean—J. W. ANDERSON.

2nd Asst. Foreman—W. T. JEWELL.
Secretary—A. C. SWEET.
Treasurer—T. IRVING BAKER.
Trustees—H. C. BASIL and J. W. WEAVER.

——: o :——

INDEPENDENT FIRE COMPANY, No. 2.

President—F. H. STOCKETT, Jr.
Vice-President—P. ELWOOD PORTER.
Secretary—RICHARD H. GREEN, Jr.
Treasurer—W. D. BASIL.
Foreman—JULIAN BREWER.
Asst. Marshal—GRAFTON MUNROE.

——:o:——

WATERWITCH HOOK AND LADDER COMPANY.

Foreman—JOHN L. BEALL.
Asst. Foreman—A. M. PARKINGSON.
1st Marshal—JOHN NASON.
2nd   "   —JAMES CANNON.
Recording Secretary—JAMES BURNS.
Treasurer—THOMAS EADES.

Annapolis, June 15, 1887.

HISTORY OF ANNAPOLIS.

[1608.] The Indians were the first to occupy the site of Annapolis. The records of their habitation remain in the occasional well-shapen arrow and finely-modelled tomahawk that the furrow of the farmer upturns in the vicinity, or the showers of heaven wash from the earth.

The white man, who first saw the fair hills of Severn, was the famous Captain John Smith, of Virginia, who, in 1608, made his celebrated voyage up the Chesapeake, and, from his description of his journey, passed the mouth of the Severn, and continued his travels to the Patapsco.

The settlement of Annapolis was due to events as novel as a romancer's imaginings.

[1648.] A Protestant governor ruled in Virginia, a Catholic proprietary reigned in Maryland. That liberality, which professors of a similar faith might be reasonably expected to exhibit to each other, was sadly wanting in the Churchmen of Virginia towards their Puritan brethren, and, in the year 1648, the authorities of Virginia, discovering that the Congregational or Independent Church, formed in 1642, had, by the aid of secret meetings, notwithstanding the laws against it, increased to one hundred and eighteen members, began a rigorous execution of their penal statutes against the Puritans. Their conventicle was broken up, and the members of it were scattered in different directions.

Near the close of the year 1648, the elder of the Independents, Mr. Durand, took refuge in Maryland. Negotiations for a settlement of the Independents very soon began, and the persecuted Puritans were offered an asylum in Maryland, provided they, who would hold land, would take the oath of allegiance to Lord Baltimore.

This was the oath :

"I do faithfully and truly acknowledge the right honorable Cecilius, lord baron of Baltimore, to be the true and absolute lord and proprietary of this province and country of Maryland and the islands thereunto belonging, and I do swear that I will bear true faith unto his lordship and to his heirs as to the true and absolute lords and proprietaries of the said province and islands thereunto belonging, and will not at any time by words or actions in public or in private, wit-

2

tingly or willingly, to the best of my understanding, any way derogate from, but will at all times as occasion shall require, to the utmost of my power defend, and maintain all such his said lordship's and his heir's right, title, interest, privilege, royal jurisdiction, prerogative, proprietary and dominion over and in the said province of Maryland and islands thereunto belonging, and over the people who are and shall be therein for the time being as are granted, or mentioned to be granted to his said lordship and his heirs by the king of England in his said lordship's patent of the said province under the great seal of England. I do also swear that I will, with all expedition, discover to his said lordship, or to his lieutenant, or other chief governor of the said province, for the time being, and also use my best endeavors to prevent any plot, conspiracy, or combination, which I shall know, or have cause to suspect, is, or shall be, intended against the person of his lordship, or which shall tend any ways to the disinherison or deprivation of his said lordship's or his said heir's their right title, royal jurisdiction, and dominion aforesaid, or any any part thereof, and I do swear that I will not either by myself, or by any other person, or persons, directly or indirectly take, accept, receive, purchase, or possess, any lands, tenements, or hereditaments within the said province of of Maryland, or the islands thereunto belonging, from any Indian or Indians to any other use, or uses, but to the use of his said lordship and his heirs, or knowingly from any other person or persons not deriving a legal title thereunto by, from, or under some grant from his said lordship or his said heirs legally passed, or under his or their great seal of the said province for the time being. So help me God, and by the contents of this book."*

[1649.] A small company from Richard Bennett's plantation, at Nansemond, in all about ten families, was the first to arrive on the Severn. At Greenbury's Point they made a settlement—a tract of two hundred and fifty acres was surveyed and divided into lots of fifteen acres, each settler receiving one lot, and Bennett securing the balance. As the Puritans came to the Chesapeake they took possession of unoccupied lands, and there was quite speedily a line of plantations extending from Herring Bay to Magothy river, a distance of twenty-five miles.

George Lynn Lachlin Davis says the town was originally intended to be erected at Greenbury's Point, and bases his opinion on the fact that the lots there were spoken of as the "Town Land at Greenbury's." The events that led to the subsequent selection of the present as the location of the town, have not been preserved.

Among those who had land surveyed in or about Annapolis at this period, was Matthew Howard, whose lot was surveyed July 3, 1650, on "ye south side of Severn river." Then came these allotments: For William Grouch, on Dec. 11, 1650, on "ye south side of Severn river," for Thos. Todd, July 8, 1651, "on ye south side of Severn river." "This," says the present Roll Book,† "is part of Annapolis Town, and part the Libertys begins at ye n. e. point of the town and extends along the river to ye first creek to ye west and then with back lines to ye beginning." Nov. 22, 1651, Locust Neck, on the south of the Severn, was surveyed for James Horner. Nov. 22, 1651, land was surveyed for Nicholas Wyat ; Nov. 15, 1651, for Richard Acton, near

* Bozman's Maryland, vol. 2, p. 639.
† Vol. 1, p. 65.

Severn river; Nov. 20, 1651, for Peter Porter, on the south side of Severn river; Nov. 25, 1651, to Thomas Howell, on south side of Severn river; Nov. 20, 1651, for James Warner, near Severn river; Dec. 4, 1658, for Thomas Gott, on south side of Severn river, (afterwards escheated to the State and bought by William Bladen.) Nov. 3, 1658, John Norwood was given the title to tracts of land on the south side of the Severn; Aug. 27, 1659, land was surveyed for Wm. Galloway, on the south side of Severn; Nov. 2, 1659, for John Colier, on south side of Severn; Dec. 16, 1661, for Saml. Ruthers, on south side of Severn river, near Howell's creek.

There were besides these many allottments on South river, one of which on Feb. 20, 1661, was of Wardridge, "for James Warner and Henry Ridgely, on the north side of South river, possessors of 200a., Coll. Henry Ridgely, 200a., ditto for his son Henry's orphans: 200a. for Charles Ridgely." The tomb of a descendant of these Ridgelys remains to this day on the same spot, upon which the early Ridgelys first settled.

Thomas Todd's lot is the only one of the early settlers' allottments that can be recognized as part of Annapolis. The water front of his lot began at a point on the harbor line and ran up to the mouth of Spa creek.

The Puritans, who formed the nucleus of this colony, which was destined to rule the province, were with but few exceptions the sturdy sons of the English yeomanry. Warrosquoyacke county, or Isle of Wight, afterward called Norfolk county, Virginia, lying on the south of the James, was the centre of the Puritan district, from whence the settlers of Providence came. Edward Bennett, a wealthy London merchant, who had obtained in 1621, a large grant of land on the Nansemond river, south of the James, when he came to Virginia, had brought with him considerable company of Puritans. Edward Bennett was their patriarch, Rev. William Bennett, a relative, their spiritual leader, and Richard Bennett, son of Edward, became the Moses of the Virginia Puritans when they made their exodus from Virginia to Maryland.‡

Descended from this hardy stock of sturdiest English, indoctrinated in the tenets of their austere faith, inheritors of trials and persecutions, their subsequent rebellious and courageous conduct in Maryland was the natural sequence of their blood, religion, and education.

Soon after their arrival at Providence, Gov. Stone urged upon the uritans the oath of allegiance to Lord Baltimore, which he told them f they did not take, they must have no land, nor abiding in the ovince."

The Puritans peremptorily refused to take the oath of allegiance, haggling especially at the expressions "royal jurisdiction" and "absolute dominion," which latter "they exceedingly scrupled." They objected to the oath, also, because "they must swear to uphold that government and those officers who were sworn to countenance and uphold anti-Christ—in plain words expressed in the officer's oath—the Roman Catholic religion."

Lord Baltimore's friend, Mr. John Langford, very aptly replied to these objections that "there was nothing promised by my lord or Captain Stone to them, but what was performed. They were first ac-

‡ A Puritan Colony in Maryland, p. 7.

quainted by Captain Stone before they came there with that oath of
fidelity, which was to be taken by those who would have any land
there from his lordship; nor had they any regret to the oath, till they
were as much refreshed with their entertainment there, as the snake
in the fable was with the countryman's breast: for which some of
them are equally thankful. But it is now, it seems, thought, by some
of these people, too much below them to take an oath to the lord proprietary of that province, though many Protestants, of much better
quality, have taken it, and, (which is more than can be hoped for some
of these men,) kept it. As to the government there, they knew it
very well before they came thither; and, if they had not liked it,
they might have forborne coming or staying there: for they were never
forced to either. The chief officers, under my lord there, are Protestants. The jurisdiction exercised there by them is no other than
what is warranted by his lordship's patent of that province, which
gives him the power and privileges of a count palatine there, depending on the supreme authority of England, with power to make laws
with the people's consent; without which powers and privileges his
lordship would not have undertaken that plantation, and have been
at so great a charge, and run so many hazards he hath done for it."
* * * "There are none there sworn to uphold anti-Christ, as Mr.
Strong falsely suggests; nor doth the oath of fidelity bind any man
to maintain any other jurisdiction or dominion of my lord's, than
what is granted by his patent. Though some of these people (it
seems) think it unfit that my lord should have such a jurisdiction and
dominion there, yet they, it seems, by their arrogant and insolent proceedings, think it fit for them to exercise farre more absolute jurisdiction and dominion there than my lord Baltimore ever did; nor are
they contented with fredom for themselves of conscience, person and
estate, (all of which are established to them by law there and enjoyed
by them in as ample manner as ever any people did in any place in the
world,) unless they may have the liberty to debarr others from the
like freedom, and that they may domineer and do what they please."**

So obstinately did these people refuse to comply with the obligations they took to obtain an asylum in Maryland, they remained entirely outside the pale of lord Baltimore's government, and obstructed
the formation of a county, for a year.

** Bozman's Maryland, vol. 2, p 371.

CHAPTER II.

FORMATION OF ANNE ARUNDEL COUNTY.

[1650.] The Puritans of Providence by April, 1650, had recovered
sufficiently from their scruples of conscience to elect delegates to the
General Assembly, that convened at St. Mary's on the 6th of that
month.

The Governor's return from Providence was, "By the lieutenant, &c., of Maryland. The freeman of that part of this province of Maryland, now called Providence, being by my appointment duly summoned to this present assembly, did unanimously make choice of Mr. Puddington and Mr. James Cox, for their burgesses, I being there in person at the time."

The reconciliation effected by Gov. Stone promised to be permanent. The House chose Mr. James Cox, of Providence, their speaker, and the Assembly passed the following :—

"An Act for the erecting of Providence into a county by the name of Annarundell county.

"Be it enacted by the Lord Proprietary, by and with the assent and approbation of the Upper and Lower House of this Assembly, That, that part of the Province of Maryland, on the west side of the Bay of Chessopeack, over against the Isle of Kent, formerly called by the name of Providence by the inhabitants there residing and inhabiting this yeare, shall henceforth be created into a shire, or county, by the name of Annarundell county, and by that name hereafter to be ever called."

It was probably so called from the maiden name of Lady Baltimore, then lately deceased, Lady Anne Arundel, the daughter of Lord Arundel, of Wardour, whom Cecilius, Lord Baltimore, had married.*

After the adjournment of the General Assembly, Governor Stone, in July, 1650, visited Providence, and organized it into a county, under the name of Anne Arundel.

A commission was issued by the Governor to "Mr. Edward Lloyd, gentleman," appointing him "to be commander of Anne Arundel county, until the Lord Proprietary should signify to the contrary." James Homewood, Thomas Meares, Thomas Marsh, George Puddington, Matthew Hawkins, James Merryman, and Henry Catlyn were, with Commander Lloyd, appointed commissioners of the county.

The commission of Commander Lloyd gave him, with the approval of the other commissioners, the right to issue "warrants and commissions, and for all other matters of judicature, with whom you, Commander Lloyd, are to consult in all matters of importance concerning your said county."

Commander Lloyd's duties, as by his commission declared, were "to call and appoint courts to be kept within and for the said county ; in which courts you, the said commander, or your deputy, (being one of the said commissioners,) with any three or more, of the said commissioners there present from time to time, to hold pleas, and finally to determine all causes and actions whatsoever, civil, happening or arising between any of the inhabitants of the said county, of what value soever, saving and reserving to all and every, the inhabitants of said county and others, liberty of appeal from the county court to the provincial court, in any civil cause or action to the value of £20 sterling or 2,000lb tobacco, and upwards, the party so appealing first putting in sufficient security to the said county court to be answerable for treble damages in case the order of judgment of the said county court made in that cause, shall happen to be confirmed upon hearing by the provincial court ; and also to hear and determine all matters

* Ridgely's Annals o... Annapolis, p. 37.

criminal, happening and committed in the said county, which may be
heard by justices of the peace in any county in England, in their
courts of session, not extending to life or member, and further to do,
use, and execute all manner of jurisdiction and authority whatsoever,
for the conservation of the peace within the said county, as any justice of the peace in England may, or ought to do, by virtue of his
commission for the peace ; further likewise authorizing you the said
commander, or your deputy, to elect and appoint all necessary officers
for the execution of justice and conservation of the peace there, with
allowance of such fees as are usually belonging to the same or like
officers in Virginia ; and to do all other things and acts, which shall
be necessary for the execution of the powers and jurisdiction hereby
committed to you."†

This commission was signed by Gov. Stone at Providence, July 30, 1650.

The day before the above was issued, Gov. Stone had given a commission to the Commander of Anne Arundel authorizing him "to grant
warrants for land within the said county to adventurers or planters,
according to his lordship's conditions of plantation, whereupon such
land shall happen to be due to such adventurers or planters respectively." "The warrants, together with the particular demands or as-
signment upon which the same shall be granted, to be entered upon record by his lordship's secretary of the said province."

Though the political storm had calmed, all was not well in the infant
colony. The Indian was still a near neighbor, and though generally
peaceable, his savage nature had displayed itself in the murder of some
of the citizens of the new county in a most cruel and inhuman manner.

These murderers were supposed to be Susquehannocks, a powerful
and war like tribe, who inhabited all that section which extends from
the Patuxent to the Susquehanna river on the Western Shore, and all
that part that lies between the Choptank and Susquehanna rivers on
the Eastern side of the bay.

To punish the murderers and their abettors, the General Assembly
of 1650, enacted that "Whereas, certain Indians these last year have
most wickedly and barberously murthered an English inhabitant of
the county of Kent and other inhabitants likewise since, in Anne
Arundel county. Be it therefore ordered, that the Governor, with
the advice of the council, or the major part of them, shall have power,
in case such Indians, who have committed such barberous and wicked
murders, shall not be sent in, after demand made of them, to the
government here to receive such punishment as is due for such offence,
to press men, and to appoint such allowance for their pay, and to
make war upon the nations of Indians refusing to deliver up those offenders as aforesaid, as in in his and their best discretion, shall be
thought fit ; the charge of which was to be laid by an equal assessment on the persons and estates of all the inhabitants of this province."

No account has come down to us of the result of these preparations,
although the silence of our records raises the presumption that the
traditional peace of the colony with the Indians was also unbroken in
this case.

Meanwhile, with the usual activity of Englishmen, the colony
carried on a brisk trade with those Indians whose peaceable methods
led them in the avenues of barter and exchange.

† Bozman's Maryland, vol 2, p 408.
‡ Bozman's Maryland, vol. 2, p. 409.

CHAPTER III.

THE PURITANS REFUSE TO SEND DELEGATES TO THE LEGISLATURE OF 1651.

The Puritans who settled at Annapolis, were a restless set with itching ears, who seemed never so satisfied as when they were in open opposition to the powers that were.

The General Assembly of 1650 had modified the oath of allegiance to Lord Baltimore, carefully expunging the objectionable phrases "absolute lord" and "royal jurisdiction." In their place was inserted "that they would defend and maintain all such his lordship's just and lawful right, title, interest, privileges, jurisdictions, prerogatives, propriety, and dominion over and in the said province, &c., not any wise understood to infringe or prejudice liberty of conscience in point of religion."

This, for a time, tranquilized the settlers at Providence, but the next year, 1651, when they were called upon to send delegates to the General Assembly, they peremptorily refused.

The reason for this refusal has not been preserved, but it is generally thought it was because the Puritans believed that the proprietary government would be overthrown by Cromwell, who was steadily advancing to power.

Lord Baltimore heard of the conduct of the Puritans with just indignation. Under date of August 20, 1651, he wrote to "William Stone, Esq., his lieutenant of his said province of Maryland, and to his right trusty and well-beloved, the Upper and Lower Houses of his General Assembly there, and to all other his officers and inhabitants of his province," expressing his "wonder at a message which he understood was lately sent by one Mr. Lloyd, from some lately seated at Anne Arundel within his said province of Maryland to his General Assembly, held at St. Mary's in March last, and his unwillingness to impute either to the author or deliverer thereof so malign a sense of ingratitude and other ill-affections as it may seem to bear; conceiving rather, that it proceeded from some apprehensions in them at the time, grounded upon some reports in these parts of a dissolution or resignation here, (in England) of his patent and right to that province." After declaring these rumors to be false and, referring the Puritans to Mr. Harrison, their former pastor, who was then in England, for the truth of his assertions, Lord Baltimore added, "in consideration of a better compliance from these people with his government there for the future, he should not any further expostulate, or make any further reflection on that message, till further occasion given him by them, and if such admonition did not prevail, then that he would make use of his authority, with the assistance of well-affected persons, to compel such factious and turbulent spirits to a better compliance with the lawful government there." He accordingly willed and required "his lieutenant to proceed with all such as shall be for the future refactory on that kind ; and in case any of the English inhabitants of that province should at any time hereafter refuse or neglect to send burgesses to our General Assembly there, being lawfully summoned for that purpose, he wills and requires all the members of the said Assembly, which shall lawfully meet upon such summons to proceed, as they ought, as they may lawfully do, in all business belonging to the General Assembly there, notwithstanding any such refusal, or neglect as aforesaid, and to fine all such refusers or neglectors according to their demerits ; and moreover, in case of their persistency in such refusal or neglect, then, that they be declared enemies to the public peace of the province, and rebels to the lawful government thereof, and be proceeded against accordingly.''*

The conduct of these Puritans was especially ungrateful, since, received by Lord Baltimore when professors of the Protestant religion had refused them domicil, their asylum in Maryland had cost Lord Baltimore the enmity of Charles II, then in exile upon the continent. So great was the displeasure of the young king, that Lord Baltimore had given the Puritans a settlement in Maryland, that he, the natural friend of the proprietary, in spite of Lord Baltimore's undoubted right to name his lieutenant in the province, appointed Sir William Davenant, Governor of Maryland, alleging in the commission that Davenant was so appointed ''because the Lord Baltimore did visibly adhere to the rebels in England, and admitted all kinds of sectaries and schismatics, and ill-affected persons in that province.''†

* Bozman's Maryland, vol. 2, p. 416.
† Same p. 410.

CHAPTER IV.

THE ANIMOSITIES OF THE OLD WORLD TRANSPLANTED IN THE NEW.

[1649.] In 1649, when Charles I was executed, Thomas Greene, who was acting Governor during the absence of Governor Stone, caused the Prince of Wales to be proclaimed in Maryland as the ''undoubted, rightful heir to all his father's dominions.'' This proclamation was issued on the 15th of November, and on the same day another was published ''to further the common rejoicing of the inhabitants upon that occasion,'' declaring a general pardon to all the inhabitants of the province, who had committed any criminal offence.*

This proclamation and the general rejoicing were not in consonance with the sentiments of the Puritan adventurers on the banks of the Severn, and this latent feeling was exhibited in their refusal to send delegates to the General Assembly, and, a little later, a more forcible proof of their political animosities was given.

The cause of the commonwealth triumphant in England, Cromwell turned his attention to the American plantations, and commissioners were sent out to take possession of all that were unfavorable to the Protector. Maryland was not named in the Act of Parliament, but Lord Baltimore's enemies contrived to have that colony mentioned in the instructions to the commissioners.

* Ridgely's Annals of Annapolis, p. 35.

Richard Bennett and the notorious William Claiborne, who had given so much trouble to the infant colony of Maryland, were two of the commissioners.

[1652.] In March, 1652, at the head of an armed force, the commissioners entered Maryland. They proposed to Governor Stone and the council of the province, "that they should all remain in their places, conforming themselves to the laws of the commonwealth of England in point of government only, and not infringing the Lord Baltimore's just rights." Governor Stone and the balance of Lord Baltimore's officers of government "declared that they did in all humility submit themselves to the government of the commonwealth of England, in chiefe under God."

From the proposition, however, to issue writs in the name of the commonwealth instead of Lord Baltimore, Gov. Stone and his counsellors "desired to be excused, because they did conceive the parliament intended not to divest the Lord Baltimore of his right in his province, and that they understood out of England, that the Council of State intended not, that any alteration should be made in Maryland; that the King's name was never used heretofore in said writs, but that they had always been in the name of the lord proprietary, according to the privileges of his patent ever since the beginning of that plantation."

"Whereupon," says Mr. John Langford, "the said commissioners demanded of Captain Stone the Lord Baltimore commission to him; which he showed them; and, then without any other cause at all, they detained it, and removed him and his lordship's other officers out of their employment in the province under him, and appointed others to manage the government of Maryland, independent of his lordship."

Bennett and Claiborne ordered "that all writs, warrants, and process whatsoever, be issued forth in the name of the keepers of the liberty of England; and that they be signed under the hand of one or more of the council hereafter named, viz :—Robert Brooke, Esq., Col. Francis Yardley, Mr. Job Chandler, Captain Edward Windham, Mr. Richard Preston, and Lieutenant Richard Banks."

The new council, or any two or more of its members, was empowered to hold courts, and to direct and govern the affairs of the province.

Thus the disaster, that Lord Baltimore, by his personal intercession with parliament, had been able to ward off in the legislative branch, was consummated by his enemies through the executive power of the Council of State.

Maryland reduced to subjection, the commissioners returned to Virginia, where Bennett was made Governor, and Claiborne, Secretary of State.

Handsomely provided for in Virginia, the commissioners visited Maryland to rivet more firmly their hold upon it. Discovering that Governor Stone was exceedingly popular with the people, as well as affable to the commissioners, Bennett and Claiborne resolved to make him Governor once more. In order to justify their actions in ousting him at their previous visit, they declared, in their proclamation restoring Governor Stone to his office, and Mr. Hatton as Secretary of State, that these were left out of office "upon some misapprehension or misunderstanding, as they alleged, in that particular of issuing out writs and all other process whatever, in the name of the liberties of England by authority of parliament," that Captain Stone was "contented to reassume his former place," on condition that he might "reserve and save to himself, as also to the aforesaid Mr. Thomas Hatton, Robert Brooke, Esq., and Captain John Price, their oaths made to the Lord Baltimore, lord proprietor of this province, until the pleasure of the State of England be further known."†

The proclamation bore date of June 28th, 1652.

† Bozman's Maryland, vol. 2, p. 447.

CHAPTER V.

PROVIDENCE SENDS A PETITION TO THE COMMISSIONERS OF THE COMMONWEALTH.

[1653.] Whilst Maryland was made a shuttle-cock in the hands of opposing forces, the Puritans of Severn addressed a petition—

"To Honorable, Richard Bennett and Col. William Claiborne, Esqrs., Commissioners of the Commonwealth of England for Virginia and Maryland." It was styled: "The Humble Petition of the Commissioners and Inhabitants of Severne, *alias* Ann Arundel county, sheweth." It read: "That whereas, we were invited and encouraged by Captain Stone, the Lord Baltimore's Governor of Maryland, to remove ourselves and estates into his province, with promise of enjoying the liberty of consciences in matter of religion, and all other privileges of English subjects. And your petitioners did upon this ground, with great cost, labor, and danger, remove ourselves, and have been at great charges in building and clearing: Now the Lord Baltimore imposeth an oath upon us by proclamation, which he requireth his Lieutenant forthwith to publish; which, if we do not take within three months after publication, all our lands are to be seized for his lordship's use. This oath we conceive not agreeable to the terms on which we came hither, nor to the liberty of our consciences as Christians and free subjects of the Commonwealth of England: Neither can we be persuaded in our consciences by any light of God, or engagement upon us, to such an oath; but rather humbly conceive it to be a very real grievance and such an oppression as we are not able to bear; neither do we see by what lawful power such an oath, with such extreme penalties can by his Lordship be exacted of us who are free subjects of the Commonwealth of England, and have taken the Engagement to them. We have complained of this grievance to the late Honorable Councel of State, in a petition subscribed by us, which never received an answer, such as might clear the lawfulness of such, his proceedings with us, but an aspersion cast upon us of being factious fellows; neither have we received any conviction of our error in not taking the said oath, nor order by that power, before whom our petition is still depending, to take it hereafter; neither can we believe that the Commonwealth of England will ever expose us to such a manifest and real bondage (who assert themselves, the maintainers of the lawful liberties of the subject,) as to make us swear absolute subjection to a Government, where the Ministers of State are bound by oath to countenance and defend the Roman Popish Religion, which we apprehend to be contrary to the Fundamental Law of England, the covenant taken in the three Kingdoms, and the conscience of true English, subjects and doth carry on an arbitrary power, so as whatever is done by the people at great costs in assemblies, for the good of the people, is liable to be made null by the negative voice of his Lordship. But affirmative propositions and commands are incessantly urged, and must not be denied.

"In Consideration, whereof, we humbly tender our Condition and Distraction, upon this occasion, falling upon the hearts of the people, to your view and consideration, intreating your honors to relieve us according to the Cause and Power wherewith you are entrusted by the Commonwealth of England. We rather, because upon such an exigent at this, we have none to flie to but yourselves, the Honorable Commissioners of the Commonwealth of England; not doubting but God will direct you into what his mind and will is in this matter concerning us, and that you will faithfully apply yourselves to our redress in what is just and our lawful liberty, which is the prayer of your poor petitioners. Severn River, the 3d of January, 1653."*

This petition was signed by Edward Lloyd and seventy-seven others of the housekeepers, freemen, and inhabitants of Severn.

The people of north Patuxent sent a similar petition under date of March 1st, 1653. This was signed by Richard Preston and sixty others. On March 12, 1653, Bennett and Clarborne returned an encouraging answer to the petitions from Severn and Patuxent, in which reply they counselled that the settlers "continue in your due obedience to the Commonwealth of England, in such manner as you, and they, were then appointed and engaged; and not to be drawn aside from the same upon any pretence of such uncertain relations as we hear are divulged among you. To which we expect your real conformity, as you will answer the contrary; notwithstanding any pretence of power from Lord Baltimore's Agents, or any other whatsoever to the contrary."

* Force's Tracts, vol. 2, ch. IX. p. 28.

------------◄ ● ►------------

CHAPTER VI.

Gov. Stone Proclaims the Puritans to be Rebels.

[1654.] Information of Cromwell's elevation to the protectorate having been received Governor Stone proclaimed him protector on the 6th of June, 1654. The same year, on the 4th of July, Governor Stone, in public proclamation, charged the commissioners, Bennett and Claiborne, and the whole Puritan party, mostly of Anne Arundel, with "drawing away the people, and leading them into faction, sedition, and rebellion against the Lord Baltimore."

This proclamation is not now extant, but Mr. Leonard Strong, a Puritan writer and a leading citizen of Providence, contemporaneous with the document, says that the paper called ''that which was done by commission from the Council of State in England, rebellion against the Lord Baltimore; and those, that were actors in it, factions and seditious persons, which was done by a proclamation full of railing terms, published at Providence in the church meeting.''[*]

Bennett and Claiborne promptly returned to Maryland. Eleven days from the date of Gov. Stone's proclamation, ''they applied themselves to Captain William Stone,[†] the Governor, and Council of Maryland,'' ''in a peaceable and loving way to persuade them into their due and promised obedience to the commonwealth of England.''[‡]

The commissioners, in their published statement of the occurrence, declared that Governor and Council, ''returning only opprobious and incivil language, presently mustered his whole power of men and soldiers in arms, intending to surprise the said commissioners, and (as could be imagined) to destroy all those that had refused the said unlawful oath, and only kept themselves in their due obedience to the commonwealth of England under which they were reduced and settled by the parliament's authority and commission. Then the said commissioners, in quiet and peaceable manner, with some of the people of Patuxent and Severn went over the river of Patuxent, and there at length received a message from the said captain Stone, that the next day he would meet and treat in the woods; and thereupon being in some fear of a party come from Virginia, he condescended to lay down his power, lately assumed from the lord Baltimore and to submit, (as he had once before done) to such government as the commissioners should appoint under his highness the lord protector.''

* Bozman's Maryland, vol. 2, p. 501.
†Statement of the Commissioners.
‡Leonard Strong.

CHAPTER VII.

AN INDIAN TREATY MADE ON THE SEVERN.

[1652.] The dissensions of the Maryland colonists did not prevent them from looking to the peace of State with the Indians.

The Governor and Council, sitting as a court, on the 28th of June, 1652, Wm. Stone, Governor, Thomas Hatton, Secretary, and Robert Brooke, Col. Francis Yardley, Job Chandler, and Richard Preston, members, being present, passed the following:

''Whereas, this court is informed, that the Susquehanna Indians have a long time desired, and much pressed for the conclusion of a peace with the government and inhabitants of this province, which as is now conceived, may tend very much to the safety and advantage of the inhabitants here, if advisedly effected: It is, therefore, ordered,.

and the court doth hereby give full power and authority unto Richard
Bennett, Esq., Mr. Edward Lloyd, Captain William Fuller, Mr.
Thomas Marsh and Mr. Leonard Strong, or and three or more of them
whereof the said Richard Bennett, Esqr., to be one, at such time and
place as they may think convenient, to consult and treat with the said
Susquehanna Indians, and by the use of all lawful and fitting means,
(if they can,) to conclude a league and peace, on the behalf of this
government and the inhabitants thereof, with the said Susquehanna
Indians, so as the peace, safety, and advantage of the inhabitants
here may be, (so far as in them lies,) thereby advanced, settled, and
preserved."

All of the persons named as commissioners were, with the exception
of Richard Bennett, inhabitants of Providence.* The commissioners
proceeded at once to their work. On the fifth of July following, a
treaty of peace was concluded with the Susquehannas, "at the River
of Severn, in the Province of Maryland."

It is not difficult to picture the canoe of the formidable Susquehannas, decked with feathers and paint, armed with bow and tomahawk,
dashing with daring skillfulness from Greenbury's to Sycamore point,
and thence to Windmill, and out again to the offing, and fading in the
dim sunset up the Chesapeake before the steady gaze of the sturdy
Puritans, nor the ripple of excitement that moved the little settlement when these formidable savages appeared in its midst.

The following is an exact copy of the treaty made on the Severn,
and the quaint style of expression and homely phrases cast a ruddy
glare of information upon the environs of the early inhabitants
of the capital :

"Articles of peace and friendship treated and agreed upon the 5th
day of July, 1652, between the English nation in the province of
Maryland on the one party, and the Indian nation of Sasquesahanogh
on the other parties, as followeth :

"1stly. That the English nation shall have, hould, and enjoy to
them, their heires, and assigns for ever, all the land lying from Patuxent river unto Palmer's island on the western side of the bay of
Chesapeake, and from Choptank river to the northeast branch, which
lyes to the northward of Elke river on the eastern side of the said bay,
with all the islands, rivers, creeks, ——† fish, fowl, dear, elk, and
whatsoever else to the same belonging, excepting the isle of Kent and
Palmer's island, which belong to Captain Claiborne. But, nevertheless, it shall be lawful for the aforesaid English or Indians to build a
house or fort for trade or any such like use or occasion at any tyme
upon Palmer's island.

"2dly. That if any damage or injury be done on either side at any
tyme hereafter, either by the English or Indians aforesaid, or by any
other allies, confederates, tributaries, or servants, that reparation be
made and satisfaction given from each other from tyme to tyme as the
case requires, and as in reason should be done between those that are
friends, and that desire soe to continue.

"3dly. That if any the people or servants belonging to the English or to the Indians shall goe away or run away from either side, they
shall not be concealed, or kept away from each other. But shall, with all

* Now Annapolis.
† A word not legible in the record.

convenient speede, be returned back, and brought home. And satisfaction to be made in a reasonable way for transportation by land or water to those that bring them in.

"4thly. That, upon any occasion of business to the English, or any message or the like, the Indians shall come by water and not by land. That there shall not be above eight or ten at the most at one tyme. And that they bring with them the token given them by the English for that purpose, by which they may be known and entertained. As also that the English on their partes, when they send to the Indians the messenger shall carry the token which wee have received from them.

"5thly. And lastly, these articles and every particular of them shall be really and invioably observed, kept, and performed by the two nations, before named, and by all the people belonging to them, or that are in amity with them, for ever to the end of the world. And that all former injuries being buried, and forgotten from henceforward, they doe promise and agree to walke together and carry one towards another in all things as friends, and to assist one another accordingly. But if it so happen at any tyme hereafter that either party is weary of the peace, and intends war, then that the same shall be signified and mode knowne each to other by sending in, and delivering up his writing before any Act of hostility or enmity be done or attempted, and that twenty days warning thereof be given beforehand.

"These several articles were solemnly and mutually debated and concluded at the river of Severne, in the province of Maryland, by Richard Bennett, Esquire, Mr. Edward Lloyde, Capn. William Fuller. Mr. Thomas Marsh, and Mr. Leonard Strong, commissioners, authorized and appointed by the governor and councell of the aforesaid province. And by Sawahegeh, treasurer, Auroghtaregh, Scarhuhadigh, Ruthchogah, and Nathheldianch, warr captaines and councillors of Sasquehanogh, commissionors, appointed and sent for that purpose by the nation and state of Sasquehanogh. All were fully ratified, done, and confirmed by several presents, gifts, and tokens of friendship mutually given, received, and accepted on both sides. In witness whereof the aforesaid commissioners, in behalf of the aforesaid nation have hereunto sett their hands and seales the day and the yeare above written.

"Ri. Bennett—Edw. Lloyd—Thos. Marsh—Will. Fuller,—Leo. Strong.   Locus

The mark of ⊐   X
        Sawahegeh   Sigilli.
The mark of ⊲
        Auroghtaregh."
The mark of   F   Ruthchogah.
                     V
The mark of |
                     Λ   Scarhuhadigh.
The mark of WW Nathheldianch.

                                              Locus
William Lawson,   X
                                              Sigilli.

Iafer Peter—for the Sweades's Governors Witness."‡

‡ Council Proceedings, Lib. II. II., p. 62.

CHAPTER VIII.
PREPARATIONS FOR WAR.

[1654.] Frequent and violent changes in the government of the province had their legitimate sequence.

On the last reducement of the Maryland government by Bennett and Claiborne. July 15, 1654, they had appointed. Captain William Fuller, Mr. Richard Preston, Mr. William Durand, Mr. Edward Lloyd. Captain John Smith. Mr. Leonard Strong, John Lawson, Mr. John Hatch, Mr. Richard Wells. and Mr. Richard Ewen, or any four of them, whereof Captain William Fuller, Mr. Richard Preston. or Mr. William Durand, to be always one, to be commissioners for the well-ordering, directing, and governing the affairs of Maryland. under his highness, the lord protector of England, Scotland, Ireland. and the dominions thereof, and in his name only, and no other." The commission gave authority to hold courts. to summon an assembly, and prohibited Roman Catholics from voting.

The names in, and spirit of. the commission, bear evidence that the majority of the commissioners were Puritans of Providence and its adjacent settlements.

Captain Fuller and his associates summoned a Legislature, and it began its sessions at Patuxent, October 20th, 1654, the assembly sitting as one house. The most remarkable law of this Legislature was the one that "enacted and declared that none who profess and exercise the Popish (commonly called the Roman Catholic) religion can be protected in this province by the laws of England formerly established and yet unrepealed !"

Never had the fable of the camel who asked to put his nose in the Arab's tent and who finally turned the owner out, been more completely realized than it was with the Puritans and Catholics of Maryland. Stringent laws were passed by the same assembly against drunkenness, swearing, false reports, slandering, and tale bearing, violations of the Sabbath, and acts of adultery and fornication.

An act was also passed changing the name of Anne Arundel county to the County of Providence, and prescribing the bounds thereof to be Herring-Creek, including all the plantations and lands unto the bounds of Patuxent county, (supposed to be the present Calvert,) that is. to a creek called "Mr. Marshe's Creek, otherwise called Oyster Creek."

[1655.] All was peace in the province until January, 1655, when the ship *Golden Fortune*. Capt. Tilman, arrived in Maryland. On it came a gentleman named Eltonhead, who brought the information "that the lord Baltimore kept his patent and that his highness, (the lord protector,) had neither taken the lord Baltimore's patent from him, nor his land."

By the same ship, it appears, came a letter from lord Baltimore upbraiding Gov. Stone for "resigning up his government unto the hands of the lord protector and commonwealth of England, without striking one stroke."

Gov. Stone needed no more encouragement to act. He re-assumed the duties of Governor under his former commission, and determined to make a manly struggle to obtain possession of the government of the province. He proceeded immediately to issue military commissions to officers, and to organize an armed force in the loyal county of St. Mary's.

Which of the two sides, Lord Baltimore's or the Commissioners', Cromwell sustained is difficult to tell, in view of two letters on the subject one written January 12th, 1655, and the other September 26th, which are palpable contradictions of each other.

But this conflict of rights had gone so far, war, and not words, could only decide it.

The overt act was committed by Gov. Stone, who despatched Mr. John Hammond to recover the records of the province and to seize a magazine of arms and ammunition, gathered at Mr. Richard Preston's house at Patuxent, and belonging to the Puritans.

Mr. Hammond says: ''I went unarmed amongst the Sons of Thunder, only three or four to row me, and despite all their braves of raising the country, calling in his servants to apprehend me, threatened me with the severity of their new made law, myself alone seized, and carried away the Records in defiance.''

The Puritan account of these proceedings is quaint. Mr. Leonard Strong wrote : ''Then (that is on the arrival of the news by the *Golden Fortune*,) the Lord Baltimore's officers, and the popish party began to divulge abroad, and boast much of power, which came in that ship from his highness, the lord protector, to confirm the Lord Baltimore's patent to him, and to re-establish his officers in their former places under him ; which pretended power they assumed to themselves ; Captain Stone and the rest giving out threatening speeches. That now the rebels at Patuxent and Severne should know that he was governor again : giving order. That neither Act of the said Assembly should be observed, nor writ from the power established by the commissioners aforesaid obeyed,''—(to wit, writs in the name of Captain Fuller and others, to whom Bennett and Claiborne had committed the powers of government, as before cited,) ''but what should issue forth in the name of the lord proprietary, viz., lord Baltimore. And further, the said Captain Stone gave several commissions to the papists and other desperate and bloody fellows, to muster and raise men in arms to be ready upon all occasions, giving out that he would go to Patuxent, and seize the records of the province at the place where they were appointed to be kept by an Act of the Assembly, and to apprehend Mr. Richard Preston also, at whose house they were : which shortly was effected by virtue of a warrant in Captain Stone's name, without proclaiming, or shewing and power by which he acted such high robbers, But in threatening speeches declared, that they would have the government ; and for the terror of others, would hang some of the commissioners, which were entrusted with the government by the commissioners of the commmonwealth of England, under his highness, the lord protector, namely, Captain William Fuller, Mr. Richard Preston, and Mr. William Durand.''

CHAPTER IX.
THE BATTLE OF THE SEVERN.

[1655.] About the 20th of March, 1655, Gov. Stone started from St. Mary's to bring the unruly Puritans of Providence into subjection to Lord Baltimore's government. The forces of the Governor consisted of 130 men. Part of these marched by land up the southern peninsula, and were ferried across the mouths of rivers and creeks in eleven or twelve small boats which the Governor had pressed into his service.

Advised of the advance of Gov. Stone's forces, the Puritans sent messengers to meet the Governor, whom they found near Herring Bay,* in Anne Arundel.

Roger Heameans who took part in the engagement that followed, says:

"A message having been sent to demand his power and the ground of such his proceedings.

"The second message to him being such low terms, that those that sent it were grieved at their hearts that ever it went out of their hands; which was as followeth :

"For Captain William Stone, Esq.:

"Sir :—The people of these parts have met together, and considered the present transactions on your part, and have not a little marvelled that no other answer of the last message hath been made, than what tendred rather to make men desperate than conformable; yet being desirous of peace, do once again present to your serious consideration these ensuing proposals, as the mind of the people :

"1. If you will govern us so as we may enjoy the liberty of English subjects.

"2. And that we be, and remain indempnified in respect of our engagement, and all former acts relating to the reducement and government.

"3. That those who are minded to depart the province, may freely do it without any prejudice to themselves or estate; we are content to own yourself as governor, and submit to your government. If not, we are resolved to commit ourselves into the hands of God, and rather die like men, than be made slaves.

WILL. DURAND, Secretary.

"But no answer to this was returned, but the same paper in scorn sent back again."

These pacific offers were carried by six men in a boat. The proposals of peace were not only rejected, but the messengers were seized as captives of war. Three of them, however, contrived to escape, and took back to Providence the story of their treatment, and the intentions of Captain Stone upon the settlement.

On the rejection of their offer of peace, the Puritans prepared to put in execution their resolve "to die like men, rather than be made slaves."

Gov. Stone, in the meanwhile, behaved himself in a fustian style at Herring Bay, seizing one of the commissioners of State, and forcing

* Then called Herring Creek.

3

"another of quality to fly for his life, having threatened to hang him up to his own door; and not finding the man, affrighted his wife, and plundered the house of ammunition and provision, threatning still what they would do to the people at Providence, and that they would force the rebellious, factious Roundheads to submit, and then they would show their power."[*]

Gov. Stone, moving nearer to Annapolis, sent forward Dr. Luke Barber with a proclamation which is not extant. Dr. Barber, in describing his envoyage to Cromwell, says that "in the end of this declaration the governor did protest, as in the presence of Almighty God, that he came not in a hostile way to do them any hurt, but sought by all means possible, to reclaim them by faire meanes; and to my knowledge at the sending out of parties, (as occasion served,) he gave strict command, that if they met any of the Ann Arundel men, they should not fire the first gun, nor upon paine of death plunder any. These were his actings to my knowledge upon the march."

Whilst these messages were passing between the opposing forces, the men of St. Mary's were rapidly closing the gap between them and Providence.

Dr. Barber and his companion, Mr. Coursey, were permitted to read the document they brought from Gov. Stone, "but having no other treaty to offer, they were quietly dismissed to their own company," to whom it seems they did not return. Mr. Packer, from Gov. Stone, the next day followed Dr. Barber. After Mr. Packer, came Mr. Coursey, presumably on the same errand. None of them returned to Gov. Stone, who, left in ignorance as to the intentions of the Puritans, pushed on to the Severn, at the mouth of which, on the 24th of March he arrived "about the shutting of the eve," "with eleven or twelve vessels, greater and lesser, in which their whole army was wafted."[†]

On the appearance of Gov. Stone and his fleet at the mouth of the Severn, Capt. Fuller, the commander of the Puritans, called his councillors together, and sent his secretary, Mr. William Durand, and another of his councillors, on board the merchant ship, Golden Lyon, Roger Heamans, captain, then lying in the harbor. There they made a requisition upon the captain, for the services of himself, his ship, and its crew, in defence of the town. Durand, at the same time, posted on the mainmast a proclamation by which Heamans "was required in the name of the Lord Protector and commonwealth of England, and for the maintenance of the just liberties, lives, and estates of the free subjects thereof, against all usurped power, to be aiding and assisting in this service." Heamans manifested a real or fictitious unwillingness to take part in the controversy, but says, "we are seeing the equity of the cause, and the groundless proceedings of the enemy, he offered himself, ship, and men, for that service, to be directed by the said councillors." Dr. Barber, a partizan of Gov. Stone, says, Heamans was hired by the Puritans to take the part he afterward played.

Heamans relates that, on seeing the "company of troops and boats marching towards the ship, the council on board, and the ship's company, would have made shot at them, but this relator commanded them to hold, and went himself upon the poop on the stern of the ship, and asked them several times, and no answer was made. He

[*] Hazard's State Papers, v. 2, p. 2.
[†] Langford's Refutation, B. 2, p. 22.

then charged them not to come nearer the ship, but the enemy kept
rowing on their way and were come within shot of the ship: his mates
and company having had information of their threatenings, as well
against the ship as the poor distressed people, resolved to fire upon
them without their commander's consent, rather than hazard all by
the enemy's nearer approach, whereupon he ordered them to fire a
gun at random to divert their course from the ship, but the enemy
kept still course right with the ship, and took no notice of any warning given. He then commanded his gunner to fire at them, but one
of his mates, Mr. Robert Morris, who knew the country very well,
the malice of the adversary against these people who were then near
worn out with fears and watchings, made shot at them, which came
fairly with them: whereupon they suddenly altered their course from
the ship, and rowed into the creek, calling the ship's company rogues,
round-headed rogues, and dogs, and with many execrations and railing, threatened to fire them on the morning."

Gov. Stone entered the mouth of Spa Creek, which forms the
southern boundary of the present city of Annapolis, and landed his forces
on Horn point, a peninsula opposite Annapolis, and south of Spa Creek.

Whilst the Governor was landing his men, Capt. Heamans fired
another shot at them. "The shot thereof lighting somewhat near to
them, the Governor deemed it most prudent to send a messenger on
board the Golden Lyon to know the reason of their conduct, with
directions to the messenger to inform the captain of the ship, that he
(Gov. Stone) thought 'the captain of the ship had been satisfied.'
To which, Captain Heamans, who and a younger brother, Mrs.
Stone says, were great sticklers in the business, answered in a very
blustering manner—'Satisfied with what? I never saw any power
Capt. Stone had to do as he hath done, but the superscription of a
letter. I must, and will, appear for these in a good cause.'"[*]

"The same night," says Heamans, "came further intelligence from
the enemy in the harbor, that they were making fireworks against
the ship." On this the Puritans "commanded a small ship of Captain
Cut's, of New England, then in the river, to lie in the mouth of the
creek to prevent the enemy's coming forth in the night, to work any
mischief against the ship."

The St. Mary's men evidently looked upon the campaign as one of
certain triumph, and like of Goliath of Gath, before the armies of
Israel, they defied the hosts of the Puritans.

Approaching on the morrow by a narrow neck of land, near which
their vessels were moored, the Cavaliers, with sound of drum and rail-
ings loud, called to their enemies: "Come, ye rouges, come, ye
rouges, round-headed dogs." On this the Captain of the Golden
Lyon fired his fourth and, this time, fatal shot, killing one of the St.
Mary's men.

The day, the 25th of March, was the Sabbath, but religion and
fighting are professions the Puritans always would mix. So whilst the
Governor was putting his troops in martial array, the Puritans were
already in his rear. Their little band of one hundred and twenty,
under Capt. Wm. Fuller, had marched out of town, around the head
of Spa Creek, a detour of six miles, and now appeared behind the Governor's army.

* Leonard Strong--in Bozman's Maryland, vol. 2, p. 524.

The sentry of the St. Mary's men fired the signal shot, when "Captain Fuller still expecting, that, then at least, possibly they might give a reason of their coming, commanded his men, upon pain of death, not to shoot a gun, or give the first onset, setting up the standard of the commonwealth of England, against which the enemy shot five or six guns, and killed one man in the front before a shot was made by the other." "Then," continues Mr. Leonard Strong, "the word was given, "*In the name of God fall on: God is our strength.*" The cry of the St. Mary's men was, "*Hey, for St. Mary's.*" Thus the battle of the Severn began.

The charge was fierce, but brief. "Through the glorious presence of the Lord of hosts," says the same cotemporary author, "manifested in and towards his poor, oppressed people, the enemy could not endure, but gave back ; and were so effectually charged home, that they were all routed, turned their backs, threw down their arms, and begged for mercy. After the first volley of shot, a small company of the enemy, from behind a great tree fallen, galled us, and wounded divers of our men, but were soon beaten off. Of the whole company of Marylanders there escaped only four or five, who ran away out of the army to carry news to their confederates. Capt. Stone, Colonel Price, Capt. Gerrard, Capt. Lewis, Capt. Kendall, (probably Fendall.) Capt. Guither, Major Chandler, and all the rest of the councellors, officers, and soldiers of the Lord Baltimore, among whom both commanders and soldiers, a great number being Papists, were taken, and so were their vessels, arms, ammunition, provisions, about fifty men slain and wounded. We lost only two men in the field, but two died since of their wounds. God did appear wonderful in the field, and in the hearts of the people, all confessing Him to be the only worker of this victory and deliverance."

However much the Puritans attributed the fate of battle to the Almighty, after the contest was once over, they laid aside His precepts, and proceeded to close matters after their own will. Doctor Barber, an author of that period, writing in the interests of the St. Mary's men, says: "After the skirmish, the Governor, upon quarter given him and all his company in the field, yielded to be taken prisoners, but, two or three days after, the victors condemned ten to death, and executed four, and had executed all, had not the incessant petitioning and begging of some good women saved some, and the soldiers others : the Governor himself being condemned by them and since begged by the soldiers, some being saved just as they were leading to execution."

Those who were executed, were Mr. William Eltonhead, Lieut. Wm. Lewis. Mr. Legget, and John Pedro, a German. Gov. Stone, though his life was spared, was treated with great cruelty, and, whilst in prison, suffering from a severe wound received in the battle, neither his friends nor his wife were allowed to visit him.

A year after this battle, the 23rd of October, 1656, Lord Baltimore sent instructions to his Lieutenant and Council in which he required the people of Anne Arundel to quietly and peacefully submit to his Lordship's Patents as he used and exercised the same there before the troubles began, vizt. in the year 1650, and according to the advice of the said (of Trade) committee, which had decided that Lord Baltimore was entitled to the Government of the province of Maryland.

He added, "His Lordship wills and requires his said Lieutenant and Council that the Law in the said Province instituted, An act concerning Religion and passed heretofore there with his Lordship's assent, WHEREBY ALL PERSONS WHO PROFESS TO BELIEVE IN JESUS CHRIST have Liberty of Conscience and free exercise of their religion there, be duly observed in the said Province by all the inhabitants thereof, and that the penalties mentioned in the said act be duly put in execution upon any offendors against the same, or any part thereof."*

The Province was restored to Lord Baltimore in March, 1658, he having been deprived of it six years.

------◄ ● ►------

CHAPTER X.

QUAKERS AND INDIANS DISTURB THE COLONY.

[1658.] Incessant were the disturbances in the colony. When the Puritans and the State were at peace, the Indian and the Quaker ruffled the Province. "At a Council held 23 of Julij, at Annarundell Present, The Governor, The Secretary Col: Nathaniell Vtie." The following proceedings took place :

"This morneing was sworne Of his Lordship Councell Mr. Edward Lloyd and from the Councell went to assist the Governor at the County Court.

"After the Court was ended the Councell mett againe and there being then Present The Governor The Secretary Coll : Nathaniell Vtie Mr. Edward Lloyd.

"Toke into consideracon the insolent behaviour of som people called Quakers who at the Court, in contempt of an order then made & proclaimed, would presumptuously stand Covered, and not only so, but also refused to subscribe the engagement notwithstanding the Act of Assembly in that case provided alleadging they were to be governed by Gods lawe and the light within them & not by mans lawe vpon full debate finding that this theyr refusall of the engagement was a breach of the Articles of the 24th of March last, and that theyr principles tended to the destruction of all Government.

"ORDERED

"That all persons whatsoeuer that were resideing within this Province on 24th of March 1657 should take & subscribe the said engagement by the 20th of August next or else depart the Province by the 25th of March followeing vpon paine due to Rebbells & Traitors if found within this Province after the said 25th of March, & that a Proclamacon be forthwith drawne to this effect.

"PROCLAMATION,

"By the Lieutenant & Governor of Maryland.

"Whereas vpon the Surrender of the Government to me his Lordship Lieutenant on the 24th of March last past amongst other things it was then agreed that the Oath of fidelity should not be pressed vpon the inhabitants then resideing within this Province but that in place

* Archives of Maryland. Council Proceedings, p. 325.

and stead thereof an engagement should be taken in Manner and forme as in those Articles (relation vnto them being had) more at large appeareth And whereas by Act of this last Generall Assembly the said Articles are confirmed & the said engagement by a Lawe commanded to be taken To the end the said Articles may be inviolably observed and that all Jealousies and feares be removed These are in the Lord Proprietarys name strictly to charge & Command all persons whatsoeuer to make theyr repaire to the Clarkes of the respectiue County Courts at or before the 20th day of August next ensueing to make theyr subscriptions to the said engagement or else that they provide themselues to depart this Province by the 25th day of March next and to declare that all persons who shall refuse to subscribe the engagement within the time before limited and shall be found in any part of this Province after the 25th day of March aforesaid shall be proceeded against as Rebbells & Traitors Given vnder my hand this 23rd of July 1658.   Josias Fendall.

"At Councell held 25 Julij at Patuxent Present The Governor The Secretary.

"According to the Warrant bearing date 22nd Instant Thomas Thurston was brought before the Governor, & the said Thurston being desirous to depart the Province the Governor Ordered this followeing Warrant to be drawne Whereas Thomas Thurston by himselfe & friends hath desired of me that he may passe vp to Annarundell, from whence he hath ingaged himselfe to depart this Province by Monday next being the second day of August, vntill whos departing out of this Province Josias Cole is to remaine as by Order of Court Provided These are therefore in the Lord Proprietarys name to Will & require you not to molest the said Thomas Thurston during the time limited for his stay and so soone as he shall signify to you his intention presently to depart that you sett at liberty the said Josias Cole Provided that if they or either of them shall be found within this Province after the aforesaid second day of August (vnlesse made vnable to depart by sicknes) they or either of them be apprehended and proceeded against according to lawe in theyr case provided Given Vnder my hand at Patuxent this 25th day of July 1658.   Josias Fendall." *

[1665.] In 1665, the Indians again became an element of trouble, and a Council that met at St. Mary's, June 6th, 1665, took "into debate some speedy way for the prevention of the Indian Enemyes further incursiones into this province. And how they may be suppressed for the future."

In the levy for the various counties, St. Mary's had to raise thirty men and the like number was required of Anne Arundel. Capt. William Burges, of Anne Arundel, was put in command of the troop, and he was ordered to raise them by press or otherwise, with sufficient arms and ammunition. He was also made Deputy Commander of all the forces.

The commission and instructions given to Capt. Burges, preserved in the proceedings of the council,† give a curious insight into the state of the colony regarding that still unsolved problem—the American Indian.

"THE COMMISSION READS:

"Charles Calvert &c., To Capt. William Burges Greeting Whereas

---

* Archives of Md. Council Proceedings, p. 358.
† Archives of Md. Council Proceedings, p. 523.

Diverse Forraigne Indians have of late Committed diverse murders vpon the people of this Province and Committed diverse other Outrages for repression of which I have thought fitt to raise a Competent Number of Men Now Know Yee that I reposing especiall confidence in yor fidelity Courage and Experience in Martiall Affaires have Constituted Ordained and Appointed and by these presents doe Constitute Ordaine and appoint yow Commandr in Cheife under mee of all the forces soe raised in St. Mary's, Kent, Charles. Calvert and' Anne Arundell Countys against the said Indians to make warre and pursue and by Gods Assistance to Vanquish and Kill and Generally in all things to doe all or any thing or things as any Commandr in Cheife may or of Right Ought to doe according to such Instruccons as I haue herewith sent or shall from time to time send yow Given at St. Mary's undr my hand and Seale this 6th day of June in the 34th yeare of his Lordps Dominion Ouer this Prouince Annoq Domini 1665.

Charles Calvert."

The following were the instructions given Capt. Burges :*

"Instructions directed by the Honble the Leiutennt Generall Charles Calvert Esqr &c.. To Capt. William Burges and sent wth his Comcon dated 6th day of June 1665.

"Imprimis you are to take Under yor Charge and Comand the Seuerall parties of men raised in St. Mary's, Kent. Charles and Calvert Countys as those in Anne Arundell Countys wth which men according to your Best discrecon and wth the Aduice and Consent of the major part of the Officers comanding in the Seuerall partyes yow are to Endeauour to find out the Indian Enemy in theire Quarters and them by God's Assistance to Vanquish or Otherwise driue Out of this Prouince or Otherwise uppon the place and Emergent Occasions as yow with the Aduice and Consent aforesaid shall finde it more Expedient and for the safety of the Prouince in Generall to keepe seuerall partyes ranging the woods as well to the Head of Patuxent as Patapsco & Bush Riuers or euen up to the Utmost bounds of the Prouince uppon the Sasquesahanough riuer.

"Secondly yow are to take speciall Care to see yow men want not necessary prouisiones for foode nor Armes nor Amunicon and to that end yow are to issue Orders to the Sherriffes or other Officers next to yow in the seuerall Countyes where yow shall chance to come in pursuite of yor Commission to presse any Armes Ammunicon or Provisiones Needfull : Who are to keepe exact and true accompts of such thinges so pressed as aforesaid.

"Thirdely yow are to take especiall Care of the People in Patapsco riuer and Gunn Powder Riuer and to that end yow are to keepe a Constant Correspondence with yor Colonell Lewis Stockett, whom, when yow shall Chance to meet yow are to Obey in all thinges.

"Fourthly To the end all necessary assistance may be Given to all places in danger yow are to giue notice of all yor proceedings and all intelligence yow shall receive to me twice euery weeke and Oftener if need be, and to presse messengers expressely to bring yor letters to me as also to send yor intelligence to your Collonell as often as need shall be, and Generally yow are to presse Boates men or horses either to Carry Baggage or to March after the Ennemy as yow shall see Occasion.

"Fifthly Yow are to Associate with any the friendle Indians to any number yow shall finde most Contenient for the service now in hand : but in yor march or in yor Quarters yow are to take speciall Care that noe English doe Game or wrestle with any Indians so to auoid all Occasiones of Quarrell."

No war followed this preparation of arms, and, in 1666, a treaty of peace was made with a number of Indians, in which the right was conceded to the proprietary to appoint the emperor of the Indians. For nine years the colony enjoyed exemption from Indian warfare.

CHAPTER XI.
COLONIAL LIFE.

From 1657 to 1683 there is a lamentable gap in the history of Providence, due, it is believed, to the loss of the State's Records by "the removal of the records and documents of the province from St. Mary's to Annapolis, some of which were greatly damaged," and to "the loss of some by the fire which destroyed the State House in 1704, where they were chiefly deposited."[*]

The chasm will be filled by extracts from the journals of the General Assembly and records of the Courts, from whose quaint proceedings and curious customs may be gleaned the thoughts, deeds, and characters of the men who laid the foundations of Annapolis.

UPPER HOUSE, Saturday 28th, April, 1666.

[1666.] "Then came a member from the lower house, and desired the governor,[†] from the the whole lower house, not to discharge Edward Erbery, merchant, from the *sare* of Bristol ; in regard, they had something to object against him, as well for abusing the lower house of Assembly, as his lordship, last night.

"Then came a member from the lower house, with this paper following :

TUESDAY, 1st May, 1666.

"William Calvert, Esq., motions the house,

"That, whereas there was an abuse committed last night by Edward Erbery, to the disturbance of the whole house, in their quiet and rest, and the clerk of this house informs that the said Erbery did call the whole house papists, rogues,**** rogues, &c., which the speaker is desired to take notice of, and proceed therein, either by presentment or otherwise, as to him shall seem best, and that it be the first thing this house takes into consideration or debate.

"Mr. Nicholas Piccard and Mr. Richard Blunt informed the house of certain vulgar and indecent expressions of Erbery concerning the lower house, and that they were ashamed of the place from whence they came.

* Ridgely's Annals of Annapolis, p. 54.
† Archives of Maryland. Proceedings of Assembly, p. 55.

"Mr. Richard Hall says, that amongst a great many other extravagant words, Erbery said that Charles Calvert was a rogue.

"William Calvert, Esq., saith, how that Erbery, in his hearing, said, we, viz. the assembly, were in company of pitiful rogues and puppies, and there is not one in the country deserves to keep me company but Charles Calvert, who owes me ten thousand pounds of tobacco.

"Mr. Richard Smith informs this morning, when Erbery awaked, the Erbery complained that he was bound ; that he remembered all that he had said last night, and that he was not drunk ; and in a threatening manner, said he would remember those that bound him.

"The abuse that Edward Erbery gave to the lieutenant-general and this assembly last night, being taken into consideration, and upon a full debate thereon, had in this house, they do judge the same to be a scandal to the Lord Proprietor, to his lieutenant-general, and to both houses of assembly, and a great reflection upon the province in general ; and, therefore, unanimously voted by this house, that the said Erbery be brought before this house, to give answer to the above said charge, in relation to those informations now given in against him.

"Ordered by the speaker that Mr. Edward Erbery be brought into the sheriff, &c.'

"And taxed by the speaker of all those words spoken, who making his appearance after the charge being read unto him, he answered that he remembered none of these words that is alleged, only he confesseth that he was in drink, and being further taxed about the words spoken this morning, (which were averred by a member of this house) he says that he remembers not that ever he spoken such words.

"Which answer being taken into consideration, the house do judge the same altogether unsatisfactory, and that no person of full age shall take advantage by drunkenness in such case.

"Whereupon this house do humbly present the consideration thereof to the upper house, that they would please to signify to this house their resentment of the same, and what they shall judge further necessary to be done with the said Erbery as touching the punishment or otherwise for this house's concured therewith.'

"The upper house do order that the said Edward Erbery be tyed to an apple tree before the house of assembly, and be there publickly whipped upon the bare back with thirty-nine lashes, and that the sheriff of St. Mary's county be commanded to apprehend the said Erbery and see this order put in execution, and that the said Erbery do pay the sheriff his fees before he departs out of his custody ; and further ordered, that the said Erbery be, after he is whipped, brought into both houses of assembly publickly to ask them forgiveness.

(Signed) JOHN GITTINGS, Clerk."

"UPPER HOUSE, February 17th, 1674.

[1674.] 'Came into this house, a petition of the lower house, as followeth, viz:

"To the honourable Charles Calvert, Esquire, Lieutenant General and Chief Judge of the Provincial Court of the Right Honourable the Lord Proprietary.

"The humble petition of the Deputies and Delegates of the Lower House of Assembly,

"Humbly sheweth to your excellency,

"That, whereas John Cowman being arraigned, convicte', and condemned upon the statute of the first of King James of England, &c., for witchcraft, conjuration, sorcery, or enchantment used upon the body of Elizabeth Goodall, and now lying under that condemnation, and hath humbly implored and beseeched us, your lordship's petitioners, to mediate and intercede in his behalf with your excellency for a reprieve and stay of execution.

"Your excellencie's petitioners do therefore, accordingly, in all humble manner, beseech your excellency that the rigour and severity of the law to which the said condemned malefactor hath miserably exposed himself, may be remitted and relaxed by the exercise of your excellency's mercy and clemencie upon so wretched and miserable an object.

"And your petitioners, as in duty bound, will ever pray, &c.'

·UPPER HOUSE, February 17th.

"The lieutenant-general hath considered of the petition here above, and is willing, upon the request of the lower house, that the condemned malefactor be reprieved, and execution stayed, provided that the sheriff of St. Maries' county carry him to the gallows, and that the rope being about his neck, it be there made known to him how much he is beholding to the lower house of assemblie for mediating and interceeding in his behalf with the lieutenant-general, and that he remain at the city of St. Maries, to be employed in such service as the governor and council shall think fitt, during the pleasure of the governor."

The Quakers, or Friends, who had settled in Maryland at an early period of its establishment, suffering under that system of intolerance and prosecutoin which prevailed against all dissenters at that, and down to a latter day, remonstrated against the unjust laws of the province which debarred their testimony or, "affirmation," "and subjected them to heavy penalties for refusing to take the prescribed oaths," "although contrary to their conscience, and, in their opinion the Saviour's positive injunction, declared in his sermon on the mount —'swear not at all.'" This remonstrance or petition appears upon the journals of the upper house in 1674, and is as follows:

"SATURDAY, 23d May, 1674.

"Read in the house, a petition exhibited by certain Quakers, as follows, viz:

"This we do lay before the governour and council assembly, in the wisdom of God, to consider of, from us who in scorn are called, Quakers.

"What we can say and do instead of an oath, it is in obedience to Christ's command, that we cannot swear and take an oath, and Christ our Lord and Saviour's command is, 'I say unto you swear not at all,' Though in the old time, they were not to forswear themselves, but perform their oaths to the Lord; and the Lord Jesus Christ's command is, but let your communication be yea, yea, and nay, nay, for whatsoever is more than these cometh of evil; and St. James saith, in his general epistle to the Church of Christ, above all things, my bretheren, swear not; neither by heaven, nor by the earth, nor by any other oath: mark, but let your yea, be yea, and your nay, be nay, least you fall unto condemnation. Now, here ye may see, that Christ and apostles sett us yea, yea, and nay, nay, over and above an oath and swearing, and in lieu of an oath. See, in obedience to Christ and the apostles' command, it is, that we do not, and dare not swear, least we should go into the evil, and so fall into condemnation, as Christ and the apostles saith before. But according to Christ Jesus and the apostles' command, doe keep to yea, yea, and nay, nay, wherein they do double their words to make them of more force. Christ Jesus to the deciples and the apostles to the church; and now, if, that we are called to testifie the truth, or to serve in any office or place or jurie, if that we do break our yea, yea, or nay, nay, then let us suffer the same penalty, as they, that do break an oath, or are foresworne. And this not repugnant to the laws of England, having the same penalty on the same transgression ; for, in Jamaica, their law is so, that our brethren's testimony upon yea, yea, and nay, nay, as Christ and as the apostles commanded, is taken, and the same in the same in the acts and province laws at Carolina, and the same in the patent and acts at Road Island, and the same in the new country of Jersey, is taken instead of an oath ; which the governour and his council and assembly may, by an act of assembly, let us have the same liberty here, as our brethren have in other places, colonies, or provinces, that we may not be put to inconveniences, for you do not know what trouble often many of us are put to, because we cannot swear and take oath, and do lose our rights and that which is due to us from others, and how we have been made prey upon by many, because we cannot swear, and have lost much in our estates, and cannot be so serviceable in our generation to the country, as we might be, and also what trouble we have had, who have been overseers or executors, or the like, that have been intrusted with orphans, fatherless, and widows' estates or wills, for want of an oath. And, therefore, you having power to remedie these things by making an act, we do lay them before you, and that if we do breake our yea, yea, or nay, nay, or what we testifie, then let us suffer the same punishment as they do that break their oaths or swear falsely ; and this we are willing to suffer, who profess faith in Christ, and would all that profess the same, to exercise a conscience void of offence towards God and men. So you may remove this oppression if you please, and let us have the same liberty that our friends and bretheren have in other countrys and islands, as we are creditably informed ; whose hands are hereunto subscribed in behalfs of our bretheren.

| 'WENLOCK CHRISTERSON, | Jo. HOMEARD, |
| 'WILLIAM PERRIE, | RI. BEARD, &c. |

"Ordered by the house, that the petition here above be sent to the lower house, and offered to their consideration.

"This petition was accordingly sent to the lower house, who returned it with a message requesting to be informed by his excellency and the upper house, whether, in their opinion, the assembly had the power to alter the form of the oath prescribed by the laws of England, in point of evidence between the king and his people, &c., in matters depending within the province, or not. To which message, the upper house replied, that they had resolved, that the petition should remain upon the journal till further advice from the Lord Proprietary, who declared that he 'formerly had intention of gratifying the desire of the said people, called Quakers, in that kind :' but for some reason not mentioned, his lordship desired 'that all proceedings therein be, for the present, suspended.'

"This highly respectable and long misunderstood society of christians, were not restored to the rights and privileges, so moderately, but firmly, insisted upon in the foregoing petition, until the year 1702*—when the legislature struck from the statute books this relict of intolerance."†

[1671.] On the 28th of March, 1671, when the Upper House had met at "two of the clock in the afternoon," it received "a message from the Lower House which was their desire to know whether the Deputys of Calvert county or the deputys of Anne Arundel county ought to take place. Upon examination whereof this House were of opinion that the Deputys of Anne Arundel ought to have the Precedency and sent the honorable, the Secretary to satisfy them in that particular with the Records of their Commission constituting their county Courts. And afterwards this house sent Mr. Brooks and Mr. Trueman to the Lower House for their further satisfaction therein."‡

The jurisprudence of a nation and the manner of its application to the causes which arise under it are indices of the moral and mental status of that people.

From yellow and dusty volumes, MSS. preserved among the archives of Maryland, are taken the records of some quaint trials which throw a radiant light upon those curious times.

[1656.] In 1656, the province being under the authority of the commissioners of Cromwell, Judith Catchpole was brought before the Court under a suspicion of having murdered her child. It was "a Generall Provincial court Held at Patuxent, September, 22nd, 1656," which heard the case to determine if she should be indicted. Patuxent was then the name of Calvert county.

The Court was composed of Capt. Wm. Fuller, Mr. Richard Preston, Mr. Edward Lloyd, Mr. John Scott and Mr. Michael Brooke. Judith denied even the birth of the child, whereupon the court ordered "a jury of able women to be impanelled and to give in their verdict to the best of their judgement whether she, the said Judith, hath ever had a child, or not."

The following jury was selected: Rose Smith, Mrs. Belcher, Mrs. Chaplin, Mrs. Brooke, Mrs. Battin, Mrs Cannardy, Mrs. Bussey, Mrs. Brooke, Elizabeth Claxton, Elizabeth Potter and Dorothy Day—eleven.

The testimony in the case, as recorded, was:

"James Jolly, sworne examined, saith that being at John Grammer's, a weeke before Wm. Bramhall's man died, the said servant of Bramhall said that Judith Catchpole cut a maid's skinn off her throat, and she never felt it, and the said Judith Catchpole sewed the wound up, againe, and further saith not."

"Elizabeth Norton, sworne and examined, saith that Wm. Bramhall's servant that dyed, saith that Judith Catchpole, Cut the skinn of a maid's throat when she was asleep, and the said maid never felt it, and the said Judith sewed up the wound againe, with a Needle and thread; and the said servant said, if he should divulge it, it would be worse for him, and further saith not. That Wm. Bramhall's man said that Judith Catchpole and he did grind a knife Dutch fashion, and the said Judith prickt a seaman in the back with it, and she

* Act of 1702, chapter 1, section 21.
† Ridgely's Annals.
‡ Archives of Maryland, Proceedings of Assembly, p. 240.

begged a little grease of the chirurgeon, and greased his back, and he stood up again ; and the said servant said that Judith was to kill three or four men more and further said not."

"Andrew Wilcox sworne and examined, saith, that Mr. Bramhall's man-servant that dyed said that when the murther was done all the people and seamen in the ship were asleep ; and after it was done Judith Catchpole and the said servant of Wm. Bramhall went up upon the deck, and walked a quarter of an hour, afterward off they Went. each to their Lodging ; this being at Sea in the middle of the night, and further saith not."

We the jury thereupon rendered a verdict "The Jury of women, before named, having according to our charge and oath, searched the body of Judith Catchpole, doe give in our verdict that according to our best judgment. that said Judith Catchpole hath not had any child within the time charged."

The court then gave opinion that, "Whereas, Judith Catchpole, servant to Wm. Darrington, of this Province of Maryland, was apprehended and brought before the court upon a suspicion of murdering a child in her voyage at sea, bound for this Province in the ship Mary and Francis, who set forth of England upon her intended voyage in, or about October last, 1655, and arrived in this Province in, or about January following, and her accuser being deceased, and no murther appearing, upon her examination, denying the fact ; was ordered that her body should be searcht by a jury of able women, which being done, the said jury returning their verdict to this court that they found, that the said Judith had not had any child within the time, charged, and, also it appearing to this court, by severall testimonies that the party accusing was not in sound mind, whereby it is conceived the said Judith Catchpole is not inditable. The Court doth, therefore, order that upon the reasons aforesaid that she, the said Judith Catchpole, be acquitted of that charge unless further evidence appear."

The court records of this decade bear, in severall places, the name an individual who seemed to be one of those characters, who furnish food for courts. Peter Godson is the unfortunate Marylander. One of the cases was when Peter was sued for calling a woman a witch. He confessed penitence, and escaped, in a measure, the meshes and penalties of the law.

[1665.] "At a court holden the fifth day of October, 1665," it is recorded that "Peter Godson, being convicted of stealing a bodkin from the wife of John Hambleton, and concealing the same shall according to the Act of Assembly, restore four fould in silver, which is four shillings and six pence, to the defendent, with the charges of court being four hundred and six pounds of tobacco."

In December of the same year Peter again appears in court. Thos. Ager complained "that he hath paid unto Peter Godson Tobacco for a cure, ihe said Godson undertook to perform on the said Ager, and hath left him worse than he found him. It is ordered," said the Court, "that the sai d Godson pay him his tobacco back againe except he perform his undertaking."

In the succeeding March, the following proceedings in the case were had :

"Whereas, by a former order, Peter Godson was injoyned to make a cure of Thomas Ager or else repay ye tobacco which he had received in satisfaction of his cure, and it, appearing to this Court, that the said Godson hath not performed the order, it is now ordered that the said Godson shall repay the said tobacco which is 600lb and caske, or else execution."

James Johnson for a misuse of his tongue paid severe penalties. At a court held July 15th, 1647, "the Court being informed of certaine mutinous speeches uttered by James Johnson, about ye 3d of July, viz.: that he should say unto Richard Bennett, after some discourse concerning the Government now established, that he hoped within a while, to see a confusion of all Papistry here, and further the said James Johnson said that both he, the said Richard Bennett and yt. came up with the late Governor from Virginia, (meaning the soldiers,) were rogues : for that they had undone a brave country, for had it not been for them, to witt, the soldiers, they might have enjoyed this country, to themselves, (meaning the late Rebells to his Proprietary,) and their progeney after them. And the said Richard Bennett replyed, yt. there were in the Governor's Company as honest men as himself. The said Johnson still persisted in it, saying that they were all rogues and he would justifie it, and, at the same time he, the same James Johnson, urged the said Bennett to go downe, and certifie the Governor of these speeches, saying that if he should complaine to the Governor against him, he regarded it not, for he cared noe more for the Governor, (meaning Mr. Greene,) then he did for any of the rest. Also, at the same time, speaking concerning Capt. Hill, he wished that Capt. Hill would come, and re-assume the government, affirming that, if Capt. Hill, were come, and yt. he, the said James Johnson could see Capt. John Price, pressing soldiers to resist the said Capt. Hill, and not above two others in his company, he would shott him, (meaning Capt. Price.) All which being proved by the oath of Richard Bennett, the Court judged that he should be fined in 2,000lb tobacco, and to be whipped with thirty lashes. And to remain in the Sheriff's hands, till the Corporall punishment be exequuted, and to put in security for ye payment of the said fine.

"Warrant to the Sheriff to see sentence exequuted to-morrow in the evening."

[1651.] Mrs. Brooks for an amiable piece of gossip among her acquaintances, was called to answer "at a court holden for the Province of Maryland, 16th of Oct., 1654."

The first witness Mr. Geo. Newman, testified he "heard Mrs. Brooks relate that she heard Mrs. Goulson had beaten her maid two houre by the clock, AND THEASE WERE that would take their oath that it was an houre and a hull by the clock."

"Margaret Prichard, aged twentie yeares or thereabouts," deposed, "that this Deponent heard Mrs. Brooks say that Mrs. Goulson had beaten her maid two hours," following that with the significant attestation, "by the clock." Unlike the inattentive and pozzled Newman, Margaret had not to say that Mrs. Brooke related "there were that," who could make a certain oath that, and so forth, but she could swear to the person, and give a longer period to Mrs. Goulson's active episode in her household duties. She testified that Mrs. Brooks further said: Elizebeth Tennis would take her oath that it was two hours and a half," but the important "by the clock," was not vouchsafed by this deponent. Elizebeth heard more ; Margaret had finished up with a delicious titbit of gossip respecting the conjugal relations of her unmerciful acquaintance. Margaret further continued her deposition by testifying that "Elizabeth Tennis should say" that the exasperated lord of Mrs. Goulson, "tore the hair of his head and wisht that she, the said Mrs. Goulson would kill the self-same maid, that she might never kill more."

This record follows:—"That, whereas, Mrs. Brooks reported that Sarah Goulson unlawfully punished her maid-servant, which cannot be proved. It is ordered that Mrs. Brooks shall pay the charges."

Thus the slanderer received her reward.

[1648.] Its dignity our provincial courts jealously guarded. Swearing at its sessions was punished, and perjury before it, it would, in no wise, countenance, as is attested by the sentence of one John Gonoore who was found guilty of this latter crime, "att a court held at Henry Morgan's att Kent 22nd Jan'y," sometime about 1648.

Thomas Matthews in behalf of the Lord Proprietary complained "against John Gonoore. that being called to answer upon his oath, not haveing the feare of God afore his eyes, he answered falsely and and against his knowledge, whereby he committed a willfull perjury, wherefore the said Thos. Matthews requireth in the behalf of the said Lord Proprietary, the said Goonore to be brought to condine punishment.

"John Goonore not having anything to say for his defence, more than that it was the first time he ever committed the like offence. The Court adjudged him to be nailed by both ears to the Pillory with nailes in each eare, and the nails to be slitt out. and afterwards to be whipped with 20 good lashes. *And this to be executed immediately before any other business of Court be procee le l vpon.*"

The following curious trial is found in Liber S. Folios 297 and 298, of the Provincial Court of Maryland :

[1659.] "Whereas John Wasnington, of Westmoreland county. in Virginia, hath made complaynt against Edward Prescott. merchaut, accusing ye said Prescott of felony unto ye Governor of this Province. Alleging how that thee ye said Prescott. hanged a witch in his ship, as hee was outwards bound from England hither ye last yeare. Uppon which complaynt of ye said Washington, ye Governor caused ye said Edward Prescott to bee arrested : Taking bond for his appearance at this Provinciall Court, of 4,000 ls to mee o. Giving. moreover. notice to ye said Wasnington, by letter, of his proceedings therein, a copie of which bond, with ye said Washington's answere thereto are as followeth :

"Mr. Washington,

"Uppon your complaynt to me that Mr. Prescott did in his voyage from England hither, cause a woman to bee executed for a witch, I have caused him to bee apprehended uppon suspition of felony, and doe intend to bind him over to ye Provincial Court to answere it; where I doe allso expect you to bee, to make good your charge. Hee will be called upon his tryall ye 4th on 5th of October next. att ye court to bee held then att Patunent. neare Mrs. FFenwick's house ; where I suppose you will not fayle to bee. Whitnesses examined in Virginia will be of no vallew there in this case. for they must bee face to face with ye party accused, or they stand for nothing. I thought good to acquaynt with this, that you may not come unprovided. ¶

"This at present Sr. is all from
"Your Friend,
"Josiat Fendell,
"29th September."
"Humble Sir.
"Yours, of this 29th instant, this day I received. I am sorry, yet my extraordinary occasions will not permit me to be at ye next Provinciall Court to be held in Maryland ye 4 of this next month. Because then, God willing, I intend to get my young sone baptized, all ye company and gossips being all ready invited. Besides in this short time witnesses cannot be got to come over. But if Mr. Prescott be bound to answer at ye next Provinciall Court after this, I shall do what lyeth in my power to get them over. Sir. I shall desire you for to acquaint me wheather Mr. Prescott be bound over to try, next Court, and when yr court is, that I may have some time for to provide evidence. And so I rest
"Your Friend & Servant.
"John Washington,
"30 September 1659."

"To which complaynt of John Washington, ye said Edward Prescott, (submitting himself to his tryall,) denyeth not but that there was one Elizabeth Richardson, hanged in his ship, as he was outward bound ye last year from England, and comming for this Province, near unto ye Western Islands, by his master and company, (he having appointed one John Greene, for ye voyage master. thought himself was both merchants and owner of ye ship.) but further sayth, that he understood ye proceedings of his said master and company, and protested against in that business. And that there upon both ye master and company were ready to mutiny.

"And it appearing in ye court by ye printed custom house discharge, and light house bills or acquittances produced and shewn by ye said Edward Prescott, taken or given in John Greene's name, that ye said Green was master for ye voyage, and not Edward Prescott. and no one coming to prosequnto. Ye said Prescott, therefore prays that hee may be acquitted.

"Edward Prescott, prisoner at ye bar, upon suspition of felony. stated upon his acquittal. If any person can give evidence against him, let him come in, for the prisoner otherwise will be acquitted.

"And no one appearing. ye prisoner is acquitted by the Board."

CHAPTER XII.
AN INDISCREET REPRESENTATIVE FROM ANNE ARUNDEL.

[1662.] The early annals of the province of Maryland preserve, as representatives of Anne Arundel in the General Assembly, the names of many families still to be found within the borders of this interesting county. In 1662, Anne Arundel was represented by Robert Burle, Richard Beard, and Ralph Hawkins.

The former became engaged in a serious difficulty by the indiscreet use of his pen, as will appear by the following extracts from the journal of proceedings of the General Assembly :[*]

"Wednesday, the 2d of April. Then was taken into consideration a certain paper, endorsed 'To the worshipful, the burgesses for this present Assembly, holden for Maryland. The declaration of several of the inhabitants of Anne Arundel county, which, as bearing no date, nor being subscribed by any person whosoever, was put to the vote whether it were a libel yea, or no.'

"Voted by the House that it is a libel, containing scandalous and seditious expressions, tending to the utter subversion and overthrow of the legislative power of this province, residing in the Lord Proprietary and both houses of Assembly, and, that it be sent to the lower house who are desired to join with this house in the searching out and centuring the author. "Ordered, that Mr. Daniel Jenifer, messenger, be sent from this house to the lower house, to present that seditious paper published at Anne Arundel, with the vote of this house for their concurrence."

"Thursday, the 3rd of April.

"Then the Lower House returned the seditious pamphlet sent by the Upper House to them together with the vote of this house, endorsed on the back side :

"Assented to by the lower house. William Bretton, clerk.

"And further informed this house that as a member of that house, by name Robert Burle, did acknowledged that paper would reflect upon him, and that therefore the Lower House did desire that that member might be suspended from voting as a member till he had purged himself.

"Unanimously voted by the Upper House that that person, viz : Robert Burle, should be suspended from sitting till he had purged himself, and that this vote be sent to the said Burle.

"Then came two members of the Lower House, and said that the Lower House desired that Robert Burle might be forthwith tried.

"Ordered, That a conference be desired immediately with the Lower House.

"At a conference the Upper House did satisfy the Lower House, that Robert Burle is not to be tried by an assembly, but at a Provincial Court regularly.

"Friday, the 4th of April.

"Then came Robert Burle and preferred the following petition and acknowledged his hearty sorrow for his faults concerning the mutinous and seditious expressions in the libel contained, which he penned and was published at Anne Arundel

"To the Right Honorable, the Lieutenant General and to the Honorable Philip Calvert, Esq., Councellor, and to the Honored Council.

"The humble petition of Robert Burle, showeth,

"That whereas your petitioner is adjudged by your honors and by the Burgesses to have committed great transgression, and that of a high nature, which he hath committed inconsiderately through infirmity and weakness, for which he declareth himself to be heartily sorry and humbly prayeth your honors to pardon and to pass by his great offence and conceiving himself to be the first offender since his

* Archives of Md. Proceedings of Assembly, p. 427.

4

Lordship's arrival, humbly prayeth for forgiveness which may be for the Honor of his Lop,† and shall engage your petitioner to better fidelity, loyalty, and faithful obedience, and shall ever engage the petitioner to pray for your honor's prosperity.

"Ordered, That the said Burle do forthwith go to the Lower House and ask pardon for his fault, and that the clerk of the Lower House be desired to see his submission recorded in their journal.

"The Lower House sent to desire to know whether Robert Burle might be admitted to sitt with them again.

"The Lieutenant General left it to their discretions."

The exact contents of this paper are not preserved. It is apparent the Lower House concluded to let Mr. Burle remain a member of that body, as his name appears among the list of delegates prefixed to the acts of assembly of the session of 1662.

† Lordship.

CHAPTER XIII.

The Courageous Spirit of the Maryland Settlers.

[1681.] It was not alone in the tented field that that courageous spirit, which has always characterized Marylanders, was evinced by our early settlers, but in every position where manly deeds and noble words were required, the hardy adventurers proved themselves men worthy of the stock from whence they came.

Over and over again the Legislature of Maryland, the lower house especially, showed a determined opposition to the encroachments of the proprietary upon their just rights and liberties, and evinced that determination in so marked a manner that proprietaries were compelled to submit to their imperative demands.

This determination to yield no rights and to urge no unnecessary privileges was strongly portrayed by the proceedings of the Assembly which met in August, 1681. On calling the roll, there appeared twelve vacancies in the lower house. The house thereupon addressed the Lord Proprietary requesting him to appoint some officer, to whom the speaker of their house might direct his warrants, to cause these vacancies to be filled; until which "they humbly conceived themselves greatly incapacitated to act and do proportionable to the great trust reposed in them, and sufficiently to consult the grand and weighty affairs of the province." The address also complained about his lordship having called but two members from each county when four should have been called.

His lordship asked the presence of the lower house. On entering the upper house, the Lord Proprietary said: "That by his proclamation, by which they were now called, the law for four delegates is sufficiently dissented to, and that otherwise, he would gratify their request in issuing out writs for filling up vacancies." The lower house was then requested to unite with the upper house, with their members then present, and to proceed to business.

The lower house refused. Thereupon the Proprietary agreed that writs might be issued for supplying the vacancies for the present, provided the lower house would acknowledge it as a favor from his lordship, and so enter it upon the journals.

Seeing the opportunity by a stroke of policy to secure a principle, the lower house consented to make this entry on their journal, and to agree to the election of two representatives from each county, provided his lordship would consent that in all future vacancies, the speaker should have the right to issue his warrant to the secretary of the province to order elections to fill such vacancies : otherwise they declared their unanimous resolution, "to stand to, and not to recede from the substance of their address," and for the right of their speaker to issue his warrant in case of vacancies, and that they had "made all the condescentions they can, without apparent violation of their privileges," and they hoped that the upper house would concur therein. The upper nouse refused to grant this authority which they thought "aimed at things wholly new and unheard of in this province."

The lower house answered this by declaring it a "denyal of the just and reasonable proposalls of this house for the future election of deputies, &c.," and passed a unanimous vote, "that it was the undoubted privilege of this house, that the speaker of this house issue his warrants," &c., and considered it "a very unsafe, ill precedent to proceed any further in the business of the session, and request his lordship to appoint some person to whom said warrants should be directed."

The chancellor thereupon was sent by his lordship to the lower house to acquaint them "that he cannot but wonder how the lower house of assembly assume to themselves a power here that is not only new to us, and unheard of before in this province, but not practiced in Virginia, Barbadoes, or any other of his majesties plantations," &c.

"His majesty hath the sole power to dispose of his conquests upon terms he pleases, &c., and desired to know their positive answer, whether they would join them in the dispatch of business, promising if they would, he would immediately issue writs to fill up the house with four delegates from each county."

The lower house resolved, that if his lordship caused writs to issue as promised, that they would "proceed upon such matters as shall be recommended to them from his lordship." But at the same time, they asserted "their rights and privileges, rather from the rules of England than the imperfect proceedings of the nominated colonies, the first being our inherent right—yea, and birthright, though born in this province.

"To liken us to a conquered people, we take very heavily, and wish we had not heard, and do wonder it should pass the upper house. But, if the word conquest intends that we are subjects to arbitrary laws and impositions, then we humbly take leave to believe that they are not his lordship's words, but the result of strange, if not evil council.

"That his majesty has reserved for us the rights and privileges of Englishmen, is that we insist upon."

The Lord Proprietary, in reply to the last message from the lower house, disclaimed any intention to liken the freemen of Maryland to a conquered people, or subject to arbitrary laws or impositions, and hopes that they may no way deserve that severe reflection, and assures them that he had always "been ready to oblige and show his kindness, to the good people of this province;" and, as a further testimony of it, states his willingness to issue writs as desired, if the lower h use will ask it of him "as a thing that will oblige (at this time) the inhabitants of this province, of whom they are representatives," &c.

The lower house accordingly made the request, stating their willingness "to leave off all disputations about words," saying, it "will be a matter of great content and rejoicing among to the good people of this province," &c.*

Thus the "freemen of Maryland," as they were called, proved themselves worthy of their honorable title, and gave abundant evidence of that love of liberty and courage to enjoy it which have characterized the English speaking race, at all times, the world over.

* Ridgely's Annals of Annapolis, p. 86.

CHAPTER XIV.

Providence Changed to "The Town, at Proctor's."

[1683.] Providence seems to have changed its name sometime between 1656 and 1683, for by an act of the Legislature of the last named year, chap. V,* it was spoken of as "The Town at Proctor's," and made a port of entry of the province.

The commissioners appointed by this act to execute its powers were, sometime before the 25th of March, 1684, to meet on the respective lands, and to agree with and purchase of the owners 100 acres of convenient lands, and cause the same to be surveyed, marked and staked out, and divided into convenient streets, lanes, and alleys, with open places to be left for erecting church, chapel, market-house, or other public buildings, and the remaining part of the said 100 acres, to divide into 100 equal lots, marked on posts, 1, 2, 3, &c., to 100, of which the owner of the land, to have his first choice for one lot. No person to purchase more than one lot, during four months after the 25th of March, 1684, and the lots to be purchased by the inhabitants of the county only. But if not taken up by them within the said four months, then to be free to any person whatsoever, to take up the same, paying the owner proportionably.

If the owners refused, or were disabled by legal incapacity to sell, the commissioners were empowered to issue their warrant to the sheriff, to summon a jury to value the lands, and the damage by them assessed, was to be paid to the owners, by the parties taking up lots, in proportion to their lots.

* Bacon's Laws.

The commissioners were empowered to summon the Surveyor-General, or his Deputy, in the county, to survey and lay out the "100 acres aforesaid," and to mark and stake out the same into 100 equal lots, with streets.

After such survey, laying-out, and valuations, any person making choice of a lot, and making entry thereof, with the person appointed by the commissioners, to keep the book of entries, and paying or giving security for payment of such sum, as should be by direction of the commissioners, rated upon such lot, and payable to the owner of the land, and building on such lot one sufficient twenty foot square house, at the least, before the last day of August, 1685, each respective lot to be held of the Lord Proprietary, his heirs forever, under the yearly rent of one penny current money, for each respective lot; the same, or any other manner of settlement or building thereon, according to the directions of the act, was to invest the said taker-up and builder with an estate of inheritance in the said lot to him, his heirs, and assigns forever. And also, upon tender of payment and refusal, the said buildings as aforesaid, with proof of such tender and refusal, were to be binding to all intents and purposes, against the said parties so refusing, their heirs, &c.

The commissioners for each respective county, named in this act, were to appoint a person to keep a book, wherein to enter down each man's choice of any respective lot.

The Surveyor's fee was to be 80lbs. of tobacco for each lot, to be paid by the taker-up.

In case the taker-up of any lot should refuse or neglect to build within the time by this act appointed, any person whatsoever, might take up the same, paying the tobacco first set on such lot, to the commissioner of the county, or to the person by them appointed to receive the same, for the use and benefit of the said town, provided such second taker-up begin to build such house, as was limited in the act within one month after such his entry, and finish the same within six months, which house, so built, should give and settle an estate of inheritance to him and his heirs forever, on said lot.

Lots not taken up in five years were to revert to their original owners "as in their first and former estate."

All ships and vessels trading with the province, after August, 1685, were required to "unload their respective goods and merchandise at such towns, ports and places only," as were in the "act before set down and appointed, on penalty of forfeiting all such goods and merchandizes by them landed, at any other places whatsoever, one-third to his lordship, one-third to the benefit of the next adjacent town in the county where such offence shall be committed, and one-third to the informer.

No merchant, factor, mariner, or other person, trading into the province, whether foreigner or inhabitants, was allowed to traffic, sell, or barter away any goods but at some of these legally appointed ports and towns, but it was allowed for workingmen's wages to be paid, and the inhabitants were permitted to buy at their own plantations, necessary provisions for their families, with any goods, &c., bought at any the ports, or with goods by them purchased, imported, and landed at any of the ports.

All goods and wares, of the growth, production, or manufacture of the province, intended for exportation, had to be brought to one of these ports for shipment, and all store-house keepers, having room for storage, were required under penalty, to allow goods brought for exportation to be stored, under rent of 10 lbs. of tobacco per hogshead. The store-house keeper acted by this receipt of goods as insurer of the goods, casualties by fire excepted.

"This effort to enlarge the "Town at Proctors," it appears, proved futile, for, in 1694, commissioners, with similar powers, to those given in the act of 1683, were re-appointed to do these 'first works over again."

CHAPTER XV.

THE IMPEACHMENT OF MAJOR THOMAS TRUMAN.

[1675.] The Susquehannock Indians, at one time one of the most powerful tribes in Maryland, had to retreat before the advance of the ferocious Senecas, and, in 1675, the former located themselves in the country of the Piscattoways at the head of the Potomac.

Several murders having been committed by these Indians, Maryland and Virginia united in sending a force against them. The troops invested a fort occupied by the Susquehannocks, from which during the course of the siege, five Indian chiefs were induced, under offers of friendship and promises of protection, to come into the colonial camp, in which they were treacherously murdered.

This base conduct aroused the indignation of the people of Maryland, and Major Truman was impeached and tried for murder in 1676.

The first article of impeachment declared:

"Articles against major Thomas Truman exhibited by the lower house of assembly to the right honourable the Lord Proprietary, and upper house of Assembly.*

"We, your lordship's most humble, true, faithful and obedient people, the burgesses and delegates in your lower house of assembly, being constrained, by necessity of our fidelity and conscience, in vindication of the honour of God, and the honour and welfare of your lordship and this province, do complain and shew that the said major Thomas Truman, late commander-in-chief upon an expedition against the Indians at the Susquehannah forte, hath, by many and sundry ways and means, committed divers and sundry enormous crimes and offences, to the dishonour of Almighty God, against the laws of nations, contrary to your lordship's commission and instructions, and to the great endangering of your lordship's peace, and the good and safety of your lordship's province, according to the articles hereafter mentioned, that is to say:

"We find, upon reading your lordship's commission and instructions, and the affidavits which we herewith send to your lordship and upper house of assembly, and which we humbly submit to you lordship's examination and serious consideration.'

* Archives of Maryland Assembly Proceedings, p. 185.

"The first. That the said major Truman hath broken his commission and instructions thus : that the said major Thomas Truman having received six Indians sent out by the Susquehannahs as embassadors to treat with him on the Sunday after the arrival of the Maryland forces, and received their paper and meddall,† by which we find they were received as friends, and in amity with us, and had liberty of going back to the fort. and were assured that no intention of force was to be used against them, and that no damage should be done to them, their wives, or children, and that they did, that night. go into the forte, and the next morning did return again with the like number, only one Indian changed, and supposed to come on purpose to treat, and not in any hostile manner, yet the said major Thomas Truman, without calling any council of warr of your lordship's officers under his command. as he ought to have done, did, in a barbarous and cruel manner, cause five of the said Indians to be killed and murdered. contrary to the law of God and nations, and contrary to your lordship's commission and instructions."

The upper house after a "full hearing on both sides, and after reading of the said major's commission and instructions from his lordship and council," found Major Truman guilty as impeached, and ordered a messenger to be sent to the lower house to draw up a bill of attainder against him.

The lower house prescribed in the bill a fine as punishment. The upper house objected to a fine being levied for "such broad crimes," and said ; "it will be much wondered by those who shall hear and view our proceedings thereon. what shall be the cause why the same hath been past over with so slender and slight a punishment, being no more than what crimes of a more inferior nature might have deserved."

The lower house replied to this by saying "that the said Major Truman, for his crime does not deserve death. in regard that several circumstances that appeared at his tryall, extenuated his crime very much, as the unanimous consent of the Virginians, and the eager impetuosity of the whole field. as well Marylanders, upon the sight of the Christians murdered at Mr. Hinson's, and them very Indians that were there killed. being proved to be murderers, both of them and several other Christians ; and in regard, also; that it appears to this house that the said crime was not maliciously perpetrated. or out of any design to prejudice the province, but merely out of ignorance, and to prevent a mutiny of the whole army, as well Virginians as Marylanders ; wherefore, this house do not think fitt to recede from their former vote."

Between the differences of the two houses on the subject, Major Truman appears to have escaped punishment altogether.

† Very probably those received when they made the Treaty with the Puritans on the Severn in 1652.

CHAPTER XVI.
Removal of the State Capital from St. Mary's to Annapolis.

[1694.] Plant a capital on any site, and it immediately throws out its tendrils, and takes root in the body politic and in the affections of the people. Time increases the depth of these roots, and diminishes the chances of their transplanting. History establishes the fact that capitals are not easily removed from one place to another, and that a State clings to the site of its ancient capital with almost religious veneration. Catholic Italy, for a time deprived of its early seat of government, at the favorable moment, put its armies in motion, and headed by a son of the Church, thrusts the Pope into the narrow confines of the Vatican, and seizes upon its ancient capital to the joy of a Catholic people.

Maryland, since her settlement as a colony, has had but two substantial changes of her capital. Several temporary removals of the place of the meeting of the General Assembly and the sessions of the Courts have taken place, but from 1634, the year of the settlement of Maryland, to 1683, "St. Marie's," in St. Mary's county, remained legally, and, most of the time, really, the venerated capital of Maryland.

The first evidence St. Mary's had that its treasured prerogative, the possession of the capital, could be taken from her, was in 1654, after the parliamentary commissioners, Bennett and Claiborne, had reduced the colony to obedience to the commonwealth—to which authority it was never overtly disobedient. The Assembly, called by the Puritan provincial authorities, met at one Richard Preston's house on the Patuxent River, to which place the documents and records of the colony had been removed. In 1656, whilst St. Mary's remained the residence of Lord Baltimore's Lieutenant in the Province, Gov. Fendall, Patuxent still continued the place of the regular meeting of the General Assembly. St. Mary's, in the year 1659, was fully restored to all her ancient prerogatives, and, in that year, the session of the General Assembly was held there.

St. Mary's remained undisturbed in her re-acknowledged honors until 1683, when, through the remoteness of the town from the rest of the province, its inconvenience, and expense of access, which had always been "felt and often complained of," she was once more temporarily shorn of her laurels. The will of the Proprietary and feelings of the people conspired to sustain the privileges of this ancient city; but the former, in 1683, yielded to the desires of the long-suffering people, and the Assembly was removed, with the courts and provincial offices, to a place called the "Ridge," in Anne Arundel county. One session only of the General Assembly was held here. The poor accommodations of the Ridge drove them hence, and the peripatetic capital took up its abode on Battle Creek, on the Patuxent River, from whence, after a session of three days only, it was again removed to its old site, the city of St. Mary's. The Provincial Court found it necessary to adjourn* also from the Ridge, from the want of necessary accommodations.

Once more settled at St. Mary's, the Proprietary gave the inhabitants of that town a written promise that the capital "should not be removed again during his life." Resting under this assurance the people of St. Mary's had reason to feel secure in the possession of the capital of the province, at least, for the uncertain duration of the proprietary's life. Subsequent events proved the vanity of human calculations upon this tenure.

* McMahon's Maryland, p. 251.

Providence, evidently, had a desire for the location of the seat of government within its limits very early in its history, for in 1674, when the Legislature was considering the propriety of erecting a State House, prison, and office, at the Ridge, a member of the lower house stated, and the house sent the message to the Governor and Council that "there are severall persons of qualitie in Anne Arundel county that will undertake to build a State House, prison and office at there own charge onlie to be repaid by the countrey when the buildings are finished and to build a House for his Excelency, at their own proper costs and charges." The Lower House showed that it was fully ripe for the innovation by voting "that it be necessarie and this house doe petition his Excelencie accordinglie."

The Upper House gave a sharp reply. It returned "answer to which vote the Captaine General signifieth to the Lower House that he, having by writiceing allreadic declared his choice and the public faith being allreadie passed, and conceiving that this Last Paper is noe answer to the last message of this House tuching the Buildings, doth not thinke fit to take anie further notice of the said Paper; but that the Lower House be desired to signefie to this House of what dimension the said Buildings are to be and then some persons will offer themselves as undertakers of the same."

In 1689, William of Orange mounted the throne of England, and Protestantism became the ascendant religion in that kingdom. Lord Baltimore received instructions to proclaim William and Mary, as sovereigns, in the province of Maryland. He promptly obeyed the command. His orders, however, failed to reach his agents in Maryland in proper season, and, waiting to hear his mind in the matter, the Proprietary's "timid deputies lost him his government by shirking in a moment of emergency above the ordinary restrictions of law, from the exercise of powers not nominated in their commission."†

The instrument of the revolution in the province was an organization known as "An Association in arms for the defense of the Protestant religion, and for asserting the rights of King William and Queen Mary to the province of Maryland and all the English dominions." John Coode was the leader of the association. After a brief struggle, the association, in August, 1689, obtained entire possession of the province. A convention was immediately held in the name of the association, and a full account of the proceedings and purposes of the organization was submitted to the King.

The King approved the revolution, and the province remained under the authority of the convention until April 9th, 1692. At that time, in accordance with the wishes of the convention, Sir Lionel Copley, who had appointed the first royal governor of Maryland, assumed control of the affairs of the province. He convened the Legislature immediately. Notwithstanding the governor counselled moderation in legislation, the General Assembly commenced its work by throwing a fire brand in the province, in thanking the King for redeeming them "from the arbitrary will and pleasure of a tyrannical Popish government under which they had so long groaned." A most gratuitous and unwarrantable assertion. They followed up that charge, with the establishment of the protestant religion in the province, and providing for its support by general taxation. Lord Baltimore's agents

† McMahon's Maryland, p. 236.

were then prohibited from receiving port duties, and his collection of his land rents was grievously interferred with.

The old city of St. Mary's, around which clustered all the historic associations of early settlement, and which had been the permanent seat of government since the existence of the colony, was immolated in turn upon the altar of revolution. The town at this time, 1694, contained about sixty houses—a number it had reached a few years after its settlement. It had soon obtained its full growth. Stunted in its early energies, its vital powers were sapped, and, at the period when the removal of the capital was suggested, had become "a mere landing-place for the trade of its own immediate neighborhood." St. Mary's had several disadvantages that presented the town unfavorably to the body of Legislators. Situated at the southern extremity of the province, it was remote from the rest of the inhabitants, and the expense and inconvenience, in those days of incommodious traveling, attended access to, and egress from the place. Besides its local disadvantages, it had one feature to discommend it to the partizans of that day. Its people were Catholics, whilst the Legislature was peculiarly Protestant, at least, as far as illiberal men could represent protestant principles. With all these against it, there is no wonder at the result, although a State House of respectable dimensions at St. Mary's indicated what expense would attend the loss of one capitol, and the building of another.

The place contemplated as the new capital was the "Town at Proctors," now Annapolis. This place, as we may judge from an almost contemporary description of it, was not so large even as St. Mary's but, by an act of the Legislature of 1683, it had been created as a town and port of entry. In 1694, previous to the removal of the capital, it was named, "Anne Arundel Town," and was made the residence of the district collector, the naval officer, and their deputies, "for the dispatch of shipping." Passing ahead of the period of which we are writing, we quote a description of the town penned about six years later. It reads, "Col. Nicholson has done his endeavor to make a town of that place. There are about forty dwelling houses in it, seven or eight of which can afford a good lodging or accommodations for strangers. There are also a State House and a free school, built of brick, which make a great show among a parcel of wooden houses, and the foundation of a church is laid, the only brick church in Maryland. They have two market days in a week; and had Gov. Nicholson continued there a few months longer, he had brought it to perfection."‡

The people of St. Mary's were not disposed to let this valued treasure slip from their grasp, without making the most strenuous efforts to retain it. They turned their eyes toward Gov. Nicholson, lifted up their hands, and, casting themselves at his feet in an agony of desperation, as their only hope, prayed him for succor in this, the day of their calamity. They directed a petition to him as "his Excellency," and as "Captain General and Governor in chief, in and over this, their Majestys' province and Territory of Maryland." The address began, "The Mayor, Recorder, Aldermen, Common Councilmen, and Freemen, of the city of St. Mary's in the said province, and principally, from the bottom of their hearts, they rejoice in your Excellency's happy accession to this, your Government; and sincerely

‡ Oldmixon's History of Virginia.

pray for your peaceable and quiet enjoyment thereof, and long and prosperous continuance therein for the Glory of God, their Majestys' service, the good and benefit of their subjects, and your own particular comfort and satisfaction.''

The petition then proceeds to supplicate the Governor to continue to the petitioners "their ancient franchises, rights, and privileges, granted them by their charter with such other benefits and advantages as hath been accustomed and generally allowed, and, from time to time, continued to them by your predecessors, rulers, and governors of the province, humbly offering and proposing to your Excellency these following reasons as motives inducing thereto.''

These reasons were classed under sixteen heads. The first, in full: "*Imprimis*, As that it was the prime and original settlement of the province, and from the first seating thereof for above sixty years hath been the antient and chief seat of Government.''

The second reason was because Lord Baltimore had conferred on it, in consideration of the above fact, especial privileges.

The third paragraph set forth that the capital should remain where it was, because "the situation in itself is most pleasant and healthful, and naturally commodious in all respects for the purpose, being plentifully and well watered with good and wholesome springs, and almost encompassed around with harbor for shipping, where five hundred sail of ship, at least, may securely ride at anchor before the city.'' The town also contained, this section asserted, excellent points of land on which to erect fortifications to defend the said shipping, and for the preservation of the "public magazine and records of the province.''

The fourth argument recited that the capital ought not to be removed, because, by an act of the Legislature of 1662, land was bought, and in 1674, the Legislature passed an act to build a State House and a prison, which cost the province 300,000 pounds of tobacco; and in the next asserted that the inhabitants of St. Mary's had made and paid a free offering of 100,000 pounds of tobacco to build Lord Baltimore a house adjacent to the town.

The sixth and seventh paragraphs recounted the removal of the Legislature and Courts to the Ridge in 1683, and those inconveniences that brought again the capital to the "antient seat of government.''

The eighth reason given was that, for the encouragement of the inhabitants of St. Mary's to make provision for the accommodation of the persons who would be called to the town by public business, Lord Baltimore promised the seat of government should not be removed from St. Mary's during his life.

The ninth section states that "upon which encouragement given, several of the Inhabitants of the said city have launched out, disbursed considerable estates to their great impoverishment and almost utter ruin, if they should be defeated of such, their promised encouragement, and not only so, but divers others the inhabitants for several miles about contiguous and adjacent to the said county, upon the same encouragement of his Lordship, have seated themselves upon mean and indifferent lands, and laid out their estates, and made improvements thereon, barely for the raising of stock wherewith to supply the said city for the end and purpose aforesaid, which is now become their whole and only dependence for their future support and maintenance.''

The tenth paragraph laid down the advantages of St. Mary's, as to its convenience for masters of vessels and others coming in and going out of the province, for the dispatch of letters and expresses, its accessibleness from Patuxent and Potomac Rivers, and the "Main Bay," and the colony of Virginia, "with whom" the petition affirmed, "mutual intercourse and correspondence is most undeniably necessary and material."

The eleventh reason given announced that the capital should not be removed because Gov. Copley had been required to enter upon his gubernatorial duties at St. Mary's!

The twelth set forth that "scarce any precedent can be produced of so sudden a change, as the removal of the antient and chief seat of government, upon the careless suggestion and allegation of some particular persons for their own private interest an advantage;" and evidently to array Gov. Nicholson upon the side of St. Mary's, the petitioners flattered him with the soft impeachment that the removal of the capital was invested with him as their majestys' representative, and, at his Excellency's "feet," continued the petitioners, "we humbly cast ourselves for relief and support against the calamities and ruin wherewith we are threatened, and wholly relying upon your Excellency's grace and favor therein, with whom, we also conceive, should be good manners in all persons first to treat and interceed, before they presume to make any peremptory result, in case of so high a nature as this may be."

The thirteenth and fourteenth paragraphs reminded the Governor that, in 1692, "it was put to the vote of a full house, whether the holding of the Courts and Assembly at Saint Mary's were a grievance, or not, and carried in the negative," and they, the petitioners "humbly conceive that house did well consider all difficulties and outlays, losses, and expenses to be incurred in moving the capital, besides the hazards and casualties of removing and transporting the records from one place to another, of which already some experience hath been had."

To meet all the objections of inconvenience of travel to the "antient and chief seat of government," the petitioners offered to provide as soon as possible "a coach, or caravan, or both, to go at all times of public meeting of Assemblies and Provincial Courts, and so forth, every day, daily, between St. Mary's and Patuxent River, and at all other times, once a week, and also to keep constantly on hand a dozen horses at least, with suitable furniture, for any person, or persons, having occasion to ride post, or otherwise, with or without a guide, to any port of the province on the Western shore."

The sixteenth and concluding paragraph argued that the objection that St. Mary's was not in the centre of the province, and, therefore, not suitable as the capital, was conspicuously untenable from the fact that the Imperial Court is held in London, "as far from the centre of England as St. Marie's in this province; Boston, in New England; Port Royal, in Jamaica; Jamestown, in Virginia; and almost all other, their Majesties American plantations, where are still kept and continued in their first antient stations and places, the chief seat of government and courts of judicature."

Then follow the names of the Mayor, Aldermen and Councilmen of St. Maries, with the freemen thereof, among the latter being that of John Coode.

After the signatures comes an especial sop for the governor's vanity, in which the same parties hoped that the reasons and motives herewith offered to his Excellency and the Council will prevent their assent to the contemplated law, and affirmed that they placed their reliance on "his Excellency's known experience, assisted by so worthy a council." They urged again that it was a royal prerogative only to change the seat of government, and when that authority was invaded "the State is in a confusion." Knowing their Majesties' respect for the rights of their subjects, as "sufficiently evidenced by their placing *a person of your Excellency's known regard to the same at the helm of the government*, the petitioners do humbly conceive that it is not consistent with the rules of gratitude for so great a blessing, as to pass a law which your petitioners are well informed, is an apparent incroachment upon their Majesties' prerogative."

They supplemented their lengthly review of the case with a prayer, which *showed* how solicitous the people of St. Mary's were for the reputation of the State. "Least," said the petitioners, "the province may be so blamed as to have it said that it was the first of the American plantations, that offered violence to the prerogative of so worthy a prince," they ask that the governor will reject the bill, until, at least, leave be first obtained from his Majesty. An apology for putting with so much freedom his Excellency in mind of a matter which they knew was his "chiefest care to preserve," concludes the paper. The Governor sent the petition to the lower house.

The quaint and jeering reply of that body to this petition was found in a yellow and musty MS, at the Land Office, Annapolis, Md. It is quoted entire:

"By the Assembly, Oct. the 11th, 1694.

"This House have read and considered of the petitions and reasons of the Mayor, Aldermen, and others, calling themselves Common Council and Freemen of the City of St. Maries, against removing the Courts and Assembly of, from this Corner and poorest place in the province, to the Center and best abilitated place thereof. Although wee conceive the motives there laid downe, are hardly deserving any answer at all, many of them being *against the plain matter of fact*, some against reason, and all against Generall good and wellfaire of the province ; yet, because your Excellency has been pleased to lay them before us, wee humbly returne this, our sence of the same, that as to the 1 : 2 : 3 : 4 : 5 : 6 : 7 : and 8 : Reasons, relating to what his Lord Proprietary has thought fitt to doe to the city of St. Maries, it is noe Rule, nor Guide to their Majesties, your Excellency, nor this house. *Itt seemes in some parts to reflect* on his Lord Proprietary more than this house believes is true, or deserved by his Lord Proprietary.

"2. As to the 9 : this house say that it is against the plain matter of fact, for wee can decerne noe Estate, either laid out, or to lay out in, or about this famous City comparable with other parts of this province. But they say, and can make appeare that there has been moore Money spent here, by three degrees or more, than this city and all the inhabitants for tenn miles round is worth, and say that having had 60ty-odd years experience of this place, and almost a quarter part of the province devoured by it, and still, like Pharoah's kine, remain as

at first, they are discouraged to add any more of their substance to
such ill improvers.

"As to the Tenth and Eleventh, wee conceive the being of St.
Maries soe neare Virginia, is not soe great an advantage to the province, as the placeing the Courts in the Centre and Richest part of
the same, which is noe great distance from thence of Virginia either,
and nearer New York and other Governments which wee have as
much to doe with as Virginia, if not more, and the place as well
watered and as Commodious in all respects as St. Maries, which has
only served hither to cast a Blemish upon all the rest of the province
in the Judgment of all discerning strangers who, perceiving the
meanness of the head, must rationally judge proportionably* of the
body thereof.

"To the 12: 13: and 14: they say that they doe not hold themselves
accountable to the Mayor and his Brethern for what they doe for their
countrey's service, nor by what measures they do the same, nor what
time they shall take to doe it in, nor for what reasons; and are, and
will be as carefull of the records and properties of the people, as the
proprietary.

"To the 15th: the house say the petitioners offer faire as they have
done formerly: but never yet performed any, and this house believes
that the Generall welfare of the province ought to take place of that
sugar plum of all the Mayor's Coaches, who, as yet, has not one.

"To the 16: this house conceive that the citty of St. Maries is very
unequally rankt with London, Boston, Port Royall, &c.

"All which wee humbly offer to your Excellency's juditious Consideration."

All the honeyed words of flattery that fell from the lips of the petitioners upon the ear of his "Excellency," were also unavailing. On
the reception of the answer of the House of Delegates, the council
tersely recorded its view of the matter, in this brief paragraph—"This
Board concur with the said answers made by the House of Burgesses."

The removal was consummated the ensuing winter, and the Assembly met first on the 28th of February, 1694, (old style,) in its new
capital.

The archives of the province, which were the objects of such disinterested solicitude on the part of the people of St. Mary's were ordered
to be carried "in good strong bags, and to be secured with cordage
and hides, and well packed—with guards to attend them night and
day, *to be protected from all accidents,* (!) and to be delivered to the
Sheriff of Anne Arundel County at Anne Arundel Town." These records reached Annapolis in the winter of 1694-95.

* This word is found in a later copy. In the earlier records it seems to be
"exporconably."

CHAPTER XVII.

CHRONICLES OF ANNAPOLIS FROM 1694 TO 1700.

[1694.] By chapter 8, acts of 1694, passed Oct. 18th, the name of
"Town-Land at Proctors," now Annapolis, was changed to the "Town
and Port of Ann-Arundel." The commissioners by the act of 1694

were Major John Hammond, Major Edward Dorsey, Mr. John Bennett. Mr. John Dorsey, Mr. Andrew Norwood, Mr. Philip Howard, Mr. James Sanders, and the Honorable Nicholas Greenbury, Esq. The concluding section of this act, appointing the commissioners, says: "That, at the Town and Port at Severn in Anne Arundel county, shall be bought or valued by the Jury as before in this act is mentioned, all that parcel or neck of Land within Leary Neck-Cove* and Acton's Cove† lying and adjoining, or near, to the said Town as aforesaid, or so much thereof as by the commissioners shall be found convenient, to be fenced in and called THE TOWN COMMON,'OR PASTURE, and paid for, and fenced in at the Public Charge: And shall be for the public use and service, when need shall require, and that the inhabitants of the said Town shall not raise any of cattle or hogs, horse's or sheep, more than what they can contain and raise upon their respective lot or lots, and not more, at the discretion of the commissioners."

This same act also constituted Ann-Arundel town a port of entry and place of trade, and made it the place of residence of the collector of the district, naval officer, and their deputies, "for the dispatch of shipping."

[1695.] Dignified with the seat of government, Annapolis put on its honors with the stir of a new vitality. The Legislature ordered one or more places to be laid out and reserved as ship-yards, and passed an act giving Anne Arundel the Town the more euphonious title, of Annapolis, "Chap. II of this session enacting that the port shall for ever hereafter be denominated, called and known by the Name and Port of Annapolis, and by no other Name or Distinction whatever."

The first session of the Legislature in Annapolis was held in the house of Major Edward Dorsey, begining on February 28, 1694, O. S., (or 1695, N. S.)

One day during this session, the Legislature adjourned in a body to an ale-house, if, for other than the inferential reason, is not stated : but the affair excited the indignation of Governor Francis Nicholson.

Brick clay of good quality having been discovered near Annapolis, contracts were made with Casper August Herman, a burgess from Cecil, for building the parish church, school-house, and Stadt-house.*

This Assembly voted "that a publique ferry be kept upon Severn river at Annapolis, for the accommodation of the publique." Allen Robinett was appointed keeper of the ferry and was required to reside in Annapolis, and for his services was paid 9000 pounds of tobacco a year, out of the public revenues. This ferry was maintained by the Anne Arundel county authorities to the year 1887, when it was superseded by a bridge.

In the act of 1695, "for keeping good rules and orders in the Port of Annapolis," it was enacted that "for encouragement of all sorts. of tradesmen, or men of calling, to come and inhabit the town aforesaid, * * * * * that when any baker, brewer, tailor, dyer, or any such tradesmen, that, by their practice of their trade, may any ways annoy, or disquiet the neighbors or inhabitants of the town, it shall and may be lawful for the commissioners and trustees aforesaid, to allot and appoint such tradesmen such part or parcel of land, out of the present town pasture, as to the said commissioners shall seem meet

* In Graveyard Creek.
† In Spa Creek.
* State-house.

and convenient for the exercise of such trade, a sufficient distance
from the said town as may not be annoyance thereto, not exceeding
the quantity of one lot or acre of land to any one tradesman aforesaid. And provided, the same trade and lots of land for that use,
may be as near together and contiguous as the nature of the trade will
allow, without hindering or annoying one another, which said appointment and parcel of land aforesaid, allotted by the commissioners
and trustees aforesaid, shall be to such persons, tradesmen, and their
heirs for ever, and to the maintenance of such trades and not others."

[1696.] In this year, the Legislature passed an act for "keeping
good rules and order" in the town of Annapolis, and Gov. Nicholson,
the Honorable Sir Thomas Lawrence, the Honorable Nicholas Greenbury, the Honorable Thomas Tench, Major John Hammond, Major
Edward Dorsey, Mr. James Sanders, and Captain Richard Hill, or any
five of them, were made the body corporate for the town. The same
act gave Governor Nicholson a lot of land within the town common,
"for planting or making a garden, vine-yard, and summer-house."
This land comprised all that part of the town beginning on the north
east side the present dock, (then called Nicholson's Cove,) running
with a straight line to East street, with the said street to State House
Circle, with the Circle to Francis street, then down Francis to Church,
down Church to the south east side of the dock. There stood within
the lines of this lot, until fifteen years since a house, for many years
occupied by Mrs. Richard Ridgely, which tradition says was the house
where the first Governor who lived in Annapolis resided. That Governor was Francis Nicholson. The house stood on the corner of Hyde's
alley and Cornhill street and was of frame and of an architecture
curious and ancient.

It appears from the same act that Mr. Richard Beard had made a
map, or plot, of Annapolis.

The commissioners were authorized to erect a market-house and to
hold a market once a week, and a fair every year.

At the same session it was proposed to have a Bridewell, "if any
person would undertake to build and keep it that all idle and vagrant
perpers may be taken up and put to work there."

The house declared, "that such Bridewell, or house of correction, was
very necessary and convenient, but that the present ill circumstances
of this province will not admit the beginning or carrying on of any
new building then already undertaken."

For the improvement of Annapolis, it was proposed and adopted by
the house "that ye townes poeple be empowered to purchase a common, and for the commissioners of the said town to make bye-laws,
with power to ffyne any persons, inhabitants committing breach
there[f] in such summe to be ascertained." "To assess ye conduit made
at the publique charge. That the common be well cleaned with ye
points of land, and ye place dividing the common to be well d't hed."
"That an handsome pair of gates be made at ye coming in of the towne,
and two triangular houses built for ye rangers." "To have the way
from the gate to go directly to the top of ye hill without the towne, and
to be ditched on each side and sett with quick setts or some such thing."[*]

"That part of the land which lye on ye creeke,[†] by major Dorsey's

* Ridgely's Annals of Annapolis, p. 90.
† This creek stood on King George street and entered the garden where
Dr. S. N. [illegible] Eddy now resides.

house, whereby his excellency at present lives,[*] be sett aside for public buildings, and if in case the same happen to come within any of ye said major's lotts,—propose that land be given him elsewhere for it.

"To have in the said towne two ffairs a year, and persons coming thither not to be arrested for one day before the said ffair and one day after.

"That forty foot space be left along the water side within the port of Annapolis, for any person to build warehouses upon if the owners of such lotts that front upon the same do not build thereon in such a tyme to be sett." "That the holes made by grubbing up stumps and cutting off tops of stones in the said port of Annapolis be filled up."

It was proposed this session to build a church in Annapolis, and a committee was appointed to "inspect into the proposals for building the same."

Major Edward Dorsey, from the committee, reported 'that there was in Banck for building the church at Annapolis, £458 sterling. That they had *discoursed* workmen, and the carpenter demands for his work £250—the bricklayer, having all *stuff* upon the place, £220—the brickmaker £90—that they find no other means to raise money therefor without the assistance of some charitable disposed persons. That the charge of building the said church will amount to £1,200 sterling."

An was act passed the same day imposing a tax of "three pence per hundred on tobacco, to continue and be in force until the 12th day of May, which shall be in the year of our Lord God, 1698, and to be applied to the building of ye church at Annapolis." The architect of this church was Thomas Ffielder.

This year a Mr. Gaddess arrived at Annapolis, "being sent, out by his Lordship the Bishop of London and the house appointed him to read prayers in some vacant parish, and made a provision for his support of 10,000 pounds of tobacco."

The legislature at its May session, in 1696, passed the act, establishing at Annapolis the famous "King William's School." "for the propagation of the gospel and education of youth in good letters and manners." At this school the distinguished William Pinkney was a student.

Mr. Pinkney was a native of Annapolis, and his renown is naturally linked with that of another distinguished lawyer and son of Annapolis, Reverdy Johnson, who followed him in the classic halls of St. John's, the lineal descendant of King William's school. These two men, whose talents and renown have been the glory of the nation, ought to have barbed the arrows of derision that conceited minds have often aimed at the age and size of the ancient city. When the long roll of America's illustrious names is called, the little hamlet on the Severn proves its right to existence by pointing with just pride to Pinkney and Johnson as the peers of any, in virtue, intellect, and patriotism.

[1700.] A general visitation of the clergy of the province was held at Annapolis, May 23, 1700. This was summoned by Rev. Dr. Bray[†]

* This is the house where Mrs. Margaret Marchand now lives.
† Allen's St. Anne's Parish, p. 81.

5

who had been appointed by the Bishop of London, commissary of Maryland. This convocation, the first held in America, is memorable for orginating "the first missionary effort made by any part of the church on this continent." The field selected was Pennsylvania—the people the Quakers! Three clergymen appeared at this convocation from Anne Arundel. They were Henry Hall, of St. Jame's, Herring Cre·k ; Joseph Colbach, of All Hallows ; and Edward Topp, of Annapolis.

CHAPTER XVIII.

THE FIRST STATE HOUSE IN ANNAPOLIS.

[1696.] "The foundation of the First State House in Annapolis was laid April 30, 1696.*

[1697.] On the 11th of June, 1697, the Legislature passed the following :†

"Whereas, this Province hath been at great charge and expense in the building of a State House, or Public House of Judicature, at this Port of Annapolis, which is now almost finished and completed, and to the end that the said House and the several rooms and apartments therein, may in time present and to come, be applied and appropriated to the uses and purposes the same was designed for, and no other.

"II. Be it enacted by the King's Most Excellent Majesty, by and with the advice and consent of the present General Assembly, and the authority of the same, that the said State House and the several rooms and apartments therein, for the time present and to come, be, and is hereby appointed and appropriated to the uses and purposes hereafter mentioned, and no other, that is to say,

"III. The great room below stairs, for courts and assemblies to sit in ; the little room below the stairs to be for a magazine for everything but powder to lie in ; the two rooms on the right hand above stairs, for jury and committee rooms ; the two rooms on the left hand, to be for provincial and land-office records to be kept : and the fore-porch to be for the commissary's office, and records of probate of wills and granting administrations, &c., to be kept in : the two rooms on the right hand in the upper lofts, one for the county clerk to keep the county records in, and the other for Annapolis town clerk to keep his papers in ; and the other two rooms on the left hand, one of them for keeping the records of the Chancery court, and the other for keeping the records of the Governor and Councils in one part of it, and another part of the same room for lodging of all bonds, bills, certificates, dockets and other naval papers, transmitted from the Collectors and Naval Officers of this province. * * * * The room above the back-porch to be for the Clerk of the House of Delegates to keep the

† Bacon's Laws.
* Allen's History of St. Anne's, p. 27.

Journals of Proceedings of that House in : and the loft above the fore-porch over the Commissary's office to be for hanging a lanthorn out, and for a committee room."

Thus disposing of the apartments, the Assembly enacted that the "rooms be fitted up with all necessary and convenient boxes and shelves, desks, and tables to write on, and at the door of every office a bar be made, within which no person shall come, but the clerk of such office, unless upon urgent and great occasion."

"His Excellency, Francis Nicholson, his Majesty's present Governor of this province, the Honorable Sir Thomas Lawrence, Baronet, his Majesty's Secretary, and the Honorable Henry Jowles, Esq., Chancellor of the province, and the Honorable Kenelm Cheseldyn, the Commissary General," were made a committee to carry out the provisions of this act.

[1699.] This State House had a brief and tragic history. On the journal of the House of the 13th of July, 1699, is the following :

"Memorandum, that on Thursday, July 13th, about four or five of the clock in the afternoon, a violent flash of lightning broke into the State-house at Annapolis : the House of Delegates being there sitting, which instantly killed Mr. James Crauford, one of the members of Calvert county, and hurt and wounded several other members, and shattered and broke most part of the doors and window cases belonging to the said house, and sett ye said State House on fire in one of the upper chambers, and several other damages ; but the fire was presently quenched by the diligence and industry of his Excellency, Nathaniel Blackistone, his majesty's governor."‡

[1704.] In 1704, the State House was burned down. From what cause it was ignited is left to conjecture. Gov. Seymour in his message on the subject said :

"The late melancholy accident might have been prevented had my often admonitions took place : for I never saw any public building left solely to Providence but in Maryland. I hope this sad experiment will awaken your care for time to come, and in the interim your best considerations to secure the laws and records of your country for the advantage and quiet of future generations. What is proper to be done in rebuilding your Stadt-house, so very necessary for the accommodation of the public, I leave entirely to your own serious debates and decision, for I have no other aim than the true interest and service of your country."**

This State House had been ordered to be built by the Legislature of 1694.†

‡ Ridgely's Annals of Annapolis, p. 104.
** Ridgely's Annals of Annapolis, p. 105.
‡ Ridgely's Annals of Annapolis, p. 93.

CHAPTER XIX.

ST. ANNE'S PARISH.*

1692—1887.

[1692.] This parish is one of thirty which were established under the Act of Assembly, of 1692. The loss of the first twelve pages of the parish records has robbed us of much of its valuable history. In the returns, however, of the several vestries in the province to the Governor and his Council in 1692, St. Anne's was designated by the name of Middle Neck Parish, and consisted of the territory between South and Severn rivers.

The destruction of these pages of the records of the parish has left to speculation the origin of the name of the parish. There is, however, hardly any doubt but that it was named in honor of the reputed mother of the Virgin Mary, St. Ann; and so designated because it was a happy coincidence with the name of the Princess Anne, afterward Queen Anne, of England.

[1694.] On the 8th of October, 1694, the Governor proposed to his council that, at the port of Annapolis, a lot be laid off for the minister nigh to where the church is to stand, and that the minister be obliged to read prayers twice a day. On the 7th of May 1696, Mr. Coney, supposed to be the incumbent of St. Anne's Parish, preached before the assembly, and this sermon he was desired by the assembly to have printed.

[1696.] When St. Anne's returned its proceedings, as required by ch. 2d, acts of 1696, under the name of Middle Neck Parish, the taxable persons in it were stated to number 374. The vestrymen of the parish were given as : Thomas Bland, Richard Warfield, Lawrence Draper, Jacob Harnass, William Brown, Cornelius Howard. When King William's school was established the same year, 1696, Rev. Peregrine Coney, the supposed rector of St. Anne's, was one of its trustees.

On September 30th, the Lower House sent to the Upper the following message : "To show our readiness to contribut to the utmost of our abilities to the service of God, in building a free church and school at Annapolis, we have proposed and resolved, that out of the revenue raised for the charge of the Province, by 3d per hhd. on tobacco, one year's revenue so raised be for defraying the charge of the church at Annapolis."

The Lower House, preparatory to passing this Act, appointed a committee to inspect the proposals for building the church ; which reported that there was in bank for this purpose £458 sterling. This had arisen from the sale of the tobacco which had been collected. They also reported that the church would cost £1200 sterling, about $7,000.

These were busy times in Annapolis. The State House, King William's School, and St. Anne's, for, on the 2d of October, the Governor

* For the early facts of this page I am mainly indebted to Rev. Ethan Allen's History of St. Anne's Paris .

was selected by the council to employ workmen to build the church, were all in course of erection.

This was the first brick church in Maryland, but not the first place of worship in Annapolis. There was a meeting-house of the Puritans in Annapolis thirty years before this and the records show there was also a house dedicated to the service of God on Greenbury's Point that also antedated St. Anne's.

[1697.] On the 30th of June, 1697, a petition from Ruth Gregg was laid before the Governor and his council. Rev. Peregrine Coney was defendant. This document, with Mr. Coney's defence, was ordered to be given to Mr. Carroll, "the said Ruth's procurator." The nature of the complaint has not come down to us, but Mr. Coney appears to have enjoyed, and never to have lost, the fullest confidence of Governor Nicholson, who gave him the duty of issuing marriage licenses. His sermons were frequently asked for publication by the Assembly.

[1699.] Gov. Nicholson selected the site of St. Anne's, and was the active agent in its erection. Gov. Blackiston succeeded Gov. Nicholson, and, in the former's term, July 22, 1699, an Act of Assembly imposed a fine of £333, 6 s. 8 p., on Edward Dorsey for not fulfilling his agreement to build the church ; and another Act of the same session appointed persons to treat with workmen to build it.

[1704.] Rev. Mr. Topp followed as the second rector of St. Anne's and Rev. James Wootten was the third, and, in 1704, the vestrymen were recorded as Col. John Hammond, Mr. William Bladen, Mr. William Taylard, Mr. Amos Garrett, Mr. John Freeman, Mr. Samuel Norwood. An entry on the parish records, ordering payment for altering the gallery seats, shows that the church was finished. Thomas Ffielder was the architect of the edifice. The entries in the parish records also discover to us that the first St. Anne's had both bell and belfry, and a golden ball adorned the spire.

The church was build in the shape of a T, and was neatly finished inside. The principal entrance faced east, that is toward the State House.

[1706.] In 1706, the General Assembly, ever mindful of St. Anne's, directed that, of the three lots originally laid out within the city, one should be for the rector of the Parish, one for the Sexton, and a third for the clerk of the vestry and commissary's clerk. The revenues of St. Anne's were further exhanced by an order requiring 40 shillings for every corpse buried in the church yard. This was the ground about the church and is embraced in the present circle. The graveyard extended beyond its present limits into the streets as excavations within its beds painfully proved a few years since.

The revenues at this period were exceedingly meagre, and it is estimated that in 1717 the rector did not receive over $350 per annum.

[1719.] May 15, 1719, the vestry of St. Anne's laid before the Lower House of Assembly the grievances under which the parish labored. The gravamen of their burden was that the parish church, by being built near the utmost verge of the parish, is hereby rendered very inconvenient to a great part of the parishioners, some of these living twenty miles, and others at a greater distance from it, so that were "it not that the rector voluntarily goes up at appointed times and preaches among them, a great part of them would be without the benefits of a minister ; that to add to this difficulty the church is much too little for a parish church, many of the parishoners being obliged to stay at home for want of room, but that this is most visible at public times, as we humbly conceive is apparent to the constant experience of this Honorable House, that there is no visible way to remove the first of these difficulties, but by contracting the parish into narrower bounds, or dividing it, nor is there any means to remove the latter but by enlarging the church, but no both these are rendered impracticable to us by some other difficulties which we shall take the liberty of naming to your honors."

The first remedy was open, the report continued, to the objection that the benefits of this parish are already so small, that it is but a bare support for "a single man in a parish," but to that is added that being "Chaplain to the public," he "is unavoidably exposed to much greater expense than the benfits of the parish can defray" which has often been the cause of the parish being without a minister.

The second remedy could not be applied as the vestrymen had no means with which to enlarge. The Legislature took no notice of this printed applications for an increase of revenues.

At this time one family came thirty miles to church, having to drive on Saturday into the neighborhood, so as to be able to reach Church on Sunday.

[1723.] May 7th, 1723, Alexandria Frazier, Robt. Gordon, Thomas Worthington, Vachel Denton, Joshua George and William, obtained permission to build at their own expense a gallery at the west end of the church.

[1727.] April 4th, 1727, several parishoners of St. Anne's, V. Denton, Thomas Worthington, John Beall, and Philip Hammond, with A. Frazier, rector, obtained permission to build a chapel in the upper part of the parish. This was asked on account of the inconvenience of reaching Annapolis for church. The site selected was the head of South River. No church, or chapel could be built in the province without the permission of the Lord Proprietory, and he had delegated his power to his Governor, Charles Calvert, who gave the requisite license.

May 2nd, 1727, permission was granted to Mr. Richard Claggett "to erect a pew where the font stood," and on July 4, the vestrymen granted permission "to erect a gallery over the pews appointed for the gentlemen of the Assembly." On May 7, 1728, the following petition on the same subject was presented to the vestry as the humble petition of some of the parishoners of said Parish :

[1728.] "That, in consideration of the smallness of the parish and that there was much want of room, you were pleased to encourage your parishioners by giving them leave sometimes since to build a gallery towards the north-east end of the said church, and your petitioners made provisions according thereto, but some vestries after, we understood you were inclined to enlarge the said gallery by making it extend from near the pulpit all over the assembly pews and over the chancel, until it should reach near the Governor's pew, a design very much wished for and of a general good and service, and by these contrivances the church may be made to hold almost as many above as below. And we are humbly of opinion, as we believe all good and considerate men will be likewise, that the best ornament to a church is a good pastor and a large flock, we thank God we are blest with the one, (Rev. John Humphrey,) but want of room obstructs the other. In consideration of which, we with patience waited to know your resolutions, and, at length, being ordered to go on with your first direction which we did accordingly till we were prevented by Mr. John Beale, who told us not to proceed any further until further orders We, therefore, having been at considerable charges, and loss of time in proceeding with the said work according to your orders, humbly hope your honors will take it into your consideration. And we beg leave to know your commands, being fully persuaded that it will be most consistent to the honor and praise of God, and to the great benefit and advantage of the said church and people. In hopes of which with humble submission your petitioners as in duty bound shall ever pray.

"Richard Tootell, Simon Duff, Peter Werard, Wm. Ghiselen."

The vestry ordered the petitioners to proceed with the erection of the gallery.

[1740.] In 1740, St. Anne's was enlarged, but this enlargement did not accommodate its increasing congregation, and, in 1741, leave was given to build a gallery to hold eleven pews.

[1750.] In 1750, the assembly passed a tax bill to raise a sinking fund to protect the colonists from border ravages by the Indians. In the taxables were bachelors. A list from each parish was ordered to be returned to the Government. The list in St. Anne's Parish included Gov. Sharpe and Rev. John McPherson, the rector of St. Anne's, who, not caring to determine whether they came under the list of taxables, or not, the vestry settled their status for them by ordering them on the list. All over 25 years of age, assessed under £300 and over £100 were taxed five shillings each, and the law remained in force six years. Joshua Frazier. Richard Green and Allen Quynn, paid till 1751, Baldwin Lusby paid for 1756: Caleb Davis and Emanuel Marriott for 1756-7, and Rezin Gaither, at the head of Severn, for 1756-7-8.

[1756.] Those assessed over £300, were taxed 20s. each and William Stuart, John Ridout. John Gilliss, and Daniel Wolfstenhome, Stephen Bordley, and Charles Carroll, barrister, paid it for six years. James Maccubbin, Beall Nicholson, of Annapolis, William Gaither, head of Severn, Charles Hammond, of Philip, and John Griffith paid it for five years. Col. Benj. Tasker and Lancelot Jacques; paid the tax for four years. James Johnson. John Leadler, and Zachariah Hood; paid it for three years. The last was the stamp-officer in 1765, and had to flee the city before the wrath of the people. Moses Maccubbin and John Davis paid the tax for two years; and S. Lowe, Charles Cole, William Thornton, Charles Carroll, Esq., Dr. Upton Scott, Robert Strain, Robert Conden, Benj. Beall, and John Bennett paid it for one year.

Non-attendance upon the services of the church about this time became such a serious evil, that on March 6, 1751, the wardens of St. Anne's gave this public notice in the columns of the *Gazette*:

"The Church wardens of St. Anne's Parish, in Anne Arundel county, do hereby signify that we shall be under a necessity of observing the Laws of this Province, and the Statutes of England, relating to religious worship : and more particularly the 14th section of the first Elizabeth, Chap. 2, which oblige all persons, not having lawful excuse, to resort to their Parish Church, or Chapel, on every Sunday, and other days ordained and used to be kept as Holy Days, and then and there to abide in decent manner, during the time of common prayer, preaching, or other services of God; and therefore request all concerned to take notice.

"Samuel Howard, Gamaliel Butler, Church Wardens."

On the 29th of June 1761, an organ loft was ordered, the first mention looking to the use of an organ in the church.

On the 2nd of February, 1768, the vestry ordered a search for the deed of the parsonage, lot K in Annapolis. It was found, and was dated 1759. It was from Philip Key, of St. Mary's and Theodosea, his wife, to the Rev. Alex. Williamson and vestry; consideration £20. The lot is described, as lying on the Southwest side of Hanover St., running South 156 feet, and Northwest 196, the whole corresponding with the parsonage used until the present decade, and which is now owned by Mrs. Owen A. Iglehart.

[1767.] It was at this period that St. Anne's had a notorious pastor, the Rev. Bennett Allen, the seventeenth incumbent. His was a spirit born to intrigue and violence. A graduate and fellow of Wadham College, Oxford, April 20, 1767, he presented his letters of introduction to the vestry from Gov. Sharpe. Mr. Allen was a particular friend of Lord Baltimore, who wrote Gov. Sharpe to give him whatever he wished in the province. Mr. Allen had his eye on All Saints Parish, in Frederick, which was worth nearly $5,000 per annum, and whilst he was waiting for the aged rector to drop into his grave, he accepted St. Anne's. For a year all went well, the rector being held in general esteem, and with lavish hand spending a whole year's income to improve the glebe house. On the 24th of October, Mr. Allen received from the Governor, a license as curate of St. James, Anne Arundel, and the rector soon after dying, he received letters of induction and became its rector, w..ilst still holding on to the rectorship of St. Anne's with the consent of both vestries. This permission he obtained by unfair means, and for it received a challenge from one of St. James' vestry. He also became involved in a quarrel with Daniel Dulany, Esq., it is said, who visited him with personal chastisement in the streets of Annapolis.

[1768.] In June 1768, the rector of All Saints being dead, Mr. Allen was presented with that parish. He was mobbed on the very first Sunday of his appearance, under the influence, he said, of the Dulanys. Mr. Allen resigned St. Anne's and after holding on to All Saints one year resigned that also.

Allen was a tory and, as by the bill of rights, the support of the clergy ceased in November, 1776, he returned to England. There on the 18th of June, 1782, he challenged Mr. Lloyd Dulany, formerly of Maryland, but then in London, and killed him. It is said of Allen that he died in wretched poverty, being intemperate and degraded about the streets of London. He is said to have been a man, not only of finished scholarship, but of fine personal appearance and address. He was, however, destitute of principle and piety, profane, grasping and haughty; "poor wretched man!"[*]

[1770.] Nothing went on in Annapolis at this time that escaped the eye or ear of the observant Eddis, who arrived in Annapolis,

†.Allen's History of St. Anne's.]

September 4th, 1770. "Understanding" he writes, "that I was in time for divine service, I availed myself of an immediate opportunity to offer up my fervent acknowledgement at the throne of grace. * * * * The exterior of the church, (St. Anne's,) has but little to recommend it, but the congregation was numerous. The solemn offices were performed with a becoming devotion, and my mind was in perfect unison with the important duties of the day."

[1771.] St. Anne's was the only church in the city and notwithstanding it was the protege of the State, it was allowed to fall into a ruinous condition. Its minister often remonstrated with his congregation and urged the repairing or rebuilding of it. September 5, 1771, the following poem appeared in the Maryland *Gazette*, addressed: "To the very worthy and respectable inhabitants of Annapolis, the humble petition of the old church, showeth:

"That, late in century the last,
By private bounty, here were placed,
My sacred walls, tho', in truth,
Their style and manner be uncouth;
Yet, whilst no structure met mine eye,
That even with myself could vie,
A goodly edifice I seemed, •
And pride of all Saint Anne's was deemed.
How changed the times: for now, all round,
Unnumbered stately piles abound,
All better built, and looking down
On me quite antequated grown.
Left unrepaired, to time a prey,
I feel my vitals fast decay:
And often have I heard it said,
That some good people are afraid,
Least I should tumble on their heads.
Of which, indeed, this seems a proof—
They seldom come beneath my roof.
The stadt-house, that, for public good,
With me co-eval long had stood;
With me full many a storm had dared,
Is now at length to be repaired:
Or, rather, to be built anew,
An honour to the land and you.
Whilst I alone, not worth your care,
•Am left your sad neglect so bear.
With grief, in yonder field, hard by,
A sister-ruin I espy;
Old Bladens place, once so famed,
And now too well, "the folly" named.
Her roof all tottering to decay,
Her walls a mouldering all away:
She says, or seems to say, to me,
'Such too, ere long, thy fate shall be.'
Tho', now forever gone and lost,
I blush to say, how little cost,
The handsome pile would have preserved,
Till some new perfect had deserved

A mansion here, from us, to have
As good as Carolina gave.
But party, faction (friends that still
Have been the foes of public weal)
The dogs of war against her slipped,
And all her rising honours nipped,
Of sunshine oft a casual ray,
Breaks in upon a cloudy day,
O'erwhelm'd with woe : methinks, I see
A ray of hope thus dart on me.
Close at my door, on my own land,
Placed there, it seems, by your command,
I've seen, I own, with some surprise,
A novel structure sudden rise.
There let the stranger stay, for me,
If virtue's friends, indeed one be.
I would not, if I could, restrain,
A moral stage ; yet, would I fain
Of your indulgence and esteem,
At least, an equal portion claim.
And, decency, without my prayers,
Will surely whisper in your ears,
'To pleasure, if such care you shew,
A mite to duty, pray bestow.'
Say, does my rival boast the art
One solid comfort to impart,
Or heal, like me, pour forth the strain
Of peace on earth, good will to men ?
Merit she has ; but, let me say,
The highest merit of a play,
Tho'. Shakespeare wrote it, but to name
With mine, were want of sense or shame.
Why should I point to distant times,
To kindred and congenial climes,
Where, spite of many a host of foes,
To God a mighty temple rose ?
Why point to every land beside
Whose honest aim it is, a pride,
However poor if be, yet still,
At least, to make God's house genteel?
Here, in Annapolis alone,
God has the meanest house in town,
The premises considered, I
With humble confidence rely,
That, Phenix-like, I soon shall rise,
From my own ashes to the skies ;
Your mite, at least, that you will pay,
And your petitioner shall pray."

The poem accomplished what the pastor could not. The congregation resolved to erect a new church.

[1774.] The General Assembly was appealed to for aid, and at its March Session, 1774, Chapter 11, the General Assembly appointed John Ridout, Samuel Chase, William Paca, Upton Scott, and Thomas

Hyde, trustees, for building in Annapolis, an elegant church adorned with a steeple. It was to cost £6,000, and £1,500 was to be received from the State. In return for it, there were to be provided a pew for the Governor, a large one for the Council, one for the Speaker, all to be properly ornamented, and other pews for the members of the Lower House, one for the Judges of the Provincial Court, and one for strangers. One was also to be for the incumbent, one for the Wardens, and one for the Provincial Juries. When completed, the subscribers were to choose their pews, preference being given to subscribers of the largest amounts; no one who subscribed less than £20 being entitled to a pew. Then twenty pews were to be sold to the parishioners by auction. There was to be a common gallery for the parishioners, one for servants, and another for slaves. July 1775, Mr. Woodcock was allowed £30 a year as an organist. The revolution prevented the erection of the church, and the theatre was used to worship in.

"It was now," says the faithful chronicler of St. Anne's, "a dark day for the church in Annapolis. Her church edifice had been taken down, her congregation scattered, her minister deprived of his support" and the Parish was vacant.

"In the last twenty-six years, St. Anne's had the services of eleven clergymen, not averaging two-and-a-half years to each one, yet no one of them had died while in the service of the parish. It seems to have been the Point-Look-out of the church in the province. All save one had continued in the parishes, of which they became the incumbents on their leaving here, till their death, or till the present time. Malcolm, Keene, and Boucher were certainly eminent men in their profession. One was indeed a bad man, and perhaps, two others were of doubtful character. But Myers, McPherson, Edmyston, Montgomery, and T. Lendrum, all were of fair, if not, of excellent standing. Still, what had been gained, for the church. The population of the parish had increased probably one-third during the period under review, and wealth also had increased. But the theatre had been introduced, and horse-racing, card-playing, dancing and drinking had became unrestrained, and Governors and office-holders had upheld and patronized them, not less than did the proprietaries themselves, and the church had shown itself powerless. And now, it was in the dust, a time of retribution had come, and everything was dark."

[1792.] The church was finally completed in November, 1792, eighteen years after it was commenced. It cost £6,000, nearly $30,000. The church was 110 feet long, and 90 broad, and was surmounted with a tower. On the outside were pilasters, which divided the wall into panels, and long windows gave it, with its time-colored bricks, a sombre and religious appearance. Inside, the church was frescoed. This church, with its modern panels and posts, in green and white, encircling the yard, remained until the night of Sunday, February 14th, 1858, when it was destroyed by fire. This originated [1858.] from the furnace below which ignited the flooring. About eleven o'clock the ringing of the bell of the church summoned the citizens to the destruction of this ancient edifice. At first the bell seemed to be only the nine o'clock curfew; but the doleful cry of "fire," resounding through the dark and quiet streets told another story. For two hours the flames, unseen and inaccessible, lay hidden in their lairs, pouring forth volumes of stifling smoke.

This slumber, that deceived the hopeful, suddenly ended with the flames flaring into the ceiling, darting from the roof, and leaping to the tower. The faithful bell, that had not ceased from the beginning of the fire to peal its own requiem, broke the stilly atmosphere with its doleful knell, the crackling timbers joined the dirge, the pitiless heat, sweeping through the organ, touched its keys with fiery fingers and made it sing its own death song, whilst a passing steamer's sympathizing bell and faithful women's tears attended the unexpected calamity. In a few hours only the bare walls of St. Anne's remained.

The laborers employed to remove the rubbish from the site of St. Anne's unearthed a tombstone bearing the following inscription :

"HERE LYETH THE BODY OF JOHN THE ELDEST SON OF EVAN JONES AND MARY HIS WIFE WHO DYED THE 2d of 7tber ANO d m 1716 AGED TWO YEARS.

> Pe diuch nag wyluch yn gaeth
>   Dyfaruch
> Darfu ty milwrncih
> Ifyn o gnawd i hynny gwnaeth
> Prudd alwodd i pridd cilwaeth."

The latter part of this inscription was in the Welsh language, and was cut on the stone in very rude characters in lines perpendicular to the lines of the first part of the inscription. Mr. Joseph H. Bellis translated it. He said it was a verse of Welsh poetry :

> "Do not, do not grieve to much.
> Repent :
> I have finished my course.
> This flesh of mine for that was made,
> Earth called to earth again."

The stone was of rectangular shape, about three feet long, one-and-a-half feet wide, and four inches thick, with bevelled edges. It was steatite, and in excellent preservation.

The following was copied from a stone which had been lying at the east end of the church for many years :

"Here lieth interred the body of Mr. Amos GARRETT of the city of Annapolis, in Anne Arundel county, in the Province of Maryland, Merchant, son of Mr. James and Mrs. Sarah Garrett, late of St. Olive street, Southwork, then in the Kingdom of England, now a part of Grate Brittain, who departed this life on March the 8th, 1727.

Ætatis 56."

The stone was of white marble, and the inscription is below a coat of arms consisting of fleur de lis and a griffin rampant.

This inscription possesses interest to Annapolitans, from the fact that Mr. Garrett was the first Mayor of our city. He kept a store in the house on Green street, now occupied by the Public School. It is said that after his death his body was arrested for debt, and kept for seven days, as was allowed by an old law of England.

The third St. Anne's was rebuilt the same year the second was destroyed.

Hon. George Wells, president of the Farmers' Bank, and formerly presiding officer of the Maryland Senate, was one of the Wardens of St. Anne's when the furnace was put under the church. He remonstrated against it, and when the edifice was burned, he declined to give anything to rebuild it. So the church went up and the bellless tower was finished. One day a thousand dollar bell was sent to the church. The good-hearted warden had kept his vow and also showed his generous spirit.

[1887.] A change has come over the spirit of her dreams since the days when St. Anne's dragged paltry tithes from unwilling tax-payers or threatened callous citizens with public prosecution unless they attended church services.

It is in the front rank of good works and charitable deeds; its numerous societies for the benefit of its parishioners attesting its zeal, its piety, and goodly walk.

From the report of the rector of 1886, Rev. W. S. Southgate, it is found that St. Anne's has a Parish Church and two Chapels, 3 Sunday Schools, 44 teachers, 396 scholars. During the year there were Baptisms 60; Marriages 21; Burials 44; Communicants 359: Contributions for the year (including completion of Chapel and repairs of Rectory) $11,430.

St. Anne's Chapel, East Street, was begun in 1877; lower story being used for services in 1878. The Building was completed, as a memorial of Alexander Randall, in 1886. Total cost about $9,000.

St. Philip's Chapel—a place of worship for colored people—originally built by Zion Baptists, was bought a few years ago and fitted up for the colored congregation now using it. It has about 35 communicants.

The bell, given by Queen Anne's, perished in the fire of 1858, but St. Anne's retains one proof of its honorable age. The set of communion vessels, now used in St. Anne's Church, consists of five pieces made in London by Francis Garthorne in 1695. They are all of solid silver and engraved with the arms of William III.

CHAPTER XX.

KING WILLIAM'S SCHOOL.

1696——1785.

"For the propagation of the Gospel and the education of the Youth of this province in good letters and manners," the act of 1696, chapter 17, of the General Assembly of Maryland; provided that "place or places for a free school, or place of study of Latin, Greek, writing, and the like, consisting of one master, one usher, and one writing master or scribe, to a school, and one hundred scholars, more or less, according to the ability of the said free school, may be made erected founded, propagated established under your Royal patronage." This act was addressed "to his most Excellent Majesty, &c., Dread Sovereign," William the Third of England.

This law further enacted, "that the most reverend Father in God Thomas, by divine Providence Lord Archbishop of Canterbury, Primate and Metropolitan of all England, may be Chancellor of said schools and that, to perpetuate the memory of your majesty it may be called King William's School, and managed by certain trustees, to be chosen and appointed by your sacred majesty to wit : as also by the following trustees nominated and appointed by this present General Assembly. That is to say, by your Majesty's said Governor, Francis Nicholson, Esq., the Honorable Sir Tho nas Lawrence, Baronet, Col. George Robotha 1, Col. Charles Hutchins, Col. John Addison, of your Majesty's Honorable Council on this province ; the Reverend Divine, Mr. Peregrine Coney, and Mr. John Hewett, together with R bert Smith, Kenelin Che seldyne Henry Coursey, Edward Dorsey, Thomas Ennals, Thomas Tasker, Francis Jenkins, William Dent, Thomas Smith, Edward Boothy, Jno. Thompson, and John Bigger, gentlemen, or the greatest part, or the successors of them, upon and in a certain place of this province, called Anne-Arundel Town, (now Annapolis,) upon Severn River."

The trustees were given power to hold land to the value of £1500 sterling and to accept all other personal effects given for the support of the various schools to be established under this act. The official title of the boards of management of the various schools was "the Governors, and Visitors and Trustees," who were limited to twenty and of whom "one discreet and fit Person shall be called rector." One hundred and twenty-pounds per annum was voted to each free school thus established.

In the proceedings of the House of Delegates, July 3, 1699, the following is found :

"The new elected members of this house give to the use of the free schools, to wit :

	£ tob.	
Mr. Jas. Crawford,	1,000	These gentlemen to be discharged from their own subscriptions in their several countyes."
Mr. Jenkins.	1,000	
Mr. Wm. Hutton.	1,000	
Mr. Wm. Helmsley,	800	
Mr. Geo. Ashman,	800	
Major Wm. Barber.	800	

This evidently went to King Williams school since these members were to be discharged from "subscriptions in their several countyes."

"Mr. Anthony Workman came before this house, (the same day) and gave £150 sterling to the building of a house upon a lott which his excellency had already given together with tenn pounds sterlings towards building the said house, which is to be enjoyed by the said Anthony Workman during his natural life, and remayned over to the use of the free schools. Also, the said Mr. Workman promised to leave all improvements upon said lott in good and sufficient repair."

This house was built and King William's school succeeded to the ownership of it.

King William's school was thus established at Annapolis. Gov. Nicholson gave a lot and upon this the trustees immediately began the erection of a brick school house. This was on the south side of the State House, or court-house as it was often called, very nearly, if not on the site of the De Kalb Statue. The name of School street, the street that connects State House and Church circles—is doubtless a memento of this ancient seminary of learning. It was a plain building, containing besides school-rooms, apartments for the teacher and his family. It was completed in the year 1701. The Bishop of London, sent over Mr. Andrew Geddess to take charge of the school, but, he, not finding it finished was sent to All Saints, Calvert county. The earliest mention of an officiating master of the school is found in the records of St. Anne's parish. They record, "Died, Nov. 9th, 1713, Rev. Edward Butler, rector of St. Ann's, and master of the free school, Annapolis." Mr. Butler was selected as rector April 14, 1711, and the fact, that he was a resident of Annapolis before that period, has raised the presumption that he had been master previous to being rector.

Unfortunately information regarding this interesting seminary, which educated the celebrated William Pinkney, is exceedingly meagre. The act of 1750, chapter 26, indicates, however, that the school was not without friends and supporters. By authorizing the sale of certain lands, it shows the school had some endowments beside the £120 voted it as its establishment. This act authorized the rector and visitors of said school to sell 650 acres in Dorchester county, devised to them by Thomas Swithson, late of Talbot county, and also several houses and lots in Annapolis "of which they are seized." The rector and visitors were directed to lay out the money "arising from the sale of said lands, and the said lots and houses in the city of Annapolis, at interest on good security, for the use of said school, and apply the annual interest arising therefrom towards the payment of a master, masters, or usher of the said school, and to no other use or purpose, whatever: saving to his majesty, the Lord Proprietary, and all others not mentioned in this act, their several and respective rights."

By act of 1774, chapter 15, the "rector, governors, trustees, and visitors of King William's school in Annapolis," were empowered to receive any gift of lands or chattles, provided they were not to hold beyond £200 annual income. By the same act any seven of the above board were empowered to transact business in the absence of the rector. The register of the school, also by the same act was required, under a penalty of £20, to give notice to every member of the board, residing in Annapolis or any member whom he knows happens to be in Annapolis, of any intended meeting of the corporation. This suggests there may have been secret assemblies of a clique of the trustees for special purposes, and this act was to check these ancient "ways that were dark and tricks that were vain."

The new political condition of the province required in 1778, the passage of a law enacting that any number of the visitors, not less than three, who have taken the oath of fidelity to support the State, may manage the affairs of the school, and execute all the powers of the corporation, until some three, or more, shall have met and elected so many other visitors as are required to complete their full number. This election they were enjoined to make on or before the 15th of July following, out of the inhabitants of the State, "duly qualified who have taken the oath aforesaid."

By act of 1785, chap. 39, the property and funds of King William's School were conveyed to St. John's College. Among the chattles passed to the college was a number of "quaint and curious volumes of forgotten lore," which still remain in the Library of St. John's. Few of the rectors of the school have come down to us, but about

1756, and for nine years after. Mr. Isaac Daken is mentioned as master of the school. On the 17th of August 1784, Rev. Ralph Higginbotham was appointed master of King William's School.

The record of the graduates of King William's School is lost, but one name remains—that proves its right to existence—William Pinkney's.

CHAPTER XXI.

THE SECOND STATE HOUSE IN ANNAPOLIS.

1706——1769.

After the first State House was burned in 1704, a committee of the Legislature reported that the old walls could be built upon in "form and manner as before," and it was rebuilt by Mr. W. Bladen, the architect of the other buildings. The price was not to exceed £1,000 sterling. Mr. Bladen was given the benefit of all "the materials saved out the fire which appertained to the old court house."*

During the erection of this building the House of Delegates held its sessions in the house of Colonel Edward Dorsey, in Annapolis, the assembly meeting twice a day, from 8 o'clock to 12 A. M., and from 2 to 4 P. M., and was called together by the beating of a drum.

Mr. David Ridgely, who wrote the "Annals of Annapolis" in 1841, says:

"This house," (the second State House,) "was finished in 1706, and is recollected by some few of the present inhabitants of this city —and stood where the present state house now stands. It is described as having been a neat brick building. It was in form an oblong square, entered by a hall—opposite to the door of which was the judges' seat, and on each side there were rooms for the jury to retire. Over the judges' seat was a full length likeness of Queen Anne, presenting a printed charter of the city of Annapolis. In this house the General Assembly held its sessions. A handsome cupola surmounted the building, surrounded by balustrades, and furnished with seats for those who desired to enjoy the beautiful scenery around. The portrait of Queen Anne, just mentioned, is said to have been destroyed during the revolutionary war—when everything bearing the semblance of royalty was in bad odour with our republican sires.

"About the same period, an armory was built near the court-house, on the north side of it. It is represented to have been a large hall with seats around it, above which the walls were covered with arms, tastefully arranged. It was often used as ball room—from the vaulted roof was suspended a wooden gilt chandelier, which, when lighted up, produced a brilliant effect by the reflection of the light from the arms.

* The State House was often called Court House.

The walls of the hall were also decorated with full length portraits of Queen Anne and Lord Baltimore. The governor and council held their sessions in one of the apartments of this building.

"On the south side of the court-house, stood the memorable academy of King William."†

In the Treasury Building the Governor and Council also held their sessions, and, at one time, both Houses of the Legislature met there : probably when the present State House was in course of erection.

October 1st, 1769, Mr. Eddis wrote of the State-house, then called the Court House.‡

"The court-house, situated on an eminence at the back of the town, commands a variety of views highly interesting : the entrance to the Severn, the majestic Chesapeake, and the eastern shore of Maryland, being all united in one resplendant assemblage. Vessels of various sizes and figures are continually floating before the eye ; which, while they add to the beauty of the scene, excite ideas of the most pleasing nature.

"In the court-house, the representatives of the people assemble, for the dispatch of provincial business. The courts of justice are also held here ; and here, likewise, the public offices are established. This building has nothing in its appearance expressive of the great purposes to which it is appropriated ; and by a strange neglect is suffered to fall continually into decay : being, both without and within, an emblem of public poverty, and at the same time a severe reflection on the government of this country, which, it seems, is considerably richer than the generality of the American provinces.

"The council chamber is a detached building, adjacent to the former on a very humble scale. It contains one tolerable room, for the reception of the governor and his council, who meet here during the sitting of the assembly ; and whose concurrence is necessary in passing all laws."

It was during this same year that the Legislature became imbued with sentiments similar to those entertained by Mr. Eddis, and determined to remove this " severe reflection on the government," and the second State House was pulled down to make room for the third.

————————— ◄●► —————————

CHAPTER XXII.

THE ATTEMPT OF RICHARD CLARKE, IN 1707, TO BURN ANNAPOLIS.

[1707.] In the address of Gov. John Seymour, made to the House of Delegates of Maryland, on March 27th, 1707, he stated that among other duties the members of the Legislature would be called upon to

† Ridgely's Annals of Annapolis, p. 106.
‡ Eddis ' Letters, p. 15.

6

perform, would be that of outlawing "Richard Clarke, whose crimes are so notoriously aggravated, they cry aloud for justice."

On March 31st. Col. John Contee, Mr. Robert Bradley, Mr. William Frisbey, Mr. John Watters, and Col. Pearce, were appointed a committee to investigate the crimes against Clarke.

Annapolis, at this time, was the most important town in the province of Maryland. A plot that struck at it was no small conspiracy.

On April 4th, the Lower House, in its reply to the executive, made in accordance with custom, said to Gov. Seymour:—"We are very sensible of the Great and dangerous designs which have been carrying on by wicked people, enemys to Her Majestys Government, to destroy the records, arms, and ammunition, of this town, and all that was necessary to render this Government safe and secure, and we doe, in a very deep sence thereof, returne you our hearty thanks for the great care and prudence you have showed in the preservation of all those things, and the preventing the effect of soe dangerous a conspiracy, and we doe humbly pray that your Excellency would be pleased to give order to the Atturney Generall to prosecute all such persons as now are, or shall be found to be, in the said conspiracy."

On the same day the committee, appointed to investigate the case of Clarke, elected Col. John Contee, chairman, and Mr. Richard Dallam, clerk, and after examining a large mass of testimony, worded in the quaint phraseology of those timss, and given at length in the manuscript copy of the proceedings of the Lower House of Maryland of 1707, and preserved in the Land office at Annapolis, made the following report to the House :

"The Committee having fully heard and considered the aforegoing declarations, doe humbly report to the House, that they find there was a design fram'd by Richard Clarke, Daniel Wells, and a certaine person who term'd himself a saylor, to take some vessell, and get what assistance they could, in order to disturb her Majestys peace and government, here, to make an attempt upon the Town of Annapolis, and burn some houses there, and, whilst that consternation continued, to seize the magazine and powder house to furnish themselves with arms and ammunition to goe a privateering ; that they so farr prosecuted their designe as to gain several housekeepers of desperate fortunes, and other disaffected persons to their party, and that Clarke, by his prodigality in disbursing and spreading about the counterfeit money, (which he had coined himself,) had so insinuated himself into the minds of several servants belonging to persons in and near the Towne of Annapolis and elsewhere, to joine with them in their cursed and wicked designe and intent ;

"That they had caballs together especially at Annapolis, where a time for their goeing was prefix'd to be some time in March last .

"That they had agreed to take Mr. Buff's boate and if that (was) not sufficient, Mr. Evans Jones' Shallup, or any other vessell fit for their turne, as soon as they had done their mischief here, to go to Carolina. That Clarke was assisted out of South River by Daniel Wells and him, called the Saylor, who afterwards came to Annapolis 'o prepare the others, but Wells having broke some of Clarke's money was in fear of being apprehended, whereupon he, the saylor and (William) Simpson had a meeting at the house of Smithers in Annapolis, and then Wells and the Saylor went off in a boat and pursued a shallop, wherein was Mr. Jacob Lookermann, Jr., and one Edward

Taylor, bound for South River, but not gaining their intent made their way down the Bay and came within a day's journey of Clarke, sometime after several of them were apprehended in Annapolis and committed to prison (to witt) Simpson, Cooper, Williams, Peacocke, and Keyton where they now lye by his Excellency's orders, (who we thinke deserve the utmost thanks of the House for his care therein,) for had this cursed and villainaious design taken Effect, we and our prosterity might have been ruined by burning of the Records which we are of opinion was the Chief Intent and designe of these villaines.

"As to those persons that were Runing away with Mr. Gales' sloop at the Eastern, we are of opinion, was to the same intent of the others.

"As to the money, we conceive Clarke was the maker and it's plain his wife the disburser, therefor. to Mr. Carroll.

"As to Sylvester Welch, his selling the country powder, its very plain by the declaration of John Devall and Elezabeth Finley, that three pounds of the country powder was sold by Welsh to Wells, and it is the opinion of this committee, that the several persons now in prison, and concerned in the same design and conspiracy, be prosecuted at the common law, and that the House give order to her Majesty's Attorney General, to proceed according."

The committee also reported that William Simpson, whose deposition was before the committee, was one of the "chiefe actors in the intended designe of Clarke and his accomplicies against her Majesty's Government, also that Wells and the privateer followed Clarke, came to Long Island in the Bay where Clarke had been the day before, and inquired after him, that they were in a small boat well armed, that Wells carryed powder and shot with him from home, pretended they were in pursuite of Clarke by order of Major Wilson, that Clarke pretended himself a merchant going to settle in News River in Carolina, said many people of Maryland were following him, and used many arguments to perswade the inhabitants about the Islands to goe with him."

The House concurred in the report.

Clarke's personal appearance was not prepossessing. He is described as "having a flat nose, peaked chinn, and under jaw outsetting the upper." He was also addicted to drunkenness.

The bill for the attainder of Clarke was passed by both Houses on the 9th of April.

But this was not the only proceedings had in the Legislature in regard to this nefarious plot. The records of the two Chambers show that the General Assembly was most intensely exercised over this conspiracy, which, if consummated, would have been exceedingly injurious to the colony.

Capt. Sylvester Welch, on April 3rd, was called before the Council to answer the charge of selling the country's powder to Clarke's accomplices. Capt. Welch replied that "he did spare Daniel Wells powder, but it was of his own—being asked what he had done with the country powder he had of his Excellency, he said what was left was at his house and the rest he had fired away in the summer."

"His excellency was pleased," continues the record of the proceedings of the council of 1707, "to tell him that he did not believe him, and discharged him from his command, and ordered that he should give good security for his behavior."

April 5th, Major Josiah Wilson, high sheriff of Anne Arundel county
brought before the Council, "as he had been ordered to arrest them,
John Spry and Thomas Brereton, the former the professed" skipper
of the sloop Margaret's Industry, lately arrived from Virginia in
South River, after the goods of some of the conspirators. The proceedings say "neither of the said persons offering to make an Ingenious confession, but trifling with his Excellency and the board, were
ordered to be committed to the custody of the Sheriff of Anne Arundel county untill his Excellency and the Board had further leisure to
Examine them."

It was, however, gathered that Clarke was at "Little Wicomico, in
Virginia," awaiting the return of the sloop. It was also discovered,
probably from the same source, "that Clarke haunts Cartewrights, at
the Rosey Crowne, in Norfolk Towne."

Subsequently Brereton and Spry, in council, under oath, on the 7th
of April, confessed that they had been sent by Clarke, after his wife,
children, and household goods, with an open letter to Mr. Hill, who,
in accordance with the paper, had given them assistance.

On the 8th of April, Thomas Tench, Esq., entered the House of
Delegates and delivered a bill of attainder against Richard Clarke
and the following message from the council:

"The bill herewith sent to House for the attainder of Richard
Clarke is thought reasonable by this Board, since this is the second
time your House has ordered the Attorney Generall to prosecute him
and his accomplices, and that hath been ineffectual, and although
there are now actually four bills of indictment found by several grand
juries of this province against him, yet divers evil persons have presumed to receive, comfort, and aid him, whereby he has been able to
avoid justice, according to his demerits, sculking within tenn miles of
this place, the seat of government, and practicing and carrying on his
traitorous and wicked designs."

The paper was read and referred for further consideration.

It was on this evidence that the following proceedings were had:

On the 9th of April, a warrant was issued by the council, directing
the Sheriff of Anne Arundel county, to arrest Joseph Hill for treason,
and to keep him in custody until "such time as he shall be delivered by
due course of, law therefrom." This process was recommended, or approved of, by the Attorney General. Mr. Hill was arrested on the
10th, and brought before the council to make his defence, six members of the House appearing to represent it: Messrs. Major Low,
Mr. Young, Col. Greenfield, Mr. Hall, Mr. Spinner, and Mr. Macall.
The Governor opened the interview by telling Mr. Hill, that he little
expected a man of his status and character would be guilty of aiding, and corresponding with those that were enemys to her Majesty's
Government, and disturbers of the peace thereof. The depositions of
Spry and Brereton were read to Mr. Hill, who then "denyed ever the
evidence mentioned Clarke's name to him, and says that he has not
seen him for about twelve months, nor does he know where he now is."
Mr. Hill denied ever receiving a letter from Clarke by the two witnesses who were called in, confronted him, and affirmed that they had
delivered to him the letter in question. The Council concluded their
inquiry by informing him that they would at present have nothing
further to say to him, as he had given bail.

On the 11th the depositions were sent to the Lower House, and Mr. Hill was desired to withdraw from it as "the House find" the depositions relate "some high crimes and misdemeanors supposed to be committed by Mr. Joseph Hill, a member of this House." The accused withdrew, and the House after fully considering and debating the subject resolved that Mr. Hill be expelled from the House "till he be cleared of what is lay'd to his charge." The expelled member was then called into the House, and informed of its action, when he withdrew.

It seemed that the House wished the evidence of Spry, Brereton, and Thos. Richetts entered on their Journal, probably as a justification of their actions. The Council only gave consent to put it in at the end, as they did not wish to have the Queen's Evidence Divulged before trial, as "they were unwilling to trust to Mr. Taylard, their Clark'e integrity, in that he may give out a copy." The House did not agree to this, and sent a message saying that they ought to be inserted the same day they were read in the house. The Council agreed to this on condition to which the House consented, that they "be close sealed up untill Mr. Hill's Tryall was over."

What punishment was meted out to the conspirators, their abettors, and sympathizers is not known. The Court records of Anne Arundel of that period have not been discovered after research. The act of attainder which passed this session upon Clarke, and which set forth that he "had obstinately refused to surrender himself to justice," was not the first measure that had been taken against him. In 1705, he had been outlawed for the same character of offences. It is very probable, as our records and history are so silent upon the subject, that Clarke himself never suffered the penalty of the law for his treasonable designs.

CHAPTER XXIII.

ANNAPOLIS IS MADE A CITY.

On the 10th of August, 1708, Annapolis received its charter as a city, which was granted by the honorable John Seymour, the royal Governor of Maryland. "It appears to have been one of his favourite designs, and was proposed by him to the assembly, as early as 1704. No measures being adopted by the latter to carry his wishes into effect, he at length conferred the charter by virtue of the prerogative of his office. Under this charter, besides the powers and privileges relative to the organization and exercise of its municipal government, the city of Annapolis obtained the privilege of electing two delegates to the general assembly."[*]

This privilege the city retained until 1833. That year it was reduced to one representative, and finally, in 1840, it lost this remnant

* McMahon's Md. p. 255.

of its ancient importance, and was merged into the county of Anne Arundel. By the act of 1840, Annapolis was continued as the Capital of the State and the place of holding the Court of Appeals for the Western Shore, and the high Court of Chancery. The act of 1837, made it the residence of the Governor. These honors have been incorporated in the organic law of the State and are part of the present Constitution adopted in 1867.

The following was the petition presented to Governor Seymour, by the Mayor, Recorder, Aldermen, Common Council, and sundry citizens of Annapolis, asking a charter for the city:

"To His Excellency, John Seymour, Esq.,

"The humble peticion of the Corporacion of the Citty of Annapolis, and the greater parts of the inhabitants of the same, humbly showeth:

"That, whereas, in her most gracious majesties in behalf of yor. Excellency, for the benefitt of her dutifull subjects, inhabitants in this place was pleased to grant them a Charter, incorporating thereby this late towne of Annapolis, into a Citty, it haveing formerly had the honour in Remembrance of Princess Anne, now our good Queen to be erected into a towne, and in as much as it is the seat of Government the best situated and most convenient place for trade, wherein are a greater number of inhabitants than in any other place in this her majesties Province, who are desirous that that parte of her majesties grant to this Citty, inpowering the Mayor, Recorder, Aldermen, and five of the Common Councillmen, to ellect and send two representatives to the Generall Assembly, to serve as Burgesses, for this Citty, may be enlarged. May it therefore, please yor. Excellency, see farr to enlarge the Charter that all persons being free-holders in this Citty, (that is to say, owning a whole lott of land with a house built thereon, according to law,) and that all persons actually resideing and i habitting in this Citty haveing a visible estate of the vallue of twenty pounds, sterling, and all soe, that all persons that hereafter shall serve five years to any trade within this Citty, and shall, after the expiracion of their time be actually housekeepers and inhabitants in the same, (they first taking the oath of free citizens,) may have a free vote in the ellecting such representatives or Burgesses to serve hereafter in all Generall Assemblys as in the said Charter, is expressed and further that after the Decease or Removall of any of the Common Councillmen, already ellected, and sworne by the Mayor, Recorder, and Aldermen, of the said Citty, all the freemen, inhabitants, as aforesaid, may have a free vote in the ellecting of another Common Councillman, or Common Councillmen, to serve in this or their place and stead; and it is further most humbly prayed, that noe person or persons—after the next Generall Assembly, (notwithstanding, being made freemen of the Citty,) shall have an ellection voyce in the chuseing of Burgesses, or Representatives, for this Citty, untill they have been made free three months, which is the humble desire of your petitioners, the subscribers, and as in duty bound wee will ever pray, &c.

"Amos Garrett, Mayor; Wornell Hunt, Recorder; Wm. Bladen, John Freemen, Benjamin Fordham, Evan Jones, Thomas Boardley, Josiah Willson, Aldermen.

"William Haughton, Charles Crowley, Wm. Ellott, Richard Thompson, Samuel Newill, Wm. Gaylard, John Grosham, Jr., Cha. Kill-

bourne, Math. Beard, Tho. Jones, Patrick Ogilvie, Cadder Edwards,
Common Councillmen.

"John Baldwin, John Brice, Tho. Donera. Richard Young, James
Wotton, Christopher Smithers, Joseph Humphrey, John B,——
Wm. Gwyn, Richard Bukardike, Richard Kolk, Thomas Holmes.
John Novarre, Wm. Durdan."

The petition was acted upon immediately. The records bear the
annexed endorsement:

"November the 18th. 1708. The within petticion granted and
ordered that the Corporaicon prepare a Charter as within prayed, t
be signed by his Excellency, and on her majesties, behalfe sealed, with
the greate seals of this Province,

Signed per Order,

W. BLADEN, Clerk Council."

This was the charter:

"THE CHARTER OF THE CITY OF ANNAPOLIS.

"Anne, by the Grace of God, of Greate Brittain, France, and Ireland,
and the Dominions thereunto belonging, Queen, Defender of the faith,
&c. To all and singular our faithfull subjects within our Province of
Maryland, Greeting, whereas, there is a very pleasant, healthful and
comodius place for trade, by act of the Generall Assembly of this our
Province, laid out for a towne and porte, called Annapolis, in honour
of us, which said towne and porte, hath in few years (especially, since
the accession of our trusty and well beloved John Seymour, Esq., our
Capt. Generall and Governour-in-Chiefe, of this our Province, to
the Government thereof,) very considerably encresed in the number
of its inhabitants as well as buildings, both public and private, soe
that it excelleth all other townes and ports in our said province, and
for that our present seate of Government. within our province aforesaid. is fixed att the said porte and towne, whereby the same is become
the chiefe mart of the whole countrey, wee, being willing to encourage
all our good and faithfull subjects as well att present, resideing and
inhabitting. or which hereafter shall, or may inhabitt, or reside within
the said porte of Annapolis. of our Royall Grace, good will, and meer
motion with the advice of our Councill. in our said province, have
thought fitt, and doe by these our letters pattents, constitute and
erect the said towne and porte of Annapolis. together with the circuits
and presincts thereof, includeing the lands heretofore laid out for the
said towne and porte of Annapolis, publick pasture, and towne common together, with the River and Creeks adjacient, into a Citty, by
the name of the Citty of Annapolis, and doe grant to the inhabitants
of the said Citty that the same Citty shall be incorporated a Citty, consisting of a Mayor, one person learned in the law, stiled, and bearing
the office of Recorder, of the said Citty, and six Aldermen, and tenn
other persons to be Common Councillmen, of the said Citty, which said
Mayor, Recorder, Aldermen, and Common Councillmen shall be a
body incorporate. and one comunity forever in right, and by the name
of Mayor, Recorder, Aldermen, and Common Councill, of the said
Citty of Annapolis, shall be able and capable to sue and be sued att
law, and to act and execute, doe and performe as a body incorporate,
which shall have succession forever, and to that end to have a common seale, and that Amos Garrett, Esqr., one of the inhabitants of

the said Citty, shall for the present be, and be named Mayor of the
said Citty, for the ensueing year, and Wornell Hunt, Esqr., Recorder
thereof, and William Bladen, John Freemen, Benjamin Fordham,
Evan Jones, Tho. Boardley, and Josiah Willson, Esqrs., inhabitants
of the said citty, shall be Aldermen thereof, soo long as they shall
well behave themselves therein, haveing first taken and subscribed the
test and severall oaths for security of the Government, as by Law established and allsoe the oath appointed by us or our present Governour, to be taken by the Mayor, Recorder, and Aldermen of the Citty
of Annapolis, aforesaid ; Which shall be administered to them by our
Governour-in-Chiefe, keeper of the greate seale of this our province
for the time being, or by such other person or persons as wee, our heirs,
and successors, or our Gov. aforesaid, for the time being, shall, from
time to time, authorize and appoint to administer the same, and wee
grant that the said Mayor, Recorder and Aldermen, or the Major parte
of them shall ellect and choose some others of the most sufficient of
the inhabitants of the said City, being freemen thereof, to be of the
Common Councill of the said City, for soe long time as they shall well
behave themselves, and to perpetuate the succession of the said Mayor,
Recorder, Aldermen, and Common Councill in all times to come, wee
doo grant, that, for the future, they shall assemble in some convenient
place in the said citty, upon the feast day of St. Michaell, the Archangell, in every year, and shall ellect and choose by the Major vote of
such of them as shall be then present, one other of the Aldermen of
the said citty, for the time being, to be Mayor of the said citty, for
the ensuing year, and upon decease or removeall of the said Mayor, of
the said citty, for the time being, or upon any decease, or deceasses,
removeall, or removealls, of the said Recorder, or Aldermen, or any
of them, or within one month, after such respective decease, or de-
ceases, removall, or removalls, the residue of the said Aldermen, together with the said Mayor, or if he shall be living or the major part
of them whom shall at a set time by them to be appointed within ye said
citty and presincts ellect and nominate some other person or persons
to be Mayor, Recorder, Alderman or Aldermen of the said Citty in
the place and places of such person or persons soe deceased or removed respectively as the case shall require soe as the said mayor to be
Ellected and nominated to be att the time of such Ellection and nomi-
naion actually one of the Aldermen of the said Citty and soe as the
said Recorder soe to be Ellected and nominated, be a person learned
in the law, soe as the said Alderman or Aldermen soe to be Ellected
and nominated be actually att the time of such Ellection and Nomi-
nacion of the Common Councill of the said City, the said Mayor, Recorder, or Alderman, or Aldermen, soe to be Ellected and Nominated,
first Takeing the severall and Respective Oaths before mencioned to be
appointed as aforesaid, and shall likewise then fill up by the Election of
the free Voters of the said Citty, out of and from among the Inhabittants and freeholders of the said Citty, the full number of teon persons
to be Common Councillmen, and that the said person s hereby appointed
and named or hereafter to be Elected and nominated mayor, Recorder,
or Aldermen, be Justices of the peace within the City presincts and
liberties thereof, having first taken the oaths usually appointed to be
taken by the Justice of the Peace, the said Mayor, Recorder, and Aldermen hereby named and appointed or hereafter to be Elected, nomi-

mated, or any three of them, whereof the said Mayor or Recorder, for the time being, shall be one, shall have, within the presincts of the said Citty, full power and authority to make Constables and other nessessary officers, and to rule, order, and govern the inhabitants thereof, as justices of the peace, are or shall be authorized to doe, and shall have power to execute all the Laws, Ordinances, and Statutes, in that behalfe, made as fully and amply as if they were authorized thereto, by express, commission, named therein, willing and commanding that noe other justices of the peace or quorum within our said county or province, doe att any time hereafter, take upon them or any of them to execute the office of a justice of peace within the said Citty, or in the presincts thereof ; notwithstanding any comission at large, authoriseing them thereunto, saveing the authority and jurisdiction of her majesties' justices of oyer and terminer and Goale deliver, now or hereafter to be assigned, dureing the time of their holdeing their severall respective Courts in the said Citty, and further wee will and grant unto the said Mayor, Recorder, and Common Councill of the said Citty, for the time being, full power and authority, after the space of six years, to ellect a Sherriff for the said Citty, but that untill then the Sherriff of Anne Arundell county for the time being, shall be Sherriff of the said county and to make, order, and appoint such by-laws and ordinances among themselves, for the regulacion and good Government of Trade and other matters exigences and things within the said Citty and presincts, as to them, or the major parte, shall seem meet to be consonant to reason and not contrary, but as near as conveniently may be agreeable, to the Laws and Statutes now in force, which said Bye-laws, shall be observed, kept, and performed by all manner of persons, Tradeing and Resideing within the said Citty, under such reasonable pains, penallties, and forfeitures, as shall be imposed by the said Mayor, Recorder, Aldermen, and Common Councillmen, or the major parte of them then assembled from time to time, not exceeding forty shillings sterling, the said pains, penaltys and forfeitures to be raised by distress, and sale of the goods of such person offending, and to be employed for the publick benefitt of the said Citty att their discression ; and further, wee doo grant and give full power, lycence, previllidge, and authority, to the Mayor, Recorder, Aldermen, and Common Councillmen of the said Citty, for the time being, and their successors forever, and alsoe all free-holders of the said Citty, that is to say, all persons owneing a whole lott of land with a house built thereon, according to law, and all persons actually resideing and inhabitting in the said Citty, haveing a visable estate of the vallue of twenty pounds sterling, att the least, and likewise, all persons hereafter who shall serve five years to any trade within this Citty, and shall, after the expiracion of their time, be actually housekeepers and inhabitants in the same, to send two cittizens and delegates to every one of our assembly or assemblys, hereafter to be held, or att any time or times, hereafter to be called, to be held for this, our said Province of Maryland, to be ellected and chosen out of the inhabittants, actually being and resideing within the said Citty, haveing a freehold or visable estate of the vallue of twenty pounds sterling therein, by the said Mayor, Recorder, Aldermen, Common Councillmen, Freeholders, and Freemen as aforesaid, or the major parte of them being present, by virtue of our writt or writts of action to be sent to them for that purpose, which said writt or writts, wee doe hereby grant, shall be issued out and sent to the said Mayor, Recorder, and Aldermen, soe often as occasion shall require: provided, that all such ellector or voters as aforesaid, doe take an oath to be true to the interest of the said Citty before they be admitted to such vote: and provided, alsoe, and att all times after the end of the next Generall Assembly, to be held for this province, noe Freeman, as aforesaid, not being a freeholder as aforesaid, shall have the libertie of such vote as aforesaid, until free three months, after such his freedom obtained: and when hereafter, there shall happen any Generall Assembly to be held, according as writts shall be sent to the severall and respective counties for ellecting Deputies or Delegates for their severall and respective counties in this our province of Maryland, wee further grant that the said cittizens and delegates, by them soe as aforesaid ellected and sent, shall have full and free votes and voices in all and every of our Generall Assemblys, touching or concerning all matters or things thereto, to be discoursed and handled as other, the Deputies or Delegates of the severall and respective countys, formerly have had, now have, or hereafter shall have; and further, wee grant and give lyceence to the Mayor, Recorder, Aldermen, and Common Councill of the said Citty, for the time being, and their successors forever, to have and to hold two marketts weekly within this said Citty, on every Wednesday and Saturday in the weeke, in some convenient place to be by them appointed within the presincts* Liberties of the said Citty, and alsoe two fairs yearly to be kept on Munday, otherwise, called St. Phillip and Jacobs Day, and on the feast of St. Michaell, the Archangell, or on the next Day succeeding, each or either of them, in case they shall happen to fall on the Lord's Day, for the sale and vending all mannor of goods, cattle, wares, and merchandizes whatever, on which said fair Days and first two days before and after all persons comeing to the said fairs togther with their cattle, goods, wares, and merchandizes, and returning thence shall be exampt and previllidged from any arrest, attachments, or executions whatsoever, and that the said Mayor and Aldermen shall have power to sett such reasonable tole upon such goods, cattle, merchandizes, and other comodities as shall be sold therein, respectively as shall be thought fitt, not exceeding sixpence on every beast sold, and the twentieth parte of the value of any comodity, and shall and may hold a courte of Pypowdry† dureing the said fair, for the determinacion of all controversies and quarrels which may happen therein, according to the usuall course in England, in the like cases, and wee grant unto them all profitts and perquisits due, incident, and belonging to said markett, fair, and Courte of Pypowdry; and further wee doe grant that the said Mayor, Recorder, and Aldermen, or any three or more of them, shall hold a Courte of Hustings within the said Citty where they are hereby impowered to make proper officers and to sett reasonable fees, not exceeding what are now allowed in the County Courte, and shall have

* "And" probably left out.

† The lowest—and, at the same time, the most expeditious Court of Justice known to the law of England, is the Court of PIEPOUDRE, CURIA PEDIS PULVERIZATI; so called from the dusty feet of the suitors or according to Sir Edward Coke, because justice is there done as speedily as dust can fall from the foot. It was held at markets so that attendants on the markets might have their causes heard and determined expeditiously, and they lose no time by the delays of the law. Blackstone, Vol. III, p. 31.

jurisdiction and hold-plea of trespass and Gectment for any lands or tenements within the said Citty, as alsoe of all writts of dower for the same lands and tenements, and of all other actions personall and mixt, and as a Courte of Record give judgement and award execucion thereon, according to the Laws and Statutes of England and this Province ; provided, the demand in the said action personall and mixt exceed not the sume of six pounds, ten shillings sterling, or seventeen hundred pounds of tobaccoe ; and, provided, nevertheless, that any party or partys, plaintiffs or defendants, shall be at their liberty on good grounds to bring writts of habeas corpus and certiorarie, to remove any plaints from the said Hustings to the Provinciall Courte of this Province and alsoe to appeale from the judgment of the Mayors, or bring writts of error att their choice to the Provinciall Courte under such limitacion and regulacion as is already by the act of Assembly of this Province assigned for prosecuting appeales and writts of error from the County Courtes to the Provinciall. In testimoney whereof, wee have caused these our letters to be made pattent, given att Annapolis, under the Greate Seale of our said Province. Wittness our trusty and well beloved John Seymour, Esq., Captain Generall and Governour-in-Chief of our said Province, this twenty-second Day of November, in the seventh year of our Reigne &c., Annoque Domni, 1708."*

"From the period of the grant of its charter by governor Seymour, Annapolis was continually on the advance. It never acquired a large population, nor any great degree of commercial consequence : but long before the American revolution, it was conspicuous as the seat of wealth and fashion ; the luxurious habits, elegant accomplishments, and profuse hospitality of its inhabitants were proverbially known throughout the colonies. It was the seat of a wealthy government, and of its principal institutions ; and as such, congregated around it many, whose liberal attainments eminently qualified them for society."†

A French writer in speaking of this city as he found it during the American revolution, thus describes it : "In that very inconsiderable' town, standing at the mouth of the Severn, where it falls into the bay, of the few buildings it contains, at least three-fourths may be styled elegant and grand. Female luxury here exceeds what is known in the provinces of France. A French hair dresser is a man of importance amongst them ; and it is said, a certain dame here hires one of that craft at one thousand crowns a year. The State House is a very beautiful building, I think the most so of any I have seen in America."

This forms a striking contrast to the account given of it at a much earlier date, and which is to be found in a satire, called, "The Sot-weed Factor, or a Voyage to Maryland :" in which is described the laws, government, courts, and constitutions of the country ; and also the buildings, feasts, frolics, entertainments, and drunken humours of the inhabitants of that part of America. In burlesque verse, by Eden Cook, gent., published at London in 1708.

* Liber P. C. Chancery Proceedings, p. 595.
† McMahon's p. 257.

Annapolis is thus mentioned in one part of this quaint work :

"To try the cause, then fully bent,
Up to Annapolis I went :
A city situate on a plain,
Where scarce a house will keep out rain
The buildings framed with cypress rare ;
Resemble much our Southwick fair ;
But strangers there will scarcely meet
With market place, exchange. or street :
And, if the truth I may report,
It's not so large as Tottenham court,—
St. Mary's once was in repute,
Now here the judges try the suit.
And lawyers twice a year dispute—
As oft the bench most gravely meet,
Some to get drunk, and some to eat
A swinging share of country treat ;
But as for justice, right, or wrong,
Not one amongst the numerous throng
Knows what it means, or has the heart
To vindicate a stranger's part."

Mr. Jonas Green reprinted this poem in 1731, but took care to tell the readers it was a description of Annapolis twenty years before.

CHAPTER XXIV.

THE ANNAPOLIS DELEGATES DENIED ADMITTANCE TO THE HOUSE.

The Lower House considered that the power to erect cities and grant charters was a prerogative that could be exercised only by the crown itself, and when the delegates from Annapolis made their appearance at the September Session of 1708, that body denied the authority of the executive "to confer the charter and expelled the delegates elected under it. Astonished at a measure so bold and unexpected, the governor, at first, attempted to win it to his purposes by conciliation. Its members were summoned to the Upper House, where they were addressed by him in language disclaiming all intention to interfere with their rights and privileges in determining the election of their own members; but claiming for himself also. the competency to judge of his own prerogatives, and they were urged to return to their house, and rescind their resolution. In justification of themselves, they replied that the course pursued by them was founded upon the complaint of some of the freeholders and inhabitants of Annapolis, who conceived that it affected their rights as freemen, and particularly as to the privilege of voting for delegates ; that the right to erect cities, was not expressly vested in the governor, and ought not therefore to be exercised until the Queen's pleasure was known: but that they would cheerfully concur with him in granting the charter, if all the inhabitants and freeholders of the place desired, and were secured in their equal privileges, to which they were entitled by the laws of England, and the public lands and buildings secured to the uses for which they were purchased. The Governor now tried the usual expedient with a refractory house. The Assembly was dissolved and a new house immediately summoned, which he at first found quite as unmanageable as the old. Their first message desired him to inform them, if he had received from her majesty any instructions authorizing the grant of charters and the erection of cities which were not contained in his commission; and if so, to communicate them. His brief reply was, 'that he had no doubt of his own right and if the exercise of the power was unwarranted, he was answerable to her majesty, and not to them.' To bring this difference to a close, a conference was now had between the two houses; which terminated in a compromise, and in the passage of the act of 1708, chapter 7th, to carry that compromise into effect. By this act, the charter of Annapolis was confirmed, under certain reservations as to the public buildings, and restrictions of the municipal power."[*]

This was the act the Assembly passed to settle and confirm the charter of Annapolis:

"Whereas this present General Assembly have taken into their consideration the Charter lately Granted to the City of Annapolis, and being desirous to give all due encouragement to cohabitation, have resolved to confirm the same Charter, and to explain and restrain some clauses and grants therein contained, they humbly pray that it may be enacted;

"II. *And it is hereby enacted,* By the Queen's most Excellent Majesty, by and with the advice and consent of her Majesty's Governor, Council, and Assembly of this Province, and by the authority of the same, That the said Charter to the City of Annapolis, bearing date at the said City on the twenty-second day of November, Anno 1708, in the seventh year of her Majesty's Reign, Sealed with the Great Seal of this her Majesty's Province, and signed with the Sign Manual of his Excellency John Seymour, Esq., Captain-General and Governor in Chief thereof, incorporating the inhabitants of Annapolis into a City, and Body Corporate, and the several Articles, Clauses, Grants, Powers, Authorities, and Privileges therein contained, shall, by virtue of this Act, be held, taken, stand, remain, and be firm, and valid to all intents and purposes whatsoever, within the same Charter mentioned and expressed, subject nevertheless to the several restrictions and explanations herein specified and declared, (that is to say,) That it shall in no wise be intended, construed, meant, or taken, to infringe the liberties and privileges of the public, either in regard to the public lands and buildings by them heretofore purchased and built; but that the same shall be reserved and continued forever, to the uses and purposes to which they have already been allotted: And that all and every the Judges and Justices of the several Courts of Judicature which have usually held their Courts within the same City, in the public Court-house thereof, shall and may continue so to do; and the

* McMahon's Md. p. 256.

Justices, Commissioners, and Sheriff of Ann-Arundel County shall have, hold, and exercise their Jurisdiction, in as full and ample manner, to all intents and purposes, in the Port of Annapolis, as heretofore had been usual.

"III. *And be it further Enacted and Declared,* That the Bye-Laws, to be made by the said Corporation, shall not affect or be binding to any other the Inhabitants of this Province, but wholly restrained to the Inhabitants and Residents of the said City; and that the Clause in the said Charter, impowering the Corporation to set toll on horses, cattle, and other commodities, to be sold on the two fair days, of the first of May, and of St. Michael the Arch-Angel, yearly, shall not, in any wise, enure, be construed, or extended, to impowering the Corporation to assess any toll or impost upon Cattle, Goods, or Merchandizes whatsoever, to be sold therein, if the Goods, Wares, or Merchandizes should not amount to the value of twenty shillings current money; but if it exceed twenty shillings value, and not above five pounds current money, then the sum of six-pence shall be paid for the fee or toll thereof; and for all Goods, &c., exceeding in value five pounds current money, then it shall be lawful to assess the sum of twelve pence current money for the fee or toll thereof, and no more.

"IV. *And Whereas,* the Citizens and Burgesses of the several Boroughs in England have formerly been allowed but half wages, in respect to the salary of the Knights of the Shires; *Be it therefore Enacted,* That the Citizens, representing the City of Annapolis, shall only be allowed half the wages to the Delegates and Representatives, as is and shall be allowed to the Delegates of the several Counties of this Province, and no more.

"V. *And whereas,* Wornell Hunt, Esq., the present Recorder of the said City, is not yet qualified for that trust, by reason he hath not been resident in this Province during the term of three years; nevertheless the said Wornell Hunt, by virtue of this act, shall be deemed, and is hereby qualified and enabled to hold and execute the said Office of Recorder of the City aforesaid, any Law, Statute, Usage, or Custom to the contrary in any wise notwithstanding.

"VI. *And be it enacted,* by the advice and consent aforesaid, That the Land called the Town-Common, be reserved and remain to the use of the proper Owner or Owners, unless the Citizens can make it appear to have made satisfaction for the same, the next Session of Assembly."

CHAPTER XXV.
THE FIRST NEWSPAPER IN MARYLAND.

[1727.] In August, 1727, William Parks, printer to the Province of Maryland, made the first venture in Maryland journalism. He began at Annapolis "THE MARYLAND GAZETTE." It was printed on a sheet a little larger than foolscap; had two columns to the page, and four pages to an issue. It was published once a week. The first numbers of this interesting relic of Maryland history are lost to the State, as well as the concluding issues. The Maryland Historical Society, however, is the fortunate possessor of some twenty copies of the *Gazette*, beginning with number 65 of the issue, dating from Tuesday, Dec. 3, to Tuesday, Dec. 10, 1728. The last number it has is number 97, of date of July 23, 1729. On either side of the head of the paper, was an excellent cut, and below the caption was a space left, in which the names of the several subscribers were written to take the *Gazette* on its way through the post to its destination. At the bottom of the fourth page was the announcement—"Annapolis, printed by William Parks, by whom advertisements and subscriptions are taken." The paper was made up of copious extracts of foreign news, a few local items, and sometimes one page of advertisements. There were frequently long communications written in the semi-classic style of the period. In No. 66, there were four local items, all relating to the shipping of the port of Annapolis. On January 1, 1729, is a notice recounting that a negro, belonging to William Robinson, of the county, had impudently and without provocation struck William Smith, carpenter, during a dispute over the fighting of their dogs, and that for it the said negro had his ear cropped which the *Gazette* said it noticed, because it was the first case under the law, and it published it as a warning. We can hardly believe that the said negroes intended to be forewarned by this Charitable admonition were assiduous readers of the *Gazette*.

In No. 89, there were published three advertisements, in one of which notice was given "that there is a ship arrived in South River with about two hundred choice slaves, which are to be sold by Daniel Dulany, Richard Snowden, and Peter Hume."

Mention is made in the issue of June 16, 1729, that "on Tuesday last, George Plater, Esq., was married to Mrs. Rebecca Bowles, the relict of James Bowles, Esq., a gentle woman of considerable fortune."

From the issue of June 24, 1729, are the following extracts made:

"On Friday last, died James Carroll, at the House of Charles Carroll, Esq., in this city.

"On Friday last, the Hon. Patrick Gordon, Esq., Governor of Philadelphia, attended by several gentlemen of that province, arrived here to visit our Governor. His Excellency received them very kindly, and they were saluted with the discharge of our great guns, colors flying, &c., and their entertainment has been made as agreeable as this place could afford. This morning his Honor, the Governor of Pennsylvania, departed this city under discharge of our guns, &c.

"Annapolis, March 4th, Saturday last, being the birth day of our most gracious Queen Caroline, was celebrated here in the manner following: His Excellency, Benedict Leonard Calvert, our Governor, invited the gentlemen of this city to a very handsome entertainment at dinner, and in the evening there was a ball at the Stadt House."

The price of the *Gazette* was fifteen shillings a year, and advertisements, no rule as to length, were "to be inserted in it at three shillings for the first week, and two shillings for every week after."

When the *Gazette* ceased publication, we are left to conjecture. The probability is it was discontinued in a few years. Mr. Parks, elected in 1727 State Printer, remained in that office until 1742, when he was succeeded by Jonas Green.

The *Gazette* was the sixth paper, in point of time, that was printed in the American Provinces.

CHAPTER XXVI.*

CHRONICLES OF ANNAPOLIS FROM 1707 TO 1740.

[1707.] In 1707, the Legislature passed a supplementary act for the advancement of trade. In this law it was enacted that "all the towns in Baltimore and Anne Arundel Counties, with the River, Creeks, Coves, thereunto belonging, (saving in Patuxent River) to be members of the Port of Annapolis."

[1720.] A "Prospect to Annapolis" was laid off May 24, 1720. It comprised two lots of ground, one called Durand's Place, the other Woodchurch's Rest. It was re-surveyed for Benj. Tasker. It lay on the North Side of Severn.†

[1715.] By act of 1715, ch. IV, the Legislature reiterated its agreement with Anthony, alias William Workman, in regard to giving him the privilege of building on the lots belonging to King William's School, a house which was to revert to the School at Workman's death. The act discovers that these three lots, that the school was possessed of, lay "to the foot of the Stadt House Hill, on the Eastward thereof," and that Workman was an inn-keeper, and that, for erecting and so donating the house alluded to the General Assembly, had granted him liberty and license "to keep an ordinary in said House, during his natural life, free and discharged from the payment of fine, then imposed by law therefor." Workman came from Kent Island, then declared to be "in the county of Talbot." William Freeman, bricklayer, of Philadelphia, in Pennsylvania, built the house. The same act, after reciting the difficulty of getting the board of Rector, Governors, and Visitors of King William's School together to transact business, enacted that five of the board on special occasion, could execute the powers of the school.

[1718.] In 1718, "the Honorable Colonel William Holland, Colonel Thomas Addison, Capt. Daniel Mariartee and Mr. Alexander Warfield" were made Commissioners by Act of Assembly, at the petition of the Corporation of Annapolis, to lay out ten acres of public land into half acre lots "for the better encouragement of poor Tradesmen to come and inhabit within the said city, and carry on their respective trades therein." These were laid off on Powder-House Hill and were to be donated to any person or persons not an owner of property in

† Old rent roll, vol. 1, p. 170.

* The material of this chapter is mainly drawn from Ridgely's Annals of Annapolis, pages 108-115.

the town, who would build a dwelling-house upon the same. If the lots were not taken up at the end of two years, then owners of property in the city were allowed to have them.

This addition was called "New Town."

The General Assembly, by the same Act, appointed James Stoddard, Esq., to survey and lay off the city of Annapolis, as the original plat of the town which had been made by Richard Beard, had been burned when the State House was destroyed by fire in 1704.

Mr. Stoddard's survey made the town contain one hundred and forty-two acres; one hundred and fifty-three square perches, and two hundred, nine and three quarters square feet. The State House Circle was laid down as containing 218.988 square feet, with a diameter 528 feet and a circumference of 1159. The Church Circle contained 94,-025 square feet, with a diameter of 346, and a circumference of 1087 feet.

Among those who were the first to have lots surveyed, has been well preserved by records in the Land Office. After the Public Circle, (State House Circle,) Church Circle, and Market Space had been surveyed, Dr. Charles Carroll had resurveyed his lot lying on the north west side of Duke of Gloucester street, and running to Market street. Thos. Macnemara had the second lot resurveyed. It laid on the southwest side Duke of Gloucester street. He had five other lots resurveyed, all on the southwest side of Duke of Gloucester street. Thomas Bladen, Patrick Ogleby, Robert Thomas, Amos Garrett, Benj. Tasker, James Carroll, Samuel Young, John Baldwin, Catherine Baldwin, Col. Sam'l. Young, and Philip Lloyd are among the lot-owners by the re-survey of 1718. July 25, 1718, a lot was resurved for St. Anne. It lay between Temple street and Doctor street. Temple street has passed from memory, but Doctor street remains.

[1720.] In 1720, an Act of Assembly was passed giving further time to the several tradesmen who originally took up the new lots within the addition to the City of Annapolis, to improve the same ; and at the same session a grant was made to Mr. Edward Smith of one hundred and twenty feet of ground in the City of Annapolis for a sawyer's yard.

[1723.] In 1723, the Assembly passed an Act "for the encouragement of learning and erecting schools in the several counties within this Province." Under it Rev. Mr. Joseph Colebatch, Col. Samuel Young, William Lock, Esq., Capt. Daniel Mariartee, Mr. Charles Hammond, Mr. Richard Warfield, and John Beale, Esq., were made the visitors of the schools of Anne Arundel.

[1727.] In 1727, Mr. William Parks, of Annapolis, was authorized to print a compilation of the laws of the Province. To this date there had been no printer. Mr. Ridgely who wrote in 1841, says, "this collection of the laws of Maryland is now nearly out of print—but few copies remaining—and is held by the few that own a copy of it as a rare and curious body of laws passed by our early legislators."

[1728.] In 1728, "Henry Ridgely, Mordecai Hammond, and John Welsch, gentlemen," were empowered to lay out a lot of land, 60 feet in breadth on the water, 300 feet in length, and 25 feet wide at the head of the land, being a part of a lot formerly alloted on which to

7

build a custom house. The corporation was given the fee-simple to the lot provided it built a market house thereon. This lot is the site of the present market house.

[1733.] In 1733, the Legislature passed an Act giving £3,000 for purchasing convenient ground in Annapolis, for the use of the public, and for building thereon a dwelling house for the residence of the Governor. This was for a temporary residence. The Executive, Samuel Ogle, does not appear to have used the fund, and a further sum of £1,000 was added in 1742 to this, and Governor Bladen, empowered to purchase four lots in the City of Annapolis, and to erect a building thereon as a residence for the Governor. From this act sprang McDowell Hall, St. John's College.

[1736.] In 1736, Charles Hammond, Philip Hammond, Vachel Denton, Daniel Dulany, Esq., and Mr. Richard Warfield were empowered to purchase a piece of ground within the town for a public school in Annapolis; to contract for material and to employ workmen to build it. £1,500, current money, was voted by the Legislature for this work.

[1740.] In 1740, is found the first Act of Assembly that brings to public a name that will be forever linked with the history of Maryland. Chapter 4, Acts of 1740, "was for the speedy and effectual publication of the Laws of this Province, and for the encouragement of Jonas Green, of the City of Annapolis, printer." For twenty-eight years, and until his death in 1768, Mr. Green continued the printer of the Province. He was a man of ready wit, large benevolence, and successful enterprise. His journal, the Maryland *Gazette*, is one of the fullest and most reliable sources of history left the State by the corroding touch of time.

In the act that made Mr. Green the State Printer, he was required to print, stitch, and deliver a copy of the public laws, speeches, and answers made at the various sessions, and was directed to make marginal notes to the laws of the Legislature. He was also required to reside in Annapolis. Each county court was obliged to lay a tax of £15 yearly in their respective counties for the support of the State Printer. The office was for two years.

The Legislative Records of this period contain numerous acts for the relief of languishing debtors lying in prison for their debts. There was quite a number so discharged from the Annapolis jail.

CHAPTER XXVII.

THE SECOND NEWSPAPER PRINTED IN MARYLAND.

In that repository of archives—the Maryland State Library—will be found nearly one hundred volumes of "*The Maryland Gazette*," the second newspaper printed in Maryland. The dimensions of the *Gazette* were exceedingly modest, its pages, but four in number, measuring only nine and a half inches in length and seven and a half in width.

The first issue of the *Gazette* was dated Thursday, January 17th. 1745: the publisher being "Jonas Green, Post-master, at the Printing office in Charles street," who announced that it contained "the freshest advices—Foreign and Domestic." These advices were from London in the preceding August and from Amsterdam, Frankfort, and Paris in the same month, and from Constantinople as far back as July. News from Boston bore date of November 12th, 1744, and that from New York was exactly one week later.

In the news from Paris of August 17, old style, was this item: "Six of the most noted Fish-women of this city, took the trouble to go to Metz as soon as they heard of the King's Illness, and made his Majesty a present of a Shirt and Night-Cap, which they had touch'd to the Shrine of St. Geneveve : his Majesty slept in them very comfortably, and the next day found him much better. No doubt Shirt and Night-Cap touch'd by the Shrine of so precious a Saint, contributed much towards his Majesty's recovery."

The last sentence appears to be the *Gazette's*.

Then, as now, editors like Presidents, felt incumbent upon them to offer an inaugural address. Mr. Green, in making his bow to the public, said "the advantage of a newspaper * * * being so universally known, renders it unnecessary to recommend a thing of the kind; however, since it might be looked upon as unfashionable to usher one into the world without a word or two by way of introduction, we shall * * * * give some account of our design." "Our intent," continues the editor, "therefore, is to give the public a weekly account of the most remarkable occurrences, foreign and domestic, which shall from time to time, come to our knowledge ; having always a principal regard to such articles as nearest concern the American Plantations in general, and the province of Maryland in particular ; ever observing the strictest justice and truth in relation of facts, and the utmost disinterestedness and Impartiality in points of controversy.

"And, in a dearth of news which, in this remote part of the world, may sometimes reasonably be expected, we shall study to supply that defect by presenting our readers with the best materials we can possibly collect ; having always, in this respect, a due regard to whatever may conduce to the promotion of virtue and learning, the suppression of vice and immorality, and the Instruction as well as entertainment of our readers."

The advertisements of the first issue were four in number—one offering a reward for a strayed or stolen stallion : the second, advertising a computation table for merchants ; the third placed on sale a work entitled, "A Protest against Popery, showing the purity of the church of England, and Errors of the church of Rome." This advertisement is quoted entire : "Lent sometime ago, but to whom is forgot, a bound Book in Octavo intitled, News from the Dead, or True Inteligence from the other World : On a Leaf preceding the title page is wrote : 'The Wicked borrow and never return.' The person who has it, is hereby desired to consider that Text, and restore the Book to the right owner."

The subscription to the *Gazette* was twelve shillings, Maryland currency, per annum. When the paper was furnished sealed and directed, two shillings additional were charged. "Advertisements of moderate length," were inserted at five shillings each ; subsequent insertions at one shilling each.

The *Gazette* was so much encouraged that, at the end of the second volume, it was able to enlarge ; and it continued to prosper and increase in size down to 1839, when it had become a journal of very respectable dimensions. It was, in that year, discontinued.

Its pages reflect the history of the province ; its columns show the ways and thoughts of the early Marylanders.

The first volume contains many advertisements for run-away servants, such as "a negro boy, named Edward Mills," "an Irish servant-man, Alexander McCoy." The rewards for their capture ranged from "being well rewarded," to ten pounds. The descriptions of runaways were pointed, and did not mince matters. Sarah Munro advertised Elizabeth Crowder, a run-away, "as an English convict servant, * * * upwards of forty years of age, pretty tall and round-shouldered, her hair very grey, and has been lately cut off ; but, it is supposed, she has got a tower to wear instead of it." Thomas Wood~ was advertised as being "5 feet, ten inches high, has a fresh complexion, short brown hair, and one of his teeth broken. * * * He goes by the name of John Wilson * * * * and has got a pass which he has forged, of which he is very capable, as he writes a good hand, and is a sly cunning fellow." John Jones, "a mulatto fellow," was advertised as "about 26 years old, has a deep dimple in his chin and a likely pleasant look, and is a mighty singer." The descriptions of their wearing apparel were as minute.

An advertisement in October, 1745, announced, "next Spring a caravan will be set up to go from said places, (Charlottetown and Patapsco,) to York, Lancaster, and Philadelphia, for the conveyency of Passengers, Goods, letters, &c." Six months public notice was thus given of a journey that now can be made from those points to Philadelphia in six or eight hours ;

Nostrums were duly advertised in those pastoral times. In the issue of September 13, 1745, one Francis Torres gave out in a flaming advertisement, a page and a quarter in length, that he had possession of certain Chinese stones and powders which had cured "Rheumatism, Gout, Bite of Venemous Snake, Cancers, Swellings, Pleurisy, Toothache, Headache, and numerous other diseases, simply by an outward application of the remedies." The announcement was followed by a long number of certificates of persons, (which practice continues until this day,) who had seen cures made, or had themselves been healed, by these "chemical compositions." Some certified to seeing six persons cured of rattlesnake bites, one of being cured of tooth-ache, one of pain in the feet, one of a cancer being cured, and thus, throughout the list, the marvelous healings ran.

But "Monsieur Torres" was not allowed to sell in peace his Chinese cure-alls at twenty-five shillings per stone and bag. A correspondent, in the *Gazette*, of November 8, stated that "if any one could not afford the price charged for these articles, they should go to a cutler's shop, there you will find a remnant of buck-horn, cut off probably from a piece that was too long for a knife handle, saw and rasp it into whatever shape you please, and then burn it in hot embers, and you will have Mons. Torres. Chinese stones which will stick to a wet finger, a fresh sore, &c., &c., &c., and have all the virtues of—a new tobacco pipe."

The powders were disposed of in as summary a manner by this critic.

The *Gazette* paid some attention to local matters ; considerably more to legislative proceedings. Its columns, in 1745, contained the correspondence between the Governor and the Legislature when they were at variance about the imposition of a tax on tobacco, which the Governor and council of State had imposed without the authority of the Legislature. Several sharp messages passed between them, and controversy ended in the dissolution of the Legislature by the Executive.

The marvelous pervaded the columns of newspapers then as well as in these times. Thus we hear from Dorchester county, that, in the great snow in December last, a poor man standing upon the limb of a tree, with a broad axe in his hand, cutting off some boughs for firewood, his foot slipped, and he tumbled down, and falling upon the edge of the axe, (which was kept uppermost by the snow,) his breast was cut open quite the whole breadth of the axe, and his lungs came out. A surgeon, being applied to in a few days, made a perfect cure of. him.''

In the date of June 3, 1746, the *Gazette* published this item : "The following article, having been transmitted with a desire to have it inserted in this paper, it is therefore, without any alteration, submitted to the judgment of the people :

" "On Saturday, May 24, 1746, two men of repute, fishing off Kent Island, about four o'clock in the afternoon, the weather clear and calm, they saw to their surprise, at a small distance, a man, about five feet high, walking by them on the water, as if on dry land. He crossed over from Kent to Talbot county about the distance of four miles.' ''

The attention that was paid to foreign news was very great. Almost the entire paper, number after number, was filled with news from important places of the old world. These clippings show a decidedly Protestant cast of sentiment. The following is an account of a procession observed at Deptford, England, in 1745, honor of the King's birthday :

"I. A Highlander, in his proper dress, carrying on a pole a pair of wooden shoes, with this motto :

THE NEWEST MAKE FROM PARIS.

"II. A Jesuit in his proper dress, carrying on the point of a long flaming sword, a banner with this inscription in large Capital letters :

INQUISITION, FLAMES, AND DAMNATION.

"III. Two Capauchin Friars, properly shaved, habited and accoutred with flogging poles, beads, and crucifixes, &c. One or them bore, on a high pole a bell, Mass'book, and candles, to curse the British nation with ; the other carried a large standard with this inscription :

INDULGENCES CHEAP AS DIRT.

Murder .... Nine-pence.
Adultery...... ... . Nine-pence half pence.
Reading the Bible...... .... A thousand pounds.
Fornication...... .... Four pence half penny farthing.
Perjury. .... Nothing at all.
Rebellion...........A Reward or draw-back of thirteen pence half penny Scots money.

"IV. The pretender with a ribbon, a nosegay, &c., riding upon an ass, supported by a Frenchman on the right, and Spaniard on left, each dressed to the height of the newest modes from Paris and Madrid.

"V. The Pope riding upon his bull.

"The procession was preceded and closed by all sorts of rough music, and after a march round the town, the Pope and the pretender were committed to the flames according to custom, but not 'til they had been first confessed, absolved, and purged with holy water, by the Jesuit. The several actors played their parts with great drollery, and the only token of affection to popery which the spectators gave was a liberal collection to the money-boxes of the begging friars."

The character of the education, then available in the Province of Maryland, is learned from an advertisement in the "Gazette." Mr. Peter Robinson advertised that at his school in Upper Marlborough, Prince George's county, reading, writing, arithmetic, geometry, cosmography, astronomy, merchants' accounts, "or the art of book-keeping after the Italian manner," and algebra, were taught: also the description and use of "sea-charts, maps, quadrants, forestaffs, nocturnal protractor, scales, Coggershalls' rule sector, gauging rod, universal ring dials, globes, and other mathematical instruments."

The hard, persecuting spirit of those times is evidenced by a paragraph taken from the same issue in which Mr. Robinson's advertisement appeared:

"ANNAPOLIS:—Last week some persons of the Romish communion were apprehended, and upon examination were obliged to give security."

The same mind was shown in the needless cruelties inflicted upon criminals.

In the issue of Friday, June 14, 1745, was this item: "Last week at Talbot County Court, a Negro man was sentenced to have his right hand cut off; to be hanged, and then quartered; for the murder of his overseer, by stabbing him, a few days before, with a knife."

Another—"On Friday last Hector Grant, James Horney, and Ether Anderson were executed at Chester in Kent county, pursuant to their sentence for the murder of their late master. The men were hanged, the woman burned. They died penitent, acknowledging their crimes, and the justice of their punishment." The latter sentence commends itself to the sainted murderers of today.

CHAPTER XXVIII.

ANNAPOLIS IN 1745.

The members of the House of Delegates for this year from Anne Arundel were Major Henry Hall, Dr. Charles Carroll, Mr. Philip Hammond, and Mr. Thomas Worthington. For Annapolis City, Capt. Robert Gordon, and Dr. Charles Stewart.

On Wednesday, May 15th, 1745, James Barret was executed at Annapolis for the murder of John Cain in Baltimore county, perpetrated under the following circumstances: Cain, Barret, and another man, all three of them convicts, were engaged in petty thieving, and Cain was employed to sell some wool for them. He did it for eighteen pence; and, on his refusal, after several demands to give his companions their share of it, they drew lots who should kill him. It fell upon Barret, and he inflicted a wound upon him with a knife, from which he died in nine weeks. Barret appeared at his trial about the first of April without remorse, but, at his execution, he "seemed penitent for his sins; implicitly confessed the fact for which he suffered: admonished the spectators to avoid drunkenness and passion, and declared he forgave, and died in charity with all mankind."[*]

Slave catching thrived in the province in those times. The records tell of one John Irwin, who was well known in the province, "particularly for his wonderful dispatch and integrity in taking up runaways, and his remarkable good nature in sometimes helping them off. It will be left to a certain class of moralists to determine which of these traits led him to commit a robbery and murder on the public highway in Scotland, which he expiatiated by his life at Edinburg, Nov. 1744."

On Tuesday the 16th of July, 1745, there were great demonstrations of joy, such as "firing of guns and drinkings of healths &c." made at Annapolis over the reduction of Louisburg by the New England and English troops. The newspaper of the capital gave great space to the account of this capture, showing how keen an interest the people felt in the achievement.

On the 4th of August, 1745, Sunday, a severe storm passed over Annapolis doing great damage to it. A house was struck, and a man and his wife severely injured; other persons, in and near the town, were also hurt. Several cattle were killed in the country. The storm was particularly severe towards South River. In this section three riders had just left their horses standing under a tree and had retired to the house for shelter, when all of the horses were struck by lightning and killed.

On the 13th of August, a lad, aged 12 years, William Watson was knocked overboard by the boom of a schooner within Greenbury's Point and drowned. On the 25th of the same month two "servent men," one belonging to Mr. Tootell and one to Mr. Inch were upset in a canoe on Spa Creek, and drowned.

On the 13th of September, James Briscoe, of St. Mary's county, was burnt in the hand at Annapolis pursuant to a sentence of court for manslaughter, to which he pleaded guilty.

Robt. Gordon, Esq., was chosen mayor of the city in October.

In this year the ship William and Anne, of Annapolis, Capt. Strachan was captured—it is supposed by the French—then at war with England—on her passage to London, and ransomed for 1,500 guineas.

On Thursday, December, 20th, a fire broke out about midnight in the residence of Mr. Gibson, in Annapolis, which, notwithstanding all possible assistance, entirely consumed the same, with all the furniture wearing apparel, and out houses. Two negroes, a man and a woman, perished in the flames; the rest of the family narrowly escaping with their lives. "It is thought this melancholy accident was occasioned by the negroes carrying coals up stairs to light their pipes with."

Friday, December 7, Robt. Gordon, Esq., and Walter Dulany were

* Maryland Gazette.

unanimously elected delegates to the General Assembly to represent
Annapolis.

On Monday, August 5th, 1745, the Maryland Legislature began a
called session in Annapolis. A greater number of delegates was
never known to be in attendence at the first day of the session. Col.
Edward Sprigg was unanimously elected speaker and Major William
Tilghman appointed clerk. The Governor, Thomas Bladen, Esq., approved their election. It is thus seen the Governor had an important
prerogative in the House—the rejection of its elected officers.

"The session," said the Governor in his speech to the House, "was
occasioned by a letter I have received from the Governor of New
England, which shall be laid before you. You will find by it, that
we are called upon to give our assistance towards securing to the
obedience of our Sovereign the late acquisition of Cape Breton."
After expressing his belief that the body would not be wanting in
patriotism in the matter, Gov. Bladen concluded his speech, with
"This service requiring the first place in consultations, and the
speediest dispatch, I shall postpone the mention of a. y other Matters
to you, 'til we have discharged our duties upon this point."

The Upper House of the Legislature in a brief address assured Gov.
Bladen they were ready to give all assistance in their power to aid in
securing Louisburg or Cape Breton to obedience to their common sov-
erign; and were ready to show on all occasions their duty and zeal for
his Majesty's cause.

Gov. Bladen briefly replied to the Upper House: "Gentlemen of the
Upper House of Assembly, I thank you for your address, which cannot but be very agreeable to me, as it confirms me in the good opinion
I have of your duty and affection to his Majesty, and zeal for his
service."

On Wednesday the 7th, the Lower House, or House of Delegates
made their reply. The peculiar phraseology of the first part on the
first sentence is noticeable. "MAY IT PLEASE YOUR EXCELLENCY. We
his Majesty's most dutiful and loyal subjects, the Delegates of the
Freemen of Maryland, in this present Assembly convened, take leave
to acknowledge the favour of your excellency's speech at the opening
of this session, and your goodness in communicating to us Gov. Shir-
ley's letter, whereby we have the pleasing news of the Reduction of
Louisburg or Cape Breton, to his Majesty's obedience." They added
although accepted from the call for troops, they would proceed to
raise a support, and promised to give this but less their first attention.

On Friday, Gov. Bladen returned this brief answer: "Gentlemen of
the Lower House of Assembly. It is a real satisfaction to me to find
by your address that you are resolved to act like good subjects, faithful representatives, and true lovers of your country."

This was all very well; but behind this Gov. was a party to secure
an appropriation for supplies for Louisburg expedition skel ton.
He wanted the supplies voted at once. That was all, it appears,
that he desired them to had the Legislature in his power. He had
the right of dissolution in his hand. So, if the Legislature was turbulent afterward, he could prorogue them, and not disappoint his
wishes, but to send the members home before the supplies were granted
would defeat the very object for which they were called together. The

Lower House, on which its seems devolved the burden and the honor of defending the rights of the "Freemen of Maryland" were as well aware of this pitfall, as was the Governor who set it. They did not intend to step in it.

On the evening of the 7th, probably after the other mild and agreeable address had been presented to Governor Bladen, the following additional one was passed by the Lower House : "May it please your Excellency, It appearing to this House, that there has been assessed and levied by order of your Excellency and council, the sum of one pound of Tobacco, on every taxable person within this Province : and to force the collection thereof an execution hath been put into the hands of the respective sheriffs : But in as much as it is not known to this House, by what Power or authority your excellency and their Honors have done the same, we humbly pray your excellency will please to order to be laid before this House, the authority by which the said tax hath been assessed, levied, and execution issued for the same."

On the 12th another address was sent to his excellency. It read : "May it please your Excellency, We beg leave to represent to your excellency, that, as the several Naval Officers of this province do, by virtue of sundry acts of Assembly, collect large sums of Money for the use of the public, we pray your Excellency will be pleased to acquaint us whether they give any bond for the due execution of their trusts in their offices, and if any, where lodged. As also to cause the same, or authentic copies thereof, to be laid before the House."

The Governor ignored for a time these two addresses from the Lower House, but sharply rebuked that body on the 13th by the following message :

"Gentlemen of the Lower House of Assembly. You have now sat above a week, and no bill has yet been offered to me, or by what I can find, sent to the Upper House for the purpose, I so earnestly recommended at our first meeting, and which brought us together at this season of the year. This Delay is the most extraordinary, as you have, in your address in answer to my speech at the opening of the session, made the greatest professions of loyalty to our gracious sovereign, and zeal to the common cause, and you cannot but know, that the greatest dispatch is absolutely necessary, to render whatever you shall think fit to contribute, of real use. This is a truth not to be denied, and, therefore, it is that I postpone the mentioning any other matter to you till we shall have discharged our duties upon this Point ; which might very easily have been done in two or three days. I am sensible that what is passed cannot be remedied, and that all I can do is to remind you of your duty : therefore I earnestly exhort you, as you regard his Majesty's honor and service, and your own reputation, to discharge it without farther loss of time."

Undismayed by attacks upon their loyalty to their sovereign or insinuations against their personal reputation, the members of the Lower House, under date of the 15th, made this manly reply : "May it please your Excellency, Whatever construction you are pleased to put upon our actions, we assure you, that our unfeigned loyalty to his Majesty will never permit us to give the least delay to anything that relates to his service, and this is apparent by the early and unanimous resolve of our House, to raise a sum of money for the support of his garrison at Cape Breton: And accordingly a bill to that end is in as great forwardness as the subject matter would admit, and will, with the utmost expedition, be sent to the Upper House. Were we inclined to think of any other than a fair and upright behavior in your excellency, we conceive there is equal room to suspect a delay on your part; as you have had before you our address relating to the authority by which your excellency and his lordship's council have levied upon the people one pound of tobacco per poll, near as long as the affair for support of Cape Breton hath been under our consideration, and we should think it less difficult for your excellency to say by what authority that tobacco was levied, than it is for us to find out ways and means effectually to answer the service of his majesty with the greatest ease to the people.

"As what we are about to do for the service of our most gracious sovereign is the result of our own free will, we are determined not to be diverted from that method of proceeding, whereby we hope to render it most useful and agreeable."

The quarrel was now fully inaugurated and the irate Governor was not long in making a reply to this independent address. The next day, the 16th, Gov. Bladen sent this message to the Lower House: "Were I to judge of your address by the reasoning, language, and style of it, I should put no other construction upon it, but that you were at a loss how to defeat the service you are met upon, and that you were resolved to treat me with the utmost indecency and ill manners, merely to furnish yourself with a pretence, that you were diverted from the method of proceeding that would have rendered your services most useful and agreeable to his majesty.

"But, as you say, you are determined not to be so diverted, let your proceedings give evidence of the sincerity of your words, and I shall rejoice at it, and shall willingly lose the remembrance of your extraordinary behavior towards myself in the pleasure I shall receive, when I shall see your actions correspond with the profession you make of duty to his Majesty and affection for his service: This is the great point you are met upon, and I must say, you have a very little so much time to go by, that you have no more to lose, if you really mean to act like good subjects and avoid an odious distinction that must inevitably be made between the behavior of a Maryland Lower House of Assembly and that of all the other colonies, who have been applied to on this important business.

"As for not giving you an answer to your address in relation to the levy of one pound of tobacco per poll, I have deferred it purely in respect to his Majesty's service which ought to have engrossed our whole attention, and which, if it had, would have saved the pain of answering an address of so strange a nature as what you have sent me this day, which I know to be the production of a few. So to a few, very few, do I impute it."

Three days after, the Legislature voted £1,999 towards the support of the garrison at Cape Breton. They had before made an appropriation to this service of £2,090. Thus they showed their loyalty to their sovereign, whilst they maintained their rights as freemen.

Once in the arena, the Freemen of Maryland, by their representatives, were disposed to bring their recalcitrant governor to the torture block, and to answer for real or imaginary delinquencies. On the 21st, after reciting in an address to the governor that the people of Maryland were "burthened with many taxes and charges," they reminded him there were certain fines. forfeitures and amerciaments, which ought to be appropriated to the support of the government, and, as there have been no accounts been rendered to the House of Delegates for many years, they desired accounts of them from "1715 to this time."

On the 23rd of the month, the delegates of Maryland sent his excellency another address. It was brief and pointed. It read :

"May it please your Excellency, You not being pleased hitherto to give us an answer to a former address of this House, requesting you would order to be laid before us, by what authority your excellency and his lordship's council have caused to be levied on the people of this Province one pound of tobacco per poll, we humbly presume to renew our application to your excellency for that purpose.

"And we do hope this request will be the more readily complied with, as it is the desire of the whole representative body of the people of Maryland."

That day Gov. Bladen sent three messages to the Lower House in reply to the addresses of that body. In the first he said that the tax of one pound of tobacco was levied "by virtue of an act of Assembly, for the ordering and regulating the militia of this province for better defence and security thereof, which you will find in the body of laws, page 101."

In regard to the naval officers' bond. the Governor said they were "lodged" with him, and he had ordered copies to be laid before the House.

As to the fines and forfeitures paid since 1715. that were appropriated by the Legislature for the support of the Government. the governor said that he took it "for granted, that the agents, who received them, have accounted for them to the Lord Proprietary, to whom only they were accountable." The same reasoning and manner of reply was made as to the fines and forfeitures of common law. The Governor closed his communications with "and if there was any occasion to lay such accounts before the Lower House of Assembly, as you desire. which I think there is not, it would be a very difficult task on me to procure such accounts, because several of the gentlemen who have been agents, are dead, and I am not acquainted with their executors or administrators. The same reasons will reach the amerciaments, and, therefore, I need not add anything more relating to them."

The governor's replies in regard to the bonds of naval officer. and the fines, forfeitures. and amerciaments appear to have been satisfactory ; but not that in regard to the levying of the tobacco tax by himself and council.

On September second, the Lower House sent the longest paper of the correspondence to the Governor, in which it recited the act by which the governor claimed to lay the tax, and stated that, as this act was one supplemental to one enacted to be in force for three years, its authority had long since expired. "And although," the address continued, "this be our opinion on that point, we take leave further to observe to your excellency, that if the said act were in its full force, yet it does not appear to us. that your excellency and the honorable board, have acted agreeable to the letter, meaning, or intention thereof.

"It gives us great concern to have any cause of complaint against or difference with your excellency, and that honorable board, and therefore truly wish and hope to find, that the welfare and ease of the people may, and will, be the measure and rule of acting.

"We, therefore, hope you will agree with us, that it is a high infringement on the liberties of the people of Maryland to levy any taxes on them under color of law, as not only we, but our constituents generally conceived has been done in this case."[*]

[*] This correspondence is found in the current numbers of the Maryland Gazette.

CHAPTER XXIX.
ANNAPOLIS A CENTURY OLD.

[1749.] Mr. Allen, in his brochure of St. Anne's Parish, says of Annapolis at this period:

"At this date (1749,) one hundred years had passed away since the emigrants from Virginia had settled in the territory of this parish. And it may be worth while to take passing retrospect of the changes here during this period. The original inhabitants, the Indians, were all gone. The Puritans, they too, as such, were no longer heard of, their places of worship were desolate, and their graveyards—where are they? At their Proctor's Landing, a city had grown up; it was the seat of Government for the province. The State House, the Church, the School Houses, and magnificent dwellings, some of which still remain, had taken the place of the log-hut of the emigrant and the wigwam of the Indian. Luxury, fashion, and commerce, with their attendant dissipations and extravagance, had taken the place of the severe and stern simplicity of the early settlers. The battles and wars of its first days had been forgotten, and the full congregations worshipping at the Parish Church and the Chapel at the head of the Severn, show that Puritanism had passed away. And the men mentioned change, what had produced it? The descendants of the early Puritans were not a few, and many of them were still here; but were they Puritans? How came all this? Was it that there was lacking in Puritanism the elements of perpetuity? True, in reference to the church which Christ, the sacred font, had repudiated, prayer, and belief; still, the descendants, and the forms of worship, which their ancestors had called by such harsh names, and so utterly repudiated, were the same. Certainly, then we are led to the conclusion that while the Church of England did embody whatever was needful to self-preservation and purity, the system which had here passed away, did not possess them. For could earnestness and zeal and devotion have preserved them, they had continued to flourish."

As spiritual changes had taken place in the Church—so in material matters, marked transitions had occurred. A hundred years had

[*] 1748.

given the matchlock of the Marylander for the quiver of the Indian; the pinnace for the canoe; the printing press for pictorial chronicles; skilled tillage for the unthrifty hunt; African slavery for savage liberty; the race-course for the wrestling match; the school for the war-dance; substantial edifices for the wigwam; the grand ritual of a mighty Church for the artless appeal to the Great Spirit; the busy throb of an important Capital for the still-hunt of the savage.

The out-look of the city was fair and promising—its merchants had secured the chief trade of the province; ships from all seas came to its harbor; its endowed school educated its citizens for important positions; its thought made the mind of the province; the gayety of its inhabitants and their love of refined pleasure had developed the race-course, the theatre, and the ball-room:—their love of learning the *Gazette* and King William's School:—creations and enterprises that made the province famous, in after years, as the centre of the social pleasures, of the culture, and of the refinement of the American colonies.

CHAPTER XXX.*
CHRONICLES OF ANNAPOLIS FROM 1746 TO 1773.

[1746.] January 28, the ship Aurora, Captain Pickeman, from Holland, arrived at Annapolis with nearly 200 Palatines.† Four died on the passage of twelve weeks.

Saturday, March 8, from 10 to 12 o'clock, there was a remarkable aurora borealis at Annapolis. "It extended a full quarter of the compass, and in some places resembled a red-hot oven. The coruscations, or streams of light, which were numerous, and continually changing shape and situation, reached near 50 degrees towards the zenith."

The importance of Annapolis in the province at this time can be seen from the fact that Baltimoreans were obliged to do their advertising in the Annapolis paper—the *Gazette*,—the only journal then printed in Maryland.

On Tuesday, the 6th of May, the long boat of the ship Richmond, was upset about three miles from Tolley's Point, and the boatswain, gunner, and three others were drowned. About a week afterwards their bodies washed ashore near Annapolis.

At a meeting of the corporation about this period, all by-laws were repealed, and fourteen others were enacted in their stead, constituting at that time the entire local code of the city. They were:

1. To prevent nuisances.
2. To ascertain the allowance to juries for verdicts.
3. To oblige officers to attend to their duties.

* The items of this chapter are taken mainly from the Maryland Gazette. The quaint expressions are the Gazette's own.

† Germans.

4. To prevent the dangers which may happen by the firing of chimneys.

5. For security of the peace.

6. To prohibit keeping sheep, hogs, or geese, or useless cattle, or horses within the town fence ; except in styes and inclosures.

7. To prevent accidents by fire.

8. For the encouragement of tradesmen.

9. To prevent vexatious suits for small debts.

10. To subject such persons as shall hereafter be elected Sheriffs of Annapolis to a fine, if they shall refuse to undertake the execution of said office.

11. To prevent the dangers and accidents which may arise from building, beaming, or graving ships, sloops, boats, and other vessels.

12. To prevent the entertaining and harboring of slaves

13. To prevent sundry irregularities within the city of Annapolis.

14. For repair of the public streets and other purposes therein mentioned.

15. To repeal all former by-laws of this corporation.

June 13, three persons were fined £20 each by the Anne Arundel Court, held at Annapolis, for drinking the Pretender's health.

On July 6th, the schooner Peggy, bound for Annapolis, with passengers, was struck by lightning near Sharp's Island, the mainmast was rent from top to bottom. Ten persons lay for some time as dead. On recovering their conciousness they were seized with violent vomitings. The cabin was filled with a sulphurous smell.

The *Gazette*, of the issue of July 15, says : ''The gentlemen belonging to the ancient South River Club, to express their loyalty to his Majesty, on the success of the inimitable Duke of Cumberland's obtaining a complete victory over the Pretender, and delivering us from persecutions at home, and popery and invasion from abroad, have appointed a grand entertainment to be given at their Club House on Thursday next. An example worthy the imitation of all true loyal subjects.''

On Wednesday night, September 2nd, about midnight, Dr. Charles Carroll lost a warehouse by fire, ''the third disaster of the kind,'' which had befallen him in eight months. Loss £600 sterling.

On the 15th of September, three companies set sail, in high spirits, from Annapolis, to engage in the contemplated reduction of Canada by the English. The Captains were Campbell, Croftis, and Jordan. The men had attained great proficiency in drill. The practice of appealing to the ruler of the universe for success in arms was in vogue in Maryland. The editor of the *Gazette* says of this embarkation and enterprise : ''This important affair must excite, in every true subject, a hearty zeal and ardour in his prayers, that the GREAT GOD OF HOSTS would crown their enterprise with success.'' Small caps are the editors.

Monday September 29, Michael Macnemara was elected Mayor of Annapolis.

Wednesday, November 5th, the great Whitfield visited Annapolis. It was a day of thanksgiving. He preached a sermon from Prov. XIV, 28 : ''Righteousness exalteth a nation.'' As the service ended, the ornament at the back of the Speaker's pew, gave way, and struck several gentlemen. Two were hurt severely. The fall was occasioned by a heavy gust of wind.

During this year the sloop Molly, of Annapolis. Charles Giles, commander, bound to Barbadoes, was captured by a French privateer.

[1747.] Tuesday, January 6, was launched a very fine and large ship, belonging to Mr. William Robert, of Annapolis. She was called the *Rumney* and *Long*, after the names of the Builders, and would carry 700 hogsheads of tobacco.

On January 29, Sheriff William Thornton, by order of Anne Arundel County Court, offered for sale to the highest bidder, two men in his custody, for his fees.

The Maryland *Gazette*, of March 3, says, "on Monday last week, arrived in Patuxent, Capt. Isaac Johns, from London, which place he left the 13th of December last. We have not yet learned of any news he has brought except that he left Portsmouth twenty-four hours after a Fleet bound to America, under convoy of a Man of War; whom were the Captains German Cole for Patuxent, and Grindell and Creagh for Patapsco. He also brings advice, that his Excellency Samuel Ogle, Esq., with his Lady and Family, is on board the same Man of War, bound hither, with a commission to resume the Government of this Province; his Excellency the present Governor designing for England this Spring."

On March 9, Thomas Williamson, advertised that "he gives good encouragement to men, women, and children, that can be aiding and assisting in the business of making duck and osnabrigs; especially spinners."

By letters from London, the *Gazette*, of March 17, says, we learn that the Snow Glasgow, Capt. Montgomery, and the Ship Prince George, Capt. Coulter, both bound hither, were taken the 10th of September last, about 50 leagues from the Capes, by four Frenchmen of war from the West Indies, who, after they had taken out the goods, burnt both the vessels.

Stephen West, Jr., advertised in March of this year for persons who "are skilled in spinning of Hemp for sail-cloth, osnabrigs, sacking, or cordage; and weaving of sail cloth, &c., or laying of rope, having all materials in readiness for carrying on the business."

A touch of Baltimore's growing commercial importance was felt at this time, the *Gazette* of Tuesday, March 24, argumentatively saying: "Last Saturday sailed out of Severn River, the Ship Britannia, Capt. John Hutchinson, for London, having on board 1064 hogsheads of tobacco, consigned to Mr. John Hamburg. The great dispatch which has been made in the loading of that large ship, being but little more than two months (all our navigation being stopped for many weeks in the winter,) and the dispatch which those ships that load in that river commonly made, is enough to make one wonder that so many go further up the Bay into Patapsco to load, where the navigation is so much more difficult, and must consequently take much longer time; and where we are well informed the worm bites as bad as in Severn."

The Brig, Raleigh, late the Raleigh Privateer, Capt. Samuel Allyne, from Annapolis, with 5,000 bushels of wheat for Madeira, ran ashore and bilged on Willoughly's Point in Virginia, on the 21st of March at night. The vessel and cargo were lost, and the crew saved with much difficulty.

During April of this year, "some villians broke into the Council House in this city, and stole some of the arms. His Excellency, the

Governor, has issued a Proclamation, offering a reward of fifty pounds to any one that will discover the person or persons concerned in the **fact.**"

On Friday, May 29, Dr. Alexander Hamilton, of Annapolis, was married to Miss Margaret Dulany, (daughter to the Hon. Daniel Dulany, Esq., "a well accomplished and agreeable young lady, with a handsome fortune."

On Thursday night the 12th of May, "died here, after a short illness, Miss Anne Ogle, eldest daughter of his Excellency, our Governor, a very hopeful and promising young lady, endowed with a surprising wit and every endearing quality, beyond most of her tender years; and is greatly lamented."

Wednesday May 1, a negro man, named Tom, was executed here for a burglary, of which he had been convicted at the preceeding County Court in March.

On Sunday, July 12th, last, two very hopeful children, the eldest sons of Mr. William Reynolds, hatter, of this place, one of them 7, the other 6 years of age, were drowned. Their bodies were soon after taken up.

Among the Acts, passed at the late Session, was one "for repairing and amending the public and county goal, in the city of Annapolis." Also, one for the speedy and effectual publication of the Laws of this "Provinces and for the encouragement of Jonas Green, Printer."

On Tuesday, July 28th last, "Mr. Nicholas Maccubbin, of Annapolis, merchant, was married to Miss Mary Carroll, only daughter of Dr. Charles Carroll, a young gentlewoman blessed with every good qualification, having a handsome fortune."

A number of the Rebels, imported in the ship Johnson, into Oxford, were brought to Annapolis about this time and were put upon sale.

On the 3rd of August, the body of Elisha Williams was found drowned—servant to John Senhouse. An inquest was held, the coroner, at the time, charging "the too often rigorous usage and ill-treatment of masters to servants, whereby it very often happened, that such ill-usage was the causage of many servants making an end of themselves one way or other." The jury then took evidence. What was the exact result of their labors it is difficult to say, as the only record there is at hand is the *Gazette's* account given in the following clouded style: "The jury gave the following verdict; viz: That by his having been lately ill-used by Hannah Senhouse, his mistress, he went voluntarily into the water and was drowned, whether his having been ill-used, or expectation for the future to be so, was the cause of this drowning is left to a Grand Inquest for the body of this county to enquire into; and we are informed, that the transgressor, as well as the evidences, are bound over to the next Assize-Court. It is, therefore, to be hoped, and it is the intent of this (being in print,) that all masters may, and will, for the future, use their servants according to their deserts, let the consequence of this case end in whatever manner it will."

At this period Nicholas Clouds kept "boats and hands at Broad Creek, on Kent Island, to cross the Bay to Annapolis with gentlemen and their horses, and likewise from Annapolis to Kent Island."

The Annapolis Company, Capt. Campbell, showed the white feather at Saratoga. Lieutenant Joseph Chew of that company, and who was taken prisoner, stated: "We were indeed over-matched, yet our men behaved ill; some threw away their pieces without ever firing of them; others fired once, and ran off."

On November 16th, a negro man, named York, was convicted of horse-stealing in Anne Arundel county, and sentenced to death, and, on Wednesday, December 9, was executed at Annapolis. In contradistinction to the great parade made today in the newspapers when a criminal is hung, the Maryland *Gazette* summed up the whole matter in two lines.

December 14, the General Assembly was convened in extra session by Gov. Samuel Ogle. A quorum not appearing, the Assembly was prorogued until Monday the 21st. On the 22nd, the Governor made his speech to members, excusing the necessity of calling them together at that season, but he added he "thought it my indispensible duty to obey his majesty's commands, which I shall lay before you." He further stated what his majesty desired was that money he raised to support their own colonial troops in the war against the French until the whole expenses could be laid before Parliament.

The Upper House expressed its willingness to do all it could to demonstrate their loyalty to their sovereign; the Lower House. the immediate representative of the people, was more cautious in its expressions. After stating the inconvenience with which they had assembled, they expressed their willingness to do all in their power to answer "his royal expectations." They also informed his Excellency that they would take the subject into their "serious consideration; and determine thereupon, agreeable to the present circumstances of the people we represent." They were not long in coming to a conclusion. On that very day it seems they made a further address to the Governor, in which they represented "that the vast charge and expense the people of this province have already been at, in lodging, maintaining here, and transporting to Albany in the province of New York, the place of general rendezvous, and further supplying those levies with provisions there; together with the heavy taxes, and other difficulties, under which the people we represent now labor; have rendered it altogether impracticable for us to raise or advance any sum for payment of the said forces. And as no further business lies before this House, we pray your Excellency will please to put an end to this meeting."

The Governor replied to the Lower House, "I wish with all my heart you could have thought of any way of answering his majesty's expectations at this time, in relation to our own levies, agreeable to the zeal you have hitherto shown upon the like occasions; but as you represent it impracticable for us to raise or advance any further sum for the payment of the said forces, nothing remains for me to do, but to put an end to this Assembly."

The Legislature was prorogued to the second Tuesday in May ensuing.

On the 27th of December, Mrs. Baldwin, aged 99 or 100 years, died near Annapolis on her son's plantation. She is said to have been born in Anne Arundel which would make her birth about the settlement of the county. She left behind a numerous progeny.

[1748.] Information arrived at Annapolis early in this year that the schooner Hopewell, Capt. Coulhon, of Annapolis, had been captured by the French.

8

The Judicial Proceedings of the province throw great light upon the principles of the early Marylanders. We turn out of the way to take a case from Baltimore county. On the second of that assize "one Bevis Pain, an old grey-headed sinner, was tried for blasphemy. His abominably wicked expression (to vile and horrid to repeat) was fully proved upon him, and the jury soon found him guilty, and he was sentenced to be bored through the tongue, and to pay twenty pounds sterling : the first part of the sentence being immediately put in execution, and he committed to the Sheriff's custody 'til he paid the fine."‡

At the April Anne Arundel Court, "One William Phillips, alias Gormond, was indicted for burglary and felony. Cleared of the burglary, but found guilty of the felony, he was branded with the letter R in the hand, and then committed for the want of security for his good behaviour."

On the second of June, one of the Kent Island ferry boats, that plied between Annapolis and the former place, was overset near the shore by a gale. Wm. Vickers, of Talbot county, Benjamin T. Fish, and John Donnahoe were drowned. One person saved himself by swimming ashore and another by holding on to the boat until he was taken off.

The captures, by the French privateers at this time, made an armed merchantman a valuable carrier. Thus, in July, the Ship Winchelsea, Thomas Cornish, commanding, lying in Severn River, as a carrier, advertised as an inducement to shippers that she carried 18 guns and 40 men.

On the 18th of August, Capt. Loyall from Madeira, arrived at Annapolis in a sloop that had been taken from the French by an English Man of War. Because the sloop could not be condemned at Maderia, a court of vice admiralty met on the 22nd, at Annapolis, and condemned her and her cargo as a legal prize.

In August of this year, the Annapolis prison was guarded every night by a strong watch, as numerous prisoners were in it who were to be tried at the next assize for capital offences. For all that, on Saturday morning, the third, in broad daylight, about 8 o'clock, Mark Parr, one of the prisoners charged with robbery, and "remarkable for his many infamous rogueries, having found means to get off his irons, scaled the prison walls, and walked off. He was seen walking through the town by several persons who did not know him. It was stated shortly afterward, how correctly we are unable to say, that his dead body was found in back woods."**

On Thursday, the 15th of September, court ended for Anne Arundel county. On that day "Joseph Humes; of the city of Annapolis," Jeweler, for a burglary and felony, in breaking open and entering the store of Mr. Lyde Goodwin, merchant in this city, and stealing from thence several things of value ; Mathew Lapear and Charles Higginson, for breaking open and robbing the store of Dr. James Walker, near Patapsco Ferry, were sentenced to death. On Wednesday the 21st of September, Higginson was reprieved, but the other two on that day were executed at the gallows near Annapolis. It would seem from the expression "at the gallows" that this horrid instrument was in such constant use it was kept continually erected. Humes

‡ Gazette.
** Md. Gazette.

and Lapear "were attended to the place of execution by a numerous crowd of spectators, implicitly confessed the facts for which they suffered, behaved with great decency, and declared they died in charity with all the world."†

On Thursday, the 22nd of September, the Ship Winchelsea, Capt. Thomas Cornish, sailed out of Severn River with 950 hogsheads of tobacco, consigned to John Hanbury, merchant, of London.

On Thursday, the 29th of September, John Ross, Esq., was chosen Mayor of Annapolis.

Two fatal accidents on a vessel in South River is recorded on the 6th of October—a boy belonging to it fell down the hold and was instantly killed; and in the evening one of the crew of the same ship, fell overboard and was drowned.

Felons were imported in the province as late as this period—for the *Gazette* notes that this day (the 26th of October,) the Snow Mary, Capt. Brown, arrived in nine weeks from London, with 52 felons. The same paper contains an advertisement for their sale for a term of seven years. They consisted of men, women, and boys.

On Tuesday, November 1st, Capt. John Carpenter, died at Annapolis. He "had long been a worthy inhabitant of this city, and was many years commander of a ship from London, in the tobacco trade; and who, by a diligent application and honest industry, had acquired a considerable fortune, with a fair character."

[1749.] On March 2nd, Robert Gordon, Esq., and Mr. Walter Dulany, former representatives, were unanimously rechosen delegates to the Legislature for Annapolis.

On Wednesday, March 28, "the Rev. Andrew Lendrum was inducted into this parish—Annapolis—in the room of the Reverend and Ingenious Mr. John Gordon, who is removed to the great grief of his parishioners, to St. Michael's parish, in Talbot county."‡

On the night of the 27th of March, the night after the county election, at a tavern in Annapolis, "some persons being more merry than wise, and not considering that Golden Rule of Doing to others as they would they should do unto them, made themselves sport with Mr. Vincent Stewart, one of the company, (who had been a little too free with liquor,) by throwing and tumbling him about whereby he got very much hurt and bruised; and last week he died. The coroner has had an inquest on his body, which is adjourned some days. It is a very melancholy affair, as he has left a sorrowful wife and six helpless children."

On Saturday, July 29, Wm. Rogers, Esq., a gentleman who had held many posts of honor and trust, died at Annapolis, in the 50th year of his age. He was, at the time of his death, one of the Aldermen of Annapolis.

At the assize for Anne Arundel county, which ended September 13th, Charles Elliott received sentence of death for stealing a mare.

On the 29th of September, John Bullen, Esq., was elected Mayor of Annapolis. On the election day a race was run on the race-course near Annapolis, "for the late Mayor's Plate, £20, which was won by Mr. Butler's horse, Calico.** At night there was a ball, where there

† Md. Gazette.
‡ Md. Gazette.
** Md. Gazette.

was a great number of gentlemen, and a splendid appearance of ladies.''

Joseph Wilson and Isaac Wright, in October, were sent to Jail for counterfeiting bills of credit of the province. The counterfeiting was poorly executed. They were sent to Cecil county for trial, where Wilson was soon after tried and received sentence of death, Wright having turned State's evidence against him. Wilson, however, subsequently broke jail and escaped.

On Wednesday, the 8th of November, the Ship Chester, Capt. Sedgley, from Bristol, arrived at Annapolis with about 20 passengers and a number of indented servants and some convicts.

On Wednesday, November 29th, the Ship Thames Frigate, Capt. James Dobbins, arrived at Annapolis, with 120 convicts on board.

[1750.] It will be observed by the following advertisement in the "*Maryland Gazette*," of the 7th of February, that the "servants" or time-service men were sometimes men of ordinary education :—"To BE SOLD. The time of a servant man, who has about six years to serve, understands arithmetic, writes a good hand, and would do well for a teacher of children in the country. Enquire of the Printer hereof."

Joseph Wilson, the counterfeiter, who escaped jail in 1749 from Cecil county, got into a fracas in New Jersey, was wounded, and afterward recognized and re-arrested. He was then confined in Bucks county, Pennsylvania, jail, and succeeded in escaping from it.

Thursday, May 8th, the Legislature met at Annapolis. On Wednesday 9th, the Legislature discharged from their body, Mr. Walter Dulany, a representative from Annapolis, "on account of his acceptance of the office of Deputy Commissary, for Anne Arundel county, since his election." On Wednesday the 16th, Mr. Dulany was unanimously re-elected the representative of Annapolis in the same General Assembly.

About the middle of this year, James Mitchell, a resident of Annapolis, met with a singular and fatal accident, in Rappahannock River, Virginia. He went out on a flat and became entangled "in a great number of sea-nettles and was drowned."

On Friday, August 31, a negro named Cuffee, was executed at Annapolis for horse-stealing.

[1751.] On Thursday, February 28, Mary Steadman was found dead in her bed with numerous bruises upon her body. A coroner's jury brought in a verdict of wilful murder, and her husband was arrested. On Friday the 12th of April, the husband, John Steadman, a Scotchman, was convicted of this murder. Besides many other bruises there were visible on her throat the marks of a man's thumb and finger. The evidence was entirely circumstantial. He was executed Wednesday April 17, denying to the last his guilt. He was afterward hung in chains on a gibbet near Annapolis. At the same time Daniel Sullivan, an Irishman, who was convicted of the murder of Donald McKennie in Baltimore county, was hung. His body was sent to that county to be placed in a gibbet near the spot where he committed the murder.

On Friday, April 12, two negro women were executed at Annapolis for burning down a tobacco house.

The convicts, transported to Maryland, committed numerous and alarming crimes—murder amongst them. Thomas Poney, in June, was sentenced to be burnt in the hand at Annapolis for burglary, and

,one Siphcorus Lucas, for burglary, was sentenced to be hung. He was executed at Annapolis June 26th. Both these were transported convicts.

On Tuesday night, July 2nd, a bold robbery was committed in Annapolis. Two armed men placed a ladder up to a dormer window of the house of Mr. Charles Cole, merchant, and one entered the room of Mr. Cole, with a dark lantern and pistol. Presenting the weapon to the head of Mr. Cole, he threatened, if he made a stir or noise, to blow his brains out. The robber proceeded to tie him, bruising him during the operation, and telling him his money he wanted, and that he would have. Mr. Cole's servant-man John, who was in a house adjoining, hearing a noise, looked out and seeing the robber's accomplice below, was told by him if he made a noise he would shoot him. The faithful fellow, not deterred from duty by this threat, proceeded to get his gun, and fired out of the window at the robber, but, missing him, was fired upon in return, barely escaping being shot. The robbers, being thus alarmed, made off. A reward of £80 current money was offered to the accomplice if he would inform who broke into Mr. Cole's room, and the certainty of a pardon.

Subsequently, about the middle of August, John Conner, a convict servant, confessed he was the accomplice who was engaged in the robbery of Mr. Cole, and that Thomas Bevan was the one who entered the room. Both were captured and lodged in jail. On being put on his trial Thursday, September 12th, Bevan pleaded *not guilty*, and when his accomplice was put on the stand against him, he objected to him giving evidence as contrary to the laws of England. On being told that there was a law of the province which allowed it, he "courteously," begged pardon for giving so much trouble, and entered a plea of guilty. He was sentenced to death, and was executed at Annapolis on Friday, November 2nd, manifesting much contrition for his evil life, and, in an address on the scaffold, warning others by his bad 'life and sad fate. He was transported from England for crime.

George Wilson was in September found guilty of the murder of Capt. Smith, near St. Mary's, and received sentence of death. He was afterward reprieved.

Richard Whalen, a resident of Annapolis, about this time was drowned in Bohemia River.

It was now that the authorities become thoroughly alarmed in regard to the conduct of convict servants, and the magistrates of Anne Arundel, during August, ordered that, for every convict servant hereafter imported in that county, there should be £50 security given. It was understood that other counties would do the same. The *Gazette* puns on the fact that these people were sent to America for the better peopling of the colonies.

[1752.] Green street was laid off in 1752 from Church [Main] street to Duke of Gloucester, by Dr. Chares Carroll. He offered lots on both sides of it for sale.

On Sunday morning, May 5th, Governor Samuel Ogle died at Annapolis, in the 58th year of his age. His remains were interred in St. Anne's Church. Benjamin Tasker, Esq., as the first person named of his Lordship's Council, assumed the Governorship of the province after the death of Governor Ogle. Governor Ogle had served three terms as Governor.

On Friday, May 15th, James Powells was hung at Annapolis, for burglary and robbery committed in Somerset county. He fainted at the gallows, it was supposed, by the stagnation of blood caused by his hands being tied so tightly. "On his coming to himself, he desired the executioner to make haste and, amidst some private ejaculations, was turned off."

Benjamin Tasker, Jr., and Christopher Lowndes offered for sale in Annapolis, by public advertisement a parcel "of healthy slaves, consisting of men, women, and children," directly from the coast of Africa, in the Elijah, Captain James Lowe.

[1753.] Wednesday, May 16th, Charles Campbell, Daniel Spinkfe, and John Brown, were executed at Annapolis for burglary. These frequent executions at Annapolis were not all due to the dissolute morals of the people of Anne Arundel, but the practice was to execute all the criminals of the province at the Capital.

Several times in July a large wild bear was seen in the woods on the North side of Severn, visiting plantations, and stealing hogs, and other domestic animals.

September 7th, Robert Gordon, Esq., died, aged 77, who for many years was" a reputable inhabitant of this city, having held the offices of Alderman, Representative to the Lower House of Assembly, Judge of the Provincial Court, and Commissioner of Land Office, which trusts he executed with diligence and industry."

December 6th, Hon. Daniel Dulany, died. He had been Commissary General, one of the Council of State, and Recorder of Annapolis. "He was very eminent in the profession of law, and in all his several stations, acquitted himself with strict equity and unwearied diligence." This was Dulany, the elder. It was the other Daniel Dulany that was so prominent for his ability.

[1754.] November 28th, Messrs. Walter Dulany and Stephen Bordley were chosen to represent the city of Annapolis in the ensuing General Assembly.

[1755.] March 13th, at the Anne Arundel County Court, Edward Vinn was convicted of stealing a grindstone for which he was stood in the Pillory and received thirty lashes at the whipping post, well laid on, "which convinced him of having had a hard bargain."

Penelope House was twice whipped and twice stood in the Pillory for shop-lifting.

February 28th, died here Mrs. Elizabeth Marriott, widow, who kept the Ship Tavern in South East street. She had property valued at upwards of £3,000.

February 28th, was landed here "from on board the Good, Captain Chew, for the use of the city, a very fine engine, made by Newthem and Reagg, No. 1800, London, which the inhabitants last year generously subscribed for. It threw water 156 feet perpendicular." Was not this the city's present heirloom, "THE VICTORY?"

October 30th, Jonas Green was elected Common Councilman in place of John Brice, Esq.

November 5th, the French and Indians were drawing so near the province that it was deemed expedient to fortify Annapolis. The celebrated Fort Frederick, still standing, was then built in Washington county.

November 18th, about 4 o'clock in the morning, a shock of an earthquake was sensibly felt by many.

[1755.] On the first of December, 1755, five vessels arrived at Annapolis loaded with those unfortunate exiles—that Longfellow has immortalized in verse. The people of the town were at first exercised at the thought of having a number of "French Papists" among them—the mixture being a double portion of foreign and religious evil. The poor Acadians proved objects of charity rather than of fear, and food and raiment were promptly supplied them. Three of the vessels were despatched to other points in Maryland to distribute the exiles among the people. One ship remained at Annapolis, and, no doubt, the descendants of these unfortunate people are with us to this day. It is to be regretted that the names of the exiles are not known to us that their progeny might trace their descent from them—genealogical study being a pleasure for which even our sturdiest Republicans have the keenest zest.

[1756.] February 5th, Mr. Launcelot Jacques, merchant, was chosen Common Councilmen, in place of Dr. Charles Carroll, deceased.

February 17th, the birthday of Lord Baltimore was celebrated by the Governor who gave an elegant entertainment. In the evening a public ball was given at the Council House.

March 22nd, Col. George Washington passed through Annapolis, en route for Virginia.

June 24th, there was a violent gust of lightning, thunder, hail, and wind. The lightning struck the Court House, and set it on fire, but, by the assistance of the inhabitants and the fire-engine, it was speedily put out.

July 8th, a Tannery was set up at Annapolis by Thomas Hyde.

Wednesday, the 10th of November, was celebrated at Annapolis as the birth-day of the King who, on that day, entered his 27th year.

[1757.] June 23rd, a number of young gentlemen of the place, armed, went as volunteers from here, to join what other force might be raised for immediate defence of the colony against the Indians.

This is the style in which the fair were puffed one hundred years ago:

"On Saturday last (January 1st, 1757,) Wm. Murdock, Esq., of Prince George's county, was married to Mrs. Hamilton, of this city, a most agreeable widow lady, of excellent accomplishments, and a happy temper."

During the preceding fall and present winter Annapolis was infected with the small-pox. Inoculation was practiced upon one hundred persons; all of whom recovered; whilst of those who had it in the natural way, one out of every six died. The family of Jonas Green was afflicted to such an extent that many of his customers were afraid to take the "Gazette," lest they would catch the disease. Mr. Green, whilst he expressed a doubt as to paper carrying the disease, subsequently stated that people "need not fear to catch the small-pox from the paper, as it was kept all the time a good distance from the house, and beside the disease was now eradicated from his premises."

On March 10th, the Gazette announced that, "As almost all the inhabitants of this city, who were liable to that distemper—(Small-pox,) have either had it, or are now down with it, we hope in a very little time the town will be quite clear of it, and business be carried on as usual." The small-pox was so bad on the 27th of March that the Legislature would not meet on that day in Annapolis, but was prorogued by the Governor to meet in Baltimore on the fifth of April.

February 14th, Col. George Washington stopped in Annapolis.

[1758.] March 22, "at night, at two minutes before ten, when the air was very calm and serene, we had here a very considerable shock of an earthquake, but through God's mercy, it has done no damage that we have yet heard from. For about ¾ of a minute, before the shock, there was a rumbling sound, not unlike that of carriage wheels on pavements or frozen ground, at a distance, which increased until the shaking, and that lasted about half a minute."*

September 7th, Walter Dulany and George Stewart, Esqrs., where chosen to represent this city in the Legislature.

The price of lodging at this time was about $1.00 per day, during the session of Assembly.

November 7th, during an inquiry into a contested election affecting a representative from this city, the question as to whether aldermen had a right to vote in the election of delegates was decided in the negative.

December 21, the election of George Stewart, Esq., one of the returned members of the Legislature from this city, was set aside, and a writ issued for a new election.

[1759.] August 20th, Mr. Thomas Jennings, Chief Clerk of the Land Office died here. He was succeeded by Mr. Wm. Stewart.

During this year, many dead bodies of men, were, at intervals, found floating in the dock. They were supposed to have been thrown overboard by captains of vessels, to escape the trouble of interment.

[1760.] On April 17th, a negro man, named Bristol, died at Annapolis, aged 125.

A handsome collection was made May 29th, in the Episcopal Church, for the sufferers by the late great fire in Boston.

The Windmill, built on Windmill-point, in this town, began to grind September 1st, and was reckoned to be the strongest and best built mill in the country. It ground, with a middling wind, 12 bushels in an hour. It was built of stone and stood on the site of the Naval Academy.

In November, a Stocking Manufactory was in operation in this city.

[1769.] On May 11th, a servant of Richard Mackubin made a confession that he was one of a gang of miscreants who for some time past had been plundering smoke-houses, ware-houses, cellars, etc., which they entered by false keys. Eleven of his companions were apprehended and committed to jail.

October 24th, a man, supposed to be intoxicated, went into a house and demanded grog, which being refused, he drew a sword, and stabbed a Mrs. Cumberford, who bled to death before assistance could be rendered.

In the Act, entitled "an Act for emitting bills of credit and other purposes therein mentioned," passed during the Session of 1769, and a sum of money not exceeding £7,000 stirling, was appropriated to the building an edifice in this city where the present (the second) State House now stands, sufficient to accommodate the Upper and Lower Houses of Assembly, the High Court of Appeals, Chancery and Provincial Courts of this Province.

[1770.] January 11th, Mr. James Brookes, of Annapolis, was appointed Clerk to the Commissioners for emitting bills of credit:

[1771.] January 12th, the following gentlemen were chosen to

* Md. Gazette.

represent the City of Annapolis in the General Assembly: Messrs. John Hall and William Paca.

In an "especial Court" held here, January 17th, one person was burnt in the hand, two ordered to be whipped and stood in the Pillory.

Morris McCoy and negro Daniel, the former for the murder of his master—were executed January 22nd, on the gallows near this city, pursuant to their sentences: McCoy's body was from thence removed to a place near which his master was murdered, and there hung in chains, on a gibbet erected for that purpose, in sight of the road leading to the lower ferry on Patapsco River.

As an instance of the curious matter deemed of such importance as to warrant publication, there is published on February 28th, a notice of the inoculation of the Governor's two children and their safe recovery.

Mr. Ralph Dobinton, of Annapolis, was drowned July 4th, while attempting to save another person, which person safely reached the shore.

The new theatre on West street, was opened September 9th. This was on the lot now occupied by the Express Office.

[1772.] A slight shock of earthquake was felt in Annapolis on April 25th.

Captain Dunlop, on board of a schooner bound for the Eastern Shore, was seized with a frenzy on November 11th, and leaped overboard, near Greensbury Point, and was drowned.

[1773.] On Tuesday, April 1st, as a young negro was digging away a bank in a gentleman's garden, he undermined the earth to such an extent that it fell upon him, and killed him instantly.

The same day, a dispute arising between a man and woman, both under the influence of liquor, the woman gave the man several blows on the head with a broomstick, from the effects of which he died in a few hours.

November 14th, Mr. Robert Pinkney was killed by a fall from his horse.

It was at this period the national feeling of the Annapolitans was all aglow. The famous dispute between the brilliant Dulany and the learned Carroll had taken place in the *Maryland Gazette*. Loving the mother country with all the loyalty of a patriotic people, the citizens of Annapolis were yet more loyal to their rights, liberties, and sacred privileges. The author of the letters of "The First Citizen," who sustained the extreme American side of the stamp act controversy, was entirely unknown but so grateful were the people to the author, that they instructed the members of the Legislative Assembly of Maryland, to return their hearty thanks to the unknown writer, through the public prints. This was done by William Paca and Matthew Hammond. When it transpired that Charles Carroll, of Carrolton, was the author of these letters, numbers of citizens went to him and expressed their thanks personally. The knowledge of this authorship elevated him at once in public favor.

CHAPTER XXXI.*

CUSTOMS AND CHARACTERS OF THE CAPITAL.

"William Farris, Maker. Annapolis." "Such is the inscription on the face of an old clock standing in an old hall in old Annapolis. And pray who was William Farris, the maker of this stately time-piece that, in measured cadence, still records the creeping hours marking the day of the month and showing the phases of the moon by the appearance and disappearance of that ever rubicund and amiable countenance which in obedience to the mysterious mechanism, peers over and dodges behind the dial plate with lunar punctuality?

"He must needs have been an oddity. The only record of his life, his will in rhyme, turns up from the dusty pigeon hole of a dead lawyer's office desk, legally endorsed, W. Farris, watchmaker at Annapolis, Maryland, his will—composed by Miss Charlotte Heselius, first wife of Thos. Jennings Johnson, Esq., and daughter of Heselius, the portrait limner.'" Here is

THE WILL OF WILLIAM FARRIS.

"Old Farris one day, as he sat in his shop
Revolving the chances of dying or not,
The hyppo so seized him he tho't it was best
To divide his estate ere his soul went to rest.
So to work went the goldsmith:—Dreadful the task!
But first, for advice, he applied to his flask.
The gin, ever generous, fresh spirits afforded
And the will as I heard it was nearly thus worded,
I, William Farris, being well as to health.
Knowing Death often comes to old people by stealth
And without giving caution, or caring for fears,
Will take whom he pleases, regardless of tears;
So I now think it best to be thus on my guard,
By making my will, tho' I own it is hard
To forsake all the gains I have made all my life,
And, God knows, I have made them with trouble and strife,
Many nights have I watched, dread want to defy;
Now I make my last will and prepare me to die,
Then, I give and bequeath to my dear loving wife;
In case she's a widow the rest of her life;
The plates, spoons and dishes, pots, kettles and tables,
With the red and white cow that inhabits the stables,
The landscape, and "Judith" that hangs on the wall,
And the musical clock hind the door in the hall.
My buckles and cane to son William I give.
And no more, because he's got substance to live,
His road I took care in his youth to instruct him,
Tho' I say it myself, a princess might trust him.
The dog grew ungrateful, set up for himself.

* A large portion of this chapter is the result of the research, labor, and ability of Frank B. Mayer, Esq., who, with unusual personal kindness and marked zeal in the work of saving to history the chronicles of Annapolis, placed his manuscript at the disposal of the author, who has liberally availed himself of the generous offer.

And at Norfolk, they say, he has plenty of pelf.
Since he's gone away 't will be best for his brother.
I give Hyam his portion to comfort his mother,
All the tools in my shop to said Hyam I give
And, if he minds work, he'll make out to live.
My coat, which I turned, is a very good brown
And may serve many years to parade in the town.
'Twill be good as ever if he take my advice,
And the buttons of silver will make it look nice,
The place in the back which is greased by my club
Would come out if he'd take good care to rub
It with soap and with brush or good spirits of wine
Which will freshen the cloth and make it look fine.
The coat he must wear with my corduroy breeches
When Abbey has given them a few odd little stitches.
And Ab' will be kind, I know, to her brother
Because he's the favorite of me and his mother.
A pair of silk hose I had when a boy
Intend shall be his; 'twill give him much joy.
To own these said hose he has begged for so often
But they n'er shall be his till I'm safe in my coffin.
I had always a mind to give them to Saint
'Till he, like a fool, turned Methodist quaint.
I swore at the time he never should have them;
And I know Saint would *wear*, the other would *save'em*.
For the reasons here mentioned I leave them to Hy
To wear if he pleases when walking is dry.
To my son, Charles Farris,* I have and bequeath
My watch and bird organ, and also I leave
To said son, as he pleases, a black ring or pin:
There are two ready made which I'm sure would suit him,
They're the first that I made, rather clumsily done,
But good, in all conscience, enough for my son.
The teeth he may have, rather clumsily strung;
Every tooth that I've drawn since the time I was young;
Six pair of thread stockings; two cotton, two yarn;
That my wife, poor dear woman, sat up all night to darn,
These will last him, with care, a very great while
And so money he'll save to make the pot boil.
To Saint Farris, my son, who is now on the seas
I will that he has any roots that he please;
All my garden utensils; "Swift's Polite Conversations;"
And I wish he'd leave sea to live with his relations.
I know all their minds, and they all love poor Saint,
And his brother has promised to teach him to paint.
The "History of China" and "Swift" sometimes lend
When your business or pleasure requires a friend;
Such acts, my dear children, I very well know
Are of much greater service than making a foe.
Thank God! I've but two that I hate from my heart.
And, as ill luck would have it, they're not far apart.

* In August 1765, Charles Farris is mentioned as one of many citizens to resist successfully the landing of the odious stamp paper.

I've the greatest dislike ; God forgive me the sin ;*
But indeed there's no bearing that old Louis Dinn,
There's another I hate bad as Quinn for the fraud
That his heart is so full of that is Jonathan Todd.*
This sin, as I die, I hope will be forgiven ;
Or, else, I am sure, I shall ne'er get to heaven.
My sons, if you heed me, beware of such friends :
They'll destroy all you're worth, if they have but the means.
To Nancy, the darling of me and my wife.
I give and bequeath the spinnet for life.
Once I thought she would play with the help of a master,
But, it grieves me to say, she learned not a bit faster,
Harry Woodcock I trusted to teach her to play,
But I soon found 't was money and time thrown away ;
So she did what was right, made me save all my pelf,
And picked out a tune here and there by herself.
All the town knows that Harry's a very great liar
And music from him she should never acquire,
What a time there has been for his making of money ;
Like a puppy he's missed it, like a puppy he's funny,
Poor devil, sometimes, in the midst of a gloom,
For a dinner he's forced to play the buffoon ;
But I still like old Woodcock I vow and declare ;
As a proof I shall leave him a lock of my hair.
To Abagail next ; my trunk, desk, and papers.
That's therein contained, and a large box of wafers.
The "Spectator" for her, as she reads very well,
And she'll soon learn to write, for now she can spell.
For Abb is the girl that would take the most learning
And, I flatter myself, she's a girl of discerning.
A negress, named Sylva, I leave to my Nancy,
For Sylva she'd always a very great fancy.
That woman's first child, about fifteen years old,
I give to my Abb lest for debt she be sold.
Poor thing 't was a fool from its birth, I well know,
But her mistress will teach her to spin, knit, and sew.
I leave to Sol Mogg for tolling the bell,
My old hat and pipe which he knows very well.
To my nephews and nieces my blessing I give
And entreat they will mind and learn how to live.
My thanks to the public I cannot express ;
Their goodness to me has been quite to excess,
My feelings are many but words are too few
To tell how it pains me to bid them, 'Adieu.' "

Here we have the man and his time. "He, in his brown coat and
silver buttons, the back marked by the quadrant of powder, the club
of his queue described as it moved back and forth with his head, like
one of his own pendulums, so fullfilling the resemblance men grow
to their pursuits. We have a picture of his house, his family and
his friends, the 'Landscape,' and the picture of 'Judith' in the hall
with the musical clock behind the door, the spinnet in the parlor

* These are fictitious names but the cognomens of real neighbors were in
the original will. The author of this history does not desire to hand down A
private slander.

and the red and white cow in the stable. Then there was the garden
and the shops with its many tools and few books, and its half century
accumulations ; prominently hanging among them all the trophies of
his dental skill, strung together ; for trades mingled in those colonial
days when 'specialities' were unknown. His three sons had distinct
individuality, and his daughters Nancy and Abigial were notable
girls. He had a thrifty wife and his friend Harry Woodcock was a
ne'er-do-well genius. He remembers Sol Mogg, the sexton, and does
not forget to put on record his irrepressible dislikes. In that brown
coat with its silver buttons, his corduroy breeches, and silk stockings,
'if the walking be dry,' silver shoe buckles, cocked hat, cane and
queue he paraded the town on Sundays, and on the King's birthday
for a loyal subject of King George, was he, the reproduction in the
Colony of a London craftsman, and a reader of "*The Maryland Gazette*" for the latest news, only three months old, from Europe, and in
that venerable journal this advertisement for a runaway servant or
apprentice :

"Run away from the subscriber living at Annapolis, on the 27th of
this instant August, 1745, a servant man man named John Powell,
alias Charles Lucas, a Londoner born, by trade a clock and watch
maker ; he is a short, well set fellow, has full goggle eyes, and wears
a wig : He had on when he went away an Osnabrigs shirt, a pair of
buckskin breeches, a pair of short wide trousers, two pair of white
hose and a well-worn broad-cloth coat with metal buttons.

"Whoever secures the said runaway so that he can be had again,
shall have 3£ reward, besides what the law allows ; and if brought
home, reasonable charges :—" but in the next number we find that

"Whereas John Powell was advertised last week in this paper as a
runaway ; but being only gone into the country a cyder-drinking, and
being returned again to his Master's Service ; these are therefore to
acquaint all gentlemen and others, who have any watches, or clocks,
to repair, that they may have them done in the best manner at reasonable rates."

Between one hundred and fifty years ago and and today there is no
greater change than in the matter of a gentleman's dress. "In the
male sex a fear of color and a slouchy negligence of attire charac-
terize the nineteenth century ; in the eighteenth the porte and bearing of a man indicated his social rank and a 'gentleman' was supposed to be accomplished in all knightly exercises. The dress moreover exacted attention to mein and bearing, as any lack of muscular
development was at once apparent and exposed the unfortunate weak-
ling to ridicule from the fair. We of today are disposed to measure
dress and manner by the narrow standard of utility and to forget that
ofttimes "manners make the man" and that an attire expresses as
much as words. Perhaps the old-school exaggerated the needs of
courtesy and deportment, but, when we consider what a time and
trouble a full dress toilet must have cost my gentleman, may we not
pardon that frailty of human nature which sought to display his art
to the best advantage ? To the complete gentleman dancing and
fencing were as indispensable parts of education then 'as the use of
the globes,' and a man's legs and spine were objects of critical scru-
tiny."

Mr. Charles Peale, probably the father of our Nestor of American artists, Charles Wilson Peale, advertises in the *Maryland Gazette* 1745, that,

"At Kent County School, Chestertown, Maryland, young gentleman are boarded and taught the Greek and Latin tongues, Writing, Arithmetic, Merchants accounts, Surveying, Navigation, and the use of the Globes by the largest and most accurate pair in America : also any other parts of the Mathematics.—N. B. Young gentlemen can be instructed in Fencing and Dancing by very good Masters."

The ranks of Colonial society were most sharply defined in those days and the physiognomy and costumes at once indicated the social position. Of the dress and features of the convict and hewers of wood and drawers of water, we have detailed descriptions in the rewards offered for runaway servants (both white and black,) and therefrom could reproduce a motley group of the tramps of 1745.

These white men and women were sold for a term of years to pay their passage money from England and seem to have been an uncertain kind of property. Dominick Hogan, a runaway Irish servant, wears a brown great coat, a blue jacket, shirt, and trousers, and "has an Iron collar about his neck." A highland Scotch servant wears a red pea-jacket, a double breasted white flannel vest, white ribbed stockings, a cap, a white wig, and a felt hat. Another, "a white whitney coat and breeches, a green callimanco jacket without sleeves, white thread stockings, a fine hat and a large brown wig."

"An English convict servant woman, named Elizabeth Crowder, by trade a quilter, she is upwards of fourty years of age pretty tall and round shouldered, her hair very gray and has lately been cut off, but it is supposed she has got a *tower* to wear instead of it. She had on when she went away a dark stripped cotton and silk gown, a blue quilted coat, blue worsted stockings, and black shoes newly soled. She had with her a large bundle with sundry things in it, particularly, a sprigged linen gown, shifts, caps, aprons, etc.

"A convict servant man, imported in the Sr. George, named Hugh Roberts, is a thick, likely, full faced, middle sized fellow but stoops a little ; had on a short black wig, a full trimmed, open-sleeved, blue cloth coat, almost new ; a full trimmed scarlet waistcoat with a double row of buttons, red plush breeches, and diced yarn stockings. He was born in Shropshire, has been used to farming and malting, and can write a little. Whoever takes him up and returns him to the ship shall have four pounds reward and reasonable charges from Captain James Dobbins.

"28 July 1747. A number of rebels imported in the ship Johnson, into Oxford, (Md.) are brought over here and are now upon sale." These were Scottish patriots who, having risked their lives in the cause of the "Young Pretender" of '45, were transported as their reward. 22 March, 1753, "Just imported from London in the Brigantine Grove, Capt. Robert Wilson, and to be sold by the subscribers, on board the said brigantine in West river, for sterling or current money. A parcel of healthy indented servants ; among whom there are tradesmen and husbandmen. Samuel Galloway."

Of the Ladies, except in their praise, the *Gazette* has little to say, if we except a "protest against stays," which met with the writer's unqualified disapproval, and a "history of female dress" in which says the author, "my business today is chiefly with the ladies, on whose dress I intend to treat with the same delicacy and tenderness as I should use in my approach to their pretty persons."

A English lady's dress of that day is thus described. "A black silk petticoat with a red and white calico border; cherry colored stays, trimmed with blue and silver; a red and dove colored gown, flowered with large trees; a yellow satin apron, elaborately trimmed; a muslin head-dress with lace ruffles; a black silk scarf; and a spotted silk hood or 'capuchin.'"

"To judge by cotemporary records and portraits the fashions of the colonies were no ways behind those of "home," as they persistently called old England. In those days fashions did not so rapidly vary as nowadays, and the materials were substantial, as notably the damasks and brocades, that dresses of necessity became heirlooms. We will not dwell upon the female costume of the time as we are all more or less familiar with the comparatively graceless dress of that day, the dress was stiff and graceless in those days. The stiff and unnaturally elongated stays, the immense expanse of skirt, sustained by the hoops, the high heeled shoes and the towering head gear, the short sleeve with immense cuffs, borrowed from the male dress, with the wealth of lace falling over the arms. At that period, when, in the history of every style, it seems to attain its perfection, the male dress was eminently graceful, stately, and ample, and displayed the figure to great advantage; the female fashion for a while yielded to some harmony with nature and the natural hair was worn of becoming length, the hoops somewhat curtailed and aprons, even in full dress, became the vogue. This was about 1750.

"Annapolis had then been the Capital of Maryland over fifty years, the government having been removed from St. Mary's, the place of the orignal settlement, in 1694, thus supplanting that ancient city in the honors and emoluments of official patronage and with the government transferring the commerce of the colony. Annapolis was now the rallying point of the cleverness and culture of such small population as then existed in separate colonies or provinces. Opulent men built costly, elegant houses as their city dwellings, if, as was commonly the case, they had large plantations or manors, where they dwelt at other seasons, superintending Maryland's grand staple of that time—Tobacco. Tobacco from America became smoke in the old world, but brought back very solid revenue, together with all the luxuries of life. Troops of slaves, docile as in the Orient, supplied service. Lumbering equipages, or very rickety stage-coaches, but generally *superb horses*, bore the colonists about the country. In town they visited in sedan-chairs borne by lacquers in livery. They sat on carved chairs, at quaint tables, amid piles of ancestral silverware, and drank punch out of vast, costly bowls from Japan, or sipped Madeira, half a century old, At Annapolis they laid out the best race course in the Colonies and built certainly the first theatre. Here the best law-learning of America was gathered—the Jennings, Chalmers, Rogers, Stones, Pacas, Johnsons, Dulanys. Dulany's opinions were sent for even from London. They built a superb ball room which a British traveller called 'elegant.'

"The clergy were commonly men of culture sent from England, and portioned on the province by the proprietary. Generally they were men of excellent education and manners, seldom would one of a different character be tolerated by the high-toned men who

composed the vestries. These clergymen did not abandon their classic
pursuits when they crossed the sea, and familiarly wrote Latin notes
to their boon companions of Annapolis, whose culture, in those days,
enabled them to answer in the same language. They were free hearty
livers, importing and relishing their old Madeira ; and it was in Annapolis that soft crabs, terrapins, and canvass-back ducks first obtained their renown as the greatest delicacies of the world.

"The style of the time was in winter, to enjoy the capital, but, in
milder seasons, to travel a social round among the great estates and
manors—until the principal families of Calvert, St. Mary's, Charles,
Prince George's, and Anne Arundel counties, and across the Bay, on
the Eastern Shore, were visited. They were bold riders, expert in
hounds and horse flesh ; and the daily fox-chase, in season, was as
much a duty to our systematic ancestors as it was to go to the parish
church with proper equipage and style on Sunday.

"With races every fall and spring ; theatres in winter ; assemblies
every fortnight : dinners three or four times a week ; a card party
whenever possible ; athletic fox-hunting ; private balls on every festival ; wit, learning, and stately manners, softened by love of good fellowship, it is not surprising to hear this character recorded of Annapolis in 1773 : 'I am persuaded,' says a British traveller, 'there is
not a town in England of the same size of Annapolis which can boast
of a greater number of fashionable and handsome women ; and, were I
not satisfied to the contrary, I should suppose that the majority of the
belles possessed every advantage of a long and familiar intercourse
with the manners and habits of your great metropolis.'

"Between the old colonial mansions of the Northern and Southern
colonies a striking contradiction seems to exist—while those of New England were invariably wooden structures with little use of either brick
or stone, in the colonies of Maryland and Virginia we find brick buildings of remarkable solidity and considerable architectural pretensions,
well developed and worthy examples of the style of Queen Anne and
the Georges. These interiors recall to us the Dutch taste of William
and Mary's day as seen at Hampton Court, and later we trace the influence of Sir Christopher Wren and the French architects of Louis
XV and XVI. In solidity and honesty of construction they shame
the insincerity of the builders of our day and mock the shallowness of
our modern pretension in their deep capacious window seats and noble
hearthstones—which measure the thickness of the walls. To climb to
the attic and study the joinery of the roof would delight the heart of
a true artisan. - A stairway is sometimes concealed in these thick
walls and suggests secret chambers behind the panelled wainscoting.
The stairways, ascending from halls that greet you with spacious welcome, glide rather than climb to the floor above where a large upper
hall or ball-room is often found. The walls are always panelled in
wood or stucco and the carvings which frames the high chimney pieces
and relieves the shutters and doors are evidently old-country work of
the school of Grindling Gibbons, and the decorators of Hampton
Court. The cornices both exterior and interior are borrowed from
Italian designs. A noble hospitality is expressed in the great mansions
of this time—and a similar arrangement was adopted by most builders
to insure this end. The central or main building lodged the family
and guests and two wings or out-buildings, connected by corridors,

served for kitchen, offices, and servants' quarters. The strange absence of verandah and porches in our climate can only be explained by the Englishman's tenacity to English custom and refusal to acknowledge that the sun was other than the sun of England. With our independence we began to develope a style in accordance with our climate and copied from Italy the piazza, portico, and verandah. In the less imposing houses, the homes of the people, the "hipped-roof" was almost universal, in our day revived as the Mansard or French roof. There is a look of cosy comfort in these old homes of the burghers, arranged very compactly and worthy of imitation, even if the ceilings be low and the chimneys quaintly placed in the corner of the room or windows opened with charming disregard of conventional symmetry. And can we forget those burnished brass knockers, the housewife's pride, so eminently respectable in their size and rich curvature, in their varied device and expression; nor the 6 by 4 panes in the broad sashes, the dormer windows with their heavy cornices, the noble stacks of chimneys; memorial pyramids of generous life,— and the gardens that environed all?

"An old fashioned Queen Anne's garden would now be rather a prim affair with so much box-edging and the walks so straight and Dutch-like, but the old fashioned flowers would redeem it. There you would find plenty of lilacs and snow-balls, then known as the golden-rose, privet and holly in the hedges and borders. Larkspurs, wallflowers, hollyhocks, periwinkles, snapdragons, candytufts and daffodils would abound. A damp, shady corner would be given to a bed of the lily of the valley, and ten to one, but you would find a bed of chamomile growing hard by a bed of lavender or sweet basil. Of course there would be balsam, (only called 'lady's slipper') and rocket under the name of 'dame's violet,' pansies known as ladies' delight or 'hearts' ease,' pasque flower and cowslip, and meadow-sweet, and groundsel, and feverfew, and milfoil, yarrow, thrift, spurge, loose-strife, honesty, Adam and Eve, drop-wort, dittany, daises, jonquils, monk's hood, innocence, wind flower and moss pink and the Joseph's lily and laburnum blooming in the most liberal and splendid way.

"Fancy the delightful irregularity of the quaint roofs and chimneys outlined against the warm blue sky; the sparkling leaves and soft glow of the flower beds, and listen, while you rest in the shady arbor, to the cooing of the pigeons, the whirr and twitter of the swallows and martins, and the defiant crow of chanticleers, heedless of the moving shadow of the sun-dial on the chimney side.

"In the streets you find no pavements, they are still country roads edged with green grass, and the rights of foot passengers maintained by rows of posts. Here and there a more enterprising citizen may have laid bricks and a curb-stone. Bookishness had not then blunted the intelligence of vision, and the mind was still addressed by direct appeals to the perceptive sense in the shape of signs of every description of imitative art. The dangling key, the pendant awl, the golden pestle and mortar, the hammer wielded by a swarthy arm; the symbols of good cheer, as the 'heart in hand,' or may be cheap boarding expressed by the 'spider and the fly.' A jubilant negro, a jolly tar, or a taciturn Indian, the master work of the ship carver, guarded the tobacconist's door and 'the thistle,' and 'the ship' 'near the city gate,' invited the sailor as did the sign of the 'top-sail-sheet-block'

9

near the market. The 'three blue-balls,' a rival of 'the Duke of Cumberland' and 'the Indian King,' was a tavern of Church street, and there must have been a 'golden horse,' a 'black bear,' and a 'white swan,' to creak in concert of a stormy night. The 'Annapolis *coffee-house*' was the resort of the gentry. From the '*Gazette*' we read that, 'what a grievous thing the law is shown by a sign that once hung in the rolls of liberty in London: on one side a man all in rags wringing his hands with a label importing that he had *lost his suit*, and on the other a man that had not a rag left, but stark naked, capering and triumphing that he had *gained his cause*, a fine emblem of going to law and the infatuating madness of a litigious spirit.'

"Many of these signs indicated the amphibious character of the population of Annapolis, and were evidently inspired by nautical associations complimentary to the sea-faring strangers who frequented the port, for the 'ancient city,' had its custom house: a stately brick, yet standing, but no longer the receipt of his majesty's customs. The Maryland fleet under convoy of British men-of-war and themselves, for the most part, well-armed gathered here as their port of destination, and many is the tale related by our old journal of their combats with the French men-of-war and privateers, a prolific nursery of sailors' yarns, told in sea phrase, and recording British pluck and contempt of the Frenchman.

"The two fair days of the annual fairs were the gala days of the people, as the high days and holidays of the gentry were the birth-days of Prince and Proprietary. May-day, Whitsuntide, Michaelmas and Christmas, Militia trainings, and muster-days also broke the monotony of daily duty. At the 'fairs' horse-races were included as a principal attraction and in one advertised for 'Baltimore-town,' a bounty was offerred of forty shillings to any person that produces 'the best piece of yard-wide country-made white *linnen*, the piece to contain twenty yards. On Saturday, the third day, a hat and ribbon will be cudgelled for; a pair of pumps wrestled for; and a white shift to be run for by two negro girls.' "

A triplet of advertisements further illustrate the times:

"John Wallis, chimney-sweeper, who served his time to John Kent, Esq., his most excellent majesty, King George the second, his chimney-sweeper in London; and understands that curious and difficult business as well as any man, lives near the gate in Annapolis and will sweep chimneys in the best and cleanest manner. * * Any gentlemen, or others, who shall be pleased to employ him may depend on being served with fidelity, care, and dispatch by their humble servant.

'Richard Wagstaffe, Peruke and Lady's tate-maker, and hair-cutter, will soon settle in Annapolis and follow the said business, and will sell his goods at reasonable rates. He also intends to teach reading, writing, and accounts; and will take in youth to board and educate at twenty-three pounds per year. N. B. He has a few perukes ready made which he will dispose of very cheap, such as Ramillies, Albemarles, and Bobs, &c.

"John Lammond, musician, at the house of John Lansdale, shoemaker, hereby gives notice; that if any gentlemen should want music to their balls or merry-makings, upon application made, they shall be diligently waited on by their humble servant. The said Lammond, having a good able horse, will undertake journeys to any part of the province, with the utmost expedition, and fidelity, to the full satisfaction of any gentlemen who are pleased to employ him.

"The duties of a servant are shown by one who offers himself 'to wait at table, curry horses, clean knives, boots and shoes, lay a table, shave and dress wigs, carry a lanthorn, and talk French : is as honest as the times will admit and as sober as can be.' We can fancy this man-of-all-work conducting his master home from some convivial meeting, the lanthorn swaying to and fro as the faithful domestic adjusts the old gentleman's wig and cocked hat and guides his meandering footsteps thro' the unpaved and unlighted streets of the provincial capital."

The club, invention of modern days to avoid the rigor of prohibition, was no new thing in Annapolis. It was for quite a different purpose, yet being social, after the manner of the people of those days, it embraced a large amount of drinking.

The South River Club, near Annapolis, survived almost to the present day, and of the Tuesday Club, of Annapolis, it has been said "if its records have been accurately kept, at least deserves so to have survived. The latter was an assemblage of wits, who satirized every one, and did it successfully."

Some of their squibs and portraitures even now pass current, and the incomplete memorial of their transactions is among the most interesting originals preserved in the Maryland Historical Society.

When it is read what were the proceedings of the Tuesday Club, opinions will differ as to its right of survival. The same author* in a foot-note on the same page says:

"The Homony Club, founded later, was more or less political in its membership, and purposes, but the Tuesday, the Independent, Thursday, and most of the other clubs, were exclusively social, and, as the ladies, who were generally excluded from their sessions, complained, were usually organizations of men to encourage steady smoking and hard drinking. The records of the Tuesday Club, which extend over the space of ten years, are that of a society of the most distinguished and influential men of the ancient capital, graduates of the British Universities, and wits of the first order. They kept 'high jinks,' after the manner of that society to which Guy Mannering was introduced in his pursuit of Lawyer Pleydell ; but their records, most faithfully and elaborately kept, abound with example of steadfast pursuit of wit and foes. The club met at the houses of members in regular alternation, and each member was bound to provide his own sand-box as a spittoon, in order to save the carpet. Offensive topics of conversation were dealt with by the 'gelastic' method and laughed off the floor. At suppers, it was ordered that the first toast should always be 'the ladies ;' after that, 'The King's Majesty ;' and after that, 'the deluge.' There was much singing, some of it probably very good ; and Parson Bacon, the learned and venerable compiler of the laws of Maryland, * * * * was elected to honorary membership, on account of his accomplishments as a fiddler, thus becoming, as it were, the Friar Tuck, of this jovial society, the mottoes of which were—*'libertas et natale solum,'* and *'concordia res parvae crescunt.'* It is to be regretted that we are forced to add that there was a great deal of dog-

* Scharf's History of Maryland.

gerel in the club's poetry, and of indelicacy in its conundrums and jokes. The age was coarse and the club accurately reflected it."

The only permanent club left is the Arundel. It is of recent date, having been organized in 1883. It admits none but males to its membership and festivities. Its diversions are suppers, billiards, cards, current literature, social converse and potations at the will of the individual member, as it is a rule of the club that no one shall be invited to drink. There seems to be an exception to this in favor of visiting strangers.

To return to the Tuesday Club, let the records of its Secretary tell of its witty sallies and bacchanalian pleasures.

The history of the Tuesday Club, preserved in the rooms of the Maryland Historical Society, Baltimore, is dedicated "To the venerable the Chancellor of the ancient and honorable Tuesday Club and his successors in that honorable office," and dated from the author's study September 9th, 1754, and in quaint style acknowledges all dedications to be "at best but paltry stuff," in which truth is warped "either by the power of flattery or by the pestilent inclination to party, or pusillanimous fear of the anger and resentment of men in power."

The first volume contains the first decade of the transactions of that society comprehended in 239 sederunts, viz: from May 1745, to May 1755, inclusive, with the heads of the honorable the President, and the principal officers and members, and also figures of the most material transactions of the club—with an appendix of the club music composed by Signor Lardini, the most favourite songs used in clubs, etc. The laws provide that the club shall meet weekly at each other's dwellings by turns, every Tuesday, throughout the year, that the member appointed to serve as steward shall provide a "gammon of bacon," or any one other dish of vittles and no more. That no fresh liquor shall be made, prepared or produced after eleven o'clock at night and every member to be at liberty to retire at pleasure.

Here comes

THE CLUB IN SESSION.

"Long live the Tuesday Club, so wisely framed
That 'mongst all those great Addison has named,
Not one so great—long may the members stand
And still maintain their badge of hand in hand."

"It is established as a rule of the society," "That immediately after supper the ladies shall be toasted, before any other toasts or healths go round. It is consented to—that such as are bachellor members of this society may be permitted to have a cheese instead of dressed vittles.

"Sederunt, June 18th, 1745. This night the great cheese or bachellor's was produced upon a side board. Passed into a law, That if any subject of what nature soever be discussed which levels at party matters, or the administration of the Government of this Province, or be disagreeable to the club, no answer shall be given thereto, but after such discourse is ended, the society shall laugh at the member offending in order to divert the discourse."

"June 25th, the *gelastic* law was this night put in execution against Mr. Secretary Marshe, who got into a prolix harangue about the consciences of lawyers. Ordered, that Mr. Secretary Marshe entertain this society upon Tuesday, the 2nd of July next ensuing."

July 25, 1745, "Resolved, That cheese is not any more to be deemed a dish of vittles. Therefore the use of it as such in the club is forbid."

"July 23d. This night the society before breaking up was entertained by Mr. Charles Cole, steward, with a large bowl of rack-punch, and a catch song, "The Great Bell of Lincoln.""

As the society developed, the insignia of office and various adjuncts of ceremony were adopted, badges of silver, double gilt, and engraved with the device and mottoes of the society were procured from London.

Here are some of the club's orders:

"There shall be a ball held at the Stadt-house for the entertainment of the ladies at the common expense of the club, etc." The term "Stadt-house," points to the Dutch reign of William and Mary, and is still termed the "State House."

"Ordered, That Wm. Thornton, Esq., frame a discourse to the society next meeting, upon that trite text "Omnia Vincit Amor."" Next meeting or sederunt, Mr. William Thornton delivered a discourse to the society upon the subject proposed last meeting, which met with the approbation of the society, and was so well liked, that he was desired to deliver it a second time, which he very complacently did with a singular good grace.

"Ordered, That the Rev. Mr. John Gordon prepare a discourse to be delivered to the society at next meeting the subject, Ad libitum—other "orders" follow on such subjects as

"Government," "chearfullness," "charity," "clubs," or "prudence,"—"wisdom."

The entry is made that Wm. Thornton, Esq., on account of his uncommon talent in singing, was by unanimous consent of the club appointed proto-musicus or chief musician, and it is ordained that as often as he votes in club he is to sing his vote in a musical manner, else it is to go for nothing.

"The secretary delivered a speech the purport of which was an accusation of Mr. Speaker Dorsey, of negligence in office, as not displaying his talents in oratory to the club, on such occasions as demanded his elocution, but the club let him go without censure. The Rev. Mr. Gordon congratulated the Secretary upon the late event of his marriage, which speech the club approved of, etc. Then our Speaker Dorsey, rising with that gravity and action which is his peculiar talent on all such occasions discoursed, but little upon that subject, delivering chiefly an encomium upon Mr. Gordon's discourse, in a nervous and elegant style which is natural to that gentleman upon all occasions. "June 23rd, 1747. The chief musician was accused by the Secretary of negligence in his office, which accusation was slurred over by the President and club on account of that gentleman's good performances at other times. As acknowledgement of the favour, he entertained the club with two excellent new songs, the one solus and the other in concerto with another voice, after which he had the privilege conferred on him of commanding any member of the club to sing after having first sung himself."

Here is:

"The humble petition and remonstrance of sundry of the single females of Annapolis, showeth,

"That, whereas, it has been observed by sundry persons as well as your petitioners, that a singular and surprising success has all along attended such happy females as your honor has been pleased to pitch upon as the toasts of the honorable chair, every one of whom in a short time after having been adopted by your honor has successfully and happily been provided with a much more eligible state, your petitioners, therefore, earnestly pray, that your honor instead of conferring your favors in so partial a manner, would, in commisseration of our desperate situation, include us *all* in the circle of favor that the benign influence of your honors' maritiferous notice may henceforth equally shine upon us all. *   *   *   *   *   *   *

"To the honorable Charles Cole, Esq., President of the most worshipful and ancient Tuesday Club."

"The honorable president was pleased to declare that he would grant this petition as far as lay in his power."

The anniversaries were occasions of great ceremony. The members wearing their badges proceeded to the house of the President. "As they marched along in a solemn and stately manner they were honored by a great many spectators of all sorts and ranks, and when they came within twenty paces of the honorable the president's gate, his honor made his appearance and did each member the honor of a salute by *manuquassation*, upon which they halted a little, and Jonas Green, Esq., holding up the anniversary ode in his right hand, waved it around his head in a very graceful manner by way of salutation to his honor, who made several low bows which were respectfully returned by the master of ceremonies, Sir John, and the Chancellor. Then his honor taking his place between the two latter, the procession marched into his honor's court-yard, the way being all strewed with flowers and the ensign or flag displayed as usual. After some time sitting in the court-yard the members assembled in his honor's great saloon. As his honor went to take the chair with a grand pas, a martial time was played by the chief musicion or proto-musicus, and he took the chair with a plaudite."

The Secretary in his speech reflects the sentiment of the club. "This is not a time to speak much, but to act well—that our discourse and conversation be regular, orderly, free, humorous, and jocose, without reflexion, without passion, without reserve, without clamor, without noise,—let our songs be in tune, our puns and repartees apropos, and not too poignant or satirical, our toasts loyal and amorous, our stomachs keen to relish our fare and our punch-bowls always replete with nectarious liquor, for this cordial juice taken with temperance and moderation heightens the spirit, enlivens the wit, and will conduce not only to make men a more fluent orator, but, more jolly and benevolent, long-standing members.

"Whene'er we meet
With bowl replete
    The loyal healths go round ,
And in each toast
We all can boast
    Wine honest, hearty, sound!"—

After the supper of which the "outward decoration and apparatus was as elegant and harmonious as the inward rhetoric and eloquence of the club was uncommon," several loyal healths were drank, as, his

majesty King George the Second ; the Prince and Princess of Wales;
the Duke, (of Cumberland) ; success to his majesty's arms ; a speedy
and honorable peace ; prosperity to the province of Maryland, etc.
Then they drank to the memory of the "South Sea Company," and
sang "The Great Bell of Lincoln," and that favorite song, "the Hun-
dords of Drury."

"A speech of a member being thought unseasonable, assuming, and
unpolite, had the *gelastic* law put in force against him the whole
company being seized with a most vociferous and roaring laugh in
which the culprit himself, joined with most prodigious force of lungs
—But he thinking to take the president upon his weak or blind side,
knowing his enthusiastic fondness for old England, and everything
appertaining to that happy country, he asked his honor to favour him
at least, for country's sake ; that he was his countryman and the only
Englishman now in club, besides himself and his honor's attorney, the
rest of the members being either country-born or Scotsmen.   To this
his honor made reply 'that he set no value upon that and that he
always judged of a man by his behaviour and not by his country.'
This was an excellent sentiment and came from his honor unawares,
he not being given to speak philosopically or justly when old England
was introduced into conversation which evinces that even resentment
at times may make a man utter philosophical truths."

On issuing commissions to new members January 30, 1749, "it is
thought fit to affix seals of black wax, upon the occasion of the day
being the martyrdom of that blessed Saint Charles I."

"The master of ceremonies, Mr. Jonas Green, and the Secretary are
ordered to prepare each of them a conundrum, to be proposed in club
immediately after all the toasts are drank—and in case the club should
solve or answer them the above officers are expected to drink a
bumper each to the prosperity of the club, in the opposite case the
gentlemen are declared victors.   The conundrums are ordered to be
recorded."

"To drowsy man pray how can you compare
A garment that is worn till quite thread-bare.

"The answer's easy for we all must grant
That both and each of them a *nap* does want.

Two minutes only by the watch was given to answer—
Why is a dancing master like a shady tree ?

Because he is full of *bows—boughs.*

Why is a wizard like an Ethiopian ?

Because he is a *necromancer—negroe man, sir.*

A client who has lost his cause is like a winter stocking, because he is worsted.

A pump in a well is like a firelock, because it depends upon
springs.

An almanac is like a butcher, because he deals in wethers.

Dried apples are like married people, because they are paired.

A scandalous story is like a church bell, because it is often told-toll-ed.

The city of Westminster is like a school-boy's horn-book, because it has an Abbacy—A. B. C."

A motion being made to exclude the use of long pipes in the club, excepting the president's, the same was not assented to.

Mr. Jonas Green, the printer of the *Maryland Gazette*, in acknowledging the honor of admission to the club says :

"May good fellowship dispell every cloud that may threaten us excepting only that of tobacco, *the dear specific condensator of political conceptions.*"

Although the circumspect and dignified Maryland publisher advanced to high position in the club and "his titles were expressed in the manner of the ancient Romans by five capital p's, P. P. P. P. P. important sundry officers of trust and dignity, viz. poet, printer, punster, purveyor, and punchmaker, he did not escape indictment duly preferred in law-latin and a formal trial and conviction. "After reading the sentence during which Jonas Green, Esq., stood up. His lordship knocked upon the table with a little mallet after the manner of Sir Hugh McCarty, Esq., Lord President of the *Monday Club, of New York*, and this signal being given the Sergeant at Arms immediately took Jonas Green, Esq., into custody and he was confined for a full half hour, a languishing prisoner in a remote corner of the room, being deprived of all comfort and assistance from the sparkling and enlivening board, a woeful and lamentable spectacle and a warning to all loyal members to be upon their good behavior."

What pleasure there could be in all this except only that of eating and drinking !

"After all impediments are removed and the club forms itself again around the great table to smoke and drink how dull and sleepy are the members, how flat their conversation, what yawning, what gaping, what nodding, what sleeping, what snoring ! How much better to have spent the time in witty conversation, such as punning, framing of quaint conundrums, cracking sly jokes, telling comical stories, singing old catches or composing quaint rhymes ; but alas ! all this is only preaching to the wind, and beating the air in vain for one may preach to eternity and never reform the manners of clubs.

"These quaint and lively volumes are embellished with rude drawings, not without merit in their sense of character, representing the most humorous and important events in the club's history, its anniversaries, its frolics, and its disputes. There is a series of portraits of the members in which the likenesses are evidently, in the words of a certain limner, 'strong as pison.' "

Before the Revolution the people of Annapolis were intensely loyal and preeminently convivial. The slightest pretext sufficed for an exhibition of the one and the enjoyment of the other.

Wednesday, the 23rd of April, 1746, being the festival of St. George, was observed "by a number of gentlemen of English birth, descent, and principle, in an elegant manner. The same day the exit of the rebellion (lately occurred in England,) was celebrated by firing of guns, drinking loyal healths, and other demonstrations of joy. There was a ball in the evening, the whole city was illuminated, and a great quantity of punch given amongst the populace at the bonfire, on this occasion."

It was again on October 30th, 1746, when this patriotic conviviality was exhibited, which the *"Gazete"* announced "as being the anniversery of the birth of his most sacred Majesty, our only rightful sovereign, King George the second, (who God long preserve,) when his majesty completed his 63rd (a grand climaterical) year, the same was observed here (Annapolis) with firing of cannon, drinking loyal healths, &c. &c."

The domestic circle, as now, furnished the local column with items. Only then the stately courtesy of sentiment and expression united to smooth down the indelicacy that has invaded the reports of modern journalism. On December 23rd, 1746, the editor of the *"Gazette"* announced: "At the dawn of the 21st instant, the wife of the printer of this paper, to the great joy of her husband, was safely delivered of a son; who is to have the honor of being named after that great general, his royal highness Duke William."

The arrival of dignitaries in the city was made the occasion of public and private courtesies and patriotic demonstrations. The faithful publisher of the capital, says in March 1747:

"On Tuesday last, arrived within our Capes his Majesty's Ship, the Foulkstone, Capt. Greger, with Samuel Ogle, Esq., and Lady, on board, who, some short time after, disembarked, and went on board the Neptune, Capt. Grindall, bound for this place, where he arrived about ten in the evening, and was received at his Landing by a number of gentlemen, &c., and saluted by the town guns, and from on board Sundry Ships in the river. And yesterday morning, his honor, attended by his Excellency Thomas Bladen, Esq., then Governor, and his Lordship's honorable Council, &c., went to the Council Chamber, where his commission, appointed him Lieutenant-General and Chief Governor of this Province and Avalon, was opened and published. After which his Excellency was pleased to issue his Proclamation for continuing all officers, both Civil and Military, in their respective offices, until further orders."

Although the bill of rights had not been written and the Maryland Code published, the Maryland Courts of the last century had an innate desire to adjudicate all causes before them "according to the very right and equity of the matter." For example:

On Tuesday, June 16th, 1747, "at the County Court, held here last Tuesday, Mrs. S. C. of Patapsco, was fined the sum of one penny, for whipping the R——d Mr. N——l W——n with a Hickory Switch, it being imagined by the court that he well deserved it."

In the same spirit, no doubt, the sword of justice was unsheathed in September 1747, when two servants, "Rebels lately imported," were found guilty of drinking the Pretender's health, together with "some other treasonable expressions," being incapable of paying fines, were "well whip'd at the whipping post," and were stood in the pillory.

The times were writ, when during the second week in January, 1747, a negro man in Annapolis had one of his ears cut off by the sentence of the peace, "for offering to strike his overseer.

The court then allowed no trifling with a lady's feelings, as was proved on the 12th of April, 1748, when ''a great case'' was tried at Annapolis. ''wherein a young gentle woman was plaintiff and a gentleman defendant for breach of a promise of marriage. The trial lasted about nine hours, when the jury went out, and after a short stay, returning with a verdict for the plaintiff and £50 damages.''

On May 2nd, 1752, Mary W——n obtained from Joseph W——d, after a long trial and the examination of numerous witnesses, £50 damages for a breach of promise of marriage.

Electricity had its devotees nearly a century and a half ago, who had made some progress in the subtle science, as was proved on Friday, June 9th, 1749, when a gentleman with an electrical machine made some interesting experiments in Annapolis. He placed it on the South side of a creek, supposed the Spa, ''and having set some spirits of wine in a small vessel, on a table on the North Side, he caused a spark of electrical fire to dart across in an instant, through 200 yards of water, which set the spirits in a blaze in the first attempt, and several times afterwards ; and discharged a battery of eleven guns, to the surprise and great satisfaction of the spectators.''*

The Ancient, Free and Accepted Masons were established in the city at this early date, and ''on Wednesday, the 27th of December, 1749, the festival of St. John the Evangelist, and the anniversary of the Ancient and Honorable Fraternity of Free and Accepted Masons, the Gentlemen of the Brotherhood, connected with lodge in Annapolis with several of the order from the country, celebrated the day.

At 12 o'clock, the whole company, 30 in number, ''went in procession with white gloves and aprons, from the House of their Brother Middleton, being preceded by their master, Wardens and Grand Stewards to the church, where an excellent sermon, adapted to the occasion, was preached by their brother, the Rev. Mr. Brogden : After Sermon, they returned in the same manner from Church to the Indian King, where having dined elegantly, they elected their master and officers for the ensuing year, and then proceeded in the above order to the great Council Room, where they made a ball for the entertainment of the Ladies, and the evening was spent with innocent mirth and gayety.''

The hearth-stone again furnishes the *Gazette* with a local note. On Wednesday, January 24th, 1750, it says :

''Last Saturday, being the anniversary of the birthday of his royal highness the Prince of Wales, the wife of the printer of this paper was happily delivered of a son, who will be baptized the name of Frederick.''

For the curious the colonial printer had a well-developed appreciation. There was a naivete in his quaint expressions that lent a charm to his descriptions. On December 5th, 1750, he says :

''We have an account that a few days ago, one J——W——e, in this county, as he was carrying home one of his neighbor's hogs, which he had killed with a design to make it his own, having tied the feet together, and put it over his neck, he went to rest himself by laying the hog on a dead tree, but laying it too far over, the string catch'd him by the throat and chock'd him, and they were there found ; so they proved executioner to each other.''

Emigrants, from the continent continued to arrive in large numbers, in Annapolis.

* Md. Gazette.

On October 10th, 1752, the ship Friendship, Capt. James Lucas, arrived at Annapolis, with 300 German passengers called Palatines, who were consigned to Messrs. Alexander Lawson and James Johnson, merchants. Among them were husbandmen and tradesmen, who were offered for sale at Annapolis on the 14th of October to pay their passage money.

From business to pleasure the Annapolitans of the last century turned with a keen zest; and the Annapolis Theatre is now found in full operation. Among the pieces played were The Busy Body, The Lying Valet, The Beggar's Opera, The Beaux Stratagem, The Virgin Unmasked, Recruiting Officer, The Beau in the Side, The London Merchant, The ballad Opera, Damon and Pythias. King Richard III was advertised to be played. Mr. Wyrell took the part of Richard.

In the early part of November, of the same year, 1752, Richard Buckell & Company exhibited at Annapolis, three wax figures, the queen of Hungary, her son, and a pandour in his military dress, also a curious brass piece of ordinance, that could be discharged twenty times in a minute, together with pictures of places of note in England, Scotland, France, and Italy.

A Court incident occurred about this time that does not reflect much credit upon the women jury system. At a late Provincial Court, Mary Perry, sentenced to die, pleaded that she was with child. A jury of matrons was summoned to examine her, "the foreman being an experienced midwife, which pronounced her not quick. A few days afterwards in Queen Anne's county jail, she gave birth to a lusty boy."

The intense loyalty to all that was British was constantly shown by the people of Annapolis. Saturday, the 17th of February, 1752, the birthday of Lord Baltimore, at which time he attained his majority, twenty-one, was warmly celebrated at Annapolis. "At noon cannons were discharged, in the evening the President of the province gave a public ball where there was a handsome appearance of gentlemen and ladies. The Loyal Healths, Lordship's Prosperity to Maryland, &c., &c., were drank, and the town was beautifully illuminated. There was a bonfire near the dock, and a hogshead of punch was given to the populace."

Again, on November 1st, 1759, their loyalty cropped out when there was great rejoicing at Annapolis on account of the taking of Quebec,—guns were fired, illuminations made, and a public ball was given by the Governor. Much regret was felt for death of Gen. Wolfe.

The scenes shift, and the bright picture of filial affection is marred by the ominous clouds of disapproval on the brows of the Freeman of Maryland who had never submitted, and were determined never to submit, to the levying of any taxes upon them except such as were laid by their own deputies.

On December 21, (1769,) "at ten o'clock at a numerous meeting, by beat of the town-drum, at which were many of the gentlemen committees from the several counties of this province, who in July last, entered into the articles for non-importation of British superfluities, and for promoting frugality, economy, and the use of American manufactures, resolved unanimously, that the said articles be most strictly adhered to and preserved inviolate : and that each and every gentleman, present at this meeting, will use his utmost endeavor to those laudable ends.''

This mosaic of sentiment, politics, and festivities presents Annapolis as it was a hundred years ago.

It was at this period that Eddis, the English Surveyor of Customs at Annapolis, wrote : ''I am persuaded there is not a town in England of the same size as Annapolis, which can boast of a greater number of fashionable and handsome women ; and were I not satisfied to the contrary, I should suppose that the majority of our belles possessed every advantage of a long and familiar intercourse with the manners and habits of your great (London) metropolis.''

During the winter these lovely and accomplished women had opportunity to display their graces in fortnight balls. The rooms for dancing, (the present Assembly Rooms) were large and of elegant construction, and were illuminated with great brilliancy. At each end of the room were apartments for the card tables, ''where select companies enjoy the circulation of the party-colored gentry, without having their attention diverted by the sound of fiddles, and the evolutions of youthful performers.''

It is to the credit of the citizens of Maryland that, during the gloom and distress occasioned by the Revolution, the convention prohibited balls throughout the province. The public mind, however, did not seem to need the legal prohibition for it was engaged in too serious business to pursue the phantom of social pleasures.

One of the most faithful pictures of Annapolis life immediately preceeding the beginning of the hostilities of the Revolution is drawn by the pen of Mr. Eddis who was part of what he described. In his cheerful and entertaining style, under date of January 18, 1771, he writes from Annapolis :

''In a former letter, I attempted to convey some idea of the truly picturesque and beautiful situation of our little capital. Several of the most opulent families have here established their residence : and hospitality is the characteristic of the inhabitants. Party prejudices have little influence on social intercourse : the grave and ancient enjoy the blessings of a respectable society, while the young and gay have various amusements to engage their hours of relaxation, and to promote that mutual connexion so essential to their future happiness.

''You well know, that I have ever been strongly attached to the rational entertainment resulting from theatrical exhibitions. When I bade farewell to England, I little expected that my pass'on for the drama could have been gratified, in any tolerable degree, at a distance so remote from the great mart of genius : and I brought with me strong prepossessions in behalf of favourite performers, whose merits were fully established, by the universal sanction of intelligent judges. My pleasure and my surprise were therefore excited in proportion, on finding performers in this county equal, at least, to those who sustain the best of the first characters in your most celebrated provincial theatres. Our governor, from a strong conviction that the stage, under proper regulations, may be rendered of general utility, and made subservient to the great interests of religion and virtue, patronizes the American Company ; and as their present place of exhibition is on a small scale, and inconveniently situated, a subscription, by his example, has been rapidly completed to erect a new theatre, on a commodious, if not an elegant, plan. The manager is to deliver tickets for two seasons, to the amount of the respective subscriptions; and, it is imagined, that the money which will be received at the doors, from non-subscribers, well enable him to conduct the business without difficulty; and when the limited number of performances is completed, the intire property is to be vested in him. This will be a valuable addition to our catalogue of amusements. The building is already in a state of forwardness, and the day of opening is anxiously expected."

On November 2, 1771, Mr. Eddis introduces another scene in Annapolis life. To his correspondent in England, he says:

"In this remote region, my dear friend, the phantom pleasure is pursued with as much avidity as on your side of the Atlantic; and certainly with as much gratification except by the injudicious herd who form ideas of happiness from comparison alone.

"Our races, which are just concluded, continued four days, and afforded excellent amusement to those who are attached to the pleasures of the turf; and, surprising as it may appear, I assure you there are few meetings in England better attended, or where more capital horses are exhibited.

"In order to encourage the breed of this noble animal, a jockey club has been instituted, consisting of many principal gentlemen in this and in the adjacent provinces many of whom have imported from Britain, at a very great expense, horses of high reputation.

"In America, the mild beauties of the autumnal months amply compensate for the fervent heats of summer, and the rigid severity of winter. Nothing could exceed the charming serenity of the weather during these races; in consequence of which there was a prodigious concourse of spectators, and considerable sums were depending on the contest of each day. On the first, a purse of one hundred guineas was run for, free only for the members of the club; and on the three following days subscription purses of fifty pounds each. Assemblies, and theatrical representations, were the amusements of the evening, at which the company exhibited a fashionable and brilliant appearance.

"Our new theatre, of which I gave you an account in a former letter, was opened to a numerous audience the week preceding the races. The structure is not inelegant, but, in my opinion, on too narrow a scale for its length; the boxes are commodious, and neatly decorated; the pit and gallery are calculated to hold a number of people without incommoding each other; the stage is well adapted for dramatic and pantomimical exhibitions; and several of the scenes reflect great credit on the ability of the painter. I have before observed, that the performers are considerably above mediocrity; therefore, little doubt can be entertained of their preserving the public favour, and reaping a plenteous harvest."

Mr. Eddis was disposed to give the country of his choice credit for every virtue it possessed. In these glowing sentences he depicts the conservatism of their sentiments and the beauty and accomplishments of American women, which latter opinions were founded entirely by the Maryland and Virginia ladies he had met and chiefly those of Annapolis, since Mr. Eddis appears to have been in no other parts of this continent. On December 24, 1771, he writes from the Maryland capital:

"Whatever you have heard relative to the rigid puritanical principles and economical habits of our American brethren, is by no means true when applied to the inhabitants of the southern provinces. Liberality of sentiment, and genuine hospitality, are every where prevalent: and I am persuaded they too frequently mistake profuseness for generosity, and impair their health and their fortunes, by splendor of appearance and magnificence of entertainments.

"The quick importation of fashions from the mother country is really astonishing. I am almost inclined to believe, that a new fashion is adopted earlier by the polished and affluent American, than by many opulent persons in the great metropolis; nor are opportunities wanting to display superior elegance. We have varied amusements, and numerous parties, which afford to the young, the gay, and the ambitious, an extensive field to contend in the race of vain and idle competition. In short, very little difference is, in reality, observable in the manners of the wealthy colonist and the wealthy Briton. Good and bad habits prevail on both sides the Atlantic.

"It is but justice to confess, that the American ladies possess a natural ease and elegance in the whole of their deportment: and that while they assiduously cultivate external accomplishment, they are still anxiously attentive to the more important embellishments of the mind. In conversation they are generally animated, and entertaining, and deliver their sentiments with affability and propriety. In a word, there are, throughout these colonies, very many lovely women, who have never passed the bounds of their respective provinces, and yet, I am persuaded, might appear to great advantage in the most brilliant circles of gaiety and fashion.

"In this country the marriage ceremony is universally performed in the dwelling houses of the parties. The company, who are invited, assemble early in the evening, and after partaking of tea and other refreshments, the indissoluble contract is completed. The bride and bridegroom then receive the accustomed congratulations: cards and dancing immediately succeed; an elegant supper, a cheerful glass, and the convivial song close the entertainment.

"There are few places where young people are more frequently gratified with opportunities of associating together than in this country. Besides our regular assemblies, every mark of attention is paid to the patron Saint of each parent dominion; and St. George, St. Andrew, St. Patrick, and St. David, are celebrated with every partial mark of national attachment. General invitations are given, and the appearance is always numerous and splendid.

"The Americans, on this part of this continent, have likewise a Saint, whose history, like those of the above venerable characters, is lost in fable and uncertainty. The first of May is, however, set apart to the memory of Saint Tamina, on which occasion the natives wear a piece of a buck's tail in their hats, or in some conspicuous situation. During the course of the evening, and generally in the midst of a dance, the company are interrupted by the sudden intrusion of a number of persons habited liked Indians, who rush violently into the room, singing the war song, giving the whoop, and dancing in the style of those people; after which ceremony a collection is made, and the retire well satisfied with their reception and entertainment.

"In this province there are scarce any vestiges of the original inhabitants, but it does not appear that their numbers have been reduced by any inhuman or indirect practices of the British settlers. In Dorset county, on the eastern shore of Maryland, there are indeed the remains of a nation, once populous and powerful, who, to this day, retain considerable tracts of valuable land, for which they receive an annual consideration, but by no means equivalent to the real value. When every other Indian nation thought it necessary to retire beyond the range of the European settlements, these people it seems determined to continue on their native spot. But being precluded from their former occupations and pursuits, they became totally indolent and inactive: and a different habit of living, a violent propensity to spirituous liquors, and the havock occasioned by the small-pox, and other disorders, to which they were unaccustomed, reduced their numbers to such a degree, that at this time not twenty of their descendants remain."

Politics is the child of government. America had its politics and Maryland a noted part of it before the Revolution. It had not reached exact national delineation before the throes over the Stamp Act began, but in Maryland there was a one line of policy which the citizens, on all occasions, "in season and out of season" pursued, and that was to resist with manly courage all infringements of their rights by the Crown's officers. Mr. Eddis, seeing with an Englishman's eye, portrays this determination in the following extract from Annapolis, Feb. 17,1772:

"The annual revenue of the proprietary, arising from the sale of lands, and the yearly quit rent, after deducting all the various charges of government, averages at twelve thousand five hundred pounds *per annum*. All offices, excepting those in the service of the customs, are in his gift, or in the gift of his representative for the time being. This patronage includes a very extensive range of lucrative, and respectful stations; and consequently throws great weight and influence into the scale of government.

"This influence is considered by many, as inimical to the essential interests of the people: a spirit of party is consequently excited; and every idea of encroachment is resisted, by the popular faction, with all the warmth of patriotic enthusiasm.

"I have before observed, that elections in this province are triennial. The delegates returned, are generally persons of the greatest consequence in their different counties; and many of them are perfectly acquainted with the political and commercial interests of their constituents. I have frequently heard subjects debated with great powers of eloquence, and force of reason; and the utmost regularity and propriety distinguish the whole of their proceedings.

"During the sitting of the assembly, the members of both houses receive a stated sum for their attendance on public business; and the number of days being properly certified, they are regularly paid their respective claims at the conclusion of each session.*

"Provincial and country magistrates are appointed by the governor. The former are commissioned to try capital offences, and important causes relative to property; the latter preside in the county courts. They have likewise, individually, power to determine causes

* Members of the upper house, nine shillings sterling per diem; those of the lower, about eight shilling and six-pence.

of the value of forty shillings : and to inflict punishment on servants, complaint being regularly made, and the matter proved by their employers.

"The governor has a discretionary authority to pardon persons capitally convicted ; and by the principles of the constitution, he is obliged to sign all warrants for the execution of those who suffer agreeable to sentence.

"A litigious spirit is very apparent in this country. The assizes are held twice in the year, in the city of Annapolis, and the number of causes then brought forward, is really incredible. Though few of the gentlemen who practice in the courts have been regularly called to the bar, there are several who are confessedly eminent in their profession : and those who are possessed of superior abilities, have full employment for the exertion of their talents, and are paid in due proportion by their respective clients.

"The natives of these provinces, even those who move in the humbler circles of life, discover a shrewdness and penetration, not generally observable in the mother country. On many occasions, they are inquisitive, even beyond the bounds of propriety ; they discriminate characters with the greatest accuracy ; and there are few who do not seem perfectly conversant with the general, and particulr interests of the community. An idea of equality also seems to prevail, and the inferior order of people pay but little external respect those who occupy superior stations."

By October 3rd, 1772, there was another color in the political current. This is the sneering and inappreciative language which Mr. Eddis uses, evidently with the sincerest belief that he fitly described them, towards the patriots who were in the van in opposing British encroachments upon the just rights and liberties of the colonies :

"Under pretence of supporting the sacred claims of freedom, and of justice, factious and designing men are industriously fomenting jealousy and discontent : and unless they are stopt in their progress by the immediate and determined exertions of the wise and moderate, they will aggravate the dissention which is become but too evident, and involve this now happy country in complicated misery."

In the decade preceding the Revolution and part of that contemporaneous with it, its life of fashion and frivolity reached its height at the capitol. Wealth gave leisure and education : education and leisure created the desire for refined and fashionable pleasures. The presence of a large number of officials, part of whom had come from the realm of "Merry England," and had imported its follies and pleasures, not only added to the reportoire of social amusements, but the emoluments of office gave the means of gratifying their tastes. These enlarging the fund of native resources of society, not only did the fame of the elegance and enjoyment of life at Annapolis extend to the utmost bounds of the Province, but it invaded the sister commonwealth of Virginia, and one of the frequent visitors of Annapolis, and participant in the pleasures and excitements of its race-courses, its card-parties, and its balls, was George Washington, then a colonel in the service of his State.

The only place in Maryland that offered to the devotees of fashion the opportunity to gratify a refined and cultivated taste for social pleasures, it became the rendezvous of a gay and voluptuous society. The very emptiness of their minds and lack of useful employment begat a.longing for these trivial pleasures, which they called enjoyment because it relieved "from the ennui of the moment, even by occupation in trifles." The seat of a wealthy government, the daily life of its inhabitants was softened by the refinements of art, the indolence of wealth, and the substantial benefits of opulence. The furniture of their houses was constructed of the most costly woods and the most valuable marbles, each enriched by the elegant devices of the painter's and sculptor's arts. When they paid their social debts, or gathered for the stately minuet, they came in equipages light and handsome, drawn by fleetest coursers, and managed by livried slaves in richest apparel. Three-fourths of the dwellings of the city, by their style and elegance, gave proof of the wealth of the people whilst the employment of a French hair dresser, by one lady at a thousand crowns a year, was an out-cropping of that luxury which made it the home of a gay and haughty circle of giddy voluptuaries and social autocrats.

Nor was the element of evil wanting in this dwarfed prototype of European social life. Youth, beauty, wealth, and intelligence soon chastened the rigors of the primitive virtues of the settlers of the province and city into the refinement of continental manners. The fascinating and dangerous attractions of gayety, whilst they earned for Annapolis the title of the *Athens of America*, the chronicles of those times warrant the belief, that "her pleasures, like those of luxurious and pampered life in all ages, ministered neither to her happiness nor her purity."[*]

After the Revolution, its life of fashion subsided, its commerce departed, wealth gradually took its flight from Annapolis, and the city fell into a somnolent state. In its days of dreamy slumber a Naval Commission reported that "A polar expedition is useless to determine the Earth's Axis. Go to Annapolis rather. It should be called the pivot-city. It is the centre of the universe, for while all the world around it revolves it remains stationary. One advantage is that you always know where to find it. To get to Annapolis you have but to cultivate a colossal calmness and the force of gravity will draw you towards the great centre—once there, there is no certrifugal force to displace you, and you stay. By natural evolution your hands disappear in your breeches pockets and you assume the most marked characteristic of the indigenous Annapolitan. No glove merchant ever flourished there. Annapolitans in heaven have heads and wings, their hands disappear. On old tombstones you may see them as Angels, on earth they resemble exclamation points, all heads and tails, like the fish they eat. Natural evolution developes itself in a taste for oysters, as they need no carving, and a phosphorous diet swells the brain ; they talk politics continually. Annapolis keeps the Severn river in its place. This will be useful when the harbour of Baltimore dries up. Annapolitans are waiting for this. They are in no hurry, they don't mind waiting. Two or three centennials will do it."

A fair specimen of the raillery Annapolis has outlived. This facetious description, once well-nigh historical, no longer represents Annapols of the present which begins to stir in its slumber long and profound.

The whistle of the locomotive, as it crosses the Severn, echoing

* McMahono p. 256.

10

above the hill-tops of encompassing walls, is arousing "The Ancient
City." to its advantages· The infusion of new blood, that sees with
new eyes the opportunities its location presents, indicates the renais-
sance of its importance as "a port of trade," and railroad and capital are to make of "THE TOWN LAND AT PROCTORS" what legislative
enactments, surveyor's plats and commissioners' warrants could not accomplish.

CHAPTER XXXII.

THE FIRST AMERICAN THEATRE ERECTED IN ANNAPOLIS.

1752—1887.

The first theatre in America was built at Annapolis. In the Maryland
Gazette, of June 18th, 1752, appeared the following advertisement:
"By permission of his honor the president, (Benjamin Tasker, Esq.,
then president or governor of the province,) at the new theatre in
Annapolis, by the company of comedians from Virginia, on Monday
next, being the 22nd of this instant, will be performed, "The Beggars'
Opera," likewise farce, called the "Lying Valet," to begin precisely
at 7 o'clock. Tickets to be had at the printing office. Box 10 s.
pit 1s. 6d. No person to be admitted behind the scenes."

The principal performers appear to have been Messrs. Wyrill, Herbert, Eyanson, Kean, and Miss Osborne. The company played whilst
in Annapolis, "The Busy Body," "Beaux Stratagem," "Recruiting
Officer," "London Merchant," "Cato," "Richard III," and other
dramas. This company afterward performed at Upper Marlborough
and Pisataway, on the Western Shore, and at Chestertown, on the Eastern.

At the same time the Virginia company was here, Mr. Richard
Bucknell and company exhibited some curious wax figures, representing the Queen of Hungary sitting on her throne, and the Duke, her
son, and courtiers in attendance. In 1760, the *Gazette* announced
that "by permission of his Excellency, the Governor, a theatre is
erecting in this city which will be opened soon by a company of comedians who are now at Chester Town." This company arrived March
3rd, and began performing the same evening. They remained until
May 15th.

The following show the dramas performed in that period:

Plays.	Fares.
Mar. 2. Orphans.	Lethe, or Esop in the Shades.
" . Recruiting Officer.	Miss in her Teens
" . Venice Preserved.	Mock-Doctor.
" 29. Richard III.	King and the Mil-ler.

" 13. Provoked Husband.	Stage Coach.
" 15. Fair Penitent.	Anatomist.
" 20. Stratagem.	Lethe.
" 22. George Barnwell.	Lying Valet.
" 24. Busy-Body.	Mock-Doctor.
" 27. Revenge.	Lying Valet.
" 29. Bold Stroke for a Wife.	Damon and Phillida.

(In Passion week the Theatre was closed.)

April 7.*Romeo and Juliet. Stage Coach.	
" 8. Provoked Husband.	Honest Yorkshireman.
" 9. Othello.	Devil to Pay.
" 10. Constant Couple.	King and the Miller.
" 11.† Romeo and Juliet.	Miss in her teens.
" 12. Suspicious Husband.	Mock-Doctor.
April 14. Richard III. (Ben of Mr. Douglass.)	Hob.
" 15. Fair Penitent. (Mr. Palmer.)	Lying Valet.
" 16. Venice Preserved. (Mr. Murray.)	Devil to Pay.
" 17. Provoked Husband. (Mrs. Douglass.)	Yorkshireman.
" 19. Revenge. (Mr. Hallam.)	Lethe.
" 22. Stratagem. (Mrs. and Miss Dowthaitt.)	Lying Valet.
" 23. Orphan. (Miss Crane and Comp.)	Lethe.
" 24. Constant Couple. (Mr. Morris.)	Yorkshireman.
May 5. Douglass. (Mrs. A. Hallam.)	Virgin Unmasked
" 8. Jew of Venice. (Mr. Morris.)	Lethe.
" 12. Gamester. (Mr. Scott.)	Toy Shop.

The company then went to Upper Marlboro' and played several weeks.

On Saturday, the 18th of February, 1769, a new theatre was opened by the American company of comedians with Romeo and Juliet. The company then consisted of Messrs. Hallam, Jefferson, Verling, Wall, Darby, Morris, Parker, Godwin, Spencer, Page, Walker, Osborne, and Burdett, Mrs. Jones, Walker, Osborne, Burdett, Malone, Parker and Mrs. Hallam. This company was held in high estimation in Annapolis, and especially for its performance of Richard III. Miss Hallam excited the admiration of the poets, and the Muse's flame was kindled in her honor. One of the stanzas to this star of the stage ran :

> "Around her, see the Graces play,
> See Venus' Wanton Doves,
> And in her Eye's Pellucid Ray,
> See little Laughing Loves.
> Ye Gods! 'Tis Cytherea's Face."

It was this theatre that Mr. Eddis, the ever-faithful chronicler, so quaintly described in his letter dated from Annapolis, November 2nd, 1771, and printed in the preceding chapter :

This theatre stood on the present site of the Adams Express Office, West Street, and was pulled down over fifty years ago to make room for the present building, which was erected by the Hutton Brothers, as a wagon manufactory.

* "Romeo, by a young gentleman for his diversion."
† "With the funeral procession of Juliet, to the monument of Capuletts."

The theatre in Annapolis was the miniature of the progress of dramatic art the world over. Here was the devotion to actresses and here was displayed their haughty tyranny when their royal highnesses were displeased by an exacting and capricious public. This hauteur was pointedly evinced on the last night of a season's performances by the Old American Company of Comedians. During the evening the audience desired a Mrs. Henry to perform some part of the programme which she refused to do. A local correspondent wrote to the *Gazette* that "pity it is that being so well satisfied with the company in general, the Annapolitans should at last have their indignation excited by the contemptuous and ungrateful behavior of Mrs. Henry, who not only obstinately refused to gratify them in the only way in which she is superiorly qualified to please, but had not even the compliance to offer an apology for denying their request. But if we regret that our good humor should, at length, have been tired out by the insolence of this princess, we lament still more feelingly that our displeasure should, even in appearance, have fallen on two performers so deservedly possessed of our favor and esteem as Mrs. Morris and Mr. Wignell while the audience were bent on hearing Mrs. Henry sing."

In 1828, another theatre was built of wood on Duke of Gloucester street, on the present site of the Presbyterian Church. The corner-stone of this theatre was laid on the 14th of August, 1828, by Richard I. Jones, Esq. A leaden box, containing a list of the names of the Building Committee, a copy of each of the newspapers printed in this city, and a copy of the will of General Washington, was deposited under it. An appropriate address was delivered by James F. Brice, Esq., in the presence of the Committee, and a respectable number of citizens, who had assembled to witness the ceremony. It is deserving of remark, that the stone used for the corner-stone of this edifice, was the corner-stone of the theatre which formerly stood on West street, and which was pulled down about 1818.

Of this theatre Mr. David Ridgely wrote in 1841, it "is rarely opened not having votaries of the dramatic muse sufficient to sustain it even for a season."

Annapolis since that period has had no regular theatre; but is indebted to occasional visits of artists of genius, among them John E. Owens and Madame Jannescheck, with a plenitude of strolling companies of indifferent ability—whose place of performance is the Masonic Opera House. The amateur talent of Annapolis has been occasionally displayed to the signal credit of performers and the pleasure of the public. Frequent dramatic performances at the Naval Academy have enlivened the monotonous duties of military life, and the exhibit of town-talent at the Masonic Opera House in 1879 and 1881 in the reproduction of the cantatas of Belshazzer and Joseph reflected the high musical talent and dramatic skill of our citizens, and afforded unusual pleasure to large and cultivated audiences.

CHAPTER XXXIII.
THE STAMP ACT IN ANNAPOLIS.

1765—1766.

Boston, on the 14th of August, 1765, hung and burned the effigies of Bute and Greville. Thirteen days later Annapolis to show its "detestation of, and abhorrence to, some late tremendous attacks on liberty and their dislike to a certain late arrived officer, *a native of this province!*" "curiously dressed up the figure of a man, which they placed in a one-horse cart, male-factor like, with some sheets of paper in his hands before his face. In that manner they paraded through the streets of the town, till noon, the bell at the same time tolling a solemn knell, when they proceeded to the hill, and after giving it the MOSAIC LAW at the whipping-post, placed it in the pillory, from whence they took it and hung it on a gibbet, there erected for that purpose, and set fire to a tar-barrel underneath and burnt it till it fell into the barrel. By the many significant nods of the head, while in the cart, it may be said to have gone off very penitently."

The proceedings were under the direction of "a considerable number of people" calling themselves "Asserters of British American privileges," who had assembled from all parts of the State, amongst them being that bold and aggressive spirit, Samuel Chase—in 1776, one of the signers of the Declaration of Independence from Maryland.

The man who was the appointed instrument of oppression for Maryland, was a native and merchant of Annapolis, one Zachariah Hood, who happened to be in London at the time the stamp act was passed, and who, thus early at court, and too far from home to know the dangers of the office he desired to fill, sought and received the royal gift. McMahon photographs him in one sentence : "He was a willing instrument in the hands of a tyrannical ministry for the oppression of the people amongst whom he was born and had lived."

The announcement of this appointment was made in a letter from London, published in the *Gazette* of August 22nd, 1765. "We are credibly informed," says the writer, "that Z——h H——d, late a sojourning merchant of the city of Annapolis : but, at present, Z——h H——d, at St. James', has, for his many eminent services to the King and country during the late war, got the commission of Distributor of the stamps of that province. This gentleman's conduct is highly approved of here by all Court-cringing politicians, since he is supposed to have wisely considered that if his country must be *stamped*, the blow would be easier borne from a native, than a foreigner, who might not be acquainted with their manners and institutions."

On the arrival of Hood in the latter part of August, or the first of September, with his stamps, he was met at the City Dock by the citizens of Annapolis who had repaired in a body to resist his landing. In this they were successful, and, in the scuffle which ensued, Mr. Thomas McNeir had his thigh broken—the first patriot injured in the struggle for American rights. The names of two others only who took part in this rally for liberty have come down to us. They were Mr. Charles Farris and Mr. Abraham Claude—the latter, the grandfather of our estimable Mayor, Dr. Abram Claude. The landing, prevented at the City Dock, was clandestinely made at another point.

Foiled in one assault, the people made another. On the night of September 2nd, three or four hundred people assembled in Annapolis, and pulled down a house which Hood was having repaired for the reception of a cargo of goods. Terrified at such suggestive proceedings at the hands of his former friends and the populace generally, Hood intimated to Governor Sharpe that if he thought that his resignation as stamp distributor would reconcile his countrymen to him, and would advise him to take that step, he would throw up the commission of his tormenting office. Governor Sharpe was unwilling to take this responsibility, and, as Hood and his relations felt that he would not be safe in his or the Governor's house, he retired "for a few weeks to New York." Before he went, however, he declared the office had been solicited by Thomas Ringgold, a member of the Legislature from Kent. Ringgold indignantly denied this by advertisement in public print, and said if the office had been asked for him by any one, it was without his knowledge. In the same issue of the *Gazette*, Benjamin Welsh gave public notice that he would 'pay no tax whatever but what is laid upon me by my representative.''

Hood did not purchase peace by flight. On the 28th of November, a party of citizens of the neighborhood, surrounded the house on Long Island, in which Hood was concealed. As escape was impossible, he "endeavored to excuse his conduct and desired liberty to relate his case, and read the letters he had wrote to reconcile himself to his incensed country. The request was granted. He said that some considerable service that he had done or designed his country, together with his long absence from it and his friends, on his late return from England to Maryland, had given him expectations of the most agreeable and endearing reception, and the pleasing views of a genteel subsistence for life. But that on his arrival he was every way so totally disappointed that he was really an object of compassion rather than resentment—that he was obliged to leave all his affairs in the greatest confusion and fly for the preservation of his life. That his absence had occasioned great losses, and that his life was still in danger should he offer to return. That he had been in a state of continual painful anxiety ever since his arrival in America, that even his enemies might pity." He begged that he might resign upon his honor, without oath, and "that he might be allowed to hold his office if his countrymen might hereafter desire it." Neither request was granted, and under threat of being delivered to the multitude, Hood agreed to execute, and subsequently, did, under oath, a complete and abject resignation.

The mob, its indignation now changed to gratification, cheered Hood and invited him to an entertainment which he very naturally declined on the ground that "he was in such a frame of body and mind that he would be unhappy in any company."

Whilst the Annapolis stamp-officer was undergoing such severe treatment in New York, the citizens of his native place remained as sincerely in earnest in their intention never to submit to the stamp-act as when they met Hood on the wharf of the City Dock and prevented his landing.

On the 31st of October, a supplement to the Maryland *Gazette* appeared in deep mourning. The editor announced his intention of suspending publication, rather than submit to the "intolerable and burthensome terms," imposed on all newspapers by the stamp-act, declaring, "The times are Dreadful, Dismal, Doleful, Dolorous, and Dollerless."

On the 10th of December, "an apparition of the late Maryland *Gazette*" *appeared*, the editor determining to resurrect his paper "under the firm belief that the odious stamp-act would never be carried into operation." He announced that the *Gazette* "shall be, as it had been, sacred to liberty and consequently to virtue, religion, and the good and welfare of its country." Here was a noble example of the fearless and conscientious editor who, whilst receiving the patronage of the crown offices, boldly defended the rights of the people.

The attacks of the *Gazette* upon Parliament were incessant, and came often in pithy paragraphs and pointed allusions that carried greater weight than extended arguments.

The final passage of the stamp-act it had conveyed to the people in this paragraph: "Friday evening last, between nine and ten o'clock, we had a very smart thunder gust, which struck a house in one part of the town, and a tree in another. But we were more *thunderstruck* last Monday, on the arrival of Capt. Joseph Richardson, in the ship *Pitt*, in six weeks from Downs, with a certain account of the stamp-act being absolutely passed."

The people of Maryland had never intended to submit to the stamp-act, and this determination culminated in March, 1766, when the "SONS OF LIBERTY," from Baltimore, Kent and Anne Arundel counties met at Annapolis and made a written application to the Chief Justice of the Provincial Court, the Secretary and Commissary-General, and Judges of the Land Office, to open their respective offices, and to proceed as usual in the execution of their duties. This request was granted and the stamp-act became a rigid corpse in Maryland.

The presence of his Majesty Sloop Hawke, which arrived in December, 1765, with the stamped paper for Maryland, did not cool the ardor of the patriots. There was no person to receive the paper, and Governor Sharpe had ignominiously to return three boxes of it to England by a merchant ship, the Brandon, Capt. McLachlan, in December, 1766.

Hood himself afterward returned to Annapolis and conducted business without molestation.

On the 5th of April, 1766, the glad news was received by express that the stamp-act had been repealed. The city responded to the good tidings, and the afternoon was spent by the people in mirth and congratulations, in which "all loyal and patriotic toasts were drank."

On the 11th of June, by proclamation of the Mayor, the day was given over to rejoicing and festivity on account of the "glorious news" of the absolute repeal of the stamp-act. At night the city was brilliantly illuminated.

[1765.] A few nights after the mob destroyed Mr. Hood's intended residence in Annapolis, a British officer and a Mr. Hammond had a dispute about their prowess. Midnight was the hour, a public house the place, a large company the spectators. The disputants agreed to decide the debate by a bout at boxing. Mr. Hammond was worsted, and so much so that he had to leave the company. Thereupon a cry arose that Mr. Hammond had been killed by the officers. Whereupon a mob gathered, and the British officers of the Hornet, it seems lying off the town, were in danger of being murdered upon the strength of the false cry. The gentlemen of the town interferred, and the participants in the mob were afterward ashamed to acknowledge their connection with it.

⸻ ◂•▸ ⸻

CHAPTER XXXIV.
Gov. Eden, of Maryland, the Last English Governor to Leave the Revolted Colonies.

1769—1776.

Robert Eden became Governor of Maryland in 1760, under the grant of Charles the First to Lord Baltimore. He was alike the last of the proprietary Governors of Maryland and the last English Governor to leave the revolted Colonies. It was under his hospitable roof that Washington was guest when at Annapolis and where he displayed that native dignity in conversation and broad liberality in opinion which so eminently distinguished his lofty character.

It was in the lovely month of June when Gov. Eden landed. At this season the picturesque scenery of Annapolis is particularly beautiful. On the fifth of the month the ship bearing Gov. Eden, wife, and family arrived in the harbor. On coming to anchor the ship fired seven guns which number was returned by the citzens. In the afternoon when the Governor landed he was met by all the members of the Governor's Council then in town, and a great number of citizens, the guns of the battery making the Severn resound with its salvo of welcome. On Tuesday morning, about ten o'clock, he went up to the council house, attended by his lordship's honorable council, where his commission was open and published.

The royal Governor was a gentlemen, "easy of access, courteous to all, and fascinating by his accomplishments," and so too Mr. William Eddis found him, for when he arrived in Annapolis, September 3rd, 1769, to take the position of English Collector of Customs and made his appearance before the Governor. He says: "My reception was equal to my warmest wishes. The deportment of Governor Eden was open and friendly. He invited me to meet a party at dinner, and I took leave till the appointed hour, with a heart replete with joy and gratitude. On my return to the Governor, he introduced me, in the most obliging terms, to several persons of the highest respectability in the province. He treated me with the utmost kindness and cordiality ; assured me of his strongest disposition to advance my future prosperity and gave an unlimited invitation to his hospitable table."

Not only to the select circle of a private company of his intimate friends did Governor Eden dispense his generous hospitality, but when the little city appeared in all its splendor on the anniversary of the proprietary's birth, he "gave a grand entertainment on the occasion to a numerous party ; the company brought with them every disposition to render each other happy : and the festivities concluded with cards, and dancing which engaged the attention of their respective votaries till an early hour."

Although the Governor led in the festivities of the province, he was not unmindful of the weightier cares of State. Mr. Eddis, who spoke with the unction cf a grateful heart and sanguine temperament said of him : "He appears competent to the discharge of his important duty. Not only in the summer, but during the extreme rigour of an American winter, it is his custom to rise early ; till the hour of dinner he devotes the whole of his time to provincial concerns ; the meanest individual obtains an easy and immediate access to his person ; he investigates, with accuracy, the complicated duties of his station ; and discovers, upon every occasion, alacrity in the dispatch of business ; and a perfect knowledge of the relative connexions of the country."

Not only was Gov. Eden moved by motives of principle and personal welfare to promote the well-being of the province, but being a brother-in-law of Lord Baltimore, his family interests urged him to make the commonwealth prosperous. He was not wanting in any public enterprise to further the happiness of the province. A patron of the drama, it was by his liberal example, sufficient funds were raised to erect a theatre in Annapolis on a commodious plan. He was beside the friend of education, and through his exertions a Seminary was established "which as it will be conducted under excellent regulations, will shortly preclude the necessity of crossing the Atlantic for the completion of a classical and polite education."

In June, 1774. Governor Eden made a visit to England. He returned early in November.

In the meantime the Peggy Stewart had been burned.

On the 8th of November, Eddis wrote : "The Governor is returned to a land of trouble. He arrived about ten this morning in perfect health. He is now commenced an actor on a busy theatre ; his part a truly critical one. To stem the popular torrent, and to conduct his measures with consistency, will require the exertion of all his faculties. The present times demand superior talents, and his, I am persuaded, will be invariably directed to promote the general good. Hitherto his conduct has secured to him a well-merited popularity ; and his return to the province has been expected with an impatience which sufficiently evinces the sentiments of the public in his favor."

The bearing of the Governor during this trying period is described by his ever faithful admirer. Eddis, who, March 13, 1775, wrote—"It is with pleasure I am able to assert, that a greater degree of moderation appears to predominate in this province, than in any other on the continent, and I am perfectly assured we are very materially indebted for this peculiar advantage to the collected and consistent conduct of our Governor, whose views appear solely directed to advance the interests of the community ; and to preserve, by every possible method, the public tranquility."

On May 13, Mr. Eddis wrote: "The Governor continues to stand fair with the people of this province: our public prints declare him to be the only person, in his station, who, in these tumultuous times, has given the administration a fair and impartial representation of important occurrences; and I can assert, with the strictest regard to truth, that he conducts himself in his arduous department, with an invariable attention to the interest of his royal master, and the essential welfare of the province over which he has the honor to preside."

When the regulation went forth that all must join the association against British importation and for kindred measures of opposition. Gov. Eden and his family alone were accepted.

September 26th, Mr. Eddis found the Governor in company with a few select loyal friends; where "political occurrences engrossed their conversation in which hope appeared to operate but weakly, with respect to the eventful transactions of the times."

There was one proof in spite of the Governor's title and popularity, that he, after all, was but a royal prisoner with a show of authority—all his letters had to pass the ordeal of examination by the provincial authorities. He continued, however, "to receive every external mark of attention and respect; while the steady propriety of his conduct in many trying exigencies, reflected the utmost credit on his moderation and understanding."

But the times were growing too troublous for matters to remain in this placid state with the Governor. In the early part of April, 1776, a vessel containing a packet of letters from Lord George Germaine, Secretary of State for the American Department, was seized by an armed vessel in the provincial service.

Lord George Germaine's letters acknowledged the important information which the administration had received from the governor, who was assured "of his Majesty's entire approbation of his conduct; and was directed to proceed in the line of his duty with all possible address and activity."

This packet was forwarded to General Lee, who had the command of the southern district, by whom it was immediately dispatched to Maryland, with a strong recommendation to seize the person of the governor, together with all papers and documents of office; by which it was presumed some important discoveries would be made of ministerial intentions.

The council of safety acted on this critical occasion with the utmost moderation and delicacy. Governor Eden, by the affability of his manners and his evident disposition to promote the interests of the province, had conciliated universal regard. They, therefore, avoided proceeding with that precipitate vigour so strenuously enjoined; and only required him to give his parole, that he would not take any measures for leaving the continent, till after the meeting of the next convention.

This requisition the governor, for some time, warmly resisted: but, on conviction that the measure was unavoidable, he thought it necessary to comply; therefore, on the sixteenth of April, gave every satisfactory assurance.

On the seventh of May, the convention assembled, and on the 23d, came to a determination respecting the Governor, when it was resolved, "that his longer continuance in the province, at so critical a period, might be prejudicial to the cause in which the colonies were unanimously engaged ; and that, therefore, his immediate departure for England was absolutely necessary." An address was accordingly directed to be drawn up, and presented to his excellency, which was delivered to him the next evening by a committee of that body.

In this address the sentiments of the convention were expressed in liberal terms ; they acknowledged the services rendered by the governor to the country, on many former occasions ; and they expressed the warmest wishes, that "when the unhappy disputes which at present prevail, are constitutionally accommodated, he may speedily return and re-assume the reins of government."

The Continental Congress urged the seizure of Gov. Eden's person, and the Virginia convention passed the following resolutions against the convention of Maryland :

"Resolved unanimously, That the Committee of Safety be directed to write a letter to the President of the Convention of Maryland, in answer to his letter of the twenty-fifth instant, expressing the deepest concern at the proceedings of that Convention, respecting Governor Eden ; and our reasons for not becoming accessary thereto, by giving him a passport through this colony, of the bay adjoining : that we would with reluctance, in any cause, intermeddle in the affairs of a sister colony, but in this matter we are much interested ; and the Convention of Maryland, by sending their proceedings to the Committee of Safety, has made it the duty of the Convention, to declare their sentiments thereon.

"That considering the letter from Lord George Germaine to Governor Eden, in which his whole conduct, and confidential letters are approved : and he is directed to give facility and assistance to the operation of Lord Dunmore, against Virginia, we are at a loss to account for the Council of Safety of Maryland, for their having neglected to seize him, according to the recommendation of the general Congress, and more so for the Convention having promoted his passage, to assist in our destruction. under pretence of his retiring to England. which we conceive from the above letter, he is not at liberty to do, that supposing he should go to Britain it appears to us, that such voyage, with the address presented to him, will enable him to assume the character of a public agent, and by promoting division amongst the colonies. produce consequences of most fatal to the American cause, that as the reasons assigned for his departure : "That he must obey the ministerial mandates while remaining in his government," are very unsatisfactory, when the Convention declare, that "in his absense, the government, in its old form, will devolve on the President of the Council of State," who will be under equal obligation to obey such mandates. We cannot avoid imputing these proceedings to some undue influence of Governor Eden, under the mask of friendship to America, and of the proprietary interest of Maryland, whereby the members of that Convention were betrayed into a vote of fatal tendency to the common cause, and, we fear, to this country in particular, and feel it an indispensible duty, to warn the good people of that province against the proprietary influence."

"EDM. PENDLETON, President.
"JOHN TAZWELL, Clk. Convention."

The appeal of Virginia to seize Gov. Eden, of Maryland, added to the violence of the people ; and the Whig club of Baltimore loudly proclaimed the absolute necessity to capture the Governor, as a pledge of public safely, and it was asserted that a plan was in agitation to accomplish that purpose in defiance of the legislature. Gov. Eden did not appear concerned, but relied on the honor of the convention which had solemnly pledged his safe departure.

On Sunday, June 23, 1776, the frigate Fowey, Capt. George Montague, arrived for Gov. Eden, and the first Lieutentant of the ship came on shore with a flag of truce. Every moment now brought changes, the militia were under arms, and, a general confusion prevailed.

Under date of June 29, 1776, Mr. Eddis wrote from Annapolis:

''Till the moment of the governor's embarkation on the 23d, there was every reason to apprehend a change of disposition to his prejudice. Some few were even clamorous for his detention. But the council of safety, who acted under a resolve of the convention, generously ratified the engagements of that body ; and after they had taken an affectionate leave of their late supreme magistrate, he was conducted to the barge with every mark of respect due to the elevated station he had so worthily filled.

''A few minutes before his departure, I received his strict injunctions to be steady and cautious in the regulation of my conduct ; and not to abandon my situation, on any consideration, until absolutely discharged by an authority which might, too probably, be erected on the ruins of the ancient constitution. I promised the most implicit attention to his salutary advice ; and rendered my grateful acknowledgements for the innumerable obligations he had conferred on me ; at the same time I offered my most fervent wishes that his future happiness might be full proportion to the integrity of his conduct, and the benevolence of his mind.

''In about an hour the barge reached the Fowey, and the governor was received on board under a discharge of cannon ; his baggage and provisions were left on shore, to be forwarded in the course of the ensuing day.

''During the night, some servants, and a soldier belonging to the Maryland regiment, found means to escape on board his Majesty's ship, which being almost immediately discovered, a flag was sent off, with a message to Captain Montague, demanding the restitution of the men, previous to any further communication.

''Captain Montague, in reply, acquainted the council of safety, ''that he could not, consistently with his duty, deliver up any persons who, as subjects of his Britannic Majesty, had fled to him for refuge and protection ; he had strictly given it in charge to such officers as might be sent on shore, not to bring off any of the inhabitants without the express permission of the ruling powers; but that the case was extremely different respecting those who had, even at hazard of life, given evidence of their attachment to the ancient constitution.'

''This message not being deemed satisfactory, a letter was dispatched to the governor demanding his interference in this critical business, with an intimation, that the detention of the men would be considered as a manifest breach of the regulation under which flags of truce are established.

"Governor Eden received the officer which proper attention, but replied, he had only to observe, that on board his Majesty's ship, he had not the least authority ; and that Captain Montague was not to be influenced by his opinion, as he acted on principles which he conceived to be strictly consistent with the line of his duty.

"The event of this negotiation was disagreeable in its consequence to the governor. The populace were exceedingly irritated, and it was thought expedient not only to prohibit all further intercourse with the Fowey, but also to detain the various stores which the governor had provided for his voyage to Europe. This resolution was intimated in express terms ; and, on the evening of the 24th, Captain Montague weighed anchor, and stood down the bay, for his station on the coast of Virginia."

The property, the Governor had left behind, was confiscated. In 1783, he returned to Annapolis to obtain the restitution of his property. He died soon after his arrival in the house now owned and occupied by the Sisters of Notre Dame, on Shipwright street. He was buried, says Mr. Ridgely, "under the pulpit of the Episcopal Church on the north side of Severn within two or three miles of this place. This church was some years since burned down."

I have tried by diligent inquiry to locate this church. The nearest approach to the truth is found in the fact that, on the farm of Mrs. Winchester, near the track of the Annapolis and Baltimore Short Line Railroad, is an ancient graveyard—the site of an Episcopal Church that was burned down nearly a hundred years ago. There is a grave in this cemetery, marked by a cross of bricks—and the tradition is that an English Lord lies buried here. It would not take many repetitions of oral history to change an English Governor to an English Lord.

CHAPTER XXXV.

SHIPYARDS, RACE COURSES, AND INDIANS.

In 1747, a large ship, belonging to Mr. William Roberts, was built, launched, and called after the names of its builders the "RUMNEY AND LONG." This is the year a shipload of rebels commonly called "the King's passengers," were landed in Annapolis.

The first shipyard, of which there is any record, was located a few feet below the culvert on Northwest street where it crosses Calvert. The cove then made up beyond the jail. Its name has been lost and the water has receded a quarter of a mile since then.

In other sections of the city the water has given place to land— notably where a cove came up Church street as far as Mr. James Munroe's store, and there is a lady living who has heard a gentleman say he used to tie his boat to a stake driven at the foot of Green street.

Holland street and the property adjacent to the oyster-houses between Prince George and Hanover streets are evidences that made ground grows very fast under an impetus of business or improvement.

The owner of the Rumney and Long built and lived in the house now owned by Mrs. A. Owen Iglehart. He had a blacksmith's shop north of his residence, on which was a steeple in which was the only bell of the city until St. Anne's arrived—the one tradition says was presented by Queen Anne, and which was destroyed by fire in 1858. Below this shop were sailmakers' lofts, and other workshops necessary in shipbuilding. Messrs. Kirkwell and Blackwell, ship-builders, were also in his employ.

Tradition tells us, that they built the "Brig, Lovely Nancy"—at the launch of which the following incident occurred : "She was on the stocks, and the day appointed to place her on her destined element, a large concourse of persons assembled to witness the launch, among whom was an old white woman named Sarah McDaniel, who professed fortune-telling, and was called 'a witch.' She was heard to remark—·The Lovely Nancy will not see water today.' The brig moved finely at first, and when expectation was at its height to see her glide into the water, she suddenly stopped, and could not be again moved on that day. This occurrence created much excitement amongst the spectators ; and Captain Slade and the sailors were so fully persuaded that she had been 'bewitched,' that they resolved to duck the old woman. In the meantime she had disappeared from the crowd ; they kept up the search for two or three days, during which time she lay concealed in a house."

"The 'Lovely Nancy,' did afterwards leave the stocks, and is said to have made several prosperous voyages.

"There was, at a later period, another shipyard on the Southwest side of the city, at the termination of Charles street, where the 'Matilda,' and the 'Lady Lee' were launched—the first was owned by Samuel Chase, Esq., and the latter by Governor Lee."*

At the foot of Maryland Avenue, about 1840, Benjamin Linthicum built the Severn, a large schooner, for John S. Selby, an Annapolis merchant. It was a very fine vessel. Ship-building has since gradually declined in Annapolis. There was a small shipyard near the Northeast side of the dock in which bay craft were built, and one on the Southwest side. The first commenced about the year 1850, and continued to 1860. It was also owned by Benjamin Linthicum. The Marine Railway, now owned by Haller and Matzon, was the outgrowth and continuance of Linthicum's shipyard.

About 1750, a jockey club was established at Annapolis, consisting of many "principal gentlemen in this, and in the adjacent provinces, many of whom in order to encourage the breed of the noble animal, imported from England, at a very great expense, horses of high reputation." This club existed for many years. "The races at Annapolis were generally attended by a great concourse of spectators, many coming from the adjoining colonies. Considerable sums were bet on these occasions. Subscription purses of a hundred guineas were for a long time the highest amount run for, but subsequently were greatly increased. The day of the races usually closed with balls, or theatrical amusements." The race course at this time and for many years

* ____ of Annapolis, p. 119.

after, was located on that part of the city just beyond Mr. Severe's blacksmith shop, embracing a circle of one mile, taking in all that portion of the town now occupied by the Annapolis, Washington and Baltimore railroad depot and the lands adjacent.

Severe's blacksmith shop stood where Henry B. Myers' feed warehouse and coal yard, on Calvert street, are now located.

On the 20th of September, in 1750, a race was run on this course between governor Ogle's Bay Gelding, and Col. Plater's Grey Stallion, and won by the former. For next day six horses started, Mr. Waters' horse Parrott, winning, distancing several of the running horses. "On the same ground some years after, Dr. Hamilton's 'horse Figure,' won a purse of fifty pistoles—beating two, and distancing three others. 'Figure' was a horse of great reputation—it is stated of him that, "he had won many fifties—and in the year 1763, to have received premiums at Preston and Carlisle, in Old England, where no horse would enter against him—he never lost a race." Subsequently, the race course was removed to a field some short distance beyond the city, on which course some of the most celebrated horses ever known in America have run. It was on this latter course that Mr. Bevans' bay horse "Oscar," so renowned in the annals of the turf, first ran. Oscar was bred on Mr. Ogle's farm near this city—he won many races, and in the fall of 1808, it is well remembered, he beat Mr. Bond's "First Consul" on the Baltimore course, who had challenged the continent—running the second heat in 7 m. 40 s., which speed had never been excelled.†

"Old Ranter" was "Oscar's" great, great, grand sire.

To these races Gen. Washington used to repair, and in his diary naively recounts his gains on the bets on the successful pacers.

These stirring seasons have long since ceased to occur—and the memory of them no more excites the garrulity of tradition. In 1884, an attempt was made to revive the race course, in conjunction with agricultural fair grounds ; but the effort was abortive.

Twenty-one years later, 1771, "The Saint Tamina Society," was inaugurated in Annapolis, and continued its anniversary celebrations for many years. The first day of May was set apart in memory of "Saint Tamina," whose history, like those of other venerable saints, is lost in fable and uncertainty. It was usual on the morning of this day, for the members of the society to erect in some public situation in the city, a "May-pole," and to decorate it in a most tasteful manner, with wild flowers gathered from the adjacent woods, and forming themselves in a ring around it, hand in hand, perform the Indian war dance, with many other customs which they had seen exhibited by the children of the forest. It was also usual on this day for such of the citizens, who chose to enter into the amusement, to wear a piece of buck's-tail in their hats, or in some conspicuous part of their dress.

"The first lottery drawn in this province," was at Annapolis, on the 21st September, 1753, for the purchase of a "town clock, and clearing the dock." The highest prize 100 pistoles—tickets half a pistole. The managers were Benjamin Tasker, Jr., George Stewart, Walter Dulany, and ten other gentlemen of this place.

On the 11th of August, of this year, Horatio Sharpe, Esq., governor of the province, arrived here, in the ship Molly, Captain Nicholas Coxen, from London.

† Ridgely's Annals of Annapolis.

In September, (1753,) several companies under the command of Captain Dagworthy, Lieutenants Forty and Bacon, marched from Annapolis against the French on the Ohio.

On the 3d April, 1755, General Braddock, Governor Dinwiddie and Commodore Keppel arrived here, on their way to Virginia. On the 11th and 12th of the same month, there arrived Governor Sherley, of Boston, Governor De Lancy, of New York, and Governor Morris, of Philadelphia, with a number of distinguished gentlemen. They left here accompanied by Governor Sharpe, for Alexandria, and on the 17th they returned to Annapolis on their way to their respective governments. A few days after, Governor Sharpe set out for Frederick Town.

This period, which just preceded the defeat of General Braddock, near Fort Du Queen, appears to have been a busy time with their excellencies.

On the 29th of September, of this year, Dr. Charles Carroll departed this life, aged sixty-four years—he had resided in Annapolis about forty years. For some years after his coming to this city, he "practised physic with good success; but laying that aside, he commenced trade and merchandise, by which he amassed a very considerable fortune." In 1737, he was chosen a member to the Lower House of Assembly, in which station he is said to have spared no pains or application to render himself serviceable to the country and his constituents, to the time of his death. He is represented to have been "a gentleman of good sense and breeding, courteous and affable," and was held in high esteem by his fellow-citizens. Dr. Carroll owned all of the ground on the lower part of Church street, on the South side, extending back to the Duke of Gloucester street.

Mr. Green says in his *Gazette* of the 6th of November, of this year, "we are now about entrenching the town. If the gentlemen, in the neighborhood of Annapolis, were to send their forces to assist in it, a few days would complete the work."

This measure, it would seem, was taken by the citizens, in consequence of the "dreadful murders and massacres" committed by the French and Indians upon the border country, and serious apprehensions were entertained by the inhabitants that Annapolis would fall into the hands of their "politic, cruel, and cunning enemies." It was asserted by a writer for the *Gazette*, that the Indians "were but little way from the city, and that so entire was their defenceless situation, that even a small party of twenty or thirty Indians, by marching in the night and skulking in the day time, might come upon them unawares in the dead of night, burn their houses, and cut their throats, before they could put themselves in a posture of defence." Other writers of the day, seemed to think that there was no more danger of "Annapolis being attacked by the Indians than London." The fears of the inhabitants were soon quieted, by the return of several gentlemen who had gone as volunteers to the westward, and who reported they had seen no Indians, except one, and he was "very quiet," for they found him dead.

The last Indians to visit Annapolis lived on the Potomac river. Their name has not come down to us. They exchanged their lands with the Calvert family for lands in Baltimore county where game was more plentiful, and, as the white population advanced, the tribe retired to the Susquehanna. The Eastern shore tribes occasionally visited Annapolis, and as late as 1840, there where some few residents of Annapolis who remembered the visits of King Abraham and his Queen Sarah.

———➤•⬅———

CHAPTER XXXVI.
THE THIRD STATE HOUSE IN ANNAPOLIS.

1772—1887.

THE THIRD STATE HOUSE. Corner Stone laid March 28, 1772.

In 1769, the Legislature appropriated £7,500 sterling to build the present State House. The building committee was Daniel Dulany, Thomas Johnson, John Hall, William Paca, Charles Carroll, Barrister, Lancelot Jacques, and Charles Wallace. The majority were empowered to contract with workmen, and to purchase materials, and were authorized to draw on the dual treasurers of the State for whatever further sums might be required to complete the building.

The foundation stone of the State House was laid on the 28th of March, 1772, by Governor Eden.

In 1773, a copper roof was put on the State House, and in 1775, this roof was blown off. The Market House of the city was demolished by the same equinoctial gale, during which the tide rose three feet perpendicularly above the common level.

The dome was not added to the State House until after the revolution.

11

The dimensions of the State House are:

	Feet.
From the platform to the cornice, about................	36
" " cornice to top of arc, of roof..............	23
" " top of the roof to the cornice of the facade of the dome............	30
" " cornice to the band above the elliptical windows...	24
This terminates the view internally...............	113
From the band to the balcony...........................	22
Height of the turret..................................	17
From the cornice of the turret to the floor of the campanelle, or lantern	6
Height of the campanelle, or lantern..................	14
Height of the pedestal and acorn......................	10
Height of the spire..................................	18—87

	Entire height,	200
Diameter of the dome, at its base.......		40
do. balcony.....................................		30
do. turret..............		17
do. campanelle, or lantern..................... ...		10
do. acorn.......................................		3 8 in.
Length of the front of the building....................		120
Depth, (exclusive of the octagon,)....................		82

The architect was Joseph Clarke. Thomas Dance who executed the stucco and fresco work, fell from the scaffold just as he had finished the centre piece, and was killed.

The State House is situated upon a marked elevation in the centre of Annapolis. The eminence rises in gradual terraces to the edifice, which, though simple in architecture, has a lofty and majestic appearance, and has in all times "elicited alike the admiration of the citizen, the sojourner, and the stranger for the beauty of its structure."

The main building is of brick, the dome of wood. From the dome of the State House, 125 feet from the top of the Hill, a most delightful view is obtained. The majestic Chesapeake and a hundred tributaries, their bosoms covered with endless varieties of busy water craft ; the ancient city ; its environs ; the Naval Academy—its ships of war ;— the contiguous country with its sloping hills and variegated plains, for an extent of thirty miles, gratify the eye of the delighted spectator.

The main entrance of the State House is through a modest porch, facing southeast. It opens into a spacious hall, beautifully ornamented with stucco work which was made from plaster brought from St. Mary's county.

On the right hand is the Senate Chamber, 30 by 40 feet. Its ceiling and walls are handsomely ornamented, and rich carpets cover its floors. It has accommodations for twenty-six Senators, and a contracted lobby gives room for a small number of auditors. Portraits at full length of Charles Carroll, of Carrollton, Samuel Chase, William Paca, and Thomas Stone, signers of the Declaration of Independence from Maryland, adorn the walls.

In 1876, this chamber was improved by order of the Board of Public Works. The old gallery that linked the room with the great past was torn down and carried to the cellar, and the State acquiesced in a prolongation it had ever ordered.

In the room adjoining the Senate is a portrait of the elder Pitt, in which Lord Chatham is represented at full length in the attitude and costume of a Roman orator—decorated with emblems of his lofty principles. · This portrait was painted by Charles Wilson Peale whilst in England and presented by him, in 1794, to the State.

The Senate Chamber's highest title to renown is that in it Washington resigned his Military Commission after the Revolution, and became again a civilian. In this room also was ratified by Congress in 1784, the treaty of peace with Great Britain, which treaty recognized American Independence.

In September, 1786, at the suggestion of General Washington, it is thought, as the scheme was concerted at Mt. Vernon, a convention assembled at Annapolis to propose measures to maintain harmonious commercial relations between the States. This body met in the Senate Chamber. Five States were represented. The Commissioners who arrived were from

NEW YORK—Alexander Hamilton and Egbert Benson.

NEW JERSEY—Abraham Clark, William C. Houston, and James Schureman.

PENNSYLVANIA—Tench Coxe.

DELAWARE—George Ready, John Dickinson, Richard Bassett.

VIRGINIA—Edmund Randolph, James Madison, Jr., and St. George Tucker.

Hamilton made the report that was adopted by the convention. It proposed to the several States the convocation of a convention to take into consideration the situation of the United States.

The Annapolis convention was the parent of the great convention of 1787, that framed the federal constitution.

On the left of the rotunda is the Hall of the House of Delegates. It has seating capacity for 91 members. Three small lobbies give accommodations for visitors. On the Northeastern wall hangs a painting, representing Washington, attended by General LaFayette and Col. Tilghman his Aides-de-camp, and the Continental Army passing in review. In Washington's hands are the articles of capitulation at Yorktown. This picture was painted by Charles Wilson Peale in pursuance of a resolution of the Legislature, and is one of the best portraits extant of the immortal Virginian.

Opposite the entrance of the State House is the Library, containing, duplicates included, 80,000 volumes. These are chiefly works on law and public documents, but a handsome proportion of them is a valuable collection of works on art, science, history, and fiction. The library was established in 1834, and the building was enlarged in 1859. Before the inauguration of the State Library, the room, occupied at its establishment, had been used by the General Court of Maryland. In 1804, that court was abolished.

On the second floor to the left of the staircase is the suite of rooms occupied by the Court of Appeals. On the right of the stairway the room of the Adjutant General (formerly the State Armory,) the private office of the Governor, and the Executive Chamber are located.

In the Executive Chamber the portrait of George Calvert, the first Lord Baltimore and England's Secretary of State under James and Charles, is seen. It is a copy from the painting by Mytens, now in the gallery of the Earl of Verulam at Glastenbury, England—and was presented to the State by John W. Garrett, of Baltimore, as a result

of the researches and efforts of Mr. F. B. Mayer, of Annapolis, to inaugurate a gallery of the Governors of Maryland.   A full length portrait of Charles, third Lord Baltimore, was exchanged by the city of
Annapolis for the six portraits of Governors Paca, Smallwood, Stone,
Sprigg, Johnson, and Plater. These with the full length of Frederick, the
sixth and last Lord Baltimore, and a recent gift of a portrait of Governor
Robert Wright, and one of John Eager Howard, are the only portraits
of her Governors owned by the State.

In the Senate Chamber is a large picture by Edwin White, representing "Washington's Resignation of his Commission," obtained
under an order of the Maryland Legislature in 1859.

The basement of the State House is occupied by the furnace for
heating the building, the steam ventilator, and committee rooms.

An Annex to the State Library was ordered by the Legislature of
1886, a building long needed by reason of the over-crowded condition of
the library.

CHAPTER XXXVII.
ANNAPOLIS IN THE DECLARATION OF INDEPENDENCE.

[1776.] The dramatic arraignment of George III. in the Declaration of Independence, contains two counts that Annapolis helped to
make in that unique indictment.   The Fifteenth Count that gives as
one of the causes which impelled the colonies to dissolve the political
bands that had connected them with Great Britain, reads:

"For protecting them, (armed troops) by a mock-trial, from punishment for any murders which they should commit on the inhabitants of these States."

This was literally done at Annapolis in 1768, when, in a dispute between some soldiers and citizens of the town, two citizens were killed.
As the homicides were marines, belonging to an armed vessel lying
near, they were in time of peace, on complaint of the citizens
arraigned before the Admiralty Court for murder.   The whole affair
assumed the character of a solemn farce, so far as justice was concerned, and, as might have been expected, the miscreants were acquitted.*

Another count, the 16th, was: "For quartering large bodies of
armed troops among us."

The Maryland Assembly had been slack in voting money to keep
Fort Frederick and Cumberland in the condition the provincial governor, the representative of royal authority, wanted, and in December, 1757, five companies of the Royal Americans were quartered
upon the citizens of Annapolis as a penalty for the contumacy of the
General Assembly. They remained there until March 22nd, 1758. Governor Sharpe expostulated against the severity and injustice of the
measure which punished the inhabitants of one town for the supposed
sins of a State.

* Lossing's Lives of the Signers, p. 287.

CHAPTER XXXVIII.
ANNAPOLIS DURING THE REVOLUTIONARY WAR.

The seeds of the American Revolution had been sown in 1765 by the passage of the Stamp Act. The constant and determined support, Annapolis gave to the patriot cause, had been plainly foreshadowed by its resistance to the attempted enforcement of this odious legislation, and its summary treatment of Hood, the British distributor of stamps, though Maryland was loath to break those political ties that bound her to the mother country.

When the news of the blockade of Boston Harbor reached Annapolis, a meeting of its citizens was called. On Wednesday, the 25th day of May, 1774, the people convened, when it was

"*Resolved*, That it is the unanimous opinion of this meeting, that the town of Boston is now suffering in the common cause of America, and that it is incumbent on every colony in America, to unite in effectual measures to obtain a repeal of the late act of parliament, for blocking up the harbor of Boston.

"That it is the opinion of this meeting, that if the colonies come into a joint resolution to stop all importation from, and exportation to, Great Britain, till the said act be repealed, the same will preserve North America, and her liberties.

"*Resolved*, Therefore, that the inhabitants of this city will join in an association with the several counties of this province, and the principal provinces of America, to put an immediate stop to all exports to Great Britain, and that, after a short day, hereafter to be agreed on, there shall be no imports from Great Britain, till the said . act be repealed, and that such association be on oath.

"That it is the opinion of this meeting, that the gentlemen of the law of this province bring no suit for the recovery of any debt due from any inhabitant of this province, to any inhabitant of Great Britain, until the said act be repealed.

"That the inhabitants of this city will, and it is the opinion of this meeting, that this province ought immediately to break off all trade and dealings with that colony or province, which shall refuse or decline to come into similar resolutions with a majority of the colonies.

"That Messieurs John Hall, Charles Carroll, Thomas Johnson, Jun., William Paca, Matthias Hammond, and Samuel Chase, be a committee for this city to join with those who shall be appointed for Baltimore Town, and other parts of this province, to constitute one general committee; and that the gentlemen appointed for this city immediately correspond with Baltimore Town, and other parts of this province, to effect such association as will secure American liberty."

William Eddis writing to England three days after this meeting said: "all America is in a flame! I hear strange language every day. The colonists are ripe for any measures that will tend to the preservation of what they call their natural liberty. I enclose you the resolves of our citizens; they have caught the general contagion.

"Expresses are flying from province to province. It is the universal opinion here, that the mother country cannot support a contention with these settlements, if they abide strictly to the letter and spirit of their associations."

Several citizens of influence having expressed the opinion, that if the sense of the people had been properly taken, it would not appear that the *whole* of the proceedings of the meeting of the 25th received their approval, the friends of American liberty met the statement by distributing hand-bills, earnestly requesting another general meeting of citizens. The second meeting was held May 27th, when the proceedings of the 28th were fully approved. The opposition, however, did not stop here. On Monday, May 30th, a protest, signed by one hundred and thirty-five citizens, amongst whom were some of the best names of the town and vicinity, made its appearance.

The protest was:

''To The Printers.

                                          May 30th, 1774.

''A publication of the enclosed protest, supported by the names of a considerable number of the inhabitants of the city of Annapolis, will, it is presumed, furnish the most authentic grounds for determining the sense of the majority, on a question of the last importance.

''We, whose names are subscribed, inhabitants of the city of Annapolis, conceive it our clear right, and most incumbent duty, to express our cordial and explicit disapprobation of a resolution which was carried by forty-seven against thirty-one, at the meeting held on the 27th instant.

''The resolution against which we protest, in the face of the world, is the following :

'' 'That it is the opinion of this meeting, that the gentlemen of the law of this province, bring no suit for the recovery of any debt due from any inhabitant of this province, to any inhabitant of Great Britain until the said act be repealed.'—*Dissentient.*

''First—Because we are impressed with a full conviction, that this resolution is founded in treachery and rashness, inasmuch as it is big with bankruptcy and ruin to those inhabitants of Great Britain, who, relying with unlimited security on our good faith and integrity, have made us masters of their fortunes, condemning them *unheard*, for not having interposed their influence with parliament in favor of the town of Boston, without duly weighing the force, with which that influence would probably have operated ; or whether, in their conduct, they were actuated by wisdom and policy, or by *corruption* and *avarice.*

''Secondly—Because whilst the inhabitants of Great Britain are partially despoiled of every legal remedy to recover what is justly due to them, no provision is made to prevent us from being harrassed by the prosecution of internal suits, but our fortunes and persons are left at the mercy of domestic creditors, without a possibility of extricating ourselves, unless by a general convulsion, an event in the contemplation of sober reason, replete with horror.

''Thirdly—Because our credit, as a commercial people, will expire under the wound ; for what confidence can possibly be reposed in those, who shall have exhibited the most avowed and most striking proof that they are not bound by obligations as sacred as human invention can suggest.

''Lloyd Dulany,	Robert Kirkland,
William Cooke,	William Ashton,
James Tilghman,	Robert Morrison,
Anthony Stewart,	Charles Bryan,

William Steuart,
Charles Steuart,
David Steuart,
Jonathan Pinkney.
William Tuck,
Thomas Sparrow,
John Green,
James Brice.
George Gordon.
John Chalmers,
John Anderson,
John Unsworth.
James Taylor.
William Clayton.
George Ranken.
Robert Moor,
Jonathan Parker,
Brite Seleven.
John Varndel,
John Annis.
Robert Ridge.
Robert Nixon.
Thomas Kirby,
Williams Edwards,
Robert Lambert.
William Eddis.
John Clapham,
Elie Vallette,
Robert Buchanan,
William Noke.
James Brooks.
Richard Murrow.
John Brown.
John Hepburn.
Colin Campbell,
Nathaniel Ross,
William Niven,
James Kingsbury,
James Barnes,
John Sands,
James Williams,
Joseph Williams,
John Howard.
William Munroe,
John D. Jaquet,
John Norris,
John Steele,
N. Maccubbin, Shoem.,
Thomas Hammond,
Thomas Pipier,
Thomas Neal,
William Tonry,
James McKenzie,
Nicholas Minsky,

John Haragan.
Hugh Hendly.
Richard Thompson.
Reverdy Ghiselin,
Charles Marckel.
John Randall,
William Stiff.
James Mitchell.
Charles Roberts,
Samuel Skingle.
Thomas Stiff,
Henry Jackson.
William Devinith.
James Hackman.
Charles Barber.
John Evitts.
James Maw.
Jordan Steiger.
Joseph Richards.
Edward Owens.
Thomas Pryse.
J. Wilkinson.
Robert Key.
Lewis Jones.
William Willett.
John King.
William Prew.
Thomas Towson.
William Howard.
John Donaldson.
Daniel Dulany. of Walter.
William Worthington,
Thomas B. Hodgkin.
William Wilkins.
Thomas French.
Joseph Selby.
William Gordon.
Thomas Hyde.
John Maconochie,
Philip Thomas Lee,
John Ball.
Samuel Owens,
Samuel Ball.
Thomas Braithwaite,
James Murray,
Richard Macknbin,
Michael Wallace.
William Hyde,
Nathan Hammond,
Peter Psalter,
Joseph Browning.
Thomas Hincks,
Lewis Neth.
Edward Dogan.

Martin Water,
John Warren.
William Chambers,
James Clarke,
Denton Jacques,
Joseph Dowson,
Thomas Macken,
Richard Burland.
Daniel Dulany, of Dan.,
R. Molleson,
Robert Counden,
William Alkman,
George French,
John Parker,
Archibald Smith,
Thomas Bonner,
Matthias Mae,l
Alex. McDona d,
David Crinnig,
John Thimmis,
David Atchison,
James Maynard,
William Harrison,

J. H. Anderson,
Richard Burt,
Henry Horsley,
Cornelius Fenton,
Richard Addams,
George Ranken. Sr.
Edward Wilmot,
Robert Lang,
George Nicholson,
Benjamin Spriggs,
John Horton,
Charles Wright.
Constantine Bull.
Amos Edmons.
Henry Sibell,
Joshua Cross,
John Woolford,
Samuel H. Howard,
Oliver Weeden,
Alex. Finlater,
Con. McCarty,
Jonathan Simpson.''

A meeting of the committees appointed by the several counties of the province of Maryland, was held at the city of Annapolis, on the 22nd of June, 1774. There were present for Anne Arundel county and the city of Annapolis, Charles Carroll. Esq., barrister. Messrs. B. T. B. Worthington, Thomas Johnson, Jr., Samuel Chase. John Hall, William Paca. Matthias Hammond. Samuel Chew. John Weems, Thomas Dorsey, Rezin Hammond.

The letter and vote of the town of Boston, several letters and papers from Philadelphia and Virginia, the act of parliament for blocking up the port and harbor of Boston, the bill depending in parliament subversive of the charter of the Massachusetts Bay, and that enabling the governor to send supposed offenders from thence t anoother colony or England for trial, were read,—and, after mature deliberations thereon, it was

"*Resolved*, That the said act of parliament, and bills. if passed into acts, are cruel and oppressive invasions of the natural rights of the people of Massachusetts Bay, as men, and of their constitutional rights as English subjects ; and that the said act, if not repealed, and the said bills, if passed into acts, will lay a foundation for the utter destruction of British America, and, therefore, that the town of Boston and the province of Massachusetts are now suffering in the common cause of America.

"*Resolved*, That it is the duty of every colony in America to unite in the most speedy and effectual means to obtain a repeal of the said act, and also of the said bills if passed into acts.''

The third resolution was to the effect to stop all importations from and exportations to Great Britain.

The fourth resolution asserted that this province will join in an association with the principal and neighboring colonies to stop all exportations to, and importations from, Great Britain, to go into effect on some day agreed upon by the colonists.

The fifth resolution instructed the deputies from this province to agree to any restrictions upon exports to the West Indies, deemed necessary by the colonies in the general congress.

The sixth resolution authorized the deputies from this province to admit and provide for the importation of particular articles from Great Britain as are supposed to be indispensable.

The seventh resolution recommended to merchants and vendors of goods not to take advantage of the resolve for non-importation, but to sell their goods at the rate sold within the year previous.

The eighth resolution provided for a subscription for the relief of the inhabitants of Boston.

The ninth resolution expressed thanks to the friends of liberty in Great Britain.

The tenth resolution appointed Matthew Tilghman, Thomas Johnson, Jr., Robert Goldsborough, William Paca, and Samuel Chase, Esq., deputies for this province to attend a general congress, which was recommended to be held on September 20th.

The eleventh resolution asserted that this province will break off trade and dealings with that colony, province, or town, which shall decline the common plan which may be adopted.

The twelfth resolution directed that copies of these resolutions be sent to the Committees of Correspondence, and be published in the Maryland *Gazette*.

The strong, loyal opposition to English measures, existing in Annapolis which cropped out, at this period, has made the ancient city renowned in American history.

The burning of the Peggy Stewart was one of the most remarkable events of the Revolutionary period.

The valor of this extraordinary conduct was heightened by the presence of two local English officers, and a strong English sentiment. Mr. Eddis, the English Custom House officer, quaintly says: "I attended the whole progress of the business, and was active in my exertions to prevent the extremities to which some frantic zealots proceeded."

Mr. Eddis further declares that the owners did not burn their ship willingly, but were forced to destroy it by the citizens.

According to adjournment, the State Convention met on December 8th, and continued to the 12th. There were present 85 members. Mr. John Hall in the chair, Mr. John Duckett, clerk. The proceedings of the Continental Congress were unanimously approved, and it was resolved that every person in the province ought to carry into effect the association agreed on by the Continental Congress, and the most stringent measures were adopted to repress by force the invasion of their rights.

It was now apparent that the dispute between the colonies and the mother country would be settled by an appeal to arms. Annapolis made ready for the conflict. In compliance with the recommendation of the deputies of the several counties of the province, at their convention in June, that the gentlemen, freeholders, and other freemen of this province, as are from sixteen to fifty years of age, form themselves into companies, and to select their officers, a number of the citizens of Annapolis met on December 14th, and chose their officers agreeably to the recommendation. The companies were composed of all ranks of men in the city, gentlemen of the first fortunes being common soldiers.   After one company had been formed the patriotic *Gazette* added :

"It is said that there are a sufficient number of citizens to form another company which it is hoped will be immediately done."

Whilst the people were ardent in their fidelity to the American cause, yet such was their love of liberty and their respect for personal rights, in February, 1775, Mr. Eddis is found urging through the public press, the cause of peace, and the wisdom of retaining their political affiliation with England. The times changed rapidly. In July, of the same year, Mr. Eddis plaintively wrote:

"Government is now almost totally annihilated, and power transferred to the multitude.   Speech is become dangerous : letters are intercepted : confidence betrayed : and every measure evidently tends to the most fatal extremities: the sword is drawn, and, without some providential change of measures, the blood of thousands will be shed in this unnatural contest."

Annapolis, at this time, had two military companies ; in every district in the province the majority of the people were under arms; almost every hat was decorated with a cockade ; and the churlish drum and piping fife were the only music of the times.

At a meeting of the inhabitants of Anne Arundel county and of the city of Annapolis, (those qualified to vote for representatives,) on Wednesday, the ninth day of November, 1774, it was

"*Resolved.* That Thomas Dorsey, John Hood, Jr., John Dorsey, Philip Dorsey, John Burgess, Thomas Lappington, Ephraim Howard, Caleb Dorsey, Richard Stringer, Reubin Merriweather, Charles Warfield, Edward Gaither, Jr., Greenbury Ridgely, Elijah Robinson, Thomas Mayo, James Kelso, Benjamin Howard, Ely Dorsey, Sr., Mark Brown Sappington, Brice T. B. Worthington, Charles Carroll, barrister, John Hall, William Paca, Thomas Johnson, Jr., Matthias Hammond, Samuel Chase, Charles Carroll, of Carrollton, Rezin Hammond, Charles Wallace, Richard Tootell, Thomas Harwood, Jr., John Davidson, John Brice, John Weems, Samuel Chew, Thomas Sprigg, Girard Hopkins, Jr., Thomas Hall, Thomas Harwood, West River, Stephen Steward, Thomas Watkins, Thomas Belt, the third, Richard Green, and Stephen Watkins, be a committee to represent and act for this county and city, to carry into execution the association agreed on by the American Continental Congress, and that any seven have power to act.

"*Resolved.* That Thomas Johnson, Jr., John Hall, William Paca, Charles Carroll, of Carrollton, Matthias Hammond, Samuel Chase, and Richard Tootell, be a committee of correspondence for this county and city, and that any three have power to act.

"*Resolved,* That it is the sense of this meeting, that the gentlemen appointed to represent the county and city, in the late provincial convention, together with Charles Carroll, of Carrollton, ought to attend the next provincial meeting on the 21st inst., and have full power to represent this county and city."

On Friday, the 14th day of October, 1774, the brig *Peggy Stewart,* Captain Jackson, arrived at Annapolis from London, "having on board seventeen packages containing 2,320 pounds of that detestable weed"—the taxed tea. On hearing of its arrival, the Anne Arundel county committee, which took cognizance of such matters, immediately convened. It was then three o'clock in the afternoon. The committee was informed that the brig had been regularly entered that morning, "and the duty on the tea paid to the collector by Mr. Anthony Stewart, one of the owners of said brig." This was fuel to the flame of indignation already kindled ; but, with the law-abiding spirit which is a part of the Maryland character, they did not precipitate matters. but let the question take an orderly solution. Four only of the committee were present. and the remainder, residents of the county, were inaccessible in this emergency. The committee, therefore, called a meeting of the citizens of Annapolis, to be held at five o'clock the same afternoon. As the Provincial Court was in session at Annapolis at the time, a number of persons from Anne Arundel, Baltimore, and other counties. who were in attendance on the court, joined the citizens of Annapolis to answer the question. "What was to be done ?" The assembly proceeded at once to business. The importers, the captain of the brig, and the deputy-collector of the port were called before it and examined. The consignees. Messrs. Thomas C. Williams & Co., sent the following letter, which was read :

"FRIDAY MORNING, 10 o'clock,

OCTOBER 14, 1774.

"This is to inform you that the brig *Peggy Stewart*, Captain Jackson, is just arrived from London, and agreeable to our order of the 14th of May last, have got many goods on board for us. among which are a few chests of tea. Although agreeable to our order, yet it's contrary to our expectation, as we was in great hopes the tea would not have been shipped ; but as it have unluckily come to hand, and are sensible the sale of it, at this time, will be disagreeable to our friends and neighbors. we are, therefore, willing to leave to your determination what is to be done with the said tea, and will readily acquiesce in any measures you may suggest. either in landing and storing it, reshipping it to London, the West Indies. or otherwise."

From the captain of the brig and the deputy-collector, it was learned that the duty on the tea had not been paid. The question was then put, "Shall the tea be landed in America?" It was unanimosly decided in the negative. A committee of twelve persons was appointed to superintend the discharge of the brig's cargo, except the tea, and the meeting adjourned to Wednesday, the 19th.

On the succeeding Monday a proposal was made to the consignees by Charles Carroll, one of the committee. that they should destroy the tea themselves, which he thought would satisfy the people. The consignees readily agreed to this, offering to destroy the tea in any way that was thought proper. But the matter had gone too far for such a settlement to be satisfactory. They rejected the offer ; and in the meantime handbills were industriously circulated through the county, notifying the people of the arrival of the tea. and, requesting them to meet on the following Wednesday. The principal mover in the affair, on the part of the patriots, appears to have been Mr. Matthias Hammond, of whom the consignees complained afterward that he made no mention in said bills "who gave the committee information of the tea being arrived." This intimation that the consignees themselves notified the committee of the arrival of the tea is sustained by the date of their note of Friday "morning at ten o'clock," and by the consenting witness of silence on the part of the committee, who never denied the assertion. This was a doubtful omission by the committee, but it in no respect lessens the honor due the people of Anne Arundel and Annapolis, who were kept in ignorance of the true facts, and saw only in the *Stewart* and her cargo a defiant attempt to infringe their most cherished rights.

By eight o'clock on the morning of Wednesday, Mr. Carroll received a letter from the consignees further explanatory of the arrival of the tea, which was read to the committee on their meeting at ten o'clock. The explanation was that the tea was shipped on an order of the 14th of May previous. The consignees continued: "We, in October, 1773, (as others did), imported tea, that being the first time we ever imported any from Great Britain, and finding it to meet with a ready sale and no objection to its importation, we also, with our neighbors, ordered tea in our spring cargo, which arrived in April and May last; and then (there still being no objection to its importation) we, on the 14th of May, did also order the tea now unfortunately arrived in the *Peggy Stewart*........We did not think till about the beginning of July importation of tea would be stopt........ But soon after August we was convinced that if the tea ordered was shipped it would not be allowed to be landed or the duty paid; and from that time was determined, in case it should arrive to give it up immediately to the disposal of the committee, to do with it what they thought proper. This we told many people before the tea came, which, we believe, Mr. Thos. Harwood and Mr. Hodgsin well remember......... On the arrival of the *Peggy Stewart* here with the tea, we immediately made the committee acquainted therewith, and expressed our readiness to abide by their determination with respect to it; and on Mr. Stewart's application to us for money to pay duty on the same, we absolutely refused it, or doing anything concerning it until the committee had resolved what should be done with it. And we further declare that the vessel was entered at the custom-house and the duty paid without our knowldge or consent."

The consignees expressed their willingness to give the utmost satisfaction, and with a view to mollify the exasperated feelings of the people, declared that they had had no intention to infringe the resolutions entered into by the province of Maryland nor to import tea, nor were they "actuated by any sinister motives either in favor of ministerial power, court, court-party or otherwise." In a subsequent letter to the public, the consignees stated that the committee expressed themselves satisfied with their conduct in the matter, except in regard to the large quantity ordered. This statement was denied in public print by Mr. John Duckett, clerk to the committee.

The payment of the duty on tea, which had been done since the meeting of Friday, was a matter the people could not lightly overlook. The general indignation excited by this act caused Mr. Stewart to publish a card explanatory of his part in transaction. He said: "When the brig arrived, the captain informed me she was very leaky, and that the sooner she was unloaded the better. I told him to enter his vessel, but not the tea, which I found on inquiry of the collector could not be done. Under these circumstances, the brig leaky and fifty three souls on board, where they had been near three months, I thought my self [bound,] both in humanity and prudence, to enter the vessel and leave the destination of the tea to the committee. The impropriety of securing the duty did not then occur to me; neither did I know the tea would be suffered to be lodged as a security for the payment. I had nothing in view but to save the vessel from a seizure, and of having an opportunity of releasing the passengers from a long and disagreeable confinement." Captain Jackson added to this card an affidavit in which he stated that the tea had been put on board the brig in London without his knowledge. Neither card nor affidavit, which had been published in handbill form two days previous to the Wednesday meeting, calmed the popular indignation.

Where the committee's action ended and the people's began, it is difficult to determine, owing to no definite distinction being made as to the respective parts played by each in this curious drama ; but it appears that the committee privately heard the letter of the Messrs. Williams read, then took action upon it, and adjourned to the public meeting where the proceedings following were enacted before a large assembly of people. The first was the reading of the annexed letter signed by Anthony Stewart, Joseph and James Williams, in which it will be seen sentiments were expressed by these gentlemen very different from what they had previously given out. Mr. Stewart and the Messrs. Williams read their recantation. It ran : "We, James Williams, Joseph Wiiliams, and Anthony Stewart, do severally acknowledge that we have committed a most daring insult and act of the most pernicious tendency to the liberties of America ; we, the said Williams, in importing the tea, and said Stewart in paying the duty thereon ; and thereby deservedly incurred the displeasure of the pleople now convened, and all others interested in the preservation of the constitutional rights and liberties of North America, do ask pardon for the same ; and we solemnly declare for the future, that we never will infringe any resolution formed by the people for the salvation of their rights, nor will we do any act that may be injurious to the liberties of the people ; and to show our desire of living in amity with the friends to America, we do request this meeting, or as many choose to attend, to be present at any place where the people shall appoint, and we will there commit to the flames or otherwise destroy as the people may choose, the detestable article which has been the cause of this our misconduct."

The Williamses smarted under this compulsory self-condemnation, and, in the issue of the *Gazette*, of Annapolis, of the 17th of October, justly and bitterly complained of this card as "a most ungenerous piece," which "was drawn up by Matthias Hammond, wherein notwithstanding our candid behaviour, we are most cruelly made liable to the same degree of censure as Mr. Stewart who paid the duty ; which piece was afterward produced, and we were called upon to read and acknowledge in the midst of an incensed people, wholly unacquainted with our conduct in the affair."

The indignation of the people was centered chiefly upon Mr. Stewart, for what they considered his cheerful compliance with the act of Parliament taxing the tea ; and some were very much "disposed to present him with a suit of tar and feathers." A diversity of sentiment sprung up as to what ought to be done. Some contended that the offer to destroy the tea was sufficient reparation ; others favored the destruction of the vessel that had brought "the detestable weed" to American shores. A division took place on the question. "Whether the vessel should, or should, not be destroyed?" It was carried in the negative by a large majority.

The citizens of Annapolis generally were averse to using violence ; but the minority, mainly persons from a distance, some of great influence in their respective neighborhoods, avowed their determination to collect a body of men to accomplish the destruction of the *Stewart*. At this juncture, under the advice of Charles Carroll, of Carrollton, Mr. Stewart offered "to destroy the vessel with his own hands." The proposal was gladly accepted. The people assembled in crowds at the water-side to witness the conflagration. Mr. Stewart and the Messrs. Williams the former accompanied by several gentlemen to protect him from personal violence, repaired to the brig. Her sails were set, and. with her colors flying, she was run aground on the shore between the Gas-House and the northwestern wall of the Naval Academy. It was brought up to this point that Mrs. Stewart, the invalid wife of the owner of the vessel could see the conflagration. from the window of her residence, the house on Hanover street, now occupied by Mr. Charles S. Welch. Mr. Stewart applied the match to the vessel, and, as an offering and atonement to the offended people and an open defiance to the Crown, the *Peggy Stewart* and the obnoxious tea-chests were, in a few hours, reduced to ashes.

The adjourned meeting of provincial deputies, chosen by several of the counties in Maryland, was held at the city of Annapolis, Nov. 21, 1774, and continued by adjournment to Friday, the 25th day of the same month at which fifty-seven deputies were present.

Mathew Tilghman was chosen chairman and John Duckett, clerk.

The delegates appointed to represent the province at the late continental congress, laid the proceedings of the congress before the meeting which being read and considered, were unanimously approved of.

Not only in words and sounds of war did the inhabitants of Anne Arundel show their intention to defend their rights, but when opportunity offered they put in practice the faith that was in them.

July 18th, 1775, "the ship *Totness*, captain Harding, belonging to Mr. Gildard, of Liverpool, having on board a cargo of salt and dry goods, in coming up the bay, ran aground near the three Islands at the mouth of West river ; upon this the committee immediately met, and after consideration, determined she should proceed on to Baltimore, her intended port, but before she could get off, highly resenting so daring an infringement of the continental association, a number of people met, went on board, and set her on fire."

There were opponents of these proceedings even among those who espoused the patriot cause. They had condemned the burning of the Peggy Stewart and also this, "the second burnt-offering to liberty within this province." But revolutions are not handicapped by a minority of dissenting voices.

Early on the morning of Wednesday, September 27th, Annapolis was alarmed by the beating of drums, and a proclamation for the inhabitants to assemble at the Liberty Tree. The object of the meeting was to secure the passage of the resolution : "That all persons who had refused to sign the association, and comply with the other requisitions should be obliged to quit the city, as enemies to the essential interests of America." This was in opposition to the proceedings of the convention, and the resolution was easily defeated. A report, about this time, that a British ship of war was to be ordered to the port of Annapolis caused many families to quit the city, and others think of removing. At a meeting of the citizens, it was unanimously resolved : "If a vessel, belonging to his Majesty, should be stationed in our harbor to supply the same with every necessary, at a reasonable price, and cautiously to avoid any cause of contention with the officers or the crew." An address was also prepared to be delivered to the Governor, expressing the same pacific sentiments and asking him to convey the same to the commander of any ship that may be ordered on this duty.

Private correspondence, in the latter part of 1775, began to be examined by the provincial authorities, for here in Annapolis was set up the novelty of a dual government—the King's officers on the one hand, and the local and general committees of public safety on the other—living harmoniously together, but so far as the King's representatives were concerned very much like the fox when invited to the stork's supper.

Annapolis became daily more and more deserted ; some families leaving because of apprehensions of a bombardment ; others on account of the distressing times, bad markets, and a general scarcity of money ; even tradesmen and mechanics quitted their habitations, and retired from the vicinity of navigable waters. Agriculture was neglected, the voice of peaceful industry was hushed, and military science became the universal study of the hour.

At a meeting of the deputies from the counties of Maryland, at Annapolis, on May 24, 1775, there were present 100 men.bers. The Hon. Matthias Tilghman being in the chair, and Gabriel Duvall, clerk, the following resolutions were adopted :

"Resolved, That we acknowledge King George the third, as our lawful sovereign.

"Resolved, That all exportation to the provinces in British possession be prohibited until further orders from the Continental Congress.

"Resolved, That the formation of militia be continued, and subscription for the same be levied by the several counties."

Loyalty to the King, legions for the people, voted in the same breath !

A meeting of the committee of observation for Anne Arundel county and city of Annapolis, was held on the 14th day of June, 1775, in Annapolis, Mr. Charles Wallace, chairman. Its proceedings show how vigilant the people were to maintain inviolate the regulations adopted for their defence.

A charge having been made on oath, that Thomas Chipchase, of the city, butcher, on the 23d day of May last, had killed several lambs, he was ordered to attend. He appeared, and confessed the fact, alleging, in excuse, that he understood that there was no absolute prohibition by the continental congress, and that the scarcity of provisions at that time would plead for him, and what he did was from a a desire of supplying the many strangers in town. But as he had since been informed that such procedure was contrary to a resolve of the provincial convention, he would take care to offend in that manner no more, and hoped the committee would forgive him. The sense of the committee being taken on the above, they declared it a breach of the resolve of the provincial convention, respecting the killing of lambs ; but, all circumstances considered, they were of opinion he ought to be forgiven.

It will still further be seen by the following, as well as by other instances quoted, that the committee of observation of Anne Arundel county and the city of Annapolis, was no idle form, but it was vigilant in searching out offences, and inexorable in their punishment.

On the 28th day of June, Capt. Charles Henzell, of the ship Adventure, informed the committee of his arrival with goods on board, cleared for Maryland, his cargo consisting of two hundred dozen porter, one hundred pipes in packs, 2,000 weight of cheese, and forty-two chaldron of coals, Winchester measure—also about seventy passengers, including servants. The captain testified on oath that unfavorable winds prevented landing at Madeira, where he intended to sell his goods. The committee refused to allow him to land his goods, but gave him permission to land his passengers. Those of the committee who were present, were Charles Carroll, of Carrollton, Matthias Hammond, John Bullen, Charles Wallace, John Allen Quinn, John Brice, and Dr. Richard Fostell—Charles Carroll, of Carrollton, presiding, and G. Duvall, Clerk.

At a convention of the people of Maryland, July 26, 1775, at Annapolis, a temporary form of government was established, which endured until the constitution of 1851 was adopted. While other States had acted by the advice of Congress in establishing similar forms of government, Maryland moved solely by its own volition. Charles Carroll, of Carrollton, and Charles Carroll, barrister, were members of the Committee of Safety under its first organization, from Annapolis.

At a meeting of a number of the inhabitants of Anne Arundel county and city of Annapolis, at said city, on Sept. 12. 1775;

Present, eight members of the late Convention:

Charles Carroll, barrister, in the chair, Gabriel Duvall, clerk, it was

"Resolved, That Samuel Chase, Thomas Johnson, John Hall, William Paca, B. T. B. Worthington, Matthias Hammond, Charles Carroll, barrister, Charles Carroll, of Carrollton, Capt. William Hyde, Rezin Hammon, John Bullen, Capt. Richard Fostell, John Weems, Joseph Galloway, Stephen Stewart, John Thomas, Thom. Tillard. Marmaduke Wyvill, Thomas Watkin's, son, Thomas Dorsey, John Dorsey, son of Michael, Edward Gaither, Jun., Caleb Dorsey, Richard Stringer, Dr. Chas. Alexander Warfield, John Burgess, John Davis, Benjamin Howard, Elijah Robinson, and Thomas Hammond, or any seven or more of them be, and they are here by appointed a committee of observation for this county for a term of one year.

"Resolved, That Charles Carroll, barrister, Thomas Johnson, Jun., Samuel Chase, William Paca and Charles Carroll, of Carrollton, Esq., or any three or more of them, be delegates to represent this county in convention for the said term of one year."

In committee, Annapolis, Wednesday, 13th of September it was

"Resolved, That Charles Carroll, of Carrollton, Brice T. B. Worthington, Capt. William Hyde, Matthias Hammond, Dr. Richard Fostell, John Bullen, and John Thomas, be a committee to license suits in this county during the term of one year.

"Resolved, That Charles Carroll, of Carrollton. B. T. B. Worthington, Capt. William Hyde, Matthias Hammond, and Dr. Richard Fostell be a committee of correspondence for this county for the said term of one year.

"That the parliamentary post be prohibited, and that this resolution be strictly enforced by the several committees of observation.

"That no vessel leave this province without a license from this convention, neither shall any skipper carry any person, or letter, without giving previous notice, though this does not apply to vessels going up the Potomac, or the passage of the Pocomoke ferry."

On December 28, an evidence of the zeal of the convention, was given by the publication by their order of a well established process for making crude nitre.

On January 21st, 1776, the Council of Safety, "Resolved, That Messrs. Lancelot Jacques, Charles Wallace, William Hyde, Allen Quynn, James Brice, William Whetcroft, and Beriah Marybury, or any three of them, be requested to make a chart of the land and water at the mouths of this river, specifying the width and depth of the channel between Horn Point and Greenbury's Point, and some distance without and within the same."

This chart, returned on the 16th of March following, has been lost. The convention of Maryland appropriated £5,900 to fortify Annapolis. The Council of Safety desired a larger sum, suggesting that, with an increased appropriation, batteries might be erected on Greensbury's and Wind Mill Points, and other places, between those locations and Annapolis, that would prevent men of war from approaching Annapolis. The council was thereupon given leave to draw on the treasury for whatever sums it might deem necessary to complete the fortifications and to build a number of "row-gallies or gondolas."

Fortifications were erected on Horn Point, Beaman's Hill, and Wind Mill Point, besides several breast works were thrown up at other places. They were finished with great celerity, under the direction of Messrs. James Brice, John Bullen, Charles Wallace, William Wilkins, Beriah Marybury, John Brice, John Campbell, Joshua Frazier and Allen Quynn.

Whilst these preparations were made to receive the expected men-of-war, the public mind, by dwelling upon the subject, became unusually alert to credit alarming reports. On the fifth of March, about eight in the evening, information was received, that a ship of war was on her passage up the bay, and no distance from the city.

"The consternation," says Mr. Eddis, who was present, "occasioned be this information, exceeds description. The night was tempestuous ; extremely dark ; and the rain descended in torrents ; notwithstanding which, many persons began to remove their effects ; and the streets were quickly crowded with carriages, laden with furniture and property of various kinds. A little reflection must have made it evident, that, without violent provocation, hostilities would not have commenced : and, at all events, that timely notice would have been given, previous to any bombardment. It ought to have been considered, that a governor, acting under the authority of Great Britain, was resident in the town, and, apparently, exercising the powers with which he was invested. No complaint had been transmitted, on his part, relative to the treatment experienced by him, and the adherents of the administration. His prudent and consistent conduct had greatly tended to prevent personal outrages, and under such circumstances, it was
12

manifest, that no commander in his Majesty's service, could have formed the most distant idea of proceeding to extremities, without communicating his intentions to the supreme magistrate, who was undoubtedly a valuable pledge in the hands of the people, to secure themselves and property from immediate violence.

"But as reason seldom operates under instantaneous impressions, the Governor resolved to pursue every eligible method that might effectually remove the apprehensions so universally entertained. Actuated by such motives, he made immediate application to the Council of Safety, and, in order to dissipate the general anxiety, proposed sending a flag of truce on board his Majesty's ship, the instant she made her appearance, or came to an anchor off the harbor. An offer, so evidently tending to preserve the public tranquility, was accepted with every suitable acknowledgment; and, on the seventh instant, a ship of war, accompanied by a tender, passed by Annapolis. I had the honour to be deputed to perform this service; on which occasion I thought it necessary, in order to obviate any misrepresentation, to transcribe; as follows, the substance of my negotiation, for the inspection of the Governor, the Council of Safety, and the Committee of Observation.

FRIDAY, March 8th.

"By order of his Excellency the Governor, and, with the approbation of the president of the Council of Safety, I repaired yesterday on board his Majesty's sloop, the Otter, commanded by Captain Squire, then lying at anchor in Chesapeake Bay, between Magothy River and the Bodkin; and delivered to him a letter from the Governor, to which a satisfactory answer was returned, and immediately made known, for the general information of the citizens of Annapolis."

Whilst one part of the people were alarmed at the approach of the man-of-war, which proved to be the sloop of war Otter, Capt. Squire, and two tenders, the necessary disposition of troops was made to receive the enemy in case he thought proper to land, and expresses were dispatched to Baltimore and other parts of the province to communicate the presence of the foe. The Otter continued up Magothy River where she took a ship loaded with wheat and flour, and several other prizes. These, whilst in charge of the Otter's tenders, were subsequently recaptured by the Defence, Capt. Nicholson, the Otter standing by and not offering assistance to her consorts.

Mr. Eddis gives a clear insight into the inner life of Annapolis at this interesting period. May 20, 1776, he wrote to England from Annapolis:

"In consequence of residing with the governor, I expected an exemption from any penalties inflicted on persons, who had refused to associate or enrol. But in this idea I was very materially mistaken. The committee of observation will not consider me as a member of his excellency's household; alleging in support of their opinion, that I hold offices immediately dependent on the province. These are not times to dispute nice points. I have therefore paid ten pounds for my fine, and have taken a receipt for the same. My arms have likewise been demanded. I am, however, happy to inform you, that I have constantly been treated with kind attention, even by political opponents. It is my endeavour to regulate my conduct with propriety; carefully avoiding mixed company ; taking heed that 'I offend not with my tongue ;' and not permitting my pen to expatiate on the tendency of public transactions.   I intrust this to the care of a friend, bound to Lisbon ; may it safely reach you !''

The Council of Safety, fearing that the large number of slaughter-houses then in Annapolis, would engender disease, adopted on July 22d, the following :

"*Whereas*, it hath been represented to the Council of Safety by physicians and others, that the intolerable stench arising from slaughter-houses and spreading hides to dry in the city of Annapolis, may be productive of pestilential disorders and ill consequences to the troops and others residing in the said city : Therefore, ordered, that no butcher or other person shall, after the 26th of this instant, presume to slaughter bullocks, mutton, or any kind of meat, or put up green hides to cure within the limits of said city for and during the terms of three months, thence next ensuing.''

On the 18th of December, several of the citizens of Annapolis having received letters demanding their immediate departure from the city, and the Council of Safety being informed thereof, expressed its sense of the illegality of such a measure, by the following proceedings :

"*In Council of Safety, December* 19, 1776.

"We are called upon by the duty of our station to take notice of the powers assumed by some persons yesterday evening in ordering divers of the inhabitants of the city of Annapolis into banishment, without any cause assigned, by cards transmitted them. We are of opinion such cards are contrary to our association, flying in the face of the resolves of congress and convention, and against the letter and spirit of our declaration of rights. The peace of the State ought and must be preserved, and all offenders brought before the proper judicatures for trial. Therefore we earnestly recommend to all associators and other well disposed persons to discourage such extra judicial and disorderly proceedings, tending in their consequences to prejudice the common cause, and to the destruction of order and regular government.''

On the 23d of the same month, the Council of Safety transacted the following :

" *Whereas*, we have received information that on Wednesday, 18th day of this instant, (December) in the evening, cards were delivered to sundry persons in the city of Annapolis, to the following effect :

" 'You are hereby ordered to depart this city to-morrow, 9 o'clock.
Signed, J. WEEMS.

" 'In behalf of Anne Arundel county :' ''

"Which cards we are informed were delivered by Stephen Stewart, Junior, the Council of Safety having taken the same into consideration, are of opinion that such cards are contrary to the resolves of congress and convention, and against the 21st section of the declaration of rights, which asserts

"That no freeman ought to be taken or imprisoned, or deprived of his freehold, liberties, or privileges, or outlawed, or exiled, or in any manner destroyed, or deprived of his life, liberty or property, but by the judgment of his peers or by the law of the land.''

"Ordered, therefore, that the said John Weems and Stephen Stewart, Junior, attend the Council of Safety on the thirtieth day of De-

cember, to shew by what authority the said cards were so made out
and delivered."

On the 39th of December, Colonel John Weems and Stephen Stewart, Junior, accordingly appeared before the Council of Safety, and
acknowledged that they had been active in making out and delivering
the cards mentioned in the order of the board, and having promised
that they would not intermeddle in the same manner again, but would
leave all persons to be dealt with according to the law of the land,
they were dismissed by the council, on condition that they pay the
messenger his fees.

Annapolis, the centre of State Government, felt every throb of the
revolution. Here most of the political movements and martial
preparations in the State had their initiative. Its people were strained
to the utmost tension of excitement and were sullen and inimical to
those who did not share their patriotic sentiments though always
keeping within those bounds that courage and principle outline for
the conduct of brave men against an enemy in their power.

On July 6, 1776, the Maryland Convention then in session at Annapolis issued the following :

ANNAPOLIS, *July* 6th, 1776.

"A Declaration of the Delegates of Maryland.

"To be exempt from parliamentary taxation, and to regulate their
internal government and polity, the people of this colony have ever
considered as their inherent and unalienable right : without the
former, they can have no property ; without the latter, no security
for their lives or liberties.

"The parliament of Great Britian has of late claimed an uncontrollable right of binding these colonies in all cases whatsoever, to
force an unconditional submission to' this claim the legislative and
executive powers of that state have invariably pursued, for these ten
years past, a studied system of oppression, by passing many impolitic,
severe, and cruel acts for raising a revenue from the colonists, by de-
priving them in many cases of trial by jury, by altering the chartered
constitution of one colony, and the entire stoppage of the trade of its
capital, by cutting off all intercourse between the colonies, by restraining them from fishing on their own coasts, by extending the limits of,
and erecting, an arbitrary government in the province of Quebec, by
confiscating the property of the colonists taken on the seas, and com-
pelling the crews of their vessels, under the pain of death, to act
against their native country and dearest friends, by declaring all
seizures, detention, or destruction of the persons, or property of the
colonists, to be legal and just.

"A war, unjustly commenced, hath been prosecuted against the
united colonies with cruelty, outrageous violence, and perfidy : slaves,
savages, and foreign mercenaries have been meanly hired to rob a people of their property, liberty, and lives : a people guilty of no other
crime than deeming the last of no estimation without the secure
enjoyment of the former. Their humble and dutiful petitions for
peace, liberty, and safety have been rejected with scorn : secure of,
and relying on, foreign aid, not on his national forces, the unrelenting monarch of Britian hath, at length, avowed by his answer to the
city of London, his determined and inexorable resolution of reducing
these colonies to abject slavery.

"Compelled by dire necessity, either to surrender our properties, liberties, and lives, into the hands of a British king and parliament, or to use such means as will most probably secure to us and our posterity those invaluable blessings.

"We, the delegates of Maryland, in convention assembled, do declare, that the king of Great Britian has violated his compact with this people, and that they owe no allegiance to him. We have, therefore thought it just and necessary to empower our deputies in congress to join with a majority of the united colonies in declaring them free and independent States, in framing such other confederacy between them, in making foreign alliances, and in adopting such other measures as shall be judged necessary for the preservation of their liberties: provided the sole and exclusive right of regulating the internal polity and government of this colony be reserved to the people thereof. We have also thought proper to call a new convention, for the purpose of establishing a government in this colony. No ambitious views, no desire of independence, induce the people of Maryland to form an union with the other colonies. To procure an exemption from parliamentary taxation and to continue to the legislatures of these colonies the sole and exclusive right of regulating their internal polity, was our original and only motive.

"To maintain inviolate our liberties, and to transmit them unimpaired to posterity, was our duty and first wish: our next, to continue connected with, and dependent on Great Britain. For the truth of these assertions, we appeal to that Almighty Being who is emphatically styled the searcher of hearts, and from whose omniscience nothing is concealed. Relying on his divine protection and assistance, and trusting to the justice of our cause, we exhort and conjure every virtuous citizen to join cordially in defence of our common rights, and in maintenance of the freedom of this and her sister colonies."*

At a meeting of the associators of the city of Annapolis, on Thursday, the 11th of July, 1776, WILLIAM ROBERTS, Esq., Chairman, and Jno. Duckett, Clerk, it was

"1st Resolved, That it is the duty of every inhabitant of the city of Annapolis, and all persons having property therein, to contribute every assistance in their power for the protection and defence of the city and the inhabitants thereof, and that Mr. James Brice, Mr. John Bullen, Mr. Charles Wallace, Mr. William Wilkins, Mr. Beriah Maybury, Mr. John Brice and Mr. John Campbell, or a majority of them, or of any three or more of them, be a committee to act on behalf of the inhabitants of this city, and that they wait on the Council of Safety, and inform them that the inhabitants will afford every assistance in their power for putting the city into the best posture of defence: and that the inhabitants will, in person, or by others employed at their expense, labour on any intrenchments or works, which the council shall think necessary.

"2d. Resolved, That the said committee be empowered to call on every person, having property therein, to labor in person, or to furnish some person to labor in his stead, at such time and place as the committee shall think proper, on the works as may be ordered by the Council of Safety, to be erected for the defence of the city.

* Annals of Annapolis, p. 177.

"3d. Resolved, That the said committee be authorized to execute all matters which may be recommended by the Council of Safety, for the defence of the city, or for keeping the peace and good order therein.

"4th. Resolved, That no member of this meeting will, and that it is the opinion of meeting that no inhabitant of the city of Annapolis ought, to buy from or employ, any merchant, tradesman, or any other person who hath not subscribed the association.

"5th. Resolved, That application be made by the committee to the Council of Safety not to employ in the public service any non-associator, and that they be requested to give a preference to such tradesmen and others have manifested their attachment and zeal to the liberties of America.

"Ordered, That copies of the above resolutions be transmitted by the chairman to the associators of Baltimore town for their opinion and concurrence.

"Ordered, That the names of the non-associators in this city be published and distributed among the inhabitants.

"Resolved, That this meeting be adjourned to the 10th day of August next, and that the committee have power to call a meeting at any time before, if they shall think proper.

"True copy of the proceedings,

"Test:—JNO. DUCKETT, Clerk."†

July 10th, six companies of the first battalion of Maryland troops, stationed at Annapolis, and commanded by Col. Wm. Smallwood, embarked for the head of Elk in high spirits, and three companies of the same battalion, stationed in Baltimore town, embarked the same day for the same place, from thence they were to proceed to Philadelphia.

[1777.] In the latter part of June, 1776, Gov. Eden left Annapolis; but Mr. Eddis and another English officer continued to discharge their duties to May 30th, 1777, eleven months after the Declaration of Independence, when they were given a most "ample and honorable discharge from that employment." June 7th, Mr. Eddis took leave with a distressed mind of a few faithful friends in Annapolis, and set sail for England.

March 5th, Martha, wife of George Washington, passed through Annapolis, on her way northward.

On Friday, March 21st, 1777, Thomas Johnson, the first republican governor of Maryland, was proclaimed the executive of the State at the State house, in the presence of a great concourse of people "all of whom expressed the highest pleasure in the proceedings."

The procession began at the assembly house, and proceeded in the following order, to wit:

High Sheriff.
The Hon. the President of the Senate.
Senators.
Governor.
Council.
Sergeant at Arms with the Mace.
The Hon. the Speaker of the House of Delegates.
Delegates.

Mayor of the city and Recorder.
Aldermen.
Common Council.
Military Officers.
Gentlemen Strangers.
Citizens.

Silence being commanded, the high sheriff then proclaimed the governor.

On the signal three vollies of small-arms from the soldiers, who were paraded in front of the State house, and thirteen cannons were fired.

The procession then returned as follows:

High Sheriff.
His Excellency the Governor.
The Council.
The Hon. the President of the Senate.
Senators.
The Sergeant at Arms with his Mace.
The Hon. the Speaker of the House of Delegates.
Delegates.
Mayor and Recorder of the city.
Aldermen.
Common Council.
Military Officers·
Gentlemen Strangers.
Citizens.

and repaired to the coffee-house, where an entertainment was provided, the field officers of the army and strangers the.. in town being all present.

After dinner the following toasts were drank .

1. Perpetual union and friendship between the States of America.
2. The freedom and independency of the American States.
3. Prosperity to Maryland.
4. The Congress.
5. General Washington and the American army.
6. The American navy.
7. The arts and sciences.
8. Agriculture.
9. Trade and navigation.
10. The friends of liberty throughout the world.
11. The memory of the brave patriots who have fallen in the cause of America.
12. General Lee and our other friends in captivity.
13. Wisdom and unanimity in the councils of America, and undaunted courage in her forces to execute her measures.

The whole concluded with an elegant ball in the evening.

A matross, belonging to one of the companies stationed here, getting in the smoke before one of the cannons, just as it was fired, unhappily lost his life.

About 9 A. M., on Thursday, the 21st of August, a considerable number of British men of war, transports and other vessels, passed the mouth of the Severn, and stood up the bay. Immediately after the fleet had passed Annapolis, Governor Johnson issued a proclamation calling on all the county lieutenants, field and other officers of the militia of Maryland, of the United States, to march at least, two full companies of each battalion at once, to the neighborhood of the Susquehanna River, in Cecil and Harford counties. He concluded his proclamation : "To defend our liberties, requires our exertions : our wives, our children, and our country, implore our assistance : motives amply sufficient to arm every one who can be called a man." The Governor was encouraged in his patriotic efforts by information that the Eastern Shore militia were collecting in great numbers, determined to make the most obstinate resistance against the invasion of the State.

The British fleet proceeded to Turkey Point, on Elk River, near which the British army, under Sir William Howe, was quartered.

October 9. Samuel Chase and John Brice, Esq., were chosen to represent this city in the General Assembly—the first gentleman declining to serve, Allen Quynn, Esq., was elected.

[1778.] Early in 1778, Count Pulaski's legion of cavalry and infantry, raised partly in this State, was organized at Annapolis. The corps suffered severely in New Jersey the same year, and the next lost their heroic leader in Georgia.

Allen Quynn and Samuel Chase were elected this year delegates from Annapolis to the Legislature.

The *Gazette*, in consequence of the high price of provisions, raised its subscription to five pounds per annum.

During this year, a considerable number of citizens of Annapolis, assembled in meeting, Charles Carroll, of Carrollton, in the chair, and passed resolutions that a certain Mr. John Lawrence of the State of Pennsylvania, "ought to depart the city and not return without permission of the Governor and Council," for having made threats of violence and attempted to put them in execution against Governor Johnson, for carrying into operation against him a law that looked to the ascertainment of the fact, or not, if the person has taken the oath of fealty required by this State, and to require him to take the one prescribed by Maryland, or be fined, imprisoned, or returned to his own State. Mr. Carroll, Mr. Jenning, Mr. Brice, Mr. Davidson, and Mr. Paca were appointed a committee to present the respective parties with the meaning of the resolution. On the certificate of the ill-health of Mr. Lawrence by Dr. Murray, he was allowed to remain in the city until he could be removed with safety.

The Legislature which adjourned December 30th, passed an act to enable the corporation of the city of Annapolis to sell certain lands, to lay a further tax on property, within the said city and its precincts, to regulate and license ordinaries and retailers of spirituous liquors within the said city and precincts thereof.

[1780.] The *Gazette* of January 28th, 1780, reduced by the war to a half sheet, said "several persons have gone from this to Poplar Island, Rock-Hall, and Baltimore-Town, on the ice, and are crossing to and from Kent Island every day, which has not been known before by our oldest inhabitants, nor has the like ever happened, we believe, since the memory of man."

On the 4th of February, the *Gazette* office was burned. The printers returned their sincere thanks ' to their fellow-citizens for their assistance on that unhappy occasion, and in a particular manner to those, whose exertions preserved their goods and rescued their dwelling-house from the flames.''

An elaborate discussion, by means of communications in the *Gazette*, took place in the early part of this year upon the question of confiscating the property of British subjects. It was participated in by a number of correspondents under various signatures such as "A Senator," "Publicola," "A Plebian," "A Sentry," and "A Native of North-Britain." To show the warmth, with which the contest was carried on, the following is extracted from a communication published under date of February 27th:

"It is justly alarming to see principles like the Senator's (the Senator defended the action of the Senate in not agreeing to the House Act to confiscate the property in question.) spread in a free country, when two years ago, if any man had talked in that manner, he would as soon have dared to put himself in the fire, and be tarred and feathered, especially a member of our assembly. Good God! What is this State come to, to be the subjects of Great Britain? and we cannot take the property of our enemies to pay our taxes when, if it was in their power, they would take our lives. It is time for men to trim and make fair weather on both sides; but I can say this, though I cannot write, I can think; and I have borne a firelock; and I can say it is *toryism*. The Plebian is the echo of his voice, and the hot-bed of a furnace in all diabolical plots and conspiracies. God deliver this country from them. I am, your humble servant, a SENTRY, ELK RIDGE, FEBRUARY 27, 1780.''

In the same paper, "*A Native of North-Britain*," exhibited in himself the great personal liberty enjoyed in this intensely patriotic commonwealth by writing under date of February 28, and saying that by the bill of rights of this county "we are still the subjects of Britain, and under the realm of that kingdom;" and remarks that "it would be a great force put on any who have come to my time of day, to cast off their native country." He naively adds: "I would give the best coat on my back to see a termination of the dispute." Whether it was the debate or the Revolution itself, for which this handsome sacrifice would be made, is not known.

"*A Maryland Officer*," under the same date as the above says: "The Senator, I take to be a scary fellow. * * * France and Spain will not suffer us to confiscate British property! I would see France and Spain to——before they should hinder us from doing what is right. * * * Was I of the legislative body I would have him cashiered for his mean spiritedness. He may do well enough in private life, but I'll be——, if he is fit to wear a commission in a public station.''

Notwithstanding the wide margin the editor allowed for doubtful personal epithets, it seems that even his doubtful taste was put to a great strain, for, in the issue of March 3rd, he says: "SCOEVOLA to the Senator, contains several questionable passages, and will be returned to the author." "VINDEX is likewise too personal and cannot be published." For the most part, however, it seems the discussion was carried on in a proper, though animated, spirit.

Major-General Nathaniel Greene and Major-General Baron De Steuben, with their suites, arrived in Annapolis on Wednesday, November 7th, 1780, on their way southward, the former to relieve General Gates of the command of the Southern Troops.

'On the 8th of September, 1780, the news of Baron De Kalb's death reached Annapolis. He died from wounds received at the battle of Camden, South Carolina. DeKalb was leading his troops, his beloved Marylanders, in a vigorous attack, when he fell pierced with eleven wounds. Col. DuBuysson his aid-de-camp, embraced him, and, announcing his rank and nationality to the encircling foes, begged them to spare his life. The gallant Englishmen responded with a soldier's answer to the generous comrade, who, in protecting his General, received several dangerous wounds, and who, with DeKalb, was taken prisoner. Although the brave officer received the most considerate attention from his captors, he died in a few days. His latest moments were spent in dictating a letter declaring his warmest affection for the officers and soldiers of his command; of the intense pleasure it gave him to hear from British officers the bravery of his troops; of his own admiration of the heroic stand they made against superior numbers, after being forsaken by the remainder of the army; of the unmeasured delight he experienced from the gallant conduct of the Delaware regiment and the companies of artillery of his command, and of the affectionate regard he entertained for his entire division.

The citizens of Annapolis particularly mourned DeKalb; for his manly virtues, exhibited whilst he sojourned in the city recruiting his troops together with his patriotic conduct, had greatly endeared him to them.

Congress, from a deep sense of gratitude for his gallant services, in October, 1780, "Resolved, That a monument be erected, to the memory of the late major-general, the Baron DeKalb, in the city of Annapolis, in the State of Maryland." with the following inscription:

"Sacred to the memory of
The Baron DeKalb,
Knight of the royal order of military merit,
Brigadier of the armies of France,
and
Major-general in the service of the United
States
of America.
Having served with honour and reputation for three years,
He gave a last and glorious proof of his
attachment to the liberties of mankind,
and the cause of America,
In the action near Camden, in the State of
South Carolina,
on the 16th August, 1780:
Where, leading on the troops of the Maryland
and
Delaware lines, against superior numbers,
and animating them by his example to deeds
of valour,
He was pierced with many wounds and
on the 19th following expired, in the 48th year
of his age,
The Congress of the United States of America,
in gratitude to his zeal, services and merit,
have erected this monument."

This debt of one hundred years standing was paid by the Congress of 1883, and on the 16th of August, 1886, the statue of DeKalb, by Ephraim Keyser, was unveiled with appropriate ceremonies.

[1781.] In March, 1781, Annapolis was blockaded by the Hope and the Monk, British sloops of war. These prevented the French troops from reaching the Head of Elk. La Fayette found on arriving at Annapolis, the people greatly alarmed at the proximity of the British vessels, and very anxious to retain the French troops in the city. Meanwhile La Fayette contemplated making a land march to the Elk ; but wagons and horses were scarce and a trip that could be made in a day by boat, promised to consume ten days by the frequent ferriages across the mouths of rivers. The brave soldier obtained a small sloop and on it placed two 18-pounders, and, with this ridiculously unequal force, under Commodore Nicholson, sallied forth to meet the foe.

The little sloop that had excited the contempt of some of the timorous citizens, accompanied by another vessel, alarmed the British so that after several manœuvers they dropped so far down the Bay, that La Fayette was enabled to embark with this army.

On July, 18, 1781, a meeting of the citizens of Annapolis was held Charles Wallace in the chair, George Ranken clerk, to take into consideration the late law of the general assembly, for the emission of two hundred thousand pounds, to defray the expenses of the present campaign ; and the subscription and association recommended by the legislature, to support the credit and value of said emission—it was among other things, resolved by the said meeting—that, as sufficient means could not be raised to carry on war by taxes—that the emitting of bills of credit was necessary, and deemed it to be the duty, and real interest of every citizen of the State—who was determined to prosecute the war in defence of his property and liberty, to exert every effort to support, the value of the said bills of credit, at par with gold and silver—and that every man ought to associate to receive the said bills at par.

James Brice, Jeremiah T. Chase, Allen Quynn, Frederick Green, Nicholas Maccubbin, Jr., Samuel H. Howard, and Thomas Harwood, Esqrs , were appointed a committee, to attend to the conduct of associators, and to see that none of them violated their faith and honour, by wilfully depreciating the said bills of credit—and that they should publish the name of any such offender, who should be deemed infamous, and that to deal or associate thereafter with such an one, should be considered as dishonourable. That the credit of the paper money depended solely on public opinion, and must receive its value from the association of the principal merchants and inhabitants of Baltimore town, and the principal farmers in the several counties—all of whom were earnestly recommended to receive it at par with specie.

The scenes at Annapolis at this period were well calculated to excite the populace to the utmost of patriotic resolve. At one day's notice twenty three hundred militia assembled at Annapolis from Baltimore to meet an expected attack of the British fleet, regiment after regiment of that glorious old Maryland line was recruited at Annapolis and sent to the front. French frigates sentinelled the mouth of the Severn, and thousands of French auxiliaries passed through the city towards Yorktown.

The British fleet, however, August 1781, passed up York River, and landed the British troops at York and Gloucester.

On the 28th of August, the third Maryland Regiment, Lieut. Col. Peter Adams, commanding, marched from Annapolis to join the Southern army. This regiment was recruited here, and had all the appearance of a veteran corps. They were enlisted for three years, and were well equipped for the field. The friendships, engendered by the agreeable social relations between officers and citizens, whilst the recruiting was in progress, made the departure of the regiment one of general regret. The ardor of the soldiers on the prospect of meeting the enemy, and the martial appearance of the regiment inspired the sincerest anticipations that the Third would render marked service to their country and prove an honor to its State. It did not disappoint the hopes it had created—but these Maryland troops proved, as they had the instincts of gentlemen at home, they possessed the mettle of soldiers in the field.

The recruiting service at Annapolis was under the direction of that intrepid soldier, Major-General Smallwood, whose distinguished qualities on the field, especially fitted him for this important part of the service. He gave it his unremitting attention.

On the 7th of September, ten days after the Third, the Fourth Maryland Regiment, Major Alexander Roxburg, marched from Annapolis to join La Fayette. The Regiment numbered 600 men, its full complement. Washington was concentrating his forces for the decisive blow at Yorktown. All was ardor and zeal in Maryland—a State that never flinched in its duty during the whole of the fiery ordeal of the Revolution. Annapolis was a focal point in its patriotism and preparation. On the 12th of September, transports with the artillery, the grenadiers, and the Light Artillery, of the allied army, arrived from the Head of the Elk, en route for James River. On the 8th, four thousand French troops, with a train of artillery, marched into Annapolis from the North, on their way also to join Washington in Virginia. It was at this time, off the mouth of the Severn, were the Romulus, the Gentile and several other French frigates. The very air was martial and the inspiriting scenes in the busy and throbbing little city well foreshadowed the final victory of the Revolution.

In the meantime, September 8th, the battle of Eutaw had been fought and the Maryland troops, under the command of the "Hero of Cowpens," Gen. John Eager Howard, added new lustre to their already glorious name.

The news of Cornwallis' surrender reached Annapolis Saturday evening, October 20th. It was communicated by Count de Grasse in a letter sent by express to the Governor. The citizens hailed with acclamations of joy and volleys of artillery. On Monday afternoon, feu de joie was fired by the "red artillery," and "selected militia," and in the evening the ancient city was brilliantly illuminated.

CHAPTER XXXXIX.

A POLITICAL PRISONER IN ANNAPOLIS DURING THE REVOLUTION.

The English Collector of Customs of Annapolis had an experience rarely allotted to an officer in an enemy's country. For nearly three years after violent retaliatory measures had commenced, and for two years after open hostilities were carried on, he had been allowed to remain in Annapolis as the King's officer, and collect the royal customs. His personal experience as found in his published letter, describes the vibrations of public sentiment and the march of events in a graphic manner. On Monday, June 10th, 1776, he writes:

"Tomorrow I must obey the summons of the Committee. My colleague and I have drawn up the following representation of our case, which we mean to deliver to the chairman of that body, in order to obviate the necessity of entering into bond.

"'To the chairman and members of the Committee of Observation for Anne Arundel county.

"'*Gentlemen*,

"'We flatter ourselves that the following representation will engage the committee's candid, and dispassionate consideration; and that when the personal liberty of even an individual is concerned, his endeavours to preserve it will be received with indulgence.

"'You will please, gentlemen, to observe, that it is not ordered by the convention, that the Committees of Observation take bonds of all non-associators, but it is left to their discretion, whether to require bonds or not; and, in the exercise of this power, though the committees are not held, as magistrates are in similar cases, by the obligation of an oath, yet we presume they are bound in honour, not to demand security unnecessary for the public good, and inconvenient and embarrassing to the persons called upon.

"'From the above consideration we inferred, on being required to give up our arms, without any demand or hint respecting the entering into bonds, that the Committee of Observation, in their discretion, did not deem it necessary, or conducive to the public good. Had we been called upon for that purpose, we should have had an opportunity of appealing immediately to the convention. To that respectable body, we could have represented our peculiar circumstances: that we are officers of the Crown; that we have given security in London for the faithful discharge of our duty, agreeable to instructions from time to time received, respecting the revenue of customs; that we are not entitled to our salaries without a nihil account, transmitted quarterly of our proceedings; and, that though a correspondence of this nature could be no way injurious to America, yet it might, perhaps, be deemed a breach of the proposed bond, and consequently deprive us of the means of subsistence for ourselves and families; for by the condition of this bond, "no correspondence, directly or indirectly, by letter, message, or otherwise, with any person holding a civil office under the crown," is allowable, even a demand for, and receipt of our salaries, would be a breach of the condition prescribed.

"'Although we are not natives of this country, we are animated with the warmest attachment for its interest and happiness; and we flatter ourselves, that our conduct, for a term of years, has been generally approved, both as servants of the public, and members of the community. We are determined to persevere, faithfully and honourably, in discharging the duties of our respective offices, as long as with propriety we can act in the same ; but we cannot sacrifice our honour, or prostitute our oaths, for temporary indulgences. Should we be obliged to depart from this continent, we hope we shall be permitted to take leave, with security to our persons and property, agreeably to a resolve of the convention, in that case provided ; and wherever we may fix our residence, we shall retain the most affectionate regard for Maryland, without deviating from our allegiance to our Sovereign, which has been, and will ever continue to be the invariable rule of our conduct. Not to trespass, gentlemen, upon your time, permit us to assure you, that we cannot, consistent with our peace of mind, enter into the proposed bond. We act solely from principle, and the dictates of conscience. Relying, therefore, on your impartiality, we shall cheerfully submit to whatever you may please to determine ; and however Providence may dispose of us in future, our prayers shall be continually offered for the prosperity of this once happy province, most ardently wishing a permanent and constitutional reconciliation may speedily take place, and that Great Britain and America may remain, to the latest period, one happy, free, and undivided empire.

"We are, gentlemen,

"Your obedient, humble servants.

"John Clapham,
"Wm. Eddis."

" 'Should the Committee be pleased to determine, agreeable to the resolve of the convention, and grant us passes to depart the country, we have only to desire that a sufficient time may be allotted us, to settle the various and intricate concerns of the loan-office, which we need not observe, are of the utmost importance to the community in general. It is also highly incumbent on us, to leave the business of that department in a clear state, so that our securities, who are engaged in very large sums for our fidelity, may be honourably discharged from the obligations entered into on our behalf.

"We are by no means sanguine, with regard to the above application ; on the contrary, we are prepared to encounter every disagreeable consequence. It is possible a few weeks may be allotted, to adjust provincial and private concerns : we must then give up every flattering expectation ; every late cherished hope. We must forsake all, or act inconsistently with the dictates of honour and of conscience."

The committee required Messrs. Eddis and Clapham to give bond of £10,000 each, not to communicate with the enemy. On their refusal they were ordered to leave the province before the first of August.

June 16th, he wrote "I look forward with extreme impatience to the hour of my departure from this country, where every surrounding prospect is dreary and uncomfortable."

On the 1st of October he writes :

"My worthy colleague and his family are preparing to remove from Annapolis to a house belonging to Mr. D——, on Hunting Ridge, about six miles distant from Baltimore to which place I intend to accompany them. We propose to attend alternately in this city, until discharged from employments, or confirmed in them."

HUNTING RIDGE, November 1.

"I write to you from one of the most delightful situations on the continent of America, where I have obtained an occasional retreat from the noise, the tumult, and the miseries, of the public world. From the back piazza of our habitation, we command a truly picturesque view into several fertile counties : a distant prospect of the eastern shore : the magnificent waters of the Chesapeake, and the river Patapsco, from the entrance at the Bodkin Point, to its apparent termination at the town of Baltimore. After this inadequate description, I need not observe, that we reside on a lofty eminence where

"——— the air
Nimbly, and sweetly recommends itself
Unto our gentle senses.'

"As Mr. C—— and myself are not superseded in our office we attend in rotation, every other week, in Annapolis, from which this place is about thirty miles distant. The contrast we experience on these occasions is hardly to be described : from the churlish sounds of of hostile preparation to the calm enjoyment of peaceful retirement. Though in the vicinity of a large and populous town, agitated with uproar and confusion, and rumours of approaching calamities, here, sheltered by surrounding woods, we are entirely secluded from the busy haunts of men, and are benevolently permitted to enjoy our retirement without dread of molestation. It is well known that we have never attempted, by any injudicious steps, to incur the resentment of those who conceive they are warranted by justice and by duty, to take a contrary part ; and while we thus continue to regulate our conduct, we shall surely experience attention, with the most perfect security."

January 1st, 1777, he says :

"Myself and colleague are not yet superseded in our provincial employment : but the day is assuredly at hand. When the event has taken place, I am persuaded I shall be at liberty to revisit England : and have reason to believe, I shall be necessitated to shape my course by way of the West Indies. I think it possible we may be restored to each other early in the ensuing summer."

April 2, he writes, "We are at length superseded in our department as commissioner of the loan office."

Saturday, June 7, he embarked to return to England by way of the West Indies, permission having been refused him by the Americans to enter the British lines. On that date he wrote :

"I have taken leave of the few faithful friends still residing in Annapolis. Perhaps a final one ! It is a painful distressing idea ! But I am hastening to those, my separation from whom I have so long felt, and lamented. That thought will firmly support me under every anxious trial it may be yet my fortune to encounter. I shall embark in a few minutes. So will Mr. D——, as his vessel is likewise in the harbour, and ready for sea. Our projected route, though aiming at the same point, is widely different. I shall deliver this to his care.

Should he accomplish his passage, agreeable to his wishes, he must reach England long before 1 can possibly expect that happiness. Adieu!"

CHAPTER XL.

ANNAPOLIS AFTER THE REVOLUTION.

1781—1784.

In the minds of the people the battle of Yorktown had closed the war. On his way northward, General Washington arrived in Annapolis, on Wednesday, November 21st, 1781.

"When the citizens received the pleasing information of his Excellency's arrival, all business ceased, and every consideration gave way to their impatience to behold their benefactor, and the deliverer of his country. On his appearance in the streets, people of every rank and every age eagerly pressed forward to feed their eyes with gazing on the man, to whom, under Providence, and the generous aid of our great and good ally, they owed their security, and hopes of future liberty and peace; the courteous affability, with which he returned their salutes, lighted up ineffable joys in every countenance, and diffused the most animated gratitude through every breast.

"You would have thought the very windows spoke, so many greedy looks of young and old through casements darted their desiring eyes upon his visage; and that all walls, with painted imagery, had said at once, 'God save thee, Washington.'

"The general's arrival was announced by the discharge of cannon, and he was accompanied to his Excellency the Governor, by the honest acclamations of the whigs: a few tories, to expiate their crimes and shuffle off the opprobrium of their characters, feebly joined in applauding the man whose successes had annihilated their hopes, and whose conduct was a satire on their principles. The President of the Senate, Speaker of the House of Delegates, Members of the House of Delegates, Members of the General Assembly and Council, and many of the citizens, hastened to offer their tribute of affection, which was richly repaid by the engaging frankness and affectionate politeness of the reception. The evening was spent at the Governor's elegant and hospitable board with festive joy, enlivened by good-humour, wit, and beauty.

"On the next day the General partook of a public dinner given by the legislature, as a mark of their respect, and to render the participation of his company as general as possible. In the evening the city was beautifully illuminated, and an assembly prepared for the ladies, to afford them an opportunity of beholding their friend, and thanking their protector with their smiles.*

* Md. Gazette.

"His Excellency, to gratify the wishes of the fair, crowned the entertainment with his presence, and with graceful dignity and familiar ease so framed his looks, his gestures, and his words, that every heart overflowed with gratitude and love, and every tongue grew eloquent in his praise. When he retired from the assembly—with one united voice, all present exclaimed,

"Unrivalled and unmatched shall be his fame
And his own laurels shade his envied name."

The day on which General Washington reached Annapolis, the following address was presented by the citizens:

"To his Excellency General Washington.

"The citizens of Annapolis feel themselves happy in having an opportunity, personally, to express their affection for, and gratitude to, your Excellency. Your private character forces admiration from the foes of virtue and freedom.

"We derive peculiar pleasure from the contemplation, that the successes at Trenton and Princetown laid the corner stone of our freedom and independence, and that the capture of Earl Cornwallis and his army has completed the edifice, and secured the temple of liberty to us and our posterity. These brilliant and important events are the more agreeable to every American, from the reflection that they were planned by, and executed under, the immediate command of your excellency.

"The love of your country alone, which induced you to accept the command of our armies at the expense of domestic happiness: the persevering fortitude and equanimity of soul you have displayed on every occasion, and the very important services rendered America, justify us in saluting you as the patriot, the hero, and the saviour of your country.

"Our prayers, with those of millions, are daily offered up to the Supreme Ruler of the Universe, for your health, safety and happiness.

(Signed.)   JOHN BULLEN, Mayor.
"ANNAPOLIS, November 21st, 1781."

To which address General Washington made the following reply:

"Sir,—I am obliged by the polite and affectionate address of the citizens of Annapolis. Nothing can be more flattering to me than to know, that my general conduct has met the approbation of my countrymen; it is the most grateful reward for those services which I have ever, in the course of my command, endeavoured to render them, but which their too great partiality has oftentimes over-rated. That the State in general, and this city in particular, may long enjoy the benefits which they have a right to expect from their very spirited exertions in the prosecution of this just war, is the sincere wish of,

"Sir, your most obedient and very humble servant,
"GEORGE WASHINGTON.

"The Worshipful JOHN BULLEN, Esq.,

"Mayor of the City of Annapolis.

"ANNAPOLIS, November 21st, 1781."

On Friday, the 23rd, General Washington resumed his journey Northward.

13

Annapolis was at this period a city of great importance. On the direct line of travel to the North, by way of Rock Hall on the Eastern shore. it received all the prominent generals of the war who passed from North to South or the reverse. Loyal to its principles, hospitable to a fault, ample in resources, the distinguished stranger who chanced in its midst or the historic or patriotic event that happened in their hearing, were certain to be awarded the honors of a cannonade or the convivialities of the banquet.

On the 25th of June, 1781, the birth of a Dauphin was celebrated in the city by a public dinner given in the State House where a numerous and respectable assembly gathered and many toasts were drunk suitable to the occasion. At intervals during the day there were five hundred discharges of cannon, and at night a splendid ball was given.

[1783.] "On the 4th of January, 1783, count Rochambeau, with this suite, arrived in Annapolis, and the next morning embarked on the "Le Emerande" for France.

On the 24th of April, Annapolis celebrated the signing of the treaty of peace between England and America. An extensive building sufficient to accommodate many hundreds was erected on Carroll's Green, thirteen pieces of artillery planted, and an elegant dinner provided. The proclamation of peace was then read, and thirteen cannon announced the white-winged messenger. The gentlemen then repaired to dinner, at which were present, his Excellency, the Governor, the honorable council. Members of the Senate and Delegates of the Assembly, and a large number of gentlemen, both of town and country : who "with unfeigned satisfaction congratulated each other on the blessings of peace—the rising glory of their country—the prospects of her commerce—her future grandeur and importance in the scale of nations.

"After dinner the following truly liberal, generous. and patriotic toasts were drunk, each attended with thirteen cannon :"

1. The third of February. 1783—in perpetual memory, on which day a virtuous war was concluded by an honourable peace.

2. The United States—may their confederacy endure forever.

3. Friendship with France—may every nation imitate the depth and moderation of her policy. by which the freedom of navigation has been secured, the liberty of these States confirmed, and the blessings of peace and commerce diffused throughout the globe.

4. His Excellency, General Washington.

5. The generals, officers and soldiers of our army—may their services be remembered, and generously rewarded by a grateful people.

6. The French generals, officers, and troops, who served in America.

7. The Marquis of Fayette—may our posterity ever retain a grateful sense of his strong attachment to this country, and of the important services rendered it in the field and cabinet.

8. The immortal memory of the gallant soldiers and virtuous citizens who gloriously fell in the late war.

9. The patriots of America—honour crowns their labours ; may future ages revere their memory, and emulate their fame.

10. The United Netherlands, and the friendly powers in Europe.

11. May the influence of the present revolution be extended to all the nations of the earth, by introducing among them that spirit of

humanity, and religious toleration, which has so peculiarly distinguished this country, and united the efforts of all denominations of Christians in the support of freedom.

12. The Commissioners of the United States at Paris.

13. The State of Maryland—may she ever support religion, learning, and virtue; preserve justice, public faith, and honour; give every encouragement and attention to agriculture and commerce; and on all occasions maintain with dignity her national character."

At night, the State House was beautifully and brilliantly illuminated and an elegant entertainment given at the ball-room to the ladies.

Major-General Greene and his suite arrived in the city from the South on their way North on September 25th, 1783. On the next day the Corporation met, and presented the following address:

To the Hon. Major-General Greene:

"Sir.—We, the Mayor, Recorder, Aldermen, and Common Council, of the city of Annapolis, impressed with the most greatful feelings for the eminent services rendered these United States, and the cause of liberty, by the Southern Army under your command, beg permission to congratulate you on your arrival in this city, and to testify, with the sincerest respect and regard, the lively sense we entertain of the invaluable blessings secured to us, by your conduct and unremitted assiduity, in the noblest cause that ever graced a soldier's sword.

"Justice would wear the aspect of adulation, were we to enumerate the many signal endowments which endear you to the inhabitants of this city, and inspire us with the warmest and most respectful gratitude. They are such as will ever engage our prayers to Divine Providence, that you may long continue to possess the affections of a generous republic; to share the sweets of domestic felicity; and to experience the happy reward of your distinguished virtues.

"This address springs from the heart; and we solicit your acceptance of it, as the genuine sentiments of a grateful people.

"Signed by order and in behalf of the corporation.

"JAMES BRICE, Mayor.

"ANNAPOLIS, September 26th, 1783."

To which the General returned the following answer:

"ANNAPOLIS, September 27th, 1783.

"Gentlemen.—It is with the highest satisfaction I receive your affectionate address, and feel my bosom glow with gratitude upon the occasion.

"The happy termination of the war affords the most pleasing field for contemplation, and while it promises the richest harvest to the good citizens of America, it gives the sweetest pleasure, and most desirable repose to the soldier. If the operations of the Southern Army have answered the expectations of the public, or have had any influence upon this great event, I shall consider it one of the most happy employments of my life. And if to this I may venture to flatter myself, that my conduct either merits, or meets in the smallest degree, the approbation of the public, I shall be still more happy. The honour you have done me, and the troops under my command, are too sensibly felt to be fully expressed, or properly acknowledged.

"I beg leave to return my most sincere thanks to the corporation, for the interest they take in what concerns my future happiness, peace, and prosperity.

"I have the honour to be, gentlemen,

"Your most obedient, humble servant,

"NATHANIEL GREENE.

"To the Corporation of the City of Annapolis."

November 21st, 1783, the order of the society of Cincinnati, for Maryland, was inaugurated in Annapolis: Otho H. Williams in the chair; John Eccleston, Secretary. The order elected: Major-General Smallwood, president; Brigadier General Gist, vice-president; Brigadier General Williams, secretary; Col. Ramsey, treasurer; and Lieut. Col. Eccleston, assistant treasurer. Annapolis was appointed the place for their annual meeting.

On Monday, November 29th, 1784, Generals Washington and La-Fayette arrived in Annapolis. The next day the Legislature ordered a ball to be given in honor of the visitors. The *Gazette* says:

"The evening was crowned with the utmost joy and festivity, the whole company being made happy by the presence of two most amiable and all-accomplished men, to whom America is so deeply indebted for her preservation from tyranny and oppression."

The following addresses were presented by the executive and legislative bodies respectively to the Marquis, during his visit at Annapolis:

"ANNAPOLIS, November 30th, 1784.   ⎫
In Council.   ⎬

"Sir.—We, the Governor and Council of Maryland, beg leave with the most entire respect and heart-felt satisfaction, to embrace this first opportunity of your presence in the metropolis of this State, since the establishment of our peace, to offer you our warmest congratulations, and to express our high and grateful sense of the illustrious share which you bore in the accomplishment of that happy event.

"The early and decided part which you took in the cause of American liberty and glory, your generous services for us in the court of your august monarch, our great and good ally, and your wise and magnanimous conduct in the field, upon many of the most arduous occasions of the war, have endeared your name to America, and enrolled it high in the list of patriots and heroes, the supporters of her liberty and founders of her empire.

"May, sir, your future days be as great and honourable as the past, and may heaven take under its peculiar care and protection, a life so eminently distinguished for its attachment and devotion to the rights and liberties of mankind. With every sentiment of regard and respect, we have the honour to be, sir, your most obedient humble servant,

"WILLIAM PACA.

"The honourable the Marquis de la Fayette."

La Fayette replied:

"To his Excellency the Governor and the honourable Council of the State of Maryland.

"Sir.—In the polite attention of your Excellency and Council, I find myself equally obliged to your attachment, and honored by your approbation.

"To have been early adopted among the sons of freedom, to have seen French and American standards united in the cause of mankind, to have so peculiarly shared in the confidence and friendship of the United States, are ideas the more pleasing to me, as I am assured, when I reflect upon the difficulties this country overcame, that she will attend to the means of splendor and happiness, which now, thank God, are in her disposal.

"I beg, sir, your Excellency and Council will accept the warmest acknowledgments, and sincerest wishes that an affectionate heart can most respectfully bestow.

"LA FAYETTE."

"November 30th, 1784.

"Sir,—The General Assembly of Maryland, are happy in having an opportunity of personally testifying the grateful sense they and their constituents entertain of the important services which you rendered these United States during the late war. The strong attachment which you have manifested to its interests in situations the most trying and difficult, still continues to actuate your conduct; to this attachment and predilection we partly attribute the commercial arrangements lately adopted by his Most Christian Majesty, which bid fair to perpetuate and extend the friendly intercourse and connexions between his subjects and the citizens of these United States.

"May the Great Ruler of the Universe long preserve a life which has been so early dedicated to the service of humanity, and engaged in the most useful and brilliant actions.

"GEORGE PLATER,

President of the Senate.

"THOMAS C. DEYE,

Speaker of the House of Delegates.

"The Marquis de la Fayette.

"To the Honorable the General Assembly of Maryland:

"Gentlemen,—On this opportunity so pleasingly anticipated, of my respectful congratulations to your General Assembly, I meet such precious marks of your partiality, as most happily complete my satisfaction.

"Amidst the enjoyments of allied successes, affection conspires with interest to cherish a mutual intercourse; and in France you will ever find that sympathizing good will, which leaves no great room for private exertions. With the ardor of a most zealous heart, I earnestly hope this State, ever mindful of the public spirit she has conspicuously displayed, will to the fullest extent improve her natural advantages, and in the Federal Union so necessary to all, attain the highest degree of particular happiness and prosperity.

"While you are pleased, gentlemen, to consider my life as being devoted to the service of humanity, I feel not less gratified by so flattering an observation than by your friendly wishes for its welfare, and the pleasure I now experience in presenting you, with the tribute of my attachment and gratitude.

"LA FAYETTE."

During the sitting of this legislature, the following act was passed:

"An act to naturalize Major-General, the Marquis de la Fayette and his heirs male forever.

"Whereas, the General Assembly of Maryland, anxious to perpetuate a name dear to the State, and to recognize the Marquis de la Fayette for one of its citizens, who, at the age of nineteen, left his native country, and risked his life in the late revolution; who, on his joining the American army, after being appointed by congress to the rank of Major-General, disinterestedly refused the usual rewards of command, and sought only to deserve, what he attained, the character of patriot and soldier; who, when appointed to conduct an incursion into Canada, called forth by his prudence and extraordinary discretion, the approbation of Congress; who, at the head of an army in Virginia, baffled the manœuvres of a distinguished general, and excited the admiration of the oldest commanders; who early attracted the notice and obtained the friendship of the illustrious General Washington; and who laboured and succeeded in raising the honour and name of the United States of America; therefore,

"*Be it enacted, by the General Assembly of Maryland*, That the Marquis de la Fayette, and his heirs male forever, shall be, and they and each of them are hereby deemed, adjudged, and taken to be natural born citizens of this State, and shall henceforth be entitled to all the immunities, rights, and privileges of natural born citizens thereof, they and every one of them conforming to the constitution and laws of this State, in the enjoyment and exercise of such immunities, rights and privileges."

CHAPTER XLI.

ANNAPOLIS WANTS TO BE THE CAPITAL OF THE UNITED STATES.*

[1783.] In the proceedings of the corporation of Annapolis, Monday the 12th of May, 1783; at which were present, James Brice, Esq., Mayor; Samuel Chase, Esq., Recorder; Allen Quynn, Esq., John Bullen, Esq., John Brice, Esq., Aldermen; Frederick Green, Esq., John Davidson, Esq., William Goldsmith, Esq., Samuel H. Howard, Esq., Beriah Maybury, Esq., John Chalmers, Esq., Common Councilmen.

"It being represented to the Corporation, that the welfare and interest of the United States require that Congress should have a fixed place of residence, and with jurisdiction and Executive and Judicial powers within the same, and over all persons inhabiting or residing within the district allotted for their residence; and this city from its central situation to the federal States, and the convenience of the members of Congress to repair thither by land or water; the facility of receiving and conveying intelligence to Europe; and its remarkable healthiness; and capacity of defence from any attack of an

* From Council proceedings of 1783.

enemy : being. in the opinion of this corporation, the most eligible place in the United States, for the residence of the Honorable Congress. and their officers and foreign ministers,

"*Resolved*, That the members of this Corporation be directed to consult the citizens thereon and report the same to this Corporation on Wednesday next.

"Ordered, That the following notice be set up at the State House and Market House and other public places in the city, to wit :

"A meeting of the citizens of Annapolis is requested by the Corporation on Wednesday, at 10 o'clock in the morning, at the house of Mr. Charles Ridgely to express their sentiments, if the General Assembly will offer this city and its precincts to Congress for their permanent residence ; whether they will agree to such offer and consent to be subject to such jurisdiction and power within the city and its precincts and over the inhabitants and residents thereof as the General Assembly shall think proper to grant to the United States in Congress Assembled."

On the 14th, the Corporation met again.

"The members of the Corporation having reported that they had consulted the citizens and taken their opinion, whether this city and its precincts. ought to be offered to the Honorable Congress for their permanent residence, with jurisdiction over the same and the citizens having unanimously agreed thereto,

"*Resolved*, Unanimously, that if the Honorable the General Assembly will offer this city and its precincts containing about three hundred acres of land to the Honorable Congress for the permanent residence of that body and successors, that this corporation. and their constituents most cheerfully agree to such offer and consent to be subject to such jurisdiction and power within the city and its precincts, and over the Inhabitants and residents thereof as the General Assembly shall think proper to grant ; to the United States in Congress Assembled.

"*Resolved*, That the Worshipfull the Mayor, authenticate this Act under the Seal of the Corporation and present the same to the General Assembly."

On the 7th of July at another session of the City Council :

"The Worshipfull, the Mayor, laid before the Corporation a letter to him from the Honorable James McHenry, Delegate of this State to Congress, Dated the 30th of last month, requesting to be furnished with an accurate account of the births and deaths in this city for the last 15 or 20 years which was read, and it appearing on enquiry that no regular and complete register of deaths or births has been kept before the war, and that no register of any kind has been kept since that time,

"Ordered. That Messrs. Goldsmith, Fairbrother. Chalmers, Mills, and Reynolds be appointed to inquire and report to the Mayor the number of births and deaths of the inhabitants within this city and its precincts between the 1st day of July. 1778, and the 1st day of this present month ascertaining as far as can be the number of whites and blacks, infants and grown persons. and the cause of death, and that they report the number of inhabitants in this city during the last year,

"Mr. Mayor is requested to transmit the said report to Mr. McHenry.

"Ordered, That a plat of this city and its precincts be made out and Mr. Mayor is requested to transmit the same to Mr. McHenry."

The proceedings were continued on a kindred subject on Saturday, the 1st of November, 1783, when

"The Mayor laid before the Corporation a letter from the Honorable James McHenry and Daniel Carroll, Delegates of Congress for this State, dated the 23rd day of October last, to the late Mayor enclosing the resolution of Congress of the same date respecting the temporary residence of Congress in this city and also a letter from the Hon. James McHenry requiring suitable provision might be made for the reception of the Members, Ministers, and Officers of Congress—all which being considered, it was ordered that a committee of the Members of the Corporation be appointed to inquire what houses can be procured for Congress and for what rent, and also how many boarding houses are in town, the accommodation of each and the sums upon which members can be boarded."

"Messrs. Allen Quynn, John Brice, John Davidson, and John Chalmers were accordingly appointed."

The council loaned Isaac McHand £100 Continental Currency "to enable him to provide for the accommodation of members of Congress."

The legislature of Maryland appears to have taken no steps to further the ambitious aspiration of Annapolis. On Tuesday, October 21st, Congress settled the question as to the seat of government, so far as Annapolis was concerned by the passage of the following:

"WHEREAS, there is reason to expect that the providing buildings for the alternate residence of Congress in two places, will be productive of the most salutary effects, by securing the mutual confidence and affections of the States:

"Resolved, That buildings likewise erected for the use of congress, at or near the lower falls of Potowmack or Georgetown, provided a suitable district on the banks of the river can be procured for a federal town, and the right of soil, and an exclusive jurisdiction, or such other as congress may direct, shall be vested in the United States; and that until the buildings to be erected on the banks of the Delaware and Patowmack shall be prepared for the reception of Congress, their residence shall be alternately, at equal periods of not more than one year and not less than six months, in Trenton and Annapolis; and the president is hereby authorised and directed to adjourn congress, on the 12th day on November next, to meet at Annapolis on the 26th of the same month, for the dispatch of public business."

CHAPTER XLII.

GENERAL WASHINGTON RESIGNS HIS MILITARY COMMISSION AT ANNAPOLIS.

1783.

Annapolis became the scene of the resignation of General Washington's military commission not from any peculiar fitness of things, but from one of those accidents that sometimes makes places, as well as men, famous.

Congress had resolved that, until the public buildings then in course of erection on the Delaware and Potomac were finished, it would hold its sessions alternately at Trenton and Annapolis. The latter place was selected because it had a commodious State-House. It was chosen for the first six months of the session of 1783. Thus it became the scene of a renowned event.

Hastening from the affecting incidents of his farewell audience with the officers of his army, by a triumphal journey Washington arrived, on the 19th of December, in the City of Annapolis.

The news of General Washington's approach had preceded him, and a few miles from Annapolis he was met by Generals Gates and Smallwood, "and several of the principal inhabitants, who attended him to Mr. Mann's, where apartments had been prepared for his reception. His Excellency's arrival," continues the local authority from which we quote, "was announced by the discharge of cannon. After receiving the heartfelt welcome of all who had the honor of knowing him, His Excellency waited on the President of Congress (General Mifflin, of South Carolina,) with whom he and the members of that body, together with the principal civil and military officers of this State, dined on Saturday."

Mann's Hotel, at which Washington had been provided quarters, still stands in Annapolis, an imposing structure even in this day of improvements. It is now the City Hotel, and is situated on the corner of Conduit and Main streets. The room, which Washington occupied, yet remains, and is in one of the wings. "No. 9" is its designation. It is about sixteen feet by sixteen, with a ceiling of about twelve. There are two great windows in it that look out upon the court-yard of the hotel. Until a few years ago the very bedstead that the Commander-in-Chief occupied remained in the room. When the hotel passed from the heirs of Colonel John Walton, who was for many years "mine host" of the City Hotel, his son, Dr. J. Randolph Walton, took the illustrious relic away. He lives in Washington and when last heard from on this subject still had the bedstead in his possession.

Annapolis, at the time of this interesting event, was a quaint and agreeable city. The hip-roofs and odd gables still left here bear evidence of the picturesque period of 1783. Mr. William Eddis, the English surveyor of the port, who wrote of it in 1769, said that then it had "more the appearance of an agreeable village than the metropolis of an opulent province, as it contains within its limits a number of small fields which are intended for future erections. But in a few years it will probably be one of the best built cities in America, as a spirit of improvement is predominant, and the situation is allowed to be equally healthy and pleasant with any on this side the Atlantic. Many of the principal families have chosen this place for their residence, and there are few towns of the same size in any part of the British domains that can boast of a more polished society. * * * Several modern edifices make a good appearance. There are few habitations without gardens, some of which, planted in decent style, are well stocked." *

Washington, with his accustomed promptness, set himself at once to the business he had in hand. On Saturday, December 20th, 1783, he addressed a letter to Congress, informing that body of his arrival in Annapolis, with the intention of asking leave to resign the com-

---

* Maryland Gazette.

mission he had the honor of holding in their service. and desiring
to know their pleasure in what manner it will be most proper to offer
his resignation : whether in writing or at an audience.

Congress resolved "that His Excellency the Commander-in-Chief
be admitted to a public audience on Tuesday next at 12 o'clock, M."

It was further resolved "that a public entertainment be given to the
Commander-in-Chief on Monday next."

The State of Maryland was not behind in offering to Washington the
courtesies demanded by the auspicious occasion. The Council of
State began the formal addresses of the ceremonies with the following :

"Annapolis, December 29, 1783. }
　　　　　　　　In Council. }

"Sir:—Amidst the general joy on the happy and honorable termination of the war, we beg leave to welcome your Excellency's return to
this city, with hearts full of gratitude and affection.

"As long, sir, as mankind shall return a proper sense of the blessings of *Peace, Liberty, and Safety,* your character in every country,
and in every age wills, be honored, admired, and revered ; but to a
mind elevated as your the consciousness of having done great and
illustrious deeds, from the purest principles of patriotism of having by
your wisdom and magnanimity, arrested the arm of tyranny, saved a
dear country and millions of fellow-citizens, and millions yet unborn,
from slavery and all the horrors and calamities of slavery, and placed
their rights and liberties on a permanent foundation, must yield a
satisfaction infinitely superior to all the pomp and eclat of applauding
ages and admiring worlds.

"Attached to your excellency by the strongest obligations : and
feeling the most lively impressions of your unequalled worth and public usefulness : we beg you to accept our warmest wishes that your life
may be prolonged to a far distant period : and that it may be as happy
in your retirement as it has been glorious in the field."

The letter was signed with the usual prolonged and courteous
protestations of affection and respect by Wm. Paca, President of the
Council and Governor of Maryland.

General Washington replied to this prophetic and eloquent address :

"Sir:—I shall ever cherish a pleasing remembrance of the welcome
reception I have experienced from your excellency and the Council, on
my return to this city after the happy and honorable termination of
the war.

"The flattering sentiments you entertain of my exertions in defence
of our country, and the favorable point of light in which you place my
character, too strongly demonstrates your friendship, not to claim the
most grateful return from me.

"Convinced from experience, of the wisdom and decision which have
signalized the government of Maryland, I cannot form a better wish
for the future prosperity of the state than that the same spirit of justice and patriotism, which actuated its councils during a long and
eventful war, may continue to dictate its measures through a durable
and happy peace."

The following morning, (Sunday.) General Washington devoted to
the return of the visits of citizens of Annapolis and others who had
waited on him. He then dined, with a number of others, with Mr.
Ga

Monday, the 22d of December, had a great deal crowded into it. There were the formal addresses of the city Annapolis, those of the Senate and House of Delegates of Maryland, a public dinner to General Washington, the illumination of the State House and a Ball by the General Assembly of Maryland.

Annapolis, by its Mayor, J. T. Chase, said "The Mayor, recorder, aldermen, and common council of the city of Annapolis congratulate your excellency on the restoration of peace, and the establishment of the freedom and independence of the United States of America. The citizens feel themselves particularly happy in this opportunity afforded them, of expressing their sincere approbation of your most disinterested and unexampled conduct through every stage of the war, and the high sense they entertain of your excellent virtues, fortitude, and unremitting perseverance, under the pressure of the greatest difficulties. To you they esteem themselves principally indebted under the favor and smiles of Providence, for the inestimable blessings of peace and freedom. This acknowledgement flows from hearts filled with gratitude and the most perfect respect and veneration for your person and character.

"In your retirement to the peaceful and pleasing scenes of domestic tranquility, may America long experience the benign influence of your example, and benefit by the salutary suggestions of your wisdom and may you sir, long enjoying your health and the heavenly sensations arising from a consciousness of having done every thing for your country, and wrested her from the oppressive hand of unrelenting tyranny, without the hope of any reward, but the approbation of a free people."

To this flattering and very personal address, General Washington replied :

"To the worshipful, the Mayor, Recorder, Aldermen and Common-Council of the city of Annapolis :

"Permit me, Gentlemen, to offer to you my sincere thanks for your congratulations on the happy events of peace, and the establishment of our independence.

"If my conduct throughout the war has merited the confidence of my fellow citizens, and has been instrumental in obtaining for my country the blessings of peace and freedom—I owe it that Supreme Being who guides the hearts of all—who has so signally interposed his aid in every stage of the contest, and who has graciously been pleased to bestow on me the greatest of earthly rewards—the approbation and affections of a free people.

"Though I retire from the employments of public life, I shall never cease to entertain the most anxious care for the welfare of my country. May the Almighty dispose the heart of every citizen of the United States to improve the great prospect of happiness before us ! And may you, Gentlemen, and the inhabitants of this city, long enjoy every felicity this world can afford !"

The State of Maryland, through its General Assembly, then in session, followed with another congratulatory address. The surprise is that all being upon the same theme—the glories of Washington's personal character and his military achievements, there should be found so many variations of the subject ; but the object glowed and the changes rung with every one that began the note of praise. Maryland said :

"The General Assembly of Maryland embrace this opportunity, of expressing the grateful sense which they and their constituents entertain of your distinguished services; services which, under the smiles of Divine Providence, have secured the peace. liberty. and independence. of these States! Your retirement to private life is a full evidence of that true patriotism which induced you to draw your sword in defence of your injured country, and made you persevere to the end of the arduous struggle. in which you have surmounted difficulties, that. with prudence less than yours. could not have been surmounted. Having. by your conduct in the field. gloriously terminated the war, you have taught us. by your last circular letter, how to value, how to preserve. and to improve that liberty, for which we have been contending. We are convinced that public liberty cannot be long preserved. but by wisdom. integrity. and a strict adherence to public justice and public engagements. This justice and these engagements, as far as the influence and example of one State can extend, we are determined to promote and fulfil ; and if the powers given to Congress by the confederation, should be found to be incompetent to the purposes of the Union. we doubt not our constituents will readily consent to enlarge them. In expressing these sentiments. and by thus engaging to comply with the dictates of public faith and justice, and to satisfy the just demands of a meritorious army. we make the most acceptable return for all those cares which you have felt. and all the toils you have undergone. during your command. Permit us. in addressing you for the last time in your public character. to express our warmest wishes that you may long enjoy the sweets of domestic ease and retirement. and that cordial satisfaction which must arise from a consciousness of having merited and gained the universal love of your countrymen."

The reply of General Washington. to this patriotic address of the State whose representative. Thomas Johnson, had nominated him in 1775 for command of the Continental Army, was "particularly happy." Here it is in full :

"Gentlemen :—I feel myself particularly happy in receiving the approbation of the General Assembly of Maryland, for those services which my country had a right to demand, and which it was my duty to render in defence of it.

"Having happily attained the object for which we had drawn the sword. I felicitated myself on my approaching return to private life. and I must acknowledge, I anticipated an unusual degree of self-gratification, in that retirement. which you are pleased to consider as an evidence of patriotism.

"You have rightly judged. gentlemen. that public liberty cannot be long preserved, without the influence of those public virtues, which you have enumerated. May the example you have exhibited. and the disposition you have manifested. prevail extensively, and have the most salutary operation! For I am well-assured, it is only by a general adoption of wise and equitable measures, that I can derive any personal satisfaction. or the public any permanent advantages, from the successful issue of the contest.

"I am deeply penetrated with the liberal sentiments and wishes contained in your last address to me as a public character; and while I am bidding you a final farewell in that capacity, be assured. gentlemen, that it will be my study in retirement not to forfeit the favorable opinion of my fellow-citizens.''

Charles Carroll, of Carrollton, delivered, in person, Washington's reply to the address of the Maryland Legislature.

The public dinner that Congress had tendered to General Washington was given on Monday, December 22nd, at the ball-room.

The building still remains, and strangers are shown with pardonable pride the place where Washington, the grave and dignified Commander-in-Chief of the Continental armies, was wont, in ''the piping days of peace,'' to come and dance, perhaps, the stately minuet. ''Upwards of two hundred persons of distinction were present at the dinner,'' says the local chronicler of that period, and ''everything was provided by Mr. Mann in the most elegant and profuse style.''

Dinner over, the roar of artillery began, and to its salvos the following interesting and patriotic toasts were drank :

1. The United States.
2. The Army.
3. His Most Christian Majesty.
4. The United Netherlands.
5. The King of Sweden.
6. Our Commissioners Abroad.
7. The Minister of France.
8. The Minister of the United Netherlands.
9. Harmony and a flourishing commerce throughout the Union.
10. May virtue and wisdom influence the Councils of the United States, and may their conduct merit the blessings of peace and independence.
11. The Virtuous Daughters of America.
12. The Governor and State of Maryland.
13. Long health and happiness to our illustrious General.

At night the State House was beautifully and brilliantly illuminated, in which building a ball was given by the General Assembly of Maryland. There were many ladies present, and General Washington opened the ball with Mrs. James Maccubbin, one of the most beautiful women of her day, as his partner.

The building in which this gay and renowned assembly danced the brilliant hours by, and which on the morrow was to be made forever famous, was erected between 1769 and 1773. Among those charged with its construction were Charles Carroll, barrister, and William Paca, the latter of whom signed the Declaration of Independence.

The last act of General Washington's official life was to write a letter to Baron Steuben. It ran :

''ANNAPOLIS, 23rd December, 1783.

''*My Dear Baron :*

''Although I have taken frequent opportunities, both in public and private, of acknowledging your great zeal, attention, and abilities in performing the duties of your office, yet I wish to make use of this last moment of my public life to signify, in the strongest terms, my entire approbation of your conduct, and to express my sense of the obligations the public is under to you for your faithful and meritorious services.

''I beg you will be convinced, my dear sir, that I should rejoice if it could ever be in my power to serve you more essentially than by expressions of regard and affection; but, in the meantime, I am persuaded you will not be displeased with this farewell token of my sincere friendship and esteem for you.

"This is the last letter I shall write while I continue in the service of my country. The hour of my resignation is fixed at twelve today, after which I shall become a private citizen on the banks of the Potomac, where I shall be glad to embrace you, and testify the great esteem and consideration with which I am, my dear Baron, &c."

Washington and his aids arrived at the State House at noon, and entered the Hall of Congress. A messenger announced their arrival to the Secretary of Congress, who introduced Washington to Congress and conducted him to a chair, where he was seated. Colonel Benjamin Walker and Colonel David Humphreys, his aids, stood beside him. It was a memorable assembly. In it were four future Presidents of the infant Republic—Washington, Jefferson, Madison and Monroe; John Eager Howard and General Smallwood, of Maryland; Eldridge Gerry, of Massachusetts; Stone, Paca, Chase, and Carroll, Maryland's signers of Independence; Joshua Barney and Alexander Hamilton, with beauty and grace unnumbered and unchronicled.

The hum of incident disorder being hushed, General Mifflin, with covered head, as he and his fellow-members observed in token of the sovereignty of the States they represented, addressed General Washington:

"Sir—The United States, in Congress assembled, are prepared to receive your communications."

With his native dignity, augmented by the grandeur of the occasion, Washington arose and delivered that address, so renowned for its wisdom and patriotic foresight. He said:

"Mr. President: The great events on which my resignation depended, having at length taken place, I have now the honor of offering my sincere congratulations to Congress, and of presenting myself before them, to surrender into their hands the trust committed to me, and to claim the indulgence of retiring from the service of my country.

"Happy in the confirmation of our independence and sovereignty, and pleased with the opportunity afforded the United States of becoming a respectable nation, I resign with satisfaction the appointment I accepted with diffidence: a diffidence in my abilities to accomplish so arduous a task, which, however, was superseded by a confidence in the rectitude of our cause, the support of the supreme power of the Union, and the patronage of Heaven.

"The successful termination of the war has verified the most sanguine expectations, and my gratitude for the interposition of Providence, and the assistance I have received from my countrymen, increases with every review of the momentous contest.

"While I repeat my obligations to the army in general, I should do injustice to my own feelings not to acknowledge, in this place, the peculiar services and distinguished merits of the gentlemen, who have been attached to my person during the war. It was impossible that the choice of confidential officers to compose my family should have been more fortunate. Permit me, sir, to recommend in particular those, who have continued in service to the present moment, as worthy of the favorable notice and patronage of Congress.

"I consider it an indispensable duty to close this last solemn act of my official life, by commending the interests of our dearest country to

the protection of Almighty God, and those who have the superintendence of them to his holy keeping.

"Having now finished the work assigned me, I retire from the great
theatre of action ; and, bidding an affectionate farewell to this august
body, under whose orders I have so long acted, I here offer my commission, and take leave of all the employments of public life."

At its conclusion Washington advanced toward General Mifflin and
delivered to him his commission and a copy of his address. The President made the following answer :

"Sir :—The United States in Congress assembled receive with emotions too affecting for utterance, the solemn resignation of the authorities under which you have led their troops with success through a
perilous and doubtful war. Called upon by your country to defend its
invaded rights, you accepted the sacred charge, before it had formed
alliances, and whilst it was without funds or a government to support
you. You have conducted the great military contest with wisdom
and fortitude, invariably regarding the rights of the civil powers
through all disasters and changes. You have, by the love and confidence of your fellow-citizens, enabled them to display their martial
genius, and transmit their fame to posterity. You have persevered,
till these United States, aided by a magnanimous King and Nation,
have been enabled, under a just Providence, to close the war in freedom, safety and independence ; on which happy event we sincerely
join you in congratulations.

"Having defended the standard of liberty in this new world : having
taught a lesson useful to those who inflict and to those who feel oppression, you retire from the great theatre of action, with the blessings
of your fellow-citizens—but the glory of your virtues will not termi-
nate with your military command—it will continue to animate re-
motest ages.

"We feel with you our obligations to the army in general, and will
particularly charge ourselves with the interests of those confidential
officers who have attended your person to this affecting moment.

"We join you in commending the interests of our dearest country to
the protection of Almighty God, beseeching him to dispose the hearts
and minds of its citizens to improve the opportunity afforded them,
of becoming a happy and respectable nation. And for you we address
to Him our warmest prayers, that a life so beloved may be fostered
with all his care ; that your days may be as happy as they have been
illustrious ; and that He will finally give you that reward which this
world cannot give."

The Secretary of the Senate then delivered to Washington a copy of
General Mifflin's address, Washington arose and, with affecting dignity, bowed to Congress. The members uncovered before him. He
withdrew from the Chamber leaving beauty's eye dimmed with affection's tear.

Washington, accompanied as far as South River, three miles from
Annapolis, by the Governor of Maryland, immediately set out for
Mount Vernon where he arrived on Christmas Eve.

CHAPTER XLIII.
St. John's College.

1784—1887.

Before the Revolution, Maryland had felt the necessity of larger facilities for advanced learning. Mr. Eddis, writing under date of Oct. 4, 1773, from Annapolis, says :

"The Legislature of this province, animated by sentiments which reflect the highest credit on their patriotism and wisdom, have also determined, by a recent law, to endow and form a college for the education of youth in every liberal and useful branch of Science.

"An institution of this nature was most strongly recommended to their confidence by our worthy governor, (Eden,) at early period after his arrival in this country ; and to his laudable and persevering exertions, the public are materially indebted for the establishment of a seminary which, as it will be conducted under excellent regulations, will shortly preclude the necessity of crossing the Atlantic for the completion of a classical and polite education." This college was incipient St. John's. Gov. Bladen's unfinished residence was to be repaired and used as a college. The Revolutionary war came on and education was neglected in the struggle for political existence. The war was barely concluded before the long-cherished hope of the State was realized. By chapter 37, Act of 1784, funds were provided "for founding a college on the Western Shore of this State and constituting the same, together with Washington College on the Eastern Shore, into one University, by the name of the University of Maryland."

It is not possible for the most prejudiced mind to read the nineteen sections of this memorable Act and not be convinced of the large and wise provision the State intended to make to advance the cause of liberal education.

The preamble recited that, as "many public-spirited individuals" have subscribed and procured subscription to form a college on the Western Shore of this State, that, therefore :

"*Be it Enacted by the General Assembly of Maryland,* That a college, or general seminary of learning, by the name of St. John's, be established on the said Western Shore, upon the following fundamental and inviolable principles, namely : first, the said college shall be founded and maintained forever upon a most liberal plan, for the benefit of youth of every religious denomination, who shall be freely admitted to equal privileges and advantages of education, and to all the literary honors of the college, according to their merits without requiring, or enforcing any religious or civil test, or urging their attendance upon any particular religious worship, or service, other than what they have been educated in or have the consent or approbation of their parents or guardians to attend ; nor shall any preference be given in the choice of a principal, vice-principal, or other professor, master, or tutor, in the said college on account of his particular religious profession, having regard solely to his moral character and literary abilities, and other necessary qualifications to fill the place for which he shall be chosen."

For every thousand pounds subscribed by any individuals, who choose to class themselves together, one member of the Board of Visitors and Governors, was to be selected by those who formed the class.

Rev. John Carroll, Rev. Wm. Smith, and Patrick Allison, Doctors of Divinity, Richard Sprigg, John Steret and George Diggs, with power to appoint others, were made agents to collect the individual subscriptions to the College.

The seventh section enacted, "That, if the city of Annapolis should be fixed upon as a place for establishing the said intended college, this General Assembly give and grant, and that, upon that condition, do hereby give and grant to the Visitors and Governors of said college by the name of 'The Visitors and Governors of St. John's in the State of Maryland,' and their successors, all that four acres, within the city of Annapolis, purchased for the use of the public and conveyed on the second day of October, 1744, by Stephen Bordley, Esq., to Thomas Bladen, Esq., then Governor, to have and to hold the said four acres of land, with the appurtenance, to the said Visitors and Governors, and their successors, for the only use, benefit, and behoof of the said college and seminary of universal learning for ever." Section thirteen granted the sum of £1,750 annually and forever thereafter as a donation by the public to the use of the college.

The singularity of the formation of the Board of Governors and Visitors and the widely separated residences of the members of it, created some difficulty in securing a meeting of the managers, but on May 25, 1789, a committee of the Board, announced that the Board had appointed John McDowell, A. M., professor of Mathematics, and that the committee intended to have two rooms "pushed with all convenient dispatch." This committee was James Brice, Charles Wallace, Richard Sprigg, Thomas Hyde, and Thomas Harwood.

On Wednesday, the 11th of November, 1789, St. John's College, was opened, and dedicated with much solemnity, in the presence of "a numerous and respectable concourse of people. The honorable the members of the General Assembly, the honorable Chancellor, the judges of the General Court, together with the gentlemen of the bar, the worshipful corporation of the city, and the principal inhabitants thereof, preceded by the scholars, the professors, and the Visitors and Governors of the college, walked in procession from the State House to the college hall. An elegant sermon, well adapted to the occasion was preached by the Reverend Doctor W. Smith, who presided for the day. An oration was also delivered by the Reverend Mr. Ralph Higinbothom on, "The advantages of a classical education." As a method of instruction, the *Gazette*, in its account of the college stated that— "an acquaintance with the learned languages being considered as the surest and most proper ground on which to lay the foundation of other branches of literature, it is intended in this seminary, the strictest attention shall be paid to the students in that particular. Grammar, in all its parts, will be taught with critical exactness, and the more strongly to impress a thorough knowledge of this preparatory branch of study on the minds of the pupils, daily exercise will be performed therein. Each lesson will be accompanied with an examination into the rules and principles by which the order and construction of language is regulated in which the connexion and de-

14

pending of its various parts on each other, will be explained. By the above method the student will not only be informed in the particular language, which at the time engages his attention, but he will be enabled with ease to acquire a knowledge of other tongues, especially those of modern date, by the assistance derived from this mode of instruction.''

The *Gazette* added—''It is expected that the rooms will be ready in a few weeks for the different professors, by whom youth will be instructed in all the sciences usually taught in colleges. The tuition is fixed at five pounds per annum, and good board, lodging and washing may be had, as the public is already informed, in respectable families, at the rate of £30 current money, per annum.''

Before this early date the uncertain tenure of the appropriation by the State was already indicated. In November, 1788, the Legislature resolved that the annual appropriation be suspended until ''the professors and other officers thereof be appointed and actually engaged in the exercise of their several duties.''

On Monday, January 11, 1790, the grammar and mathematical schools were removed to the apartments prepared for them in St. John's College, which were ''fitted up in a commodious and neat manner.''

On November 21, 1793, was the first commencement. There were two graduates—John Addison Carr, of Maryland and Charles Alexander, of Virginia. The former delivered a Latin oration, and another ''On the Advantages of Agriculture.'' Mr. Alexander delivered the valedictory. On both graduates was conferred the degree of Bachelor of Arts. ''The principal then closed the business of the day by an address to the graduates, respecting their future conduct in life, and concluded with commending them to the care and protection of the Almighty Governor of the Universe.''

''These young gentlemen, on their private and public examinations acquitted themselves to the satisfaction of the visitors and others who attended, and their public exhibition, was received with the approbation of a polite and discerning audience.''*

The College early had its enemies and so industriously had they been at work that in March, 1803, the Governors and Visitors deputized A. C. Hanson, Charles Carroll, of Carrollton, and Richard Ridgely, ''to publish an account of the state of the College, and of the advantages it possesses and may afford.'' From this paper the following is extracted:

''St. John's College was founded, and has been carried on, under an Act of Assembly, passed in 1784, by private contributions, by a public annual donation of £1,759, and by tuition money. Various untoward circumstances delayed the opening and dedication until November, 1789. But in the course of 18 months from that period, the plan of the college, and the regulations in the several schools, were completed, and professors and teachers employed in the discharge of their offices.

''It is notorious, that from that time methods have been essayed to destroy, or suppress a seminary, the institution of which had been considered as reflecting a permanent honour on the State. It notwithstanding soon acquired a reputation scarcely exceeded by that of

* Md. Gazette.

any other college within the United States ; and although reports industriously circulated, have lately impaired its credit, no seminary on the continent has afforded superior advantages to students of every description.

"It is Incumbent on us to notice these reports.

"It has been bruited through the country, that young men and even boys, belonging to the college, have been corrupted, or at least rendered idle and dissipated, by the attentions paid to them by the citizens of Annapolis.

"It is indeed to be wished, that students be so far controlled as that they shall not neglect their college duties.   But what is it that a wise parent or guardian comprehends in liberal education ? Does he not wish something more than languages, and abstruse science, to be attained by his child, or ward, whilst at college ?   Can he be insensible of the vast importance of early acquired manners ?   Let him then believe all that with probability, can be told of those attentions.   He may nevertheless, be persuaded, that the respectable houses which have been reported as the haunts of collegians, confer on them at least the advantage of polishing their manners, and of preventing, in some instances, a more pernicious dissipation of their time. Besides, it cannot be denied, that valuable connexions may be formed in the polite societies, to which the address or good fortune of some of the students has introduced them, and which prejudice or ignorance alone represent as baneful to the rising youth.

"And now, admitting that students have heretofore been allowed to consume too much of their time in certain genteel, amiable circles of society, is it to be imagined, that no remedy will be found for the grievance ?   The bare report through the country will be sufficient to bring about a correction of the evil.

"The truth is, that in Annapolis, where every person is known to every other, and where there are constantly men unfriendly to the college, viewing everything about it through the medium of prejudice, the conduct of a few irregular young men may fix a reproach on the whole body of students, as well as the trustees and faculty.

"Can it be necessary to suggest to our intelligent fellow-citizens, that final advantage, enjoyed by the students in St. John's College of attending, at times, the debates in the General Assembly, and in the several supreme courts ? It is at Annapolis, that listening to the eloquence of the bar, the Senate, and the House of Delegates, an ingenuous ardent young man may catch the flame of patriotism, imbibe a laudable ambition, and lay the best foundation for future eminence.

"Let us be permitted, then, barely to hint at a comparison between this seminary and a college fixed in the country, or at an obscure place.   What are the superior advantages to be derived from the latter ? It is, beyond a doubt, that youthful innocence will be there better preserved ? No! but the latter seminary is cheaper.   This consideration is indeed important to men of scanty fortune.   But, to men of easy circumstances, it surely cannot have weight sufficient to give ponderance to the scale, into which it is triumphantly thrown.   We will not pursue a subject, which may be invidious, further than by giving a plain, correct statement of expenses at St. John's College :

"Of a youth, boarding in the College Building, board, including washing, fire and candle, both in the public
and bed rooms...................... ....£50 00
Tuition, fire-wood in the schools, pens and ink...... ...   6 10 0

Total, £56 10 0

"To which add £3 to each boy in the higher classes learning French.

"At the last meeting of the trustees, it was resolved, that the next
summer vacation, every student entering the college, who has not in
Annapolis, a parent, or guardian, or a friend who will give him board,
or in whom his parent or guardian reposes a confidence, and who will
receive him as an inmate, shall board in the college building. And the
cases in which a dispensation is to be allowed are to be judged by the
principal. Inferior teachers, who are not married men, or housekeepers, are likewise to board there, for the purpose of superintending
the students. Mr. Duke, the professor of languages, already boards
there. All the rooms are spacious, airy, and convenient: and the
family which keeps the house is respectable, and affords such fare and
treatment in every respect, as ought to give satisfaction. Students
now boarding in private house are not to be compelled to board in the
college, although they are earnestly invited to make that exchange,
which must be salutary to themselves and to the institution.

"We presume, that there are few seminaries in town, where the
whole expense, exclusive of cloaths, pocket money, and books, does
not exceed £56 10 0 or £59 10 0, and where a student shall not, to the
mortification of himself and his fond parents, subsist scantily on un-
palatable food and be stinted even with respect to clean linen, &c. It
is certain that whenever board is fixed too low, either it must in a
short time be raised, or the boarder must submit to hard fare, and
other inconvenience.

"Reports injurious to St. John's College have originated from an
unhappy difference between a teacher and a professor. We content
ourselves with remarking this most extraordinary circumstance, that
the professor, who is indeed eminent for his knowledge of the learned
languages, and who has voluntarily guided the college, without censures from the trustees, has lately been appointed to an high station
in a seminary of rising importance and reputation, in the prosperity of
which every enlightened liberal citizen must feel an interest, although
he may not wish the downfall of St. John's College."

The faculty at this time was:
John McDowell, A. M., Principal.
Reverend Ralph Higinbothom, Vice Principal.
Rev. William Duke, Professor of Languages.
Mr. John Connell, Professor of English and Grammar.
Mr. Philip Curran, Assistant Professor of English and Grammar.
Mr. Richard Owen, Master of Writing and Arithmetic.
Mr. Marin Detargny, Professor of French.

St. John's survived unscathed this attack of its enemies, and for
years realized the most sanguine hopes of its broad and liberal founders. Poets, jurists, scholars, and statesmen were sent forth from her
classic halls, "who have been the pride of her own and the admiration
of other States, and who have earned for the State reputation,
and reflected honor on their *alma mater*."

From 1793, when the first class was graduated to 1806, there appears in the registry of the Alumini of the College, four Governors of Maryland, one Governor of Liberia, seven Members of the Executive Council, six United States Senators, five Members of the House of Representatives, four Judges of the Court of Appeals, eight Judges of other Courts, one Attorney-General, one United States District Attorney, one Auditor of the United States Treasurer, six State Senators, fifteen Members of the House of Delegates, besides foreign Consuls, Officers of the Army and Navy, Physicians, and Surgeons, and distinguished Lawyers, including one Chancellor of South Carolina. There were many others who left the College before completing its course and engaged in agriculture and commerce.

In 1806, though a political feud, the nature of which has not been handed down to us, the State appropriations to St. John's and Washington College were withdrawn.

The necessary buildings had been erected, the Professors appointed, a number of young men from all parts of the State and from some of the sister States had been drawn to it; and thus, when the fondest hopes of its friends were more than realized, the Legislature so far ignored its solemn obligations as to pass an Act for the revocation of the grant made to St. John's in the Act of incorporation. "Each party," says Francis Scott Key, the author of our great national hymn, "The Star Spangled Banner," and an alumnus of St. John's, referring to this action of the General Assembly—"caught at the advantage to be gained by the apparent popularity of the measure, and the real interests and honor of the State were sacrificed by each." The distinguished William Pinkney, who eloquently, but vainly, remonstrated against the passage of this Act, predicted that "the day which witnessed the degradation of St. John's College, in the very dawn of its promise, would prove the darkest day Maryland had known." For some time the usefulness of the college seems to have been almost entirely destroyed, as no lists of graduates appear until 1810. Nothing seems to have been done to repair what is now conceded to have been a great wrong, until 1811, when the sum of $1,000 was restored. In 1824, a lottery was granted to the college, the proceeds of which, amounting to $20,000, were invested in bank stock, from which an annual income of $1,200 was derived, until about thirty years afterwards, when the whole fund was expended in erecting a dormitory for students and dwellings for professors.

It was not until 1832, that the Board of Visitors and Governors of the College, in a memorial to the General Assembly, having set forth in a most clear and forcible way the unanswerable character of their legal claim, the Legislature was led to increase the grant to $3,000, at the same time, however, providing that the Board should agree to accept this sum "in full satisfaction of all legal or equitable claims which the College might have, or be supposed to have, against the State." Here was, if not a plain case of duress at least a case of "Might vs. Right." "There is no question," says President Garnett, in 1880, "that if, at any time before 1819, when the Dartmouth College decision was rendered, and 1832, suit had been brought, the full amount of the arrearages (then over $100,000) might have been recovered; but, in defense of the Board of Visitors and Governors, it may be said that they believed their rights were entirely in the power of the State and without any means of being enforced ; so the deed of release was executed and entered upon the records of the Court of Appeals.''

The Board of Visitors and Governors, however, having become convinced of the arbitrary character of this settlement of their claim against the State, submitted, in 1859, with the consent of the Legislature, the following points to the decision of the Court of Appeals :

''1. Whether the appropriation made in the charter constitutes a contract on the part of the State which could not be legally repealed by the Act of 1805.

''2. Whether this latter Act is not a violation of the Constitution of the United States.

''3. Whether the charter constituted such a contract as, if entered into between individual citizens, would be legally binding upon them.''

All three of these points (Vol. 15, Md. Reports p. 330) were unanimously decided in the affirmative. When, however, a few years thereafter, suit was brought to recover the amount of their claim—over $390,000, inclusive of interest—it was held by the Court that the Board of Visitors and Governors could not avoid the release given in 1833, and the suit was accordingly decided against them. Inasmuch, however, as eminent lawyers, among them the Hon. Reverdy Johnson, himself an alumnus of St. John's, maintained that under the terms of the charter itself (Acts of 1784, Chapter 37, Section 16), the Board had transcended its powers in granting this release, measures were taken for an appeal to the Supreme Court of the United States. Pending this proceeding, however, the Board, feeling reluctant, as they affirmed, to seek redress for the wrongs of a Maryland College in a tribunal beyond its jurisdiction, addressed a memorial to the Legislature of 1865, in response to which, and, doubtless, in recognition of this appeal to their sense of justice, the General Assembly appropriated the sum of $12,000 annually for five years from June 1st, 1868.

Humphrey Hall, standing to the right of McDowell Hall, was erected in 1834, for the accommodation of students, and for the improving and extending the library and philosophical apparatus of the institution. ''This was done by the exertions of the Principal, Rev. Hector Humphreys, D. D., who by visits to different parts of the State, succeeded in obtaining donations aggregating over $12,000.''

The building soon after its erection was described as being ''designed for one of the professors, and the students ; there are twenty private rooms in it, intended for the separate studies for members of the advanced classes, and two large dormitories for pupils in the preparatory branches. A building like this had long been needed. It will accommodate at least sixty students in all the departments.''

During the war between the Federal Government and Seceded States, the buildings and grounds of St. John's College were seized by the Government for military purposes. Its commons were turned into a camp, its halls into quarters, and its laboratory into a stable. During this period the educational functions were suspended and the State's appropriation withdrawn. It was revived and restored in an aggregate sum by Chapter 101, Acts of 1866.

The College buildings were soon put in thorough repair, and Dr. Henry Barnard, of Connecticut, late Commissioner of Education, was elected Principal, by whom the College was reopened in September, 1866.

By Chapter 393, Acts of 1872, the College, in addition to the $3,000, already received it was given a further grant of $12,000 per annum for six years. This was a renewal of the grant of 1868.

The same Act gave $5,000 for "increasing and improving the College library, laboratory, philosophical apparatus and cabinet." This Act also directed to be paid to the Visitors and Governors of St. John's "the sum of $10,000 per annum, payable quarterly, to be applied by them in furnishing board, fuel, lights, and washing, to two of the students, educated free of charge for tuition, from each Senatorial District of this State, and appointed by the Commissioners of the Primary Schools, by and with the advice and consent of the Senator in their respective Senatorial Districts, after a competitive examination of the candidates, provided, that the said appointment shall not be held by the same student for more than four years, and that each student, receiving such appointment, shall give his bond to the State of Maryland for such amount, with such security, as may be approved of by the Principal of said College that he will teach school within this State for not less than two years after leaving College."

By Chapter 315, Acts of 1878, the appropriation of $12,000 additional to the $3,000 of contract, was voted the College for two years: and the ten thousand to Senatorial Scholars was reduced to $7,500 per annum. The candidates for Senatorial scholarship, by this Act were required to produce before the School Commissioners of their respective counties and the city of Baltimore "satisfactory evidence of their moral character and of their inability, or the inability of their parents, or guardians, to pay the regular College charges."

The appropriations of $7,500 per annum for Senatorial scholarships, and $3,000 for general expenses continues to the present.

The College, during its existence of a century presents a long array of honorable names that acknowledge St. John's as their *alma mater*. Among them are:

Daniel Clarke, Associate Judge of the First Judicial District ; John Done, Judge of the General Court, Judge of the Fourth Judicial District, and of the Court of Appeals of Maryland : Clement Dorsey, Judge of the First Judicial District : Benjamin Ogle, Governor of Maryland ; Ninian Pinkney, Clerk of the Executive Council, of the class of 1793 ; Richard Harwood, Adjutant-General of Maryland ; John Carlisle Herbert, Member of Congress and Speaker of the House of Delegates of Maryland ; Alexander Contee Magruder, Judge of the Court of Appeals, Reporter of the Decisions of the same Court ; John Seney and John C. Weems, Members of Congress, of the class of 1794 ; Robert H. Goldsborough, United States Senator : Francis Scott Key, author of "Star Spangled Banner ;" John Ridgely, Surgeon United States Navy ; Washington Van Bibber, Member of Congress, of the class of 1796 ; John Leeds Kerr, United States Senator ; John Tayloe Lomax, Judge of the Court of Appeals of Virginia, of the class of 1797 ; Alexander Hammett, Consul at Naples : Thomas U. P. Charlton, Chancellor of South Carolina ; William Rodgers, Surgeon United States Navy ; Tobias Watkins, Auditor in United States Treasury, and Assistant Surgeon United States Army ; John Wilmot, Adjutant-General of Maryland, of the class of 1798 ; Thomas Beale Dorsey, Attorney-

General of Maryland and Chief of the Court of Appeals; Dennis
Claude. M. D., Treasurer of Maryland: George Washington Parke
Custis, of the class of 1799: Nicholas Harwood. M. D., Surgeon United
States Navy; George Mann, Lieutenant United States Navy; James
Thomas. Governor of Maryland, of the class of 1800: James Murray,
Examiner General: Charles W. Hanson, Judge of the Sixth Judicial
District: Alexander C. Hanson, Member of the House of Representa-
tives and United States Senator; David Hoffman, Professor of Laws
in the University of Maryland; Charles Sterrett Ridgely, Speaker of
the House of Delegates, class of 1802; John Contee, Lieutenant
U. S. Marine Corps; William Grason, Governor of Maryland; Christo-
pher Hughes, Charge to Sweden; Thomas Williamson, Surgeon
United States Navy, of the class of 1804; George Mackubin, Treasurer
of Maryland; John Wesley Peaco, Surgeon U. S. Navy and Governor
of Liberia; Daniel Randall, Deputy Paymaster General, U. S. Army;
Hyde Ray, Surgeon U. S. Navy; John R. Shaw, Purser U. S. Navy;
Seth Switzer, Consul to Guayaquil; William T. Wooton, Secretary of
State, of the class of 1805; Thomas Randall, Judge of the District
Court of Florida; John Ridout, Visitor and Governor; John Gwinn,
Captain U. S. Navy; William Latimer, Admiral U. S. Navy; Wil-
liam H. Marriott, Collector of the Port of Baltimore, of the class of
1810; Nicholas Brewer, Judge of the Circuit Court of Anne Arundel;
William Caton, Surgeon U. S. Navy; Reverdy Johnson, United States
Senator, Attorney-General, of United States, Minister to England;
David Ridgely, State Librarian, author of ''Annals of An-
napolis,'' William Greenbury Ridgely, Chief Clerk in the Navy De-
partment at Washington; John Nelson Watkins Adjutant-General of
Maryland, of the class of 1811; Thomas S. Alexander, L. L. D.,
George G. Brewer, Register of the Land Office; John Denny, Surgeon
United States Navy, John Johnson, Councellor of Maryland, London
Mercer. Lieutenant United States Navy; Richard Randall, M. D.
U. S. A., and Governor of Liberia; Francis Thomas, Member of Con-
gress, Governor of Maryland, Minister to Peru; Ramsay Waters,
Register in Chancery; John B. Wells, Surgeon in United States
Army; George Wells, President of the Maryland Senate; William
Williams, M. D., President of the Maryland Senate, of the classes
from 1811 to 1821; Alexander Randall, Member of Congress and At-
torney-General of Maryland, of the class of 1822; Nicholas Brewer, of
John, Adjutant-General of Maryland; Burton Randall, Surgeon
United States Army, of the classes from 1822 to 1825; John Henry
Alexander, L. L. D.; William Harwood, State Librarian, Professor at
the Naval Academy, School Examiner of Anne Arundel County;
William Pinkney, Bishop of the Protestant Episcopal Church in
Maryland; William H. Tuck, Judge of the Court of Appeals; John
Bowie, Lieutenant United States Navy, of the class of 1827; John
Randall Hagner, Paymaster United States Army; Thomas Karney,
Professor of Ethics and Librarian in the United States Naval Aca-
demy; Ninian Pinkney, Medical Director, U. S. Navy; Augustus
Bowie, Surgeon U. S. Navy; Sprigg Harwood, Clerk of the Circuit
Court; John H. T. Magruder, State Librarian; Richard Swann, State
Librarian, of the class of 1830; Rev. Orlando Hutton, John Greene
Proud, Poet before the Alumni; F. W. Green, Member of Congress;
Peter V. Hagner, U. S. Army, of the class of 1831; Abram Claude,
Professor of Chemistry St. John's College, Mayor of Annapolis, of

the class of 1835; William R. Hayward, Commissioner of the Land Office; Rev. Samuel Ridout, class of 1836; William Tell Claude; Henry H. Goldsborough, President of State Convention of 1864, Comptroller, Judge of Eleventh Judicial Circuit; William H. Thompson, Professor of Grammar in St. John's College; Marius Duvall, Medical Director of the U. S. Navy; William R. Goodman, M. D.; Philip Lansdale, Medical Director U. S. Navy; William Lewly, Surgeon United States Army, of the class of 1835; Frederick Stone, Judge of the Court of Appeals, of the class of 1939; Luther Giddings, Major of the United States Army; George S. Humphrey, Lieutenant, United States Army; Richard Grason, Judge of the Court of Appeals of Maryland, class of 1841; Llewellyn Boyle, Lieutenant United States Army and State Librarian; John Thomas Hall, Lieutenant United States Army; James Kemp Herwood, Purser United States Navy; Thomas A. M. Perlin, Surgeon United States Army; John Schaaff Stockett, State Reporter of the Court of Appeals, of the class of 1844; Nicholas Brewer, State Reporter of the Court of Appeals; Richard M. Chase, Secretary of the Naval Academy; James Munroe, Mayor of Annapolis, class of 1846; James Shaw Franklin, Clerk of the Court of Appeals; John Mullan, Captain United States Army; Charles S. Winder, Captain U. S. Army, and Brigadier General Confederate States Army; class of 1847; James Revell, State's Attorney for Anne Arundel County; Thomas J. Nelson, Paymaster U. S. Army, class of 1846; Charles Brewer, Surgeon in U. S. and C. S. Armies; William Sprigg Hall, Judge of the Court of Common Pleas for Ramsey County, Minnesota, class of 1852; Daniel R. Magruder, Judge of the Court of Appeals, class of 1853; John H. Sellman, Paymaster United States Navy, Collector Internal Revenue, class of 1857; Andrew G. Chapman, Member of Congress, class of 1858; John W. Brewer, Assistant Surgeon United States Army; William Hersey Hopkins, Vice Principal of St. John's College, President Female College of Baltimore, class of 1857; Samuel T. McCullough, Lieutenant Confederate States Army, class of 1860.

In 1857, there was added to St. John's College Pinkney Hall, containing 46 rooms. When in thorough repair it will accommodate 140 to 150 students. Its floorings were greatly damaged during the occupancy of the College by the United States troops in the civil war. Its dimensions are 36 feet front, 95 feet deep, and is four stories. The Gymnasium is in the rear of the space between McDowell and Pinkney Halls. The two professors' houses to the right of Humphrey Hall were built in 1855, the fine double house, intended for the use of the Principal and Vice-Principal, was built in 1857.

The following was the faculty of 1886:

Thomas J. Fell, University of London, England; Acting President, Professor of Ancient and Modern Languages, and Lecturer on Metaphysics, Moral Philosophy and Evidences of Christianity; A. Sager Hall, Graduate and Doctor of Philosophy of Michigan University, Professor of Natural Philosophy, Astronomy, Chemistry, Zoology and Botany, and Lecturer on Mineralogy and Geology; C. W. Reid, Professor of the Greek and German Languages; Charles W. Foster, U. S. A., Professor of Military Science and Tactics, and Lecturer on International and Constitutional Law; J. H. Baker, Assistant Engineer U. S. N., Professor of Higher Mathematics and Mechanical Engineering: C. W. Cain, Professor of Mathematics and Acting Professor of English Literature: C. W. Reid, Superintendent of the Preparatory Department and Librarian: J. E. W. Revell, Tutor in the Preparatory Department; John L. Chew, Tutor in the Preparatory Department.

CHAPTER XLIV.

PRESIDENT WASHINGTON'S VISIT TO ANNAPOLIS.

On Friday morning, March 25th, 1791, President Washington, accompanied only by his private Secretary, Major Jackson, arrived in Annapolis. Intelligence having been received of his intended embarkation at Rock Hall, he had been anxiously expected on Thursday evening—but the Governor, and several other gentlemen, who had failed to meet him, were compelled to return without tidings. "The vessel, which contained the chief treasure of America, did not enter the river Severn until ten o'clock, in a dark tempestuous night. She struck on a bar, or point, within about a mile from the city; and although they made a signal of distress, it was impossible, before day-light, to go to her relief. The guardian angel of America was still watchful; and we are happy in assuring our countrymen that the health of their dearest friend has not been at all affected by an accident far more distressing to those who were apprised, or rather apprehensive, of his situation, than to himself."[*]

At 10 o'clock on the same day attended by the Governor, and a number of respectable citizens, he visited St. John's College, and expressed much satisfaction at the appearance of this rising seminary. He then pursued his walk to the government house. At three o'clock he sat down to a public dinner at Mr. Mann's with a numerous company of the inhabitants, and continued at table until there had been circulated the following toasts, each of which was announced by the discharge of cannon—

1. The People of the United States of America.
2. The Congress.
3. The dearest Friend of his Country.
4. The State of Maryland.
5. Wisdom, Justice and Harmony, in all our Public Councils.
6. Agriculture Manufactures, Commerce and Learning; may they flourish with Virtue and true Religion.
7. The King of the French.
8. The National Assembly of France.
9. The Sieur la Fayette, and the other generous Friends to America in the day of her Distress.

[*] Md. Gazette.

10. To all those who have fallen in the Cause of America.

11. The Patriots of Nations and Ages.

12. The Powers of Europe friendly to America.

13. May all the inhabitants of the Earth be taught to consider each other as Fellow Citizens.

14. The Virtuous Daughters of America.

15. The Perpetual Union of distinct Sovereign States under an efficient Federal Head.

On Saturday the President again dined with a large company at the Government House : and in the evening his presence enlivened a ball. at which was exhibited everything which the little city contained of beauty and elegance.

The little city was in a whirl of delightful excitement during the entire stay of its illustrious visitor. all care seemed suspended, and the inhabitants of the whole town were made "happy in contemplating him whom they considered as their fastest friend, as well as the most exalted of their fellow-citizens, and the first of men."

On Sunday, the 27th, the President left Annapolis on horseback, escorted, as far as South River, by a company of gentlemen. Here the most of them took leave of him, but Governor Plater accompanied him to Georgetown, where the President stayed some days before he began his arduous and patriotic journey through the Southern States.

A pleasant outgrowth of President Washington's visit to Annapolis was the following correspondence :

ANNAPOLIS, April 7th.

To The President of the United States.

Sir :—We, the Faculty of St. John's College, beg leave to express the sincere joy which the honour of your presence in our infant seminary afforded us. In common with all those who superintend the education of youth. we must feel a lively gratitude to the defender of liberty, the guardian of his country, and consequently the great patron of literature. But as this seminary was begun since the united voice of our America called you to preside over its most important interests, and ensure to them the continuance of those blessings which your calm foresight and steady fortitude had been the happy means of procuring. it seems in a peculiar manner to look up to you with filial respect. That it dates its birth from this grand era, which has placed you at the head of fifteen distinct Sovereign States united into one mighty republic, is regarded by its friends as an auspicious circumstance and flattering assurance of its future eminence and usefulness. To the friend of virtue and his country, the rise of a college. where the youth of generations, yet unborn, may be taught to admire and emulate the great and good, must give a heart felt delight, as they promise perpetuity to the labours and renown of the patriot and hero.

Our earnest prayers, that a kind Providence may constantly watch over you, and preserve a life. long, indeed, already, if measured by deeds of worth and fullness of honors, but too short as yet for your country.

Signed in behalf, and at the request, of the Faculty.

JOHN McDOWELL, President,

To the Faculty of St. John's College,

Gentlemen :—The satisfaction which I have derived from my visit to your infant seminary, is expressed with real pleasure, and my wishes for its progress to perfection are preferred with sincere regard.

The very promising appearance of its infancy must flatter all its friends among whom I entreat you to class me, with the hope of an early, and at the same time, a mature manhood.

You will do justice to the sentiments, which your kind regard towards myself inspires, by believing that I reciprocate the good wishes contained in your address, and I sincerely hope the excellence of your seminary will be manifested in the morals and science of the youth who are reared with your care.

GEORGE WASHINGTON.

President Washington gave a proof of his friendly sentiments towards St. John's by installing his ward, George Washington Parke Custis, a student in the institution. Two nephews of Washington were also students of the College.

～～～

CHAPTER XLV.

CHRONICLES OF ANNAPOLIS FROM 1777 TO 1850.

[1777.] The General Assembly, at its February Session, 1777, passed a resolution, under which, the Court of Appeals was to be composed of five Judges. The first Judges were Benjamin Rumsey, Chief Judge; Benjamin Mackall, Thomas Jones, Solomon Wright, James McCray, Associates. They were appointed December 12th, 1778.

The Acts of February Session, 1777, Chapter 15, made the "Talbot Court House" and Annapolis, the places of the meeting of the Provincial Court, afterward changed into the General Court. It was a Court of original jurisdiction. The first Justices appointed March 9th, 1778, were William Paca, Chief Judge; Richard Thomas and Alex. Contee Hanson, Associate Judges. The Court sat in the room which, in the State House, gave place to, and is now occupied in part by the State Library.

[1783.] In 1783, one I. Chalmers, a goldsmith, of Annapolis, Maryland, issued silver tokens as a speculation venture of his own. They consisted of shillings, six pences, and three pences, however, the two smaller pieces particularly so. Dr. John David Schœpf, who visited this country in 1783-4, gives the following account of these coins:

"In the United States, Annapolis has the honor of having furnished the first silver money for small change. A goldsmith of this place coins on his own account, though with the consent of the government. After the depreciation of the paper money, it became customary and necessary, throughout America, to cut the Spanish dollars, in two, four and more pieces for change. This dividing became soon a profitable business in the hands of expert cutters who knew how to cut five quarters, or nine and two-eighths out of a round dollar, so that shortly every one refused to take this kind of money otherwise than by weight or at discretion. To get over this embarrassment the said goldsmith assists in getting the angular pieces out of circulation, by taking them in exchange, with a considerable advantage to himself, for pieces of his own coinage."*

[1783.] At Washington's reception, the day before he resigned his commission, Mr. Mann furnished the supper at the State House. Ninety-eight bottles of wine, two and a-half gallons of spirits, nine pounds of sugar, a lot of limes, music and waiters, and a dozen packs of cards were supplied, and the Governor directed Col. Mills of the Annapolis Coffee House, to furnish the people with punch and grog to the value of £10 10s.

[1783.] The festivities of the day that celebrated peace between England and America were substantial. The State bought that day from James Makubbin a hogshead of rum (116 gallons at 6s. 6d. per gallon) and from George Mann, 49 gallons of claret, 32 gallons of Maderia, 35 port, 6 of spirit. It also purchased 151b of loaf sugar, 176lb of bacon, 284lb of salt beef, 52lb of shoat, 129lb of mutton, 272lb of veal, 183lb of beef, 7 lambs and 12 fowls. For the ball that closed the day there were 8 gallons of wine, 4 of spirits, beef, hams, tongues, chickens, turkeys, tarts, custards, cheese-cakes, 502 loaves of bread, 24 shillings worth of cards, and a box of candles. The State had to pay Mr. Mann for 35 knives and 29 forks lost, and 28 plates, 43 wine glasses, 1 dish, 61 broken bottles—an index of what a day it was.

[1786.] Noah Webster, the lexicographer, began his life-work as an itinerant lecturer on the English language.† This was in 1785, in which course he visited the principal cities of America, Annapolis being one of the places in which he lectured.

In 1787, William Clark, established a stage route between Baltimore and Annapolis. The coach ran three times a week. It set out from Annapolis every Monday, Wednesday and Friday precisely at five o'clock in the morning. On the return it started from Mr. Wm. Evans at the Golden Bacchus, the corner of Calvert and Banks streets, in Baltimore, on Tuesdays, Thursdays and Saturdays, precisely at five o'clock in the morning. Fare—15 shillings, way passengers, six-pence per mile.

December 6th, a lady, whose name was not given, delivered a lecture on "Poetry" in the Ball Room.

[1788.] In 1788, Judge Samuel Chase, removed from Annapolis to Baltimore, on the urgent solicitation of Col. Howard, a large property-holder, who, as an inducement to reside in Baltimore, offered Mr. Chase one full square for city building lots, if he would make Baltimore his residence. The offer was accepted, the property was conveyed to him, and is now within the heart of the city, a valuable estate. It remains in the possession of the descendants of Judge Chase.

While on a visit to Baltimore, towards the close of the Revolutionary War, he stopped, from curiosity, in a debating society, where he was astonished at the eloquence of a young man. He proved to be a druggist's clerk. Judge Chase ascertained the young man's name, searched him out, and advised him to study law. The young man disclosed to his admirer that poverty was an insurmountable difficulty in the way. Mr. Chase offered him at once the use of his library and

* Scharf's History of Md. vol. 1, ps. 178-179-180.

† Appleton's Encyclopedia, vol. 16. p. 533.

at his seat table. The offer was accepted with gratitude, the young man pursued a course of legal studies, and, on his admission to the bar, passed his examination with marked ability. That obscure young drug clerk was afterward the distinguished William Pinkney.

[1788.] The *Gazette* of date of January 31st, publishes a list of seventeen vessels that had arrived at Annapolis. The magnitude and the importance of the commerce of this port are evidenced by the fact that one vessel was from each of the following places:

Barbadoes, Limington, Demarara, Aux-Cays, Amsterdam, Dublin, St. Croix, Salem, Belfast Port-au-Prince, Charleston, St. Bartholomews, Rhode Island and Norfolk; and three from New York.

Nicholas Carroll and Alexander Contee Hanson were elected delegates to represent Annapolis in the Convention called to determine whether Maryland would accede to the proposed plan of a Confederate Government for the States. The Convention met at Annapolis Monday, April 21st, and on the following Thursday by a vote of 63 to 11, passed a resolution that "the Convention assent to and ratify the proposed plan of federal government for the United States." The nays on this important question form an interesting morsel of history. They were Jeremiah T. Chase, John T. Mercer, Benjamin Harrison, Charles Ridgely, Charles Ridgely, of Wm., Edward Cockey, Nathan Cromwell, John Love, William Pinkney, and Luther Martin.

The first ballot for the first United States Senators from Maryland, took place at Annapolis on December 9. The two houses met in joint session and it required a majority of the members in attendance to elect. There were thirteen Senators present and seventy members of the House of Delegates. Forty-two votes were necessary to elect. On the first ballot, John Henry received 41; George Gale 41; Ninah Forrest 41: Charles Carroll 40: The second ballot resulted, Henry 42: Gale 40: Carroll 41: Forrest 41. The Assembly then adjourned until Wednesday the 10th. On this day the first ballot resulted Charles Carroll 42: Ninah Forrest 39.

[1789.] On Tuesday, the 13th, of October, the Jockey Club of Annapolis had its fall races. The forty guinea purse was won by Mr. Wm. Morgan's black horse Shakespere. The £50 purse by Mr. John Lee Gibson's bay mare Cub, and the £30 stake by Mr. Wm. Campbell's bay horse Sloven.

[1790.] On Monday, February 11, about three o'clock in the afternoon the "Government House," (the Governor's residence,) was set on fire by a defective chimney. The citizens promptly repaired to it and extinguished the fire after it had injured the second story. Messrs. Andrew Brown, Alex. Thompson, James M'Faden, Dennis Dunning, John Sullivan, Patrick Dunn, Cornelius West, Thomas Clark and Charles Caton displayed judicious zeal in repairing to the roof and cutting a hole in which so as to admit the free passage of water by which the fire was extinguished.

The same day, (old style,) was celebrated as the birthday of General Washington. An elegant dinner was set at Mann's Hotel, by which the Governor, citizens, and strangers honored the illustrious hero. The *Gazette* warms with the scene and says "it exhibited a striking picture of social and elevated joy. The name of Washington operated like a charm upon the minds and spirit of the whole company. Reverence, gratitude, and love were depicted on every face, and the affections of the heart were disclosed in all the external expressions of ardent passions. The powers of beauty could only complete this joyful festival. And these were not wanting, for, at the evening assembly, the animating presence of the ladies gave a fresh spur to the feelings of the day. *Vive le President* shone in the countenance, was inscribed in the dress, and engraved on the heart of every fair attendant. In a word such an occasion alone could excite feelings so general, and so sincere." After dinner a gentleman favored the company with an original song, depicting the birth of Washington at the command of Jove.

[1790.] Henry Ridgely, of Annapolis, on November 9, was elected one of the Governor's Council.

In the *Maryland Gazette's* issue of November 11, appeared a communication, signed "A Freeman," which strongly denounced negro slavery.

On the 16th of November, Daniel of St. Thomas Jenefer, a prominent citizen of Annapolis, died aged 67 years.

Charles Carroll, of Carrolton, was re-elected Senator of the United States.

On December 9, a communication signed "Citizen" appeared in the Gazette in which the writer wanted the firing of guns in the streets on Christmas Day broken up. The practice, however, obtains to this day.

[1792.] On Friday, the 10th of February, Governor George Plater died in Annapolis. In his public character which began with his earliest manhood, and terminated with his death, he was the firm advocate of the rights of man, and was distinguished by warm and zealous adherence to the principles of the American Revolution. In private life, he lived an honest man and was above suspicion in the transactions of business. "He was warm in his affections and unbounded in his philanthropy." His remains were attended the next day by the honorable members of the council, the officers of State, and a numerous company of citizens to South River, on the way to Sotterly, his seat in St. Mary's county. James Brice, being the first name of the Governor's Council, became Governor.

In January, 1793 the Lodge of Antient York Masons, installed at their Lodge-room in the city of Annapolis in due form, by authority of Peregrine Letherbury, esq., grand-master of Maryland, and who have entitled themselves the Amanda Lodge, assembled to celebrate St. John's the Evangelist, A. L. 5792, at the house of Mr. Vachel Stevens, where, "with Masonic and convivial happiness, whilst decorum and philanthropy presided at their meeting, they drank the following toasts :"

1. Our Sublime brother, the president of the United States.
2. The Day.
3. Our grand-master of Maryland, Peregrine Letherbury, Esq.,
4. The Amanda Lodge.
5. The P. grand-master of Maryland, John Coates, Esq.,
6. Our Masonic brethern.
7. The United States.
8. The Secretary of State.
9. The Governor of Maryland.
10. The Chancellor of Maryland.

11. The Chief Judge of Maryland.
12. Col. Francis Mercer.
13. The National Assembly of France.

On February 22nd, one of the Annapolis packets on its way to Baltimore, upset off Magothy river, and the following persons from Annapolis were drowned: Mr. Thomas Pryfe, saddler; Mr. John Ross, Mr. John Hammond, Mr. Benjamin Buckland, cabinet-makers; Mr. Thomas Carstin, and Mr. Wm. Lockerman, owners of the vessel; and Mr. James Denning, Mr. Thomas Coats of Greensbury's Point, and a colored boy were also drowned. There were ten persons on the vessel and nine were drowned.

On February 24th, Thomas Dance, a plasterer of Annapolis, whilst at work on the inside of the dome of the "Stadt-house," made a false step, and fell to the floor. He died in a few hours.

July 31st. The Muse's flame was lit by adorers to burn incense to their idols in ancient Annapolis as well as in the modern days. In the *Gazette* of July 31st, appears the following acrostic:

"Skilled in science, formed without art to please.
As bright as glory, yet as mild as ease.
Refined in politeness, as in carriage nice,
Altho's she's fair, she's diffident tho's wise.
Her brilliant eyes a hermit would entice.
Merry, tho' not light; against flattery a test.
Unknown to intrigue, of female fair the best.
Range from the Northern to the Southern pole
Retrace your footsteps, e'en pervade the whole.
And view the beauties of each various clime
You'll see none so fair, as my nymph divine!"

[1795.] There lived at Annapolis at this period, one William Caton, a hair-dresser and barber, whose chief claim to renown is that he shaved General Washington. Caton was an unctious tradesman, and when he opened a grocery and dry-goods store, he closed his advertisement with:

"The said Caton, actuated by a due regard to the sacred principles of gratitude, tenders his grateful thanks for that liberal patronage which a generous and indulgent public has offered him, and he flatters himself, that, while his mind is animated by a lively sense of preceding favors, his future conduct will entitle him to the claims of universal approbation.."

[1800. On Sunday, January 26th, the Almshouse, a large and commodious building, near Annapolis, burned down. None of the inmates were injured.

Saturday, the 22d of February, by proclamation of the Governor, observed at Annapolis, "as a day of mourning, humiliation and prayer," in respect to the memory of Gen. Washington. The officials of State, City and College, the military and citizens, attended church in a body. Rev. Mr. Higinbothem preached in the morning and Rev. Mr. Roberts in the afternoon.

The text in the morning was "It is appointed for all men once to die." In the afternoon, "Know ye not that there is a Prince and a Great Man fallen this day in Israel."

Act 75, of the session of 1880, was a supplemental Act to an Act to lay out and establish a road from the city of Annapolis to the city of Washington, and to repeal the Act therein mentioned.

[1801.] In October. Allen Quynn and Richard Ridgely were elected to represent Annapolis in the Legislature.

In December of this year the proprietor of the *Gazette* had to defend himself against slanderous reports circulated about the partiality of his charges to some of his Federal friends, whilst he made his demands very heavy upon the Republicans who brought him printing. Mr. Green was thoroughly vindicated by the Republicans who were charged to have suffered.

[1802.] Act 104, of the Acts of 1802, was an Act to vest the funds heretofore belonging to the Rector, Governor, Trustees, and Visitors of King William School, in the city of Annapolis, in the Visitors and Governors of St John's College.

Allen Quynn and Richard Ridgely were elected Delegates to the Maryland Legislature from Annapolis.

[1803.] On Saturday, September 15th, there was given a dinner at Mrs. Urquhart's spring where a discussion of politics followed by candidates for the Legislature. This is the first notice found of the present barbecue.

On the 8th of November, 1803, Allen Quynn died at the ripe age of 77 years. He had been a member of the Legislature of Maryland for 25 years. and it is not out of place, to presume that his age was the cause of his retirement from service in the General Assembly.

[1804.] In the *Gazette* of February 16th. a writer who signed himself Juvenus, and who declared he desired to imitate Addison and Steele in correcting the foibles of his fellow-citizens, took up the custom of whittling, which he condemned as a destruction of property prevalent in Annapolis.

On the Frigate Philadelphia, which was captured in the Tripolitan harbor, October 31st, by the Tripolitans, Dr. John Ridgely, of Annapolis. was surgeon. Dr. Ridgely was taken with sixty-three other Americans to prison in Tripoli. Whilst there, he was sent for by the Governor to attend his sick daughter. On the convalescence of the patient, the Governor graciously offered his daughter in marriage to the young American. This honor, having an affianced at home, he had to decline. The Governor then offered the Surgeon the freedom of the city. This the gallant doctor refused unless his companions were also allowed their liberty. When Dr. Ridgely returned to Annapolis, he brought with him a fine white Arabian horse and other valuable gifts which had been presented to him by the grateful Governor.[*]

In August the articles of association to establish the Farmers' Bank of Annapolis were first printed. The Bank contemplated fifteen directors and a president. The solicitors for subscription to the capital stock at Annapolis were John Gibson, James Williams, John Muir, Robert Denny. Lewis Duvall. and William Alexander, and books were opened in every county in the State. The plan contemplated a powerful Maryland *private* banking institution.

In May, 1805, the Act of Assembly to incorporate the Farmers' Bank of Maryland was passed. There were an Annapolis subscription committee and an Easton committee. Thomas J. Bullitt, John Leeds Keer, Hall Harrison, Bennett Wheeler, Joseph Haskins, Wm. Mealing. James

---

[*] Related to me by his niece Mrs. Eliza Bonsall, then, 1886, in her 82nd year.

15

Earle, Jr., constituted the executive body to organize the bank. The books were opened July 16th, and in two days 1690 shares of the two thousand alloted to Annapolis were subscribed. On August 15th, the election for directors to the bank took place. The following were elected directors: John Gibson, Arthur Shaaff, John F. Mercer, Richard H. Harwood, James Maccubin, Horatio Ridout, William Stewart, Louis Duvall, for Annapolis and Anne Arundel County; William Wilkerson, for Calvert County; Robert Bowie, for Prince George's County; Henry H. Chapman, for Charles County; Wm. Somerville, for St. Mary's County; Thomas Davis, for Montgomery County; John Tyler, for Frederick County; Lusby Tilghman, for Washington County; James J. Wilkerson, for Baltimore County; Benedict E. Hall, for Harford County; Upton Brice, for Allegany County. The directors elected John Muir, of Annapolis, president of the bank. The bank at Easton was organized at the same time, directors elected, and Nicholas Hammond made president.

At the Annapolis Theatre, in August, 1803, Alfonso, King of Castile, Love-a-La-Mode, or the Humors of the Turf, were played, also Hearts of Oak and Raising the Wind, the Cure for the Heart-Ache, with the Tale of Mystery were played.

At the election October 4th, for two Members of the House of Delegates for Annapolis, the following was the vote: John Muir, 188 votes; Arthur Shaff, 171; Thomas Jennings, 70.

October 5th, General John Hoskins Stone was buried at Annapolis with military honors. Among the participants were officers of the Revolutionary Army and members of the Society of Cincinnati.

[1804.] May 3rd, the *Gazette* adopted the present style of editorial sub-head.

This year a lottery was inaugurated to raise money to improve the streets of Annapolis, to purchase "a large and forcible fire-engine, and to deepen the basin."

As a matter of local interest the names of the managers are appended: James Williams, Absalom Ridgely, Wm. Alexandria, John Barber, Joseph Sands, Lewis Neth, Jonathan Pinkney, John Shaw, Frederick Green, Frederick Grammer, John Muir, William Caton.

[1807.] Nicholas Brewer was appointed Register of the Court of Chancery in May.

On the 29th of June, a public meeting was held in Annapolis, at which resolutions were passed denouncing the attack of the British Frigate Leopard. upon the U. S. Ship Chesapeake, on the 22nd of June, off Norfolk, and promising to "support such measures as should be adopted by the Government." The participants refused also to have any intercourse with British vessels and appointed the following committee to carry out the resolutions: Governor Robert Wright, John T. Shaff, Jeremiah T. Chase, Reverdy Gheselin, Wm. Kilty, John Gassaway, Nicholas Carroll, Richard H. Harwood, John Muir, Lewis Duvall, Burton Whetcroft, and Nicholas Brewer.

On the 4th of July following, the city celebrated the day in an unusually animated manner. The tenth toast drank was: "The memory of our unfortunate citizens who fell in the late wanton and dastardly attack on the Chesapeake—may their brother tars be ready to avenge it."

On the 26th of August, 1807, information was received at Annapolis that a piracy had been committed in the Chesapeake, 30 miles below the city, by a French pirate, in the capture of the ship Othello, Captain Glover, bound to Baltimore.

The "Holy-Hawk," packet, with two brass four-pounders, under command of Captain Muir of the artillery, and Captain Duvall of the infantry, with a detachment of their respective companies, armed with muskets and boarding pikes, accompanied by a boat from the 'L'Eole,' (then lying in our harbor,) with thirty-three volunteers, French and American under the command of Lieutenant Mann, of the United States Navy, and an officer of the 'L'Eole,' sailed in pursuit of the pirate. They proceeded some distance down the bay, but returned without encountering the bold buccanneer. Captain Samuel and John Sterrett, in conjunction with Captain Porter, of the United States Navy, were more successful, and the pirate was captured and taken to Baltimore. Five of the crew, who had passed through Annapolis, were captured by our citizens a short distance from town. These were also taken to Baltimore. Such was the pitch of popular excitement over this affair that a high official gravely informed the captors of these five unarmed Frenchmen "that they deserved well of their country."

[1808.] Congressman Van Horn, on the 12th of January, presented a memorial from the Mayor, Aldermen, Common Council, and citizens of Annapolis, urging the great importance of the place to the trade of the Chesapeake, and praying Congress to take measures to have suitable fortifications erected there. The petition was referred to the Secretary of War. In March, proposals were advertised for the purchase of 100,000 good bricks, 200 tons of good foundation stone, and 2,000 bushels of good shell lime for the fortification of Annapolis.

The advertisement was signed by John Randall.

The Annapolis United Guards were at this time perfecting themselves in the military art.

The First Volunteer Company also drilled at this period.

On Monday, the 3rd of October, the city election for two delegates to the Legislature took place. It resulted, John Muir, 162; James Boyle, 138; A. C. Magruder, 111.

[1809.] In May, counterfeits on the Farmers' Bank appeared. They were $1 notes clumsily altered into $10.

[1810.] On the 30th of August, John Muir, president of the Farmers' Bank, died in the 60th year of his age. He was a native of Scotland but came to America when quite young. He was a warm advocate of American Independence, and took an active part in the Revolution. He represented Annapolis six years in the Legislature. He enjoyed a high reputation for charity, patriotism, and particularly for devotion to the interests of Annapolis.

Mr. Absalom Ridgely, an Annapolis merchant of the seventeenth century, appears to have been a public-spirited citizen. The following is extracted from the Annapolis Council proceedings of the 10th of May, 1788:

"The committee, appointed to report on the petition of Absalom Ridgely, made the following report, viz:

"We, your committee. appointed for the purpose of examining the situation of Prince George's street, adjoining Mr. Ridgely's, do report, that the filling up and completing the said street, will be both useful and necessary and beg leave to recommend an acceptance of the terms

for filling up and compleating the work of said street offered by Mr.
Ridgely, which we have herewith transmitted for your consideration
and approbation.

"Mr. Absalom Ridgely's proposition :

"To the worshipful the Mayor, Recorder, Aldermen, and Common
Councilmen of the City of Annapolis. The proposal of Absalom
Ridgely. to fill the public wharf at the end of Prince George's street,
as far as the logs that are now down.

"Your proposer will undertake at his own immediate expense to fill
in the wharf aforesaid, in any manner that shall be directed, by the
corporation or a committee thereof, will engage laborers for that
purpose upon the most reasonable terms they can be procured for ready
money.   Will deepen the water in front as much as possible by throwing the mud at low tides within the logs.   Will superintend the work
himself without any compensation, that it may done as expeditiously
as possible, and will wait for reimbursements of the expence in which
he means to include the cost of the wharf logs, until it will amply suit
the conveniency of the corporation to repay it without interest.   Or
if the corporation would rather choose to employ persons themselves
for the above purposes, he will advance the money and wait for the
return of it as aforesaid.

"The corporation, taking the same into consideration. do accept the
first proposal of Mr. Absalom Ridgely."

CHAPTER XLVI.

THE ANCIENT REGIME DISAPPEARS.

[1790.] Annapolis began to slough its distinctive features as a town
of the colonial regime soon after the close of the revolution. though
traces of these earlier customs remained until near the middle of the
present century. One of the attempts of the friends of the capital to advance its importance was the establishment of its Court of Hustings.
It excited at the time, 1708, the envy of the Anne Arundel officials
and a compromise of duties. no doubt born of a struggle for fees, had
to be made between the city's and county's sheriff and other officers,
before the right was given the Mayor to hold a court.

The duties of this court are indicated by a leaf from its docket :[*]

"At a meeting of the Mayor's Court on Tuesday. the 26th day of
January, 1790.

WERE PRESENT :

"Nicholas Carroll, Esq., Mayor.
"Allen Quynn, }
"Robert Conden, } Esqrs., Aldermen.
"John Bullen, }

* Minute Book of the Mayor's Court, MSS. p. 25.

"Mr. George Jennings is admitted an Attorney of this Court, and qualifies as such in the usual manner.

"The Court adjourns till 3 o'clock.

"Post Meridien, the Court met.

Present:

"Nicholas Carroll, Esq., Mayor.

"Allen Quynn,
"James Brice,   } Esqrs., Aldermen.
"Robert Conden,

"The Sheriff makes return of his pannel of Jurors, out of which, the Court appoint the following as Grand Jurors, to wit:

"Beriah Maybury, Foreman.	"Thomas Simpson,
"Joseph Clark,	"John Long,
"Henry Whetcroft.	"Joseph Rowles,
"William Middleton,	"Gilbert Middleton,
"Thomas Dalziell,	"Alexander Thompson,⁻
"Joseph Burneston,	"William Wells,
"Richard Frazier.	"George Johnson,
"John Hannah.	

"John Hyde—Bailiff.

"Who, being sworn and charged, retire to their chamber and afterwards return and present to the court the following presentments, to wit:

"Richard Thompson, Jr., for an assault on free negro Tom; same, for an assault on Wm. Williams; John Keith. for an assault on free negro Tom; James Reid, for an assault on Wm. H. McPherson; Charles Beard, for firing a gun in the street; Henry Sypolls. for same; negro Tom, slave to Mr. James Williams. for an assault on Wm. Caton; Charles Faris, for an assault on Jonathan Pinkney. of Robert: John Wiseham, for suffering his chimney to blaze out at the top; Thomas Brewer, for an assault on negro Tom; Benjamin Fairbain, for dealing with a slave; James Murray, for chimney blazing out at the top; Archd. Golder, for an assault on Wm. Grant; George Tumblert. for same on John Tootell; Samuel Hutton, for chimney blazing out at the top; Richard Thompson, Jr., and John Keith, for entering the dwelling house of Mrs. Susannah Brewer, in a riotous and disorderly manner; Benjamin Fairbain, for an assault on Richard Fleming; John Gutroy. for same on Wm. Foss; Thomas Adams, for selling liquor without licence; Richard Jones, for same at four different times; John Rea. for harboring slaves; William Alexander, for an assault on Elizabeth McMechen; same, for a riot; John Rea, for selling liquor under a pint—three different times; same, for harbouring negro Moses; same, for selling liquor and suffering it to be drank in his house; Sampson Salmon, for suffering his hogs to go at large; Daniel Fowler, 2, for same; Robert Tysalel, for same; Wm. Alexander, for dealing with negro Ruth; John Brice, of Robert, for procuring liquor for negro Ruth; William Ross, for an assault on Robert Gutroy; John Gutroy, for an assault on John Hyde; James Carroll, for chimney blazing out at the top; negro Ruth, for keeping a disorderly house; Thomas Adams, for same; Thomas Jennings, for leaving his well open; John Keith, for an assault on negro James; Allen Quynn, Jr., for same on Matthew Truine; Jane Thompson, for keeping a disorderly house, &c."

By chapter 194, passed February 13th, 1819, the charter of Annapolis was altered so as to give the electors, qualified to vote for delegates to the General Assembly, the right to elect the Mayor, Recorder, five Aldermen and seven Common Councilmen.

The Board was to be elected every third year on the first Monday in October. By this act the city's right to hold a "Court of Hustings," was annulled.

CHAPTER XLVII.
WILLIAM PINKNEY BANQUETTED IN ANNAPOLIS.

[1804.]   The *Gazette* of November, 29, 1804, says :

"On Wednesday, the 21st instant, the Honourable William Pinkney, Esquire, who has lately returned from a long residence in England, under a public appointment from the United States, and recently under a special appointment also from the State of Maryland, arrived in this city, and was immediately waited upon at Caton's tavern by a large concourse of respectable citizens, members of the legislature, &c., whose looks, still more than their declarations evinced the satisfaction felt at the safe return of this distinguished and highly accomplished gentleman. Among others the persons whose names are subscribed thereto waited on Mr. Pinkney, and presented him with the following note :

"*To the Honourable William Pinkney, Esquire.*

ANNAPOLIS, November 21, 1804.

"SIR :—We are deputed by a number of your old friends and fellow-citizens of Annapolis, to congratulate you on your safe arrival in this country, and to express the pleasure they feel at your appearance in this your native city. We are desired also to declare their impressions in regard to the honourable manner in which you are understood to have fulfilled the objects of your late mission to Europe, and the service which you have incidentally been enabled to render to the State of Maryland in the successful termination of an affair of great importance to its rights and interests. Those impressions we are authorised to say are as gratifying to the pride of your fellow-citizens as they are respectful and affectionate towards yourself. We are further deputed, Sir, to request that you will give your friends an opportunity of personally welcoming you to Annapolis, by favouring them with your company at a public dinner at Mr. Caton's tavern on Friday next, at three o'clock.

"Desiring to be considered as sharing most cordially in the sentiments here expressed, we have the honour to be, with great esteem, Sir,

Your obedient servants,

John Kilty,	John Gassaway,
John Davidson,	John Muir,
Burton Whetcroft,	Samuel H. Howard.

"To which Mr. Pinkney, on the next day, (having in the interim signified verbally his acceptance of the invitation,) returned the following answer:

ANNAPOLIS, November 22, 1804.

"GENTLEMEN:—I have read with peculiar sensibility the kind and flattering testimonial of approbation and esteem which you have done me the honour to deliver to me on the part of my fellow-citizens of Annapolis. After an absence of more than eight years from my country to meet with such a reception from the inhabitants of my native city, to which in every vicissitude of life and fortune I have always felt, and shall continue to feel, the most lively attachment, is more grateful to my heart than I am able to express.

"I beg you, gentlemen, to accept, with my best wishes for the future prosperity of this city, my sincere acknowledgments for the terms in which you have been so good as to convey its sense of my public conduct during my residence abroad. I shall take great pleasure in availing myself of your polite invitation.

"I have the honour to be, with unfeigned respect and regard, Gentlemen,

Your most obedient humble servant,

WILLIAM PINKNEY.

John Kilty, John Davidson, Burton Whetcroft, John Gassaway, John Muir, Samuel Harvey Howard, Esq'rs.

"The following card of invitation was, on the same day, presented to the President of the Senate and the Speaker of the House of Delegates, and communicated by them (from the chair) to the members of their respective houses:

ANNAPOLIS, November 21, 1804.

"SIR:—A number of the inhabitants of Annapolis, desirous of giving to their fellow-citizen, William Pinkney, Esquire, who has lately returned to this country from the successful discharge of important public functions in Europe, a testimony of the satisfaction they feel at his arrival among them, and of the high esteem they entertain for his character, have deputed us to request his presence at a dinner to be given for that purpose at Mr. Caton's tavern on Friday next: this invitation having been accepted by Mr. Pinkney, we obey with pleasure a further injunction by requesting, Sir, to be favoured at the said public dinner with your company and that of the members of the Honourable House in which you preside.

. With great respect, we have the honour to be, Sir,

Your most obedient servants.

[Signed as before.]

"Agreeably to this arrangement a great number of the citizens, the members of the Legislature generally, with the Judges of the Court of Appeals, several other gentlemen of distinction who had also been invited, and the Honourable Mr. Pinkney, assembled on Friday at Mr. Caton's tavern, and partook of an elegant dinner, at which the utmost degree of conviviality and harmony prevailed. After dinner the following toasts were given alternately by the Honourable

Mr. Harwood of the council, who (in the unavoidable absence of the Excellency the Governor) presided and Nicholas Carroll, Esquire, who acted as vice-president.

1. The people of the United States.
2. The President of the United States.
3. The Congress of the United States.
4. The memory of General Washington.
5. The ever memorable day of the Declaration of Independence.
6. The memory of Benjamin Franklin and other departed Statesmen of America.
7. The memory of Warren, Montgomery, Mercer, and other departed soldiers of America.
8. The late revolutionary army and navy of the United States.
9. The heads of departments in the government of the United States.
10. The militia of America.
11. The army and navy of the United States.
12. A speedy enlargement to our countrymen in captivity.
13. The State of Maryland.
14. Agriculture, commerce, and manufactures.
15. Peace, union, and public confidence.
16. The cause of freedom throughout the world.
17. The American fair.

After Mr. Pinkney had retired, by Mr. Montgomery of the House of Delegates,

"William Pinkney, Esquire, the successful agent for the recovery of the bank stock belonging to the State of Maryland in the British funds."

"On Saturday the following resolution being propounded to the House of Delegates was read and concurred with:

"*Resolved*, That Mr. Stephen and Mr. Montgomery be a committee to wait on Mr. Pinkney to present him with the compliments of this house, and to congratulate him on his safe return to his native country, and to inform Mr. Pinkney, that the House of Delegates will receive any further communications or elucidations which he may be pleased to make to them in person relative to the affairs of the bank stock, for the recovery of which the State of Maryland is so much indebted to his personal attention and exertions.

"Mr. Pinkney, having received the aforegoing communication by the gentlemen named for the purpose of making the same, immediately attended the House of Delegates, and being conducted to a chair within the bar, gave, with his accustomed precision and elegance, the elucidations required relative to the recovery and transfer of the bank stock, on the subject of which his lengthy and able communications, comprehending his correspondence with the ministers and law officers of the British government, and with the American Secretary of State, had already been read in both Houses of the Legislature with every mark of interest and approbation. After receiving such private civilities as the shortness of his stay would permit, Mr. Pinkney left Annapolis on Tuesday morning, intending, it is supposed, to visit the seat of the general government, where it is not doubted his reception will be such as is due to acknowledged merit, highly cultivated talents, and faithful public service."

CHAPTER XLVIII.

ANNAPOLIS DURING THE WAR OF 1812.

The period of the war of 1812 was one of alarm, dissension, and excitement in Annapolis. Two parties were arrayed against each other with all the bitterness born of political strife, intensified by the clash of arms before their very doors.

The Federalists of Maryland were sympathizers with England in the war and bitter opponents of the policy of the administration. The republicans, or democrats, were intense haters of every thing British and firm and loyal supporters of Congress and the President in the prosecution of the war.

Peace meetings were held in the county, Peace tickets voted for at elections, and the *Gazette*, the organ of the Federalists, rang with bitter denunciations of the President, the results of the war, and the republican party generally. The *Maryland Republican*, a democratic paper, had been established a few years before the war. It was edited by Jehu Chandler, and it proved a brave and merciless advocate of its principles. The editor was rewarded for his zeal in the end by an office at Washington and a knock-down at Annapolis.

The free and fearless utterances of the *Gazette* against the war and the administration shows that a high appreciation of the principles of liberty animated the people of the Republic in the early days of its history.

On July 29, 1813, the *Gazette* in an editorial declared:

"Mr. Madison may well call this "a season of trial and calamity" for never, since the struggle which united these states into a republican government, did the citizens of this country witness such a scene of difficulties as now stare them in the face, and threaten a subversion of their liberties. Whence do their difficulties arise, and who have been their authors? From the imprudence of our own rulers they may be easily traced, notwithstanding all the arts made use of to cloak their designs. Could it for a moment be supposed, that this state of thing proceeded from measures which were unavoidable, there would then be some consolation for all of our troubles; but this excuse cannot, with any justification, be pleaded. Can any one believe that our differences would not be immediately accommodated, and that upon the most honorable terms, provided a proposition to that effect was made by our government? By a continuance of the war, they can never, with any reason, expect to obtain the object, the only object, which is now in dispute: but it is, day after day, plunging us deeper into disgrace and rendering us tenfold more contemptible in the eyes of all foreign nations. It may, indeed, be well to set apart days of humilition, fasting, and prayer."

Whilst these denunciations of the war and the administration were weekly heralded in the city, Annapolis was turned into a military camp, with the enemy frequently before its harbor, and its citizens constantly excited by expectations of attack and calls to arms.

The Governor of Maryland wrote, in the early part of this year, to the secretary of war acquainting him with the defenseless situation of Annapolis. The letter was lost on the way which gave rise to many suspicions of bad faith.

On April 9, the citizens of Annapolis were alarmed at an early hour by the discharge of cannon from the fort, (Fort Madison,) and the drum beating the town to arms. The alarm was caused by the arrival of several privateers who reported that they had been pursued some considerable distance up the bay by the blockading squadron. The people responded to their rendezvous with an alacrity that did credit to their promptness and patriotism.

During this period of excitement the records of the State were removed from Annapolis to a place of greater safety, boats were pressed into the service of the State, and Major Charles S. Ridgely and his squadron hastened to Annapolis with great rapidity. Several companies of militia were also called to the place: but their services were not needed.

During these trying times William Ross, of Annapolis, was charged with treasonbly making bad cartridges for the soldiers.

In the early part of May, a British sloop went aground on Thomas' Point bar. The patriots of Annapolis were very anxious to attack it, but the Governor prudently forebore as five British frigates were near to protect it. The publication that the Governor said he was glad that the sloop got off, caused considerable correspondence and a lively newspaper war. The weight of evidence was that the words were not used.

On the evening of August 3rd, three of the enemy's ships came up the bay and anchored within three miles of Annapolis. Nineteen other vessels stood a short distance below, and were distinctly visible from the State House. Every preparation was made for an attack. A large body of military and drafted men, with detachments of regulars and volunteers, under Col. Carbury. were in the town. Most of the families of the city fled to the country with the principal part of their goods, and the town assumed the air of a military post awaiting the immediate onset of the enemy. In a few days the scenes shifted. Two 74's and, and one 64, seven other ships, frigates, and sloops of war, and three tugs, lay between Hackett's and Sandy Points. One large frigate dropped down immediately opposite the city, and a smaller one lay about two miles farther down. Below, were two 74's and two frigates, besides several smaller vessels. tugs, schooners. and tenders. There were constant calls to arms made on the citizens and the town was in a state of feverish excitement, not knowing at any moment when at attack would begin. The forces of the city were augmented by the arrival of Capt. Morris, of the frigate Adams, who was given command of both forts. He brought a large body of prime sailors. Capt. Miller, from Washington, came with a detachment of marines, and Capt. Getzendanner. from Frederick. with a company of riflemen. In the midst of these exciting times. soldiers in arms and the enemy in front, the *Gazette* was denouncing in the most vindictive manner the war and the authors of it. This imprudent conduct at a period so calamitous proved the great forbearance and love of free speech and a free press that prevailed amongst the people of the enlightened city. At the same time peace meetings were being held all over Anne Arundel.

In the latter part of August. the British squadron sailed down the bay, and the excitement at Annapolis subsided.

Internal dissensions, however, did not cease with the departure of the British, and they culminated from a remote cause in January,

1814. From the chord of sympathy touched for the English in the war with their own country, the Federalists despised Napoleon. When he fell, they rejoiced. At Annapolis they celebrated his downfall at the hands of the allied armies by a banquet on the fifteenth of January.

A large concourse of gentlemen from different parts of the State and from the District of Columbia, assembled for that purpose and a procession formed at twelve o'clock at the City Tavern,* and marched to St. Anne's Church, headed by a band of music, "where the throne of grace was addressed in an appropriate manner by Rev. Mason L. Weems, and an oration pronounced by the Hon. Robert Goodloe Harper, replete with political knowledge and the eloquence of truth."†

The distaste, which the democratic or republican portion of the community felt to these proceedings, was shown by the boys disturbing the ceremonies of the church by throwing stones at the windows and making other violent demonstrations whilst men in the gallery expressed their opposition to the proceedings by behavior that added to the general confusion. Major Alexander Stuart, commanding a detachment of United States troops in the garrison at Annapolis, ordered the national flag to be lowered to half-mast and minute guns fired to show his regret at the discomfiture of Napoleon.

"After the performances at the church were over," the company joined, by an illustrious deputation of their friends from Congress, Messrs. Pickering. Grosvenor and Hanson, who had just arrived in the city, formed into a procession, and marched back to the City Tavern, and then to the Assembly Rooms, where they sat down to a sumptuous repast prepared by Mr. Isaac Parker. J. C. Herbert, Esq., Speaker of the House of Delegates, presided at the table, assisted by Col. Plater and Samuel Ridout, Esqr., as vice presidents. The local chronicler says: "A spirit of unanimity reigned throughout the company, for they all felt the importance of the events they had convened to celebrate, and nothing occurred to mar the pleasures and enjoyment of the day. Actuated by the purest motives, and governed by the most laudable feelings. a heartfelt gratitude to the great heroes who had stayed the arm of the oppressor. all hearts united in responding these sentiments. and imploring aid from the great arbiter of the world for their patriotic exertions. When they were ground to the dust by the iron hand of ruthless power, we sympathized in their situation ; now they have burst the chains which enslaved them, we rejoice at it. Can there be feelings more philanthropic, more worthy of freemen, who estimate liberty above all things, even life itself ? The influence of events of such moment will not be confined within the limits of Europe. but their beneficial effects will be bounded only by the universe. This then is another cause of rejoicing."

It was natural that such sentiments, and especially the assertion that "the influence of events of such moment will not be confined within the limits of Europe," would produce the greatest indignation to the advocates of the war with England, when that influence was none other than England's hand off Napoleon, could come down all the heavier on the United States.

* City Hotel.
† Md. Gazette.

After the cloth was removed, a number of toasts were drunk, interspersed by songs, and music by the band.

Among the toasts were:

"The Union of these States—May it be preserved on sure and just foundations.

"The Principles of our Constitution—Which have taught us to sympathize in the common cause of national independence.

"Alexander of Russia—The magnanimous emancipator of nations.

"The Coalesced Powers of Europe—Whose banners have waved in triumph over the ruthless enemy of the liberties of mankind.

"The active, indefatigable, and glorious Blucher—The worthy pupil of the Great Frederick.

"The Return of Peace—Its light is only to be reflected to our land from the blaze of Bonaparte's funeral bier.

"Our National Councils—Purse and brain both empty, the brain the heavier for being too light, the purse too light for being drawn of heaviness.

"Our Country a Volunteer—May the emancipation of the nations of Europe be the harbinger of her deliverance from the bane of French influence."

By Mr. Grosvenor—A Volunteer—"Maryland the Ararat of the Southern States—In the deluge of democracy, there the ark of Federalism finally rested."

By Mr. G. Calvert—A Volunteer—"May Bonaparte never receive more agreeable dispatches from this country than the toasts of this day."

This banquet augmented the animosities existing in the city, the democrats going so far as to charge that the Federalists, who inspired the occasion, huzzaed for the Prince Regent.

After dinner, when nearly half the company had retired, those who remained formed themselves into a procession, and, headed by a band of music, marched through several of the principal streets. Whilst thus marching the procession was met by a mob, and assailed with clubs, brick-bats, and other miscellaneous weapons. Several of the processionists were injured but not seriously. They, however, turned tables on the ringleaders of the riot, says the *Gazette*, and administered to them summary punishment.

The bitterness of the factions led not only to political, but personal, polemics. The *Gazette*, which had maintained a dignified silence under numerous attacks of the Republican, finally broke into severe invective. On Wednesday, January 26th, 1814, it wrote: "We had, as heretofore expressedly determined not to notice any of the infamous paragraphs which might appear in that contemptible chronicle, the *Maryland Republican*, wherein, 'every third word is a lie duer paid than the Turk's tribute'—nor would we now be diverted from our proposed course, were it not that the falsehoods which marked the two last numbers, might acquire a circulation from their very malignity. We know not, nor do we care, whether they be the venenous effusions of the vulgar scoundrel (Jehu Chandler) who professes to edit the paper, or of his associates in the school of defamation, who occasionally exercise themselves in the wanton butchery of character. We have, indeed, seen and we have noticed too, a certain puffed up, conceited, swollen fool, who is ever first to laugh at his own folly, chuckling with apparent self-gratulation at the appetite excited among the vulgar, for the gross ailment weekly published by this cannibal editor. From these circumstances and the brutal sympathies of his nature which would necessarily impel him to the association, we strongly suspect him to be a member of the Jacobin club, which conducts that Journal. * * * * * * * * * *

"We have been led to these remarks, by the notice taken of the festival of Thursday last in the *Maryland Republican*; which, we are happy to learn, has met with the decided disapprobation of the more decent and respectable of the Democratic party. * * * * * *

"The celebration of their Master's defeat has set in motion all the sullen humors of Democracy, and has excited them so far as they dare, to acts of violence and outrage."

Not only were specific acts made the bases of editorial amenities between Mr. Green and Mr. Chandler, but articles, upon public matters, became the texts for most vindictive tirades. In the issue of August 10th, 1815, the editor of the *Gazette* said: "When a graceless scoundrel, like the editor of the *Maryland Republican*, a villainous compound of knavery and folly, promises not to be too familiar with us, we feel indebted to him for the only obligation which it is in the power of such a reptile to confer. What could induce him to take such particular notice of our remarks on bribery we cannot divine; perhaps experience had rendered the subject familiar to him, and habit had endeared it. But the burthen of his song seems to be, that, in the proposed distribution of bribes, not one was offered to the poor wretch himself. The unlucky fellow ! after toiling in the work of defamation with the most unremitting veniality, after selling malicious slanders, libels, and lies, by the square; after having acquired the contempt of the world, and after having excited the blushes of his friends, if there be any so mean-spirited as to hold friendly communion with him, to find himself at last almost hopeless, has he not a right to whine and whimper, and pitifully to beg the legislature to let him put his finger in the treasury for services for the not doing of which he should have been prosecuted? He seems to think it an instance of unbending integrity that a poor man should refuse the enormous bribe of five dollars, and, by his astonishment, he seems to doubt whether he could have withstood the temptation. We believe, however, that any attempts to bribe this worthy editor would, in all probability remain a secret, unless, at any time, it might serve his purposes to publish his own shame. We dismiss the fellow without inquiring whether money is the root of his evil propensities, or whether they proceed from a native villainy and obliquity of principle."

Mr. Chandler was apparently as caustic and far more industrious in his personal editorials than Mr. Green, and, it is not surprising that such offensive paragraphs had their natural result—a rencounter. Not, however, between the two editors. Mr. Chandler gave great offence in his issue of June 22nd, 1816, to Mr. J. N. Watkins by referring to him in the following enigmatical sentence—" I have a very curious and important law case, which I shall report in my next. "Blue Light vs. Blue Light." Mr. Watkins, considering that he was personally alluded to, and the term Blue Light* applied to him, pub-

---

* The name given certain New England opponents of the war of 1812, who were accused of sen ling up rocket signals from land to the British Fleet hovering off the coast.

licly declared the same day, that he would call upon the editor the first opportunity that offered, and make him declare whether he alluded to him, and what he meant by the term Blue Light as applied to him, and to chastise him if his explanation was not satisfactory. On Monday morning he met the editor in the street, and made the demand. Mr. Chandler informed him it was the case of the warrant of J. Howard against himself and Mr. Bowie, which was tried in the chancery office. Mr. Watkins then demanded what he meant by the term Blue Light as it applied to him? Mr. Chandler replied—''Wait until next Saturday's paper appeared and he would see.'' Mr. Watkins answered, ''I will not wait, and I am determined to have an immediate explanation, or I will whip you on the spot.'' Mr. Chandler was at this time moving off, but Mr. Watkins seized him by the breast, and told him he should not move a step until he had made the explanation demanded. Mr. Chandler immediately struck Mr. Watkins a violent blow over the head with a stick that staggered him, but recovering before the blow was repeated, he struck Mr. Chandler with his fist, and knocked him down, and made his stick fall from his hand. This Mr. Watkins seized, and alternately, with his fist, used the stick until Mr. Chandler was severely beaten.

These vindictive attacks on private character and personal rights had no other foundation than the attritions of rivalship in legitimate business and the unavoidable differences on political questions.

Whilst these internal dissensions were agitating Annapolis, external appearances were anything but agreeable.

The British once more hovered near Annapolis. On Sunday night, June 26th, 1814, a British barge supposed to belong to the Jasseur, a brig lying at Plumb Point, about thirty miles below Annapolis, captured several vessels, one of them being a regular packet between Annapolis and Haddaway's Ferry.

On July 9th, the British Frigate, Narcissus, accompanied by a schooner and two smaller vessels, passed the mouth of the Severn, on its way up the bay. On the 13th, the frigate returned with twelve bay crafts, which it had captured.

The proximity of the British again transposed Annapolis into a military post. A considerable body of militia arrived from Frederick and Washington counties, and the upper part of Anne Arundel. They displayed great patriotism.

On August 25th, a British frigate, a schooner, sloop, and a fleet of barges were in sight off Annapolis. On Sunday, September 18th, the enemy, having between sixty and seventy sail, again appeared off Annapolis. Their bows were down the bay. They had discovered there was a North Point and a Fort McHenry. Two of the vessels grounded on Kent Island, and that delayed them until Tuesday. On Wednesday they anchored ten miles below Annapolis.

On the night of November 15th, Annapolis was thrown into a state of intense excitement by the firing of the alarm guns on Horn Point by the guard. Citizens flew to arms, and in a brief period the town was ready to meet the attack of the enemy. The alarm proved a false one created by two bay vessels entering the mouth of the harbor and refusing to notice or answer the repeated calls of the guard. It was then announced that, after this alarm, those vessels which refused to notice the hail of the guard would be fired upon.

In February, 1815, the news of peace arrived and on the 22nd Annapolis celebrated the welcome intelligence. The city was brilliantly illuminated, the joy of the people was unbounded, all former political differences were buried, all past dissensions forgotten, and all was "peace and good will towards men." In the midst of this brilliant spectacle stood the State House, conspicuous for its elevation and splendor. The great hall was decorated with a full length portrait of Washington, suspended from the centre of the inner dome, the devices were tasteful and numerous, and the whole illumination brilliant and magnificent.

CHAPTER XLIX.

LA FAYETTE'S VISIT TO ANNAPOLIS.

[1824.] On Friday, December 17th, 1824, by invitation of the Maryland Legislature, the Marquis de La Fayette visited Annapolis. The enthusiasm excited amongst the citizens by the arrival of the distinguished visitor was indescribable "every eye beamed with pleasure, every heart throbbed with mingled emotions of gratitude, affection, and delight." His approach was announced by a national salute, and the display of the Federal colors upon the spire of the State House. It was three in the afternoon when he made his appearance in the city, accompanied by his son George Washington La Fayette, Mons. Vasseur, his Secretary, the Hon. Joseph Kent, the Hon. George E. Mitchell, Representatives in Congress from Maryland, Samuel Sprigg, Esq., late Governor of Maryland, and the deputation from Annapolis, consisting of Hon. Jeremiah T. Chase, late chief justice of Maryland, Hon. Theodorick Bland, chancellor of the State, Col. Henry Maynadier, an officer of the Revolution, and John Randall, Esq., collector of the port; who had received him at the divisional line between Anne Arundel and Prince George's counties.

Judge Chase delivered there the following address to Lafayette:

"General Lafayette, the citizens of Annapolis, ardently solicitous to demonstrate the feelings of their hearts on this happy occasion, have requested me, with one voice to express them to you—Welcome General Lafayette, thrice welcome, as the revered guest of citizens who rejoice to see you. They rejoice to see you, as the friend of America, they rejoice to see you as the friend of the illustrious Washington—they rejoice to see you receiving the congratulations of a free people; whose hearts from one end of the continent to the other, are filled with the most lively gratitude, for the great, the important services rendered by you in the Revolutionary war. To you, Illustrious Chief, they are indebted for that aid you afforded, at a time the most perilous, by which, under the favour and smiles of Providence, and under the guidance of the patriotic Washington, the freedom and independence of America was established.

"To you and your glorious acheivements they owe those rights, which they are now in the full enjoyment of—Liberty, the rights of conscience, the rights of property, and the security of all personal rights, and that high and exalted station America holds among the nations of the earth. Your noble, disinterested conduct, as the devoted friend of liberty, and your timely aid in her cause, will long be remembered by Americans. They are deeply engraven, indelibly impressed, on their hearts, and will be transmitted from father to son, from generation to generation, until America be lost and swallowed up in the never ceasing flood of time.

"May the Almighty God, the Great Jehovah, take you in his holy keeping, prolong your days, and may they be prosperous and end in peace, that peace of mind which passeth all understanding ; and may you finally be fitted for and received into those mansions of bliss prepared by our Lord and Saviour Jesus Christ, for his happy followers, is the ardent prayer of the sons of freedom."

To the above address General Lafayette made the following reply :

"The welcome I receive from you, gentlemen, in the name of the citizens of Annapolis, the pleasure to meet you again, my dear and venerated sir, and the remembrance of one of my earliest friends, and co-patriots, in the cause of America, your excellent brother, are sentiment which I am happy to express. I thank you for the testimonies of your esteem and friendship. I rejoice with you in the admirable results of our glorious revolution, and feel an affectionate eagerness to re-enter the metropolis where I am so kindly invited, and where so many old obligations have been conferred upon me."

Lafayette was escorted by Captain Bowie's elegant company of mounted riflemen from Nothingham, Prince George's county and Captain Sellman's troop of horse from South River, Anne Arundel county.

At Miller's Hill, the procession, in spite of the rain which continued from morn till night, was formed under the marshalship of Colonel Jones, of the United States Army. It presented a creditable military appearance, and consisted of :

Two companies of the Annapolis riflemen ;
Two companies of Annapolis infantry ;
One company of Annapolis artillery ;
Captain Dooly's company of riflemen from West River ;
Captain Bruce's company of mounted riflemen from Nothingham ;
Captain Watson's, Captain Warfield's, and Captain Sellman's troops of horses ;
The troops from Fort Severn ;
Colonel Charles S. Ridgely, of the cavalry, and the officers of Captain Hollingsworth's troop of horse from Elk Ridge.

The procession passed through West Street, down Church Street, up Frances to the eastern gate of the circle where the General alighted from his carriage and was conducted to the State House. Upon entering the hall, he was greeted by about thirty little girls, each about twelve years old, formed in a semi-circle, all dressed in white, with wreaths of evergreen entwined around their heads, and holding in their hands banners with the following inscriptions :

"LaFayette—The friend of our fathers will always be welcome to the hearts of their children," and

"The cannon's roar proclaims the gratitude of warriors ;

"More peaceful emblems must tell of ours."

The General was conducted to the Senate Chamber of historic renown—where, in the presence of the corporate authorities of the city, the members of the Legislature, a numerous assemblage of ladies, citizens, and strangers, he was addressed by Colonel James Boyle, the Mayor of the city, in the following terms:

"On the part of the corporation and my fellow-citizens, I greet you with a hearty and affectionate welcome. You have been in this city before, during the gloomy period of that war, which severed one-half of the British empire from the other, and placed these states on an equality with the independent nations of the earth. We rejoice to see you now. The children have inherited the grateful affections of their fathers.

"We do not know which to admire most, that bold and chivalric spirit, which prompted you to leave the quiet of repose, the joys of a splendid court, where youth and beauty cheered even the dim lustre of the aged eye, and the soft endearments of an early love, or that spirit of benevolence, which urged you to gird on the warrior sword to battle for an infant land just struggling to existence. You came like Achilles, not the leader, but the young hero of the host, to bind upon your youthful brow your earliest laurels, and the myrmidons* of your country fought untired and victorious by your side. You have been reserved for a nobler and a better fate. He fell upon the very threshhold of victory. You have survived to see the maturity of that rich boon your gallant sword assisted to achieve. The Grand Master of the Universe would not summon you from your frail lodge of clay to his celestial and eternal lodge above, until you should behold these fair fields the permanent abode of rational liberty. We have seen you retire from our shores with the nation's blessings and the nation's prayers; we have known you in your own country to reap a rich harvest of glory, and we have sighed with you when the dungeon doors of the prison of Olmutz closed and shut you from the world, your tender spouse, and infant offspring. Believe me, Sir, through this wide extended country, washed by the Atlantic on the one side, and the Pacific on the other, there is not an human bosom, old enough to distinguish right from wrong, which at the sound of your name throbs not with mingled emotions of gratitude and pleasure; not an infant prattler but has learned to lisp the name of our illustrious guest and disinterested benefactor.

"General! You have lately seen the place where the sword of the revolutionary war was drawn. You now stand in that very chamber, and on that very spot, where the father of his country returned it to the scabbard; an act which stands alone among the recorded annals of the world. High in the affections of the army, the valiant chieftain of a mighty people, reposing on the love and confidence of the nation, he might, had he been ambitious, have desolated his native land with war and bloodshed, he might perhaps have seized upon the crown through the misguided feelings of the many, and have stained to late posterity the bright escutcheon of his fame. The greatness of his character was preserved to the last as an entire whole. He would not suffer the glittering bauble to cross the bright-

* Evidently a misprint in the Gazette.

16

ness of his path, nor for a moment swerve him from the line of duty. His throne is of an imperishable nature, his crown more honorable than the richest diadems of emperors, and his sceptre cannot be broken by the united efforts of the world. They are placed upon the purest page of history, and form the brightest halo round its loveliest disk.

"Permit me again, Sir, to welcome you to Annapolis, and to assure you that your arrival is a source of unutterable pleasure."

To which General Lafayette replied :

"I had eagerly anticipated the pleasure I now enjoy, to revisit this metropolis, and to find it in the possession of those blessings of independence and freedom, for which we have had to contend. My gratification is completed by the affectionate and flattering welcome, with which I am honored, and by the kind manner in which you, Mr. Mayor, have been pleased to express it.

"This city has been the theatre of resolutions most important to the welfare of the United States, and indeed to the general welfare of mankind. It has witnessed the affecting scene, when our unparallelled chief resigned the powers he had exercised with so much civil moderation and military glory, at the head of our patriotic army, an army in every heart of whom, be assured Sir, the lofty principle of unshaken and unalloyed republicanism was as warmly felt and as firmly fixed as in the breast itself of our beloved commander.

"Amidst those solemn recollections, there are personal remembrances, endearing and honorable, which the view of this State House, most particularly impress upon my mind, and which mingle with the sense of my actual obligations, when I request you, Mr. Mayor, the gentlemen of the Common Council, and all the citizens of Annapolis, to accept the tribute of my most respectful and affectionate thanks."

He was then introduced to the members of the Corporation, and to as many other persons, as the lateness of the hour would admit. The ceremonies in the Senate Chamber being finished, the procession was again formed, and moved on to Fort Severn, where a national salute was fired, and other appropriate honors paid to the illustrious visitor by the excellent officers attached to that garrison, Colonel Jones, Lieutenants Lendrum and Davidson. The general and his suite were then conducted to the Government House, where, in compliance with an invitation from his Excellency, the Governor, his quarters were fixed. In the evening the general and his suite were escorted to the college, which had been selected as the most convenient place for the ball, which had been prepared, under the direction of the committee of arrangements, by Mr. James Williamson. The hall had been previously, tastefully ornamented by a committee of ladies, selected for the purpose, and was pronounced to be the handsomest room which had ever been appropriated to an occasion of the kind in this country. It was ornamented with wreaths of flowers, natural and artificial, transparencies of Washington and Lafayette, and many military insignia. In the centre was suspended a large chandelier, of a circular form, but gradually decreasing in its circumference from bottom to top, beautifully ornamented, and illuminated with nearly one hundred lights. The Ball was rich and elegant—and was attended by an unusually large number of ladies from various parts of the State, and by a large concourse of gentlemen. The Marine Band from Washington was procured for the occasion.

On Saturday morning there was a review on the college green—and the evolutions performed were highly creditable, both to the commanding officer, (Col. Jones,) and the soldiers under his command. A pavillion was erected on the green, for the accommodation of the General and his suite, the Governor, his aids, and other gentlemen, to whom places were assigned. After the evolutions were executed, a trial of skill was exhibited by the three Rifle Companies, commanded by Captains Dooly, Neth, and Hobbs, in shooting at a target, for a Silver Cup. His Excellency, the Governor, and Colonel Jones, were appointed the Judges, and they assigned the prize to "The First Annapolis Sharp Shooters." The cup was then presented by General Lafayette to Captain Neth, who received it in behalf of his company. In this exhibition Captain Dooly's company, (which is a remarkably fine one, and is commanded by an able officer,) distinguished themselves as expert marksmen (as did also Captain Hobbs' company.) The prize was "nobly lost, and nobly won."

At 5 o'clock in the afternoon the General and suite were conducted to the college hall, where a most sumptuous and splendid dinner had been provided by the committee of arrangements under the superintendence of Mrs. M. Robinson, of the city. The ornaments and decorations which were placed in the hall, preparatory to the hall, were found to be equally appropriate for the dinner, and the hall upon this occasion presented a scene of splendor and elegance, "seldom, or perhaps never surpassed in this country. The dinner was truly sumptuous, and the table presented not only every delicacy to gratify the palate, but was arranged with a degree of taste and elegance, which contributed to increase the temptations which it presented. The toasts which were drank upon the occasion, were very appropriate. At night a general illumination took place throughout the city, and the night being fine it had a very pleasing effect. The lower stories of the State House were illuminated, and a variety of appropriate transparencies exhibited."

On Sunday morning the General, by invitation, attended divine services at the Methodist Meeting House.

On Monday the committee, appointed by the Legislature, claimed the privilege of entertaining Lafayette. He was introduced to the Senate and House of Delegates where addresses were made to him, by the President and the Speaker. At 5 o'clock he dined with the Legislature at the College.

On Tuesday morning, he left the city for Washington, escorted by Captain Sellman's troop of horse, and accompanied, as far as the limits of the city, by Captain Neth's Rifle Company, the regulars from Fort Severn, and a large concourse of citizens and strangers, "who lamented his departure, and were penetrated with a deep sense of gratitude for the eminent services he rendered our country, and with a profound respect for his character, and a sincere affection for his person."

CHAPTER L.

"THE GLORIOUS NINETEEN."

Annapolis was the scene of a bloodless revolution in September, 1836. The constitution of Maryland was an attenuated relic of colonial times with a dash of republican spirit permeating it. By it, was an extraordinary mode of electing one branch of the Legislative body preserved.

An Electoral College, composed of forty electors, was elected by the people according to certain defined electoral districts. Of these it required twenty-four to make a quorum. The State, since the adoption of the State Constitution in 1776, had gained so in population that these districts, which at first fairly represented the population of the State and the will of the people, had become a huge, political monstrosity by which less than one-fourth of the people of the State elected one entire co-ordinate branch of the legislative department and had a large influence in choosing the Governor of the State.

As it happened, the whigs were strongest in these numerically smaller districts, and, whilst not representing the fourth of the State, were enabled to dictate to the other three-fourths in two important branches of Government. Against this the democracy of Maryland revolted, and, assisted by many whigs who were opposed to the unequal system, had called loudly for reform.

The whigs, loath to give up power, resisted the appeals of party and people for redress. In the elections of 1836, the whigs elected 21 members of the Senatorial College, and the democrats 19. On this the democrats resolved to stop the wheels of government itself or obtain the redress they asked.

From Major Sprigg Harwood, who represented Annapolis in the College, on August 18th, 1886, then in his 78th year, the sole survivor of "the glorious nineteen," as the democrats were wont to call them, I obtained the following:

"We had a little caucus at the Baltimore House, corner Baltimore and Hanover streets, Baltimore, and then agreed that we would assemble at Annapolis and send a communication, as we did on the 19th of September, to the twenty-one whig electors who were in the Senate Chamber, and who had qualified, and were waiting for all of us, requiring at least three before a quorum could be formed to transact business. When we sent our communication to them, they would hold no communications with us until we qualified. If we had qualified, they could have then proceeded to business with their majority of twenty-one.

"I first heard of the intended proceedings some days before the Baltimore meeting by Mr. Dick Higgins coming out to the country at Mr. Evans, and telling me of the letters written to the Democratic and Reform electors to meet in Baltimore. Before going, I consulted with my people here to learn their views. I said they could instruct me now, but if I went to Baltimore, and committed myself it was then too late, I would have to stand by it. They said 'Go, the principle is right, and we will stand by you.' This they did although they had a representation equal to Baltimore's—two delegates in the Legislature.

"We met in Baltimore about a week previous to the meeting of the College here on the 19th of September, and agreed on the outlines of the proposition as indicated by the letter dated on the 19th.

"There was no personal animosity among the participants. I used to associate with the whig electors outside, and they would ask me to go up to the Senate, but I would say—"No, you will lock me in." The outsiders were very much alarmed. They thought no rights were left in property as there was no legislature, the whig judges actually taking this view, and the people generally thought the country was gone.

"Afterwards, when three of the nineteen concluded to participate in the organization of the College, John S. Sellman wrote to us to meet at Annapolis, but all declined save Marcy Fountain, Enoch George, George A. Thomas, and Wesley Linthicum. Messrs. Thomas and George regretted coming, but finding three were going in, (enough to make a quorum,) they also consented to go, but not then until the basis of electing a Senate and the reforms to be given had been agreed upon.

"The whigs gave the election of Governor to the people and altered the representation in the Legislature so as to equalize it somewhat in the State.

"The democrats thereupon elected the Governor—the whigs only succeeded in getting in Gov. Pratt in 1843, and the Know Nothings, Thomas Holliday Hicks, in 1857. The whigs often, however, had the Legislature.

"Our people were satisfied, but the whigs were excited here. They did not like giving up the State. Several steamers came here daily from Baltimore and the counties, filled with whigs, who hoped to make an impression on the nineteen. Everybody had gone away then except myself."[*]

The following is the correspondence that took place on the 19th of September :

"GENTLEMEN.—It is duty which we owe to our constituents, that before we take our seats in the College of Electors of the Senate of this State, we should have a distinct and positive understanding, as to the course to be pursued by that body.

"You are apprised, that, a crisis has occurred, when neither of the political parties of the State have elected Electors, having the constitutional power to form a Senate. Of the nineteen counties and two cities, into which the State is divided, we represent the two cities and eight of the counties, having a white population of 205,922, and federal numbers 267,669. You represent ten of the counties, having a white population of 85,179 ; and federal numbers 138,002 ; and the vote of the remaining counties is divided. Of the Electoral Body, we are nineteen in number, while you are twenty-one. But, although you are a majority (the smallest possible) of the College, it is to be recollected that we represent nearly three-fourths of the free white population, and two-thirds of the federal numbers of the State, and very much the largest portion of its territorial extent and wealth : we shall, therefore, expect that you will concede to us the nomination of eight members of the Senate to be chosen, and that you will vote for the persons whom we may nominate to the College, although they may be favourable to a convention to revise and amend the Constitu-

[*] Annapolis was his home.

tion of the State, if, in all other respects, in your opinion well qualified. The counties and cities we represent ought to have, upon any political principle which governs the appointment of members of a Legislature, a majority of the Senate to be formed, greater than that which is sought to be obtained.   To force upon them, then, being the majority of the people, an entire Senate, against their will, would be unjust and Anti-Republican ; and we, their agents, cannot participate in such a violation of their rights as freemen ; neither can we become passive members of Electoral College, and thereby enable you to select for the people, we have the honor to represent, Senators residing in the district from which we come.   The people of those counties and cities have elected us to make choice of their Senators, presuming that we who reside among them are better qualified than strangers can be, to choose those who know their rights and interests, and will protect them.   If our constituents are to be subjected to a Senate opposed to their will, it would be an aggravation of the evils they will be compelled to endure to have some of the members of that body taken from the midst of communities whose confidence they do not enjoy, and whose wants and wishes they are not willing cheerfully to gratify. From these considerations, we feel compelled to take the position above assumed. Moreover, our constituents, who desire to see radical changes made in their present constitution have a right to expect that we will not fail to exert all the powers reposed in us under our form of government to make the institutions of the State more republican and conformable to the will of those for whose happiness and safety they were designed.

''The friends of reform in Maryland have sought repeatedly to obtain from the Legislature, by an exertion of the powers confided to that body by the fifty-ninth section of the Constitution, such amendments of that instrument as are indispensable, and it is with regret we say that all their applications were in vain, and indeed it may be said, they were not even treated with that respectful deference to which the remonstrances of a large majority of the people are justly entitled. It would be needless for us here to spread out in detail, the several applications for reform which have been made.

''You know the history of many petitions which have been presented to the Legislature ; and we have felt the manner of their rejection. Each instant is fresh in the recollection of our constituents, and they believe as we do, that no redress of grievances can be had through the ordinary forms which the framers of our Constitution provided. Under this solemn consideration, we have determined not to be willingly instrumental in perpetuating institutions that work such bitter injustice, and if, gentlemen, you will give us your pledge of honour to accede to our proposal, and give to the majority of the people a majority of one branch of the Legislature to prevent future violations of their rights and privileges, it will afford us great pleasure to meet you in the Electoral College today. Should, however, your views as to our relative rights and duties not accord with ours, we shall most deeply regret it, and be compelled by a high and holy sense of duty to our constituents and to the whole State, not to meet you in College, and thereby, we shall entirely avoid the odious responsibility of assisting to form a Senate obnoxious to the people we represent.

''We are aware that your rejection of this proposition, and the State of things which may grow out of it, will give some alarm to the timorous. But upon the most calm and deliberate examination of the whole subject in all its bearings, we can discover none of those causes for deep and lasting excitement, which endanger the peace and good order of the community, if the legislative functions of the government should cease for a season, that will be found to arise, should we assist to organize a Senate, which would perpetuate, possibly, all existing evils, and secure for five years, at least, that oppressive dominion, of a small minority over the majority, which has been so long reluctantly endured by the people of Maryland. We perceive no cause for apprehensions and alarm in the temporary suspension of the powers of the Senate. Thereby, the whole Constitution would not be abrogated. The Governor would remain in office long enough to afford time to form a new Constitution, and perform the function of the Executive Department.

"The Judiciary and the officers connected with the Courts would experience no interruption of their powers, and all the officers who derive their appointments annually from the Executive are impowered under the forty-ninth article of the Constitution, to hold their offices until they are superseded by the appointments of others.

"The laws, therefore, would be administered—civil rights and private property properly protected, and the peace of the community preserved, by all the means now employed for that purpose. In the mean time the powers which have been delegated to us, will revert to the people, in whose integrity, virtue, patriotism, and intelligence, we have the most entire confidence; and we doubt not but that they, guided by the spirit that animated our fathers in seventy-six, will provide for every exigency that may arise. Before any inconvenience can be experienced, the sovereign power of the people of Maryland will be employed, by means of a convention to reform our Constitution, so as not to justify a recurrence of a similar contingency, by basing all its departments on sound Republican principles, so as to secure equality of political rights, and a just responsibility in all public officers, to popular will.

"To prevent misapprehensions, we have submitted our propositions in writing, and its manifest justice gives us every reason to expect that you yield to it, a ready assent. We hope you do not desire to leave the State without a Senate, unless you are permitted to select all its members,—as well for counties you represent as those counties and cities represented by us. Nor can we believe that you will ask us to join you in the Electoral College, and be passive spectators of your proceedings, merely to witness the degradation of our constituents, by your choice of a Senate for 205,922 people, whose representatives you are not. We ask only what we think is right, and are determined to submit to nothing that is wrong. To our propositions we respectfully ask an answer at your earliest convenience.

"And whatever may be your response, we cannot doubt your concurrence with us in the perfect conviction of the competency of the people to accept a surrender of the Legislative functions of the Government, and that deeply embued with the spirit of patriotism and justice, and guided by the lights of experience they will, through the instrumentality of a Convention, so adjust and apportion them as to secure the inestimable blessings of a republican government. We are, very respectfully,

Gentlemen, Yours, &c.,

Charles Macgill,	Ephraim Bell,
Robert Wason,	Robert T. Keene,
Caspar Quynn,	Enoch George,
John Fisher,	M. Fountain,
Joshua Vansant,	John B. Thomas,
Thomas Hope,	Sprigg Harwood,
Samuel Sutton,	John S. Sellman,
John Evans.	Wesley Linthicum,
George A. Thomas,	Wash'n. Duvall.
George Ellicott,	

"To Messrs. Heard, Leigh, Vickers, Gale, Gaither, Kent, Dalrymple, Williams, Handy, Spence, Franklin, Dickinson, Dudley, Hicks, Lake, Pratt, Duvall, Merrick, Brawner, Bruce, and Beall."

"ANNAPOLIS, September 16th, 1826, P. M.

"Gentlemen, We are anxious to elect a Senate, and for the promotion of this object, we sent certain propositions to you, for your consideration, and selected Colonel Heard as the organ of communication, knowing him to be an old member of the Legislature, and an Elector returned for the County of St. Mary's which is always first called from priority. Colonel Heard returned this paper stating that he had no authority to act, and, therefore, declined presenting it to his political associates. We have, therefore, to request of you, whether you will receive any communication from us—and to indicate the manner in which you would prefer to receive communications from us.

We are Gentlemen,
Very Respectfully Yours, &c.

Charles Macgill,	Robert T. Keene,
Robert Wason,	M. Fountain,
Casper Quynn,	John Evans,
John Fisher,	George A. Thomas,
George Ellicott,	Washington Duvall,
Ephraim Bell,	John B. Thomas,
Joshua Vansant,	Enoch George,
Sprigg Harwood.	John S. Sellman.
Thomas Hope,	Wesley Linthicum,
Samuel Sutton,	

"To Messrs. Heard, Leigh, Vickers, Gale, Gaither, Kent, Dalrymple, Williams, Handy, Spence, Franklin, Dickinson, Dudley, Hicks, Lake, Pratt, Duvall, Merrick, Brawner, Bruce, and Beall."

"ANNAPOLIS, September 21st, 1836.

"At one o'clock, p. m., the Democratic Republican members of the Electoral College again assembled, when Charles McGill, of Washington county, resumed the Chair, and George A. Thomas, of Cecil county, acted as Secretary, whereupon the following proceedings were had:

"Contrary to our reasonable hopes and expectations, the other Electors having refused even to receive or reply to the propositions which we have thought proper to submit, formally and informally, in letters addressed to all of them, and in conversations held by individual members of this meeting, with individual members of the other branch of the Electoral College, and other Electors having moreover, made to us, or to any one of us, no propositions whatever, calculated to restore to the people of Maryland, through the medium of the Legislature, the right to revise and amend the constitution; and this meeting being fully convinced that we have no alternative left but to adjourn, or to submit to the selection of a Senate opposed to those reforms, both of the constitution and of the administration of the government of the State, which our constituents desire to see accomplished—Therefore,

"Resolve this meeting do now adjourn.

CHARLES McGILL, President.

GEORGE A. THOMAS, Secretary."

The calm at Annapolis whilst this peaceful revolution was in progress was in strong contrast with the excitement prevailing in other parts of the State. People generally felt a political catastrophe was at hand which threatened the destruction of property and government, and with these direful forebodings the timid saw impending and overwhelming evil, whilst the courageous prepared to meet the coming danger with heroic effort.

In many places in the State public meetings were held. At Baltimore, an immense gathering of citizens denounced the nineteen in forcible terms, and similar meetings followed in Washington, Frederick, and Allegany counties, at which all pledged themselves to sustain the supremacy of the law. On the 18th of October, the grand jury of Allegany county presented the nineteen electors "as unfaithful public agents and disturbers of the public peace."

In the interim, whilst the whig electors remained out of the College, and awaited events, the presidential election was held. On the day following, November 8th, Governor Thomas W. Veazey issued a proclamation denouncing in severe terms the conduct of the "recusant electors and their abettors," calling on the civil and military authorities to be in readiness to maintain the law, and convening the old Senate and House of Delegates to assemble on the 21st of November.

The proclamation added greatly to the excitement in the State, and was responded to cordially. One company, the Planter's Guards, tendered their services to the executive to support the authority of law. Happily their aid was never required.

Although the nineteen, Major Sprigg Harwood, who lived at Annapolis, alone excepted, had left the capital, steamboat load after steamboat load of people came to the city, in the spirit of some vague knight errantry, hopeful that they might by some means influence the nineteen to absolve their resolve.

The strain, as shown by Major Harwood's statement, proved too great for the nerves of John S. Sellman, of Anne Arundel, or else the specific promises he received were inducement enough to make him repent, early in October, his determination not to take part in the election of a Senate. He was followed by Wesley Linthicum, of the same county, on November 12th. Sellman signified this intention by letter to his associates in the communication of the 19th of September to the twenty-one whig electors.

The election of Delegates to the House hastened the dissolution of the combination. Sixty whigs and but nineteen Van Buren, or democratic delegates, were returned. The Anne Arundel, Queen Anne's, and Caroline county electors regarded the elections in their counties, as instructions from their constituents, and November 19th, Mr. Wesley Linthicum, of Anne Arundel county, Dr. Enoch George and John B. Thomas, of Queen Anne's county, and Marcy Fountain, of Caroline county, all of "the glorious nineteen," appeared, and also qualified as Senatorial electors. The College, then composed of twenty-six members, proceeded to elect a Senate.

On the 25th of November, Governor Veazey sent a special message to the General Assembly on this subject in which he declared "the annals of party contention and political errors and aberations from duty" * * * "would be searched in vain for a case of such plain and palpable violation of constitutional duty and moral obligations as the conduct of the recusant electors of the Senate of Maryland exhibits." He regretted no statue existed to meet such an emergency and suggested the passage of one.

But the revolt had crystalized public opinion on the subject of the needed reforms in State government and the measures for which the democrats contended were generally conceded by the Legislature. One was the election of the Governor by the people. The democrats thereupon held this office, with but one exception, from that date down to 1857. There being no statutory punishment for their offence, the whigs who generally had control of the Senate, visited an unwritten penalty on "the glorious nineteen." No matter to what office one of them was ever appointed by the Governor, a whig Senate would invariably reject the appointment.

CHAPTER LI.

"JOE MORGUE."

The *Maryland Republican*, of August, 1836, contained the obituary of a very remarkable character. The article read :

"Mr. Joseph Simmons, the oldest inhabitant of this city, departed this life on Sunday evening last, at the moment the church bell tolled for three o'clock—that bell which from time immemorial he had himself tolled regularly five or six times every day. There lives not this day a native of Annapolis, nay, hardly any one that has ever dwelt amongst, or sojourned within our borders, that will not on meeting this melancholy note, recall the well known sound of our church bell and the striking figure of the old man that has so punctually attended to the precise moment of ringing the hour ever since the oldest of us can remember. 'Ere the church was a ruin,' on the spot where the present venerable edifice now stands, old Joseph was bell ringer. Not one man that ever has been a member of the Legislature, Executive, or Superior Judiciary of the State of Maryland, not a student of St. John's College, or a scholar of our humbler schools, but will remember the well known summons which his bell gave them alternately to duties and to relaxation. Alas! old Joseph rings no more.

"Whether it was by the influence of association that he had acquired the habit of punctuality, we pretend not to determine, but Mr. S. had deservedly obtained the reputation of being one of the most punctual of men.

"This estimable quality he carried into the several departments of his pursuits in life. As a collector of accounts, which before he became too infirm he was considerably employed in, he was proverbial for recollecting and attending to the very moment appointed.

"The same valuable precision was carried by him into the performances of the duties of Sexton, which he filled perhaps for the last forty years.

"But it was at grave digging, that the deceased enjoyed the distinction of having held an office longer than perhaps any man ever did, may, possibly ever will do, in this State. Undisturbed by the violence of those party contentions which would seem to spare no place however humble, unmoved even by the tide of revolution itself, by which allegiance was dissolved and a new and glorious nation was created, he held the prerogatives and performed the duties of grave digger to our community ; for with honest pride we record it, we have here but one general receptacle for the dead. In that single field is buried all social distinctions. Long before this field, now studded over with grave stones, on many of which the thick moss of a former century has accumulated, was disturbed to deposit the relics of the dead, was this old man our grave digger. Of all the vast concourse in this grave yard reposing, his hand has prepared and rounded the graves. At length, sinking under the accumulated weight of nearly one hundred years, he is quietly deposited as one amongst the multitude his labours had gathered together. Accordingly to his last, and often repeated injunction, he is laid close by the side of him that in this life he loved the most, and, at whose death, was well known all over America, fifty years ago, as the famous inn keeper at Annapolis, and for whose ample table, it was the province of this, his then faithful steward, to market and provide.

"Amidst the many peculiarities of character that distinguished the deceased, some of which no doubt grew out of an occupation that seventy or eighty years had made perfectly familiar to him, though spoken and even thought of with a strange superstition, awe and aversion by some "grown up children,"—amidst all his peculiarities we say, none were more distinct than his strict veracity, honesty, and sobriety."

This obituary of Simmons sharply defines the aged sexton's character. There come down to us to color the silhouette, anecdotes of his oddities and peculiarities.

Simmons is yet remembered by some who live in Annapolis. When he had reached a centennarian's age, he was an object of interest to all. With his white hair flowing over his shoulders, his aged form tottering with the weight of years, his shackling step, and the sombreness of his occupation, he presented to the mind the apparition of Old Time himself, lacking only the emblematic scythe to make the picture complete.

It was such a character that gave a thrill of terror to the juvenile mind whenever he came in sight, for it was the belief of the children that if Simmons looked at one and said: "I want you," the day of doom for it was fixed. Having occasion then to pass the aged sexton, the children were wont to don their most courteous graces, and with unusual politeness to simper in softest accents—"How do, Mr. Morgue?" This nickname, and that it was one the children were quite ignorant of, always infuriated Simmons, as the astonished children found by the sexton's vigorous replies that they had missed their mark, and had produced an effect just opposite from what they had intended.

The spirit of Simmons' occupation became more and more a part of him as his years grew apace. He had been known after somebody had offended him to pass an innocent gentleman on the street and to take a ghastly satisfaction in hissing at him, "I'll have you some day," in a tone that indicated that he thought, with him, remained the issues of life and death.

Simmons, however, had a genial side to that grim nature that made him a terror to young people and an offence to older folk. Amongst other duties that appertained to that of sexton of St. Anne's, was the ringing of "the one o'clock bell." On one occasion, as he was going into church on that duty, a lady said to him, "Oh, Mr. Simmons, do not ring that bell until I get home. Mr. —— likes everybody to be ready to sit down to dinner at one." "Well, then," replied Simmons brusquely, "walk fast." As the lady put her foot on the first step of the porch of her house which was in the extreme end of the town, the bell of Old St. Anne's rang out the hour of one. Simmons had arrested the march of time to please his fair petitioner.

It was Simmons' habit when the clergyman ended the service for the dead at the grave to give a hearty, "Amen." There lived at Annapolis at this period, the Rev. Mr. Wyatt. He was of the Episcopal Communion with strong Methodistic tendencies. On one occasion when Parson Wyatt, as he was familiarly known, was reading the service, some boys offended Simmons and he vented his wrath in language not permitted by the decalogue. The minister and sexton finished speaking together, and Simmons ejaculated "Amen." Parson Wyatt waited until the attendants at the funeral had departed, and, taking his cane in hand, shook it in Simmons' face, saying—"Don't you ever dare to stand along side of me again and say amen to any service I perform." Simmons, pointing to the other side of the grave as if the question at issue was one of position only, angrily retorted—"Well then go over on the other side."

Col. Mann, whom Simmons had faithfully served for years as caterer to Mann's Hotel, had touched the chords of his affection. Over his grave alone, of all the human dust he had interred, Simmons wept.

One incident has come down to us that does not reflect his character in an enviable light. There was in Annapolis one familiarly called, "Jeffrey Jig," (from whom Jeffrey's Point took its name,) who with "Jinny Corneracker," his wife, lived at the foot of Duke of Gloucester street in a little hut so small they could not stand in it erect. Jeffrey periodically fell into a comatose state and was several times prepared for interment. but always awoke in time to prevent the funeral. On one occasion his resuscitation was deferred until he was placed in the grave. Then as the grim sexton threw in the clods of the valley, a noise was heard in the coffin. The bystanders said Jeffrey was alive. Hardly realizing, let us believe, that the dead was alive. Simmons continued to fill up the grave. tradition says with the remark: "He's got to die sometime ; and if he was not dead, he ought to be."

* * *

CHAPTER LII.

CHRONICLES OF ANNAPOLIS FROM 1810 TO 1839.

[1810-12.] During the years 1810-12, tradition tells us George Frederick Cooke. the brilliant and dissolute English actor played in the Annapolis theatre.

[1813.] Rev. Ralph Higginbotham, vice-principal of St. John's College. died April 21.

In October, Dr. D. Claude and Lewis Duval were elected delegates from Annapolis to the Legislature. The vote was Dr. Claude 157 ; Lewis Duvall 157 : T. H. Bowie 90. The two first were Democrats; the last a Federalist.

[1814.] Dr. Upton Scott, aged 90 years. died in Annapolis, on the 23rd of February. He was a native of Ireland, but had resided in Annapolis 60 years. His career was one of unbroken virtue, dignity, and usefulness. He was the chosen friend of Gen. Wolfe.

[1815.] On Saturday, February 25, 1815, a company of Pennsylvanians, from the neighborhood of Brownsville, and commanded by Capt. Giesey. was honorably discharged from the service. They won a high reputation among the citizens of Annapolis for their good conduct and scrupulous regard for the rights of the citizens.

[1816.] On Saturday, the 16th of March, His Britannic Majesty's frigate Niger, of 32 guns, Capt. Jackson. arrived off Annapolis. with the Hon. Henry Bagot, Minister to the United States. his lady and suite. The frigate gave the town a salute of 17 guns. which was returned by the City Battery. The Ministerial party landed the next day. under a salute from the ship. and proceeded to Washington.

Public feeling ran very high in the spring of this year over an alleged attempt on the part of the federalist to colonize the town with permanent residents of federal proclivities so as to carry the city for the Federalist Party. The democrats held a public meeting, in which the scheme was denounced in a string of resolutions. Party animosities were so bitter when the pedagogue of the town, one Mr. Bassford, changed his politics from democrat to federalist, his school became so reduced in numbers he had to quit the town.

On Thursday, May 23, the U. S. S. Washington. 74 guns, Com. Chauncey arrived off Annapolis. President Madison and wife, the

Secretary of the Navy. Commodores Rogers and Porter came to Annapolis, stopping at Caton's, (now the City Hotel,) and visited the frigate. On June 7th, the Washington sailed, having on board the celebrated William Pinkney and his family. Mr. Pinkney went as minister to Naples.

At the election for delegates to the Legislature from Annapolis this year the federalists reduced the democratic majority. The vote was:

Federalists, Alex. C. Magruder, 91 : Richard Harwood, of Thos. 90. Democrats. Lewis Duvall 109 ; Dennis Claude 109.

[1817.] The question of removing the capital to Baltimore was agitated in the Legislature of 1817 and referred to the next assembly.

The strongest point made against proposed removal was the mob in Baltimore in 1812, when Lingan was killed.

Christopher Hohne, at the same session, was voted fifty dollars for venturing his life by going on the roof of the State House to extinguish a fire.

Fort Severn at this period was put in an excellent state of repair under the supervision of Capt. James Reed, assisted by Lieuts. Bache and Smook. Fort Madison, at same time lay, in a state of dismantled desuetude.

On the 14th of August, Mrs. Ann Ogle, died at the advanced age of 94 years. Her remains were interred in the family vault at White Hall, at the seat of Horatio Ridout, Esq.

The quaint cut of a steamboat appears in the *Gazette* of September 18, 1817. It seems there was a very just suspicion in the minds of the public that steamboats were not altogether the safest mode of conveyance. So the proprietors, George Stiles & Son, of Baltimore, advertised that the Surprise's boilers, which steamer ran between Baltimore and Annapolis, "will be proved every month to bear double the pressure at which they are worked." It was propelled by an engine on the rotary motion, and moved "with more ease and swiftness than any steamboat in the United State."

The subject of a naval depot at Annapolis was agitated in November, 1817. A committee, consisting of Messrs. Hughes and Stephen, was appointed by the corporation to memoralize the general government on the subject and the President of the United States was addressed a long communication in which it was stated that "Annapolis is, from its situation, more accessible from the ocean than any other port within a convenient distance from the city of Washington. It has been spontaneously selected by the ministers from foreign provinces for their places of landing and our own envoys have generally made it the point of their departure."

The memorialists also told how the French 74, L'Eole, drawing twenty-one feet, seven inches, had come in the harbor of Annapolis in 1807, when the tide was not at its height, and that one mile above, Fort Severn, the river was 50 feet deep.

[1818.] January 24, a meeting was held in Annapolis looking to the formation of a branch society to colonize, with their consent the free colored people of the United States in Africa.

The Legislature of 1818 showed no disposition to move the capital to Baltimore, although the corporation of Baltimore pledged all the funds necessary to erect public buildings in case the capital was removed. An effort to remove the capital to Baltimore, was also made in 1864. It was again unsuccessful. The location of the seat of government at Annapolis is now a part of the organic law of the State.

On the 28th of May, President Monroe visited Annapolis and was received by John Randall, Mayor of Annapolis, and presented with a series of complimentary resolutions by the City Council, and was given a banquet by the citizens. The President visited Fort Severn where he was saluted with cannon. He then sailed up the Severn on the revenue cutter Active, as far as Round Bay, to obtain a view of the river. He remained until Saturday morning, the 30th.

At the election in October to select delegates to the Legislature from Annapolis, the following was the vote ; Democrats—Dr. Dennis Claude 143, John Stephen 135 ; Federals—Robt. Welch of Ben. 113, Addison Ridout 107.

[1819.] The question of changing the charter of Annapolis, which had remained almost untouched since its grant by Queen Anne in 1708, arose in 1819. A writer declared "its provisions are of the most odious kind, and in the highest degree repugnant to the sentiments, the feelings, and the wishes of the independent citizens of a free republic. In the true spirit of aristocracy, it permits none but freeholders to hold the office-of mayor, alderman, or common councilman, and denies to our citizens the privilege of election more than one of the branches of government." Vacancies in the board of aldermen were filled by the common council, out of their own body, and also the Mayor was elected by a joint vote of the two branches, out of the board of common council. The charter was pronounced "one of the most aristocratical and absurd charters that ever disgraced the land of freedom." The movement was successful, and by act of December session, 1818, chapter 194, the charter of the city was altered and amended. On the fifth, the first Monday in April, 1819, the first election under the new city charter occurred, and the following were elected to fill the respective offices :

Mayor—Lewis Duvall.

Recorder—Thomas H. Carroll.

Alderman—James Hunter, Francis Hollingsworth, John Randall, Sr., Henry Duvall, Alex. C. Magruder.

Common Councilmen—John T. Barber, Geo. Schwrar, Joseph Sands, Washingron G. Tuck, William M'Parlin, Henry Magruder, James Shaw.

Sunday schools were opened in Annapolis, in April, 1818. The number of scholars entered during the year was 64. The colored scholars numbered over 20. The schools were under the charge of one directress and four superintendents, with a number of ladies, acting in rotation, as teachers. The school does not seem to have been denominational.

In this year, the time appears most vague from the indefinite terms used by the correspondents from whom the facts are taken, the collector of the United States, at Annapolis, had possession of certain goods, taken from a British vessel, on a charge of smuggling. The state court issued a writ of replevin. The high sheriff of Anne Arundel proceeded to serve the writ, and the collector sent to Fort Severn, and when the sheriff attempted to take the goods, he and his posse were met by a United States officer and a file of soldiers standing between him and the goods. The excitement amongst the citizens of Annapolis was intense. A number armed themselves, and executed the writ in spite of the soldiers, "nor was it without considerable personal exertion on the part of gentlemen holding high judicial and executive offices under the state, that the tumult was prevented from becoming more serious and fatal."

[1820.] The Religious and Literary Repository was commenced in Annapolis on Saturday January 15, 1820. It was edited by a Society of Laymen, members of the Protestant Episcopal Church. Its life seemed to have been of short duration.

February 28, Charles Carroll, of Carrolton, living then at Annapolis, at the ripe old age of 82, was represented as a striking instance "of activity of body, and energy of mind, evidencing a constitution preserved by the strictest discipline. which promises him long to this country and the community of which he has long been considered the most venerable and distinguished ornament. His mansion has given celebrity to the hospitality of Maryland, by being open to distinguished visitors from every quarter of the union and every civilized country of the globe. The utility of his public life is gilded by the peaceful beams of his declining years. A worthy associate of those men whose names are engraved upon a bolder monument than the pyramids of Egypt."

On Tuesday morning, September 28, the H. B. M. Frigate Spartan, arrived at Annapolis having on board Stratford Canning, Esq., the British Minister, and Mr. Charles F. Wilmot, his secretary. Fort Severn and the frigate exchanged saluts.

[1821.] Acts of December session. 1820, chapter 67, provided for the building of the present Court House in Annapolis. The commissioners to superintend the building were Richard Ridgely, Thomas B. Dorsey. Samuel Brown, Jr., Henry Woodward, Lancelot Warfield, Thomas Hodges, Rezin Estep Joseph McCeney, Jamer P. Soaper, Francis Hancock, John T. Barber, and Richard Harwood, of Thomas. Twelve thousand dollars was the limit of the levy to be made for the Court House.

October 10th, Wm. Kilty, aged 64 years. Chancellor of the State, died. Hon. John Johnson was appointed Chancellor in his stead.

[1822.] It is not uninteresting and will have a mollifying effect on those who believe that rings political. only in these latter days, encircled the body politic, to hear Mr. John C. Weems, of Elk Ridge, openly under his own signature declare against the "Star Chamber of Annapolis, where it is believed by those few keepers of the State, and more particularly of this congressional district, that no man can be found as well calculated to support their contest, as my friend Doctor Kent, who by Mr. Howard's account, has been brought out in direct opposition to myself, although he assured me four years ago, he never would be again in my way, and although he last year assured General Marriott, he would not be in his way." The writer further indicates that the "Annapolis-Junto," as he styles the unnamed State Managers of that day. had already laid out a plan of elections by the people precisely in the order. it is currently reported and generally believed, that the political leaders parcel out beforehand posititions and places to-day.

September 15th, at the early age of 38. John Chandler, a native of Delaware, but for the previous thirteen years a resident of Annapolis, and editor of the *Republican*, died.

The city election on Monday, October 1822, presented the curious incident of two men running before the people for two offices each on the same day. Lewis Duvall was a candidate for Mayor of Annapolis and delegate to the Legislature for Annapolis. To the former office he was elected. For the latter he was defeated by the following vote : Caucus—Jeremiah Hughes 152. Thomas H. Carroll 147. Anti-Caucus—Col. Lewis Duvall 139. Thomas H. Carroll was also elected recorder of the city the same day.

September 24th, Dr. Rafferty, Vice Principal of St. John's College, advertised a course of lectures upon Natural Philosophy, to be illustrated with experiments. The Philosophic Apparatus of the College at this time had cost nearly $5,000, and "was made by the first artists in London." The apparatus, however, did not arrive in time and the course was postponed until the next year.

November 2, Jeremiah Hughes took charge of the *Maryland Republican*, as proprietor.

[1823.] In December Session, 1822, a bill was passed to incorporate a company to build a bridge over the Severn River. Reverdy Johnson was among the directors to open books for subscription. Thirty-five thousand dollars was the amount of capital stock in 1400 shares at $25 each. The structure was to be at Annapolis and was to be a toll bridge. The draw was to be forty feet wide. The bridge was not then built. It was not until 1886 that this bridge was finally erected. The County Commissioners who executed the work were Wm. Brewer Gardiner, Arthur Carr, Wm. P. Baldwin, Wm. A. Shipley, and Wm. Jones.

In this year Strawberry Hill Farm, now the Government Farm, opposite Annapolis, on which stood for many years the Alms House of the county, was sold by the trustees of the poor for $6,000. The trustees then purchased the commodious house and ten acres on the south side of South River, now in use, as the Alms House, from Mr. Larimore. This is on the site of a town projected in the early history of the province under the ambitious title of New London.

In June of this year the committee, to which was referred the annual report of the Mayor, dismissed the question of police for the city saying that "if, instead of one city constable, three men of good, energetic, firm, and respectable standing, could be obtained, and give them $80 per annum each, who should at all times, by night as well as by day, patrol the city, and particularly on the Sabbath, and that their salary should be made payable quarter yearly, by an order from the Mayor to him, they should weekly report, and be accountable for the peace of the city. But when your committee view their fellow-citizens, with respect to having this service performed, as it should be to our city, they confess themselves under conviction that it would be extremely difficult to find men possessing the necessary qualifications." A further insight into the state of local affairs is seen by the statement of a writer in the public press, that "one-third of the revenue of this city is pocketed by those holding appointments under the corporation."

Resolutions were introduced in the Corporation of Annapolis in January, by Mr. Shaw, for subscribing for shares of stock in the company, incorporated to build a bridge over Severn River.

17

As an evidence of the scarcity of ready money in the Spring of 1823, and the morality of the county, at the April term of Court. over 680 suits were brought and only one indictment found by the Grand Jury and that of petty larceny. Anne Arundel at this time was the third in population in the State, having nearly 30,000 inhabitants. It was before Howard had been carved out of Anne Arundel.

By the report of the Mayor. Lewis Duvall, made in April of this year, it is learned ''that the Police of the city is too much weakened, within the last few months. by the discontinuance of, or from reducing the number of city-constables. from which period the city appears to have relapsed into its former propensities, by indulging in riots and noise at nights, and gambling on the Sabbath and other days, to the annoyance of sundry parts of the city.''

An article written for the *Maryland Republican* of June 21st, raises the question, and parenthetically answered it, whether, or not, the celebrated Marshal Ney of France, was not ''a certain Michael Rudolph,'' of Cecil county, Maryland, who had served with distinguished bravery as a Captain in Lee's dragoons during the American Revolution. Ney's nephew, Edward C. Genet, gave the true place of his birth as one of the German departments of France, in 1769.

The pleasures of the turf in Annapolis were attended with evils that afflict them in modern days. The *Maryland Republican*, of October 18th, says: ''It is with pleasure we announce that the members of the Jockey Club have reconsidered their articles of association and abandoned the proposed races this season. If there be any advantage to the breed of horses, in such sports we have certainly been paying too dear a price for that advantage in the sacrifice of time, money, character, and morals which the race week costs.''

[1824.] A census of the population of Annapolis was taken February 1824. The population was 2,500 including the United States Troops, in Fort Severn. In 1820, the census had made the number 2,260.

During the December Session of the Legislature, of 1823, protracted until March, the question of the right of the soldiers, stationed at Fort Severn, to vote in Annapolis at the State and national elections arose in the General Assembly. The question came to the Legislature under a petition from the fifty-one men stationed at the Fort. The Fort was then in the corporate limits of Annapolis. The judges of election in the preceding October election ''refused to receive the votes of certain soldiers who had been in Fort Severn a longer term than six months, and who were citizens of this state at the time they entered into the service of the United States.'' Some of the very men who were not allowed to vote at this election had voted at former elections. The indignation on the subject was further heightened by the fact that the officers had been allowed to vote. The Legislature adopted the report of the committee on the subject that it was then inexpedient to legislate on this question.

On the first Monday of April, the city election occurred between the Caucus and Anti-Caucus party. The vote stood for Mayor—anti-caucus, R. Harwood, 161 ; caucus, James Boyle—152. For Recorder—anti-caucus, E. D. Ridgely, 159 ; T. H. Carroll, caucus—156. For Aldermen, the following anti-caucus party men were elected: T. Anderson, 161 ; J. N. Watkins, 162 ; J. W. Duvall, 159 ; caucus—D. Claude, 159 ; J. Williamson, 157. For Common Councilmen—the anti-caucus men elected J. Randall, Jr., 161 ; Geo. Shaw, 160 ; Bennett

Hurst. 159; the caucus—W. G. Tuck, 158; B. B. Brewer, 158; J. Hughes, 158. W. R. Thompson, P. Schwrar and Jona Hutton, anti-caucus, and J. Boyd, caucus, each received 157 votes, and a new election had to be held to elect one Common Councilman. At that election the vote stood W. P. Thompson, 154; J. L. Boyd, 135. These parties represented on one side a party opposed to the caucus system of nomination and on the other the advocates of it.

August 12th, H. B. M. Frigate Phæton, 44 guns, Captain Sturt, arrived in Annapolis with Mr. Vaughin, minister plenipotentiary from the Court of St. James to America. The usual salutes were exchanged between Fort Severn and the ship. The Mayor, General Harwood, and others waited on the minister, and congratulated him on his arrival. The Minister, whilst in the city, gave a dinner to Capt. Sturt, in honor of his attentions during the voyage.

March 9th, Dr. Wm. Rafferty, was chosen Principal of St. John's College.

In April, the Baltimore Medical College, awarded the first premium medal to Dr. Edward Sparks, of Annapolis, for the best medical Latin thesis.

On Monday, April 19th, the boiler of the Steamboat Eagle, on her first trip from Annapolis to Baltimore, exploded off North Point. A soldier from Fort Severn was killed, four persons were scalded, and Captain Weems and all his crew, more or less injured. Among the scalded was Henry M. Murray, of Annapolis, aged 34 years, who subsequently died of his injuries. The explosion set the Eagle on fire but it was extinguished by the crew and passengers. The son of Captain Weems, a lad of 12 or 13 years, was blown through the sky-light from the cabin without sustaining serious injury.

[1825.] At the foot of Maryland Avenue, on the Severn, now part of the Naval Academy, run transversely the highest hills in and about Annapolis. They remained until that part of the city was taken into the Naval Academy. About the year, 1825, Daniel H. Wiggins, an ingenious inventor of various implements, one of which was a wheat drill, which successfully accomplished the work, conceived the idea of erecting on this prominent elevation a wind-mill that would run on any quarter from which the wind would blow. The idea conceived, the mill was built. On the day for it to start, the assembled citizens gathered around the ingenious contrivance, the sails were set, the wind filled their open wings, and the latent machinery began to move. Around and around it went obedient to the currents, but utterly uncontrollable by the inventor. He had neglected to provide means by which to throw off the power, and to render the mill subservient to his will. There it went on whirling and whirring to the chagrin of the inventor, who had to abandon his creation to the elements as a monument of misdirected genius.

The power was taken from the wind and conveyed to the mill by means of sails rigged to the spokes of a wheel that any wind would revolve.

[1827.] In this year the act was passed which established the State Library. The law restricted the use of the books to members of the executive or legislative departments.

In October, George Wells, Jr., and John N. Watkins were elected delegates from Annapolis to the Legislature. It seems to have been a purely personal contest and party lines were not drawn. The vote was George Wells, Jr.. 151 ; John N. Watkins, 143 ; Henry Hobbs, 142 ; Richard J. Crabb, 141.

In April of this year, Dr. Dennis Claude, was elected Mayor by this vote : Dr. Dennis Claude, 154 ; Richard J. Crabb, 138.

[1828.] In Annapolis this year, national politics showed itself in the election for delegates to the Legislature. The vote was :

Jackson ticket—Richard J. Crabb, 158 ; Thomas Anderson, 148. Adams ticket—John N. Watkins. 153 : George Wells, Jr., 149.

Jeremiah Townley Chase, an ex-member of Congress, and Chief Judge of the Court of Appeals of Maryland, died in Annapolis, May 11th, aged nearly 80 years.

Jeremiah Townley Chase was from early manhood until nearly the close of his long and active life, a public man in many important offices, in all of which he acquitted himself with honor and distinction. Mr. Chase was born in Baltimore in 1748, and removed to Annapolis in 1779. He was Mayor of Annapolis in 1783, and delivered the address of welcome to General Washington when he came to resign his commission in 1783. He also enjoyed the honor of meeting and welcoming Lafayette, when he crossed the Prince George's border and entered Anne Arundel in 1824, on his way to visit Annapolis. Judge Chase took an early and decided part in the arduous and doubtful contest with Great Britain, supporting with vigor the rights of his country. During the whole of that trying conflict, he exhibited the most active and patriotic zeal and unshaken firmness.

The beginning of his public services was his appointment upon the first Committee of Safety in Baltimore. and he enlisted as a private in one of the first military companies in Maryland. In February, 1775, he was elected by Baltimore county, of which the town was then a part. a member of the Convention which framed the Constitution, and formed the Governmeno of the State, and was one of that body which united in the Declaratint of Independence for Maryland.

He continued to be a representative from Baltimore until he removed to Annapolis. He was at that time elected a member of the Executive Council, in which capacity he served to the close of the Revolutionary War. It was this Governor, Thomas Johnson, in whose council Judge Chase served, who received the acknowlegements of General Washington for procuring supplies of flour and cattle for the American Army. Judge Chase was a member of Congress in 1783, and, in 1784. was appointed one of the Executive Committee of that body to act in the recess of Congress.

In 1789, Mr. Chase was appointed a Judge of the General Court of the State. On the abolition of that Court, he was appointed Chief Judge of the Third Judicial District, and Chief Judge of the Court of Appeals.

In June, 1824, Judge Chase resigned the office of Chief Justice. In the administration of justice, Judge Chase was firm, dignified, and impartial ; in the domestic circle, amiable ; in society, brilliant ; in private conduct, kind and temperate ; exhibiting in all his acts, public and private, the benign influence of a sincere Christian life.

Judge Chase died in 1828, and was buried in the City Cemetery, Annapolis.

[1829.] In December Session, 1828, an act was passed incorporating the Annapolis and Potomac Canal Company to connect the city of

Annapolis and the Chesapeake and Ohio Canal Company. The project came to naught.

At the election for the Legislature this year, the following was the vote in Annapolis:

Administration, (Jackson's Administration,) Richard J. Crabb, 150; James Murray, 137; Anti-Administration, George Wells, Jr., 167; Dr. Dennis Claude, 162.

[1830.] The following extract, taken from the Maryland *Gazette*, of May 13th, 1830, shows that the freemen of Annapolis early put the temperance question in politics:

At a meeting of sundry individuals, held on the 14th of April, 1830, in the city of Annapolis, the following Preamble and Resolutions were adopted:

"*Whereas*, the manner in which elections have been for a long time conducted in the city of Annapolis, is viewed by us, as having a pernicious tendency to corrupt the morals of youth, as well as fraught with evil to our citizens in general: And, *whereas*, the baneful effects of such conduct cannot be counteracted successfully but by taking a decided stand against it; Therefore:

"*Resolved* by the undersigned, that we solemnly pledge ourselves to vote for no candidate or candidates for any office, for which we are entitled to vote, who shall himself give, or who shall for him, directly or indirectly suffer to be given, any kind of ardent spirits, fermented liquors, money, clothing or any thing else, to any voter or voters, at any election, for the purpose of obtaining their votes.

"*Resolved further*, That the course adopted by this meeting be recommended to our respectable fellow-citizens, and that they are invited to unite with us in putting down an evil as degrading as it is desolating.

"*Resolved*, That in order to carry our object more fully into effect, we agree to reserve our votes to 4 o'clock in the afternoon, unless the business or circumstances of any of us should require him or them to vote earlier.

"*Resolved*, That the above proceedings be published in the different newspapers printed in this city.

Signed by

Edward Williams,	Samuel Goldsmith,
Lewis Gassaway,	Grafton Munroe,
Basil Shephard,	Thomas G. Waters,
Andrew Slicer,	M. W. Conner,
Samuel Peaco,	Jacob Bassford,
William Ross,	Peter Saussac,
Vachel Severe,	Samuel Parrott,
Daniel H. Wiggins,	Daniel Dorsey,
Thomas Sands,	W. J. Goldsborough,
Charles Henshaw,	N. J. Watkins,
Thomas King, Jr.,	Philip Clayton,
Thomas King,	William M'Parlin."
William Kirby,	

They are dead, but around the names of many of them there lingers the odor of a holy sanctity of life that has made their memory precious to their descendants and an honor to the community.

[1831.] The startling episode of American slavery, Nat. Turner's revolt, alarmed the people of Anne Arundel, and companies of infantry were organized and night patrols established to defend the people from an expected uprising. Whilst the whites were preparing for belligerent measures, the following pacific action was taken in this city :

At a numerously attended meeting of the Free People of Colour of the city of Annapolis, and its vicinity, convened in the African Methodist Episcopal Church, on the evening of October 4th, 1831,—to take into consideration the propriety and expediency of adopting certain resolutions, expressive of their views, wishes, and desires, the object of the meeting having been explained by the Chairman, the following Preamble and Resolutions were adopted :

'' *Whereas* certain rumors, accompanied with suspicions of an unfavorable character, have been in circulation through the country respecting the colored population, calculated to destroy the confidence which the white population have reposed in them.

''*Resolved therefore*, That we deeply and sincerely regret that any circumstance should have transpired to create those suspicions.

''*Resolved*, That we who reside in this city, and its vicinity, who now compose this meeting, cannot refrain from expressing our grateful acknowledgments in possessing the assurance that the confidence of their white friends is still reposed in them, and that no rumor has been able to impair the same.

''*Resolved*, That, as we are not insensible of the friends we have among the white population, and that many of them have labored to ameliorate our condition, we pledge ourselves, that our future conduct and deportment shall continue to be such as will be calculated to increase and continue their confidence and good wishes.

''*Resolved*, That should anything occur contrary to our views of good order, peace, and tranquility, as inculcated in the word of God, we will use every means and all our influence, to put it down.

''*Resolved*, That we be grateful to Almighty God for the revelation of his will to man, and that revelation teaches us, that it is our highest wisdom to live soberly, righteously and godly, in this present world, that in the world to come we may be sharers of eternal life.

''Editors friendly to the above resolutions, will confer a favor on this meeting, by giving them a few insertions, particularly those of our city.

Signed,

HENRY PRICE, Chairman.

JOHN SMITH, JR., Secretary.''

It was in November of this year, 1831, that the project to build a railroad between Baltimore and Annapolis was inaugurated. At the same time the practicability of making the road connect Washington, as well as Baltimore, was suggested, hence came the twenty miles of road, known from its charter in 1836, as the Annapolis and Elk Ridge Railroad. It was not, however, until February 6th, 1832, that the bill was passed to incorporate the Baltimore and Annapolis Railroad Company. Nothing appears to have come of this. In December 1836, another act passed, naming Amos A. Williams, Leonard Iglehart, Alexander Randall, Somerville Pinkney, George Wells, and Elias Ellicott, as Commissioners to take subscriptions to the capital stock of the Annapolis and Elk Ridge Railroad Company, which was placed at $450,000. The State subscribe $300,000 to the company's stock provided first, it was to be certified to the Treasurer for the Western Shore that before the State's subscription was formally made that its quota would complete the road. The Governor and his Council were to appoint a State director for every $100,000 of stock subscribed by the State. The private stockholders were given six directors by the act. In May, 1837, it was publicly announced that sufficient stock had been subscribed to organize the company, and the State's subscription was thereupon made.

The first passenger train left Annapolis for the Annapolis Junction, Christmas Day, 1840. Henry H. Bush, now living, was the engineer, and James Miller, the conductor.

[1834.] A monument was suggested in January, to Charles Carroll, of Carrollton, at Annapolis, on the hill on the Priests' property, east corner of Gloucester street, where a large walnut tree stood which tradition says sheltered Washington and Carroll.

In August, the young men of Annapolis crystalized their indignation at the "dispositionto deprive them of any participation in the political benefits of the city," and nominated Sprigg Harwood and Frederick Louis Grammer, as candidates for the Legislature, representing the young men of the city. The nomination led to the usual bitter newspaper warfare that follows a new departure. The opposition put up Nicholas Brewer and George Wells. It was charged that these nominations were coached by William B. Curran, a young man in the employment of Mr. Blair, editor of the Washington *Globe*. The election, in October, resulted :

Opposition—Sprigg Harwood, 135 ; Fred. L. Grammer, 133. Nomination—Nicholas Brewer, 168 ; George Wells, 164.

[1835.] June 25th, the corner stone of Humphrey Hall, St. John's College, was laid. John Johnson, delivered an eloquent address on the occasion. The building committee were Ramsay Waters, John Johnson, and Nicholas Brewer. R. C. Long, was the architect, and Elijah Wells, the builder.

[1837.] The political titles of candidates for the Legislature this year show that there was another change in political shibboleths. The result was : Van Buren candidates—Richard J. Jones, 128 ; John H. T. Magruder, 127. Whig candidates—Richard Swann, 154 ; Thos. S. Alexander, 152.

[1839.] On Sunday, April 14th, 1839, Nicholas Brewer, father of the late Judge Nicholas Brewer, died. The following obituary appeared in the next issue of the *Maryland Republican*, evidently from the pen of Jeremiah Hughes, the veteran editor of that Journal :

"Thus in the 68th year of his age, closes the earthly career of another of the most active, firm, steady, and undeviating politicians of this State, and of this age. A man who, as an *opponent*, was always a MAN, open, undisguised, straight-forward, and high-minded. As a friend, no man was ever more ardent, whole-hearted, and sincere.

"For several years, and until attacked by the disease which finally carried him off, Mr. Brewer, represented this city in the House of Delegates, of which he was one of the most useful and influential members. He seldom spoke in the House : when he did his speech was always brief, to the purpose—and never failed to command attention. It may be truly said, that a delegate more devoted to the interests of his constituents has never represented any people. Twice or thrice, at earlier periods of his life, he served as Elector of the Senate—a station usually appropriated to the most popular man in each community.

"As a next door-neighbor and most intimate friend—as an associate for the third of a century in every political struggle—in peace and in war—through good and through evil report—in prosperity and in adversity—sickness and health—we have known and can truly testify of Nicholas Brewer, as a high-minded, public-spirited, patriotic, amiable man—a man of inflexible integrity in public as in private life."

Mrs. Baldwin, who died in 1749, one hundred years old, the supposed first person born in Anne Arundel, was the progenitor of Mrs. Jeremiah Townley Chase, *nee* Hester Baldwin and Mrs. Samuel Chase, *nee* Ann Baldwin.

————— ‹•›—————

CHAPTER LIII.

LOCATION OF THE UNITED STATES NAVAL ACADEMY AT ANNAPOLIS.

[1845.] As early as November 15, 1814, Hon. William Jones, Secretary of the Navy, under President Madison, suggested the expediency of establishing a Naval Academy. This recommendation, from its inception to the establishment of the Naval Academy, in 1845, was followed by the persistent and intelligent effort of the leading minds in naval knowledge, and the best informed as to the maritime wants of the country.

In 1823, two bills were before Congress, proposing the inauguration of a naval school. Whilst these were pending, the Maryland Legislature January, 1826, passed the following :

"*Resolved* by the General Assembly of Maryland. That our Senators and Representatives in Congress be, and they are hereby requested to call the attention of their respective houses to the superior advantages which the city of Annapolis and its neighborhood possesses as a situation for a Naval Academy, and that they use their best exertions in favor of the establishment of such an institution."

This resolution reached the United States Senate February 7, 1826.

Repeated efforts at legislation had failed, once in 1826 by a single vote in the Senate, to give the United States a Naval Academy, when the illustrious historian George Bancroft became Secretary of the Navy in 1845. "His own profound scholarship, his rich and varied culture, and his personal familiarity with educational methods, enabled him to appreciate the want of the service and to devise a way in which it might be supplied. To him the Navy owes the foundation of the Naval Academy. He saw, as his predecessors had also seen that a dozen separate schools without organization or intelligent supervision, constituted as appendages to navy-yards and seagoing men-of-war, could produce no satisfactory results. He had seen, moreover, the failure of many efforts at legislation with a view to reforming the systems. But he discovered what those before him had failed to see, that with him lay the authority to remedy the evils, and that the means were already provided. By placing a large number of professors upon waiting orders—that is, by dispensing with their services —a large part of the annual outlay for instruction might be saved ; and by concentrating a few of the best men of the corps of instructors at a suitable place, a school might be formed with an independent organization."*

On June 2d, 1845, a board of naval officers met at the Philadelphia Naval Asylum for the examination of midshipmen for promotion. The board consisted of Commodores George C. Read, Thomas Ap Catesby Jones, and Matthew C. Perry, and Captains E. A. F. Lavalette and Isaac Mayo.

Amongst the instructions of the board was the following :

"NAVY DEPARTMENT.

"Washington, June 13, 1845.

"Sir : I desire the assistance of your board in maturing a more efficient system of instructions for the young naval officers. The opportunity which your present arduous and responsible duties as examiners of the school afford you of giving practical and useful advice leads me to solicit your co-operation by as full a communication of your opinion as is consistent with your convenience.

"Fort Severn has been recommended to me as a more suitable place for such a school than the Naval Asylum, especially as a vessel could be stationed there to serve as a school in gunnery.

"The present term of instruction is too short. Might it not be well to have permanent instruction, and to send all midshipmen on shore to the school? What plan of studies is most advisable? I hope your board will find time and will be disposed to aid me by their suggestions.

"I wish, also, that they would nominate, for my consideration, a board of three experienced officers, whose qualifications incline them to give long-continued attention to this subject, and who could have the permanency necessary to assist me until a plan can be matured. If, from your own number, you would select such a board, or would take a wider scope in your selection, it would be acceptable to me."

"I am, respecfully, yours,

GEORGE BANCROFT.

Commodore George C. Read,

President Board of Examiners, &c., Philadelphia, Pa."

After a thorough examination of, and deliberation over, the subject, the Board made a lengthy report, in which there occurs the following :

"Three of the undersigned are ignorant of the precise situation of Fort Severn, and its fitness for a naval school in regard to its accomodation. in healthiness of location, and conveniences of the vicinity for gun-practice, but they are told by their associates, Commodore Jones and Captain Mayo, that the fort embraces sufficient space and the harbor and neighboring shores offer all the requisite advantages for gun-practice and evolution of steamers and boats. Supposing, then, that Fort Severn is selected. and there is ample accommodation within its walls for the officers and students of the establishment, it may be re-

* History of the Naval Academy. Soley. p. 42.

marked that the Government already possesses all the necessary means for commencing at once a naval school, which may be enlarged and perfected at some future time."

Shortly after this Secretary Bancroft, Governor Marcy, then Secretary of War, and Commodore Warrington, chief of the Bureau of Navy Yards and docks, visited Annapolis, the object of their visit being understood to be to examine the condition of Fort Severn and the improvements commenced the previous fall. The rumor was also afloat that it was the intention of the government to remove the Naval School from Philadelphia to Fort Severn, which be one of the reasons of this visit.†

Some after this visit, the Secretary ordered a board, composed of Commanders McKean, Buchanan, and Du Pont, to consider the subject, and to recommend a location and officers. The board decided upon Annapolis as the site, and Ward, Chauveult, and Lockwood as professors. Commander Franklin Buchanan, a Baltimorean, had already been selected as superintendent.

Fort Severn was an army post, the site of which had been purchased in 1808, at a period when Annapolis was deemed a place of military importance. The ground consisted of ten acres, almost square, inclosed on the west end and northern side by brick wall, and on the southern and eastern sides by the Severn. At the angle of the water front stood the battery, a small circular rampart, mounting *en barbette* ten heavy guns, with a magazine in the water. In the grounds was a Wind-mill built here in 1760, and on the shore of the fort the Peggy Stewart was run aground and burned by its owner, to satisfy the demands of the patriots of 1774.

The buildings consisted of officers' quarters and barracks. Buchanan row, (the new building for the Superintendent excepted,) the house opposite the southern end of the row, and the dwelling occupied by Secretary Richard M. Chase, are all that remain of those that existed when the Fort was transferred Aug 15, 1845, to the Navy Department.

October 10th, the school was opened.

The State of Maryland acted promptly in the cession of every right and privilege required by the government.

The young stripling began to grow apace. In 1847, the first addition was made to the grounds. It comprised three lots—one from F. Buchanan and others, the second from Rebecca Nicholson, with a collateral deed from Edward Lloyd and R. Nicholson to secure the title of Miss Nicholson's lot. The third from A. Randall, trustee for W. O'Hara and others.

This included land adjacent to the school and lying between Scott street and the Severn, and reached to Northeast street, now Maryland Avenue. This was under Commander Upshur.

The second addition, commenced in 1853, under commander Stripling was completed after the arrival of Com. Goldsborough. One part consisted of land lying between Scott street, Governor street, Hanover street, and Northeast street now occupied by the Academy Chapel, and by the row of officers' quarters numbered from one to eleven, and includes the lawns in front as far as the line of Scott street ; and the other part of land lying along the Severn River on the opposite side

† Annapolis paper.

of Northeast street and between it and Tabernacle street. the fourth side being the line of Hanover street extended. The buildings on it are known as Goldsborough row.

The Third addition was Scott street and Northeast street between Hanover and the river. This was in 1853.

The fourth addition was made in 1866, Admiral Porter, superintendent. The executive mansion of the state, the residence of the governors since the time of Robert Eden, with the garden adjoining, a place where Washington had been guest, was bought by the United States, and a square's length of Governor's street was taken in with it. This comprised four acres. The Governor's house is now used as the Academy library, and Porter row has been built on part of the fourth acquisition.

The fifth addition was made in 1867, by the purchase of ten acres of land from St. John's College between the College and Graveyard Creek. This tract has never been joined to the Academy, there being land intermediate between it and the Academy. Another tract of land, Strawberry Hill farm. on which the Alms House of Anne Arundel county once stood, was bought in 1868. This is not a part proper of the Academy. It adjoins the grounds of the Naval Hospital. (thirty-two acres in extent,) one part being reserved as a naval necropolis.

The sixth addition was accomplished in 1874, being four acres from that part of Lockwoodsville lying on the Severn, between, then Tabernacle, now College Avenue, Hanover and Wagner Streets.

The following is the summary of land in use by, and under the control of, the Naval Academy authorities :

	ACRES.
Grounds about Fort Severn	9
Purchases of 1847 and 1853, including streets	33
Purchase 1866, (Governor's Mansion)	4
Purchase of 1874, Lockwoodsville	4
Within the Academy	50

	ACRES.
Hospital Grounds	32
Strawberry Hill	67
College Lot	10
Outside of Academy	109

During 1883, one of the ancient landmarks of the State fell. It was the one occupied to that period from 1845, as the residence of the Superintendent of the Naval Academy.

It was built by John Duff, an architect who settled in the colony in 1728. This house was built, at least, in 1751, and probably much earlier. It was the residence of that talented family, the Dulanys, and was occupied by it from 1753 to 1808, and on the cession of the ground to the government as the site of Fort Severn, became the residence of the commander of the fort and so remained to 1845. In 1883, by a commission of officers, Captain Francis M. Ramsay being Superintendent, the house was condemned as unsafe, and was torn down, and the Superintendent, by funds reserved from the supplies voted the Academy, proceeded to build a residence for the Superintendent. Congress that had refused specific monies for this building, resented the action of the Superintendent, and, by proviso inserted, declared no money should be used to complete the offensive structure. There it remained until the end of the term of the offending Superintendent, a monument of autocratic independence and congressional indignation.

The location of the Naval Academy at Annapolis has been of large advantage to the business of the place. The social benefits have been well appreciated by its people, and the constant succession of interesting events occuring at the Academy, has added to the enjoyment and culture of an already polished community.

——— ·•· ———

CHAPTER LIV.

A Riot in Annapolis.

]1847.]   On the 5th of July, 1847, the steamboat "Jewess," was chartered by Mr. C. C. Philips, of Baltimore, to make an excursion to St. Michaels, in Talbot county, with the express understanding that the steamer would accommodate at least seven hundred passengers comfortably.   About that number took passage on the steamer including whom were the Eagle Artillerists, Col. Geo. P. Kane, commanding, and the Columbian Riflemen, Capt. Robert McAllister, commanding.   The military companies were on their way to join with the military of Talbot county in celebrating the National holiday, and the latter had made appropriate preparations to receive the expected visitors.

Before reaching the county wharf at Fell's Point, it was discovered that the boat could not accommodate those that were already on board, and on arriving at the county wharf there were the military and several hundred who desired to take passage on the boat.   The military alone were allowed to embark.

With this large crowd on board, composed, no doubt, of the motley company that generally gathers on general holidays on cheap excursions, the "Jewess" started for St. Michaels, and steamed slowly down the bay.   After being out four hours, the captain found it impossible with the large number of passengers he had on board, and the cranky condition of the steamer, to cross the bay.   The charter party to the contrary notwithstanding, Captain Sutton determined that the lives of seven hundred passengers were in his keeping, and he was responsible if any accident occured.   He, therefore, decided that he would put into Annapolis, and if one hundred and fifty passengers would land, he would then proceed to St. Michaels with the balance.

After a passage of five hours, the "Jewess" reached Annapolis. Not a man would go ashore with the understanding that "he had the privilege of finding his way back to Baltimore the best way he could." On this Capt. Sutton decided to proceed no further, tied his boat to the wharf, and let off steam.

"After the boat had been made fast," says an eye witness,* who spoke from a Baltimore standpoint, "and the passengers found they could go no further. they generally went on shore for the purpose of amusing themselves as might best suit their fancy, and were received with every mark of respect by some of the citizens. Those who visited the Naval School were kindly received by the officers, as were also those who went up to the State House, but with some of the community there appeared to be something wrong, as if some past offence had not beeen forgotten or some new aggression had been committed." In contradiction of any bad spirit being shown by the citizens, it is asserted by a citizen living at this day that a part of the excursionists behaved very disorderly. If there was ill-feeling rankling, or bad temper provoked, by fresh affronts, it found some vent when on Church street, a Baltimore youth broke a window, and whilst William F. Smith, of Baltimore, was paying for it, one of the crowd was arrested by an Annapolis constable. Mr. Smith persuaded the balance of the Baltimore boys to return to the "Jewess;" and the culprit was rescued by his friends.

At the City Hotel Col. John Walton, proprietor, testified, several of the party from the steamer entered the kitchen, took possession of it, and insisted upon helping themselves to dinner. They behaved in the same riotous manner at the bar, and he had to threaten to commit them to jail before they would leave. In other parts of the town. pistols were fired, and curses rent the air. At the Western Hotel kept by Mr. E. A. Davis, some of the party amused themselves pitching the bread out of the windows.

A significant fact bearing on the character of the people who composed the crowd on board the "Jewess" was brought out in the testimony of Col. Geo. P. Kane, in the examination that followed the affray : "He had left the boat at Annapolis, and had procured a citizen's dress from a friend, which he had exchanged for his uniform, and had determined to come up in the cars in the morning ; the conduct of a portion of those who were on board the boat having been so disorderly and riotous as to deter him from returning with them."

Whilst Col. Kane was at dinner in Annapolis, he heard the report of fire-arms. He started for the "Jewess." Before he reached there another prominent character who was to figure in the subsequent proceedings, Judge Nicholas Brewer, who had heard that a friend's son had become involved in a difficulty, and had come down to persuade him out of it, had arrived at the wharf.

At the examination before Justice Walton Gray, in Baltimore, July 9th, Judge Brewer testified that he "saw by the soiled state of the clothes of the young man and injury he had received on his nose, that he had been engaged in a fight. He remonstrated with him, and persuaded him to leave the wharf. Seeing that there was considerable excitement among those on the wharf, and every probability of a riot ensuing, he decided to remain there and endeavor to prevent it.

"Nothing of any moment occurred from this time for nearly an hour while preparations were making for the departure of the boat, and nearly all belonging to her had got on board."

The testimony of Mr. Daniel T. Hyde, a prominent citizen of Annapolis, then takes up the thread of the story : "He was sitting in his porch, (his house being about a hundred yards from where the boat

* Balto. American of July 7, 1847.

lay,) when he saw Judge Brewer go down to the wharf. The crowd on the boat began to hiss and hoot at him and some one of them called out "bring that big-bellyed man, with a straw hat on board." Thinking that violence might be offered to the Judge, and that it was his duty to endeavor to prevent it, he immediately went down towards the wharf. There was, however, when Mr. Hyde reached the steamer, no attempt to offer violence to Judge Brewer."

Mr. Hyde used his good offices to promote peace and to suppress the disturbance and was in imminent danger from the ill-feelings of the citizens on the wharf and the visitors on the steamer. The billingsgate and profanity between the two crowds at this moment was terrible. The noise and confusion were so great that it was almost impossible to distinguish what was said. In preparation for the coming fray several boys from the boat ran on shore, and picked up stones and retreated to the steamer. An old man, whom Judge Brewer thought was William F. Smith, in company with a young man, advanced on the gangway leading to the wharf and seemed ready to fight. Judge Brewer persuaded them to return to the boat. The lines were now cast off. Mr. Hyde advised Mr. Waters, the Mate of the boat and asked him to say the same thing to Capt. Sutton to move off. Mr. Hyde assisted in casting the lines of the steamer loose from the shore.

"At this time two halves of a lemon were thrown from the boat among the crowd on shore." This was the signal of battle. The crowd on the wharf gave way, a dark object was seen to fly from the boat to the shore, and the Annapolitans returned the attack with a volley of bricks. The Baltimoreans replied with stones and pistols.

The bricks that had come from the shore had fallen amongst the ladies and children, and a cry was made for the rifles of Capt. McAllister's company. The captain tried to prevent the men from getting the rifles out of the room in which they had been stowed. He sent James L. Wallace to take charge of this. Mr. Wallace, when he arrived at the temporary armory, found it filled with passengers taking away the rifles. Some of the company attempted to assist Mr. Wallace but they were "thrown aside like an old check shirt," and those in the room helped themselves to the rifles and cartridges and went on deck and used them on the citizens of Annapolis.

The ladies on the boat were now in a state of great alarm, some attempted to throw themselves overboard, whilst the work of getting them below proceeded with a haste born of urgent necessity.

Judge Brewer and Mr. Daniel T. Hyde who were in the dangerous position of being between two fires bravely endeavored to stop the Annapolitans from continuing the affray. Mr. Hyde, finding two colored boys throwing stones at the boat, kicked them away, and turned to the boat to hurry it out of danger. Fearing the boat would ground on an old stone wall in the water near the wharf, and thus make a continuance of the riot more certain, he went to the end of his own wharf, and called to Captain McAllister if he would send the stern line ashore, the steamer would be able to pull out. That is, it would make the steamer turn around from the wharf so as to head to the river—the dock here being extremely narrow and the work of steering a steamer exceeding difficult. In reply, Capt. McAllister shook his sword and said—"He was responsible for all he said and did." In vain Mr. Hyde tried, again and again, to make the captain accept his friendly offers. He was either not understood or his motives were suspected.

Judge Brewer, at the same time, was driving some away and entreating others not to interfere. Seeing a young man on shore with a pistol, preparing to discharge it in the direction of the boat, the Judge endeavored to prevent him, but was unable. Again seeing the young man preparing to fire, he seized him and called for help. Mr. John W. Brady came and took the young man. Meantime the firing from the boat continued, and glasses, bottles, and stones were hurled at the crowd on the wharf. Mr. Brady was shot whilst taking an assailant of his assailants from the fray. Judge Brewer was assisted alone by constable John Lamb, and whilst thus endeavoring to preserve the peace heard some person on the boat exclaim, with an oath, "Shoot that officer, I mistrust him." Three rifles were instantly levelled at the Judge. He jumped behind a wood-pile, whilst a friendly hand on the boat knocked up two of the rifles ; but the third, the Judge thought, was discharged at him. In all besides the bricks and other missiles exchanged between the combatants there were, it was estimated, twenty rifle shots from the boat and two pistol shots and two guns fired from the shore, but these not until after the volley from the rifles on the steamer.*

The visitors were better prepared for the attack than the citizens and their aim was good, for five citizens fell wounded, fortunately none of them fatally :

T. C. Loockerman, shot in the leg, slightly wounded ;

Basil McNew, shot in the side, badly wounded ;

John W. Brady, shot through both legs, seriously hurt ;

Watkins Hall, two toes shot off ;

Edward Barroll, wounded very dangerously in the thigh.

When Hall and Loockerman, who were actively engaged in throwing stones at the boat fell, "the people on board the boat hurrahed enough for an election day."†

Rifles are far more effective weapons than pistols and bricks and none of the excursionists, it appears, were hurt.

The report of the riot had spread through Annapolis, and, with powder contributed by the merchant and cannon seized from the State, citizens hurried to the wharf to avenge the assault on their fellow-townsmen, the fray the meanwhile being unabated, and to add to the calamities of the day, the steamer became wedged in between the two sides of the narrow wharf, and to escape the volleys of stones and bullets from the wharf most of the passengers ran to the opposite side. The steamer careened and for a moment was in danger of capsizing.

On the opposite side of the wharf was a vacant mill. The "Jewess" as she came to that side of the dock to turn was within a few yards of this untenanted house. In it a young citizen‡ had now secreted himself and was about to pour a deadly fire from his gun into the passengers, when happily his prudent father came in and drove him away, and saved one or more of the excursionists from almost certain death.

The State's cannon was then brought into position by the now thoroughly aroused Annapolitans. Col. Geo. P. Kane immediately made his way to it, and remonstrated against firing it. Finding his appeals of no avail, he threw one arm over the breech of the piece,

* Testimony of Daniel T. Hyde, in the Balto. American of July 13, 1847.

† Testimony of Daniel T. Hyde.

‡ Daniel Hollidayoke :

and placed the other hand over the muzzle and declared that the gun should not be fired without blowing him to pieces. Col. Kane was warned by those standing around that the cannon was double shotted and loaded, (which, however, was not the case.) The parties in charge of the gun then attempted to pull him away by force, and the struggle continued until some one whispered in his ear that the gun had been spiked.

This was the voice of Judge Brewer who had repaired to the cannon and spiked it with his tooth-pick. Two attempts were afterwards made to load it, but Judge Brewer succeeded in stopping both efforts.

In the attempt to prevent the cannon from being loaded Richard Cowman used his fist with such good effect on William Shuman, a shoemaker, who was endeavoring to charge the gun, as to make him bite the dust.

Mr. Hyde, in his testimony, considered the loading of the cannon ''a mere farce, and he stood by and laughed at it. It was a complete scene of confusion, some wanting to do one thing and others another and, in the meanwhile, the boat was fast getting out of their reach, even if they had been loaded.''

Judge Brewer did not escape calumny that day as one witness declared he saw the Judge looking at two negroes throwing stones at the boat and did not attempt to stop them. This the Judge contradicted in his own testimony and Mr. Hyde quaintly corroborated it with saying that the Judge ''did all that any man could do, and more than he thought a man could have done to suppress the riot and restore peace. He saw him at different parts of the wharf, driving some away and entreating others not to interfere. He had no one besides the witness to help him but a constable, who received a severe blow in the face by a brick during the early part of the affray.

''The story of the Judge standing by and seeing two negroes throwing at the boat without an effort to prevent them, the witness regarded as entirely untrue. There were no negroes in Annapolis who would dare to break the law in any way if they thought Judge Brewer was looking at them. If the duties performed that day by Judge Brewer pertained to his office as Judge, the witness thought he would not like to have it for twice its salary. He thought he was that day, whilst endeavoring to preserve the peace, in imminent danger of his life.''

The judicial investigation fastened the guilt on no one, and no punishment was meted out to the rioters.

CHAPTER LV.
CHRONICLES OF ANNAPOLIS FROM 1845 TO 1847.

[1845.] On Saturday, November 30th. Rev. Thos. Robinson, a local minister of the Methodist Episcopal Church, residing near the head of Severn River, whilst duck-shooting was thrown into the water by the upsetting of his boat. He swam ashore, and, in intense cold, dragged himself to a house close by, where he died from exhaustion.

[1846.] On Thursday, February 19th, about 7 p. m., flames were discovered issuing from the ventilator of the cellar of the State House, under the House of Delegates. On getting the cellar-door open the smoke, from immense quantities of coal and charcoal in the apartment, was so dense and stifling, there was great danger of suffocating any who entered. Notwithstanding, some brave men ventured in, and the fire, which had made considerable progress, was discovered and reached with great difficulty and extinguished.

At the City Election in April, 1846, the following was the vote:

For Mayor.

Richard Swann, Whig, 150 ; D. S. Caldwell, Dem., 120.

For Recorder.

William Tell Claude. w., 154 ; Jonathan Pinkney, d., 117.

For Aldermen.

Dr. Abram Claude, w., 158 ; Dr. Wm. Brewer, Sr., w., 146 ; Edward A. Davis, w., 144; Captain John Philips, w., 141 ; James B. Steele, w., 137 ; Daniel Caulk, d., 131 ; Wm. Bryan, d., 126 ; John M. Davis, d., 122 ; James H. Iglehart. d., 120 : James Sands, d., 120.

Richard H. Hanlon, a native of Annapolis, a volunteer against Mexico, died September 6th, at Camargo, Mexico.

The Democratic Star ceased publication in October 21st, 1846, "after a life," said the proprietors, Messrs. Daily and Taylor, "of four years hardship and incessant toil."

Theoderic Bland, Chancellor, of Maryland, died in Annapolis November 16. He was born in Dinwiddie county, Virginia, December 6, 1776.

On Wednesday, December 14, a gale blew at Annapolis. Nine vessels were driven ashore between Chink and Tolley's Points. Between Hackett's and Greenbury's Points a sloop was sunk. A few days after the gale five bodies, two of whites and three of blacks, were found at Tolley's Point.

December 21, John Johnson, of Annapolis, was appointed Chancellor of Maryland by Gov. Pratt.

[1847.] There was no opposition this year to the Whigs in the city election. The vote was:

For Mayor :

Richard Swann, 126 ;

For Recorder :

William Tell Claude, 139.

For Aldermen :

Elihu S. Riley, 141 ; John Philips, 132 ; Ed. Hopkins, 131 ; James Steele, 127 ; P. C. Clayton, 107. Mr. William Davis, independent, for alderman, received 74 votes.

One of the ancient landmarks of Annapolis a colonial dwelling, occupied by Miss Hester Chase and situated on King George st., was destroyed by fire, April 12.

May 8th, George Johnston, Esq., proprietor of the *Democratic Herald*, of Annapolis. aged 40 years, died of a pulmonary complaint. On account of his death the publication of the *Herald* ceased.

18

Major Luther Giddings, a graduate of St. John's, class of 1841, was presented with a $500 sword on April 2, by the rank and file of his regiment, the 1st Ohio, as an appreciation of his conduct in acting colonel of the regiment.

CHAPTER LVI.
A RETROSPECT OF TWO CENTURIES.

[1849.] Two hundred years after its settlement found Annapolis with thirty-five hundred inhabitants, the seat of a Naval University, the home of a College of large usefulness, and still ''the ancient capital'' of the State. The day of its commercial glory had departed, but the remnant of its traditional intelligence remained. Its bar contained the names of Tuck, Randall, and Alexander, worthy survivors of men who had made its name illustrious, and though the ball and banquet of former generations had passed away, the opening social glories of the Naval Academy forshadowed the harvest of pleasures that have proved unbounded sources of enjoyment to the young who participate in, and the elders who periodically witness, these brilliant assemblages in the Armory and Gymnasium.

The Puritan who settled the capital, might chance invoke the wrath of heaven on the *Providence* he had established where the curling smoke of the wigwam had once ascended.

The card-table, the ball-room, the pot-house, the lottery shop, and the gambling-hell were indices of the frivolities and evils that afflicted the capital, although the theatre and the race-course had ceased to find remuneration out of the depleted coffers of a city whose chief sources of revenue were the scant trade of the sparsely settled country that surrounded it, and the modest compensation awarded to the servants of the State and Nation.

The canoe of the Indian had disappeared before the pinnace of the Puritan; the pinnace had given place to the schooner; the schooner, in its turn, had been pushed aside by the steamer; the trail of the Indian had been lost in the roadway of the coach, and the locomotive had made the lumbering stage the attenuated monument of an out-ridden generation.

But the glory of her fair ones yet remained, and the ancient city still maintained its wide renown for the beauty and grace of its women.

In Church, the Puritan had long since disappeared. In his place the Churchman, the Methodist, and the Presbyterian boldly proclaimed the truth, whilst the handful of Catholics feebly held their own in the little chapel that Carroll of Carrolton's beneficence had built.

Politics, that a hundred years before displayed itself alone in manly opposition to encroachments of the provincial governors, had now become a heroic game, and, through various stages, had been formulated into Whiggery and Democracy, and stood face to face against each other on the momentous issues of tariff and slavery.

The Chesapeake and its freely given wealth of oysters lay almost unruffled by the tongs of the industrious oysterman, and the quiet of the streets of "the Ancient City," and the paucity of its business and commerce were sadly emblematic of a place whose chief adornment was the general virtue of its inhabitants, untarnished by the chicanery of trade and unblessed by the fruits of industry.

CHAPTER LVII.
A GALAXY OF ILLUSTRIOUS ANNAPOLITANS.

CHARLES CARROLL, OF CARROLTON,

Was born at Annapolis, Maryland, September 20th, 1737. In 1745, he was taken to the College of English Jesuits at St. Omer, France, where he remained six years, and then was sent to the Jesuit College, at Rheims. After one years' study of civil law at Bourges, he went to Paris, studied two more years, and began the law in the Temple. At 27 years of age, he returned to America, and, at the breaking out of the Revolutionary War, was considered the richest man in America, being worth $2,000,000. Although, by the illiberal laws of that period, he was robbed of the privilege of the elective franchise, because he was a Catholic, he ardently espoused the American cause, and began his opposition to the arbitrary measures of the British Government, by publishing in the Maryland *Gazette*, a series of articles under the signature of "THE FIRST CITIZEN," against the right of the Governor of Maryland, to regulate fees by proclamation.

In 1775, he was made a member of the first committee of observation established at Annapolis, and during the same year he was elected a delegate to the Provincial Convention. In February, 1776, he was sent to Canada, by Congress, to induce the people of that province to unite with the States. He returned to Philadelphia, in June, and found the Declaration of Independence under discussion. The delegates from Maryland were hampered by instructions "to disavow in the most solemn manner all design in the colonies of Independence." He repaired to Annapolis immediately, and, with the assistance of Judge Samuel Chase, on the 28th of June, succeeded in having these instructions withdrawn and the delegates left free to join in the Declaration of Independence.

On August 2nd, the Declaration was formally signed. As Mr. Carroll wrote his name, a member observed, "Here go a few millions," and added, "however, there are several Charles Carrolls, the British will not know which one it is." Carroll immediately added, "of Carrolton," and was ever afterward known by that cognomen. He was placed by Congress in the Board of War. In 1776, he helped to draft the Constitution for Maryland, and was the same year a member of the State Senate. In 1777, he was again a delegate to Congress. In 1781, and 1786, he was a Senator of Maryland, and in 1788, was chosen a United States Senator, to which office he was again elected in 1797. In 1799, he was one of the Commissioners to adjust the boundary line between Maryland and Virginia. On July 4th, 1828, then, in his 90th year, Mr. Carroll, in the presence of an immense concourse of people, and attended by imposing civic ceremonies, laid the corner-stone of that important Maryland enterprise—the Baltimore and Ohio Railroad. Towards the last of his life, Mr. Carroll removed to Baltimore—I have it by tradition—because the city fathers here offended him by making the taxes too high. November 14th, 1832, Mr. Carroll died, the last of the signers of the Declaration of Independence.

WILLIAM PINKNEY

Was born at Annapolis, Maryland, March 17th, 1764. His family was a branch of the South Carolina Pinkneys, who early settled at Annapolis. He studied medicine, but left that for the law, and was admitted to the bar in 1786. In 1788, he was a delegate to the Convention which ratified the constitution of the United States, and he subsequently held various State offices, as member of the House of Delegates, Senate, and the Council. In 1796, he was sent to London, as Commissioner, under the Jay treaty, remaining abroad until 1804. In 1805, he became Attorney-General of Maryland. In 1806, he was sent as Minister extraordinary to England to treat, in conjunction with Monroe, with the British Government, and was resident Minister from 1807 to 1811, when he was appointed Attorney-General of the United States, which office he held two years. He commanded a volunteer corps in the war of 1812, and was severely wounded in the battle of Bladensburg. In 1815, he was elected a member of Congress, and, in 1816, was appointed Minister to Russia, and, Special Minister to Naples. In 1818, he returned home, and, in 1819, was elected a United States Senator. He died February 22nd, 1822.

REVERDY JOHNSON

Was born at Annapolis, Maryland, May 21st, 1796. He was educated at St. John's College, and, at the age of 17, began the study of law in Prince George's county, in the office of his father, who was the Chief Justice of the Judicial District of which that county formed a part. In 1815, he was admitted to the bar, and by way of encouragement to all who do not achieve success at once, be it written, he made a lamentable failure in his first speech in Court. In 1817, he removed to Baltimore, and devoted much of his time to arguing cases before the Supreme Court of the United States, where he won renown as a profound student of the legal profession, not only in America, but his fame reaching Europe, he was called to argue before the French tribunals. In conjunction with Mr. Thomas Harris, he reported the decisions of the Maryland Court of Appeals, known as "Harris and Johnson's Reports," (7 vols. 1820-27.) In 1821, he was elected a State Senator, and re-elected in 1825. In 1845, he was chosen United States Senator, which office he resigned in 1849, on being appointed by President Taylor Attorney-General of the United States. In 1861, he was a member of the Peace Convention in Washington, which tried to prevent the Civil War. In 1862, he was again elected to the United

States Senate, and was a member from 1863 to 1868.   In June of the latter year, he was appointed Minister to England, where he negotiated a treaty for the settlement of the Alabama claims. This treaty was rejected by the Senate.   He was recalled in 1869.

During the entire Civil War, when many illegal acts were committed under the plea of "military necessity," Reverdy Johnson, whilst an ardent supporter of the Union, eloquently raised his voice against every usurpation by the military power.

On the evening of February 10th, 1876, when in his 80th year, with a mind yet undimmed by mental incapacity, and a body that gave promise of many years of usefulness, he met with a fatal accident at Annapolis.   He was at a social gathering at the Executive Mansion, John Lee Carroll being then Governor and host. Mr. Johnson started to go out the main doorway. He was offered assistance but refused it. Passing down the granite steps of the front porch, he turned to the left of the entrance and fell into a paved area, five feet below, where he was found shortly afterward in an unconscious state.   He expired soon after being discovered.   He died almost within a stone's throw of the house in which he was born, and well nigh under the shadow of his *alma mater*.

JOHN D. GODMAN

Was born at Annapolis, December 20th, 1794. He was apprenticed to a printer in Baltimore, but, at the age of twenty. enlisted in the Navy and was present at the defence of Fort McHenry.   After the war he studied medicine, and practiced until 1821, when he became professor in the Medical College of Ohio at Cincinnati, and commenced there the "Western Quarterly Reporter." In 1822, he removed to Philadelphia, and devoted himself to the science of Anatomy, of which he became, in 1826, professor in Rutger's Medical School, New York. He prepared the Zoological articles for the "Encyclopedia Americana" up to the end of the letter C.   His principal work was "American Natural History." He died at Germantown, Pa., April 17, 1830.

STEWART HOLLAND.

By one act this man made his name immortal. He was born at Annapolis. September 24th, 1854, found him a member of the engineering department of the Steamer Arctic, that, with hundreds of passengers, was sinking in mid ocean, from the effects of a collision. "About two hours after the Arctic was struck, the firing of the gun," said the third mate of the Arctic, "attracted my attention, and I recollect when I saw Stewart, it struck me as remarkably strange that he alone, of all belonging to the engineering body, should be here.   He must have had a good chance to go in the chief engineer's boat and be saved ; but he did not, it seems, make the slightest exertion to save himself whilst there was duty to be done on shipboard. I recollect that about an hour before the ship sunk, I was hurriedly searching for spikes to make a raft with. I had just passed through the saloon. On the sofa were men who had fainted, and there were many of them too ; the ladies were in little groups, clasped together, strangely quiet, and resigned. As I came out again, the scene that presented itself was one that I hope never to see again. Here and there were strong, stout men on their knees in the attitude of prayer, and others, who when spoken to, were immovable and stupefied. In the midst of this scene, Stewart came running up to me, crying "Donan, my powder is out: I want more. Give me the key." "Never mind the key," I replied. "take an axe, and break open the the door." He snatched one close beside me, and down into the ship's hold he dived, and I went over the ship's side to my raft. I recollect distinctly his appearance as once more he hailed me from the deck, the right side of his face was black with powder, and when he spoke, his face seemed to me to be lighted up with a quaint smile." So the gallant youth continued to fire "the minute gun" that booming over the sea might catch the ear of some passing vessel and bring relief to the perishing. As the ship, which carried three hundred people with it to watery graves, went down Stewart Holland was seen "in the very act of firing as the vessel disappeared below the waters."

A lot was donated in Washington, where he lived at the time of the disaster, and money subscribed to build him a monument, but the funds were embezzled by the trustee.

CHARLES WILSON PEALE.

The eminent American painter, was born in Annapolis,* April 16th, 1741. Peale had a checkered career. He was first a saddler and harness-maker, then watch and clock tinker, and, in their order, silversmith, painter, modeller, taxidermist, dentist, and lecturer. In 1770, he visited England, and, for several years, was a pupil of West. Returning home, he settled first in Annapolis and then in Philadelphia, and acquired celebrity as a portrait painter. Among his works were several portraits of Washington, and a series forming the nucleus of a national portrait gallery. He commanded a company of volunteers in the battles of Trenton and Germantown, and also served in the Pennsylvania Legislature. About 1785, he commenced a collection of natural curiosities in Philadelphia, founding "Peale's Museum," in which he lectured on natural history. He aided in founding the Pennsylvania Academy of Fine Arts.

LIEUTENANT JAMES BOOTH LOCKWOOD, U. S. A.,

Was born at Annapolis, Maryland, October 9th, 1852, and died at Cape Sabine, Smith's Sound, April 9th, 1884. To Lieutenant Lockwood belongs the distinction of having attained, during the Greeley Expedition, the point nearest to either pole, ever reached by any human being. It was on Lockwood's Island in north latitude, 80° 24'; longitude 44° 5'.

DANIEL DULANY.

A history of Annapolis would be incomplete without a biographical sketch of Daniel Dulany, who, under the *nom de plume* of Antion, carried on the memorable newspaper controversy in 1772, with Carroll, of Carrollton, the "First Citizen" of that literary prologue of the American Revolution.

Daniel Dulany, son of Daniel Dulany, was born at Annapolis, July 19, 1721, and was educated at Eton and at Clare Hall, Cambridge, England.

* Ridgely's Annals of Annapolis.

He entered the Temple, and, returning to the colonies, was admitted to the bar in 1747. Mr. McMahon, of this brilliant man, says : "For many years before the downfall of the proprietary Government, he stood confessedly without a rival in this colony, as a lawyer, a scholar, and an orator, and, we may safely regard the assertion that in the high and varied accomplishments which constitute these, he has had amongst the sons of Maryland but one equal and no superior. We admit that tradition is a magnifier, and that men even through its medium and the obscurity of half a century, like objects in a misty morning, loom largely in the distance, yet with regard to Mr. Dulany, there is no room for illusion. ' *You may tell Hercules by foot*,' says the proverb ; and this truth is as just when applied to the proportions of the name, as to those of the body. The legal arguments and opinions of Mr. Dulany that yet remain to us, bear the impress of abilities too commanding, and of learning too profound to admit of question. Had we but these fragments, like the remains of splendor which linger around some of the ruins of antiquity, they would be enough for admiration. Yet they fall very short of furnishing just conceptions of the character and accomplishments of his mind. We have higher attestations of these in the testimony of cotemporaries. For many years before the Revolution, he was regarded as an oracle of the law. It was the constant practice of the courts of the province to submit to his opinion every question of difficulty which came before them, and so infallible were his opinions considered, that he who hoped to reverse them was regarded 'as hoping against hope.' Nor was his professional reputation limited to the colony. I have been credibly informed that he was occasionally consulted from England upon questions of magnitude, and that, in the southern counties of Virginia, adjacent to Maryland, it was not unfrequent to withdraw questions from their courts and even from the Chancellor of England, to submit them to his award. Thus unrivalled in professional learning, according to the representations of his cotemporaries, he added to it all the power of the orator, the accomplishments of the scholar, the graces of the person, the suavity of the gentleman. Mr. Pinkney himself, the wonder of his age, who saw but the setting splendor of Mr. Dulany's talents, is reputed to have said of him, that even amongst such men as Fox, Pitt, and Sheridan, he had not found his superior.

"Whatever were the errors of his course during the Revolution, I have never heard them ascribed, either to opposition to the rights of America, or to a servile submission to the views of the ministry : and I have been credibly informed, that he adhered, throughout life, to the principles advanced by him in opposition to the Stamp Act. The conjecture may be hazarded that had he not been thrown into collision with the leaders of the Revolution in this State, by the proclamation controversy, * and thus involved in discussion with them, which excited high resentment on both sides, and kept him at a distance from them until the Revolution began, he would, most probably, have been found by their side, in support of the measures which led to it."

Mr. Dulany was Secretary of the Province when he conducted the famous controversy with Charles Carroll, of Carrollton. He was also a member of the Upper House under the proprietary Government †.

* Over Gov. Eden's proclamation regulating fees in the Colony.
† Chronicles of Baltimore, Scharf, p. 284.

The political differences of the Revolution survived its conclusion. Mr. Dulany held no public office after it, and the brilliancy of his talents, displayed alone in the forum of provincial courts, did not shed its effulgence in national councils, and his fame, reflected from the humble pedestal of State history, has not depicted to the nation the phenomenal proportions of his intellect. Such was the iron-heel of public opinion upon the political fortunes, of a man ''whose opinions were thought to have moulded those of William Pitt, by whom they were publicly noticed with great honor.'' These opinions, (which were published October 14, 1765, and which looked to ''a legal orderly, and prudent resentment'' to be expressed aginst the Stamp Act ''in a zealous and vigorous industry,'') widely prevailed in America. ‡ This course was urged until that time might come ''when redress may be obtained,'' **.

Mr. Dulany died in Baltimore, March 19, 1797, aged 75 years and 8 months, and was buried in St. Paul Cemetery, corner of Lombard and Fremont Streets, Baltimore ††.

‡ Bancroft's History of the U. S. vol. 5, p. 329.
** Dulany's Pamph'et, Scharf.
†† Scharf vol. 1, p. 519.

CHAPTER LVIII.

CHRONICLES OF ANNAPOLIS FROM 1860 TO 1861.

[1860.] On the 12th of September the Governor's Guards paraded for the first time, and were inspected by Adjutant-General Nicholas Brewer, of John. The company appeared to be well drilled. This company was disbanded during the Civil War, but, after it, was recuscitated. Its present commissioned officers. (1887,) are Louis Green, Captain ; John H. Wells, First-Lieutenant : James C. Porter, Second Lieutenant.

In September, 1861, the oyster catchers of Annapolis, then represented to be some fifty or sixty in number, formed themselves into an association to further the execution of the laws against oyster pirates. The sheriff of the county, Thomas Ireland, requested them to notify him of any infraction of law, and promised ''to use all his power to arrest and punish the pirates.''

By the census of 1860, the population of Annapolis was 4,658. Of these 1,643 were white males, and 1,484 white females ; 551 free colored males ; 505 free colored females ; 220 male slaves ; and 255 female slaves.

By the census of 1850, Annapolis contained, 3,011 inhabitants. Increase to 1860, 1,647. Of the inhabitants in 1850, 913 were white males ; 913 white females ; 236 free colored males; 297 free colored females ; 249 male slaves ; 403 female slaves. The large increase in the population from 1850 to 1860 is due to the enumeration of the 300 inhabitants of the Naval Academy in the census of Annapolis.

On the 5th of October, 1860, John Brice died. He was the grandson of Thomas Jennings, Attorney-General of the then Province of Maryland. The deceased was a defender of Baltimore in 1814.

On the 14th of October, John Stalker, aged 80 years, one of the defenders of Baltimore, died at Annapolis.

The Annapolis *Gazette* of Thursday, December 6, 1860, said :

"WHO WILL BELIEVE IT?"—"Nobody. And yet it is a fixed fact that we are to have a telegraph from Annapolis to the Junction. We actually saw the first coil of wire laid on last Saturday. We looked on in a sort of dreaming, wondering, doubting uncertainty ; but had finally, to yield to the patent, tangible reality. We saw the poles, and the wire, and we saw the workmen putting them in their proper places, therefore, we were compelled to believe. The work is under the management o.' Mr. Joshua Brown, and will be pushed to completion wieh the utmost despatch."

Lieut. Horace Gambrill, of Annapolis, was on the Revenue Cutter "Aiken" that was surrendered by her captain to the South Carolina authorities in December, 1860.

On Christmas Eve a patrol guarded the South River section by reason of the groundless rumor of an intended insurrection of slaves.

[1861.] The *Gazette* of February 28, announced the completion of the Annapolis, Baltimore, and Washington telegraph line.

CHAPTER LIX.

OPENING OF THE CIVIL WAR--ANNAPOIS SEIZED BY THE FEDERAL GOVERNMENT.

[1860.] The exciting contest of 1860 had just closed in the election of Lincoln. The political movements in the extreme Southern States vibrated in Maryland—a commonwealth identified with these States by its institutions, its traditions, and its interests.

The tone of the people of Anne Arundel and Annapolis, in the momentous political contest that preceded the civil war, is found in the vote in the Presidential election.

After an exciting campaign, Anne Arundel gave Bell for President, 24 majority over Breckinridge. The vote was Bell, 1041 ; Breckinridge, 1017 ; Douglas, 98 ; Lincoln, 3. Lincoln received his three votes : in Annapolis, one ; First District, one ; Second District, one. In Annapolis the vote was Bell, 261 ; Breckinridge, 227 ; Douglas, 36 ; Lincoln, 1. Mr. William Taylor, the present head carpenter of the Naval Academy, has been generally credited with the courage that made him give the lone vote for Lincoln at a time when public sentiment in Annapolis did not take kindly to Republicanism.

The State authorities as well as the people generally felt a crisis was at hand.

In his proclamation for a day of Thanksgiving on the 29th of November, 1860, Gov. Hicks among other things asked the people to pray "that dissension and strife may depart from among us; that concord and love of country may prevail; that those in authority may have his guidance; so disposing the hearts of the people and ordering the State, that the happiness and peace, the power and abundance, with all the unnumbered blessings, which this Union, which the God of our fathers gave to them, and to us, may suffer no diminution, through our follies, or our crimes; but, safe-guarded through His mercy and multiplied by His favor. descend to our children's children."

The martial spirit in the people as this time shows an undefined desire to prepare for the arbitrament of the sword.

On November 22, there was a great military display in Annapolis. The following companies took part:

The Governor's Guards, Major Wm. H. Thompson, commanding; St. John's College Cadets, Adjutant Hopkins. commanding; Union Guard, Cavalry, Capt. Iglehart, of West River, commanding; West River Guard, Cavalry, Capt. Stewart, commanding; the Southern Guard, Cavalry, Capt. Lyles, commanding; the Severn Guard, Capt. Claytor, commanding; the Vanville Rangers, Capt. Snowden, commanding. The Governor's Guards were presented by Miss Eliza Murdock, on behalf of the ladies of Annapolis, with a beautiful flag. Major Thompson responded. Lieut. John R. Magruder, of the Governor's Guards, acknowledged the compliment paid the Guards. He said the gift was appropriate, "The Star Spangled Banner now, as I trust it and ever will be, the proud symbol to the world of the united power of the people of more than thirty sovereign States. in their union one great and mighty nation." At the close of the proceedings Col. Spencer, Chief Marshal proposed "three cheers for the Union, which were given with a hearty good will and enthusiasm seldom excelled." The line, 500 strong, marched through the city and into the Naval Academy where the battalion of cadets was drawn up in full uniform and offered and received the military salute. This unexpected compliment gave eclat to the occasion.

Gov. Hicks was petitioned at this period by Thos. G. Pratt, Sprigg Harwood, J. S. Franklin, N. H. Green. Llwellyn Boyle, and J. Pinkney to convene the Legislature "to consider of the present momentous crisis,"—the dissensions in the Union. Gov. Hicks declined.

In December, 1860, South Carolina and other States had given full intention of dissolving their relations with the Federal Government. and Marylanders were debating what was the proper course for them to pursue. The editor of the Annapolis *Gazette*. Mr. Thomas J. Wilson, published the following as his sentiments:

"Our own opinion is that Maryland should declare that her soil shall not be the battle ground for the fanatics who are so eager to dye their hands in each other's blood. To declare that, whilst her borders are free of transit to all who are on missions of peace, they shall never be crossed by Northern men or Southern men in arms.

"To maintain such a position it is necessary that the Old Maryland Line be re-organized and equipped. Her sons are numerous enough and courageous enough to defend the State lines. But they must learn the soldier's life and the soldier's skill, or their courage will be unavailing. The volunteer soldiery. though admirably drilled, and well equipped, are not numerous enough for the services we have indicated. Arms and ammunition must be provided, and men of undaunted courage must be put in command of the army that can be speedily raised." * * * * We no longer urge hope for the Union. We now counsel men to look to the defence of the State, and to provide for her welfare when strife shall cease."

Events sped along at too rapid a rate for the editor to hold long to his separate sovereignty theory, and, in the winter of 1860-61, the *Gazette* is found violently denouncing the secessionists who were attempting to draw the State, as it alleged, into secession. It was especially denunciatory of them for calling, outside of Gov. Hicks, a sovereign convention "to declare the position of the State of Maryland in the present crisis." This extraordinary project accomplished no definite results. The *Gazette* rapidly drifted from its passive policy, and on February 21, 1861, is found calling the Southerners "Hotspurs," and asking this question: "Has it ever occurred to you, reader, that our present troubles might never have come but for the overweening pride and audacity of the Southern politicians?" The *Gazette* spoke very contemptuously of Mr. Lincoln's night flight through Baltimore, and, in a subsequent editorial, declared that Mr. Lincoln intimated to Gov. Hicks that he could have any office he wished.* March 28, the *Gazette* says: "Let Maryland be kept in the power of true Union men. Let secession, and all other hideous isms be kept in the dust." April 4, the *Gazette* said: "He who is not for the Union is against it. There is no half way place—no middle ground."

The *Gazette* grew more and more furious with sympathizers with the South, saying on April 18: "Men in high office now-a-days have a queer way of shutting their eyes to the obligation of their official oaths. We know of several high in office in our city, who have solemnly sworn to support the Constitution and Laws of Maryland and of the United States, who, nevertheless, are openly preaching rebellion against the State and Federal Government, and urging men to join them in their diabolical crusade. Those men too, go to church, and pray God to deliver us from 'all sedition, piracy, conspiracy, and rebellion,' and with holy prayers on their impious lips, button-hole the first man they meet and pour into his ear inducements for sedition."

April 25. The 19th of April had been passed. The *Gazette* says: "It seems to be the impression that the Legislature will pass an ordinance of secession. The feeling hereabouts is almost unanimous on the subject. * * * * The excitement here is terrible. No man seems to know what should be done to avert the evil that has come upon us; and all admit that we are utterly powerless to offer any resistance." It was a few days previous to this that Gov. Hicks said in Monument Square, Baltimore, that "I will suffer my right arm to be torn from my body before I will raise it to strike a sister State." May 9, 1861, the editor indignantly denied he had pandered in his issue of April 25, to the secession element, and declared himself unreservedly in favor of the Union.

December 6, 1860, Gov. Hicks wrote to John Contee:

"In all my feelings and interests as a Southerner, I am ready to stand by the interests and honor of the South."

Soon after, December 20, the Governor approved of, by proclamation, the appointment by President Buchanan of January 4, 1861,

---

* Mr. Wilson, the editor, and Gov. Hicks were very intimate and Mr. Wilson became afterwards the Governor's Secretary of State.

as a day of Humiliation, Fasting, and Prayer for a restoration of friendship among the States of the Union, adding a prayer be directed to Almighty God that "we may all again realize 'how pleasant it is for brethren to dwell together in unity.'"

The Governor was at this moment besieged with importunities to convene the Legislature. He had been elected as a candidate of the American party, and the Legislature was democratic. He resisted these incessant petitions with a rare courage until the tragic events of the 19th of April in Baltimore.

In the meantime two parties were rapidly forming in the State— one for immediate secession, the other urging the maintenance of the Union and indorsing the course of Gov. Hicks. The *Gazette* was a valiant champion of Gov. Hicks' sentiments.

January 4, 1861, the day appointed by President Buchanan and endorsed by Gov. Hicks, was observed in Annapolis by religious services at St. Anne's, Salem Methodist Episcopal, St. Mary's Catholic, and the Presbyterian Churches. Rev. Mr. Davenport preached at St. Anne's. He argued that the national troubles were brought upon us mainly by the corruptions of politicians, and by a sort of *sans culottism* that had mastered the minds of the people, causing them to look to a "higher law," and to, consequently, be wanting in proper respect to our Rulers. He urged that this was contrary to the teachings of the Bible, and exhorted his hearers to yield their political passions and prejudices by submitting to the will of those who rule us by our own elections, and whose authority over us had the divine sanction taught in the Bible." Mr. Davenport was of northern birth, and continued to hold his strong Union sentiments, as long as he stayed in Annapolis, which was sometime after hostilities commenced; but his opinions, cropping out in church service, begot him a host of opponents. Rev. Mr. Clemm preached at Salem Church.

January 17, a meeting was held in Annapolis, of which Dr. Dennis Claude was appointed President, Col. John Walton and Dr. Edward Jacob, Vice-Presidents. Hon. Alex. Randall offered a series of resolutions on the State of the Union which were adopted. The resolutions denied the authority of a State to secede, declared the duty of the General Government to protect itself if any State should attempt to withdraw from the Union, and that, whilst they regret the election of Abraham Lincoln, they could see nothing in it that should impair the integrity of the Union.

On Tuesday, February 5, a Palmetto Flag was hoisted near St. Anne's Church. It was soon hauled down and torn in pieces.

On January 31, a meeting of the workingmen of Annapolis was held. Mr. L. W. Seabrook was made president ; Col. John Walton, Vice-President, and Norman Leslie, Secretary ; John E. Stalker, James E. Hopkins, John R. Magruder, Benj. Hopkins, and Andrew E. Chaney were made a committee to draft resolutions. The resolutions which were adopted, declared unalterable attachment to the Union ; that secession was "no remedy for the grievous ills under which the slaveholding State have been so long suffering ; that the citizens assembled had full confidence in the patriotism and integrity of Gov. Hicks." The resolutions approved of the Crittenden Compromise.

Monday, April 1st, the municipal election was held. So soon in the struggle had party names been assimilated to political opinions. Only one ticket was voted for—the "Union ticket." By this John R. Magruder was elected Mayor by a vote of 180, and Thomas J. Wilson recorder by 184 votes.

April 11th is the first date in which a headline appeared in the *Gazette* with war in it. It was "The War Excitement."

The Naval Academy began to pulsate to the war news. Under orders from Washington the authorities removed the cannon and ammunition from the battery to the practice ship Constellation. The ship took in a supply of oil and candles. The watchmen were armed with revolvers. During this period Annapolis experienced a new sensation in obtaining the stirring news of the times by telegraph.

Immediately after the 19th of April, Gen. Butler began to land the troops en route for Washington, in Annapolis; thousands of troops passed through the city, and the town assumed the appearence of a military outpost, and to experience the results of this distinction in a scarcity of provisions. There was now not three days supply on hand.

By the 1st of May, the excitement in Annapolis had subsided, and troops, munitions of war, and provisions, arrived and departed daily from the Naval Academy which had been made a depot, on their way, *via* the Annapolis and Elkridge Railroad, to Washington. Their passage through the city no longer stirred up any excitement. The soldiers were well-behaved, and treated the citizens with every courtesy.

This was not accomplished without political throes that threatened to make Maryland the theatre of the war itself.

Gov. Hicks, had, in view of the extraordinay circumstances in and out of the State, on the 22d of April, called the Legislature to meet at Annapolis on the 26th of April in special session, "to deliberate and consider of the condition of the State, and take such measures as in their wisdom, they may deem fit to maintain, peace, order, and security within our limits." Annapolis being, subsequent to the date of the proclamation occupied by Federal troops, on the 24th Gov. Hicks changed the place of meeting to Frederick city, Frederick county.

Lincoln had called for Maryland's quota of troops to defend the capital from a real or supposed advance of the Southern forces upon Washington. There began immediately a diplomatic correspence between Gov. Hicks and the Federal authorities as to the use of Maryland's levy. Whilst this was proceeding, the people of Maryland, whose sympathies were deeply aroused for the South, began to grow restive and threatening under the intention of the Federal government to force its troops through Maryland to Washington. The 19th of April came with its startling episode in the streets of Baltimore. The correspondence changed from diplomatic to dramatic. These letters and telegrams bring the actors on the stage and shift the scenes with living vividness. The first letter on the subject was this :

WAR DEPARTMENT,
April 17th, 1861. }

His EXCELLENCY,

    THOS. H. HICKS,

        Governor of Maryland.

DEAR SIR :—The President has referred me to your letter of this day, and, in reply, I have the honor to say that the troops to be raised in Maryland will be needed for the defense of this Capital, and of the public property in that State and neighborhood. There is no intention of removing them beyond those points.

Very respectfully,

SIMON CAMERON,

Secretary of War.

This note was followed by the annexed correspondence :

BALTIMORE, April 17th, 1861.

To the President of the United States :

SIR :—From the conversation I had yesterday, in Washington, with the Secretary of War, and with Lieutenant-General Scott, I understood that the four regiments of militia to be called for from Maryland were to be posted and retained within the limits of this State, for the defense of the United States Government, the maintenance of the Federal authority, and the protection of the Federal Capital. I also understood it was the intention of the United States Government not to require their services outside of Maryland, except in defense of the District of Columbia.

Will you do me the favor to state, whether I am right in this understanding, so that, in responding to the lawful demands of the United States Government, I may be able to give effective and reliable aid for the support and defence of this Union.

I have the honor to be your obedientt servant,

THOS. H. HICKS,

Governor of Maryland.

WAR DEPARTMENT,   }
WASHINGTON, April 17th, 1861. }

To His Excellency,

THOS. H. HICKS,

Governor of Maryland.

SIR :—The President has referred to me your communication of this date, in relation to our conversation of the previous day, and I have the honor to say, in reply, that your statement of it is correct.

The troops called for from Maryland are destined for the protection of the Federal Capital and the public property of the United States within the limits of the State of Maryland ; and it is not intended to remove them beyond those limits except for the defense of this District.

I have the honor to be yours, &c.,

SIMON CAMERON.

Secretary of War.

WAR DEPARTMENT,   }
WASHINGTON, April 18th, 1861. }

To His Excellency,

THOS. H. HICKS,

Governor of Maryland.

SIR :—The President is informed that threats are made, and measures taken, by unlawful combinations of misguided citizens of Maryland, to prevent by force the transit of United States troops, across Maryland, on their way, pursuant to orders, for the defense of this capital. The information is from such sources and in such shapes, that the President thinks it his duty to make it known to you, so that all loyal and patriotic citizens of your State may be warned in time, and that you may be prepared to take immediate and effective measures against it.

Such an attempt could have only the most deplorable consequences: and it would be as agreeable to the President, as it would be to yourself that it should be prevented, or overcome by the loyal authorities and citizens of Maryland, rather than averted by any other means.

I am very respectfully, yours, &c.,

SIMON CAMERON,

Secretary of War.

STATE OF MARYLAND,

EXECUTIVE CHAMBER, }
ANNAPOLIS, April 20th, 1861. }

HON. S. CAMERON,

SIR:—Since I saw you in Washington last, I have been been in Baltimore City, laboring in conjunction with the Mayor of that city to preserve peace and order, but I regret to say with little success. Up to yesterday there appeared promise, but the outbreak came, the turbulent passions of the riotous element prevailed, fear for safety became reality, what they endeavored to conceal, but what was known to us, was no longer concealed but made manifest; the rebellious element had the control of things. We were arranging and organizing forces to protect the city and preserve order, but want of organization, of arms, prevented success. They had arms, they had the principal part of the organized military forces with them, and for us to have made the effort, under the circumstances, would have had the effect to aid the disorderly element. They took possession of the Armories, have the arms and ammunition, and I therefore think it prudent, to decline, (for the present,) responding affirmatively to the requisition made by President Lincoln, for four regiments of infantry.

With great respect I am your obedient servant,

THOS. H. HICKS.

FREDERICK CITY, MD., April 20th, 1861.

HIS EXCELLENCY,

THOMAS H. HICKS,

Governor of the State Maryland,

Annapolis, Md.

SIR:—In obedience to Special Orders, No. 106 Adjutant General's Office, Washington, D. C. of April 15th, 1861, (detailing me to muster into the service of the United States, the troops of this State called out by the President's proclamation of that date,) I have the honor to report to you my arrival at this place.

I would be pleased to receive from you, at your earliest convenience, information and instructions you may have to communicate to me, in reference to this duty.

I am sir, very respectfully,

Your obedient servant,

R. MACFEELY,

1st Lieut. 4th Infantry.

———

STATE OF MARYLAND,

Executive Chamber, }
Annapolis, April 23d, 1861. }

R. MACFEELY, Esq.,

1st Lieut. 4th Infantry.

Sir :—Your letter of the 20th inst. was received this morning. I am directed by the Governor to inform you that no troops have been called out in Maryland, and that consequently your mission is at an end. And you will therefore report to the Secretary of War, who has been informed of the Governor's views in this matter.

Your obedient servant,

GEORGE W. JEFFERSON,

Private Secretary.

———

Annapolis, April 20th, 1861.

To the Secretary of War :

I have understood that it is contemplated to send Northern Troops to garrison Fort Madison.

I would earnestly advise that none be sent.

Respectfully,

THOS. H. HICKS.

———

TELEGRAPHIC DISPATCH.

Washington, April 20th, 1861.

GOV. HICKS,

I desire to consult with you and the Mayor of Baltimore, relative to preserving the peace of Maryland. Please come immediately by special train, which you can take at Baltimore, or if necessary one can be sent from hence. Answer forthwith.

LINCOLN.

———

STATE OF MARYLAND,

Executive Chamber, }
Annapolis, April 22d, 1861. }

To His Excellency,

A. LINCOLN,

President of the United States.

Sir :—I feel it my duty most especially to advise you that no more troops be ordered or allowed to pass through Maryland, and that the troops now off Annapolis be sent elsewhere, and I most respectfully urge that a truce be offered by you, so that the effusion of blood may be prevented. I respectfully suggest, that Lord Lyons be requested to act as mediator between the contending parties of our country.

I have the honor to be, very respectfully,

Your obedient servant,

THOS. H. HICKS.

DEPARTMENT OF STATE, }
April 22d, 1861, }

HIS EXCELLENCY,

THOS. H. HICKS,

Governor of Maryland.

SIR :—I have had the honor to receive your communication of this morning, in which you inform me that you have felt it to be your duty to advise the President of the United States to order elsewhere the troops then off Annapolis, and also that no more may be sent through Maryland, and that you have farther suggested that Lord Lyons be requested to act as mediator between the contending parties in our country, to prevent the effusion of blood.

The President directs me to acknowledge the receipt of that communication, and to assure you that he has weighed the counsels which it contains with the respect which he habitually cherishes for the Chief Magistrates of the several States, and especially for yourself. He regrets, as deeply as any magistrate or citizen of the country can, that demonstration, against the safety of the United States, with very extensive preparations for the effusion of blood, have made it his duty to call out the forces to which you allude. The force now sought to be brought through Maryland is intended for nothing but the defense of this Capital. The President has necessarily confided the choice of the national highway, which that force shall take in coming to this city, to the Lieutenant-General commanding the army of the United States, who, like his only predecessor, is not less distinguished for his humanity than for his loyalty, patriotism, and distinguished public service.

The President instructs me to add, that the national highway thus selected by the Lieutenant-General has been chosen by him upon consultation with prominent magistrates and citizens of Maryland as the one which, while a route is absolutely necessary, is farthest removed from the populous cities of the State, and with the expectation that it would therefore be the least objectionable one.

The President cannot but remember that there has been a time in the history of our country, when a General of the American Union, with forces designed for the defense of its Capital, was not unwelcome anywhere in the State of Maryland, and certainly not at Annapolis, then, as now, the Capital of that patriotic State, and then also one of the Capitals of the Union.

If eighty years could have obliterated all the other noble sentiments of that age in Maryland, the President would be hopeful nevertheless that there is one that would forever remain there and everywhere. That sentiment is, that no domestic contention whatever, that may

19

arise among the parties of this Republic ought, in any case, to be referred to any foreign arbitrament, least of all to the arbitrament of an European monarchy.

I have the honor to be,

With distinguished consideration,

Your Excellency's most obedient servant.

WILLIAM H. SEWARD.

———

[Telegram from Mayor Brown.]

BALTIMORE, April 20, 1861.

To Governor Hicks :

Letter from President and Gen. Scott. No troops to pass through Baltimore, if, as a military force, they can march around. I will answer that every effort will be made to prevent parties leaving the city to molest them ; but cannot guarantee against acts of individuals not organized. Do you approve ?

GEO. WM. BROWN.

———

[Telegram in Reply.]

ANNAPOLIS, April 20, 1861.

To the Mayor of Baltimore :

Your dispatch received. I hoped they would send no more troops through Maryland ; but, as we have no right to demand this, I am glad no more are to be sent through Baltimore. I know you will do all in your power to preserve the peace.

THOS. H. HICKS.

———

[Telegram to the Mayor of Baltimore.]

ANNAPOLIS, April 20, 1861.

I have received the following dispatch :

"I desire to consult with you and the Mayor of Baltimore relative to preserving the peace of Maryland. Please come immediately by special train, which you can take at Baltimore, or, if necessary one can be sent from here. LINCOLN."

Have you received a similar dispatch ? If so, do you intend going, and at what hour ? My going depends upon you. Answer at once.

THOS. H. HICKS.

———

[Telegram in reply, without signature.]

To the Governor of Maryland :

The Mayor is in Washington. We have no knowledge of any such movement.

———

[Telegram to Mayor Brown..]

ANNAPOLIS, April 21, 1861.

To the Mayor of Baltimore ;

It is rumored here that men have been sent for from Baltimore to come here to prevent the landing of troops. Do not let them come. The troops will not land here.

THOS. H. HICKS.

STATE OF MARYLAND,
Executive Chamber, ANNAPOLIS, April 20, 1861.

To the Commander of the Volunteer Troops on Board the Steamer:

SIR :—I would most earnestly advise that you do not land your men at Annapolis. The excitement here is very great, and I think that you should take your men elsewhere. I have telegraphed to the Secretary of War, advising against your landing your men here.

Very respectfully,

Your obedient Servant,

THOS. H. HICKS,

Governor of Maryland.

———

SEAL OF THE STATE OF }
   MASSACHUSETTS. }

OFF ANNAPOLIS, April 22d, 1861.

His Excellency Thos. H. Hicks, Governor of Maryland:

In reply to the communication from you on the 21st, I had the honor to inform you of the necessities of my command, which drew me into the harbor of Annapolis. My circumstances have not changed. To that communication I have received no reply. I cannot return, if I desire so to do, without being furnished with some necessary supplies, for all which the money will be paid. I desire of your Excellency an immediate reply, whether I have the permission of the State authorities of Maryland to land the men under my command, and of passing quickly through the State, on my way to Washington, respecting private property, and paying for what I receive, and outraging the rights of none—a duty which I am bound to do in obedience to the requisitions of the President of the United States?

I have received some copies of an informal correspondence between the Mayor of Baltimore and the President of the Baltimore and Ohio Railroad, and a copy of a note from your Excellency, enclosing the same to Capt. Blake, Commandant of the Naval School. These purport to show that instructions have been issued by the War Department as to the disposition of the United States militia, differing from what I had supposed to be my duty. If these instructions have been in fact issued, it would give me great pleasure to obey them.— Have I your Excellency's permission, in consideration of these exigencies of the case, to land my men—to supply their wants, and to relieve them from the extreme and unhealthy confinement of a transport vessel not fitted to receive them? To convince your Excellency of the good faith towards the authorities of the State of Maryland, with which I am acting, and I am armed only against the disturbers of her peace and of the United States, I enclose a copy of an order issued to my command before I had the honor of receiving the copy of your communication through Capt. Blake. I trust your Excellency will appreciate the necessities of my position, and give me an immediate reply, which I await with anxiety.

I would do myself the honor to have a personal interview with your Excellency, if you so desire. I beg leave to call your Excellency's attention to what I hope may be pardoned for deeming an ill-advised designation of the men under my command. *They are not Northern troops—they are a part of the whole militia of the United States, obeying the call of the President.*

I have the honor of being your Excellency's obedient servant,

BENJ. F. BUTLER,

Brig. General in the Militia of the United States.

P. S.—It occurs to me that our landing on the grounds at the Naval Academy would be entirely proper, and in accordance with your Excellency's wishes. B. F. B.

———

SEAL OF THE STATE OF }
MASSACHUSETTS. }

Special Brigade, Order No. 37.

HEADQUARTERS SECOND DIVISION MASS. VOL. MILITIA, }
On board steamer Maryland, off Annapolis, April 22d, 1861. }

Col. Munroe is charged with the execution of the following order : At five o'clock A. M. the troops will be paraded by company and be drilled in the manual of arms. Especially in loading at will, firing by file, and in the use of the bayonet, and these specialties will be observed in all subsequent drills in the manual. Such drill to continue until 7 o'clock, when all the arms will be stacked upon the upper deck—great care being taken to instruct the men as to the mode of stacking their arms, so that a firm stack, not easily overturned, shall be made. Being obliged to drill at times with the weapons loaded, great damage may be done by the overturning of the stack and the discharging the piece. This is important. Indeed, an accident has already occurred in the regiment from this cause, and although slight in its consequence, yet it warns us to increased diligence in this regard. The purpose which could only be hinted at in the orders of yesterday has been accomplished. The frigate Constellation has lain for a long time at this port substantially at the mercy of the armed mob, which sometimes paralyzes the otherwise loyal State of Maryland. Deeds of daring, successful contests, and glorious victories had rendered "Old Ironsides" so conspicuous in the naval history of the country, that she was fitly chosen as the school ship in which to train the future officers of the navy to like heroic acts.

It was given to Masschusetts and Essex county first to man her ; it was reserved for Massachusetts to have the honor to retain her for the service of the Union and the laws.

This is a sufficient triumph of right, and a sufficient triumph for us. By this the blood of our friends shed by the Baltimore mob is in so far avenged. The Eighth Regiment may hereafter cheer lustily on all proper occasions, but never without orders. The old Constitution, by their efforts, aided untiringly by the United States officers having her in charge, is now safely "possessed, occupied, and enjoyed" by the government of the United States, and is safe from all her foes.

We have been joined by the Seventh Regiment of New York, and together we propose peaceably, quickly, and civilly, unless opposed by some mob, or other disorderly persons, to march to Washington, in obedience to the requisitions of the President of United States. If opposed, we shall march steadily forward.

My next order I hardly know how to express. I cannot assume that any of the citizen soldiery of Massachusetts or New York could, under any circumstances whatever, commit any outrages upon private property in a loyal and friendly State. But fearing that some improper person may have by stealth introduced himself among us, I deem it proper to state, that any unauthorized interference with private property will be most signally punished, and full reparation therefore made to the injured party, to the full extent of my power and ability. In so doing, I but carry out the orders of the War Department. I should have done so without those orders.

Col. Munroe will cause these orders to be read at the head of each company before we march.

Col. Leffert's command not having been originally included in this order, he will be furnished with a copy for his instruction.

By order of

B. F. BUTLER,
Brig. General.

{ Signed }   WILLIAM H. CLEMENS
Brig. Major.

STATE OF MARYLAND,
[Executive Chamber, Annapolis, April 22, 1861.

To Brig. Gen. B. F. Butler:

Sir—I am in receipt of your two communications of this date, informing me of your intention to land the men under your command at Annapolis, for the purpose of marching thence to the city of Washington. I content myself with protesting against this movement, which, in view of the excited condition of the people of this State, I cannot but consider an unwise step on the part of the Government. But I most earnestly urge upon you that there shall be no halt made by the troops in this city.

Very respectfully,

Your obedient servant,

TH. H. HICKS.

STATE OF MARYLAND,
Executive Chamber, Annapolis, April 23, 1861.

To Brig. Gen. B. F. Butler:

Sir: Having, in pursuance of the powers vested in me by the Constitution of Maryland, summoned the Legislature of the State to assemble on Friday, the 26th instant ; and Annapolis being the place in which, according to law, it must assemble ; and having been credibly informed that you have taken military possession of the Annapolis and Elk Ridge Railroad, I deem it my duty to protest against this step ; because, without at present assigning any other reason, I am informed that such occupany of said road will prevent the members of the Legislature from reaching this city.

Very respectfully, yours,

THOS. H. HICKS.

SEAL OF THE STATE OF }
    MASSACHUSETTS.   }

   HEADQUARTERS THIRD BRIGADE, }
    UNITED STATES MILITIA,   }
    Annapolis, Md., April 23, 1861. }

To His Excellency Thos. H. Hicks,

      Governor of Maryland:

You are credibly informed that I have taken possession of the Annapolis and Elkridge Railroad. It might have escaped your notice, but at the official meeting between your Excellency and the Mayor of Annapolis, and the authorities of the government and myself, it was expressly stated as the reason why I should not land, that my troops could not pass the railroad, because the company had taken up the rails, and they were private property. It is difficult to see how it could be, that if my troops could not pass over the railroad one way, the members of the Legislature could pass the other way. I have taken possession for the purpose of preventing the carrying out of the threats of the mob, as officially represented to me by the Master of Transportation of this city "that if my troops passed over the railroad, the railroad should be destroyed."

If the government of the State had taken possession of the railroad in any emergency, I should have long waited before I entered upon it. But, as I had the honor to inform your Excellency in regard to insurrection against the laws of Maryland, I am here armed to maintain those laws, if your Excellency desires, and the peace of the United States, against all disorderly persons whatever. I am endeavoring to save and not to destroy ; to obtain means of transportation, so I can vacate the capital prior to the sitting of the Legislature, and not be under the painful necessity of occupying your beautiful city while the Legislature is in session.

   I have the honor to be,

    Your Excellency's obedient servant.

      BR. GEN. B. F. BUTLER.

   HEADQUARTERS THIRD BRIGADE }
    MASS. VOL. MILITIA.   }
   Annapolis, Md., April 23, 1861. }

To His Excellency Thos. H. Hicks,

     Governor of the State of Maryland:

I did myself the honor, in my communication of yesterday, wherein I asked permission to land the portion of the militia of the United States under my command, to state that they were armed only against the disturbers of the peace of the State of Maryland and of the United States.

I have understood within the last hour that some apprehensions were entertained of an insurrection of the negro population of this neighborhood. I am anxious to convince all classes of persons that the forces under my command are not here in any way to interfere with or countenance any interference with the laws of the State. I am, therefore, ready to co-operate with your Excellency in suppressing most promptly and effectively any insurrection against the laws of Maryland.

I beg, therefore, that you announce publicly that any portion of the forces under my command is at your Excellency's disposal, to act immediately for the preservation and quietness of the peace of this community.

And I have the honor to be,

Your Excellency's obedient servant,

B. F. BUTLER,
General of Third Brigade.

STATE OF MARYLAND, }
Executive Chamber, Annapolis, April 23, 1861. }

To Brig. Gen. B. F. Butler :

Sir—I have the honor to acknowledge the receipt of your letter of this morning, tendering the force under your command to aid in suppressing a rumored insurrection of the slaves of this county.

I thank you most sincerely for the tender of your men ; but I had, before the receipt of your letter, directed the Sheriff of the County to act in the matter ; and am confident that the citizens of the county are fully able to suppress any insurrection of our slave population.

I have the honor to be,

Your obedient servant,

TH. H. HICKS.

COPY OF DISPATCHES FROM BRIG. GEN. BUTLER TO GOVERNOR CURTIN.

To His Excellency, Andrew Curtin, Commander in Chief of the Forces of Pennsylvania :

Sir : Should this dispatch be forwarded to you, countersigned by His Excellency Thomas H. Hicks, Governor of Maryland, you will please to understand that the insurgents have surrendered Pikeville Arsensal, and that it, therefore, will not be necessary to advance your troops, as you were yesterday requested by me.

B. F. BUTLER,
Brigadier General.

Annapolis, April 24th, 1861.

STATE OF MARYLAND, }
Executive Chamber, Annapolis, April 24th, 1861. }

To Brig. Gen. B. F. Butler :

Sir :—A despatch signed by you, addressed to Gov. A. Curtin, has been received by me, with a verbal request that I countersign it, and have it forwarded to its address.

In reference to the Arsenal at Pikeville, I have no official information. I do not know who is now in possesion of it. I am cut off from all communication with other parts of the State ; and have no means to forward your dispatch, if I were willing to countersign it.

I am compelled, therefore, to decline to accede to your request.

Very respectfully,

Your obedient servant,

TH. H. HICKS.

These rapid and warlike events, Gov. Hicks, in his message to the Legislature, April 27, thus depicted to that body then in session at Frederick:

"On Sunday morning last, I discovered that a detachment of troops, under command of Brig. Gen. B. F. Butler, had reached Annapolis in a steamer, and had taken possession of the practice ship Constitution, which, during that day, they succeeded in getting outside the harbor of Annapolis, where she now lies. After getting the ship off, the steamer laid outside our harbor, and was soon joined by another steamer, having on board the Seventh Regiment from New York City.

"Brig. Gen. Butler addressed me, asking for permission to land his forces. It will be seen, from the correspondence herewith submitted, that I refused my consent. The Mayor of Annapolis also protested. But both steamers soon afterwards landed at the Naval Academy and put off the troops. Subsequently, other large bodies of troops reached here in transports and were landed. I was notified that the troops were to be marched to Washington. They desired to go without obstruction from our people; but they had orders to go to Washington, and were determined to obey those orders. In furtherance of their designs, they took military possession of the Annapolis and Elk Ridge Railroad; in regard to which act I forwarded to Brig. Gen. Butler the protest, and received the reply herewith submitted. On Wednesday morning the two detachments first landed took up the line of march for Washington. The people of Annapolis, though greatly exasperated, acting under counsel of the most prudent citizens, refrained from molesting or obstructing the passage of the troops through the city.

"Seriously impressed with the condition of affairs, and anxious to avoid a repetition of events similar to those which had transpired in Baltimore, I deemed it my duty to make another appeal to the authorities at Washington. Accordingly, I sent a special messenger to Washington, with a despatch to the administration advising that no more troops be sent through Maryland; that the troops at Annapolis be sent elsewhere; and urging that a truce be offered with a view of a peaceful settlement of existing difficulties by mediation. I suggested that Lord Lyons, the British Minister, be requested to act as mediator between the contending parties. The result of the mission will be seen from the correspondence herewith submitted.

"These events have satisfied me that the War Department has concluded to make Annapolis the point for landing troops, and has resolved to open and maintain communication between this place and Washington."

Annapolis thus became an important military station, and so remained to the close of the war.

[1861.] Although the editor of the *Gazette* had abandoned the lone star policy for Maryland, Gov. Hicks, up to April 25, 1861, had not given up the hope that Maryland would not be a battle ground. Writing from Annapolis on that date to the Legislature at Frederick, the Governor said: "I can give no other counsel than that we shall array ourselves for Union and peace, and thus preserve our soil from being polluted with the blood of brethren." Gov. Hicks' remedy was of one kind and the editor of the *Gazette's* another. Both were equally inefficacious as the battles of Monocacy, Sharpsburg, and Antietam well attest.

May 9, 1861, the *Gazette* had to defend its assertions made April 25. Amongst these were that "the people of Annapolis are highly indignant at the occupation of our city. But were powerless to oppose them. Yielding to the advice of the more prudent, our people have refrained from any open demonstration against the troops." Also, that "the feeling hereabouts is almost unanimous on the subject"— that is, on secession. He asserted that "at the time we penned them they were undoubtedly true, so far as we were able to ascertain." He added that "no doubt *now* (May 9,) secession is at a discount in Annapolis, because such a thing makes a disagreeable impression in the minds of the troops," and because it is "the thing" now to be a Union man.

A town meeting was held May 4, of which John R. Magruder was President, Dr. Dennis Claude and Col. John Walton, Vice-Presidents, and Oliver Miller, Secretary, "to take into consideration the proposed action of the Legislature to appoint a committee of Public Safety. The committee on resolutions were: A. Randall, Dr. John Ridout, Frank H. Stockett, and Wm. L. Seabrook. The meeting resolved that "the proposed bill was an act of lawless despotism, and that the passage thereof would be calculated to bring the people of this State in conflict with General Government."

By May 13, the Government had a track laid from the Naval Academy, via the College Avenue, to the Annapolis and Elk Ridge Depot, and munitions of war were landed at the Naval Academy, and carried to Washington without change of cars.

Col. Smith of the 13th New York was, at this period, given command of the Naval Academy, the cadets having taken their flight to Newport, Rhode Island. Col. Smith, May 14, treated the citizens to a parade of the regiment through the town, a stratagem adroitly laid to allay any latent feeling of secession in the city. The little assumptions of authority of the colonel commanding the post brought out one of the local poets to declare in print :

"That Colonel Smith is a mighty warrior,
He commands our Naval School,
And he acts both judge and lawyer,
Though sometimes he acts the fool."

There were several other verses, and they found their way into the hands of the colonel, who, instead of resenting this rhythmic criticism, enjoyed the effusion, and complimented the unknown author on his wit and verse.

The older heads that held secession views found it wise to be quiet, but a young company of secession youths boldly dressed in red, with wooden guns, paraded the town without fear or molestation, and on the night of July 21, 1861, when the news of the battle of Bull Run reached Annapolis, a crowd of young Southern sympathizers marched down town singing and rejoicing over the defeat of the Federal troops. But that was the last of it, the Federal authorities found they had earnest work on hand and open sympathy was met with the same vigor that was displayed in the field against the Southern Confederacy. The Marylanders even found it was a dangerous combination to put the colors red and white in juxtaposition in their articles of dress.

May 30, the *Gazette* says: "By order of Gov. Hicks the National Flag will be displayed every day from the dome of the State House. The cheering sight, will, we hope, add fervor to the Union cause, and will shame away the remnant of treason which is yet skulking in the 'Ancient City,' waiting its opportunity to again suppress free speech and free action, and to inaugurate a new 'reign of terror,' in our midst. There need be little fear of this, however, for the traitors are known, every man of them, and, we trust, condign punishment will be meted out, to every one who shall again dare to raise his hand against our liberties."

The extreme carefulness of the Federal troops to show that they had not come to take away the Southerner's slaves or to give liberty to those in bondage is shown by the following from the Gazette of the same date:

"CAPTURED.—A runaway slave, belonging to *Dennis Orme, Esq.*, of this county, was captured on Thursday last by a picket guard of National Soldiery on the line of the Annapolis and Elk Ridge Railroad, and promptly taken to our county jail. Such an act is a rebuke to those who denounce the Northern soldiers as our enemies." A little later than this one of the citizens of Annapolis received very different treatment from that accorded to Mr. Orme. Mr. Danl. T. Hyde went into the Naval Academy to secure one of his slaves who had taken refuge there. The commander was willing to render him up, but when the soldiery discovered Mr. Hyde's mission, they closed around him with a ferocity that threatened the mobbing of the slave-owner. He safely escaped the danger, but, without Sam Foulks, who was hidden in a hogshead by the soldiers.

On May 23, the *Gazette* reproduced an article from the Philadelphia Inquirer, which said it had received it from "an intelligent correspondent who is one of the oldest and most estimable citizens of Annapolis, who suggests a plan by which the City of Baltimore can be made to feel the proper retribution for her unwillingness or inability to control the lawless element of her population. It is simply to make Annapolis the commercial emporium of the State of Maryland, for which purposes it far surpasses Baltimore in natural advantages. It is located in a spacious and sheltered harbor, easily accessable from the sea to ships of the greatest draught; it is the natural outlet, by descending grades, for the vast coal fields of Virginia whose development gives employment to the Baltimore and Ohio Railroad, which has now a branch to Annapolis. It is already the seat of a wealthy and refined population, which only needs an infusion of business men to inaugurate an era of commercial activity and consequent prosperity. We learn that a number of merchants who were driven from Baltimore for their devotion to the Union, will permanently locate themselves at Annapolis, supported by the unswerving loyalty of the people of that city, and that Northern business men who, within the past few weeks, have been compelled to pass through Annapolis, have declared that, before years, it would rival Baltimore in the struggle for commercial supremacy."

The faithful historian must relate that neither record nor recollection bear witness of the settlement in the 'Ancient City" of any "merchants, who were driven from Baltimore, for their devotion to the Union," and, after twenty-seven years' opportunity to realize the prophesies of this "intelligent correspondent," Baltimore still remains the emporium of Maryland.

June 10, four companies of the 13th Regt. N. Y. S. M., left Annapolis and proceeded to Easton, Md., where they seized 1700 stand of arms, six pieces of artillery, and a quantity of ammunition. A soldier was accidentally killed on the expedition.

In the Congressional election in June, Chas. B. Calvert, Union man, received at Annapolis 296 votes ; Benj. G. Harris, Democrat, 127. In Anne Arundel, Calvert received 915 votes and Harris 674.

June 15th, the Union men of Annapolis had a pole raising and flung the stars and stripes to the breeze. The 13th New York took part and speeches were made by W. L. W. Seabrook, Major Gen. Morse, of Mass., and Oliver Dayton, of New York. The artillery gave a salute of 34 guns.

Considerable excitement was created in Annapolis by the seizure, June 25, by the Federal government of Philadelphia oyster vessels in the hands of the State authorities for violations of the dredging laws. It seems the owners represented to the authorities at Washington, that their "vessels had been unlawfully captured by the secessionists from Annapolis, who had torn down the national flag from their masts, trampled it under foot, and cheered lustily for the traitor Jeff Davis."

W. H. Russell, the celebrated correspondent of the London Times, reached Annapolis, on Monday, July 14, from Fortress Monroe and remained until Tuesday.

July 25 appears to have been the day on which the vanguard of that great army of sick and wounded that was located in Annapolis during the civil war, arrived. Fifty such soldiers were brought from Georgetown.

The *Gazette*, of August 1st, complains of encroachments on the rights of the people by the Federal government, saying that "most of these incidents are totally unnecessary, totally uncalled for by any exigency and are perpetrated by fanatical and incompetent officers of the General Government, who take unconscionable advantage of circumstances to carry out some fanatical theory or revengeful feeling."

Col. R. Riddle Roberts, now in command of the Naval Academy, caused three negroes who had come by boat, and landed at the Naval Academy, and had asked shelter, to be delivered "to the Sheriff of Anne Arundel county to be dealt with according to law."

A Union Home Guard was organized in Annapolis. Its officers were Captain Roger Bellis; Lieutenant, William Hubbard, Jr.; Orderly Sergeant, Norman Leslie; 2d Sergeant, Michael Kernin, Corporals, Wm. H. Bellis, John Ireland, and Julian Brewer.

The military spirit cropped out strongly in Annapolis. The Union members of the Governor's Guard seceded and formed a new company under Capt. W. G. Tuck. A Zouave corps of 80 was formed under the command of Capt. William Hubbard. That part of the Governor's Guard, alleged to be affected with Southern sentiments, still paraded without arms, and the *Gazette* suggested it was "a great outrage to permit them to keep up their organization," as they would join the Confederates if opportunity presented itself.

September 1, eleven Confederate prisoners were brought to Annapolis. The ladies of Southern proclivities paid them marked attention. Col. Augustus Morse of the 21st Mass., had now command of the troops at the Naval Academy. He afterward settled at Annapolis, and purchased the City Hotel.

[1862.] Burnside's expedition to Roanoke Island made its rendezvous at Annapolis, and a camp for paroled prisoners was established
on the College Campus in the rear of the buildings. This camp was
eventually removed to Camp Parole, two miles from Annapolis, where
thousands of paroled prisoners were constantly quartered during the
war. From this camp was named the Station of that name on the
Annapolis, Washington, and Baltimore railroad.

' The Assembly Rooms were made the head quarters of Provost
Guard, and during their occupancy, was set on fire. The Federal
government paid for the damage and with this money the building
was repaired.

The Annapolis *Gazette*, which had been established in 1852 by
Thos. J. Wilson and Richard Sellman, ceased publication, it appears,
in August 1861. September 10, 1863, it was recuscitated with Rich.
P. Bayly, well-known in the fraternity as "Deacon Baily", as
editor and proprietor. The *Gazette* still maintained its strong union
sentiments, the new editor declaring, "with me it is the Union—the
whole Union—first, last, and all the time."

[1863.] Sept. 5, the Steam Ferryboat "Ready" arrived for use on
Severn River Ferry.

Paroled prisoners from the camps near the city who were found in
town "without a pass," subsequent to the 1st inst., were ordered to
be arrested by the Provost Guard and returned to the camp to which
they belonged. Annapolis was now thoroughly policed by a
military guard, the provost marshal being superintendent of police.

The *Gazette* expressed its gratification that the enrollment of
Anne Arundel, preliminary to a draft, was nearly completed. The
work was done under Thomas N. Pindle, Esq. The *Gazette* added :
"It is a source of pleasure to know that the work has been effected
without any violence. There were rumors that *Seresh* would not permit the enrollment to be quietly and peaceably made. In fact, so
strong was this opinion, that nearly all the persons first appointed
to make the enrollment refused to act."

It revives with breezy freshness the old war time scenes in a border
State to con over the *Gazette*.

From its local column is taken this daguerreotype of the times:

"ARRESTED.—Basil NcNew, residing near this city, was arrested on
Thursday evening, (Sept. 10,) for uttering disloyal sentiments in our
streets. He was taken to the Guard House, where he was detained
until Saturday morning, when he was taken to Fort McHenry.
Whilst in the Guard House, he vociferously hurrahed for the
Southern Confederacy and Jeff Davis, and it was with difficulty the
firm and efficient, yet kind Provost Marshal, Capt. F.J. Keffer, could
prevent the paroled prisoners in the same room from doing him personal injury."

Mr. McNew survived his temporary imprisonment in Fort McHenry,
and is now the efficient keeper of the Anne Arundel Court House.

The authorities at the same time sent Samuel Topper, *alias* Wm.
McIntosh to Fort McHenry on the charge of being a spy. He had
been arrested by the Colonel of the 109th N. Y. Volunteers at the
Annapolis Junction on the third of July, and had been in the Annapolis jail since that date. There seemed to be some difficulty in
determining whether, or not, Topper was a spy or a lunatic. The
authorities put themselves on the safe side by locking him up in prison.

The *Gazette*, at this time, published several communications whose evident object was to intimidate the democrats from taking any part in the politics of the day. The democrats were spoken of as traitors, and the publications made against them tended to make the Federal Government lay its hands on them. The animosities of that day can be easily conceived when in its issue of Sept. 24, the *Gazette* says: "THE BALL IN MOTION.—At a meeting of the Secesh Democracy, held in this city on the 15th instant, the gentlemen named below were appointed as delegates to represent this Election District (Annapolis,) in a Convention to be held in Bladensburg on‸this day,(Sept. 24,) to nominate a candidate for this Congressional District—Messrs. Passmore McCullough, Wm. Bryan, John Duvall, and Wm. Watts. These gentlemen are all well-known to have been ardent supporters of the measures of the Legislature that met at Frederick in 1861, the majority of which (*sic*) labored to the utmost of their power to unite Maryland with South Carolina, and the other Cotton States in their rebellion against the Government of the United States. That they still occupy the same position we have every reason to believe, and so far as their action relates to the said Congressional Convention we may expect the nomination of a violent secessionist, an enemy to the prevailing Government, and decidedly opposed to forcing the Rebels to lay down their arms. * * * * The question then arises, will the Government permit a party to organize in loyal Maryland, (and that too in the only Congressional District secessionism dare rear its standard,) whose chief object will be to obstruct and embarrass every effort that may be made to put down the accursed rebellion, and restore the Union and the blessings of peace? We shall see."

The county delegates to the Congressional Convention, Benj. Tongue, Dr. J. W. Waugh, Sprigg Harwood, and James Sandford, the *Gazette*, snappishly declared were "in favor of the dissolution of the Union and the recognition of the Southern Confederacy." These embarrassing charges had apparently one object in view—the arrest of democratic leaders and the utter overthrow of the party by the military power of the Federal Government.

The enrollment of Annapolis showed there were in the first class, 545 whites and 147 colored, subject to military duty, and in the second class, 163 whites and 22 colored.

The democratic Congressional Convention of the 5th district, nominated no candidate, but recommended Benj. G. Harris, of St. Mary's county.

The provost guard was no idle form, but prohibited liquor to the soldiers in a manner to do the most advanced temperance advocate's heart a boundless amount of good. October 5, it seized the stock of liquor of the proprietor of the American House and placed a guard there on the ground that liquor had been sold at the hotel to the soldiers. The hotel stood on the vacant lot above Andrews' alley leading from Main street to State House Circle.

The democrats of Anne Arundel made their contest this year under many difficulties and with the fear of military interference constantly before their eyes. In Annapolis the Union vote on State's Attorney was, H. M. Murray, 302 ; James Revell, dem., 147. In the county the

vote was, Murray, 635; James Revell, 1,119. The closest vote was
on Register of Wills—Benj. E. Gantt, independent. 853; Richard
I. Duvall, dem., 898.

Sick prisoners, out of Confederate hands were now frequently arriving in Annapolis. They were in a suffering and emaciated condition.

PUBLIC BUILDINGS, CHURCHES, AND ANCIENT LANDMARKS.

FOUR GUBERNATORIAL RESIDENCES.

Annapolis contains four houses that have served, or were intended
to serve, as the residences of the governors of Maryland.

The earliest built is that now owned by Mr. Francis T. Marchand,
formerly the residence of Judge A. B. Hagner, No. 83 Prince
George street. The house is a well preserved evidence of the taste
and solidity of the architecture of that interesting period. To this
house a few years since an addition was made on the right wing. The
outlines and proportions of the ancient building are easily discerned.

This building belonged to Major Edward Dorsey, and was occupied
by Governor Francis Nicholson, who was the Executive of the province from 1694 to 1709. The exact date of the erection of the building is not known. This house is most probably the one that was occupied for the sitting of the Legislature after the burning of the
State House in 1704.

The next in age is McDowell Hall, St. John's College. In 1744, the
College Green, containing four acres of land, was conveyed by Stephen
Boardley to Thomas Bladen, governor of Maryland, who projected
the main and central building, as a palatial residence for the governors of Maryland. Its site, the commodious grounds, the spacious
building conspired to make the mansion a desirable home and a prince-
ly public residence. Mr. Duff, the architect, came from Scotland to
superintend the construction of the building, materials of every kind
were provided in a most liberal spirit, and the edifice was nearly
finished in a style of magnificence, suitable to the prosperity and enterprise of the province, when a disagreement took place between the
governor and the legislature, that reached such a fervor, that, at a
period, when a nominal sum would have made it a fitting mansion for
the executives of Maryland, all work was stopped, and it remained
until 1784, "a melancholy and mouldering monument" of the results
of political dissensions. It appropriately received the cognomen of
"the Governor's folly."

By chap. 37, 1784, this property was voted by the State to St.
John's College, provided the college was established at Annapolis.

The third gubernatorial mansion is the one now occupied by the
Naval Academy as a library. The main building of this house was

erected by Edmund Jennings, from whom it was purchased by Gov·ernor Robert Eden who was executive of Maryland from 1769 to 1776. Governor Eden built the wings and the long-room. There are many living in Annapolis who will readily recognize Mr. David Ridgely's description of it as it appeared in 1840:

"This edifice has a handsome court and garden, extending, with the exception of an intervening lot, to water's edge. From the portico looking to the garden, a fine prospect regales the vision. The building consists of two stories, and presents an extensive front; there are on the lower floor a large room on each side of the hall as you enter; and several smaller ones; the saloon, on the same floor, is nearly the length of the house. On each side of the edifice are commodious kitchens, carriage-house, and stables, with spacious lots. Towards the water, the building rises in the middle in a turreted shape. It stands detached from other structures, and is altogether a delightful and suitable mansion for the chief magistrate of our State."

By act 1866, chap. 46, this house and grounds were sold to the United States Government for an addition to the Naval Academy.

This act provided for the purchase of a site for, and the erection of, another Gubernatorial Mansion. The Governor, Comptroller, and Treasurer, Thomas Swann being governor, were authorized to have this work executed. One hundred thousand dollars were appropriated. The site selected was a quintangular lot, fronting on State House Circle, College Avenue, (Tabernacle street,) Church Circle, Lawyer, and North streets.

To make room for the present Governor's mansion, two fine old colonial residences had to be torn down. One was the house of the late George E. Franklin, and the other of Mrs. Green. The last house was formerly the residence of Absalom Ridgely, and of his son Dr. John Ridgely, who was surgeon on the U. S. Ship Philadelphia when it was captured in the harbor of Tripoli in 1804. This house was built by Gen. Geo. H. Stewart's grandfather.

The lot and building of the new executive mansion cost $69,296.28 over the appropriation which the Legislature was called upon to meet. The Legislature investigated the matter and made a detailed report of the expense, but a wise and friendly State printer neglected to bind the report among public documents of the session, and this interesting statement is therefore lost to history and posterity.

FIRST METHODIST EPISCOPAL CHURCH.

The first trustees of the Methodist Congregation of Annapolis, of whom there is any record were Absalom Ridgely, Joseph Evans, George Wells, and John Miller. When the church was incorporated in 1833, all of the original trustees were dead save Joseph Evans who then was no longer a member of the church.

The first church of Methodism stood near the site of the present Record office on the State House Hill. The circle did not extend as far then as it does now. The church was a frame building and was known as "the old blue church," so designated from its color. It had a stairway on the outside, up which the colored part of the congregation went to the gallery set apart for them. After it ceased to be used as a church, it became a school-house.

When the Methodists became a corporate body in 1833, the following were the trustees : Nicholas J. Watkins, Basil Shephard, Louis Gassaway, Geo. McNeir, Thos. G. Waters, Grafton Munroe, Andrew Slicer, and Philip Clayton.

The Second Church, in which the' Methodists worshiped was built about 1820. It was a neat brick building, with pressed brick front, and remained until 1859, when the present church was built on the same site. It was in this second church that Gen. La Fayette attended divine service Annapolis in 1824.

The building committee of the present church was J. Wesley White, James Andrews, and James Munroe. The committee on funds: J. Wesley White, Joshua Brown, Philip Clayton, Edward Hopkins, Solomon Philips, Isaac Brewer, James Andrews, R. R. Goodman, and James Munroe.

The congregation as early as 1834 bought a parsonage on Cornhill street, on the north side near the corner. It was burnt down about 1851. The present parsonage was built in 1852.

PRESBYTERIAN CHURCH.

The first Presbyterian Church of Annapolis was organized May 2d, 1846, by the Rev. Dr. Laurie and the Rev. Mr. Dunlop, members of the congregation appointed by the Presbytery of Baltimore for that duty. The elders elected at that time were Prof. A. N. Girault and Dr. John Ridout.

On the 25th of July, 1846, the corner-stone of the church edifice was laid by Rev. Thomas Peck, D. D., at which time an address was delivered by him at the Assembly Rooms.

On the 11th of July, 1847, the Church was dedicated, Geo. W. Musgrave, D. D., preaching the sermon. On the same day, the first pastor, Rev. Chas. H. Ewing, was installed.

The following succeeded Mr. Ewing as pastors: Rev. J. J. Graff, 1849 to 1861. Rev. J. M. Patterson from 1861 to 1866. Rev. J. J. Henderson from 1867 to 1875. Rev. H. O. Gibbons from 1876 to 1881. Rev. Robt. H. Williams, the pastor now in charge, was installed in October, 1882.

ST. MARY'S CATHOLIC CHURCH.

The present Catholic Church was erected in 1858, when the Rev. Father Michael Miller was pastor.

The first Catholic Church was erected on the site of St. Mary's Parochial School. It was built mainly through the instrumentality of the venerable Charles Carroll, of Carrollton, during the later period of his life, probably somewhere about 1830. It was torn down a few years since on account of its unsafe condition. Near the parochial school is a house that was formerly used as the residence of the Catholic clergymen. It is one of a row of buildings that previously stood there, then known as "Mac Namara's row," and this house is said to be one of the oldest in the city. MacNamara was one of the earliest to have his lot surveyed when the town was re-surveyed in 1718.

The property, now owned by the Redemptorist Order, formerly belonged to Charles Carroll, of Carrollton, and was donated to this religious body by the descendants of this illustrious patriot.

WESLEY CHAPEL

Was erected in 1870. The building committee were Joseph S. M. Basil, J. Wesley Robinson, and Josiah Russell. The pastor in charge was J. H. Swope.

ST. MARTIN'S CHURCH.

St. Martin's Evangelical Lutheran Church was founded April 6, 1874. On June 7, 1875, the corner-stone of the church was laid. The building committee of the church was: M. R. Casler, Henry Kaiser, John Dressel, Jerry W. Kalmey, and John Steip. The trustees at present are : Christian Boessell, Martin M. Smith, William Haller, Henry Matzen, Frederick Vollmer, and Charles Ziehlke.

ASBURY M. E. CHURCH, (COLORED CONGREGATION.)

This church was built in 103. The trustees were John Wheeler, George Martin, Saml. Hackney, Matthias Robertson, Francis Tray, John Forty. The church was rebuilt in 1838, and at that time was connected with the Baltimore Conference. The trustees at present are Thomas Jones, Louis Lomack, David Johnson, Benj. Little, Wiley Bates, Joseph Pinkney, Arson Tyler, and Henry Hebron. The pastor is Rev. Alexander Dennis.

MOUNT MORIAH CHURCH. (COLORED CONGREGATION.)

Was built in 1876 under the pastorage of Rev. Jonathan Hamilton.

THE BALL ROOM

Is the same building that Eddis described in 1770. One room is now used for the meeting of the City Council, other apartments for balls and social gatherings, and one portion as the department headquarters. The supper room was formerly the revenue office of the province. During the erection of present State House, the Legislature met in the Ball Room.

THE OLD CITY HALL

Is the house now occupied by Worthington & Co. It was used formerly as the place of meeting of the corporation, and as a fire engine house. It was sold about fifteen years since to William T. Iglehart.

THE CITY HOTEL

Was originally the residence of Mr. Lloyd Dulany. That part was two stories high and in it is the room occupied by Gen. Washington, the night before he resigned his military commission. A new building of three stories was added afterward, and, about 1830, the buildings, from the large one on Conduit street to the corner of Conduit street and Duke of Gloucester, were erected. The first proprietor of

20

it as a hotel was Col. Mann. This was during the Revolutionary period, and it was known as Mann's Hotel. Then William Caton became proprietor, and it was Caton's Hotel and City Tavern. Messrs. Iglehart and Swann were afterward proprietors. Then Col. John Walton. Next Col. Morse. The property lately passed into the hands of William H. Gorman and Luther F. Colton.

SALVATION ARMY BARRACKS.

A corps of the Salvation Army, consisting of Captain Samuel Gully and wife, made its appearance in Annapolis in 1885. They made slow progress at first, but, in the course of the year, the corps, which had received the help of other officers gathered together about fifty recruits. Their unique accompaniments of triangle, tamborine, and cornet to draw the attention of sinners, excited the amusement and oftentimes the disfavor of the public, but their earnest words and sober lives won the respect and brought success to the Army. They were able in the fall and winter of 1885-6 to erect a plain but comfortable "Barracks" on King George street, at the foot of East.

THE CHASE MANSION.

The house, on the north side of Maryland Avenue, corner of King George, built in 1770, by Judge Samuel Chase, (known in the family as Judge Samuel Chase, the Signer,) has been described as "probably the most stately house in Annapolis, being the only colonial residence which is three stories high. The main feature of the house is its hall of entrance opening on a lofty porch and extending through the house from front to back, a distance of over forty-five feet, and being over fourteen feet wide, the large double front door being arched with glass transome and a window on each side. The stairway, opposite the front door, begins with a single flight of steps, and, rising to nearly half the height of the stairway, ends with a platform from which a flight of steps on each side diverges, ascending to a gallery which is supported by Ionic pillars. Above the first platform of the staircase rises a triple window, the central of which is arched and the whole is of magnificent porportions, reminding one of some ancient church. At each end of the gallery above is an arched door with glass transome. Opening on this gallery from the front, is the door of an apartment, and on each side of the door a niche intended for statuary. The dining room is handsomely ornamented in carved wood, and the marble mantel piece of this room represents a scene from Shakespeare in sculpture." It was intended to have had wings upon this house, but it was sold, before being finished, to Governor Lloyd, who was the executive of the State from 1809 to 1811. Mr. Henry Harwood, his son-in-law, bought the house from Gov. Lloyd. It was afterward purchased by Captain Edward Gibson, U. S. N. The next purchaser was Miss Hester Ann Chase, who bought it in 1847. She was the daughter of Jeremiah T. Chase. It is now in the possession of Mrs. Hester Ann Chase Ridout, grand daughter of Samuel Chase and Jeremiah T. Chase.

THE HARWOOD RESIDENCE.

The house, with wings, on the south side of Maryland Avenue at the intersection of King George, was designed by Mr. Buckland, architect, for Mr. Wm. Hammond, a famous Annapolis lawyer, of ye olden times. It was built between the years 1770 and 1780. It was first occupied by Jeremiah Townley Chase, Chief Justice of Maryland in 1781, and was unfinished when he went into it. The house is of brick with stone foundation, some of the foundation walls being five feet thick. The house is handsomely decorated with carved wood. The parlor, a room nineteen by twenty-seven, has a carved wainscot surrounding the room, and the mantel-piece, window, and door frames, shutters and doors are carved in arabesque, and is said to be the handsomest specimen of its kind in Maryland. In 1811, the house was purchased, together with the ground extending from King George street to Prince George street, by Chief Justice Chase for his oldest daughter, Frances Townley, wife of Richard Loockerman. The garden was designed by Mrs. F. T. Loockerman, and was laid off under her direction, and the box walk was planted by herself. The outside corridor of the south wing was added by the family and many interior improvements have been made. The house is now occupied by Wm. Harwood and family. Mrs. Harwood being a grand-daughter of Judge Jeremiah T. Chase. Mr. Hammond, for whom the house was built, it is said, was engaged to be married to a lady, and he went to Philadelphia to get his furniture, but the engagement was broken off, and he lived a bachelor.

THE OGLE HOUSE.

The house, on the corner of King George street and College Avenue, now owned by Mrs. Judge John Thompson Mason, formerly the residence of Gov. Thomas G. Pratt, was built by Gov. Samuel Ogle, who was Governor at three different periods—first in 1732 and the third time in 1746 and '47.

THE PACA DWELLING.

The house, on the northeast side of Prince George street, near East st., now owned by Mrs. Richard Swann, was built by Gov. Paca, who was Governor in 1782. Arther Schaaf purchased the house from the Governor. Louis Neth became owner after Mr. Schaaf. About 1847, Chancellor Theodoric Bland lived there, but was not the owner of it. This garden, perhaps, more than any other spot, indicated the delightful life of Annapolis a century ago. The spring house, the expanse of trees and shrubbery, the octagonal two-story summer house, that represented "My lady's bower," the artificial brook, fed by two springs of water, that went rippling along to the bath house that refreshed in the sultry days, and gave delight to the occupants, form a picture tradition loves to dwell upon to this day.

THE IGLEHART HOUSE.

The dwelling, now occupied by Mrs. William T. Iglehart, was owned by Thomas Jennings, barrister, who also lived there. He it was who built the house on East st., now owned by ex-Mayor Thomas E. Martin, for his daughter Mrs. James Brice. Apropos of this daughter, she was noted for entertaining her guests with a famous kind of cake, called Naples biscuit, the recipe for which has come down to this generation. Mr. William T. Iglehart purchased the Jennings' house, from John T. Barber's estate about 1870, removed a wing of the house, and improved its appearance, but did not alter the architecture of the main building.

AUNT LUCY SMITH'S HOUSE.

The old house on the northeast side of Prince George street, adjoining the Protestant Episcopal Chapel, is an interrogation to every passer by. Its exact date is lost in the misty clouds of age, but its appearance and ancient architecture mark it as one of the oldest houses in venerable Annapolis. Part of its history has been preserved. Many years ago there lived in it an ancient colored dame, known as Aunt Lucy Smith. She was a famous cook who served to good account on State occasions the grand dames of the former regime. At other times she supplied from her house or from her basket on the street, the choice morsels that her art divined in the kitchen. John Smith, her husband, kept a livery stable in the rear of the house, a business John's lineal descendents continue to this day in Baltimore.

THE PINKNEY HOUSE.

The Pinkney House, on College Avenue and Bladen street, was built by John Callahan, register of the Land office. It is one of the oldest houses of our city. It is now owned by Mrs. Mary Pinkney, a relative of the celebrated William Pinkney.

OTHER ANCIENT HOUSES.

The property now owned by Charles S. Welch, Esq., on Hanover street, was built in 1763, and was at one time the residence of Anthony Stewart, the owner of the famous brig Peggy Stewart.

The main residence of Mrs. Alex. Randall, situated in the five-sided lot, opposite the State House, is one the most ancient buildings of the city. It is known positively to have been in existence in 1752, and very probably in 1737. In this house Reverdy Johnson was born.

The house on the north-west of Market Space and Randall street, is an ancient building erected by John Randall, grandfather of J. Wirt Randall.

The house occupied by Ex-Mayor Thos. E. Martin, on East street, near Prince George's is also one of the landmarks af our early history. It was erected by Mr. Edmund Jennings for his son-in-law, one of the Brices.

The house, ocsupied by Mrs. Eliza Bonsall, No. 55 Duke of Gloucester street, is one of the oldest in the city. In this house Jehu Chandler, the founder of the *Maryland Republican*, lived and died.

The three houses at the lower end of Duke of Gloucester street, now owned by John R. Magruder, Lieut. Albert Ross, and Philip R. Voorhees and sister, were built by John Ridout, great grandfather of Dr. William G. Ridout. He also built the residence of Dr. William G. Ridout. The first three were built respectively for Mr. Ridout's children: Horace and Samuel Ridout and Mrs. Gibson. This John Ridout was the first of the Ridouts in the country.

Mrs. Nicholas Carroll was Miss Ann Jennings, daughter of Mr. Thos. Jennings, the great lawyer. They lived in the house now used as the Annapolis Public School Building. This house was altered during the ownership of Frank H. Stockett and also since it has been a public school building.

"THE LIBERTY TREE."

The earliest tradition, handed down to us of the imperial poplar that adorns the College Campus, is that it served as the canopy under which the colonists and Indians made a treaty of peace. As history records only one document of this kind signed here—this treaty must have been the one agreed between the colonists and the sturdy Susquehannocks in 1652.

The next public use of it we find in Eddis' Letters was when the inhabitants assembled under it to determine whether, or not, persons who had not joined the association of patriots should be driven out of the colony.

In 1825, Gen. LaFayette was entertained under it, and after that there are frequent mentions in the Maryland Gazette of Fourth of July celebrations taking place under its ample shade.

About 1840, several youths were playing under this tree with that very dangerous, but frequent adjunct of juvenile sports—gunpowder. They had about two pounds of it. They placed it in the hollow of the tree where it was ignited and exploded, setting fire to the grand old tree. The citizens of Annapolis repaired in force for its rescue. the firemen bringing out the city engine and deluging the tree with water. The boys' escapade was, no doubt, greatly denounced; but the juveniles had done better than their denunciators thought or the juveniles intended. The tree had fallen into a state of decay that threatened its life. The next year it put forth its branches with its youth renewed. The explosion had destroyed the worms that were gnawing away its vitals!

How long this monarch of a primeval forest has existed, none can tell. An octogenarian tells me he remembers it in 1812—and it seemed as large then as now. If, in 1652, it was of such imposing growth that it was selected as the scene of so important an event as the making of a treaty of peace by the Puritans with their savage foes, may we not infer it lived before Columbus saw America? On the 30th of July, 1886, it was, two feet from the ground, twenty-nine feet, four inches in circumference, and stood about 150 feet high. One third of the trunk is gone, and is now boarded up. The body of the tree is a mere shell—a marvel how its life can be maintained and thousands of tulips bloom on its branches in their season.

Its identity with Eddis' Liberty Tree is preserved to us alone by tradition, but its use and size corroborate the truth of oral testimony.

A NOTABLE BOWL.

FIRST USED AT A COLLATION GIVEN BY LLOYD DULANY.

The famous bowl that for a century graced the counter of the Old City Hotel in this city on festive occasions, such as the Fourth of July, New Year's, and Christmas, around which at the social board have gathered the sages and heroes of the Revolution and the great lights of our day, still exists. It has been in the possession of its present owner, Edward Walton, about ten years, and is sacredly guarded as a link in that great chain that connects the present with the heroic past. The bowl, which is 16 inches in diameter, 4 inches deep, and 7 inches wide at the bottom, has an interesting history. It is stated that it was first used at a collation given by Lloyd Dulany, at his private residence, now the City Hotel, a few evenings after the burning of the brig Peggy Stewart, and that among his guests was

Charles Carroll, of Carrollton. Mr. Dulany explained to his company how he became possessor of this, then much admired, bowl. He said it had been sent to him by a friend in England and had arrived in the Peggy Stewart. He also stated at the time that the captain had assured him that in no way was it a part of her cargo, that it was not on her manifest; that he had it placed in his cabin along with his private property, and that, after he had fired his brig, he recollected that he had promised to deliver the bowl in person. To this statement Mr. Carroll is represented as having smillingly replied: "We accept your explanation, provided the bowl is used to draw always this same kind of tea."

Many thousands of Marylanders and numerous statesmen of America have drank out of it.

CHAPTER LXI.

ELECTIONS IN ANNAPOLIS DURING THE CIVIL WAR.

The right of elective franchise was capricious in Annapolis during the war, and depended entirely upon the orders issued by the general of the military department of Maryland. These new qualifications for voters were formulated in test oaths whose chief objuration was that the elector had no sympathy for the South or secession. When these failed to prevent the obnoxious elector from voting, questions, yet more effectual in searching the conscience of the voter, were put until the desired disenfranchisement was accomplished. One spectacle was amusing, if it had not been disreputable. Somebody inspired the soldiers at the Naval Academy with the idea that they had a right to vote and, on being placed on their *voir dire*, two hundred enlisted soldiers of the Federal government, non-residents of the State, swore that they had come into the State of Maryland thirteen months previous with the intention of making this their residence! On this the judges of election, in the city of Annapolis, received their votes.

[1863.] The election in November, developed an anomalous state of things. The Constitution and Laws of Maryland prescribed certain qualifications for voters; the General Commanding the Department of Maryland by his pronunciamento demanded another test for the right of franchise—an oath unknown to the laws of the State. A number of citizens of Annapolis refused to qualify under this new regulation. The *Gazette* tersely says:

"During the past week* our city has been thrown into considerable excitement in consequence of the arrest of a number of persons, citizens of this city. Captain Keffer, Provost Marshal of this district, who obeys orders to the letter, addressed the following letter to Col. Waite after the election:

" '*Col. C. A. Waite, 1st Infantry, U. S. A.,*

Commanding at Annapolis:

" 'COLONEL:—I have the honor to submit to you the following names of persons, who, upon their votes being challenged on the ground of

* Issue of November 26, 1863.

Disloyalty, on the day of the election at Annapolis, refused to take the oath of allegiance, and consequently left the polls, being denied the right of voting:

"'Geo. M. Duvall, Jos. H. Nicholson, Oliver Miller, D. Claude Handy, Robt. W. Tate, James E. Tate, Wm. Tell Claude, candidate on the Secession† Ticket for the House of Delegates, Thomas G. Pratt, Thomas Franklin, James Revell, candidate on the Secession Ticket for State's Attorney ; Martin Revell, Nicholas H. Green, candidate on the Secession Ticket for Clerk of the Circuit Court ; and Edward Boyle.

"'Many of these men are members of the Bar, and express their determination on Monday, next, or as soon as possible thereafter, to have the Judges of Election indicted before the Grand Jury of Anne Arundel county, for refusing to receive their votes in accordance with the election laws of the State Maryland.

"'I would most respectfully ask what course I shall pursue in the event of the Judges of the Election being arrested.

I am Colonel, with great respect,

Your obedient servant,

'FRANCIS I. KEFFER.

Capt. 71st, P. V., Provost Marshal.''

A copy of Col. Waite's answer is not extant : but the text may be inferred by the sequence. All of the gentlemen, who refused to take the oath, were arrested and required to report to Baltimore to Major-Gen. Schenck, where, after some days' delay, they were all paroled, save Gov. Pratt and Col. Nicholson, to give no aid and no comfort to the Southern Confederacy. They were then allowed to return home. Their paroles continue to this day. Gov. Pratt and Col. Nicholson got as far south as Fortress Munroe, when the latter took the oath required of him, and returned home. Gov. Pratt refused to take any oath whatever, and was finally released by the Government.

———•◆•———

CHAPTER LXII.

CHRONICLES OF ANNAPOLIS FROM 1863 TO 1887.

[1863.] Dr. Dennis Claude died December 9th, at an advanced age. He had filled many honorable positions, amongst them State Treasurer and Comptroller.

Roger Bellis, of Annapolis, lost a leg at Gettysburg and was afterward made a Second Lieutenant in the Invalid Corps.

December 22, a fire broke out at the house of Smith Price. The military effectively aided the citizens in extinguishing the fire. The *Gazette* called on the Legislature to aid the city to secure a fire en-

† Democratic.

gine. Twenty years later under the administration of Dr. Abram Claude, Mayor, this engine was obtained by the city—the ladies having contributed by a fair $600 to the engine.

Under the Constitution adopted in 1864, a prominent citizen of Annapolis, Hon. Alex. Randall, was elected Attorney General. He was a son of John Randall, who, for many years, had been collector of the port, and who occupied a prominent position in the city. Alexander Randall early showed his ability, taking at graduation at St. John's College, the first honor of his class. He was in early life sent to represent his district in Congress. He died in 1881. After his decease his family beautifully completed the interior of St. Anne's Mission Chapel as a memorial.

The *Gazette* failed this year to obtain the State printing contract. This loss of party printing, conceded in part to the home paper, was borne with an equanimity of mind that betokened a lofty spirit. He says January 14:

"OUR PAPER.—Our readers will excuse the want of the usual variety in today's issue. The length of the advertisement in relation to the mail contracts excludes much Legislative and other news we would be glad to publish if we had time to prepare it. But being obliged to be mostly our own type-setter and pressman (as well as editor) we must ask indulgence for a week or two. We think it pertinent to remark here that the fears or hopes of those persons who think the *Gazette* will be suspended in consequence of not obtaining any of the Legislative work are groundless. Our first object, when consenting to take the proprietorship of the *Gazette* was that the Union party in this city, and in the congressional district should have a paper devoted to the holy cause of preserving this great and free nation from the terrible results that would follow upon its dissolution. Our mind has undergone no change and the *Gazette* will continue to be published, if we are blessed with health, at least, so long as this unnatural war last, even should circumstances compel us to beg or borrow a couple of blankets and made our bed with the types and our daily food be bread and potatoes."

[1864.] Jan. 21, Prof. Wm. H. Thompson, A. M., professor of the Preparatory Department of St. John's College advertised that "studies, as prescribed by the prospectus of the college will be resumed at the City Hall, (now Worthington & Co's., Drug Store,) on the first day of February, and continue there until the Government may deem it proper to vacate the College. * * * No student admitted who has not been vaccinated. By order of the Board of Visitors and Governors."

The small-pox had prevailed at Annapolis for some time past but was now abating.

The *Gazette* gives January 28, this tid-bit of local "war news:"— "SENT SOUTH.—Mrs. Davidson, who was some time since captured while crossing the Potomac from Virginia to Maryland, and who has since been confined in the Old Capitol at Washington, was on Friday last sent to the commanding officer at Fortress Munroe to be returned South. Mrs. S. is the wife of Lieut. Hunter Davidson, formerly of the U. S. Navy, but who deserted the Old Flag and joined the Traitors soon after the rebellion shew its strength."

During the early part of February three Russian vessels arrived at Annapolis. During their stay a Russian sailor Demidorf was killed by an Annapolitan. Demidorf was buried in the National Cemetery near Annapolis.

Sunday, February 14th, about half-past four in the afternoon a destructive fire visited Annapolis. A large three-story building, foot of Main street, called Noah's Ark caught on fire. A violent wind was blowing. The inside was completely ruined; two frame houses adjoining, belonging to Mr. John Slemaker were wrecked, and considerable damage done to the store and brick-dwelling of Mr. Nicholas Killman. In removing the goods and chattels of the Killman residence, three flags of the Southern Confederacy were brought to light. This highly incensed the soldiers who were untiringly working to put out the fire. Noah's Ark was reduced one-story, and the walls rebuilt upon.

A company of negro soldiers, on their way to Baltimore, were obliged to put into Annapolis on account of the ice during the latter part of February. They encamped at St. John's College. They paraded the streets of Annapolis, and it aroused the military spirit amongst the colored people, who flocked to the camp and enlisted. One hundred and twenty went from Annapolis, about twenty of whom were rejected as disqualified. The *Gazette* says it learned that between two and three hundred slaves had left their masters with the determination to enlist. The *Gazette* approved their conduct.

During the last week in March, Col. Carros A. Waite of the U. S. Infantry, was relieved of the military command of Annapolis, and Col. A. R. Root appointed in his stead. Capt. Keffer, Provost Marshal, was also relieved, and Capt. Thomas Watkins, of Company B., of the Purnell Legion, was put in his place. Capt. Watkins' company performed the duties of Provost Guard.

The local election in Annapolis in April, developed a new party cry. The tickets were Union and Anti-Huckster. The Union ticket received a support of 168, and the Anti-Huckster 97. The excitement was small, the vote light. Solomon Philips was elected Mayor.

The *Mayland Republican* passed a high enlogy, at the retirement of Hon. Geo. Wells from the Presidency of the Annapolis and Elk Ridge Railroad, on his management of it, which had elevated the Road from a very low estate to one of great prosperity and usefulness. In 1863 the State received from the road $14,286.72, being nearly 5 per cent. on the State's investment in the road. Joshua Brown, Esq., succeeded Mr. Wells.

April 12, Gen. Grant and several of his staff were in Annapolis.

Anne Arundel by an overwhelming vote elected Eli J. Henkle, Oliver Miller, Sprigg Harwood, and A. S. Bond, democrats, as delegates to the State Convention which had been called by the people. The Convention met April 27. Its chief acts were the proposed emancipation of slaves without pay and the enactment of qualifications for voters by which a large part of the white male citizens of the State were disfranchised. The constitution, with the aid of the Maryland soldiers' votes in their camps in the field, was adopted by 400 votes.

Col. Thomas J. Wilson, late editor of the *Gazette*, was sent to Annapolis in May, as Paymaster U. S. Army.

In June subscription books were "to be seen" for the Annapolis waterworks.

The barbers determined this month and thereafter to work no more on Sunday.

In July, 1864, General Early of the Confederate Army, made an invasion of Maryland. The alarm extended to Annapolis, and the military authorities began to fortify the city. The long line of redoubts, extending parallel with the Annapolis and Bay Ridge Railroad from the Annapolis, Washington and Baltimore railroad to the public road, was thrown up to meet the expected advance of the Confederates. To build the works citizens were impressed by the provost-guard and marched in double files daily to the earth works. This duty was obnoxious to many who were strongly southern in their sentiments, and who did not relish the idea, of fighting against people whom they thought were in the right. Nor was the impressment of Southern sympathizers altogether approved of by the Union side, one of them saying afterward if the fight had come off, he "would have had to keep one eye on the Southern sympathizers in his ranks and one eye on the Confederates." On this occasion the only bitterness of spirit of the war, outside of newspaper utterances and political communications, was exhibited. Some citizens were found so despicable as to buckle on a sword, and, at the head of squads of military, to search out southern sympathizers hidden in their homes in the town, to drag them out to the earthworks. Some of these rancorous spirits were among the first to turn (democrats?) when that party came into power in 1867.

During the three days of alarm a few of the fugitives were able to hide, one finding refuge in the belfry of the First Charge Methodist Episcopal Church, where he safely remained until the impressment was over.

The various drafts for conscripts were sources of deep trouble to the city. Mr. Frank H. Stockett was the draft officer and Dr. William Brewer the medical examiner. Men, conscripted to fight in a cause they disapproved of, made miserable men and women. It was surprising to find how many people developed hidden ailments. Unsuspected sources of pain and impediment were suddenly created by the drawing of the unlucky number. One man developed a lameness that entirely disappeared on the cessation of hostilities. Those citizens who had money, liberally subscribed for the unfortunates to purchase substitutes.

A border city, Annapolis sent representatives to both armies. These met in deadly array against each other at Front Royal and Winchester, Virginia, and at Gettysburg, Pa.,—the Annapolis Confederates being in the celebrated charge up Culp's Hill.

In the latter part of July Annapolis was highly excited over an alleged haunted house. Violent knocks and noises drove a family that had rented the house from the premises and coal, bricks, and clubs flew through the air to the great fear of the superstitious. The arrest of one colored man ended the ghost theory manifestations. The impression prevailed that the negro who had heretofore occupied the house, free of rent, had ingeniously, with the assistance of friends, labored to create the impression that the house was haunted that he might return to his old lodgings without charge for rent in arrears.

Annapolis was on the alert, through a committee, to see that it was not called upon to furnish more than its quota in the proposed drafts of the government for soldiers.

On the 18th of August, Henry Frazier, Jr., of Co. B. Punell Legion, was killed in a fight on the Weldon Railroad. Capt. T. H. Watkins was wounded in the head at the same time.

[1865.] The war being over, those who went from Annapolis, and who survived, returned to their former homes. The Confederates and Federal veterans fraternized like brave men and some of the firmest friendships in the city have been cemented between those who wear the palms of victory and those who maintained the "Lost Cause."

Such was the friendly feeling existing between the heroes of the two armies and such the lofty impulses of a genuine patriotism that, on May 30, 1883, Meade Post of the Grand Army of the Republic, invited S. Thos. McCullough, a lieutenant of the Confederate Army, to deliver an oration at a joint decoration of the graves of the Federal and Confederate soldiers at Annapolis. The invitation was accepted in the same generous spirit in which it was tendered, and Federal and Confederate marched together to the silent city of the dead and laid their immortelles on the graves of those who had died for their convictions on both sides of the great conflict.

A new picture presented itself at Annapolis. By September 21st, Annapolis and its surroundings had ceased to be a military department and dropped down to the humble pedestal of *Post*. The military had dwindled to four companies, one at Annapolis and three at Camp Parole. "The Naval Academy," said the *Gazette*, "is rapidly assuming its former beauty, and the midshipmen in our streels have a look of the olden time.

"Perhaps, never within the remembrance of the oldest inhabitants, has Annapolis exhbited so much of the spirit of improvement. Some forty houses are being erected and several undergoing useful and handsome improvement. The dealers in building material are as busy as bees. * * * * Many applications are made for dwellings, but there are none vacant to supply the demand."

Annapolis caught the base ball fever prevalent in the country and inaugurated the Annapolis Base Ball club with Edward C. Gantt, as President; Dr. D. C. Handy, Vice-President: Secretary, P. S. Schwrar; Treasurer, John II. Thomas; Directors—John C. Regan, John T. Wright, John S. Maley.

The Naval Academy resumed operations at Annapolis Monday October 1, under the Superintendency of Rear Admirel D. D. Porter.

The election in Anne Arundel this year resulted in the selection of the democratic ticket. The vote on sheriff shew the strength of the two parties. Rignal D. Woodward, Union, received 484, votes ; Wm. Bryan, democrat, 654.

At a special election December 28, George Wells was elected Senator from Anne Arundel county by the following vote: Wells, Union, 436, James Deale, of James, D., 391.

In January the town clock was placed in St. Anne's and was considered an acquisition to the city.

January 22, Henry Barnard, L. L. D., was installed as President of St. John's in the hall of the House of Delegates.

The Wesley Chapel congregation purchased in Feburary the lot on East street, extending to Cornhill, of Geo. M. Taylor, for $5000, for a parsonage. This is Gallilean Hall now owned by the colored people.

The Enterprise Building Association was organized in March 1st, the first Building Association in Annapolis. W. O. Bigelow was President. From this company grew the Horn Point settlement. The company erected the Bridge over the Spa and to it is due the inception of this creditable annex to Annapolis.

In the winter of this year Annapolis was the scene of numerous petty burglaries and arsons. Among the attempts to do damage to property was one to blow up the Steamer Ferry Boat, Capt. Stephen Chase, on Febuary 7, by firing up the steamer after it had concluded her trips for the day.

On the 12th. of January, George Colton was elected President of the Maryland Hotel Company with R. Swann, W. H. Tuck, Robt. Fowler, and I. M. Denson as directors.

On the 16th of January the following were elected officers of the First National Bank of Annapolis. President—Wm. H. Tuck : Directors—Robt. Fowler, James Andrews, J. Wesley White, and Johns Hopkins.

[1869.] On Thursday March 25, Hon. A. E. Borie, Secretary of the Navy, Vice Admiral D. D. Porter, and a number of ladies from Washington, arrived at Annapolis in a special train to visit the Naval Academy. They were met at the depot in carriages and driven to the Academy. The Secretary was received with the usual honors. The officers, midshipmen, and marines were drawn up in full dress, and were reviewed by the Secretary and Admiral Porter. The party was much pleased with its visit, and returned to Washington at a late hour in the evening. The Secretary was greatly gratified at the situation and the discipline of the Academy.

At the municipal election on Monday April 5, the vote was :

FOR MAYOR.

W. O. Bigelow, Rep. 109.   Augustus Gassaway, D. 335.

FOR RECORDER.

Nicholas Brewer, R. 116.   S. T. McCullough, D. 326.

FOR ALDERMEN.

J. Guest King, R. 123.	John H. Thomas. D. 317.
Grafton Munroe, R. 114.	John Hammond, D. 333.
Thos. K. Jones, R. 111.	John T. Hyde, D. 325.
C. A. Sullivan, R. 104.	Dr. Geo. Wells, D. 339.
M. R. Casler, R. 108.	W. B. Gardner, D. 333.

The Gazette, republican, explained the one-sidedness of the election thus :

"The Republicans fought this fight squarely upon the 15th Amendment to the Constitution. It was talked of before the election to bring out a citizens' ticket, but some of the Republicans being opposed to any compromise with the democrats, a straight-out Republican ticket was nominated, and the above was the result. It will be seen that the ticket did well, as a large number, who always voted our ticket, having no hope of success, did not go to the polls. This is the first election in this city, since the adoption of the amendment. We say to the Republicans of this city, to continue in the good work. and 'fight it out on that line, if it takes a life time,' and we will surely triumph."

[1870.] St. John's College, in this year, reached its acme of prosperity under the presidency of James C. Welling. On Wednesday, January 19. Dr. Welling made this report to the Legislature :

"He said that the whole number of students during the scholastic year ending on the 28th of July last, was 225, the average attendance being about 200, the present number being 181. The whole number of students nominated by the School Commissioners of the several counties for admission into the college or its preparatory department without any charge for tuition or text books, is 170. The average attendance on this basis during the last and the present year has exceeded 100. The college has offered during this period to receive the full quota of 150, and has made preparations to do so, but it sometimes happens that the pupils selected by the county boards to enjoy these free scholarships fail to enter the college with punctuality. The college has, in fact, been prepared to receive 160 additional pupils, without charge for tuition or text books, being ten in excess of the number required by the existing statutes, which enjoin upon institutions receiving State aid to provide gratuitious instruction at the rate of one student for every $100 of the State donation. Every county in the State has been represented on this basis. The accomodations of the college have been strained to their utmost capacity by the number of students seeking admission. Should the number be materially increased, it would be necessary to procure additional accommodations in the city of Annapolis, until a new college edifice could be erected. The want of such a building is already sensibly felt. It may not be generally known that the present real estate of the college (representing a money value of at least $250.000,) is purely the result of private munificence. The public bounty of the State now generously co-operates with this private munificence by granting to the college, for a limited term, an annual donation of $15,000, being in fact a sum equal to the annual interest on the investments made by private munificence for the founding of the college at the Capital of Maryland. If the endowment of the college were only placed on a *permanent* basis, its present prosperity would be but a pledge of its higher usefulness in the future.

"The whole number of teachers now comprised in the Faculty is thirteen, but the main burden of instruction is borne by nine professors and tutors, who alone receive a salary for their services. In the college classes now comprising sixty-one students, instruction is given in the branches of learning taught in American colleges. and the standard of attainment has been raised to the highest point at which it is fixed by any similar institution in the country. The attention of the General Assembly is particularly invited to the course of study pursued in the several classes of the college, as it is believed to be unusually broad and practical. as well as thorough in the methods employed to secure proficiency in scholarship. No degree of any kind is conferred except on the evidence of adequate attainments.

"The Preparatory Department of the College corresponds, in the grade and quality of its studies, to a High School. During the last few years this department has engrossed the larger share of the Faculty's attention, but as it is the wish and purpose of the Board of

Visitors and Governors to build up a College in the fullest sense of the term, and one that shall be worthy the State, it is obvious that the proportions of the Preparatory Department must hereafter be reduced, that the College proper may be developed on the liberal and comprehensive plan designed by its founders. It should be the paramount aim of the College to impart that higher education which cannot be imparted by the State, and to do this on terms which shall not make that higher education the exclusive property of the rich. And it is in this view that the College has placed itself in sympathy with the cause of public education in Maryland.

"We should not, perhaps, omit to mention that military tactics are taught to all students who desire instruction under this head, and that three military companies have been formed in connection with the College."

Dr. Welling ends by saying:

"With the expression of gratitude due as well to the Legislature as to the people of Maryland for the generous patronage awarded to the College (and the fruits of which are seen in its present unwonted prosperity), I beg leave, on behalf of the Board of Visitors and Governors and in the name of the Faculty, most cordially to invite the members of the General Assembly to visit the College, and to inspect the method used for the maintenance of order and the promotion of diligence in regularity and study." The report was referred to the Committee on Education.

The political corruptions following the Civil War reflected upon the Naval Academy. The shamelessness of the flaunting evils is evinced in this advertisement that appeared in a New York daily :

"UNITED STATES NAVAL ACADEMY.—A cadet vacancy to be filled before June. Parties of means address Congressman. Address, Box No.— office."

The *Gazette* reproduced the advertisment in its news columns.

March 10, Robert F. Bonsall, in the 63rd year of his age died. He was for many years printer to the Court of Appeals, and was a man of high principle.

The Legislature of this year passed the Act to authorize the Mutual Building Association of Annapolis to build a bridge over Spa creek to connect at Annapolis and Horn Point.

The Court House of Annapolis has been made the scene of many important trials by the removal of cases from other jurisdictions. Amongst them the Wharton trial in 1872, the Hoffman trial for the Harnden Express robbery in 1870, Nicholson and Hollahan for murder in 1873, and Hance, for murder in 1885.

During the trial of Nicholson and Hollahan, whilst State's Attorney Revell was addressing the jury for the State, Hollohan made an attack upon Assistant Marshal Frey. The marshal was sitting within the rail with his back to the prisoner's dock, and his bald crown within reach of Hollohan, who rose up suddenly and dealt him a terrible blow upon the head with an improvised slung-shot made of a stocking and a piece of coal, nails, and an iron staple. The marshal was severely wounded, Nicholson jumped up on the rail as if to dash out of the Court House, whilst Hollohan was seized in the throat by J. Randolph Walton and Detective Shaffer, a friend of Marshal Frey, clubbed his revolver and beat Hollohan over the head. People fled from the Court House in the excitement, and a general uproar ensued.

Judge Hayden, the only one that seemed to understand that Hollohan's life was being choked out of him, in stentorian tones cried out, "Let that man go!" Mr. Walton, who had some traces left of the Samsonian strength of his youth, took his hand from the throat of the well-nigh dead brute, who defiantly demanded that they kill him. The prisoners were then ironed, and the trial proceeded. When he was sentenced, Chief Judge Miller ordered the irons off the prisoners, saying, that "No man should be sentenced in this Court in chains."

[1883.] On the morning of Monday, October 18, 1883, a disastrous fire occurred in Annapolis. It began from some unknown cause, about 2 A. M., in a store on Market Space, occupied by Mr. Lewis S. Clayton, and destroyed three large brick houses on Market Space, injured another, and partially or wholly destroyed five or six others on Main street. Over Mr. Clayton's store was the residence of Mr. James Legg. When the fire was discovered, Mr. Legg's family hurried to the street. His son, Mr. Charles Legg, when the fire was threatening to overwhelm him, sought the room of his aged aunt, Miss Eleanor Watkins, to save her from the flames. Their charred bones, the next day, mutely told the heroic and futile sacrifice. The citizens of Annapolis erected a monument to Mr. Legg in the City Cemetery. He was forty-four years old when he died.

[1886.] After the Revolution the trade of Annapolis rapidly declined. The commerce which it had enjoyed, took its flight to Baltimore where all the traffic of the State centered, and fortunes were no longer made in the mercantile trade at Annapolis. What that trade once was is illustrated in the history of one of its merchants, Absalom Ridgely, son of Henry Ridgely. Mr. Ridgely was born in 1742, and began his mercantile ventures in the little house on Flat-Iron corner, at the inter-section of Fleet and Cornhill streets. His capital at marriage was $150. When he died, at the ripe age of 76, he was able to give each of his eight children, eight thousand dollars a piece in cash, besides leaving real property to be divided amongst them, Nor was this the chief heritage, he bequeathed them—he left them that which is greater than riches—a good name. His epitaph so sums up the whole matter.—"He calmly resigned his soul to Him who gave it, after having faithfully discharged his duties as a man and as a christian." His sons rose up to do him honor. John, David, Richard, Charles and Nicholas. Richard was a merchant of Annapolis; David was State Librarian and the author of the Annals of Annapolis; and John was a surgeon in the United States Army, who, after his resignation of that position, was a prominent physician in civil life.

Annapolis, however, retained some traces of its former important business up to the beginning of the war between the States. The planters of Anne Arundel came regularly to the city, at the proper seasons, and laid in supplies for their slaves and families. These bills of five and six hundred dollars each, were covered by notes that were promptly met at maturity. With the abolition of slavery, this trade was taken away from the merchants, and the mercantile trade has little outside resources. The Naval Academy, in some measure, supplies the benefits of a foreign trade. The oyster-packing establishments, of which there are about ten, bring considerable money into the city, which, with the home trade in oysters, redeems the mercantile business from annihilation.

Once since the period of the ancient commercial prosperity of Annapolis, its mercantile trade received a decisive impulse. The Civil War having made Annapolis a military rendezvous, thousands of soldiers were always quartered in and about the city and the private supplies bought by them gave any merchant who would improve it. opportunity to secure a competence. Some of them took advantage of the occasion and markedly bettered their fortunes.

Monday, December 27, the Anne Arundel Historical Society celebrated its first anniversary. Gen. Bradley T. Johnson read a paper on ''The Battle of the Severn,'' fought opposite Annapolis, March 25th, 1655. The society requested the paper for publication. Officers of the Society for the ensuing year were elected :—President—Nicholas Brewer ; Vice-President—Frank B. Mayer ; Secretary—J. Harwood Iglehart ; Treasurer—J. Schaaf Stockett. Board of Directors—Rev. Robert H. Williams and Daniel R. Randall.

[1887.] The Amateur Dramatic Association of the Naval Academy gave its first entertainment on Saturday, January 15. Gov. Lloyd and wife were among the guests. The play was entitled :—''The Shakespeare Water Cure.'' The cast was :—Ophelia, Mrs. Lieut. Bartlett ; Portia, Mrs. Lieut. J. T. Smith ; Lady Macbeth, Miss Harrington : Juliet, Miss Sampson ; Macbeth, Ensign Knapp ; Romeo, Ensign Gibbons : Othello, Ensign Lloyd ; Hamlet, Lieut. Mitchell : Shylock, Lieut. Mahan.

Louis H. Rehn, Collector and Treasurer of Annapolis, made his annual report Monday night, February 14, to the Corportion for the year ending December 31, 1886. The report showed the finances of the city to be in a most healthful condition. The revenue of the city for the year was $26,201.49 ; the disbursements, $23,371.42. Balance in treasury, $1,829.77. Debts due by the city, $14,213.89, bonded debts, $7,750, total debt, $26,801.18. Debts due the city, $17,571.50. Bonds, stock, &c., credited to the sinking fund, $8,562.90. The debts due the city and the credits to the sinking fund will almost pay the floating and bonded debt of the city. The city has personal and real property the value of $57,665.00. The city's business is now carried on a cash basis—a bill passed one night by the Board will be paid the next day.

The local sensation at Annapolis, Wednesday, March 9th, was the running of the first regular trains on the Annapolis and Baltimore Short Line railroad. One train left here at 6.40 A. M., with twenty-five passengers for Baltimore. It reached Baltimore at 8 A. M. It returned here at 9.30, A. M., leaving Baltimore at 8.20, A. M. The train was under the care of Conductor George Bender, with James Hull, engineer, and Christopher Carl, fireman. The second train left here at at noon under the conductorship of E. T. Divens, with John McCardy, engineer, J. T. Newell, brakeman. G. W. Spalding, baggage-master and express messenger, P. Dowlin, fireman. It carried thirty-one passengers to Baltimore. There was a number of citizens out to give the new venture a good send-off. The third train left Annapolis at 4.20, P. M.

March 12, Jacob V. Dolman, captain of the oyster schooner, Oliver M. Ruark, was brought into Annapolis on the charge of killing William Stanley, one of his crew, in the Chesapeake, off Hackett's Point. Bartley and Stanley, two of the crew, were afraid the boat would turn over and lowered the sail two or three times against the captain's order. On the last time, the Captain shot and killed Stanley.

March 28, the venerable poplar on St. John College Campus was accidently set on fire by some boys. Another set of youths, after considerable effort, extinguished the flames.

Tuesday, April 4. Dr. George Wells, of Annapolis, was elected by a unanimous vote of the County Commissioners, treasurer of Anne Arundel county.

Lieut. John W. Danenhower, one of the survivors of the Jeannette Expedition to the Polar regions, committed suicide at the Naval Academy, Wednesday, April 20th, by shooting himself in the temple. He was laboring under a melancholy, produced from the grounding of the U. S. Ship Constellation in the Cheasapeake whilst he was in command.

April 25. Wm. H. F. Wilson, a prominent citizen of Annapolis, died in his 76th year.

------◆------

CHAPTER LXIII.

A DISASTROUS ACCIDENT.

1866.

On Monday afternoon, July 9th, 1866, four Fathers and three students, Fathers Louis Classeans, James Bradley, John Gerdemann, and Timothy Enright, and students John Kenny, John B. Runge and ——— Guhl, left the Redemptorist College in this city on a sailing expedition.

In a secluded place, about five miles from Annapolis, two or three concluded to take a bath, when student John Kenny, who was convalescing from a recent illness was taken sick and came near drowning, but was rescued by Mr. Guhl. Whilst the latter was rescuing Mr. Kenny, Father Gerdemann, attempting to help them, was seen to disappear. This occurred between five and six in the afternoon. Although called for, and searched for, Father Gerdemann was never seen again alive.

The rain now began to pour in incessant showers, and the wind to blow with appalling violence. The faithful party remained until ten o'clock endeavoring to secure the body of the dead priest, but all in vain. The storm of rain and wind still continued, when the sorrowful company set out upon their return home. When they had gotten some distance from the shore, an effort was made to put up the sail. Too many were on one side, and, a sudden flaw striking the sail; the boat was capsized. As the boat went over, Father Enright jumped off into the water, and getting on the bottom of the boat was the only one who was not caught under the vessel.

21

Mr. Kenny was the first to appear, but sank immediately saying: "Jesus, Mary, Joseph, assist me!" Mr. Runge next appeared, ejaculating—"Oh, my God, have mercy on me."

Father Enright helped Father Classeans from under the boat and heard his confession. In the meanwhile Father Bradley had come from under the boat and was clinging to the rudder, whilst Mr. Guhl was all this time under the boat living by breathing the air that was between the bottom of the boat and the water.

This state of affairs lasted about fifteen minutes when the boat, upturning, freed Mr. Guhl from his dangerous situation, but this broke the hold of Father Classeans, and he sank, and rose no more. Whilst the boat was righted the survivors endeavored to take in the sail, but, before it was accomplished, the boat was again overturned. The anchor dropping out of the boat and fastening in the bottom produced a reactionary motion from the force of the waves that kept the boat constantly rolling, and what was worse kept the boat from drifting ashore, as it would have done since the wind blew to the land.

The boat was a round bottomed one, and Father Enright and Guhl, on opposite sides, clasped hands and in that manner kept themselves on the boat and steadied it somewhat, Father Bradley still clinging to the rudder. Here these brave and holy men encouraged each other by praying and making confessions of sins, expressing their willingness to die, and yet declaring they would make every effort in their power to save themselves. Mr. Guhl was affected with sleep, and had to be constantly called to be kept awake. When help was offered Father Bradley, he refused it declaring that each had sufficient to do to save himself. Their strength was wasting every moment, and when one hour before daylight, Father Bradley lost his hold by the boat overturning, he was unable to regain it and perished. Father Enright also lost hold and was sinking when rescued by Mr. Guhl, and they once more clasped hands across the boat.

So through that direful night, the terrible hours wore on, and at daylight the two survivors found they were a half mile from shore, and, on trying the depth, found they could touch bottom, a thing, many believe with every reason, they could have done at any time during the accident, since the boat would not likely drift from its first position after the anchor fell from the boat.

On gaining the shore Father Enright and Kenny went to the house of Aunt Charity Brashears who gave them restoratives, and offered to convey them to Annapolis, but being chilled the two preferred to walk, and made their way to Barber's farm on the opposite side of Spa Creek, and made their melancholy signal to their associates in the Redemptorist College. Here their signal was seen, and the survivors were brought to the Institution to tell their sorrowful story. It was 9.30 a. m., when they arrived greatly exhausted, and fears were entertained for their recovery.

Father Classeans was pastor of St. Mary's Church in this city, and Professor of Moral Theology in the College. He was only 38 years old. He came from Holland to America in 1851. Father Gerdemann was from Cumberland, Md., was Professor of Rhetoric, English, and German Literature. He was conductor of the colored Catholic School here, and pastor of the Catholic Church of West River. He was 27 years old. Father Bradley was here recuperating.

He was 37 years old. Mr. Kenny was studying Moral Theology, and would have been ordained the following Easter. Mr. Runge was just finishing his course of Philosophy.

Search was actively and instantly instituted for the recovery of the bodies, which were eventually recovered ; and carried amidst a sorrowing city to the College, St. Mary's bell ringing a dirge as each successive corpse was recovered.

This was the first accident of any kind that had ever occurred to the members of the Society of Redemptorist. This order was founded in Italy, November 9, 1792..

CHAPTER LXIV.

ANNAPOLIS OF THE PRESENT.

In 1870, Annapolis had a population, exclusive of the Naval Academy, whose average is 500 inhabitants, of 5,744 ; in 1880, 6,642.

The city has doubled its population since 1845, the date of the location of the Naval Academy at Annapolis. The pressing want of the city has been the establishment of manufactories. They have never flourished and the fine harbor of the city has been comparatively of little use. In 1885, the Annapolis Glass Works, situated at Horn Point, were finished, and are, at present, in successful operation.

The opening of the summer resort, Bay Ridge, some five years since, attracted attention to Annapolis, and the building of the railroad from Annapolis to the resort, consummated in July, 1886, was the direct result of the inauguration of this popular excursion place.

By the Annapolis and Baltimore Short Line Railroad, between the capital and the metropolis of the State, railroad communication has been shortened one-third in one case, and in the other nearly one-half. This road gives promise of large advantage to Annapolis, in its traveling facilities, and in bringing to the attention of capitalists the magnificent harbor of Annapolis and its almost entire exemption from obstruction from ice in winter. The slow growth of Annapolis has been the constant gibe of the unthinking. The city, however, in late years has shown a spirit of improvement. In 1877, the lots in the rear of Market street to South street were placed on the market. They were sold with great rapidity and in the course of a year, over three hundred houses were built. This was largely due to the liberal spirit of the Workingmen's Building and Loan Association which, proving an exception to most associations of that character, made it possible for many to build homes for themselves who had no means otherwise. In 1879 and 1880, the houses on Prince George street, between Maryland and College Avenues were built, and also the fine residences of Mrs. Commodore Thornton and John II. Thomas, Esq., on Maryland Avenue.

The bridge over the Spa, connecting the village of Horn Point with Annapolis. was built in 1868, and the one over College creek about the same period. In 1887. the citizens of Horn Point resolved to call their village Severn City.

Annapolis has telegraphic and telephonic facilities, gas, and fine water-works, and is noted as an excellent place of residence. Its chief disadvantage is a lack of opportunity to advance the financial interests of its residents.

St. John's College affords unusual educational facilities, and the presence of the Naval Academy, the Court of Appeals of the State, and the Legislative Body induces an acquaintance with public affairs that is at once entertaining, improving, and valuable.

Many of the inhabitants count their progenitors, generation after generation, back to the earliest settlers of Providence. They yet emulate the manly qualities and heroic spirit of their sturdy ancestors, untarnished by their bigotry and austerity.

In December 10, 1872, the Taney Statue, located on the State House hill. was unveiled. The work was done by William Rinehart, a native of Maryland. The presentation was made to the State, from the committee in charge, by S. T. Wallis. The oration, on the occasion in the Senate Chamber, was one of the most brilliant efforts of that golden-tongued orator.

August 16, 1886, the DeKalb Statue was unveiled with imposing Masonic and Military ceremonies. The Statue was the work of Ephraim Keyser, a young Baltimore sculptor, and has met the best anticipations of the public. Mr. Keyser presented the statue to the United States, and Secretary of State, Thomas F. Bayard, received it in an eloquent address. Col. J. Thomas Scharf was orator and reviewed the historic phase of DeKalb's career.

The State Museum, daily growing in importance, owes its conception to a resident of Annapolis, Mr. Frank B. Mayer, who on February 19, 1885, in the Anne Arundel *Advertiser*, suggested its establishment. Col. J. Thomas Scharf, Commissioner of Maryland at New Orleans, and Commissioner of the Land Office of Maryland, acted upon the suggestion, and when he returned from New Orleans, he placed the Maryland exhibits, that belonged to the State, in one of the rooms of the Land Office. To this nucleus an interested and patriotic people are constantly adding woods, minerals, and curiosities.

The Newspapers of Annapolis.

The Maryland *Republican* is now the oldest. It was established in 1809. Jehu Chandler was its first editor, followed by Jeremiah Hughes. He was succeeded in 1842 by Elihu S. Riley and Samuel Davis. Mr. Davis about 1856 sold his share to Absalom Ridgely, who died in 1858, and whose part was purchased by Elihu S. Riley. In 1867. the *Republican* was purchased by George Colton and Elihu S. Riley. Jr. In 1867, the share of the junior partner was purchased by Mr. Colton, who yielded the publicatication about 1878, to his son, Luther F. Colton. After the latter's death, in 1885, the *Republican* was sold to William S. Ridgely and George T. Melvin. In 1886, the new proprietors started a daily afternoon edition.

The *Evening Capital*, published by William M. Abbott, commenced in 1883 as a daily afternoon paper.

The Maryland *Gazette*, established as the Annapolis *Gazette*, some years after the death of the original *Gazette*, is a weekly paper, published by J. Guest King.

The Anne Arundel *Advertiser* is a weekly, now in its 18th volume. and is published by the estate of William T. Iglehart.

The *Record*, a weekly, is printed by Elihu S. Riley. It was established in 1875.

In December, 1882, the question of prohibition of the sale of liquor was submitted to the votors of Anne Arundel county. Annapolis gave 550 of the 650 majority in favor of prohibition. At first some of the liquor dealers proceeded in a surreptitious manner to violate the law. The Court was severe in its sentences upon convicted violators of the law. The city, for eighteen months, became noted for its peace, good order. and sobriety. Then came the invention of the system of incorporated clubs, by which, each member pleading his right to protection from criminating himself, the State was deprived of witnesses of the violations of law. The clubs increased and, according to the testimony of those who spoke, as of knowledge, there was great debauchery in private. In public there were good order and peace ; on the criminal docket of the city there were few cases. In the three years of prohibition not one murder from drink had been committed in the county. But the liquor men were on the alert and persuaded the people that the second evil of clubs was greater than the first, and promised an era of temperance and good order if the liquor saloons were allowed to be opened again. With their arguments of speech and silver, in April, 1886, Annapolis was induced to reverse, by over five hundred majority, the verdict of 1883. The business of the city has not improved as was prophesied would be done under a return to license.

In 1884, the Local Improvement Association of Annapolis was formed, F. B. Mayer, President ; L. G. Gassaway, M. Oliver, and C. E. Munroe, Vice-Presidents ; J. Wirt Randall, Secretary ; and Julian Brewer, Treasurer. In the face of many discouragements, but with final success, the society aroused an interest in public improvement and directly, or indirectly, advanced and effected, such works as the "City Circle," the planting of avenues of trees at St. John's College and marking the graves of the French Revolutionary dead, and the placing of shade trees in our streets, the formation of a continuous drive around our city by obtaining the building of the Back creek bridge, and projecting the shore road to Bay Ridge. It has endeavored to obtain from Congress the making of an avenue to connect the Government Naval Cemetery with the Soldiers' Cemetery and the City, the establishment of a signal station, and a public building for Federal uses ; the adoption of a plan for future streets and avenues, and has suggested numerous other projects incidental to the objects of the association.

Annapolis has been loath to give up its ancient ways. Up to 1854. it had but two watchmen to patrol its streets at night, one of whom remains to tell, that like the beadles of old, he used to cry the hours of the night. There are hundreds who recollect the ringing of the curfew bell of St. Anne's at nine o'clock when well-regulated youths hastily left their plays and scampered off to the parental roof.

The town is not dead. It has only slept. Thirty years ago there ~ as but one house on the north side of Prince George street from College avenue to East street, and from Prince George street to Hanover, on Maryland avenue, there were but three houses. The intervening lots afforded fine and convenient hunting grounds.

The earthquake of the 31st of August, 1886, so disastrous to Charleston, S. C., was experienced in Annapolis and vicinity. The feelings excited were those of surprise rather than of alarm. Chairs rocked and houses trembled, but no damage was done.

In closing the annals of the Ancient City, the review of the labors incident to the work is a pleasant retrospection. Removing the mouldy dust from crumbling records, touching the inner webs of outer woofs, lifting up that which had fallen from its place in the chronicles of a city, have brought the writer so close to the men who made the history of a capital, guided the destinies of a State, and helped to build a nation, that he has seen them act again the drama of their day, heard the intonations of their voice, well-nigh fathomed the secret springs of their thought and action.

In breathing upon these dry bones of fact, the writer has found his chief recompense in seeing that "the breath came into them, and they lived, and stood upon their feet, an exceeding great army.''

APPENDIX.

————:0:————

ABRIDGEMENT OF FATHER ANDREW WHITE'S JOURNAL.*

————(:o:)————

"*A Report of the Colony of Lord Baron of Baltimore, in Maryland, near Virginia, in which the quality, nature, and condition of the country and its many advantages and riches are described.*

"There is a province near the English colony in Virginia, which, in honour of Maria his queen, his majesty the king of England wished to be called Maryland, or the land of Mary.

"This province his majesty, in his munificence, presented to the lord Baron of Baltimore, in the month of June, 1632. This distinguished nobleman immediately resolved to settle a colony, with the particular intention of establishing the religion of the gospel and truth in that and in the neighbouring country, where, as yet, the knowledge of the true God had never existed. He was encouraged in his enterprize by the favourable account of the country left by his worthy father, whose testimony, founded upon actual observation, was worthy of the utmost confidence, and was corroborated by the reports of others who had visited the same region, as well as by the published narrative of captain Smith, who first described it." After alluding to the liberal conditions of settlement proposed by Lord Baltimore, Father White continues:

"The interests of religion constituted one of the first objects of Lord Baltimore, an object worthy indeed of Christians, of angels, of Englishmen; than which, in all her ancient victories, Britian never achieved any thing more honourable.

"Behold those regions waiting for the harvest. They are prepared to receive the fruitful seed of the gospel. Messengers have been sent to procure suitable persons to preach the life-giving doctrine, and regenerate the natives in the sacred waters of baptism. They are those now living in this city. (St. Mary's) who saw ambassadors from the Indian nations to Jamestown in Virginia, sent there for the purpose of effecting these objects. May we not suppose that many thousands were brought into the fold of Christ in so glorious a work.'

After a glowing and minute description of the country, with its trees, fruits, and other productions, its rivers and the various kinds of fish, he proceeds to give the

"NARRATIVE OF THE VOYAGE TO MARYLAND.

"On the 22d of November, being St. Cæcilia's day, under the gentle influence of an eastern wind, we dropped down from the Isle of Wight.

"Having placed our ship under the protection of God, the Blessed Virgin Mother, St. Ignatius, and all the guardian angels of Mary

* Ridgely's Annals of Annapolis, p. 18 to 32.

land, we had progressed but a short distance, when we were obliged
for the want of wind, to cast anchor off the fortress of Yarmouth,
where we were welcomed by a salute. While lying here we were not
without some apprehensions from our sailors, who began to murmur
among themselves, alleging that they expected a messenger from
land with letters : and because none arrived, they seem disposed to
create delays. A kind providence put an end to our fears ; for during the night a strong but favourable wind sprang up, and our pinnace, * which apprehended an attack from a French brig, that kept
within a short distance of her, took advantage of the wind and put to
sea. We, not willing to lose sight of her, followed her with all
speed, and thus frustrated the evil designs of our sailors; this was on the
night of St. Clement's day, 23d of November. On the next morning,
about 10 o'clock, after receiving a second salute from the fort at
Hurst, we were carried beyond the breakers at the extremity of the
Isle of Wight, and narrowly escaped being driven on shore. Taking
advantage of a strong fair wind on that day and the next night, we
left the western point of England, slacking sail, lest running ahead
of the pinnace, she might fall into the hands of the pirates and Turks
who then infested these seas. On the 24th of November, we made
great headway until evening, when a violent storm arose, and our
sloop being diffident of its strength, being only of 40 tons burden,
hove to, and informed us that in case of danger, she would carry
lights at her mast-head. We were in a well built ship † of 400 tons,
as strong as iron and wood could make her, and our captain was one
of great experience. The storm was so violent that we gave him the
choice of returning to England or pursuing the voyage. His in-
trepidity and confidence in the untried powers of his ship, induced
him to choose the latter. But in the middle of the night, in a boiling
sea, we saw our sloop at a short distance from us, showing two lights
at her mast-head. Then, indeed, did we fear for her, and on losing
sight of her we all supposed she had been swallowed up in the stormy
sea. Six weeks elapsed before we again heard from her. But God
had preserved her. Fearing that she could not survive the storm,
she changed her course, and took refuge in the Scilly Isles. She
afterwards sailed in pursuit of us, and we met at the Antilles. On the
27th and 28th, we made but little progress. On Friday 29th, a most
dreadful storm arose, that made the most fearless men tremble for
the result. Among the Catholics, however, it made prayer more
frequent, vows were offered in honour of the B. V. Mother, and her
immaculate conception, of St. Ignatius, the patron Saint of Maryland, St. Michael and all the guardian angels. Each one prayed
earnestly to expiate his sins through the sacrament of penance. For,
having unshipped her rudder, our vessel was tossed about at the
mercy of the winds and waves. At first, I feared that the loss of our
ship and death awaited me, but, after spending some time in prayer
and having declared to the Lord Jesus, and to his Holy Mother, St.
Ignatius, and the protecting Angels of Maryland, that the purpose
of this voyage was to pay honour to the blood of our Redeemer, by
the conversion of barbarians, I arose with a firm confidence that
through the mercy and goodness of God, we should escape the dan-

* The pinnace appears to have been a sloop of forty tons, and was called
"The Dove."
† 'The Ark.'

gers that seemed to threaten our destruction. I had bowed myself down in prayer, during the greatest rage of the tempest, and, let the true God be glorified ! Scarcely had I finished, before the storm was ceasing.

"I felt myself imbued with a new spirit, and overspread with a flood of joy and admiration at the berevolence of God to the people of Maryland, to whom we were sent. Blessed forever be the merciful charities of our dear Redeemer. The remainder of the voyage, which lasted three months, was prosperous; our captain affirmed that he never witnessed a more pleasant and happy one. The period of three months included the time we spent at the islands of the Antilles, but we were in fact only seven weeks and two days at sea.

"In sailing along the Spanish coast we were apprehensive of falling into the hands of the Turks, but we never met them. Having passed the pillars of Hercules and the Madeira islands, we were able to scud before the wind with full sail. The winds are not variable in those regions, but always blow in a southwest direction, which was our exact course. At the distance of about three leagues from us we described three sail of vessels, the smallest of which appeared to be larger than ours. Fearing they were Turkish pirates we were careful to avoid them, though we prepared our vessel for action. But as they showed no disposition to engage us, we concluded they were merchantmen, bound for the fortunate islands, and as much afraid of us as we were of them."

Father White, after some philosophical reasoning to account for the trade winds, some interesting descriptions of the tropical birds, and the flying fish. &c., &c., seen on their passage, remarks that, "during the entire voyage no person was attacked with any disease except that at Christmas, wine having been freely distributed in honour of that festival, several drank of it immoderately ; thirty persons were seized with a fever the next morning, of whom about twelve died shortly after ; of these two were Catholics, namely, Nicholas Fairfax and James Barefoot."

The route taken by the pilgrims is described to have been by the Azores, and to Barbadoes, at which latter island they landed on the 5th of January, 1634, new style. Instead of the hospitable reception which they expected from the governor and inhabitans. who were English, Father White says, "the governor and inhabitants plotted together to exact unreasonable prices for provisions and other necessary supplies." From the great abundance of potatoes in the island they received a wagon load gratis. At the time of the arrival of our pilgrims the slaves had rebelled, and determined to seize the first vessel that should arrive, but being discovered, the ringleaders were executed ; and, says the narrator, "our vessel being the first that touched the shore, was the destined prize, and the very day we landed we found eighty men under arms, to check the startling danger."

After describing the island of Barbadoes and its productions, the writer says, "on the 24th of January we weighed anchor, and passing the islands of St. Lucia at noon on the following day, we arrived in the evening at an island inhabited by savages only. A rumour had been caught by our sailors, from some Frenchmen who had been shipwrecked, that this island contained an animal in whose forehead was a stone of uncommon brilliancy, called a carbuncle." Father

White dryly remarks, "its author must answer for the truth of this report." At dawn on the following day they reached Guadaloupe, and at noon arrived at Montserrat, inhabited by Irishmen driven from Virginia, on account of their profession of the Catholic faith.

Thence they sailed to another island, where they spent one day; thence to St. Christophers, where they remained ten days, by the friendly invitation of the English government and two captains, "who were Catholics." The governor of a French colony in the same island also welcomed them warmly. Father White continues: "having at length weighed anchor hence, we pursued our voyage until we reached a point on the coast of Virginia, called 'Comfort,' on the 27th of February. We were under a good deal of dread from the unfriendliness of the English inhabitants of Virginia, to whom our colony had been an unwelcome theme. We brought, however, letters from the king and the high constable of England to the governor of the province, which contributed very much to appease their feelings, and to procure us future advantages. After receiving kind treatment for nine or ten days we set sail, and on the 3d of March, having arrived in the Chesapeake bay, we tacked to the north to reach the Potomac river, to which we gave the name of St. Gregory. We called the point which stands on the south St. Gregory, * that on the north of St. Michael, † in honour of the choir of angels. A larger and more beautiful stream I never have seen. The Thames compared with it is but a rivulet. Bounding on the sides by no marshes, it runs between solid and rising banks. On either side are splendid forests, not overgrown by weeds or briars; you might drive a four-horse carriage, with the reins loose in your hands, through them. We found the natives armed at the very mouth of the river. That night fires were blazing throughout the country, and as they had never seen so large a ship as ours, messengers were sent around to announce the arrival of a *canoe* as large as an island, and numbering as many men as the trees in a forest. We passed on to the Heron Islands, so called from immense flocks of those birds. We touched at the first of them, which we called St. Clements, on which owing to its sloping banks, we could only land by fording. Here the maids who had landed to wash the clothes, were almost drowned by the upsetting of the boat. I lost a large portion of my linen—no small loss in this part of the world. This island abounds in cedar trees, sassafras, and all those herbs and flowers entering into the class of salads, and the walnut tree with a heavy shell, and a small but very delicious kernel. A scope of four hundred acres did not appear sufficient for our new plantation. We desired a place which might preclude the commerce of the river to strangers, and also the possibility of their infringing on our boundaries. This was the most narrow crossing of the river.

"On the day of the annunciation of the B. V. Mary, (25th of March,) we first offered the sacrifice of the mass, never before in this region of the world. After which, having raised on our shoulders an immense cross, which we had fashioned from a tree, and going in procession to the designated spot, assisted by the governor, * commissary, and other Catholics, we erected the trophy of Christ the Saviour, and humbly bent the knee in reverence during the devout recitation of the litany of the holy cross. Our governor, however, having understood that the great chief of Piscataway was obeyed by many petty chiefs, determined to visit him, to explain the objects of our coming ; that having conciliated his good will, our settlement might be more favourably regarded by the rest. Having, therefore, joined to our pinnace another, which he had procured in Virginia, and leaving the ship at anchor off St. Clements, retracing his course, he sailed up the southern bank of the river. Finding the savages had fled into the interior, he proceeded to the village, which, taking its name from the river, is yet called Potomac. Here he found Archihu, the uncle and tutor of the king, who was yet a boy. The regency was in prudent and experienced hands. Father Altham, who accompanied the governor, (for I was detained with the baggage,) explained, by means of an interpreter, the truths of the Christian religion. The chief listened to him willingly, after acknowledging his own faults. Being informed that no hostile motives had brought us among them, but that feelings of benevolence prompt us to impart to them the advantages of civilization, and to open the path of Heaven to them, and to the more distant regions, he expressed himself not only well satisfied, but very grateful at our arrival. The interpreter was from the Protestants of Virginia. As the Father could not explain every thing at once, he promised to return in a short time. 'I think,' said Archihu, 'that we should all eat of the same table ; my young men will visit the hunting grounds for you, and all things shall be in common with us.' From hence we went to Piscataway, where all immediately flew to arms. About one hundred, armed with bows, were drawn up with their chief at their head. On learning our pacific intentions, laying aside his fears, the chief stepped into the pinnace, and on understanding our benevolent views in their regard, gave us liberty to settle in any part of his kingdom we might select. In the meantime, while tha governor was on his journey to the emperor, the savages of St. Clements becoming more bold, mixed familiarly with our sentries. We were accustomed to keep up a patrol day and night, to protect our wood-cutters, and our vessel, which was now undergoing repairs, from any sudden attack. The natives expressed their surprise at the size of our vessel, and wondered what part of the earth produced a tree large enough to make such a boat ; for they thought that it, like an Indian canoe, was hewn out of the trunk of a single tree. The report of our cannon struck them dumb with fear.

"In his visit to the emperor, our governor carried with him as a companion, one Henry Fleet, a captain among the settlers in Virginia, a man much beloved by the natives, and skilled in the knowledge of their language and settlements. In the beginning he was very obliging to us, but being seduced by the malicious counsels of a certain Claibone, he became very hostile, and, in the most artful manner, inflamed the minds of the natives against us. However, while he was our friend, he pointed out to our governor a suitable place for a settlement, than which a more heavenly and lovely spot Europe could not furnish. Having proceeded from St. Clements about nine leagues to the north, we glided into the mouth of a river, to which we gave the name of St. George.* This river flows from south to

* Now called St. Mary's river.

north about twenty miles before it loses, like the Thames, the salt water taste. In its mouth are two harbours, in which three hundred ships of the line could ride at anchor. We placed one of them under the protection of St. George, the other, more interior, under that of the B. V. Mary.' †

"On the left side of the river was tne settlement of Yaocomico. We ascended on the right side, and having halted about a thousand paces from the shore, we selected a site for the city, to be designated by the name of St. Mary. And to avoid all imputation of injury and occasion of enmity, having given in payment hatchets, axes, hoes, and some yards of cloth, we bought from the king about thirty miles of that part of the country now called Augusta Caroline. *

"A fierce and warlike nation of savages called the Susquehannahs, particularly hostile to king Yaocomico, made frequent incursions into his territory and devastated his settlements. The inhabitants, through fear of these savages, were forced to seek other homes. This was the cause of our having so promptly obtained possession of that part of his kingdom : God, in his goodness, opening a path for his law and eternal light by these means. The natives emigrate here and there daily, leaving behind them the fields and clearings that surrounded their homes. It amounts almost to a miracle that savages, who but a few days before arrayed themselves in arms against us, should now with the meekness of the lamb throw themselves on our mercy, and deliver up every thing to us. Here the finger of God is evident, and doubtless Providence has some good in store for this nation. A few have been permitted to retain their dwellings for one year, but the lands are to be delivered free into our hands the next year.

"The natives are tall and handsome in their persons, their skin is naturally of a copper colour, but they daub it over with red paint mixed with oil, to protect them from the flies.‡ This practice, which is decidedly more of a convenience than an ornament, gives them a hideous appearance. They daub their faces with other colours, at one time sky blue, at another red, and occasionally in the most disgusting and terrific manner. Being deficient in beard, at least until late in life, they draw painted lines from the corners of their mouths to the ears, in imitation of it. The hair, which is generally black, is tied around with a fillet, and drawn in a knot to the left ear, with the addition of any ornament in their possession which they consider valuable. Some wear as an ornament a copper plate with the figure of fish engraved upon it, placed upon the forehead. Others wear necklaces of glass beads ; beads are esteemed of less value by them, and do not answer the purposes of traffic so readily. They are dressed generally in deer skins, or something of that nature, which hangs from the back in the fashion of a pallium, and is bound round the navel like an apron, the rest of the body is naked. Boys and girls move about perfectly uncovered ; they tread on thorns and thistles, without sustaining injury, as if the soles of their feet were horn. Their arms are the bow and arrow, two cubits long, pointed

† This harl or must be either the mouth of what is called St. George's river, or the entrance to St. Inigce's creek.

 * Now St. Mary's county.

 ‡ Moschettoes.

with a piece of buckhorn, or sharp edged flint. They shoot these with such dexterity, as to transfix a sparrow at a considerable distance. Their bows are not very tightly strung, and they are unable to strike objects at a very great distance. By the use of these arms, however, they secure a sufficient quantity of food, as squirrels, partridges, turkeys, &c., of which there is a great abundance. They live in huts of an oblong and oval form, nine or ten feet high ; an opening of a foot and a half in size, through the roof, admits light and allows the smoke to escape. They construct a fire on a pavement in the centre, and sleep in a circle around it. The kings and principal chiefs have each a hut of his own, and a bed made by driving four stakes in the ground and laying poles over them. A tent of this description is allotted to my companion and myself, in which we are comfortably enough accommodated until a better house can be erected. *This may be considered the first chapel in Maryland;* it is, however, furnished in a more becoming manner than when it was inhabited by the Indians. In our next voyage, should Providence smile on our undertaking, we shall be supplied with all that is necessary for furnishing houses generally. The disposition of the tribe is sprightly and ingenious ; their taste is very discriminating, and they excel the Europeans in the senses of sight and smell. Their food consists of certain preparations of corn, which they call *pone* and *ominy*, to which is added fish and any thing that they have caught in hunting or in their snares. They have neither wine nor spirits, nor can they be easily induced to taste them, except such as the English have infected with their vices. As to their deportment, it is extremely modest and proper. In neither male nor female have I seen any action contrary to chastity. They come voluntarily and mingle with us daily, offering us, with a joyful countenance, what they have caught in hunting or fishing, and partaking of our food with us, when invited by a few words in their language. As yet we are able to converse with them very little except by signs. Many of them have wives, and preserve their conjugal faith unsullied. The countenances of the women are sedate and modest. The natives seemed possessed of generous dispositions, and reciprocate liberally any acts of kindness. They decide on nothing rashly, nor are they affected by any sudden impulses of feeling ; but when any thing of importance is submitted to their consideration, they reflect on it in silence, as if anxious to be governed entirely by reason : then having formed their determination, they express it briefly, and adhere to it most obstinately. If they were once imbued with the principles of Christianity (for which indeed nothing seems to be wanting but a knowledge of their language) they would certainly become examples of every moral and Christian virtue.

"They are much pleased with the courteous language, as well as the dress of the Europeans, and would now be clothed in our manner, if the avarice of our traders did not prevent it. Our ignorance of their idioms has hitherto prevented us from learning accurately their opinions on religion. We have, however, through the aid of interpreters, (not always to be relied on,) caught these particulars : They acknowledge one God of heaven, whom they call our God. They pay him no external honours, but endeavour in various ways, to propititate a certain evil spirit whom they call *Ochre*, that he may not injure them. I understand they worship also grain and fire, as deities very benevolent to mankind. Some of our men say they saw the following ceremony in the temple *Barcluxen*. On a certain day, all the men and women of all ages, from many villages, assemble around a large fire ; the younger ones are in advance, nearer the fire ; then having thrown some deer's fat on the fire, they raise their hands aloft and cry out with a loud voice, 'Taho, Taho !' During an interval, some one holds out a large bag, which contains a pipe, similar to those we use for smoking tobacco, though much larger, and some powder which they call *potu*. The bag is then carried around the fire, followed by boys and girls singing alternately in an agreeable voice, '*Taho, Taho.*' The circuit being finished, the pipe and the powder are drawn out of the bag. The potu being distributed to each one standing around, and lighted in the pipe, each person present smokes it, and consecrates every member of the body by blowing it over them. We are not in possession of other facts, except that they seem to have some knowledge of a flood in which the world was destroyed, on account of the sins of mankind.

"We have been but one month here : the remainder must consequently be reserved for another voyage. I can, however, assert that the soil is especially rich. The earth, soft and black to the depth of a foot, is overspread with a fat and reddish coloured clay, covered everywhere, with widely spreading trees, of great value and surpassing beauty, except here and there a small patch of cultivated ground. The land is also refreshed by abundant springs of excellent drinking water. The only quadrupeds we have seen, are the deer, beaver, and squirrels which equal in size the European rabbit. The flocks of birds are innumerable, such as eagles, herons, swans, geese, ducks, and partridges. Hence, you may suppose there is nothing wanting here which may minister to the necessities or the pleasure of its inhabitants."

The town of Saint Mary's became the capital of the province : and the first legislative assembly of the province was called and held there, about the commencement of the year 1635—(to wit, on the 26th of February, 1634—5, old style.)

——— :o: ———

THE CHARTER

—OF THE—

CITY OF ANNAPOLIS.

AS NOW EMBODIED IN ARTICLE TWO OF THE CODE OF PUBLIC LOCAL LAWS OF MARYMAND, TITLE ANNE ARUNDEL COUNTY, SUB-
TITLE, ANNAPOLIS.*

SEC. 30. The boundaries of the City of Annapolis shall be follows: Beginning at the water's edge at Windmill Point; thence by a

* From the Revised Code, 1881.

straight line to Sycamore Point; and thence again by a straight line from Sycamore Point to the wharf at Fort Madison; and thence by a drawn line from the wharf at Fort Madison, to the south wall of the Naval Academy, at the eastern terminus of Hanover street, and following the present enclosures of the Naval Academy to the Severn River, at the north-eastern terminus of Tabernacle street; thence along the south shore of said river and College Creek, to the head of said creek; thence by a stright line from the head of said creek, to the head of Acton's Cove on Spa Creek; and thence following the northeast of said creek to the place of beginning; and the said city shall be divided into three wards by the Corporation of said city, and the citizens of Annapolis, qualified to vote for members of the General Assembly of Maryland, shall, on the second Monday of July, in the year eighteen hundred and seventy-seven, and every two years thereafter, elect by ballot, a Mayor, Counsellor, and the voters in each ward shall at the same time elect by ballot two residents thereof as Aldermen, who shall constitute the Corporation of said city, under the name and style of the Mayor, Counsellor, and Aldermen of the City of Annapolis.

SEC. 31. The Corporation shall appoint three persons judges of said election, any two of whom shall be competent to hold such election, and shall also appoint the necessary clerks of said election, and the judges and clerks shall qualify in the same manner as judges and clerks of elections are required by law to qualify, and shall in the execution of their respective duties, and in the manner of conducting elections, conform in every respect to the provisions of Article thirty-five of the Code, and shall be subject to the same penalties as other judges and clerks of elections in this State.

SEC. 32. The Mayor, Counsellor, and Aldermen shall designate the place of holding elections, and the polls shall be kept open from nine o'clock in the morning until six o'clock in the evening, and the returns shall be made to the Mayor, Counsellor, and Aldermen, and recorded among their proceedings.

SEC. 33. All persons, qualified to be members of the General Assembly, shall be eligible as Mayor, Counsellor and Aldermen.

SEC. 34. In case of the death, refusal to serve, disqualification or removal out of the City of any of the members of the Corporation, a majority of the remaining members shall fill the vacancy for the residue of the term.*

SEC. 36. The Mayor shall qualify as directed by section six of article sixty-eight of the Code; the Aldermen, Counsellor, and judges and clerks of elections, and all other officers of the City, shall, before they enter upon the duties of their respective offices, take and subscribe before the Mayor the following oath: "I do solemnly swear that I will faithfully execute the office of ——— to the best of my knowledge and ability, without favor, affection, or partiality."

SEC. 37. The Mayor, Counsellor, and Aldermen shall hold their first session in Annapolis on the second Monday in April, and shall meet on the second Monday in each month thereafter, but the Mayor may summon them to convene whenever and as often as it may appear to him that the interests of the City require their deliberations, and a majority of the whole Board shall be a quorum to do business, but a smaller number may adjourn from day to day.

* By Act of 1867, c. 240, secs. 34 and 35 were repealed, and the present sec. 34 enacted in lieu of both.

Sec. 38. They may compel the attendance of absent members in such manner and under such penalties as they may by ordinance provide: shall settle their rules of proceedings; appoint their own officers and remove them at pleasure.

Sec. 39. They shall judge of the election returns and qualifications of their own members, and may, with the concurrence of their whole number, expel any member for disorderly behavior or misconduct in office, but not a second time for the same cause.

Sec. 40. The Mayor, Counsellor, and Aldermen shall have power to enact all laws and ordinances necessary to preserve the health of the City; to prevent and remove nuisances; to prevent the introduction of contagious diseases within the City; to establish night watches and patrols: to light the City; to establish new streets, lanes, and alleys, and to widen, straighten, extend, stop up, or discontinue any streets, lanes, and alleys; and when any street, lane, or alley is opened, widened, straightened, extended, stopped up or discontinued by the Corporation, the full value of all property taken and used for public street, lane, or alley, or damages to be sustained in closing the same, shall be assessed by a jury of twelve citizens, and the said full value so assessed first paid or tendered to the proprietor of said property; and if, in opening, widening, straightening or extending any street, lane or alley in said city, any benefit shall thereby accrue to the owner or possessor of any ground or improvement, within or upon said street, lane, or alley, for which such owner or possessor ought to pay compensation, said benefits shall be assessed and paid by the owner or possessor in like manner as above provided; to erect and repair bridges: to have, construct, and keep in repair all necessary drains and sewers, and to pass all necessary regulations for the regulation, repair, and preservation of the same: to regulate and fix the assize of bread; to provide for the appointment, and define the duties of City Commissioner, Police Officers, Market Masters, Gaugers, Wood Corders, Harbor Masters, Hay Weighers, Coal Weighers, and Inspectors, and all other officers which they may create, and to define the duties and compensation thereof; to provide for the safe keeping of the standard of the weights and measures, fixed by Congress, or by an Act of the State of Maryland, and for regulating thereby all weights and measures used within the City; to regulate party walls and partition fences; to erect and regulate markets; to provide for licensing and regulating the sweeping and burning of chimneys, and fixing the rates thereof, and to prescribe the size of those to be built in the City; to establish and regulate fire wards and fire companies; to restrain or prohibit gaming; to license bowling saloons, bowling alleys, nine or ten pin alleys, billiard tables, rondo tables, bagatelle tables, or any other tables or devices, or structures of a similar kind; to license carriages of pleasure and burden, and to provide for licensing, regulating, or restraining theatrical or other public amusements within the limits of the City; to license hawkers, pedlers, travelling physicians, venders of patent medicines or other articles, and their vehicles, to sink wells; to make and regulate pumps, water pipes, hydrants, water plugs, fountains, sewers, and so forth, in the streets, lanes, and alleys of the City, and to pass laws to protect the same: to impose and appropriate fines, penalties and forfeitures for the breach of their by-laws and ordinances; to levy and collect taxes; not ex-

ceeding one per centum per annum on all the assessabl e property in
the City; to pass ordinances for the prevention and extinguishment of
fires; and for paving and keeping in repair the streets, lanes, and
alleys in said city; and in addition to the power aforesaid, to tax any
particular part or district of the City for paving the streets, lanes
and alleys therein, or for constructing sewers, sinking wells, making
pumps, water pipes, fountains, hydrants and water plugs therein,
which in their judgment may appear for the benefit of such particular
part or district, in a sum not exceeding one per centum on the assessable property in said particular part or district; and to make a new
assessment of all the assessable property in said city not exempt from
taxation by the laws of this State, as often as they may deem the same
necessary; to borrow money on the credit of the Corporation for the
purpose of promoting or effecting any important and permanent public improvement in the City, or for paying its present debts; and to
issue from time to time, as they may deem proper, the bonds of the
said Mayor, Counsellor and Aldermen, payable at such times and in
such sums as may deem proper, not exceeding in the aggregation the
sum of fifty thousand dollars, and to pledge their property for the
payment thereof, and the interest thereon; *provided*, however, that a
majority of the legal voters shall approve the act at an election to be
held on a day at a place to be named by the Mayor, Counsellor, and
Aldermen of the City of Annapolis, when the legal voters of said **city**
shall express by ballot their assent or dissent to the loan proposed;
and *provided*, that the entire public debt of said city shall not exceed
the sum of fifty thousand dollars; to provide for taking up, fining or
committing to the jail of Anne Arundel county, all vagrants,
drunken, loose and disorderly persons and such as have no visible
means of support and livelihood, and common disturbers of the peace,
that may be found within the jurisdiction of the City, and the keeper
of said jail shall receive and safe keep all persons so committed, according to the tenor of the commitment; to cause a survey, as often as
they may think necessary, of the City, its harbor, streets, lots, and the
additions thereto to be made; to establish and fix permanent boundaries and stones at such places as they may think necessary, with
proper marks and devices thereon; to ascertain the lines of the City
and the additions thereto; and the survey of the said city and additions thereto, and of the streets, lanes, alleys, and harbor thereof,
when made shall be signed by the Mayor, and the seal of the Corporation thereto affixed, and shall be deposited with the Clerk of the
Corporation of the City, and received as evidence of the boundaries of
the said city, and of the harbor, lots, streets, lanes, and alleys therein;
to declare and adjudge as nuisances any encroachments on the streets,
lanes, and alleys, and cause the same to be removed at the expense of
the person offending; to lay off and divide the City into election districts, and to define their bounds and limits, and correct the same
from time to time, so as to preserve as accurately as may be an equal
number of inhabitants in each of said districts, and to designate
places for taking the vote at all elections to be held in each of said
districts; to prevent the running at large of dogs, and to impose an
annual tax on the owners and keepers thereof in the City not exceeding five dollars; to restrain or prohibit the running at large of horses,

ows, sheep, goats, or other animals; to direct in what parts of the City buildings of wood shall not be erected, and to regulate the construction of the same; to pass ordinances for preserving order, securing persons and property from violence, danger or destruction; for protecting the public and city property, rights and privileges from waste or encroachment, and generally for promoting and securing the good government of the City.

Sec. 41.   Before the Mayor, Counsellor, and Aldermen of the City of Annapolis shall pass any ordinance to open, widen, straighten, extend, stop up, or discontinue any streets, lanes, or alleys, or any part thereof, in pursuance of the authority herein delegated, at least thirty days' notice shall be given before the passage of such ordinance, in some newspaper or newspapers published in said city, and before any street, lane, or alley shall be so opened, straightened, extended, stopped up or discontinued, in whole or in part, the proprietors of lots or any part or section of the streets, lanes, and alleys so to be opened, widened, straightened, extended, stopped up, or discontinued, in whole or in part, whose property will be depreciated by the act of the Corporation, may apply to any Justice of the Peace in said city, who is hereby empowered, upon an affidavit of facts, to summon a jury of twelve citizens, whose duty it shall be to examine the premises and assess the damages sustained by the complainant; the full value of such assessment shall be paid or tendered to the complainant, as hereinbefore provided, before the final execution of such ordinance, and any Justice of the Peace shall have the same power to summon a jury for the assessment of benefits.

Sec. 42.* They shall keep a journal of their proceedings, and enter the yeas and nays upon any question, resolve or ordinance, if required by any one member, and their deliberations shall be public.

Sec. 45.* The Mayor, Counsellor, and Aldermen may repair any private wharves belonging to persons who shall refuse, after two month's notice, to repair the same, and they may receive the wharfage of such wharves until such repairs are paid for, or until the owners thereof shall pay the same.

Sec. 49. The Mayor may take the acknowledgment of any deed or instrument of writing required to be acknowledged, and receive therefore the sum of fifty cents ; all by-laws and ordinances of the said Corporation shall be signed by the Mayor ; the Mayor shall during the first ten days in the month of January of each and every year, cause to be prepared and printed, for the information of the citizens, a statement of the finances of the said Corporation ; he may call upon any officer of the City, entrusted with the receipt and expenditure of public money, for a statement of his accounts, as often as he may deem it necessary ; he shall see that the ordinances are duly and faithfully executed.

Sec. 50. They may appoint from time to time, at such periods as they deem most proper and convenient, certain persons as Wardens of the Port of the City of Annapolis, nor more than five in number, who shall be removed at their pleasure.

Sec. 51. The persons so appointed shall, each, take the following oath : ''I, A. B., do swear that I will discharge the trust of Warden

* The original Sections 42, 43, 44, 45, 46, 47 and 48 repealed by Act of 1867, c. 210.

of the Port of the City of Annapolis to the best of my ability, without favor, affection, or partiality."

Sec. 52. The Wardens, or a majority of them, shall have power to determine upon and regulate all matters relating to the erection or building of wharves in the said port, so far as respects the distance said wharves may be extended into the water, and the materials of which they shall be constructed, and the manner and form of construction, always keeping in view the preservation of the navigation of said port by not permitting any wharf to be carried out in such manner as to render the navigation of the same too close and confined, or to be built of such materials or constructed in such manner as may be deemed not sufficiently substantial and lasting.

Sec. 53. No person holding lands on the waters of said port, nor any person whatever, shall build any wharf, or carry out any earth or other material for that purpose, without license from said Wardens, or a majority of them, to do the same ; and if any person shall offend against the provisions of this section, or if any person shall build any wharf a greater distance into the waters of said port, or in a different form, or of different materials than determined and allowed by the Wardens, or a majority of them, he shall be subject to such fine as the Mayor, Counsellor, and Aldermen may ordain.

Sec. 54. In all differences that shall arise between any citizen of Annapolis and the said Wardens, touching the discharge of their duty, an appeal shall lie to the Mayor, Counsellor and Aldermen.

Sec. 55. It shall not be lawful for any person, whether licensed to sell spirituous liquors or not, to sell, dispose of, barter, or give, directly or indirectly, within the corporate limits of the City of Annapolis, or within five miles thereof, any spirituous or fermented liquors or cordials of any kind, or in any quantity whatever, to any youth or minor under the age of twenty-one years, without the written order or consent of the parent or guardian of such minor ; nor to any Midshipman or Student connected with, or attached to the Naval Academy at Annapolis, or under orders to join or leave the said Academy ; nor to any seaman, ordinary seaman, landsman, marine, or boy, or any employee of the Navy, without a written order from a commissioned officer of the Navy, (not excluding hired laborers,) nor to any Student of St. John's College without the written order of some Professor of said College : and any person violating the provisions of this section shall be liable to indictment in the Circuit Court for Anne Arundel county, and, upon conviction thereof, shall be fined a sum of not less than fifty dollars, and not more than four hundred dollars, and shall be confined in jail until the said fine and costs of prosecution shall be paid ; *provided*, said confinement in jail shall not exceed sixty days ; but if any minor or person referred to in this section shall willfully misrepresent that he is of full age, or that he is not prohibited by this section, and thereby shall obtain any spirituous liquors, and the person selling the same shall be able to prove such misrepresentation, the said person selling to the said minor or other person so falsely representing himself shall not suffer any penalty, but shall pay all the costs incurred in such case ; *provided*, that the act of any agent under this section shall not be binding upon his principal, if the court or jury shall believe that the said act was committed against the *bona fide* instructions of said principal.

Sec. 56. If any person having a license of any kind, authorizing the sale of spirituous liquors, shall violate the provisions of the preceding section, or permit any person in his employ to violate the same, at or in his tavern, shop, house, or place of business, or in or upon his premises, with his knowledge and consent, such license shall be suppressed by the Judge of said Court, and be declared null and void.

SEC. 57. The Judge of said Court shall, whenever complaint may be made to him by any two or more respectable citizens of said city, or any officer of the county or city, that any person having a license, as aforesaid, is or has been violating the provisions of Section 55 of this Article, examine witnesses and inquire into such alleged violation ; and if, upon such examination and inquiry, it shall appear to his satisfaction that the party complained against has been guilty of such violation, the said Judge shall have full power immediately to suppress the license of such person, and no new license shall be granted to him or her.

SEC. 58. Any one order which may be given to any minor under the provisions of the fifty-fifth Section of this Article, shall not be available for the purpose for which it was given, for a longer period than two days from its date.

SEC. 59. It shall be the duty of the Sheriff of Anne Arundel County and his deputies, and of the Constables of the City of Annapolis, to exercise the utmost vigilance in order to detect all violations of this Article in relation to the sale of liquors to minors and others as forbidden by Section fifty-five, and to report immediately any such violation to the Judge of the Circuit Court for said county, who shall forthwith direct the offending party to be brought before him, and snall require him to give adequate security for his appearance at the next term of said Court, and shall commit such party to jail in default of such security ; and if any Sheriff or Constable shall neglect to report to the Judge any such violation of the said section as soon as the same shall come to his knowledge, he shall be liable to a penalty of fifty dollars for each case of such neglect, to be recovered by any person in the name of the State by action of debt in said Court.

SEC. 60. All fines imposed and collected under the provisions of Section fifty-five of this Article shall go, one half to the informer (who is hereby made a competent witness) and the other half shall be divided equally between the State's Attorney and the Sheriff or other officer who shall have made report in the case to the Judge under the fifty-ninth Section of this Article.

SEC. 61. The Mayor, Counsellor, and each Alderman shall, in virtue of their office, have and exercise, within the limits of the Corporation, all the jurisdiction and powers of a Justice of the Peace.

SEC. 63.* The Mayor may take the acknowldgement of any deed or instrument of writing required by law to be acknowledged, and shall receive therefor the sum of fifty cents.

SEC. 64. The Collector of Taxes in said city shall have the same power to collect the city taxes as the collectors of county taxes, and shall be governed by the same rules.

SEC. 65. When any tax shall be due upon real estate, and no personal property shall be found thereon liable to the payment thereof the Collector shall report the fact to the Corporation at their monthly meeting in December, annually, and the Mayor, Counsellor, and

* Sec. 62 repealed by Act of 1867, c. 210.

Aldermen shall thereupon direct the real estate to be sold by the Collector for the payment of the said taxes, after giving notice in the public newspapers in the same manner as Collectors of County and State Taxes are required to do.

SEC. 66. The property in the City of Annapolis belonging to the Corporation is exempt from any tax to be levied by Anne Arundel County.

SEC. 67. No ordinance of the Corporation shall impose a fine of more than twenty dollars for any one offence, or authorize a commitment to jail for more than thirty days at one time.

SEC. 68. All fines, penalties, and forfeitures for violation of any ordinance of the Corporation may be recovered before the Mayor, Counsellor, or some one of the Aldermen, or a Justice of the Peace ; and the Mayor, Counsellor, or Aldermen, or Justice, may commit the offender until the fine is paid, or he be discharged in due course of law.

SEC. 69. If any ordinance shall give part of a fine or penalty to the informer, or if such fine or penalty be discretionary, the judgment of the officer imposing the fine or declaring the penalty, shall specify how much of such fine or penalty shall be to the use of the Corporation, and how much to the informer.

SEC. 70. No ordinance of the said Corporation shall be binding on persons who do not reside in the said city, until the same shall have been published in some newspaper of the said city, unless in case of wilful and intentional violation of said ordinance after notice thereof.

SEC. 71. The said Corporation shall pass no ordinance that shall be contrary to law.

SEC. 72. The inhabitants of the said city, and all persons holding property therein, shall be competent witness in all actions arising under the Charter or Ordinances of said city, if exempt from all other exceptions than that of interest as an inhabitant of said city, or member of said Corporation.

SEC. 73. All that part of the Charter of the City of Annapolis which gives to the Mayor, Counsellor, or Aldermen the power of holding a Court of Hustings within said city, and all other parts of said Charter repugnant to, or inconsistent with, the provisions of this Article in relation to the City of Annapolis, are repealed.

SEC. 74. The public lands and buildings heretofore purchased and built by this State or Anne Arundel County, in said city, are reserved and continued forever to the uses to which they have been allotted, and the Judges of the several Courts which have usually held their courts in the said city in the public Court House thereof, shall and may continue to do so: and the Justices, Commissioners, and Sheriff of Anne Arundel County, shall have, hold, and exercise the jurisdiction in as full and ample manner in the said city as heretofore.

SEC. 246. It shall not be lawful for any person to carry concealed, in Annapolis, whether a resident thereof or not, any pistol, dirk-knife, bowie-knife, sling-shot, billy, razor; brass, iron or other metal knuckles, or any other deadly weapon, under a penalty of a fine of not less than three, nor more than ten dollars in each case, in the discretion of the Justice of the Peace before whom the same may be tried, to be collected as other fines and penalties are now collected *provided*, the provisions of this section shall not apply to any officer of the law, either of the State or City, where any pistol or other weapon is a part of the prescribed outfit of said officer ; and *provided further,* that either party, feeling aggrieved at the decision of the said Justice of the Peace, shall have the right to appeal to the Circuit Court of Anne Arundel County.

CHAPTER 496.

AN ACT to enlarge the powers of the Mayor, Counsellor and Aldermen of the city of Annapolis, by adding certain sections to the charter of said city relating to public cemeteries, and the acquisition of land by said corporation for that purpose, and the regulation thereof, and the construction and maintenance of roads and bridges leading thereto.

SECTION 1. *Be it enacted by the General Assembly of Maryland,* That the following sections be and the same hereby are added to the Code of Public Local Laws of Maryland, title "Anne Arundel county," sub-title "Annapolis," to be known as sections seventy-five, seventy-six, seventy-seven, and seventy-eight, of said title and sub-title:

SEC. 75. The mayor, counsellor, and aldermen of the city of Annapolis, shall be authorized and empowered, in their discretion, to acquire by purchase, condemnation, gift, or grant, for the purposes of a public cemetery or cemeteries for said city, so much land either within or without the limits of said city as they may consider necessary : and also to make such ordinances, by-laws, rules, or regulations relative to the same, and to the public cemeteries belonging to said city, or within its limits, as may by them be deemed right and proper.

SEC. 76. If the said mayor, counsellor, and aldermen of the city of Annapolis cannot agree with the owner or owners of the land so sought to be acquired for the purpose aforesaid, for the purchase of the same, the said mayor, counsellor, and aldermen shall be authorized to proceed to condemn said land for the purposes aforesaid, in manner as provided by sections one hundred and seventy, one hundred and seventy-one, one hundred and seventy-two, one hundred and seventy-three, one hundred and seventy-four, and one hundred and seventy-five of chapter four hundred and seventy-one, of the acts passed by the general assembly of Maryland at the January session, eighteen hundred and sixty-eight, and all the rights, powers, and privileges conferred by said sections upon the corporation therein mentioned, shall be deemed applicable to and vested in said mayor, counsellor, and aldermen for the purposes of this act.

SEC. 77. The said mayor, counsellor, and aldermen shall be authorized to open roads, ways, or streets to said cemetery or cemeteries, and condemn property for that purpose under the powers conferred by the preceding sections of this act, or to acquire title to the land necessary for that purpose by purchase, gift or grant, as provided by said sections; and they shall furthermore be authorized to erect or construct bridges over the navigable waters of College creek or of Spa creek, on either side of said city, for convenience of access to such cemetery or cemeteries.

SEC. 78. The said mayor, counsellor, and aldermen shall be authorized to lay off into burial lots the land required by them under this act, and to lease, sell, and convey said lots as they may deem right and proper. They shall be authorized to make all such rules and regulations, relative to the maintenance and use of such roads and bridges as may be constructed by them under the provisions of this act as they may deem expedient, in the same manner as by existing laws they can make and enforce relative to public streets within said city.

SEC. 2. *And be it enacted*, That this act shall take effect from the date of its passage.

Approved April 8, 1884.

INDEX.

————(:o:)————

A

Abuse of the house by Edward Erberry........... 41
A brief struggle............ 57
Abigail and Nancy....... ..125
Abraham Lincoln, election of.284
Abbott, Wm. M............324
Abridgement of Fr. White's J.327
Acknowledgement can be tak.338
Acadians in Annapolis. 119
Act of attainder of R. Clarke. 85
Accomplishments of Annapo. 91
Act of Assembly on charter.. 93
Acton, Richard.............. 19
Act of Assembly to punish Indians for murder........ 22
Academy of King William.... 80
Acts against Quakers repealed 44
Act to build State House and prison at St. Mary's...... 59
Accessibleness of St. Mary's.. 60
Acton's Cove................ 63
Advance of Gov. Stone's forc. 33
Address of Mayor, &c., of St. Mary's................. 58
Advantages of St. Mary's.... 60
Addison, Col. John.......... 78
Admittance to the House..... 92
Addison, Col. Thomas........ 96
Addition to Annapolis called New Town. 97
Addition to the city of Annap. 97
Advertisement in the Gazette. 99
Adultery....................101
Admiralty, court of, at Annap114
Adams Express Office........147
Adverse Meeting............166

Adventures cargo refused landing....................176
Adams, Lieut. Col. Peter....188
Address of Annapolis to Washington............193
Address of A. to Gen. Greene.195
Addresses to La Fayette....196-7
Address of Council of State to Washington..........203
Address of A. to Washington.203
Address of State to Wash....203
Address of Washington......206
Address of Gen. Mifflin to W.207
Advantages of St. John's Col.211
Adams, Thomas.............229
Address to La Fayette.........239
Additions to Naval Academy266-7
Adventure of Naval Academy to Annapolis.................268
A Disastrous Accident.........321
Advertiser, Anne Arundel..324-5
Adams, Richard.............168
A. & E. R. Railroad...........262
A Notable Bowl..............309
A. & E. R. R. pays to State...313
A. & B. Short Line R....320, 323
Affirmative commands urged. 27
Affirmed, charter of Annap.... 93
African slavery...................108
Affray at Annapolis..........151
Affability of Gov. Eden.......154
Agents fail to receive orders... 57
Aged rector to drop into grave 72
Agricultural fair grounds......159
Age of poplar on College Campus......................309

A Galaxy of Annapolitans....275
Allen Rev. B., a notorious
    pastor.... 72
All Saints Parish rector of
    being dead................... 72
Allen, Rev. Mr. gives with
    lavish hand........ ... 72
Allen, Mr. rec. of 2 parishes 72
Allen, Rev. Mr. personal chas-
    tisement of.................. 72
Allen, Rev. Mr. mobbed.. ... 72
Allen, Rev. M. resigns All
    Saints........... 71
Allen, Rev. resigns St. Anne's 71
Allen, Rev. returns to Eng.. 72
Allen, Rev. Mr. challenges L.
    Dulany............ .. 72
Allen, Rev. kills L. Dulany.. 72
Allen, Rev. dies in poverty 72
Allen, Rev. Mr. gifted but
    degraded................. 72
All Saints, Calvert county.... 79
Aldermen of Annapolis. 1708. 86
Allen, Mr. writes of St. Anne's 108
Allison, Patrick.............209
Alkman, William 103
Alexander, Charles...... .. 210
Allyne, Capt................ 111
All America in a flame.......164
Alumni of St. John's.......215
Almshouse burned...........224
Alexander, Wm....225, 228, 229
Alarms of citizens of A..234, 238
Alms House.................257
Alexander, Thos. S.........263
Alms House of A. A. Co.....267
Altham, Father...... 331
Alkman, Wm..................168
Alleys, powers over.........338
Amerciaments, fines, forfeit-
    ures.....................107
American women, beauty of..140
American Company.........140
American ladies, case of 142
American Com. of Comedians.147
American House.............301
American tobacco........ 127
Amateur Dramatic. A. N. A..320
Amendment to City Charter..342
Annapolis Town............. 18
Annapolis, Port of.......... 19
Anne Arundel Co., formed... 21
Anne Arundel named in honor
    of Lady Anne Arundel... 21

Anne Arundel changed to Co.
    of Providence.. 31
Anne Arundel men......... 34
Anne Arundel required to sub. 36
Annarundel................. 37
Anne Arundel County....... 39
Annapolis, 34, 35, 40, 57, 58,
    62, 63, 68. 72, 78, 82,
    95, 97.
Annapolis, not as large as St.
    Mary's..... 57
Anne Arundel Town, (now
    Annapolis.) 57
Annapolis, remv'l. of Capital. 55
Annapolis has forty dwelling
    houses 57
Annapolis, State House in ... 57
Annapolis, Free School in.... 57
Annapolis, good lodgings in.. 57
Annapolis has two market
    days in a week.......... 57
Anne Arundel Town........ 58
Annapolis, Records reach..62, 78
Anne Arundel County....... 63
Anne Arundel Town, a port
    of entry.. 63
Annapolis puts on its honors. 63
Annapolis give its pres. name.. 63
Annapolis, rules and orders..63,
    64.
Annapolis, gates of....... 64
Annapolis, Town Clerk to keep
    his papers in............ 66
Annapolis, busy times in 68
Annapolis, First Mayor of.... 76
Ancient communion vessels.. 77
Annapolis, mem. reading to.. 79
Annapolis, 2nd State House in 80
Annapolis, printed charter of. 80
Annapolis, attempt to burn... 81
Annapolis, plot that struck... 82
Annapolis, attempt upon Town
    of 82
Annapolis is made a City..... 85
Annapolis has two delegates.. 85
Annapolis merged in A. A. C.. 86
Annapolis reduced to one del. 85
Annapolis loses its delegation. 85
Annapolis cont'd. as Capital.. 86
Annapolis, petition of Cor. of. 86
Annapolis wants a charter.... 86
Annapolis wants delegates.... 86
Annapolis, Common Council-
    man of, 1708........... 87

Annapolis, Aldermen of.. ... 86
Annapolis, Charter of, grated 87
Annapolis, Charter of City of 87
Annapolis, "a very pleasant
healthful comd. place.".. 87
Annapolis, town and port of.. 87
Annapolis, Sheriff for........ 89
Anne Arundel. Sheriff for.. . 89
Anne, by the Grace of God, &c. 87
Annapolis, Free-holders of.... 89
Annapolis, two fairs yearly in. 90
Annapolis on the advance.... 91
Annapolis, accomplishments of 91
Annapolis, French writer on.. 91
Annapolis, described in verse. 92
Annapolis, description of..... 92
Annapolis, delegates denied.. 92
Annapolis, complaints from.. 92
Annapolis, port of........ 94
Annapolis, shipping of.. 95
Annapolis, members of port of 96
Annapolis, prospect to....... 96
Annapolis, Corporation of.... 96
Annapolis, area of............ 97
Annapolis, addition to 97
Anne Arundel, Schools of.... 97
Annapolis, Public School in.. 98
Anderson, Ether............102
Annapolis in 1745............102
Annapolis, delegates of......102
Annapolis, a severe storm in..103
Annapolis a century old......108
Annapolis, chief trade at.....109
Annapolis, aurora borealis in.109
Annapolis, chronicles from
1746 to 1773............109
Annapolis, importance of.....109
Annapolis, by-laws of 1746...109
Annapolis, Whitfield visits...110
Annapolis, manufacture of
osnabrigs 111
Annapolis to Kent Island.....112
Annapolis, Admiralty Court at.114
Annapolis, prison at, guarded.114
Annapolis, gallows at........114
Annapolis, convicts arrive at.116
Annapolis, robbery in........117
Annapolis, fortified......117, 118
Annapolis, Earthquake in 1755,
1758, 1772.....118, 120, 121
Annapolis, Acadians in.......119
Annapolis, small-pox in......119
Annapolis, gang of miscreants
in...................120

Annapolis, pillory in........121
Annapolis, old clock. old hall.122
Annapolis, Capital 50 years. 127
Annapolis, Latin notes in......127
Annapolis. Coffee House..130, 331
Annapolis, clubs in..........131
Anniversaries of clubs. 134
Annapolis loyal to England..136
Anniversary of King observed.137
Annapolis, emigrants to......137
Annapolis, electricity in 1749.138
Annapolis. Masons estab. in..138
Annapolis Theatre........139, 226
Annapolis belles............140
Ancient City...............146
Annapolis outlives raillery...145
Annapolis, stamp act in......149
Annapolis and B. & S. L.....157
Annapolis, Wash. & B. R. Dep.159
Annapolis entrenched, 1755..160
Annex to State Library......164
Annapolis, in Dec. of Indep'd.164
Annapolis, during Revolution.165
Annapolis sympathizes with
Boston...................165
Anderson, John..............167
Annis, Robert..............167
Anderson, J. H..............168
Anne Arundel...............172
Annapolis deserted, 1775 175
Annapolis, consternation in..177
Annapolis, Associators of....181
Annapolis blockaded........187
Annapolis after Revolution...192
Annapolis, a city of importance193
Annapolis wants to be the
Capitol of the U. S.......198
Annapolis and Trenton......200
Annapolis quaint & agreeable.201
Annapolis, address of, to
Washington.............203
Annapolis, Wash.'s reply to..203
Annapolis from 1777 to 1810.220
Annapolis first to make silver
coin....................220
Annapolis, commerce of......222
Annapolis Jockey Club. 222
Ancient Regime disappears...228
Annapolis during the war of
1812..................233
Annapolis a milit'y camp.233, 238
Annapolis riflemen..........240
Annapolis infantry..........240
Annapolis artillery......... 240

Annapolis, join to 256
Anne Arundel............... 257
Anti-Caucus party.......... 258
Anderson, T................ 258
Annapolis & Potomac Canal
    Company............... 260
Ancient Landmark burnt....273
Annapolis, population of.280, 323
Annapolis seized by the Fed.
    Government............. 281
Anne Arundel, vote in, 1860. 281
Annapolis, vote of, in 1860...291
Annapolis & E. R. R. seized..296
Annapolis an important Mili-
    tary Station............. 296
Annapolis has strong secession
    sentiment............... 297
Annapolis to rival Baltimore. 297
Annapolis Gazette established.300
Anne Arundel enrollment....300
Annapolis, enrollment of 301
Andrews, James........304, 316
Annapolis Pub. School Build-
    ing..................... 208
Anti-Huckster Ticket........313
Annapolis witnesses 314
Annapolis excited over Early's
    invasion............... 314
Annapolis fortified........... 314
Annapolis Confederates....... 314
Annapolis reduced to a post..315
Anne Arundel His. Society...320
Annapolis revenues......... 320
Annapolis of the present..... 323
Annapolis Glass Works...... 323
Annapolis, newspapers of....324
Annapolis, local option in.....325
An exceeding great army.....326
Annapolis, Charter of....... 334
Anapolis, boundaries of...... 334
Annapolis City Government.. 15
Annapolis Vol. Fire Dept..... 15
Annapolis, Mayors of........ 13
Approval of State subscription 3
Appointment of Hood, stamp
    officer.................. 149
Apparition of the Gazette....151
Appropriation to St. John's
    suspended.............. 210
Appropriation to St. John's.214-5
Appendix.................. 326
Arrival of Puritans.......... 19
Articles of Peace and Friend-
    ship.................... 29

Arms and Ammunition....... 32
Arms, ammunition, taken ... 36
Articles against Major Thos.
    Truman.............. 54
Archives carefully guarded... 62
Armory near the Court House. 80
Armory often used as a ball
    room.................. 80
Arrest, attachment, or execu-
    tion................... 90
Arrest, stayed at fairs........ 90
Area of Annapolis........... 97
Arms stolen............... 111
Architectural pretensions. ...128
Arrival of Washington in A .192
Arrival of stamped paper....151
A royal prisoner....... 154
Arrival of Washington at A..201
Arbitrary character of settle-
    ment.................. 214
Area of Naval Academy.....267
A retrospect of two centuries.274
Arsenal at Pikeville........ 295
Arrest of Basil McNew......300
Arrest of Sam'l Topper 300
Arrest of Citizens by Military.311
Army, an exceeding great..... 326
Ark, The (note)...... 328
Asylum in Maryland......... 17
Assembly called by Puritans.. 56
Assem'y meets at R. Preston's 56
Ashman, Mr. Geo...... 78
Assembly called by beating of
    drum 80
Assembly dissolved...... ... 93
Assize Court................ 112
Assizes.................... 144
Asserter of American privileg.149
Assembly at the Liberty Tree.174
Associators of Annapolis 181
Assembly Rooms set on fire....300
Asbury M. E. Church........305
Association, W's. B. & L.....323
Association, Local Improveme325
Aston, William.............. 166
Atchison, David.... 168
Attendance, members of corp.336
Attempt of R. Clarke, to burn
    Annapolis 81
Attempt upon Town of Anna. 82
Attainder of R. Clarke....... 84
Attainder, act of R. Clarke... 85
Attachments stayed at fairs... 90
Athens, The, of America.....145

Attacks of the Gazette.......151
Attack on the Chesapeake....226
Attack on Marshal Frey......318
Attainder, bill of............ 55

Authorities alarm'd at convicts117
Authority to make constables. 89
Aurora borealis, at Annapolis.109
Aunt Lucy Smith's House....308

B

Banks, Lieut. Richard....... 25
Battle of the Severn 32, 332
Barber, Dr. Luke............ 34
Barbarous and cruel manner.. 55
Battle Creek, capital remov-
   ed to.................... 56
Bachelors taxed 71
Barber, Mr. Wm............ 78
Baldwin, John............ 87-97
Baltimore county, member of
   Port of Annapolis........ 93
Baldwin, Catherine.. 97
Barrett. James. executed.....102
Baltimoreans advertise in An-
   napolis newspaper.......109
Balto. growing importance....111
Bay, Ferry, across..........112
Baldwin. Mrs., died. aged 100.113
Ball at State House.... 131
Balls in Annapolis 140
Balls discontinued during Rev.140
Bacon, Lieut..............140
Balto. Co., lands in........160
Baltimore Town....130, 133, 162
Banishment, ordered into.....179
Bay frozen..... 184
Baron, Steuben............204
Barney. Joshua............205
Barbecue first.............225
Barber. John..............226
Banque' to Wm. Pinkney....250
Ball, rich and elegant.......252
Baltimore, House............252
Baltimore..........244. 245. 254
Basis of representation......245
Bagot, Hon. Henry 253
Bassford, Mr..............253
Bache, Lieut . .. .254
Barber, John T...........255-6
Baldwin, Wm. P...........257
Baldwin, Mrs. aged 100......264
Baldwin, Hester............264
Baldwin. Mrs. Ann.........264
Bancroft, Geo. historian..264-5-6
Baltimoreans reply with stones
   and pistols.............270
Barrall, Edward, shot.......271

Baltimore, a rival for........298
Bayly, Richard P...........300
Basil, J. S. M 305
Bates, Willy..............305
Ball room.................305
Barracks of Salvation Army...306
Barber, John T., estate of....307
Barbers and Sunday work....314
Base ball in Annapolis......315
Barnard, Hy., L. L. D.......315
Bartlett, Mrs. Lieut........320
Bay Ridge. opening of......323
Bayard, Thomas F..........324
Barnes, James..............167
Barber, Chas.............167
Ball, John...............167
Ball, Samuel... 167
Bassford, Jacob............261
Baltimore, Town of 191
Barnard. Dr. Henry........ 214
Belles, of Annapolis.........140
Bedstead in which Washing-
   ton slept................201
Bellis, Roger, Capt..........299
Bellis, Wm. H., Corporal....299
Belt, Thomas, the third.. ...170
Bennett, Richard..18,19.25,29,46
Bennett, Edward............ 19
Bennett, Rev. William....... 19
Bennett and Claiborne.25.27,28,56
Bennett, Gov. of Virginia.... 25
Bennett, Hon. Richard.......26
Beard, Ri........   ......43, 49
Between the differences, Tru-
   man escape.............. 55
Bennett, Mr. John.......... 63
Beard, Mr. R., plat of Annap. 64
Bell and belfry in St. Anne's 69
Beall. John.... ....70, 71
Beall, Benj................ 71
Bennett. John.............. 71
Bell of St. Anne's tolls its re-
   quiem................. 75
Bellis, Joseph II., translates
   epitaph... 76
Bell given by Queen Anne
   burned................ 77

Beauty of the scenery of A.. 81
Beard, Math 87
Beard, R., mat of, burned.... 97
Beven. Thomas............117
Beauty of America a we sen...141
Beauties of Antamated Youths.141
Belshazzer & Joan &, Cantatas
of....................148
Bewitching of the Lovely
Nancy................158
Bell of St. Anne's...........158
Beard, Charles.............229
Beall, Ephraim.............248
Bells. Roger, loses leg at
Gettysburg.............311
Bender, Geo., conductor......320
Bills of credit to build State
House.................120
Birth announced........ ...137-8
Birth of Dauphin celebrated..194
Birthday of Washington cele-
brated...... 222
Birth of Chas. Carroll, of Car-
rollton 275
Bigelow, W. O.............316
Bigger, John...............78
Birthday of Queen Caroline... 95
Bible Reading....... 101
Birthday of Lord Baltimore...119
Birthday of King, celebrated.119
Bloody fellows........... 32
Blunt, Mr. Richard......... 40
Bland, Thomas............. 68
Blackiston. Gov........... 69
Bladen, Mr. Wm........... 69
Bladen, Mr. Wm., architect
of second State House.... 80
Bladen, Wm...........19, 86, 88
Blasphemy. Levis P. tried for.113
Bladen, Gov. Thomas.......104
Bladen, Gov. Thos., speech of.104
Bladen, Gov. and Legislature.104
Bladen, Gov., called to acct..105
Bladen, Th. s. Esq., Gov.....137
Blockade of Annapolis.......187
Bladen, Gov....... .....98, 208
Bladen, Thomas, Esq........209
Blue Light vs. Blue Light...237
Bloodless Revolution.........214
Blair, Mr. Ed. of the Globe...263
Bland, Theodoric.......289, 273
Blake, Capt. comdn't of N. A.291
Bladen, Thomas.........97, 302
Bland, Chancellor, Theodoric.307

Boardley, Wm....,...... 86-88
Bond of Naval Officers........107
Bohemia River..... 117
Board of Public Works 162
Boston, resolutions about.....165
Boston, sympathy for 168
Bodkin, The 178
Bodkin Point..............191
Bordley, Stephen, Esq.......209
Boyce, James................ 227
Bowie, Capt., Mounted Riflem240
Borst much of power......... 32
Bordley, Daniel............ 71
Boucher, rector of St. Anne's. 75
Boothby, Edward........... 78
Bowles, Mrs. Rebecca........ 95
Bowles, James, Esq 95
Bodies washed ashore.......109
Bordley, Stephen......113, 302
Boston sufferers, collection for120
Bold riders.................128
Bowie, Robert...............226
Boyle's, Col. Jas. address to
La Fayette.............241
Bowie, T. H......... 253
Boyie, James................258
Board of Naval Officers......265
Boyle, Llwellyn.............282
Boessell, Christian............305
Bonsall, Mrs. Eliza..........308
Bowl, a notable............309
Boyle, Edward..............311
Bond, A. S.........   313
Boris, A. E., visit of........316
Bonsall, Robt. F., death of...318
Boundaries of Annapolis......334
Bonsall, Mrs. Eliza, (Note.)..235
British sloop aground........234
Brooke, Robert.............. 32
Braves of raising the country. 32
Brooks, Mrs. convicted of
slander................ 47
Bretton, Wm. clerk.. 49
Brick clay discovered near A. 63
Brooks, Mr. Michael......... 44
Bridewell, or House of Cor. 64
Bray, Dr. Rev. appointed com-
missioner........ 65
Brown, William.......... ... 68
Brick school house........... 78
Bradley, Mr. Robert......... 82
Brereton, Thomas........... 84
Brice, John.................. 87
B——, John 87

Briscoe, J. burned in the hand.103
Breton, Cape, garrison at....105
Britannia. ship..........111
Broad Creek, Kent Island....112
Brevity of account of execu-
   tion...................113
Bravery of a servant........117
Brown, John, executed.......118
Bristol, dies aged 125........120
Brooks, James..............120
Broomstick kills a man.......121
British traveller............128
Breach of promise cases. 138
Brice, James F.,............148
Brig Lovely Nancy..........158
British soldiers quartered upon164
Braddock, Gen. in Annapolis..160
Bryan, Charles.............165
Brown. John...............167
Brooks, Jas.......... 167
Browning, Joseph...........167
Braithwaite, Thomas........167
British ship of war..........175
Brice, John, 170, 176, 177,
   181, 198, 129, 281.
Brice, James, 167, 177, 181,
   187, 198, 200, 223.
British men of war......183, 184
British fleet and troops.......188
Bravery of Maryland troops..188
Brice, James, Mayor........ 195
Brown. Andrew.............222
Brice, Upton...............226
Brewer, Nicholas...........226
Brewer, Thomas............229
Brewer, Mrs. Susannah......229
Brice, John, of Robert.......229
British fleet off Annapolis ...234
British hover near Annapolis..238
Brice's, Capt. company 240
Brown, Saml. Jr.............256
Bridges over the Severn......257
Brewer, B. B...............259
Brewer, Nicholas...........263
Brewer, Nicholas, Judge, 269, 270
Brady, John W. shot........271
Brewer, Dr. Wm........273, 313
Brewer, Nicholas, of John....280
Brown, Mr. Joshua.281, 304, 313
Brown, Geo. Wm............289
Brewer, Julian, Corporal.....299
Bryan, Wm........273, 301, 315
Brewer, voice of Judge.........272
Brewer, Isaac...........304, 313

Brice, Mrs. James............307
Bridge over the Spa 313, 318, 324
Brewer, Nicholas.......316, 320
Bradley, Father James.......321
Brewer, Julian........ 325
Bridges leading to Annapolis.342
Brisk trade with Indians....... 22
Burgesses, if they neglect to
   send... 23
Burges, Capt. Wm. put in
   command 38
Burges', Capt. instructions... 38
Burgess, Capt. Wm......... 39
Burle, Robert.............. 49
Burle, Robert, suspended from
   house, confesses penitence
   for slander of Lord Balto. 49
Building of State House in A.. 66
Busy times in Annapolis...... 68
Burning of St. Anne's....... 75
Butler, Ed. rec. of St. Anne's 79
Butler. Ed. master of K. W's.
   School............ 79
Burning of Annapolis........ 81
Bull's, Mr. boat.... 82
Burning of the Records...... 83
Bukardike, Richard.......... 87
Burgesses of Annapolis have
   half wages.............. 94
Bull, riding upon............102
Burnt in the hand, J. Briscoe.103
Burnt to death, negroes.. ...103
Bullen, John, Esq.. 115
Bucknell, Mr. Richard.......146
Burdett............. 147
Burland, Richard............168
Burt, Richard...............168
Bull, Constantine............168
Burning of the Peggy Stewart169,
   170.
Burgess, John...........170, 176
Bullen, John, Capt...........170
Buchanan, Robert...........167
Bullen, John, 176, 177, 198, 228
Burning of Gazette Office....184
Bullen, John, Mayor.........193
Buckland, Mr. Benj..........224
Burning of Alms-house......224
Bull'tt, Thomas I...........225
Barneton, Joseph............229
Bush, Hy. II...............263
Buchanan, Fred. Commodore.266
Buchanan's proclamation....283
Butler, Gen. lands troops in A.285

Butler, B. F. letters of to Gov.
Hicks, 291, 292, 293, 294, 295
Butler seizes the Constitution.292
Burning of Parsonage........304

Burnside's expedition rendezvous at Annapolis.......300
Buckland, Mr..............306
By-Laws of Annapolis, 1746...109

C

Catholic Proprietary........... 17
Capt. Stone's invitation to
  Puritans............. 26
Captain Wm. Stone........28, 33
Capt. Claiborne.............. 29
Captains and Councillors of
  Susquehannah. 30
Catholics prohibited from vot. 31
Capt. Fuller & his associates.. 31
Catholics and Puritans....... 31
Capt. Tilman, Golden Fortune 31
Carried away the Records.... 32
Capt. Stone..............32, 36
Capt. Heamans.............. 35
Calvert County.............. 39
Capt. Burgess to make war on
  Indians 39
Calvert, Charles..........39, 41
Calvert, Wm. Esq.........40, 41
Catchpole, Judith, charged
  with murder........... 44
Calvert, once called Patuxent. 44
Catchpole, Judith, acquitted.. 45
Calvert, Philip, Esq........... 49
Capital removed to the Ridge. 56
Capital removed to Battle
  Creek 56
Capital once more settled at
  St. Mary's.............. 56
Catholics.................... 57
Catholics, people of St. Mary's 58
Cattle, hogs, sheep on the
  common 63
Carroll, Mr., Ruth's procurator 69
Calvert, Charles............. 70
Carroll, Chas. barrister, 71, 161.
  168, 170, 176, 205.
Camaliel, Butler............. 72
Card playing, dancing, drinking................... 75
Cabals at Annapolis........ 82
Carroll, Mr................ 83
Capital, Annapolis, contn'd as 86
Carroll, James..........86, 97
Carroll, Chas. Esq.... 95
Caravan to York, &c........100
Capuchin Friars.............101

Cain, John................102
Carroll, Dr. Chas. 102, 110, 112,
  117, 119, 160.
Called Session of Legislature..104
Cape Breton, Garrison at.....105
Canoe, pinnace for...........108
Canada, three companies go to.110
Carroll, Mrs. Mary.........112
Campbell, Capt.'s Company
  act cowardly.............112
Capture of the Hopewell......113
Carpenter, Capt. John........115
Calico horse 115
Campbell, Chas. executed....118
Carroll and Dulany..........121
Carroll, Chas. of Carrollton..121,
  170, 172, 176, 184, 205, 210,
  223, 256, 304, 305, 310.
Capital customs & characters.122
Cantatas of Belshazzer and
  Joseph..................148
Capt. Montague and the deserter...................157
Calvert family..............160
Carroll, Chas.........168, 171, 222.
Carroll, Chas. of Carrollton,
  Esq....................176
Campbell, Colin.............167
Carroll, Chas. of Carrollton,
  proposes to burn Peggy
  Stewart 174
Campbell, John.........177, 181
Capital of the U. S..........198
Capital of U. S. temporarily at
  Annapolis...............200
Carroll, Daniel.............200
Carroll, Rev. John..........209
Carr, John Addison 210
Carroll, Nicholas....222, 226, 228
Campbell...................222
Caton, Charles..............222
Caton, Wm.....224, 226, 229, 306
Carston, Thomas............224
Carroll, James..............229
Caton's Tavern.........230, 231
Carbury, Col..............234
Calvert, G............ 236

Calm at Annapolis............249
Caton's Hotel, City.........254
Capital, effort to remove. 254
Carroll, Thomas H..255, 257, 258
Canning, Stratford.. 256
Carr, Arthur...............257
Caucus party.... 258
Canal Company A. &. P..... 260
Carroll, Chas. mómento to ...263
Cast loose, the Jewess.... ...270
Calumny against Judge Brewer272
Caldwell, D. C..............273
Caulk, Daniel...............273
Canoe of Indians disappears...274
Carroll, Chas. of Carrollton,
  born at Annapolis........276
Carroll, Chas. millions of.....275
Carroll, Chas.removes to Balto.276
Cameron, Simon........285, 286
Calvert, Chas. B............299
Camp Parole... 300
Catholic Church, St. Mary's...304
Casler, M. R............305, 316
Carroll, Mrs. Nicholas.. 308
Cadet vacancy offered for sale.318
Carl, Christopher, foreman....319
Catholic Priests drowned.....321
Cecilius, Lord Baltimore...... 62
Centre of Province............ 62
Century old, Annapolis, a....108
Celebration of King's anniver-
  sary...................137
Celebration of taking of Quebec139
Celebration on Treaty of Peace 194
Celebration of Peace........221
Celebration of Washington's
  Birthday...... 222
Celebration over Peace...... .239
Cemeteries, public...........342
Churchmen of Virginia 17
Chandler, Job.............25-28
Chesapeake, Bay of.......... 29
Charge fierce, but brief....... 36
Charles I................... 24
Chandler, Mayor............ 36
Charles county.............. 39
Chase, J. T.................203
Chandler, I., a goldsmith....220
Chesapeake..... 191
Chinese cure alls, criticism of.100
Chancellor sent to acquaint
  L. H 51

Chriterson, Wenlock 437
Church, Lower House ready to
  build..... .:........... 68
Charter wanted by Annap.... 86
Charter of A. granted....... 87
Charter of the City of An.... 87
Charter of Annap. affirmed.... 93
Charter, act of Assembly on... 93
Chronicles of Annapolis 1707
  to 1740 96
Chronicles of Annapolis from
  1746 to 1774...............109
Chronicles of Annapolis, from
  1777 to 1810..............220
Chronicles of Annapolis, 1810
  to 1839..................253
Chronicles of Annapolis from
  1845 to 1847..............272
Chronicles of Annapolis from
  1860 to 1861..............280
Chronicles of Annapolis from
  1863 to 1887..............311
Church Circle 97
Chinese stones and powder....100
Cheap Indulgencies..........101
Character of the education....102
Church, the 105
Chapel and Church...........108
Church of England...........108
Changes Spiritual...........108
Chew, Lieut. Jos............112
Chester, ship..............116
Chew, Capt................118
Characters and customs of the
  capital...... 122
Change in gentlemen's dress...125
Chestertown................126
Chimneys, windows, cornices.129
Chester Town............... 145
Chase, Samuel...... 149-198
Church on north side of Severn157
Church on Severn burned......157
Church st., cove up.............157
Chase, Samuel, Esq..........158
Chase, Sam'l....165, 168, 170, 176
Chipchase, Thomas, butcher..175
Channell, between Horn Point
  and Greenbury's............177
Chesapeake frozen...........184
Chase, Jeremiah.............187
Chase, Judge Sam'l., befriends
  Pinkney...................221

23

Chalmers, John..............198, 199
Chase, Jeremiah T................222
Chapman. Hy. II.................226
Chase. Jeremiah T...226, 239. 306
Chesapeake attack on............226
Charter of Annapolis altered.230
Chandler, Jehu..................233
Chandler, Mr., Editor of the
    Republican.....................237
Chandler and Watkins fight..238
Chauncey, Commodore..........253
Changing charter.................255
Chandler. Jehu, death of.......256
Chase, Jeremiah Townley......260
Chase. Mrs. Jeremiah Townley264
Chase, Mrs. Sam'l..............264
Chauvelt, Prof...................266
Chase. R. M., dwelling of....266
Chase, Miss Hester.............273
Chesapeake. The................274
Cheers of Naval Academy bat-
    talion.........................282
Chaney, Andrew E..............284
Chase Mansion, The............306
Chase. Miss Hester Ann.......306
Chase. Sam'l., Judge..........306
Chandler. Jehu.............308. 324
Chase. Capt. Stephen..........316
Chandler, Jehu.................324
Chapel First, in Md............333
Charter, The. of Annapolis....334
Charter. City's, amendment to.342
Chalmers, John......167
Chambers, William..............168
Chew. Samuel.............170-176
City of Annapolis Charter of. 87
Cities right to erect............. 92
Citizens of Long Island mob
    Hood..........................150
Citizens killed by British
    soldiers.......................164
Citizens for Military Comp's...169
Citizens desert Annapolis......175
Citizens ordered into banish-
    ment..........................179
Citizens of Annapolis uphold
    credit of province...........187
Cincinnati, Society of...........196
City Hotel invaded.............269
City Election....................273
Citizen, The First...............175
Civil War, opening of..........281
Citizens meeting on the Union.284
Civil rights encroached upon.299

City Hotel..........201. 299. 305
City Tavern.....................306
Civil War, election during.....310
City Hall........................312
Citizens impressed.............314
City Government of Annapolis.315
Claiborne. Wm..................26
Claiborne. Col. William........26
Claiborne. Capt.................29
Clerk of House of Delegates... 66
Claggett, Mr. Richard.......... 70
Clarke, Richard, to burn A.... 81
Clarke's Richard. crime cry... 82
Clerk, Mr. Richard Dallam.... 82
Clarke's wife the disburser..... 83
Clarke's. Richard. personal
    appearance.................... 83
Clark, attainder of............. 83
Clarke's accomplices........... 83
Clarke, Richard, attainder of. 84
Clarke, Richard, probably not
    executed...................... 85
Clerk, Council, W. Bladen.... 87
Clouds. Nicholas, keeps boats.112
Collier. John.................... 19
Clergymen of culture...........127
Clubs no new thing in Annap..131
Clubs in session................131
Clubs, Anniversaries of.........134
Clubs. gelastic law in..........135
Clubs. ancient doings of........136
Claude, Abraham. Mr...........149
Claude, Joseph, arch't killed...162
Clapham. John..............167, 190
Claims of St. John's, settle-
    ment of.......................214
Clarke, Wm. stage route.......221
Clarke, Charles.................222
Clarke, Joseph..................229
Claude, Dr. D.253, 254. 255, 258.
    260, 261, 284, 297
Claude. Dr. Abram.............273
Claude. William Tell......273, 311
Clayton, P. C...................273
Clayton, Captain................282
Clemm, Rev. Mr................284
Clayton, Philip.............261, 304
Claude, Dr. Dennis, death of...311
Claude, Dr. Abram, Mayor....312
Clayton, Mr. Louis S. store of.319
Classens, Father Louis.........321
Clayton, Wm....................167
Clarke. James..................168
Congregational Church.......... 17

Conventicle broken up. ... 17
County Neck........................ 18
Company of Puritans............ 19
Cox, James....................... 21
Cox, James, made Speaker of.
the House..................... 21
Catlyn, Henry.................... 21
Commander to grant land war-
rants........................... 22
Colony mentioned in the in-
structions...................... 24
Commissioners of Md. came
with armed force............ 25
Commissioners revisit Mary-
land........................... 25.
Commissioners of the Common-
wealth........................ 26
Copy of treaty made on Severn. 29
Commissioners counsel obedie. 27
Council of State in England.... 28
Council unwilling to trust Tay-
lard........................... 85
Corporation of Annapolis, peti-
tion of........................ 86
Common Councilmen of Anna. 87
Confirm Bal'o's patent to him. 32
Colonists to give notice of in-
tended war..... 30
Commissioners appointed for
Maryland...................... 30
Coursey, Mr..................... 34
Cole, Josias, bondsman for Mr.
Thurston..................... 38
Colonial Life.................... 40
Courts, Records from 40
Cowman, John, pardoned of
witchcraft.................... 42
Courageous spirit of Maryland
setters................ 50
Conquests, His Majesty power
to dispose of................. 51
Conquered people likened....... 51
Commissioners of Proctors..... 52
Commissioners reappointed in
1694.......................... 54
Coode, John, leader of the As-
sociation..................... 57
Convention held by Coode and
others......................... 57
Copley, Sir Lionel, first royal
Governor...................... 57
Copley convenes the Legisla-
ture........................... 57
Commissioners of 1694.......... 62

Corporation of St. Mary's peti-
tion........................... 57
Col. Nicholson has done his en-
deavor........................ 58
Copley, Gov. enters upon his
duties......................... 60
Coach, or caravan, to be pro-
vided.......................... 60
Common, the Town.............. 63
Cornhill Street.................. 64
Commissioners of A., to make
by-laws....................... 64
Committee to build church at
Annapolis..................... 65
Colbach, Joseph, of All Hal-
lows.......................... 66
County clerk to keep the county
records in.................... 66
Committee Room................ 67
Coney, Mr. to read prayers be-
fore the House................ 67
Coney, Peregrine, master of N.
W's. School.................. 68
Coney, Peregrine, rector St.
Anne's....................... 68
Coney, Rev. Peregrine, a de-
fendent....................... 69
Coney, Mr. has the confidence
of Governor................... 69
Coney's, Rev. Peregrine, serm. 69
Cole, Charles,.................. 71
Conden, Robert................. 71
Cost of St. Anne's in 1792...... 75
Communion vessels............. 77
Council of the Province 78
Coney, Rev. Peregrine.......... 78
Coursey, Henry................. 78
Committee report old walls
good.......................... 80
Court House.................... 80
Council Chamber................ 81
Contee, Col. Richard........... 82
Conspiracy..................... 82
Counterfeit money.............. 82
Cooper........................ 83
County pardon................. 83
Common Council to be ten per-
sons.......................... 89
Constables, authority to make 89
Common Councilmen of Annap 89
Courte of Pypowdry............ 90
Court of Record................ 91
Cook, Eden, gent............... 91
Complaints from Annapolis.... 92

Courts to continue in Annapo. 93
Corporation of Annapolis....... 96
Counties. schools in............ 97
Colebatch, Rev. Mr. Jos........ 97
Compilation of Laws........... 97
Commun. Romish, persons of.102
Controversy between Governor
　Bladen and Legislature...104
Corporation by-laws of 1746...109
Companies, three, go to Canada110
Convoy. fleet under............111
Cole, Capt. German...........111
Coulter. Capt...................111
Council House, villians broke
　into............................111
Cowardice of Capt. Campbell's
　company.....................112
Coulborn, Capt................113
Cornish. Thomas. Capt.....114-115
Court of Admiralty at Annna.114
Convicts arrive at Annapolis.116
Convicts commit crimes...... 116
Cole, Charles, robbed...........117
Conner, John, convict..........117
Courteous convict..............117
Convicts. authorities alarmed.117
Court House struck by light-
　ning...........................119
Collection for sufferers in Bos.120
Colonial Society. ranks of.......126
Colonial mansions............. 128
Cornices. windows, chimneys...129
Coffee House, Annapolis...... .130
Cole, Mr. Charles............133-134
Conundrums of Tuesday club..135
Courage of the Marylanders...143
Commission, description by
　Naval. of Annapolis.......145
Company of comedians from
　Va................................146
Comedians. American com-
　pany of.......................147
Courtesy of Governor Eden....152
Convention of Maryland.176, 154,
　222
Claiborne, Secretary of Va... 52
Committee of safety......... ...155
Congress urges Gov. Eden's
　seizure........................155
Confiscation of Gov. Eden's
　property.....................157
Cove up Church St...........157
Col. Plater's Grey Stallion.....159
Coxen, Nicholas, Capt........159

Companies from Anna. against
　French.........................160
Corner stone of State House...161
Convention of five States..... 163
Court of Appeals...............163
Committee of the Province....168
Convention 169
Correspondence, private ex-
　amined 175
Committee of observation.176, 178
Council of safety 177, 178, 179, 181,
　182.
Consternation in Annapolis....177
Count Pulaski's legion.........184
Congress orders a monument
　to De Kalb...................186
Count Rochambeau.............194
Continental currency..........200
Congress settles seat of govern-
　ment..........................200
Council of State, address of, to
　Washington.................202
Council of State, Washington's
　reply to.....................202
Congress 206
College, St. John's.............. 208
College, Washington...........208
Commencement, first of St.
　John's........................210
Condition of grant to St John's.209
Connell, John, Mr..............212
College, Presid't, of St. John's.213
College seized by government.214
Correspondence of Washing-
　ton, about St. John's Col-
　lege............................219
College, St. John's, and Wash.219
Court of Appeals...............220
Col. Mills,.......................221
Commerce of Annapolis.........222
Cockey. Edward.................222
Coates, John....................223
Coats, Thomas..................224
Counterfeits on Farmers Bank.227
Court of Hustings..........228, 230
Counden, Robert............168, 228
Corporation, election...........335
Corporation of Annapolis, pow-
　ers of.........................336
Contents........................ 9
Competent witnesses..........341
Construction of roads to Anna.342
Construction of bridges to An.342
Cooke, William................166

Conner, M. W..................261
Committee of Public Safety
   meeting......... 297
Company of secession youths...297
Confederate prisoners in Anna299
College Green............ 302
Colton, Luther F..........306, 324
College Campus, poplar on....308
College of Electors..............245
Correspondence of Elector...245,
   246, 247
Corncracker, Jenny.............252
Cooke, Geo. Frederick..........253
Company of Pennsylvanians...253
Colonization of free colored...254
Conflict bet. State and U. S..255
Court House in Annapolis....256
Cowman, Richard.................272
Contest of 1860.......... 281
Contee, John....................283
Correspondence of Gov. Hicks
   and Government.......... .285
Constitution seized by Butler..292
Collation given by Lloyd Du-
   lany................... 309-310
Counter of Old City Hotel......309
College. St. John's.............312
Colored people enlisted.........313
Convention of 1864............. 313
Constitution of 1864........ 313
Colton, Geo..................316, 324
Collector and Treasurer of An.320
Cromwell, Nathan................222
Crowder, Elizabeth, servant..261
Cromwell and the American
   plantations...... 24
Cromwell's elevation, view of. 27
Cromwell's two letters.......... 32
Cromwell.......................... 34
Cry of St. Mary's men.......... 36
Cry of Puritans.................. 36
Creek up King Geo. St.,(note) 64

Cropped negro's ear............ 95
Crowder, Elizabeth...............100
Criticism of Chinese cure all...101
Cruelties upon criminals.......102
Criminals, cruelties upon.......102
Croftis, Capt.................. 110
Cregh, Capt......................111
Crabs, terrapins, canvas-back
   ducks............ 127
Crabb, Richard J...........260-261
Cried the hours..................325
Crinnig, David.....................168
Cross, Joshua................... 168
Commission to Edward Lloyd. 21
Commissioners of Anne Arun. 21
Cuts, Capt..................... 35
Curate of St. James............ 72
Custom House, lot for............ 98
Culture and refinement.........109
Cuffee executed for horse
   stealing...... 116
Cumberford. Mrs., stabbed to
   death...................... 120
Curious items published.........121
Customs and characters of the
   capital......... 122
Customs of the times, 1765... 124
Culture, clergymen of.......... 27
Custom house of Annapolis....130
Curious Executioners..........138
Carran, Mr. Philip..............212
Custis, Geo. W. Parke.........220
Curran, William B..............263
Curtain. Gov. A., of Pa.........295
Curfew-bell in A...... 325
Customs of Indians............. 334
Crawford, James, killed by
   lightning...... 57
Crawford. James............. 78
Crime of Richard Clarke....... 82
Crowley. Charles................ 86

D

Davidson, Lieut...............242
Davis, E. A. Mr...........269, 273
Davis, John M.................273
Davis, William................273
Davenport, Rev. Mr...........284
Davidson, Mrs. sent across line.312
Davids n, Lieut. Hunter......312
Danenhower, Lieut. John W.321
Davis, Saml.................324
Davis, Benj...................176
Dead bodies floating in dock..120
Delegates in the province......143
Devotees of fashion...........144
Description of A., by Naval
    Commission............"""145
Departure of Gov. Eden re-
    quired..................155
Departure of Gov. Eden........156
Desertion of a soldier........157
De Lancey, of New York........160
Declaration of Independence...164
Delegates to Congress.........169
Declaration of Maryland......180
Delegates, Declaration of.....180
De Kalb's death.............186
Deye, Thomas C...............197
Dedication of St. John's Col-
    lege...................209
Detargny, Mr. Marin..........212
Decision, Dartmouth College...213
Denning, James..............224
Denning, Robert.............225
Democrats..............244, 250
Delegates to the House........250
Democrats of Anne Arundel..301
Dennis, Rev. Alex...........305
Demidorf, Russi'n sailor, killed312
Development of ills...........314
Decoration, Joint of graves,...315
Deale, James, of Jas..........315
Detective Shaffer............318
Description of natives of Md..332
Devenith, Wm...............167
Descended from the hardy
    stock...................19
Desperate and bloody fellows.32
Declaration of Gov. Stone.....34
Deputys of Calvert...........44
Deputys of Anne Arundel...44
Delegates constrained to com-
    plai 54
Designation of rooms in State
    House...................66
Denton, Vachel..........70, 98

Dent, William................78
De Kalb Statue........78, 186, 324
Designs, great and dangerous.82
Devall, John.................83
Delegates, two from Annap....85
Delegates, none from Annap...85
Delegate, one from Annapolis.85
Delegates, Annapolis wants....86
Delegates, mode electing......86
Delegates, estate of.........89
Description of Annapolis......92
Delegates, from Anna. denied.92
Debtors in Jail..............98
Deptford, procession at.......101
Delegates of Annapolis......102
Displeasure of Charles II.....24
Dishonor of Almighty God.....54
Dissolution of Assembly.......93
Dimensions of the Gazette.....98
Dispute between Gov. Bladen
    and Legislature...........105
Dispute between Dulany and
    Carroll..................121
Discussion of ladies dress....126
Division amongst the colonists155
Dinwiddie, Gov. in Annap....160
Dimensions of the State House162
Dinner to Washington....192, 203
    205, 218.
Diggs, George...............209
Difficulty to secure meeting...209
Dissipat'n alleged at St. Jon s.211
Disappearance of the Ancient
    Regime..................228
Dissensions, internal!........234
Disloyalty, on election day...311
Devins, E. T. Conductor......320
Disastrous Accident, A........321
Documn's and records removed.56
Dorsey, Major, Edwa'd.63, 64, 302
Dorsey, Mr. John.............63
Dorsey, Edward, fined.........69
Dorsey, Edward...............78
Donations to free schools......78
Donera, Tho.................87
Doctor Street...............97
Donnahoe, drowned...........114
Dock, dead bodies floating in.120
Dobinton, Ralph.............121
Dobbins, Capt. James.........126
Dorsey, Mr. Speaker, of club..126
Doings of the ancient clubs....136
Dogworthy, Capt............160
Dome of State House added....161

Dorsey, Thomas......168, 170, 176
Dooly's. Capt. company.........240
Dooly, Capt....................243
Dorsey, Thomas B..............256
Dowlin, P., foreman...........320
Dolman, Jacob V. Capt........320
Dove, The. (Note,)............328
Donaldson, John...............167
Dogan, Edward................. 167
Dowson, Joseph................168
Dorsey, Philip................170
Dorsey, Ely. Sir..............170
Dorsey, Caleb 170, 176
Dorsey, John, son of Michael.176
Dorsey, Daniel................261
Drunkenness. Swearing, False
    Reports...................... 31
Draper, Lawrence.............. 68
Drollery, actors played with...102
Drew les who should kill......102
Drinking pretender's health...110
Drowning of Vickers, Fish,
    Donahoe.....................114
Dress of the times, 1765.......124
Dress, gentleman's, change in.125
Dress, ladies, discussed.......126
Dress, heirlooms...............127
Drinking of pretender's health
    punished....................137
Drama patronized by Governor
    Eden........................140
Dramas 146
Drama poorly sustained.........148
Dreadful, dismal, &c...........151
Drowning of Rev. Thomas
    Robinson....................272
Dressel, John..................305
Drowning of Catholic Priests
    and students. 321
Durand, Mr.................... 17
Durand, Mr. William...31, 32, 87
Durand, Wm. Secretary..... 33
Durand, Wm. makes requisi-
    tion......................... 34
Duff, Simon................... 71
Dulany, Daniel, quarrel with. 72
Durand's place................ 96

Dulany, Esq., Daniel........ 98
Dulany, Walter, 103, 115, 118, 120
    159.
Dulany, Miss Margaret......112
Dulany, Walter, discharged
    from Legislature.........116
Dulany, Hon. Daniel.........118
Dunlap, Capt. drowns himself.121
Dulany and Carroll..........121
Dulany's opinion 127
Duties of a servant..........131
Dunmore, Lord...............155
Dulany, Daniel..............161
Dulany, Lloyd...............166
Duckett, John, clerk........169
Duckett, Mr. John, 172, 174, 181
    182.
Dual government.. 175
Duvall, Gabriel.............175
Duvall, G...................176
Du Buysson, Col.............183
Duke, Mr...................212
Dunning, Dennis............222
Dunn, Patrick..............222
Duvall, Lewis..225, 226, 263, 257
Duvall, Capt...............227
Duvall, Washington........248
Duvall, Lewis, Mayor......255-7
Duvall, Hy.................255
Duvall, J. W..............258
Dupont...................266
Dulanys, The..............267
Dulany, Dan'l., born at An...278
Duvall, John...............301
Duvall, Richard J..........302
Duff, Mr., the architect.....302
Dunlap, Rev. Mr............304
Dulany, Mr. Lloyd..........305
Dulany, Lloyd, collation giv-
    en by.............309, 310
Duvall, Geo. M.........311
Dulany, Lloyd.............166
Dulany, Daniel of Walter....167
Dulany, Daniel of Dan.....168
Duvall, Gabriel...........176
Dwelling House for Governor. 98
Dwellings, magnificent......168

E

Each settler receiving one lot 18
Early Ridgelys, first settled. 19
Earthquake in Annapolis in
    1755.......................118

Eastern Shore of Maryland.... 81
Earthquake at Annapolis 1758 120
Earthquake at Annapolis.1772.121
Earthquake in Annapolis......326

Ear cut off, sentenced to have.137
Ease of American ladies.........143
Eastern Shore tribes.............161
Earle, Jr., James 226
Eagle, explosion of the.........359
Early's invasion excites A......314
Eccleston. John....................196
Eccleston. Col....................196
Eddis, Wm. observant..........72
Eddis, Wm. attends divine
   service in Annapolis.......73
Edmyston, recto of St. Anne's 75
Eddis. Mr. writes of State
   House............................81
Edward, Cadder..................87
Education. character of the..102
Eddis writes of Annapolis......140
Eden. Gov.....152, 156, 182, 208
Eddis, Wm. Mr......152, 165, 167.
   170, 190, 199, 201, 208.
Eden, Gov. required to depart.155
Eden, Gov. prospect to return.155
Eden's, Gov. property confis·.157
Eden, Gov. return of..........157
Eddis, Mr. wrote................156
Eddis. Gov. Eden's advice to.156
Eddis', Mr. life in Annapolis...178
Edwards, William...............167
Edmons, Amos....................168
Eddis, Mr. fined................178
Eddis. Mr. leaves Annapolis..182
Eddis, Mr. summoned before
   Committee......................189
Eddis and Clapham to give
   bond............................190
Eden's Gov. Proclamation on
   fees............................279
Eden, Robert.....................303
Educational facilities in A....324
Effort to enlarge Proctor's port 54
Effigies of Bute and Greville..149
Effigy of Hood. stamp officer.149
Effort to remove Capital....254
Elder of the Independents ..17
Elk River..........................29
Eltonhead. Mr. Wm. executed 36
Election, mode of................46
Elliott. William.................86
Elliott, C. sentenced to death.115
Election of Geo. Stewart set
   aside..........................120
Electricity in 1749, in Annap.138
Erection in the province.....143
Electoral College...........244

Electors correspondence of....245,
   246, 247.
Elliott, John.....................248
Elliott, Elias....................262
Election of Lincoln......281, 284
Election in Annapolis...........284
Election in Annapolis during
   Civil War 310
Election of Corporation.........335
Election, Judges of.............335
Election returns. Judges of....336
Embassadors of the Susque-
   hannocks.......................55
Emblem of public poverty......81
Emigrants to Annapolis.........128
English yeomanry.................19
English inhabitants..............23
Encroachments resisted by Leg 50
Enormous crimes...................54
Entire possesion of the prov...57
Encouragement to St. Mary's 59
Ennals, Thomas....................78
Entrance to the Severn.........81
Entitled to privileges and laws 93
Encouragement of Tradesmen 96
Engine for city...................118
English, sun of...................129
English Lord.......................157
Entrenching Annapolis, 1755.160
English oppression, resolution
   against.........................168
English officer's representation186
Enemies of St. John's...........200
Enemy's ships off Annapolis..234
Encroachment on civil rights.299
Enrollment of Anne Arundel.300
Enrollment of Annapolis.......301
Enlistment of colored people.313
Enterprise Building Asso'n...316
Enright, Father Timothy......321
Ewen. Mr. Richard...............31
Erberry, Edward. merchant...40
Erberry, Edward. abuses the
   house, 40; tried, 41; found
   guilty, 41; punished with
   whipping 41.
Ewing. Chas. H., Rev.........304
Escheated to the State.........19
Establishment of K.W's School 77
Estate of delegates.............89
Estep. Ralph 256
Establishment of Annapolis
   Gazette.......................300
European social life............145

Evitts, John............167
Evans, Mr. Wm............221
Evans, Mr............244
Evans, John............248
Evans, Joseph............303
Extracts from Journals.........40
Exportation to be from ports. 53
Expelled from the House, Mr.
   Joseph Hill...............85
Executions stayed at fairs.......90

Executions, brevity of account113
Extra Session, Gov. Ogle calls113
Express office............121
Executioners, curious..........138
Executive Chamber............163
Exchanging of Portraits.....164
Exportation prohibited..........175
Explosion of Steamer Eagle...259
Expedition from Annapolis....299
Excited over haunted houses..314

F

Fable of the Camel and Arab
   enacted.........31
Fair to be held every year in
   Annapolis.........64
Fairs in Annapolis...........65, 90
Family comes 30 miles to
   church.........70
Fairs, processes stayed at.....90
Fair days, two.........94
Fashion, luxury, commerce...108
Farris, Wm. watchmaker......122
Farris, Wm. will of.........122
Farris, Chas. (in note)..123, 149.
   229.
Families, principal.........128
Fairs, annual.........130
Fair games.........130
Fashions, quick importation of 142
Fashions and frivolty.........144
Factious men.........144
Fashionable pleasure.........144
Fair grounds in Annapolis......159
Faculty of St. John's.........211
Farmers, Bank of Maryland....225
Fairbain, Benj.........229
Father Andrew White's Journ.327
Father Altham.........331
Fendall. Josais.........38
F. Fenwick's, his house........47
Fendall. Josiat.........48
Fendall, Gov.........56
Ffielder. T. architect of church 65
Few rectors of K. W's school
   known.........79
Feast day of St. Michaels....88
Fees, profits, perquisites.......90
Feast and frolics.........91
Fees, men sold for.........111
Ferry acros the bay.........112
Ferry boat overset.........114
Fencing and Dancing.........126

Females, single, petition of.
   Annapolis.........133
Festival of St. George observed136
Federal Goverament seizes St.214
Federalists of Maryland......233
Federalist Party.........253
Fears of a riot.........269
Fees laid by proclamation....279
Federal Government and Gov.
   Hicks.........285 to 295
Fees and penalties.........341
Fenton, Cornelius.........168
First to arrive at the Severn... 18
Fireworks against the ship.... 35
Fifty men slain.........36
Five Indians chief murdered.. 54
First evidence to St. Mary's.. 56
First session of Leg. in Annap 63
First convocation held in A... 66
First State House in Annap.. 67
Fire quenched by industry of 67
First brick church in Md..... 69
Ffielder, Thos. achitect of St.
   Anne's.........69
Fire in St. Anne's.........75
First Mayor of Annapolis. ... 76
Finley, Elizabeth.........83
First newspaper in Maryland. 94
Fine, free from.........96
First issue of the Gazette. ... 99
Fish women and the King...... 99
Fines, forfeitures,amerc'ments107
Fire, warehouse lost by......110
Fish, Benj. T. drowned..... 114
Fire engine.........118
First citizen, the letters of 121
First American Theatre erected
   in Annapolis.........146
First shipyard.........157
First commencement of St
   John's.........230

First lottery in province......159
First U. S. Senator from Md 222
Fire in government house....222
Firing off guns in the streets 223
Fight between Chandler and
  Watkins................238
Fish, John 248
First passenger from Annapolis263
Fire in State House...........273
First citizen, the............275
First M. E. Church............303
First Church of Methodism....303
First Presbyterian Church in
  Annapolis................304
Fire at Smith Price's 311
Fire, "Noah's Ark" injured...313
Fire disastrous in Annapolis...219
First regular train on Short
  Line.....................320
First accident toRedemptorists323
First Chapel in Maryland......333
Fire Department of Annapolis. 15
Finlater, Alex 169
Flattery unavailing......... 62
Flames, Inquisition, Damna-
  tion.... 101
Fleet, under convoy..........111
Fleming, Richard 229
Flags of Southern Confederacy313
Fleet, Capt. Henry..........331
Fort for trade............... 29
Four or 5 Marylanders escape. 36
Fort invested by Md. and Va.
  troops................... 54
Foundation of State House in
  Annapolis................. 66
Forty shillings for every burial 69
Form of second State House.. 80
Fordham, Benjamin..... 86, 88
Fornication 101
Forfeiture, fines, amerciament107
Fort Frederick 118
Fox chase ... .128
Fowey, the Frigate...... 156
Forty, Lieutenant 160
Fostell, Dr. Richard.........176
Form of State Government
  established...............176
Fortification of Annapolis......177
Four future Presidents......206
Forrest, Noah...............222
Fortification asked for A.....227
Fort Severn....240, 241, 254, 255,
  258, 259, 266.

Fowler, Daniel................229
Fort Severn, from, regulars..243
Fountain, Marcy........245, 250
Fountain, M 248
Fort Madison................254
Fort Severn recommended for
  Naval Academy............265
Four regts. wanted from Md..285
Four Gubernatorial residences.302
Forty, John.............. ...305
Fortification at Annapolis....314
Fowler, James...............316
Fostell, Richard.............176
Foulks, Saml. hidden in hogs-
  head......................248
Frequent and violent changes 31
Free exercise of their religion 37
Friends early settle in Md.... 42
Friends petitioning to affirm.. 42
Freemen of Maryland.......52, 105
Freeman, Mr. John......69, 86, 87
Free school of brick in A..... 58
Frazier, Alexandria 70
Frazier, Joshua.......... 71, 177
Friend of Lord Baltimore.... 72
Free schools, donations to.... 78
Free schools, subscriptions to. 78
Friends and supporters of K.
  W's school............... 79
Frisby, Col. John............ 82
Free voters of Annapolis..... 88
Free-holders of Annapolis...... 89
Free-holders and freemen...... 89
French writer on Annapolis... 91
French hair dresser in A..91, 145
Freemen, Wm. bricklayer...... 96
Friars, Capuchin............101
Frenchmen on the right........102
French privateer.............111
French men of war...........111
French capture the Hopewell.113
French and Indians...........118
Freemen of Annapolis aroused139
French troops...............187
French Frigates........187, 188
Frigate Philadelphia..........225
Frazier, Richard....... 229
Free negro Tom..............229
Frigate, Phaeton............259
Free people of color..........251
Franklin, J. S..............282
Frederick city..............285
Franklin, Geo. E............303
Franchise, right of..........310

Franklin, Thomas..............311
Frazier, Henry, Jr. killed....315
Fraternization of soldiers.....315
Frey, Asst. Marshal attacked.318
French, Thomas...............167
French, George...............168
Fuller, Capt. Wm..29, 30, 31, 32, 44.
Fuller, Capt. appears behind Gov. Stone................ 35

Fuller. Capt. calls a council... 34
Fuller, Capt. gives word to begin battle................ 36
Full hearing on both sides..... 55
Full house regrets removal of Capital................ 60
Funds of K. W's School conveyed to St. John's........ 79
Funds for Gov's. residence... 98
Funds of K. W's School......225

G

Galloway, William........... 19
Gallery for servants in St. Anne's 75
Gap in the history of Provide. 40
Gates of Annapolis 64
Gaddess. Mr., arrives in An... 41
Garrett. Mr. Amos........69, 97
Gallery of St. Anne's altered. 69
Gallery built in St. Anne's... 70
Gallery in St. Anne's, leave to build................ 71
Gaither, Rezin 71
Gaither, William........... 71
Gazette, poem on St. Anne's in 73
Gallery in St. Anne's for parishioners................ 75
Gallery in St. Anne's for slav. 75
Garrett, Amos, body of, seized 76
Garrett, James............. 76
Garthorne, Francis......... 77
Gales, Mr., sloop of........ 83
Garrett. Amos, Mayor....... 86
Gaylard. William 86
Garrett, Amos, Esq......... 87
Gazette. The Maryland...94, 125
Gazette ceased publication.... 96
Gazette, Maryland, reliable services 98
Gazette, dimensions of the.... 98
Gazette, news in............ 99
Gazette, Md., inaugural addr. 99
Gazette, advertisement in.. 99
Gazette, subscription to the.. 99
Gazette, encouraged.........100
Gazette, marvelous in........101
Garrison at Cape Breton.....105
Gazette, the........109, 323, 324
Gazette, jealous of Balto.....111
Gallows at Annapolis........114
Gang of miscreants in Annap.120
Galloway, Samuel.........126

Garden, Queen Anne's.........129
Gazette in deep mourning....150
Gale in Annapolis...... 161, 273
Garrett, John W...........163
Gazette office burned........184
Gates, General 185, 210
Garnett, President. of St. J..213
Gale, George................222
Gassaway, John........226, 230
Gazette and republicans quarr236
Garrison...................242
Gardner, Wm. Brewer....257, 316
Galaxy of Illustrious Annap..275
Gambrill, Lieut. Horace......281
Gazette, Annapolis, view.282, 283
Gazette defends itself.......296
Gazette, Annapolis, establis..300
Gantt. Benj. E..............302
Gazette fails to obtain print...312
Gantt, Edward C............315
Galilean Hall..............316
Gassaway, Aug..............316
Gassaway, L. G.............325
Gaither, Edward. Jr....170, 176
Galloway, Joseph...........176
Gassaway, Lewis........261, 304
Gov. Stone urges the Puritans to take oath............ 16
General Pardon granted..... 24
Gerrard, Capt.............. 36
General Assembly heedful of St. Anne's.............. 69
George, Joshua............. 70
George, William........... 70
General Assembly appealed to for St. Anne's........... 74
Geddess, Andrew........... 79
Geetment for any lands........ 91
Gentleman's dress, change in.125
Gelastic law in clubs........135
German passengers..........139

Germain, Lord George.......154-5
General Lee..... 154
Gen. Washington...............150
Gerry, Elbridge...................206
Getzendanner. Capt... 234
George, Enoch.......245, 248, 250
Gerdemain, Father John.......321
Gheselin, Reverdy.........167, 226
Giving out threatening speech 32
Gittings, John, clerk............ 41
Gilliss, John.................... 71
Giles. Charles, commander .. 111
Gibbetted, Morris McCoy.....121
Gist, Gen............. 196
Gibson, John...............225-6
Giddings, Major Luther, given
    a sword 274
Girault, Prof. A. N. 304
Gibbons, Rev. H. O.........304
Gibson, Capt. Edward.......306
Gibson, Mrs., nee Ridout.....308
Gibbons, Ensign.............320
Ghiselen, William............ 71
"Glorious Nineteen"...........249
Glass Works.................323
Golden Lyons................ 35
Goodall, Elizabeth, bewithed.. 42
Godson, Peter, charged with,
    slander, and medical char-
    latanism 45
Gov. from Virginia............. 46
Gov. Seymour.... 67
Good lodgings in Annapolis... 57
Gov. Nicholson. 58, 60
Gov. Copley enters upon his
    duties................ 60
Gov. Nicholson given a lot...... 64
Gott, Thomas..... 19
Gov. Stone, exceedingly popu. 25
Gov. Stone proclaims Crom-
    well........... 27
Gov. Stone censures the comr's 27
Gov. Stone submits the second
    time........................... 28
Gov. Stone attempts to sur-
    prise comr's 29
Golden Fortune, Capt. Tilman. 31
Gov. Stone re-assumes duties
    of office................ 31
Gov. Stone determines to assert
    his rights............. . 32
Gov. Stone organizes a mili-
    tary force............ ... 32
Gov. Stone directs no writs

from the Puritans shall be
    obeyed.................. 32
Gov. Stone's party threaten to
    hang.............. 32
Gov. Stone............33, 34, 35
Gov. Stone's force........ ... 33
Gov. Stone's march to Provi-
    dence.................... 33
Gov. Stone visits Providence 21
Gov. Stone organizes Anne
    Arundel 21
Gov. Stone submits to the com. 25
Gov. Stone's com. seized..... 25
Gov. Stone has a saving clause 26
Gov. Nicholson selects site of
    St. Anne's.............. 69
Gov. Nicholson active for St.
    Anne's................:........ 69
Gov. Blackiston............. 69
Golden ball on St. Anne's.... 69
Gordon, Robt........ 70
Governors and office-holders.. 75
Governors, visitors, Trustees
    of K. W's School........ 78
Governor and Council session 81
Governor. John Seymour....... 81
Gordon, Patrick, Esq. Gov. of
    Pa..................... 95
Governor of Pa. visits Gov. Md 95
Governor's, residence........:. 98
Gov. Saml. Ogle.............. 98
Gov. and Legislature, sharp
    messages between........100
Gordon, Capt. Robert........102
Gordon, Robt. Esq.103, 115, 118
Governors important peroga-
    tive. 104
Governor Bladen and Legis...104
Governor Bladen called to ac-
    count 105
Gov. Bladen's 3 messages in 1
    day 107
Gov. Ogle. calls extra session.113
Gov. Ogle's speech to Legis-
    lature...................113
Gov. Ogle, disappointed by
    Legislature.............113
Gordon, Mr. John...........115
Gordon Rev. John to prepare
    a discourse.............133
Gov. Eden, patronizes the
    drama..................140
Governor can pardon.........114
Godwin............ 147

Gov. Sharpe 150, 151
Governor Eden, of Maryland, 152.
  153, 154.
Governor Eden patronizes the
  stage........ 153
Gov. Eden establishes a semi-
  nary....................153
Gov. Eden recommended to be
  seized..... 154
Gov. Eden, parole of........154
Gov. Eden's departure required155
Gov. Eden returns 157
Gov. Eden departs 156
Gov. Eden's property confis-
  cated..................157
Gov. Lee 158
Gov. Ogle's Bay Gelding.....159
Governor....................178
Gov. Eden ... .182
Gov. Johnson..........183, 184
Goldsmith, Wm 198
Government House on fire....222
Golder, Archibald..........229
Government Farm 257
Godman, John D. born at An-
  napolis................ 277
Governor's Guards......280, 283
Gov. Hicks' proclamation....281
Gov. Hicks' convenes Legislat285
Government and Gov. Hicks
  285 to 295
Gov. Hicks' message to Legis.296
Governor's Folly, the........302
Goodman, R. R.............. 304
Gorman, Wm. H............306
Governors of Md 11
Gordon, George........ 167
Gordon, William...........167
Goldsmith, Saml 261
Goldsborough, W. J.........261
Greensbury Point............ 18
Greene, Thomas 24
Greene, Mr., Governor....... 46
Gornoore, John, punished for
  perjury........... 47
Greene, John... 48
Greenbury, Esq., Hon. Nicho-
  las....................63, 64
Great room below stairs...... 66
Greensbury's Point, church on 69
Gregg, Ruth, petition from... 69
Graveyard beyond present cir. 69
Greene. Richard............. 71

Griffith, John........ ... 71
Great and dangerous designs 82
Greenfield, Col.............. 84
Grosham, Jr., John.......... 86
Great seal of our said Province 91
Green, Mr. Jonas.....92, 96, 118
Green, Jonas, Printer....98, 112
Green, Jonas, Postmaster...... 99
Grant, Hector................102
Grindell, Capt................111
Grand Inquest to enquire....112
Green St..................117, 157
Green, Jonas, family has small-
  pox 119
Green, Jonas............134-5-6
Gregor, Capt. 137
Grindall, Capt...... 137
Great case at Annapolis....... 138
Grant of Charles I...........152
Green, Major, Gen. Nath 185
Green, Frederick. 187
Grenadiers.................188
Greene, Major General. 195
Greene's, Major Gen., reply..195
Greene, Nath............ ...196
Greene, Federick.........198. 226
Grant to St. John's on conditi209
Green, Mr., slandered.......223
Grammer, Frederick.........226
Grouch, Wm..............18, 19
Grant, Wm................229
Green, Mr., editor of the Ga-
  zette...................237
Grand Jury indict "the Glori-
  ous Nineteen".............249
Grammer, Frederick Louis...263
Gray, Justice Walton 269
Green, Louis, Captain........ 208
Green, N. H.............282
Green, Mrs 303
Graff, Rev. J. J.............304
Green, Nicholas II....... 311
Grant and staff in Annapolis.313
Graves, joint decoration of...315
Green. John................167
Green. Richard.............170
Gunther, Capt 36
Guard at Annapolis, prison...114
Gutroy, John..... 229
Gubnatorial Mansion, the third302
Gubnatorial Mansion, second.303
Guhl, Student 321
Gwyne, William............. 87

H

Hawkins, Matthew ... 21
Hatton. Mr. Secr'y of State.. 25
Hatton. Mr. Thomas 26, 28
Hatch. Mr. John............ 31
Hammond, Mr. John 32
Hall. Mr. Richard.......... 41
Hambleton, John. wife of.... 45
Hawkins, Ralph............. 49
Harbor for shipping at St.
    Mary's................. 59
Hammond, Major John....63, 64
Hall, Henry, of St. James.... 66
Hanging a lanhorn out...... 66
Harnass. Jacob............. 68
Hammond, Col. John........ 69
Hammond. Philip.....70. 98. 102
Hammond, Chas. of Philip. 71
Hanover street............. 72
Hall. Major................ 84
Hair dresser. French in...... 91
Hammond. Mr. Charles....97. 98
Hammond. Mordecai........ 97
Hall. Major Henry.........102
Hamburg. Mr. John.....111. 119
Hamilton. Dr. Alex..........112
Hamilton, Mrs..............119
Hall. John...121, 161, 165. 168,
    169, 170. 176, 316.
Hammond. Matthias.121,165.168,
    171, 172, 173. 176.
Hogan, Dominick. Irish ser-
    vant....................126
Handsome women..............128
Hawke. Sloop. his Majesty's..151
Haller and Matzen.... 158
Hanlan.............. 147
Hauteur of Mrs. Henry 148
Hallam. Miss. poetry about...147
Hallam, Mrs................147
Hamilton, Alex..........163, 206
Hall of House of Delegates...163
Hammond, Rezin..168. 170, 176
Hammond, Thomas..........167
Hammond, Nathan..........167
Haragan, John...... 167
Hackman, James..............167
Harrison, William............168
Harwood, Thomas, Jr........170
Hall, Thomas................170
Harwood, Mr. Thomas......172
Harding, Capt. ship Totness.174
Harford, Mr................202

Harwood, Thomas.170, 176, 187,
    209.
Hanson. A. C 210
Hanson. Alex. Contee.. .220, 222
Harrison. Benj..............222
Hammond, Mr. John .316, 224,
    229.
Harrison, Hall...............225
Haskins, Joseph 225
Harwood. Richard..........225
Hall. Benedict E............226
Hammond, Nicholas........226
Harper. Robt Goodloe........235
Harwood. Major Sprigg.244, 245.
    248. 263. 282, 301. 313.
Harwood, Ralph.. ....254. 258
Harwood, Thos. Richard....256
Hancock, Francis 256
Hall, Humphrey............263
Hall, Watkins, shot..........271
Hanlan. Richard H.........273
Harvest of pleasures........274
Harris. Benj. G.............299
Harris, B. G. recommended...301
Hagner, Judge A. B 302
Haller, Wm......... 305
Hackney, Saml..............305
Hamilton. Rev. Jonathan....305
Harwood, Hy..............306
Harwood, residence, the......306
Hammond. Mr. Wm.....306, 307
Handy, D. Claude.......311, 313
Haunted house in Annapolis..314
Hance's trial for murder.....318
Harnden Express trial.........318
Hayden, Judge.............319
Harrington, Miss............320
Herring Bay 18, 33
Herring Creek........... 31
Heamans, Roger.......... 33
Heamans. Roger, required to
    assist Puritans.......... 34
Heamans dissembles.......... 34
Heamans' story 34
Heamans warns Stone not to
    come nearer............. 35
Heamans' resolved to fire.... 35
Heamans shoots at St. Mary's
    men. 35
Heamans fires a third shot.... 35
Heamans. Capt.denies Stone's
    authority................ 35

Heamans' fourth shot kills a
man 35
Herman, Casper, Aug. builds
State House, Church and
School 63
Hewett, Mr. John..... 78
Helmsley, Mr. William 78
Heselius, Miss Charlotte..... 122
Heirlooms, dresses 127
Henry's, Mrs. hauteur.......148
Henzell, Capt. Chas.........176
Henry, John...............222
Herbert, J. C............. .235
Heard, Col.................248
Herald, Democratic......... 273
Henderson, Rev. J. J...... . 394
Hebron, Henry.............305
Henkle, Eli J.............313
Hepburn, John 197
Hendley, Hugh.............167
Henshaw, Charles 261
Hill, Capt................ 46
His Majesty's power to dispose
of conquests......... ... 51
Hill, Capt. Richard......... 64
Higinbothom, Rev. R. master 80
Hill, Joseph... 84
Hill, Mr. Joseph expelled from
House.................. 85
History, relic of, Maryland.... 95
Higginson, Chas. sentenced to
death................114
His Majestys sloop Hawke....151
Higinbothom, Rev. Mr. Ralph
209, 212, 225, 253.
Higgins, Mr. Dick. 245
Hicks, Thos. Holliday.......245
Hicks', Gov. proclamation...281
Hicks', Gov. proclamation of,
speech of 282, 283, 284
Hicks, Gov. and Fed. authori-
ties...... 255
Hicks, Gov. and Fed. Govern-
ment............285 to 295
Hicks, Gov. letter of Seward to 289
Hicks, Gov. letters of Butler
to....291, 292, 293, 294, 295
Hicks, Gov. refuses consent for
troops to land..........206
Hicks, Gov. still had hope ...296
Historical Society of A. A. Co.320
Hincks, Thomas............ 167
Howard, Matthew............. 18
Horner, James............. 18

Howell, Thomas 19
Howell's Creek 19
Horn Point............. 35, 323
Homeard, Jo 43
House awaits ad. as to Quakers 43
Hargans, Henry, at Kent.... 47
House asks its vacancies be
filled...... 50
House compromises with pro-
prietary................ 51
Howard, Mr. Philip... 63
House appoints Mr. Gaddess
chaplain 65
Howard, Cornelious 68
Hood, Zachariah....... 71
Howard, Samuel.... ....72, 187
House of Col. Edw. Dorsey.... 80
House of Smithers. 82
Holmes, Richard 87
Home, Peter...... 95
Holland, Col. Wm.......... 96
Horney, James....... 102
House of Delegates, mem. of..102
Horse steal'ng. York hung for.113
Hopewell, senbr. of Annapolis
captured 113
House, Penelope, whipped.....118
Horse races.................130
Homony Club..........131, 132
Hood, Stamp Officer, burnt in
effigy... 149
Hood's appointment as Stamp
Officer................149
Hood, Stamp Officer resisted..149
Hood lands the stamps 149
Hood willing to resign.... ...150
Hood's flight................150
Hood returns to Annapolis.....151
Hornet, officers of the 152
Howard, Gen. John, Eager...188
Hospitality of Gov. Eden.....153
Hope of Gov. Eden's return...155
Holland street 158
Hodgsin, Mr...............172
Howe, Sir William.. 183
Howard, Saml. H....168, 198, 230
Howard, John, Eager........206
Howard's, Col.offer to J.Chase222
Howard, J.... 238
Horn Point.................238
Hollingsworth's Capt. troop...240
Hobbs, Capt.............. 243
Hope, Thomas.. 248
Holme, Christopher.........254

Hollingsworth, Francis......255
-Hodges, Thomas............256
Howard County 257
Hollidayoke, Daniel, ...271
Hopkins, Edward........273, 304
Holland. Steward. born at A..270
Hopkins. Adjutant.........282
Hopkins. James E..........284
Hopkins, Benjamin...... .284
Houses. other ancient... 308
House of Anthony Stewart....308
Horn Point settlement. 315
Hopkins, Johns.............316
Hoffman. trial..............318
Hours, cried in..............325
Howard. William 167
Hodgan. Thos. B 167
Howard. John...............167
Horsely. Henry.............168
Horton. John..............168
Hood. John, Jr............168
Howard. Ephraim 170
Howard. Benj...........170, 176
Hopkins. Girard. Jr.........170
Humphrey, Rev. John, rector
　of St. Anne's.. 71
Hutchins, Col. Chas........ 78
Hutton. Mr. William........ 78
Hunt. Wornell, Recorder..86, 88
Hughton, William.......... 86
Humphrey. Joseph.......... 87

Hustings to the Prov. Courte. 91
Hunt, Wornell. Esq 94
Hutchinson. Capt. John......111
Humes. Jos. sentenced to
　death 114
Hutton, Bros. wagon manu-
　facturers 147
Hunting. Ridge............191
Humphrey. Col. David 206
Humphrey Hall.........214, 217
Humphreys. Rev. Hector. ...214
Hustings, Court of 228
Hutton. Samuel.............229
Hunter, James 255
Hughes. Jeremiah.257. 259, 263,
　324.
Hurst, Bennett 259
Hutton, Jona 259
Hubbard, Jr. Wm.. Lieut....299
Hull, James, engineer.......320
Hunting Grounds in Annap..326
Hyde's Alley 64
Hyde, Thomas......74, 167, 209
Hyde, Thos. set up tannery..119
Hyde, John.................229
Hyde, Mr. Daniel T.....269, 270
Hyde, Danl. T. threatened by
　soldiers 298
Hyde. J. T................316
Hyde. William.........167, 177
Hyde, William. Capt.......176

I

Iglehart. Mrs. Owen A....72, 158
Iglehart. Leonard 262
Iglehart, James H..........273
Iglehart. Capt............282
Iglehart. Wm. T 305, 324
Iglehart. and Swann........306
Iglehart House........... .307
Iglehart. Mrs. Wm. T...307, 324
Iglehart. J. Howard........320
Ill-treatment of servants....112
Illiberal laws...............275
Impeachment of Major Thos.
　Truman 54
Improvement of Annapolis for. 64
Importance of Annapolis.....109
Importation of rebels........112
Importation of fashions......143
Impressment of citizens......314
Improvement in Annapolis. .315
Improvement. spirit of.......323

Improvement, Asso. Local....325
Indians..................... 17
Independents................ 17
Indians, a near neighbor...... 22
Indians commit murder in A.A 22
Indian treaty made on the
　Severn................... 28
Inhabitants of the Providence 29
Indemnity for injuries to Ind. 29
Indemnity for injuries to col. 29
Indians. 8 or 10 only to come
　at a time................. 30
Indians to give notice of in-
　tended war.............. 30
Intentions of Capt. Stone..... 33
Insolent behavior of Quakers. 37
Indians an element of trouble. 38
Instructions given Capt Bur-
　gess.................... 38
Indians, Forraigne.......... 39

Information of K. W's School
    meagre 79
Information, Lower House
    wants.................107
Indians, how to fight........... 39
Indians, treaty of peace with. 40
Indiscreet representative from
    A. A. Co...................... 49
Indian chiefs treacherously
    murdered...................... 54
Indignation over Major True-
    man's conduct............ 54
Instruction broken by Major
    Trueman...... 55
Inn-keeper, Workman........ 96
Inaugural address of Md. Ga-
    zette........................... 99
Indulgencies, cheap. 101
Inquisition, flames, damnation101
Inch, Mr......................103
Infringement of liberties.......108
Indians, The...................108
Indian, quiver of.............108
Inquest on Elisha Williams...112
Indians volunteer against....119
Insignia of clubs.............133
Indians ravaged by small-pox.143

Indians, race courses, and In-
    dians.....................157
Indians, murders by..........160
Indians, some very quiet.....160
Indians, last to visit to Ann a160
Inner life of Annapolis.......178
Inscription on DeKalb statue.186
Incorporation of St. John's Col.208
Internal dissensions.........234
Insurrection, Nat. Turner's..261
Investigation of riot.........272
Indians make treaty under
    poplar....................309
Intention for setling Md.........327
Indians and early settlers....331
Indians pleased with Euro-
    peans... 333
Indian customs 384
Independent Fire Co......... 16
Inhabitant competent witness 84
Irwin, John................103
Ireland, Thos...............280
Ireland, John, Corporal........299
Isle of Wight................ 19
Isle of Kent................. 29
Islands, mouth of West River.144

J

Jacques, Lancelot.,71, 119, 161,
    177.
Jail, Annapolis.............. 98
Jaunescheck................148
Jackson, Capt. of Peggy Stew.172
Jackson, Major, Washington's
    Secretary..................121
Jacob, Edward..............284
Jacquet, John D..............167
Jackson, Henry..............167
Jacques, Denton............168
Jackson, Captain...........170
Jenifer, Daniel, messenger...... 49
Jenkins, Francis 78
Jenkins, Mr................. 78
Jennings, Thomas..120, 226, 229,
    231.
Jefferson....................147
Jenifer, Danl. of St. Thos....223
Jennings, Mr. George........229
Jeffrey's Point..............252
Jeffrey, Jig................252
Jewess Steamboat............268
Jewess reaches Annapolis......268

Jewess' passengers disorderly.269
Jewess overcrowded..........268
Jewess cast loose............270
Jefferson, George W.........228
Jennings, Edmond............303
Jennings, Thomas, barrister .307
Jennings, Mrs. Ann..........308
Journals, extracts from...... 40
Johnson, James, charged with
    slander, convicted...... 46
Johnson, Reverdy student of
    St. John's................ 65
Jowles, Esq., Hon. Henry.... 67
Johnson, James.............71, 139
John, Leadler. 71
Jones, Evan.............76, 86, 88
Jones', Evan, shallup.......... 82
Jones, Thos...........87, 220, 305
John, Beall, Esq............ 97
John, Jones, a "mulatto fel-
    low"....................100
Jordan, Capt...............110
John, Captain Isaac......... 111
Johnson, ship.. 112

Johnson, Thos. Jennings, Esq.122
Jockey Club in Annap....141, 158
Joues, Miss. 147
Jones, Richard, J.......148, 263
Joseph & Belshazzer, cantatas
　　of............................ 148
Johnson, Thomas.........161, 176
Johnson, Thos. Jr...165, 168, 169,
　　170, 177.
Johnson, Thos. first Rep. Gov.182
Johnson, Gov..................183
Johnson, Gov. threats against.184
Joy over Cornwallis's surrend.188
Johnson, Reverdy.......214, 257
Journey of Washington.........219
Jockey Club of Annapolis....222
Johnson, George..... 229
Jones, Richard..................229
Jones, Col. U. S. A.............240
Joues, Col...................242, 243
Johnson, John......256, 263, 273
Jones, William..................257

Johnson. Thomas, Gov.......260
Jones, William, Hon............264
Jones, Com. T. Ap Catesby....265
Johnson, George, death of......273
Johnson, Reverdy, born at A.276
Johnson, David..................305
Johnson, Reverdy, house in...308
Jones, Thos. R..................316
Johnson, Gen. Bradley T....320
Journal of Father White.....327
Journal to be kept.............338
Jonathan, Pinkney.............166
Jones, Lewis..................167
Jury of able women............ 44
Jury and Committee Rooms... 66
Jury, verdict of..................112
Judicial proceedings............113
Judges of the Court of Appeals 231
Judges of Election threatened.311
Judges of Election...........335
Judges of Election returns.....336

K

K. W's. school empowered to
　　receive...................... 79
Kane, Col. Geo. P.......268, 269
Kane, Col., in front of cannon272
Kaiser, Henry................305
Kalmey, Jerry W. 305
Keepers of the liberty of Eng-
　　land...................... 25
Kent, Isle of 29
Kendall, Capt. (probably Fen-
　　dall.).................... 36
Kent county................... 39
Kennedy, Dr. S. D. (note)... 64
Key, Philip................. 72
Key, Theodoric.........　......... 72
Keene, rector of St. Anne's.. 75
Keyton... 83
Kent Island, Broad Creek....112
Kent Island to Annapolis....112
Kent Island, ferry boat overset114
Kent county school..........126
Kent, John. Esq.............130
Keppel, Commodore.........160
Keyser, Ephraim.. .....187, 324
Key, Francis Scott............213
Kerr, John Leeds............225
Keith, John.................229
Kent Island.................238

Kent, Hon. Joseph...........239
Keene, Robt. T...................248
Kent, Doctor.....................256
Kernan, Michael, sergeant....299
Keffer, Capt., Provost Marshal310
Keffer, Thos., Provost Marshal313
Kenny, John student.........321
Key, Robert......................167
Kelso, James................170
King's name not in commissio 25
King submitted to........... 57
King approved the resolution. 57
King thanks for redeeming
　　Maryland from "a tyran-
　　nial Popish government". 57
King William's school estab.. 65
King William's school..68, 77, 78,
　　96, 109
King William's school's friends 79
King William's school re-or-
　　ganized... 79
King William, Academy of... 80
Killbourne, Chas............ 86
King and the fish-women....... 99
King Birthday 101
King's anniversary.........137
King's, the, passengers......157
King George, the Third......175

Kirkwell and Blackwell, ship-builders..................158
King Abraham and Queen Sa-ㅋ rah...................161
King William's school funds..225
Kilty, William.........226, 256
Kilty, John.................230
Killman, Mr. Nicholas......313
King, J. Guest.........316, 325
Killing of William Stanley...320

Kirkland. Robert 166
Kirby. Thomas..............167
Kingsbury, James...........167
King, John.................167
King, Thomas, Jr.,.........261
King, Thomas...............261
Kirby, William.............261
Know Nothings..............245
Knapp, Ensign..............320
Kolk, Richard.............. 87

L

Langford's, John, defence of Capt. Stone................... 19
Langford, John............. 25
Lawson, John.............. 31
Lawrence, Hon. Sir Thos..64, 67
Lanthorne to be hung out...... 67
Lawrence, Sir Thomas......... 87
Lands, gectment and tres. for 91
Laws and privileges.......... 93
Laws of the province......... 97
Lapear, Matthew, sentenced to death.................114
Ladies dress discussed.......126
Law learning of America.....127
Latin notes in Annapolis.......127
Lammond, John, musician....130
Landsdale, John, shoemaker.130
Law sign...................130
Dawson, Alexandria..........139
Last English Governor.........152
Landing of Gov. Eden........152
Launch of the Lovely Nancy 158
Lady Lee and Matilda.........158
Landing of cargo refused.....176
Lawrence, Jno. ordered to de-part.....................184
La Fayette's stratagem.......187
La Fayette, Gen.....196, 197, 198
La Fayette naturalized........197
Lady lectures...............221
La Fayette's visit to Annap..239
La Fayette's reply to Mayor of Annapolis...............243
Larimore, William 257
Lavalette, Capt. E. A. T.....265
Landmark, ancient falls......267
La Fayette, Gen.............304
Laurie, Rev. Dr............304
La Fayette entertained under poplar..................309

Labors of writing History......326
Lanes, powers over..........338
Lambert, Robert.............167
Lang, Robert...............168
Lappington, Thomas..........170
Legislature at Patuxent........ 31
Lewis, Captain.............. 36
Lewis, Lieut. Wm. executed. 36
Legget, Mr. executed.......... 36
Levies to fight Indians......... 38
Legislature resist encroachm't 50
Legislature peculiarly Protest 58
Legislature gives the denial due it....................61
Legislature's reply to Saint Mary's...................
Leary Neck Cove.............. 61
Legislature first session in A.. 63
Legislature adjourns to an ale 68 house....................
Legislature fails to help St. 63 Anne's................... 70
Leave to build a gallery in St. Anne's................... 71
Lendrum, T. rec. of St. Anne's 75
Lendrum, Montgomery........ 75
Legislature receives severe re-flection................... 82
Legislature and Gov. Sharp, messages between..........101
Legislature and Gov. Bladen.104
Legislature resists taxation...105
Legislature appoints Gov. Ogle113
Legislature prorogued..........113
Lendrum, Rev. Andrew........115
Letters of the first citizen......121
Legislature, Assembly of Md..121
Lee, General...............154
Lee, Gov...................158
Lecture by a lady...........221

Lee, John..................222
Letherbury, Peregrine.........223
Leonard vs. Chesapeake 226
Loudrum, Lieut..............242
Lemon, two halves cause a riot..270
Legislature convened by Gov.
  Hicks....................285
Letter of Seward to Gov. Hicks 289
Letters of Butler to Gov. Hicks.291
  292, 293, 294, 295.
Leslie, Norman O. Sergeant...299
Legg, Charles, heroic act of...319
Legg, Mr. James...............319
Lee, Thos. Philip.............167
Line of plantations........... 18
Liberty's........ 18
Life in the colony............ 40
Likened to a conquered people 51
Lightning broke into the State
  House.....................67
Lightning kills and wounds
  several delegates............ 67
Lightning injures State House 67
License to build a chapel....... 70
Library of St. John's.......... 79
Likeness of Queen Anne's...... 80
Library, Maryland State....... 93
Liberties, infringement of.....108
Lightning, schr. Peggy struck
  by....................110
Lightning strikes Court House 119
Litigious spirit..............144
Life of fashion and frivolty....144
Linthicum, Benjamin...........158
Library of the State.......... 163
Liberty tree at Annapolis 174
Licensed vessels..............177
Licenses......................184
Linthicum....................245
Linthicum, Wesley.248, 249, 250
Lincoln, election of...........281
Lincoln's calls for Md. quota.285
Lincoln, A.......... 288, 290
Liquor seized by Provst Guard.301
Little, Benjamin.............305
License to sell liquor in Anna.339
Liquors, sale of, in Annapolis.339
Lloyd, Edw. made Commander 21
Lloyd, Edward, and 77 others 27
Lloyd, Edw....29, 30, 31, 44, 266
Lloyd, Philip................. 97
Lloyd, Governor 306
Lloyd, Gov. and wife...........320
Lloyd, Ensign.................320

Lord Baltimore.................. 17,
  19, 24, 25.
Lord Baltimore indignant at
  Puritans....................... 23
Lord Baltimore writes to Gov.
  Stone........ 23
Lord Baltimore directs Gov.
  Stone to proceed against
  Puritans...................... 23
Lord Baltimore charged with
  adhering to rebels.......... 24
Lord Baltimore's enemies....... 24
Lord Baltimore's agents....... 27
Lord Balto. kept his patent... 31
Lord Baltimore upbraids Gov.
  Stone 31
Lord Baltimore's officers begin
  to divulge 32
Lord of Hosts manifested....... 36
Lord Baltimore's instructions. 36
Lord Baltimore's declaration
  on freedom of religion.... 37
Loss of State's Records...... 40
Lord Proprietor, a scandal to
  the......... 41
Lord Proprietary to be con-
  sulted about................. 43
Lord Proprietary seeks an inter-
  view with Lower House.. 50
Lower House take very heavily
  to be liken to a conquered
  people....................... 51
Lower House insists on their
  rights....................... 51
Lots to be laid off, 1683........ 53
Lots to revert, 1683.......... 53
Lower House refuses to concur
  in punishment of Major
  Truman....................... 55
Lord Baltimore, residence of. 56
Lord Baltimore orders his Gov.
  to proclaim William and
  Mary........ 57
Lord Baltimore promises not
  to remove Capital.......... 59
Loss of Records of St. Anne's. 68
Lower House ready to build a
  church 68
Lowe, S... 71
Lord Baltimore, friend of...... 72
Lord Baltimore intercedes for
  Rev. Mr. Allen.............. 72
Lord Proprietary.............. 79
Lord Baltimore, portrait of.... 80

Lord's Day.................. 90
Lots of K. W's. School........ 96
Lock, William, Esq............ 97
Lot for Custom House........ 97
Lots who should kill, drawing.103
Louisburg, rejoicing over....103
Lower House wants information.................108
Loyall, Captain...............114
Loundes, Christopher..........118
Lowe, Captain James.........118
Loyalty in Annapolis..........136
Loyalty, intense in Annap....139
Long Island, citizens of......150
Lord Baltimore................152
Lord Dunmore.................155
Lovely Nancy..................158
Lottery, first in province.....159
Lottery for St. John's......213
Loockerman, William.........224
Lottery, public in Annapolis.226
Long, John....................292
Location of the Naval Academy at Annapolis......264

Long, R. C...................263
Lockwood, Prof...............266
Loockerman, T. C. shot..... 271
Lockwood, Jas. Booth, born at Annapolis..............278
Lord Lyons suggested as mediator................289, 296
Lomack, Louis.................305
Loockerman, Richard.........307
Loockerman, Mrs. F. T......307
Local Election in Annapolis...313
Local Sensation at Annapolis.320
Local Option in Annapolis....325
Local Improvement Ass'n....325
Loockerman, Jr., Mr. Jacob.. 82
Low, Major.................... 84
Lusby, Baldwin............... 71
Luxurious habits of Annap... 91
Luxury, fashion, commerce... 92
Lucas, Sipheorous, executed...117
Lucas, Chas. alias Powell, Jno.125
Lucas, Captain James........139
Lutheran Church..............305

M

Made a settlement........... 18
Magothy River......... 18, 178
Marsh, Thomas.......21, 29, 30
Maryland. made a shuttle-cock 26
Magazine of arms............ 32
Matthew, Thomas.......... 47
Maryland and Virginia united against Indians.......... 54
Major Thos. Trueman....... 54
Major Trueman broke his instructions.............. 55
Major Trueman guilty as impeached.............. 55
Mayor, the, of St. Mary's...... 57
Mayor, &c., of St. Mary's, address of.............. 58
Market in Annapolis........ 64
Major Dorsey's house........ 64
Marchand, Mrs. Margaret... 65
Magazine for everything but powder............... 66
Marriage licenses, 1697....... 69
Marriott, Emanuel.......... 71
Maccubbin, Moses........... 71
Maccubbin, James... 71, 221, 226
Malcome, rector, of St. Anne's 75
Mayor of Annapolis............ 76

Masters of K. W's. school, Daken & Higginbotham.... 80
Maryland, Eastern Shore of.. 81
Magazine and powder-house.. 82
Macall, Mr................. 84
Maryland. voyage to........ 91
Maryland Gazette........... 94
Maryland History, relic of..... 95
Mariartee, Capt. Dan'l....96, 97
Macnemara, Thomas.......... 97
Market House, site for....,.. 98
Maryland State Library...... 98
Marvelous in Gazette...........101
Maryland, the Treasurer of....106
Magnificent dwellings...........108
Material transitions.............108
Matchlock of Maryland.........108
McNemara, Michael............110
Manufacture of osnabrig.......111
Maccubbin, Mr. Nicholas.......112
Masters ill-treat servants.......112
Mayor's plate..................112
Marriott, Mrs. Elizabeth.......118
Manufactory, stocking.........120
Mackubin, Richard, servant of120
Man killed by a woman........121
Mayer, Frank B. (in note) ...122

Maryland, the, Gazette.........125
Marshe, Mr., Secretary...182, 133
Martyrdom of St. Charles I....135
Masons established in Annap.138
Masonic celebration in Annap.138
Marriage ceremony in America142
Maryland Politics............... 143
Magistrates.........................143
Malone...... 147
Masonic Opera House............148
Maryland Convention..154, 180, 222
Maryland, Virginia Convention to........................155
Matilda and Lady Lee..........158
Maryland Avenue................158
Marine Railway...................158
May-pole..........................159
Mayer, F. B...........164, 320, 325
Marybury, Beriah...167, 181, 189, 229
Maryland, declaration of.......180
Maryland troops...............182
Martha, wife of Gen. Washington...... 182
Maccubbin, Nicholas, Jr.......187
Mann, Mr..........................201
Mann's Hotel...201, 222, 252, 306
Maccubbin, Mrs. James.........205
Macall, Benj.....................220
Martin, Luther....................222
Masonic celebration..............223
Mann, Lieut., U. S. N.........227
Magruder, A. C...................227
Mayor's Court......................228
Maryland Republican....233, 324
Madison, Mr........................233
Madison, Fort....................234
Magruder, Col. Hy........239, 255
Marine Band......................242
Magill, Charles.................249
Mann, Col...................252, 305
Magruder, Alex. C 254, 255
Madison, President and wife..254
Magruder, John H. T............263
Madison, President................264
Mayo, Isaac......................265
Marcy, Gov., Secretary of War265
Martial Spirit in Annapolis in 1860........................282
Magruder, John R., speech of.282
Magruder, John R..284, 297, 308
Macfeely, R., Lieut., reports to Gov. Hicks................288

Mayor of Annapolis protests..296
Marchand, Francis T., house.302
Matzen, Henry.................305
Martin, George.................305
Mason, Mrs. Judge J. Thomp.307
Martin, Ex-Mayor, Thos. E. 307, 308
Mally, John S..................315
Maryland Hotel, Co............316
Market Space 319
Mahan, Lieut...................320
Maryland reduced to submission........................ 25
Maryland, Governors of...... 11
Mayors of Annapolis......... 13
Maintenance of bridges to Annapolis.....................342
Maintenance of roads to Annap342
Maryland, voyage to..........327
Maryland reached............330
Mayor shall qualify as........335
Maconochia John...............167
Mackubin, Richard...........167
Maw, James.....................167
Mackel, Charles...............167
Macken, Thomas...............168
Mael, Matthias................168
Manard, James.................168
Mayo, Thomas.................170
McPherson, Rev. John, rector of St. Anne's......... 71, 75
McDowell Hall...98, 214, 217, 302
McCoy, Alex., Irish servant...100
McKennie, Donald, executed..116
McCoy, Morris, executed for murder......................121
McCoy, Morris, gibbeted.....121
McCarty, Hugh, Sir...........136
McNeir, Thos., thigh broken..149
McLachlan, Capt..............151
McDaniel, Sarah..............158
McHenry, James..........199, 200
McHand, Isaac, loaned money by city 200
McDowell, John A. M...209, 212, 219
McPherson, Wm. H...........229
McMechen. Elizabeth..........229
Md. Gazette, poem in, on St. Anne's.................. 73
M'Faden, James..............222
McCency, Joseph 256
McKean, Commodore 266
McAllister. Capt. Robt.......268

McAllister's, Capt., company.270
McNew, Basil, shot.........271
McNew, Basil, arrested........300
McCullough, Passamore.......301
McNeir, Geo.....................304
McNamara's Row............304
McCullough, Lt. S. T., delivers oration..............315
McCullough, S. T................316
McCurdy, John, engineer.....320
McKenzie...........................167
McDonal.......................... 168
McCarty, Con.....................168
Merryman, James...... 21
Meet and treat in the woods... 28
Men of quality force to fly.... 33
Messengers between Stone and Puritans..................... 34
Men of St. Mary's.............. 34
Merchants, factors, and mariners to trade at ports.... 53
Meeting-house of Puritans.... 69
Members of Port of Annap... 96
Men walking on water.......101
Members of the House of Delegates.........................102
Men sold for fees 111
Meeting of freemen of Annap.139
Memory of St. Tamina. 141
Meeting of County and City...176
Meeting to offer jurisdiction to Congress.....................199
Mercer, John T...................222
Mercer, Col. Francis..............224
Mercer, John F......226
Mealing, Wm.....................225
Methodist meeting house.......243
Meeting, public..................249
Meeting of workingmen.........248
Message of Gov. Hicks to Leg.296
Message to Washington.........296
Methodist Episcopal Church..303
Methodist Church, second......304
Memorial, St. Anne's Mission Chapel....................312
Melvin, Geo. T...................324
Members who voted for State subscription.................. 7
Merriweather, Rueben..........170
Missionaries sent to Quakers.. 66
Mills, Edward, negro boy ...100
Mitchel, James, drowned.....116
Miscreants, gang of, in Annap.120
Militia training.................130

Miss Hallam, poetry about....147
Military Commission resigned by Washington...............163
Militia, formation of.........175
Militia called out.............183
Mifflin, Gen.............201, 206
Mifflin's, Gen., address to Washington....................207
Military art.....................227
Middleton, William..............229
Middleton, Gilbert...............229
Military camp at Annap.233, 238
Miller, Capt....................234
Mitchell, Geo. E..............239
Miller's Hill....................240
Miller, James...............263
Mill, deadly fire about to be made from................271
Millions, Charles Carroll's......275
Military display in Annapolis.282
Military possession of A. & E. R. R......................296
Military Station, an important296
Miller, Oliver.........297, 311, 313
Miller, John.............. 303
Miller, Chief Judge..........319
Mitchell, Lieut..............320
Minor liquor law............339
Mitchell.............167
Minsky, Nicholas...............167
Morris, Mr. Robert, shoots at Puritans...................... 35
Mobbed, Rev. Mr. Allen....... 72
Montgomery, rector of St. Anne's.................. 75
Mode of electing delegates..... 86
Montgomery, Capt...............111
Mogg, Sol., the sexton.........125
Mosaic of sentiment...........140
Morris..........................147
Morris, Mrs.....................148
Mobbing of Hood..............150
Mourning, Gazette in...........150
Mob gathers.....................152
Montague, Geo., Capt.........156
Montague, Capt., refuses to give up deserter.............157
Morris, Gov. of Philadelphia.160
Mount Vernon...................207
Morgan, Wm......................222
Mourning for Washington......224
Morgue, Joe.....................250
Monroe, President..............255
Morality and ready money......257

Monument to Chas. Carroll....263
Morse, Col. Augustus...........299
Monument to Charles Legg...319
Morrison, Robert..............166
Moor, Robert..................167
Molleson, R...................168
Mr. Lloyd..................... 23
Mr. Harrison.................. 23
Mr. Richard Preston's House. 32
Mr. John Hammond seizes
    records................... 32
Mrs. Stone.................... 35
Mrs. Henry's hauteur..........148
Mr. Waters' horse Parrott.....159
Mr. Mann's, public dinner at.218
Mr. George Mann.............. 221
M'Parlin, William......255, 261
Mt. Moriah Congregation......305
Murders having been commit. 54
Munro, Sarah..................100
Murder........................101
Murderers hanged..............102

Murdock, Esq.. Mrs............119
Muster days...................130
Munroe, James, store of.......157
Murders by Indians............160
Murray, James.168, 220, 229, 261
Murray, Sarah. acrostic to....224
Muir, John......225, 226, 227, 230
Muir, Capt....................227
Murray, Henry M...259, 301, 302
Murdock, Miss Eliza...........282
Municipal Election in Annap.284
Munroe, Grafton..........261, 304
Munroe, Grafton, Jr...........316
Munroe, James.................304
Musgrave, Geo. W., D. D......304
Museum, The State.............324
Munroe, C. E..................325
Murrow, Richard...............167
Munroe, William...............167
Myers, rector of St. Anne's... 75
Myers, Hy. B..................159
"My Lady's Bower".............307

N

Nansemond River............. 19
Naval Officers of the province.105
Naval Officers' bond..........107
Nancy and Abigial............108
Native shrewdness............144
Naval Com. description of A.145
Naval Academy................148
Native of North British......185
Naturalization of La Fayettte.197
Naval Depot at A. agitated...254
Nat. Turner's insurrection...261
Naval Academy at Annapolis.264
Naval Academy, resolution on264
Naval Academy opened.........266
Naval Academy, additions to..267
Naval Academy, area of.....267
Naval Academy of advantage
    to Annapolis..............268
Naval Academy, battalion
    cheer.....................282
Naval Academy pulsates with
    war news..................285
National Flag on State House298
Naples biscuit................307
Naval Academy reserves.......315
Naval Academy helps trade...319
Narrative of the voyage to Md 327
Natives of Maryland..........332
Negotiations for a settlement. 17

Negative voice of his Lordship 27
News of the Golden Fortune.. 32
New political condition of Prov 79
Nefarious plot............... 83
Neivill, Samuel.............. 86
Newspaper, the first in Md.... 94
Negroes ear cropped.......... 95
New Town..................... 97
Newspaper, second in Md...... 98
News in the Gazette.......... 99
Newest make from Paris.......101
Negro man's land cut off by
    sentence..................102
Negroes burnt to death.......103
Negro women executed........116
Negro, Bristol, aged 125.....120
Negro, Daniel, executed for
    murder 121
Negro accidentally killed.....121
News of Cornwallis's surrend..188
Nephews of Washington.......222
Neth, Lewis......167, 226, 307
Negro, Ruth...................229
News of Peace celebrated....239
Neth, Captain.................243
New London...................257
Ney, Marshal of France......258
Negro fugitives delivered to
    Sheriff...................299

Negro Soldiers............ 313
Newell, J. T. brakeman.........320
Newspapers of Annapolis....324
Neal, Thomas.... 167
Nicholson, Col. (Governor)... 57
Nicholson, Col................... 58
Nicholson, Gov...............60, 78
Nicholson, Gov. indignant.... 63
Nicholson, Gov. given a lot.. 64
Nicholson's cove 64
Nicholson, Francis, Gov.67, 78,
302.
Nicholson, Gov. selects a site
    of St. Anne's 69
Nicholson, Gov. active for St.
    Anne's.................... 69
Nicholson, Beall......... ... 71
"Nineteen, The Glorious"......244
Nicholson, Rebecca...........266

Nineteenth of April............ ..284
Nicholson, Jos. II............311
Nicholson and Hollahan........318
Nicholson, Richard........ 167
Niven, William..................167
Nicholson, George.............168
Norfolk county..... 19
No oath, no land............ 19
No answer to Pur. poposals... 33
No precedent for sudden re-
    moval of Capital........... 60
Norwood, Mr. Andrew. 63
Norwood, Mr. Samuel......... 69
Non-attendance upon church. 71
Novarre, John.... 87
North side of Severn......96, 118
"Noah's Ark,"injured by fire.313
Noke, William.................167
Norris, John..................167

O

Oaths of allegiances............ 17
Oath modified for the Puritans 23
Oaths usually appointed...... 88
Oath unknown to the Laws...310
Obedient to commonwealth.... 28
Observing festival of St. Geo.136
Obituary of Nicholas Brewer.263
Objects of L. Balto's settlem't 327
Offer of A. A. no answer to
    Legislature's proposal.... 57
Officers of the province,
    residence of.............. 58
Offices open in spite stamp act..151
Officers of the Hornet........152
Offer for U. S. Capital..........199
Ogilvie, Patrick............... 87
Ogleby, Patrick............... 97
Ogle, Saml. Gov.....98, 111, 307
Ogle, Miss Anne, dies............112
Ogle. Gov. calls extra session.113
Ogle's, Gov. speech to Legis...113
Ogle, Gov. disappointed by
    Legislature..............113
Ogle, Gov. Samuel, dies......117
Ogle, Samuel, Esq. and lady.137
Ogle, Ann, Mrs............. 254
Ogle, House, The....... 307
O'Hara, W..................266
Old clock, old hall, old Annap.122
Old gallery torn down........162

Oldest inhabitants. 250
Old Blue Church 303
One hundred acres to be laid
    off......... 53
One of the signers 149
Opening of Naval Academy....266
Opening of the Civil War......281
Opening of Bay Ridge........323
Orders in Annapolis.......... 63
Organist in St. Anne's, Mr.
    Woodcock.............. 75
Orme, Dennis, slave of.......298
Oration of S. T. Wallis......324
Osnabrigs manufactured in A.111
Osborne......... 147
Otter, the sloop 178
Other Ancient Houses 308
Out-look of the city.........109
Overt act committed by Gov.
    Stone............... ... 32
Overcrowding of the Jewess .268
Owens, John E..............148
Owner of Rumney and Long..158
Owen, Mr. Richard.............212
Owen, Edward 167
Owens, Saml.................167
Oyster creek................ 31
Oyster House.................158
Oysters, wealth of..............275
Oyster vessel seized by Gov....299

P

Part of Annapolis.............. 19

Puritans...................... 20

Parishioners' gallery in St.
    Anne's.................. 75
Patuxent and Severn.........28, 32
Patuxent River...........20, 56, 96
Palmer's Island 29
Patuxent county.................... 31
Packer, Mr.................. 34
Papist taken prisoners.......... 36
Papistry...................... 46
Patuxent....................38, 111
Paper and Meddall.................. 55
Parliamentary commissioners. 56
Patuxent, place of meeting of
    Assembly.................. 56
Papers of collectors and Naval
    Officers.......... 66
Papers of clerk of House of
    Delegates.................... 66
Parishioners 20 miles from St.
    Anne's................ 69
Parsonage in Annapolis........ 72
Paca. William.74, 121, 161. 165,
    168, 169, 170, 176, 196, 202,
    205, 220.
Parks, William, printer....94, 95
Parks, William.................... 97
Pages of Gazette reflect history 100
Parish of St. Anne's........... 108
Palatines, 200.................. 108
Patapsco....................111, 191
Pain, B. tried for blasphemy. 114
Pain, Bevis, bored through the
    tongue................ 114
Parr, Mark, a remarkable rogue 114
Pannelled walls................ 128
Pavements, no.................. 129
Palatines offered for sale...... 139
Party prejudices waived......... 140
Pardons......... 143
Pay of members, (note)........ 143
Passion week................. 147
Page....................... 147
Parker....................... ...147
Parole of Gov. Eden............ 154
Packet of letters seized........ 154
Parliament........ 172
Packet upset off Magothy...224
Parker, Mr. Isaac.............. 255
Patrol on South River......... 281
Palmetto flag hoisted in A....284
Parole, Camp.............. 300
Parsonage burnt 304
Pattterson, Rev. J. M..........304
Paca Dwelling, The............307

Paca, Governor...............307
Parker, Jonathan............. 167
Parker, John.................. 168
Parrott, Samuel............... 261
Peace of the Colony............ 22
People of North Patux. petit. 27
Peaceable and loving way.... 28
People of Patuxent & Severn. 28
Peter, Jafer.................. 30
Peace in the Province.......... 31
People of Providence........... 34
Petition, save lives of St. Mary's
    men............................ 36
Pedro, Jno. a Ger. executed... 36
Peace, treaty of with Indians
    in 1666 40
Perrie, William 43
People of St. Mary's make
    stern effort 57
People of St. Mary's beseech
    Gov. Nicholson.......... 57
People of St. Mary's try to
    keep Capital 58
People of St. Mary's raise stock 59
Petition from Ruth Gregg..... 69
Permission asked to build a
    chapel...................... 70
Petition for a gallery, 1728.... 70
Personal chastisement, Rev.
    Mr. Allen...... 72
Pearce, Col..... 82
Peacocke 83
Petition of Cor. of Annapolis. 86
Petition of Charter of Anna-
    polis acted upon.......... 87
Perquisites, fees, profits........ 90
Perjury...................... 101
Persons of the Romish Com...102
Peggy, schnr. struck by light-
    ning........................ 110
Pew gives way................. 110
Peale, Mr. Charles.............. 125
Peale, Charles Wilson........ 126
Petition of single females of A.133
P. P. P. P.................. 136
People of Annapolis loyal....136
Perry, Mary, sentenced to die. 139
Peace, celebration of............ 221
Performers, dramatic.......... 146
Pendleton, Edw.............. 155
Peggy Stewart, burning of...169,
    170, 174.
Peace, treaty of, celebrated...194
Peace meetings.................233

Peace celebration............239
Pennsylvanians, company of...253
Peale, Chas. W. born at A....278
Peck, Thomas, D. D........304
Porter, Rear Admiral, D. D..315
Petty burglaries and arsons...316
Peaco, Samuel..............261
Philip, William, branded.....114
Phantom pleasure pursued...141
Photograph of Hood..........149
Philip, Capt. John..........273
Philadelphia, U. S. Ship.....303
Philips, Solomon.......304, 313
Piccard, Mr. Nicholas......... 40
Piscattoways.................. 54
Pinkney, Wm. student of K.
    W's School............... 65
Pinkney, Wm. native of An.. 65
Pinkuey and Johnson, peers
    of any.................... 65
Pinkney, Wm....79, 80, 203, 222,
    231, 232.
Pinnace for the canoe.........109
Pickeman, Capt 109
Pillory in Annapolis..........121
Pinkney, Mr. Robert........121
Pitt, portrait of.............163
Pinkney, Hall................217
Piracy on Chesapeake........226
Pinkney, Joathnan of Robt....229
Pinkney, banqutted in Anna.230
Pinkney, Wm. and family....254
Pinkney, Somerville.........262
Pinkuey, Wm. born at Annap.276
Pikesville, arsenal at........295
Picket guard captures a slave.298
Pindle, T. N. enrolling officer.300
Pinkney, Joseph...............305
Pinkney House, The..........308
Pinkney, Jonathan.167, 226, 273,
    282.
Pipier, William 167
Plantations, line of............ 18
Place, ought to take, deputies 44
Plot that struck at Annap... 82
Pleasure, Queen's known..... 93
Plater, George, Esq........... 95
Pleasure pursued..............141
Plays on the board...........147
Plebian 185
Plater, George...............197
Plater, Gov. George..........220
Plater, Col..................245
Planter's Guards..............249

Porter, Peter................ 19
Popish party begin to divulge 32
Port made at Town of Proctors 52
Ports, exportations to be from 53
Poor accommodations of the
    Ridge 56
Poem on St. Anne's in Gazette 73
Poem accomplishes rebuilding
    of St. Anne's............ 74
Portraits of Queen Anne and
    Lord Baltimore.......... 80
Port of Annapolis.......87, 94
Port of Annapolis, members of 96
Powder-house Hill........... 96
Powders and Chinese stones....100
Pope riding upon his bull......101
Poney, Thomas, burnt in hand.116
Powell, James, hung........117
Point, Windmill.............120
Powell, Jno. alias Chas. Lucas.125
Politics.....................143
Populace irritated...........157
Potomac River...............160
Portraits in Senate Chamber..162
Portrait of Pitt..............163
Portrait of first Lord Balto....163
Portrait in Senate Chamber....164
Portrait of 3rd Lord Balto....164
Post, Parliament prohibited..176
Political prisoner in Annapolis.189
Political fued injures St.John's213
Porter, Capt. U. S. N........ 237
Porter, Com 254
Police for the city...........257
Population of Annapolis.258, 280
    323.
Politics a heroic game.......274
Porter, J. C. 2nd Lieut 280
Poet, local on Col. Smith.....237
Poplar on College Campus......368
Poplar set on fire... 309
Porter, V. A'l, D. D...........316
Poplar on St. John's set on
    fire.....................321
Powers of the Cor. of Annap..336
Powers of Port Wardens.....339
Powers of incorporate officers.339
Providence.................19, 34
Protector, The............... 24
Preston, Richard.25, 28, 31, 32,
    44.
Providence sends a petition... 26
Preston, Richard and 60 others 27
Providence, in church meeting 28

Preparations for war 31
Proposals of Puritans to Stone 33
Price, Col...................... 36
Province restored to Lord
    Baltimore................. 37
Prescott, Edward, arrested, ac-
    quitted................47, 48
Providence changed to the
    Town at Proctors 52
Preston's house, Rich. assem-
    bly meets at.............. 56
Provincial Court removes to
    the Ridge.............. 56
Provincial Court removes from
    the Ridge 56
Proprietary promises not to re-
    move Capital from St.
    May's in his life... 56
Providence desires the capital 57
Protestant religion established
    in Maryland.............. 57
Protestant..................... 57
Protestant, Leg. peculiarly.... 58
Proctors, Town at........... 58
Province, centre and riches
    part of...................... 62
Protection for colonists......... 71
Protege of the State, St. Anne's 73
Price of second State House.. 80
Printed charter of Annapolis.. 80
Provincial business in the Court
    House.................. 81
Processes stayed at fairs........ 90
Profits, perquisites, fees..... 90
Privileges and laws.............. 93
Printer, Jonas Green.....98, 112
Pretender's Health, drinking
    of, punished..............137
Preface......................... 5
Prospect to Annapolis........ 96
Protest against Popery......... 99
Procession at Depsford...101, 102
Pretender, The................101
Prerogative, important of, Gov102
Proctor's Landing.............108
Printing press................108
Province famous as centre of
    social pleasures, &c......109
Pretenders health............110
Prorogation of Legislature....113
Prison at Annapolis...........114
Principal families...............128
Prototype of European social
    life...... 145

Proprietary, revenue of the....143
Proctor's, Town Land at.......146
Presbyterian Church..........148
Prisoner, a royal 155
Proprietary interest of Md......155
Prince George street..........158
Protest by citizens of Anna-
    polis on Boston resolutions166
Proposal to burn Peggy Stew.174
Private corres. examined....175
Proclaimed Governor..........182
Procession at Inauguration of
    Governor....................182
Proclamation call'g out Militia183
Prisoner in Annapolis..........189
Presidents, four future........206
President Wash.'s visit to A..218
Pryfe, Thomas................224
Prince George Street, wharf...228
Pratt, Governor.............245, 273
Price, Henry..................263
Proclamation on fees.......... 279
Proclamation of Thanksgiving 281
Pratt, Thos. G........282, 307, 311
Proclamation of Buchanan....283
Protest of Mayor of Annapolis.296
Provost Guard................301
Provost Guard seizes liquor....301
Presbyterian Church in Anna.304
Provost Marshal.............310
Price's, Smith, fire at............311
Printing, Gazette fails to obtain313
Preparatory department St.
    John's College............312
Prosperity of St. John's Col..317
Progenitors of inhabitants of A324
Property of City exempt......341
Prew, William.... 167
Pryse, Thomas...................167
Psalter, Peter..................137
Puritans...17, 19, 24, 32, 35, 36,
    37.
Puritan district.............. 19
Puritans refuse to take oath
    of fealty................. 19
Puritans compared to snake in
    fable.................... 20
Puritans charged with desire
    to domineer................ 20
Puritans send delegates to
    Legislature, 1651.... 20, 23
Providence....................... 20
Puddington, Mr.............. 21
Puddington, George........... 21

Puritans who settled Annap... 23
Price, Capt. John.............. 26
Puritans petition the Com.... 26
Puritans charge terms of settlement and oath of fealty do
 not agree................. 26
Puritans complain to Council
 of State................... 26
Puritans called factious fellows 26
Puritans defend their conduct. 26
Puritans beg and bemoan...... 26
Puritans of Providence....31, 33
Puritans and Catholics......... 32
Puritans sends mes. to Stone.. 33
Puritans grieved at their humble message................ 33
Puritans' proposals to Stone... 33
Puritan messengers seized by
 Stone.................... 33
Puritans get in rear of St.
 Mary's men............. 35
Puritans win the battle of the
 Severn.................... 36
Puritans lose four in battle of
 Severn.................... 36
Puritans close matter after
 their own way............. 36
Puritans execute 4 St. Mary's 36

Puritan Assembly.............. 56
Publique Buildings, lots set
 aside for................... 64
Public Buildings left solely to
 Province.................. 67
Puritans, meeting-house of... 69
Publication of sermon of Mr.
 Coney.................... 69
Pulled down 2nd State House 81
Publication. Gazette ceased... 95
Public Circle................. 97
Public School in Annapolis.... 98
Puritans, The................108
Puritanical ideas not prevalent142
Public meeting about Boston..165
Pulaski's legion of cavalry.....184
Pungent correspondence........185
Publicola.......................185
Public Dinner to Washington..192
Public dinner at Mr. Mann's.218
Puritan disappears...........274
Public Buildings. Churches
 and Ancient Landmarks..302
Public School Building in A..308
Public Lands and Buildings
 reserved...................341
Public Cemeteries 342
Pypowdry, Court of.......... 90

Q

Quakers and Indians disturb
 the Colony.................. 37
Quakers, early settlement in
 Maryland.................. 42
Quakers petitioning to affirm. 42
Quakers, acts against repealed 44
Quaint and sneering reply...... 61
Quakers. missionaries sent to. 66
Quarrel with Daniel Dulany... 72
Queen Anne's bell burned...... 77
Quaint and curious volumes... 79
Queen Anne, portrait of...... 80
Queen, defender of the faith. 87
Queen's pleasure known......... 93
Queen Caroline, birthday of. 95
Quarrel between Gov. Bladen
 and Legislature.......105, 106

Quiver of the Indian............108
Quarters, servants'..............129
Queen Anne's garden............129
Queen bee. taking of, celebration.139
Queen Sarah and King Abraham..........................161
Quynn, John Allen..............176
Quaint and agreeable...........201
Queen Anne.....................255
Qualification of members of
 corporation..................335
Quynn, Allen...71, 177, 187, 198,
 199, 225, 228
Quynn, Jr., Allen..............229
Quynn, Caspar................248
Quota for drafts................315

R

Raleigh, brig,.................111
Ranks of Colonial society......126
Races.................128, 159

Races in Annapolis.........141, 156
Ravages by small-pox...........143
Raillery, Annapolis out-lives...145

Race course, shipyard and In-
dians................157
Ramsey, Col...............196
Ramsay, Benj., Chief Judge...220
Randall, John........167, 227, 237,
255, 308
Randall, J. Jr..............258
Rafferty, Dr. Wm.........257, 259
Railroad between Balto. and
Annapolis......... 262
Randall, Alex...262, 284, 297, 313
Ramsay, Capt. Francis M......267
Railroad built to Naval Acade.286
Randall, Mrs. Alex., residence308
Randall, J. Wirt.... ......308, 323
Randall, John, Alex. R., son of312
Randall, Daniel............320
Railroad, A. & B. S. L.........323
Ranken, George.............167
Ranken, George, Sir............168
Reconciliation of the Puritans. 21
Refusal to issue writs in Com-
monwealth's name....... 25
Rebellion against Lord Balto. 28
Rebels at Patuxent and Severn 32
Religious Liberty in Maryland 37
Records of Courts..........40, 91
Rebels to his Proprietary..... 46
Representative, Indiscreet,
from A. A. Co........... 49
Refuses to concur, Upper
House.................. 51
Removal of capital to Annap. 53
Residence of Lord Baltimore. 55
Revolution of Coode approved
by the King............. 57
Religion supported by taxation 57
Residence of officers of prov. 58
Removal of Legis. to Ridge... 59
Removal of Courts to Ridge... 59
Removal of capital, full house
regrets................. 60
Reputation of province, St.
Mary's solicitous for....... 61
Reply of Legis. St. Mary's... 61
Removal to Annap., consumat 61
Records reach Annapolis..... 61
Report of Com. to build a
church in Annapolis 65
Records of Chancery Court,... 66
Rector, second, of St. Anne's. 69
Rector, third, of St. Anne's.. 69
Rector, receives $350 salary
in .717................. 69

Revenues of St. Anne's......... 69
Rector preaches outside of St.
Anne's............. 69
Rector All Saints being dead. 69
Rector of St. Anne's........ 75
Retribution had come....... 75
Rector, report of, St. Anne's. 77
Report of rector of, St.Anne's 77
Rector of King William school 78
Rector, Governors, &c., of K.
W's. school............. 79
Register of K. W's. school to
give notice.............. 79
Records of K. W's. school lost 80
Records, burning of the...... 83
Relic of Maryland history..... 95
Residence, house for Governor 98
Residence, fund for Governors 98
Records, legislative.......... 98
Reading the Bible...........101
Rebellion...........101
Rejoicing over Louisburg....103
Reward of £50 offered......112
Rebels imported and sold.....112
Reynold, Mr. Wm., drowned.112
Rebels for sale..............126
Records of the club..... 131, 132
Reverend, a, whipped........137
Revenge of the proprietary...143
Repeal of Stamp act.........151
Rejoicing over repeal of Stamp
act....................151
Recommendation of Congress.155
Return of Gov. Eden........157
Rebels, ship load of.........157
Resolutions about Boston.....165
Resolutions of Md. against
English oppression.........169
Respect of personal rights....170
Representation of Eug.officers'
cases...................189
Reply of Washington to Annap193
Reply of Annap.to Gen. Greene195
Replies of La Fayette....196, 197
Resignation by Washington of
military commission.....200
Reply of Wash. to council of
State......... 202
Reply of Washing. to Annap 203
Reply of State to Washington204
Registry of Alumni of St.
John's.................213
Reception of Washington....221
Reid, James................229

Rea, John.. 229
Republican, Maryland....233, 324
Republican's and Gazette's
    quarrel...............236
Regulars from Fort Severn....243
Reform Electors.............244
Representation, basis of......245
Reform of Maryland.........246
Reed, Capt. James..........254
Repository, Regl. & Lit'y......256
Resolutions of colored people.262
Resolutions on Naval Academ.264
Read, Commodore, Geo. C....265
Report of the riot.............271
Retrospect of two centuries...274
Remnant of treason.........298
Revell, James......301, 302, 311
Redemptorist Order..........304
Residence of Mrs. A. Randall.308
Revell, Martin..............311
Representatives in both armies314
Regan, John C..............316
Report on St. John's College.316
Revell, State's Attorney.....318
Rehn, Louis H..............320
Revenues of Annapolis..... 320
Record, The.................325
Review of labor of writing
    History..................326
Returns, election, judges of...336
Rescue Hose Co.............. 15
Real estate, taxes on.........340
Regulation of sale of liquors.339
Richard Bennett's plantation. 18
Ridgely, Henry.......... 19, 97
Ridgely, Col. Henry.......... 19
Ridgely, Charles.19, 199, 222, 319
Ridgelys, Tomb of........... 19
River of Severn............. 30
Richardson, Eliz., hanged as
    a witch................. 49
Rights of Lower House insists 51
Ridge, the capital, removed to 56
Ridge, capital removed from,. 56
Richest part of the province. 62
Ridgely, Mrs. Richard....... 64
Ridout, John............71, 74, 308
Ridgely, Mr. David..80, 148, 319
Richetts, Thomas............ 85
Right to erect cities......... 92
Ridgely, Mr................. 97
Richmond, the ship..........109
Riders, bold..................128
Richard Buckell & Co., exhib139

Riot over stamp act in Annap149
Rioters pull Hood's house
    down..................150
Ringgold, Thomas...........150
Richardson, Capt. Joseph....151
Ridgely, Richard...210, 225, 256,
    319
Ridgely, Charles,of Wm......222
Ridgely, Henry,of Annapolis.223
Ridgely, Absalom...226, 227, 303
Ridgely, Major Chas. S 234
Riot in Annapolis, ...236, 268
Ridout, Sam'l..............235, 308 -
Ridgely, Charles S., Col......240
Ridout, Horatio..........226, 254 -
Ridout, Addison.............255 -
Ring$, political...... 256
Riots and noise 257
Ridgely, E. D..............258
Right of soldiers to vote.....258
Riot, fears of...............269
Riot, State's cannon used in...271
Riot, investigation of........272
Riley, Elihu S..........278, 324
Richest man in America......275
Ridout, Dr. John....297, 303, 304 -
Rival for Balto...............298
Ridgely's, David, description
    of Third Gov's. residence.303
Ridout, Miss Hester A. Chase.306 -
Ridout, Dr. Wm. G.........306 -
Ridout, Horace.............308 -
Ridouts, the............. ...308 -
Right of Elective Franchise..310
Ridgely, Abslaom, merchant.319
Ridgely, John..............319
Ridgely, Nicholas..........319
Ringe, student John B......321
Rinehart, William..........324
Riley, Elihu S., Jr..........324
Ridgely, Absalom, the, 2nd...324
Ridgely, Wm. S.............324
Ridge, Robert..............167
Richards, Joseph............167
Ridgely, Greenbury 170
River, West... 170
Roll-book...................... 18
Roundheads to be forced to
    submit.................. 34
Roundheads................. 34
Robinett, Allen, keeper of Sev-
    ern Ferry.............. 63
Rooms of the State House to
    be fitted up............ 67

Room wanted in St. Anne's... 71
Royal patronage of K. W's.
    school 77
Robotham, Col. Geo.......... 78
Royalty in bad odor......... 80
Rosey, Crowne, in Norfolk
    Towne...................... 84
Robinson, William............... 95-
Robinson's, Peter, school......102-
Romish, communion, persons.109
Robert, Mr. William 111
Rogue, a remarkable........114
Ross, John, Esq........115, 224
Rogers, Esq., Wm...........115
Robbery in Annapolis............117
Roberts, Hugh...............126
Royal prisoner................154
Roberts, Mr. William....157, 181
Row-gallies or gondolos......177
Roxburg, Major Alex.....188
Rock Hall..............194, 218
Rochambeau, Count........194
Roberts, Rev. Mr................224
Ross, Wm............... ...229, 261
Rowles, Joseph.............229

Ross. Thomas...................234
Robinson, Mrs. M............ 243-
Rogers, Com.....................254
Robinson, Rev. Thos. drowned272
Robinson, J. Wesley...... 305
Robinson, Matthias......... 305
Ross, Lieut. Albert............308
Root, Col. A. R..................313
Route of Md. settlers.......329
Roads to Annapolis............342
Ross, Nathaniel 167
Roberts, Charles..................167
Robinson, Elijah........170, 176-
Ruthers, Samuel............. 19
Runaway servants to be retur 29
Rules and orders in Annapolis 62
Rumney and Long......111, 157
Russell, Wm. H., in Annap...299
Russell, Josiah..............305
Russian sailor killed........313
Ruark, Oliver M., schooner..320
Rumors of Balitmore's patent
    to be taken from him.... 23
    House.................... 81

S

Sanders, Mr. James..........63, 64
Saylor, A...................... 81
Sale, rebels for..............126
Sanitary measure............175, 179
Sands, Lewis..................226
Salmon, Simpson..............229
Sands, Joseph.................255
Sands, James..................273
Sandford, James...............301
Salvation Army and Barracks.306
Sale of Cadet vacancy offered.316
Sampson, Miss.................320
Sale of liquors in Annapolis..329
Sands, John...................167
Sappington, Mark Brown......170
Sands, Thomas.....,.........261
Sanse, Peter.................261
Scott, Mr. John............... 44
Scott, Dr. Upton...........71, 253
Scott, Upton.................. 75
School, King William's77, 96, 109
School street a memento...... 78
Schools in the counties....... 97
Schools of Anne Arundel..... 97
School House...................108
School, Kent county.........126

Scottish patriots.............126
Scoevola.......................185
Scenes at Annapolis............187
Schoff, Dr. John David......220
Schwrar, George..............255
Schwrar, P....................259
Scott, Lieut. Gen............285-
Schaaf, Arthur................307
Schwrar, P. S.................315
Scenes in Court House of An..318
Scharf, Col. Thos. J..........324
Severn.......17, 34, 145, 152, 183
Settlement of Annapolis........ 17
Severn River....18, 111, 114, 115,
    218.
Settlement of South River..... 19
Settlers at Providence tranquil-
    ized........................ 23
Sectaries and Schismatics...... 24
Severn, Battle of............. 33
Servants gallery in St. Anne's 75
Second State House, form of.. 80
Severn, entrance to the....... 81
Seymour, Gov. John.......81, 93
Seymour, Gov................ 82
Seymour, John, Royal Gov.... 85

Seymour, Gov. John, gives charter to Annapolis...... 85
Several persons of qualitie in Anne Arundel offer to erect public buildings...... 57
Severn Ferry instituted........ 63
Sermons of Rev. Peregrine Coney 69
Severn, head of.............. 71
Second State House in Annap. 80
Second message of Puritans to Gov. Stone.............. 33
Sentry of St. Mary's fires signal..................... 36
Senecas..................... 54
Several murders committed ... 54
Seymour, John, Esq..... 87, 91
Severn, North side of........... 96
Second Newspaper in Md....... 98
Sentence to cut off man's hand 102
Seat of Government............ 108
Senhouse, John............... 112
Servants ill-treated............ 112
Senhouse, Hannah, blamed.... 112
Sedgley, Capt................ 116
Servant, bravery of.. 117
Servant of Richard Mackubin 120
Sexton, the, Sol. Mogg....... 125
Servants............. 126
Secret chambers............. 128
Servants' quarters..... 129
Servant, duties of.............. 131
Session, club in.............. 132
Secretary, speech of Tuesday club..................... 134
Sentenced so have ear cut of.. 137
Seminary at Annapolis........ 153
Severn, the schooner........ 158
Selby, John S., merchant...... 158
Severe's blacksmith shop..... 158
Senate Chamber, portrait in... 163
Second buurt offering to liberty 174
Senator................. 185
Sentry..................... 185
Seat of Government settled... 200
Settlement of claims of St. John's................ 213
Seizure of St. John's........ 214
Sellman's, Capt., troop. 240, 243
Senate................244, 245
Sellman, John S:...245, 248, 249
Sexton's character.......... 251

Severn River bridge........ 257
Severn Guard................ 282
Separate sovereignity for Md. 282
Seabrook, W. L. W.284, 297, 299
Seward, Wm. H., letter of, to Gov. Hicks.......... 289
Seventh Regt. from New York 296
Secession feeling strong in A.. 297
Secession Youths........... 297
Sellman, Richard........... 300
Severn River Ferry........... 300
"Secesh Democracy" berated. 300
Second Gubernatorial Mansion 303
Second Methodist Church... 304
Settlers reach Md........... 330
Settlement of Md 330
Settlers and the Indians..... 331
Session of Corporation...... 335
Seleven, Brite............ 167
Selby, Joseph............/... 167
Severe, Vachel............. 161
Sherley, Gov. of Boston..... ...100
Ship, Winchelsea, armed....... 114
Shrewdness of the Natives.. 144
Ship Tavern, in South east st. 118
Shipwright Street............ 157
Shipyards, race courses, and Indians................ 157
Ship load of rebels........... 157
Shipyard, First............ 157
Ship building declined........ 158
Sharpe, Horatio, Gov., arrives 159
Sharpe, Gov., expostulates... 164
Ship Totness................ 174
Shaff, Arthur.............. 226
Shaw, John ...., 226
Shaff, John T.............. 226
Shaw, James................ 255
Shipley, Wm. A............. 257
Shaw, Geo................. 258
Shurman, William.......... 272
Shephard, Basil........ 261, 304
Shaffer, Detective.......... 318
Shakespeare Water cure.... 320
Short Line Railroad........ 320
Shoem, Maccubbin N... ...167
Should know he was Gov. again................. 32
Ship Mary and Francis..... 45
Ship required to unload at ports 53
Shipyards to be reserved..... 63
Sharpe, Gov. 71, 72, 150, 151, 160

25

Shallup, Evans Jones'......... 82
Sheriff of Anne Arundel. ..84, 89
Shumer. Mr..... 84
Sheriff for Annapolis..... ... 89
Sheriff of Anne Arundel co.,
   entitled to jurisdiction in
   Annapolis 94
Shipping of Annapolis.......... 95
Ship with slaves.................. 95
Sharp messages between Gov.
   and Legislature..............100
Ship William and Anne.........103
Ship captured................104
Ship ransomed.................103
Ship, the Richmond 109
Site of St. Anne's selected by
   Gov. Nicholson............ 69
Sinking fund 71
Site of King William's school 78
Situation of Court House.... 81
Simpson, William..... ...82, 83
Simpson. Cooper, Williams,
   Peacocke. and Keyton.... 83
Site for Market House...... 98
Sign. Tavern...............129
Sitting of the Assembly......143
Site of Theatre.............147
Sisters of Notre Dame, house of157
Situation of State House....162
Simpson, Thomas 229
Simmons. Joseph............250
Sick prisoners arrive at Annap302
Simpson, Jonathan..........168
Sibel. Henry...............168
Sketch of William Pinkney..276
Sketch of Reverdy Johnson..276
Sketch of John D. Goodman.277
Sketch of Stewart Holland...277
Sketch of Chas. Wilson Peale.278
Sketch of Jas. B. Lockwood..278
Sketch of Daniel Dulany....278
Skingle. Samuel...............167
Slaves gallery in St. Anne's.. 75
Slaves. ship with............ 95
Slaves. catching. 103
Slee Molly. captured 111
Slate. Capt. ... .158
Slanders against Mr. Green..225
Slaves captured by a picket
   gu. 298
Sliver. Andrew.........304, 201
Slemaker's. Mr. Jno., houses.313
Smith, Rev. Wm.............209

Smith, Joan... 17
Smith, Capt. John 31
Smith, Mr. Richard 41
Smith, Robt.... 78
Smith, Thomas.............. 78
Smithers, house of.......... 82
Small boat well armed 83
Smithers. Christopher........ 87
Smith, Wm., carpenter...... 95
Smith, Edward.............. 97
Small-pox in Annapolis..119, 313
Small-pox ravages Indians...143
Smallwood, Col. Wm.......182
Smallwood, Major Gen......188
Smallwood, Gen.......201, 206
Smith, Rev. Doctor W.......209
Smook, Lieut................254
Smith, John, Jr............262
Smith, Wm. T 269, 270
Smith, Col. 13th N. Y......297
Smith, M. M.... 305
Smith's house, Aunt Lucy...308
Smith, John, husband of A.
   L. Smith................308
Smith, Mrs. Lieut. J. T 320
Smith, Capt...................327
Smith, Archibald............168
Snowden, Richard........... 95
Snowden, Capt...............282
Society of Cincinnatti.........196
South River, 19, 70, 82, 84, 95,
   115, 209, 219
Sons of Thunder............. 82
Sop for Governor's vanity...... 60
Sot-weed factor............. 91
South River, storm toward...108
Social pleasures 109
South River Club... ....110, 131
Society Colonial, ranks of....126
Southern provinces, not puri-
   tanical.....................142
Sons of Liberty..............151
Soldier deserts.............157
Soaper, James P.............256
Soldiers, right of, to vote......258
South River, patrol on.........281
South Carolina...............282
Soldiers vote in Annapolis....310
Soldiers, negro 313
Soldiers of A. meet in conflict.314
Soldiers, fraternization of......315
Society, A. A. Co. Historical.320
Spa Creek.................19, 85

Space on water side for ware-
house in A.............. 65
Speculation as to origin of St.
Anne's 68
Spry, John..................... 84
Spaniard, on left 102
Sprigg. Col. Edward, speaker.104
Spinkfe. Daniel, executed....118
Speech of Sec. of Tuesday Club134
Spencer...................... 147
Sprigg. Richard..............209
Spriggs. Saul................239
Sparks. Dr. Edward...........259
Spencer, Col 282
Speech of Gov. Hicks........283
Spirit of improvement in An..315
Spa Bridge............... ..316
Spa, Bridge over the....318, 324
Spaulding, G. W., baggage-
master................320
Spirit of Improvement........323
Sparrow, Thos..................167
Sprigg, Benjamin............168
Sprigg, Thomas..............170
Stone, Captain............... 19
Stone, Gov., proclaims Prince
of Wales................. 24
Stone made Gov. by com'r...... 25
Stone removed under misun-
derstanding............... 25
Stone's men execrate the Puri-
tans 35
Stone proclaims the Puritans
rebels 27
Strong, Leonard, Mr............ 28
Strong, Leonard...29, 30, 31, 32
Stringent Laws................. 31
Stone, Gov...................... 32
St. Mary's men declare they
will have the government 32
Stone, Capt. William.......... 33
Stone's men plunder a house.. 34
Stone. Gov., in ignorance of
intentions of Puritans .. 34
Stone, Gov., arrives at the
Severn................. 34
St. Mary's men defy Puritans. 35
St. Mary's men kill a man...... 36
St. Mary's men routed....... 36
Stone, Gov., yields on quarter
given...................... 36
Stone. Gov., condemned to death 36
Stone, Gov., wounded........... 36

St. Mary's county 39
St. Mary's..................39, 40
State's Records, loss of...... 40
State House destroyed by fire. 40
St. Mary's, removal of capital
from......................... 55
St. Mary's, the venerated capi-
tal...................... 56
St. Mary's undisturbed until
1683........................ 56
St. Mary's, capital, once more
settled................... 56
St. Mary's has a life tenure
in the capital............. 56
Struggle, a brief............. 57
St. Mary's, hope of.......... 58
St. Mary's immolated......... 58
St. Mary's, a mere landing
place....................... 58
St. Mary's has several disad-
vantages........ 58
St. Mary's Catholic, Legisla-
ture Protestant......... ... 57
State House at St. Mary's..... 57
State House in Annapolis...... 57
St. Mary's petition Gov. Nich-
olson 57
St. Mary's rejoices at Gov.
Nicholson elevation......... 58
St. Mary's prays for the quiet
of Gov. Nicholson.......... 58
St. Mary's asks to claim an-
cient franchises........ . 58
St. Mary's people Catholics... 58
State House at St. Mary's.... 58
St. Mary's, State House, at... 58
State House at Annapolis...... 58
St. Mary's tries to keep capital 58
St. Mary's capital for 60 years 59
St. Mary's, spring, at........ 59
St. Mary's, advantages of.... 60
St. Mary's, accessibleness of... 60
St. Mary's uncentral position
for capital................. 60
St. Mary's solicitous for reputa-
tion of....................... 61
St. Mary's, reply of Legis. to. 61
St. Mary's compared to Pha-
roah's Kine............. 61
St. Mary's unequally ranks.... 62
St. Mary's called ill-improvers 62
Stir of a new vitality in Annap 63
State House, first in Annap.... 66

State House has a tragic history 67
St. Anne's Parish estab. 1692. 68
St. Anne's once Middle Neck
      Parish...................... 68
St. Anne's....................... 68
St. Anne's, selection of its site 69
St. Anne's finished............ 69
St. Anne's built in shape of T. 69
St. Anne's faces east.......... 69
St. Anne's. General Assembly
      needful of.......... 69
St. Anne's three lots.......... 69
St. Anne's inconvenient to
      parishioners...... 69
St. Anne's too little 70
St. Anne's, room wanted in... 71
St. Anne's enlarged, 1740...... 71
Stuart, William............... 71
Stamp officer, in 1765......... 71
Strain, Robert 71
St. Anne's, wardens of. threate 71
St. James, curate of 72
St. Anne's, protege of State.. 73
St. Anne's falls into ruin ... 73
St. Anne's poem on, in Gazette 73
St. Anne's, Assembly asked to 74
St. Anne's, trustees of, 1774. 75
State gives £1500 to St. Anne's 75
St. Anne's. State gives £1500 to 75
St. Anne's with steeple 75
State pew in St. Anne's...... 75
St. Anne's, State pews in.... 75
St.   Anne's subscribers to
      choose pews in.......... 75
St. Anne's, Gallery's for pa-
      rishioners, slaves, and ser-
      vants.................... 75
St. Anne's, organist of....... 75
St. Anne's, dark day for ... 75
St. Anne's, the Point Look Out 75
St. Anne's, rector of, Malcolm,
      Keene................... 75
St Anne's, cost of. in 1792 ... 75
St. Anne's burned............ 75
St. Anne's bell tolls its requiem 75
St. Anne's rebuilt............ 76
St. Anne's, change of spirit.. 77
St. Anne's in front ranks...... 77
St. Anne's, report of rector... 77
St. Anne's Chapel........... 77
St. Philip's Chapel........... 77
St. Anne's ancient communion
      vessels 77

St. John's, Library of.......... 79
State House, second in Annap 80
State House, emblem of pov-
      erty...................... 81
St. Michaels. feast day of ... 88
St. Philip's day.. 90
St. Jacob's day 90
St. Michael, the Arch angel... 90
State House, very beautiful... 91
Stoddard's, James, survey of A 97
State House destroyed by fire. 97
State House Circle........... 97
State Library 98
Stewart, Dr. Chas.............102
Storm towards South River...103
St. Anne's Parish.............108
State House. 108
Stewart, Mr. Vincent, killed...115
Steadman. Mary, murdered...116
St. Anne's. Gov. Ogle interred117
Stewart, Geo., election of, set
      aside.....................120
Stewart, Wm..................120
Stocking manufactory.........120
State House, bills of credit for120
Styles of the time...........128
Streets with no pavements......129
St. George's festival...........136
Stage in Annapolis 140
St. Tamina......................142
Stamp act in Annapolis.........149
Stamped paper returned 151
Stage patronized by Gov. Eden153
St. Anne's bell.................158
St. Tamina society.............159
Stewart, George 159
State House, the third in An.161
State House, dimensions of...162
State Convention 169
Stewart. Mr. Anthony..171, 172,
      173
Steuben, Major-Gen. Baron..185
Stratagem of Lafayette.......187
State, address of. to Washing.203
State, reply of Wash. to...... 204
Steuben, Baron, Washington's
      letter to....................205
St. John's College...........208
Steret, John.....................209
St. John's injured by a politi-
      cal fued....................213
St. John's, Lottery for.........213
St. John's claim, settlement of214

St. John's, appropriation to...214
St. John's seized 214
St. John's, Wash. visit to....218
St. John's College and Wash.219
Steven. Vachel 223
Stone, John Hoskins..........226
Sterrett, Sam'l. Capt.......227
Sterrett. John...............227
St. Anne's Church stoned......235
Stuart, Major Alex.... 235
State public meeting.........249
Steamer Surprise..............254
Stiles. Geo. & Son............254
Stephen. John................255
State and U. S.. conflict bet..255
Star Chamber of Annapolis...256
State Managers. unnamed ...256
Strawberry Hill farm..........256
State Library 259
Stewart, Peggy...............266
States' cannon used in riot...271
State House, fire in..........273
Steele. James B 273
Star. the Democratic...........273
St. John's College cadets.....282
Stewart, Capt 282
Stalker, Jno. E 284
Stockett. Frank H.... 297
Steam Ferry Boat "Ready"..300
Stewart, Dr. Geo. H 303
St. Mary's Catholic Church..304
St. Martin's Church...........305
Steip, John...... 305
Stewart, Anthony, house of..308
Stewart, brig Peggy.bowl from309
Steam fire engine in Annap....311
St. Anne's Mission Chapel, a
  memorial..............312
St. John's College...........312
State receives from A.&E.R.R313
Stockett, Frank H.,staff officer313
Steam Ferry boat..... 315
St. John's College, report on..317
St. John's College, property of317
Stockett, J. Schaaf..........320
Stanley, William, killed......320
Statue of Taney.............324
Statue of De Kalb............324
State Museum...............324
Storm overtakes settlers......328
State subscription approved... 3
Sypolls, Henry..............229

State subscription, members
  who 7
Streets. powers over...........338
Stewart, Chas 167
Steuart, David................167
Steele, John 167
Stiff. Wm....................167
Stiff, Thomas................167
Steiger, Jordan......... 167
Stewart, Anthony 167
Stringer, Richard..........170, 176
Steward, Stephen..........170, 176
Susquehannock Indians 22
Susquehanna Indians......... 28
Susquehannas desire peace... 28
Susquehannock embassadors.. 55
Submitted to the King......... 57
Sudden removal of capital... 60
Sugar Plum of all the Mayors
  coaches...... 62
Subscribers to choose pews in
  St. Anne's.............. 75
Subscription to free schools.... 78
Susscription to the Gazette....99
Support of garrison at Cape
  Breton 105
Sullivan. Daniel, gibbetted....116
Sufferers. collection for Boston120
Sun of England.................129
Susquehanna.......... 161
Suggestion of Gen. Wash....162
Suspension of St. John's ap-
  propriation 210
Sullivan, John................222
Somerville, Wm..............226
Sutton, Sam'l...............248
Sunday Schools..............255
Sutton, Capt., decided to put
  into A......... 268
Sunday work and barbers......314
Sullivan, C. A...............316
Suicide of Lt. Danenhower...321
Susquehannahs................332
Swithson, Thos., donates to K.
  W's. school. 79
Swann. Richard............263, 273
Swann, Thomas................303
Swope, J. H...............305
Swann, Mrs. Richard..........307
Swann, R...........316
Sympathy for Boston...........168

T

Tax to build church in Annap. 65
Taxable persons in St. Anne's 68
Taylard. Mr. William......... 69
Tax bill to raise sinking fund. 71
Tasker, Col. Ben. 71, 96, 97, 146
Tasker Thomas.............. 78
-Taylor. Edward............. 83
Taylard. Mr. Clarke. mistrusted 85
Tax on tobacco...............101
Tax imposed without authority105
Tasker. Esq.. Ben. acts as Gov.117
Tasker. Benj.. jr.. ...... 118. 159
Tannery set up by Thos. Hyde119
Tavern. Signs................129
Tamina. St 142
Tatswell. John...............155
Tar and feathers.............178
Talbot Court House 220
Tate. Robt. W................311
Tate. James E................311
Taylor. Geo. M 315
Taney statue 324
Taxes on real estate... 340
Terms of purchase of lots.... 53
Temporary removals of capital 56
Tenure vain, for St. Mary's.. 56
Tench. Hon. Thomas........ 64
Tench. Esq , Thomas......... 84
Ten persons to be common
    councilmen................ 88
Temple street............... 97
Ten persons struck by light-
    ning 110
Tea burnt at Annapolis.......171
Temperance in politics.........261
Testimony of Dan. T. Hyde.269
Telegraph to Annapolis........281
Telephone and telegraph in
    Annapolis...... 324
Threatening speeches.......... 32
The Battle of the Severn...... 33
Thurston, Thos., before the
    Governor 38
Thurston, Thos., desires to
    leave Province 38
Thomas Trueman, impeach-
    ment of.... 54
Three clergymen from Anne
    Arundel.................. 66
Three lots for St. Anne's...... 69

Thorton, William................ 71
Theatre had been introduced.. 75
Thomas, archbishop of Cantr'y 77
Thompson, John.............. 78
Thompson, Richard............ 86
The first newspaper in Md.... 94
The Maryland Gazette.......... 94
Thomas, Robert............. 97
The second newspaper in Md.. 98
The Pretender.................101
The Freemen of Maryland....106
Three Governor's messages in
    one day......................107
The Indians.......................108
The Puritans....................108
The Gazette 109
Three companies go to Canada110
Thornton, William, sheriff.....111
The legislature prorogued......113
Thames. Frigate 116
Theatre on West street.........121
The First Citizen, letters of...121
The sexton, Sol. Mogg..........125
The Maryland Gazette........125
Thornton, Wm., Esq., to frame
    discourse....................133
Theatre in Annapolis...........139
The first American theatre....146
Theatre, the first American....146
Theatre opened...................147
Theatre, site of..................147
Theatre on Gloucester St.....148
The stamp act in Annapolis...149
The King's passengers........157
Thornton, Mrs. Commodore ..323
Thomas, John........315, 316, 323
The St. Tamina Society.......159
Third State House in Annap..161
The third State House.........161
Three islands, mouth West
    River 174
Thousands of French auxilia-
    ries......................187
Thomas, Nicholas 220
Thompson, Alex.........222, 229
Theatre. Annap.226, 140, 141, 148
The Ancient Regime disap-
    pears.....................228
Thompson, Richard. Jr......229
Thompson, Jane............229

Thomas' Point, British sloop on234
"The Glorious Nineteen,"....244
Thomas, Geo. A............245, 248
Thomas, Jno. B............248, 250
Thompson, W. R............ ...259
Three rifles leveled on Judge
  Brewer................271
The Democratic Star............273
The First Citizen....... 275
Thanksgiving, proclamation of281
Thompson, Wm. H..............282
The College Green...........302
The Governor's Folly.......302
The third Gubernatorial Man-
  sion..................302
Third Gubernatorial Mansion.302
"The Old Blue Church,"..... 303
The Ball Boom..................305
The Old City Hall.............305
The City Hotel..............305
The Gazette and State Printing312
Thompson, Prof. Wm. H.....312
The Gazette explains defeat..316
The Court House of Annapolis 318
The Chase Mansion...........306
The Harwood Residence.....306
The Ogle House..............307
The Paca dwelling.............307
The Iglehart House...........307
The Pinkney House 308
The Liberty Tree..............308
The Dove, (Note)...........328
The Ark, (Note)..................328
The Charter of Annapolis....334
Thompson, Richard.........167
Thimnis, John.....................168
Thomas, John................176
Timid deputies lose the gov-
  ernment.................... 57
Tilghman, Maj., Wm., clerk..104
Times. customs of the, 1765...124
Times, dress of the time 1765.124
Times are dreadful, &c.........151
Tilghman, Mathew.169, 174, 175
Tilghman, Lusby.............226
Tilghman, James.... 166
Tillard. Thomas.............176
Took possession of unoccupied
  lands.................... 18
Town originally intended...... 18
Town laid at Greensbury's.... 18
Todd, Thomas................. 18
Tomb of the Ridgleys......... 18

Todd, tomb of...... 19
Token to be brought by In-
  dians.................... 30
Town at Proctors, made a port 52
To draw up a bill of attainder. 55
Town at Proctors..........57, 58
Town Land at Proctors....62, 146
Town at port of Anne Arundel 62
Town and port at Severn.... 63
Topp, Edwd., at Annapolis... 66
Town clerk of Annapolis...... 66
To treat with workmen to
  build 69
Topp, Rev. Mr............... 69
Tootell, Richard.... ....71, 170
Tombstone of Evan Jones...... 76
Tombstone of Amos Garrett... 76
Town of Annapolis, attempt
  upon.................... 82
Town and port of Annapolis.. 87
Town-common................ 94
Torres, Francis, advertisement100
Tobacco, tax on.............. ..100
Tootell, Mr. 103
Tobacco, taxed without law....105
Tolley's Point 109
Tom, a negro, executed.....112
Tobacco from America..........127
Totness, ship, burned...........174
Toasts at inauguration of Gov183
Toasts on treaty of peace.......194
Toasts at dinner to Wash205, 218
Toasts at dinner to Wash....218
Toasts at Masonic celebration223
Tootell, John 229
Toasts at banquet to William
  Pinkney...................232
Toasts at banquet on downfall
  of Napoleon 236
Topper, Samuel, arrested......300
Tongue, Benjamin...........301
Townley, Francis...........307
Town clock in Annapolis......315
Town not dead.... 325
Tonry, William 167
Towson, Thomas.............167
Tract of 250 acres surveyed.... 18
Trade committee decides for
  Lord Baltimore......... 36
Treaty of peace with Indians
  in 1666 40
Trade to be done at ports.... 53
Troops invest a fort.......... 54

Trueman, Thomas, impeachment of 54
Trueman, Major, found 55
Trueman escapes punishment. 55
Tradesmen given land in Annapolis 63
Tradesmen put outside city limits 64
Tradesmen not to annoy one another 64
Trustees of St. Anne's, 1774.. 75
Trustees of King William's school 78
Treasurer's Building 81
Trespass and ejectment 91
Trade act to advance 96
Tradesmen, encouragement of 96
Transition material.......... 108
Trying period for Gov. Eden.. 153
Trade at Annapolis 109
Troops, Maryland 182
Trenton and Princeton 139
Treaty of peace celebrated..... 194
Trenton and Annapolis 200
Truine, Mathew 229
Tray, Francis 305
Treaty of peace under poplar.. 309

Trade of Annapolis declines... 319
Traces of trade in Annapolis.. 320
Trade revives in Annapolis... 320
Treatment of Indians 331
Tuesday club 131
Tuesday club, conundrums of. 135
Tuition at St. John's 210, 211
Tumblert, Geo 229
Tuck, Washington G 255
Turf, the, in Annapolis..... 258
Tuck, W. G 259
Tuck, W. G., Capt 299
Tuck, W. H 316
Tuck, Wm 167
Two substantial changes of capital 56
Two market days in a week.... 57
Two fairs a year in Annap, 65, 90
Two fair days 94
Two hurt severely 110
Two military companies at Annapolis 170
Two halves of a lemon........ 270
Two centuries, a retrospect of 275
Tyler, John 226
Tysalel, Robt 229
Tyler, Arson 305

U

Union pole and Flag raising... 299
Union Home Guard formed... 299
Union members of Gov. Guards secede 299
Union Ticket 313
Unsworth, John 167
Unwilling to trust Mr. Tayland 85
United States and State officers 255

Upshur, Commander 266
Upper House refuses to concur 51
Upper House gave a sharp repl 57
Upper House disclaim any inte 92
Upper Marlboro 147
Urquhart's, Mrs., Spring 225
Utie, Col. Nathaniel 37

V

Van Horn, a congressman.... 227
Vansant, Joshua 284
Vanville Rangers 282
Vanguard of sick arrive...... 299
Vacancies, how filled 335
Varndel, John 167
Vallette, Eli 167
Vessels licensed 177
Vessels, arms, ammunition tak 36
Vestrymen of St. Anne's in... 68
Vestrymen of St. Anne's, 1704 69
Vestry of St. Anne's lays its grievances 69

Vestry of St. Anne's order a 72
Verse, Annapolis described on 93
Verdict of Jury 112
Verling 147
Very quiet Indians.......... 160
Veazey, Gov. Thomas W. 249
Veazey, Gov 250
Virginia 19
Visitation of the clergy 65
Villianous designs 83
Villians break into Council .. 84
Vinn. Edward, in pillory. 118
Violence of the people 156

Virginia Convention to Md....155
View from State House.........162
Vindex.............................185
Visitors and Govs. of St. Jno's.209
Visit of La Fayette to Annap.239
Vindication of Judge Brewer.272
Views of Annap. Gazette on
   crises....................282, 283

Visit of A. E. Borie.............316
Volumes, quaint and curious.. 79
Voyage to Maryland....... 91, 327
Volunteers against Indians...119
Vote of Annapolis in 1860.....281
Vollmer, Frederick..............305
Voorhees, Philip R..............308

W

Warner, James.................. 19
War could only decide it....... 32
Washington, John................ 47
Warfield, Richard........68, 97, 98
Wardens of St. Anne's threat-
   en non-attendents.......... 71
Walls of St. Anne's alone re-
   mained............ 76
Walls of second State House
   good...... 81
Waters, Mr. John..... 82
W. Bladen, clerk of Council... 87
Warfield, Mr. Alex..... 96
Water, men walking on.........101
Watson, William.................103
Warehouse lost by fire..........110
Walker, Dr. James.........114
Washington, Col. Geo........119
Wallis. John, chimney sweep.130
Wagstaffe, Richard.............130
Wax figures in Annapolis....139
Washington. George......144, 220
Wall..............................147
Walker.......................147
Wagon manf. of Hutton Bros.147
Washington, guest at.........152
Water gives place to land....157
Water and made land......... 157
Washington resigns military
   commission........ 163
Washington, suggestion of....163
Wallace, Mr. Chas., chairman175
Wallace, Charles...161, 170, 176,
   177, 181
Washington in Annapolis.....192
Washington, Gen............196
Washington resigns his mili-
   tary com. at Annapolis...200
Washington arrives at Annap.201
Washing's. room in City Hotel201
Walton. Col. John..............201
Walton. Dr. J. Randolph.201, 318
Washington............. 201, 203

Washington, address to......202
Washington reply to Council
   of State............. 202
Washington, address to An. to203
Washington, President, visit
   to Annapolis.............218
Washington visit St. John's...218
Washington's reply to Annap.203
Washington address of State to203
Washington, reply of, to State204
Washington's letter to Baron
   Steuben..... 205
Washington and his aids.......206
Walker, Col. Benj...........206
Washington's address...... .206
Washington, Gen. Mifflin's ad-
   dress to...... 207
Washington College..............208
Washington, dinner to..218, 219
Washington, journey of......219
Washington and St. John's
   College.................. 219
Washington, nephews of....220
Washington's reception..... 221
Washington, mourning for....224
War of 1812........ 233
Watkins. J. N.237. 258, 259. 260,
   261, 304
Watkins and Chandler fight...235
Watson's, Capt., troops......240
Warfield's. Capt., troops.....240
Watson, Robert..............248
Warfield, Lancelot..........255
Waters, Ramsay..............263
Warrington, Commodore.......266
Ward. Prof......................266
Walton, Col. John, testifies...269
Wallace. James L...270, 297, 306
Walton. Col. John...............284
War excitement in Annap....285
Watts, Wm....................301
Waugh, Dr. J. W..............301
Waters, Thomas G...... ...304

Walton, Col., has notable bowl309
Waite, Col. C. A., U. S. A....310
Watkins, Capt. Thos., Provost
   Marshal.................313
Waterworks, Annapolis......314
Watkins, T. H., wounded....315
Wallis, S. T.. oration of......324
Waterwitch Hook and Ladder
   Co.................. 16
Wardens of the Port..........338
Water, Martin...............168
Warren, John............ 168
Watkins, Thomas............170
Watkins, Stephen.............170
Warfield, Alex., Dr. Chas....176
Waters, Thomas G............261
Warrosquoyacke county......... 19
Wells, Mr. Richard............ 31
Werard, Peter............ 71
Welsh epitaph.............. 76
Wells, Hon. Geo., presents a
   bell......................... 76
Wells, Hon. George, protests
   against furnace............. 76
Wells, Daniel................. 82
Welsh, Sylvester........ ... 83
Welsh to Wells......... 83
Wells to We'sh.............. 83
Wells, Daniel........ 83
Welsh, Capt., discharged.... 83
Welsh, John............... 97
West, Jr., Stepney, manufac.111
Wealthy Government..........145
Welch, Benj., will pay no tax.150
Weems, John..................168
Welch, Chas. S...........,......174
Webster, Noah, visits Annap..221
Wells, Wm..................229
Weems, Rev. Mason L.... 235
Welcome address to La Fayette239
Welch, Robt..................255
Weems, Mr. John C.........259
Weems, Capt.................250
Wells, Geo. Jr........259, 260, 261
Wesley Chapel..................305
Welch's, Chas. S., property...308
Wells, Hon. Geo., President
   A. & E. R. R.............. 313
Wesley Chapel congregation..315
Welling, James C.............316
Wells, Geo......262, 263, 303, 315
Wells, Elijah.................263
Western Hotel invaded........269

Wealth of oysters................275
Wells, John H., 1st Lieut......280
West River............... 282
West River Guard..............282
Wesley Chapel..............305
Wells, Dr. Geo............316, 321
Weapons, not lawful to be
   carried.................. 341
Weeden, Oliver......... 168
Weems, John.............170, 176
Whipped publicly, E. Erberry 41
Wholesome springs at St.
   Mary's................. 59
Workman, Anthony, donates. 78
Whitfield visits Annapolis....110
Whalen, Richard..............117
Whipping of a reverend......137
Whig Club of Baltimore.....157
Whetcroft, William.........177
Whitting, condemned.......225
Wheeler, Bennett................225
Whetcroft, Burton....... 229, 230
Wharf at end of Prince
   George's street..... 228
Whetcroft, Henry..............229
Whigs were strongest..........244
Whigs..............245. 250
Why Senate rejects nomina-
   tions..... 250
White, J. Wesley..........304. 316
Wheeler, John................ 305
Wharton trial................318
White's, Father Andrew,
   Journal..................327
Wharves may be repaired....338
Witch hanged on shipboard... 49
Williamson, Rev. Alex.......... 72
William III, of England..... 77
Williams......................... 83
Wilson, Major................. 83
Williams, a conspirator...... 83
Wilson, Josiah................86. 88
Wilson, John......................100
William and Anne, ship......103
Williamson, Thos., manufact'r111
Williams, Elisha, drowned....112
Wilson, Joseph, conterfeiter..116
Wilson, Geo..................117
Winchelsea, ship, armed..113, 115
Wild bear.................118
Windmill on Windmill Point.120
Will of William Farris......122
Wilson, Capt. Robert..........126

Will of Gen. Washington......148
Wignell, Mr.... ... .148
Williams, Thos. C. and Co.....171
Williams, Jas., 167, 172, 173,
   225, 226, 229
Williams, Joseph........172, 173
Wilkins, William...167, 177, 181
Williams, Otto H..... 196
Williams, Gen.................196
Wilkerson, William...........226
Williams, Wm.................229
Wisepam, John.................229
Williamson, James..............242
Wilmot, Mr. Chas. F..........256
Williamson, J..................258
Wiggins, Daniel H............259
Windmill of D. H. Wiggins...259
Williams, Amos A.............262
Windmill, a.................266
Wilson, Thos. J., proposes
   Maryland to set up sepa-
   rate sovereignty..........282
Wilson, Thomas, elected re-
   corder.... 285
Wilson, Thos. J..............300
Williams, Rev. Robt. H. 304, 320
Wilson, Col. Thos. J., pay-
   master..................313
Wilson, W. H. F., death of...321
Williams, Joseph............167
Wilkinson, J................167
Willatt, William............167
Wilmot, Edward.............168
Williams, Edward..........261
Wiggins, Daniel H.........261
Women, able, jury of....... 44
Workmen to build St. Anne's 69

Wooten, Rev. James.......... 69
Worthington, Thomas.......... 70
Wolfstenhone, Daniel.......... 71
Woodcock, Mr., organist of St
   Anne's 75
Wootton, James.............. 87
Woodchuck's Rest............. 96
Workman, Anthony, alias
   William... 96
Wood, Thomas............... 100
Worthington, Mr. Thomas.....102
Worm bites in Patapsco........111
Women, negro, executed.....116
Woman kills a man........ 121
Woodcock, Harry.............125
Woman and The Lovely
   Nancy 158
Worthington, B. T. B........168
Wolfe, Gen........ 253
Woodford, Henry..............256
Workingmen's meeting in An-
   napolis............ 284
Worthington & Co............312
Woodward, Regnal D..........313
Workingmen's B. & L. Ass'n.325
Worthington, William..........167
Woolford, John...............168
Worthington, Brice T. B.170, 176
Wright, Isaac, counterfeiter.116
Wren, Sir Christopher......128
Wright, Solomon.............220
Wright, Robt., Gov...........226
Wright, John S 315
Wright, Charles.............168
Wyat, Nicholas............. 18
Wyat, Rev. Mr...............252
Wyvill, Marmaduke,..........176

Y

Yarley, Francis........... 25, 28
Young, Mr................... 84
Young. Richard............. . 87
Young, Sam'l............... 97

Young, Col. Sam'l............ 97
York hung for horse stealing.113
Yorktown...................187

Z

Zielke, Charles................305
Zouave Corps.................399

ERRATA.

—:o:—

Page 213, Sec. par., 1st line, read through, for though.

Page 292, sec. par., 15th line, read Constitution, for "Constellation."

Page 78, Thomas Lasker, should be Thomas Tasker.

Page 152, "Robt. Eden became Governor of Maryland in 1760," should be 1769.

Page 154, second paragraph, 3rd line. read excepted, for accepted.

Page 224, last paragraph, 1st line, read 1800, for 1880.

Page 243, in date of card, read 1836, for 1826.

Page 308, 6th paragraph, 3rd line, read Thomas Jennings, for Edmund.

www.ingramcontent.com/pod-product-compliance
Lightning Source LLC
Chambersburg PA
CBHW030857270326
41929CB00008B/455